KT-529-726

KING
HENRY VI
PART 2

Edited by
RONALD KNOWLES

The Arden website is at
http://www.ardenshakespeare.com

The general editors of the Arden Shakespeare have been
W. J. Craig and R. H. Case (first series 1899-1944)
Una Ellis-Fermor, Harold F. Brooks, Harold Jenkins and
Brian Morris (second series 1946-82)

Present general editors (third series)
Richard Proudfoot, Ann Thompson and David Scott Kastan

This edition of *King Henry VI, Part 2*, by Ronald Knowles,
first published 1999 by Thomas Nelson and Sons Ltd
Reprinted 2001 by Thomson Learning

Editorial matter © 1999 Ronald Knowles

Typeset in Ehrhardt by Multiplex Techniques Ltd

Arden Shakespeare is an imprint of Thomson Learning

Thomson Learning
Berkshire House
168-173 High Holborn
London WC1V 7AA

Printed in Singapore

British Library Cataloguing in Publication Data
A catalogue record for this book is available from the British Library
Library of Congress Cataloguing in Publication Data
A catalogue record has been requested

ISBN 1-903436-62-1(hbk)
ISBN 1-903436-63-X (pbk)

NPN 9 8 7 6 5 4 3 2 1

THE ARDEN SHAKESPEARE

$8.99

THIRD SERIES

General Editors: ... n Thompson

Associate General Editor ... Williams

KING HENRY VI
PART 2

THE ARDEN SHAKESPEARE

*Second Series

The Editor

Ronald Knowles is Senior Lecturer in English Literature at the University of Reading. He is author and editor of several books, including *Henry IV Parts 1 and 2: 'The Critics Debate'* (1992) and *Shakespeare and Carnival: After Bakhtin* (1998).

For Daniel and Jessica
as ever

CONTENTS

LIST OF ILLUSTRATIONS

GENERAL EDITORS' PREFACE

The Arden Shakespeare is now over one hundred years old. The earliest volume in the first series, Edward Dowden's *Hamlet*, was published in 1899. Since then the Arden Shakespeare has become internationally recognized and respected. It is now widely acknowledged as the pre-eminent Shakespeare series, valued by scholars, students, actors and 'the great variety of readers' alike for its readable and reliable texts, its full annotation and its richly informative introductions.

We have aimed in the third Arden edition to maintain the quality and general character of its predecessors, preserving the commitment to presenting the play as it has been shaped in history. While each individual volume will necessarily have its own emphasis in the light of the unique possibilities and problems posed by the play, the series as a whole, like the earlier Ardens, insists upon the highest standards of scholarship and upon attractive and accessible presentation.

Newly edited from the original quarto and folio editions, the texts are presented in fully modernized form, with a textual apparatus that records all substantial divergences from those early printings. The notes and introductions focus on the conditions and possibilities of meaning that editors, critics and performers (on stage and screen) have discovered in the play. While building upon the rich history of scholarly and theatrical activity that has long shaped our understanding of the texts of Shakespeare's plays, this third series of the Arden Shakespeare is made necessary and possible by a new generation's encounter with Shakespeare, engaging with the plays and their complex relation to the culture in which they were – and continue to be – produced.

THE TEXT

On each page of the play itself, readers will find a passage of text followed by commentary and, finally, textual notes. Act and scene divisions (seldom present in the early editions and often the product of eighteenth-century or later scholarship) have been retained for ease of reference, but have been given less prominence than in the previous series. Editorial indications of location of the action have been removed to the textual notes or commentary.

In the text itself, unfamiliar typographic conventions have been avoided in order to minimize obstacles to the reader. Elided forms in the early texts are spelt out in full in verse lines wherever they indicate a usual late twentieth-century pronunciation that requires no special indication and wherever they occur in prose (except when they indicate non-standard pronunciation). In verse speeches, marks of elision are retained where they are necessary guides to the scansion and pronunciation of the line. Final -ed in past tense and participial forms of verbs is always printed as -ed without accent, never as -'d, but wherever the required pronunciation diverges from modern usage a note in the commentary draws attention to the fact. Where the final -ed should be given syllabic value contrary to modern usage, e.g.

> Doth Silvia know that I am banished?
> (*TGV* 3.1.221)

the note will take the form

> 221 **banished** banishèd

Conventional lineation of divided verse lines shared by two or more speakers has been reconsidered and sometimes rearranged. Except for the familiar *Exit* and *Exeunt*, Latin forms in stage directions and speech prefixes have been translated into English and the original Latin forms recorded in the textual notes.

COMMENTARY AND TEXTUAL NOTES

Notes in the commentary, for which a major source will be the *Oxford English Dictionary*, offer glossarial and other explication of verbal difficulties; they may also include discussion of points of theatrical interpretation and, in relevant cases, substantial extracts from Shakespeare's source material. Editors will not usually offer glossarial notes for words adequately defined in the latest edition of *The Concise Oxford Dictionary* or *Merriam-Webster's Collegiate Dictionary*, but in cases of doubt they will include notes. Attention, however, will be drawn to places where more than one likely interpretation can be proposed and to significant verbal and syntactic complexity. Notes preceded by * involve discussion of textual variants in readings from the early edition(s) on which the text is based.

Headnotes to acts or scenes discuss, where appropriate, questions of scene location, Shakespeare's handling of his source materials, and major difficulties of staging. The list of roles (so headed to emphasize the play's status as a text for performance) is also considered in commentary notes. These may include comment on plausible patterns of casting with the resources of an Elizabethan or Jacobean acting company, and also on any variation in the description of roles in their speech prefixes in the early editions.

The textual notes are designed to let readers know when the edited text diverges from the early edition(s) on which it is based. Wherever this happens the note will record the rejected reading of the early edition(s), in original spelling, and the source of the reading adopted in this edition. Other forms from the early edition(s) recorded in these notes will include some spellings of particular interest or significance and original forms of translated stage directions. Where two early editions are involved, for instance with *Othello*, the notes will also record all important differences between them. The textual notes take a form that has been in use since the nineteenth century. This comprises, first: line reference, reading adopted in the text and closing square bracket; then: abbreviated reference, in italic, to the earliest edition to adopt the accepted reading, italic semicolon and noteworthy alternative reading(s), each with abbreviated italic reference to its source.

Conventions used in these textual notes include the following. The solidus / is used, in notes quoting verse or discussing verse lining, to indicate line endings. Distinctive spellings of the basic text (Q or F) follow the square bracket without indication of source and are enclosed in italic brackets. Names enclosed in italic brackets indicate originators of conjectural emendations when these did not originate in an edition of the text, or when this edition records a conjecture not accepted into its text. Stage directions (SDs) are referred to by the number of the line within or immediately after which they are placed. Line numbers with a decimal point relate to entry SDs and to SDs more than one line long, with the number after the point indicating the line within the SD: e.g. 78.4 refers to the fourth line of the SD following line 78. Lines of SDs at the start of a scene are numbered 0.1, 0.2, etc. Where only a line number and SD precede the square bracket, e.g. 128 SD], the note relates to the whole of a SD within or immediately following the line. Speech prefixes (SPs) follow similar conventions, 203 SP] referring to the speaker's name for line 203. Where a SP reference takes the form e.g. 38 + SP, it relates to all subsequent speeches assigned to that speaker in the scene in question.

Where, as with *King Henry V*, one of the early editions is a so-called 'bad quarto' (that is, a text either heavily adapted, or reconstructed from memory, or both), the divergences from the present edition are too great to be recorded in full in the notes. In these cases the editions will include a reduced photographic facsimile of the 'bad quarto' in an appendix.

INTRODUCTION

Both the introduction and the commentary are designed to present the plays as texts for performance, and make appropriate reference to stage, film and television versions, as well as introducing the reader to the range of critical approaches to the plays. They discuss the history of the reception of the texts within the theatre and scholarship and beyond, investigating the interdependency of the literary text and the surrounding 'cultural text' both at the time of the original production of Shakespeare's works and during their long and rich afterlife.

ACKNOWLEDGEMENTS

Though a single editor's name may appear on the title-page, a volume such as this draws on the work of many scholars and critics, past and present, as the reference section below makes apparent. I am deeply indebted to all editors of *King Henry VI*, *Part 2*, most particularly to those who have provided annotated editions of all three parts of the *Henry VI* plays, namely Michael Hattaway, Norman Sanders, John Dover Wilson and my Arden predecessors H. C. Hart and Andrew S. Cairncross. Access by microfilm to William Montgomery's unpublished edition of *The Contention of York and Lancaster* has been invaluable. Throughout the commentary I have referred to modern historians and I would like to thank, as representative, Ralph A. Griffiths, I.M.W. Harvey and Roger Virgoe. I have worked closely with the Arden senior General Editor, Richard Proudfoot, and with the advisory editor for Shakespeare's English histories, George Walton Williams; both have given generously of their knowledge of Shakespeare's texts and contexts. With their patience, encouragement and experience, they have been, in the words of the play, 'my stay, my guide and lantern to my feet'. David Scott Kastan gave me the benefit of his comments on the Introduction. My thanks are due to those individuals and institutions who gave permission to reproduce the illustrations (detailed acknowledgement is made in the List of Illustrations).

The publishing team at Nelson has been crucially supportive, particularly Jessica Hodge whose unfailing affability has sustained me at timely moments. A special acknowledgement must be made to the copy-editor for the bulk of this volume, Roger Fallon, and to his successor Judith Ravenscroft, whose exacting meticulousness and tenacious eyes prevented many a slip. With great forbearance, my long-suffering medieval and renaissance colleagues in the English and History departments at Reading have listened to my questions and offered advice: thanks to Cedric Brown, Anne Curry, Andrew Gurr, Ralph Houlbrooke, Christopher Hardman and David J. Williams. I am indebted to Reading University Library, the British Library, the Bodleian Library, and the many libraries which have contributed to this edition by way of the inter-library loan facility at Reading, whose staff on many occasions have acted well beyond the call of duty. For several years all my published work has been processed by Cheryl Foote who, faced with the multiple problems of an Arden text, once again rose to the challenge and solved everything with her customary professionalism. I am deeply grateful for her work.

This book is dedicated to my son and daughter, but in concluding these acknowledgements I would like to express my profound respects for Sydney Anglo, the teacher and scholar whose unique undergraduate course in renaissance civilization and ideas laid the foundation that I have built upon throughout an academic lifetime.

Ronald Knowles
Reading

INTRODUCTION

The Introduction discusses the three topics of performance, criticism and text. 'Performance' offers a survey from the very sketchy details of staging indicated by the first Quarto, known as *The Contention*, to the productions after the Second World War which draw on the full Folio text not only of *2 Henry VI* but of the other plays of the trilogy. The 'Criticism' section provides a historical survey of earlier criticism of the play and then analyses the influence of, and reaction to, arguably the most influential commentator on Shakespeare's English history plays in the twentieth century, E. M. W. Tillyard. I focus on the leading critical questions of the debate, and look at alternative developments in more recent years. Following the sections 'Seneca, Rhetoric and poetry' and 'Feminism', in 'History, justice, drama', I take up the essential issues deriving from the Tillyard debate and re-explore them through the lens of the carnivalesque.

The 'Text' of the play exists in both Quarto (Q) and Folio (F) editions the nature of which has given rise to a fraught dispute among textual scholars and editors. This edition takes the longer F version as the control text but refers often to the Quartos, the importance of which is emphasized here. The 'upstart Crow' sneer was part of the playwright Robert Greene's warning about the new young rival William Shakespeare in relation to the *Henry VI* plays, and I begin my discussion of the text by looking at the controversy concerning the first Quarto: was it an old play of mixed authorship which Shakespeare revised for the much longer *2 Henry VI*, or was it actually a garbled report from actors' memories of *2 Henry VI*? 'Date, sequence and authorship' seems a simple enough subheading, but as with most issues

1

concerning *2 Henry VI* it is, in fact, extremely complex since the available evidence is far from sufficient to establish comprehensive and unchallengeable certainty. 'From revision to report' follows the two sides of the textual controversy, between revisionists–collaborationists and memorialists, up to the turning point of 'Acceptance and reaction'. 'Acceptance' indicates the triumph of the 'reporter' or memorialist school, while 'reaction' is twofold: those few who could not accept *The Contention* as a memorial report, or as Shakespeare's, and those contemporary textual scholars who are re-examining the methodological bases of the New Bibliography which had in large part developed from a theory of the derivation of the Quartos.

This Introduction contributes to an edition which has been prepared in the conviction that had a barely known young Warwickshire playwright been carried off by the London plague of 1592, *2 Henry VI* would remain as the greatest history play in early modern drama and one of the most exciting and dynamic plays of the English Renaissance theatre. Furthermore, as post-war productions have shown, and modern critical theory has emphasized, the power politics of personality and institutions and the social revolution of demagogue and ideologies in *2 Henry VI* are as relevant to our contemporary world as to past history.

PERFORMANCE

Abridgement and adaptation

Apart from the evidence of staging recorded in the first Quarto of *2 Henry VI* (see Montgomery, 'Staging') there are no further records of production until John Crowne's Restoration adaptations entitled *The Misery of Civil War* (printed 1680, acted 1681) and *Henry the Sixth, the First Part* (1681) (Odell, 1, 63–7; Spencer, 298–303).

The Misery of Civil War takes the Jack Cade material from *2 Henry VI* and also adapts much of *3 Henry VI*. Crowne was an ardent royalist and used his adaptation of Shakespeare to warn

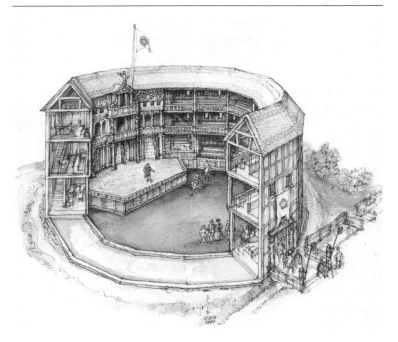

1 The Rose Theatre, where *2 Henry VI* was first performed

against the dangers of Whiggism leading to civil war, and adds scenes to Act 3 of raping and looting, 'Houses and Towns burning, Men and Women hang'd upon Trees, and Children on the Tops of Pikes'. *Henry the Sixth, the First Part* draws on Shakespeare's *2 Henry VI*, Acts 1 to 3. Writing at the time of the Popish Plot hysteria, Crowne takes every opportunity to vilify the Cardinal's role in the murder of the good Duke Humphrey, which had a topical significance, since the assassination, in 1679, of Sir Edmund Berry Godfrey, an upright London magistrate, was assumed to have been by popish hirelings. Consequently, Crowne expands considerably on Shakespeare's assassins.

Two more adaptations of *2 Henry VI* appeared in the eighteenth century, by Ambrose Philips and Theophilus Cibber. As with Crowne's version, their adaptations reflect aspects of contemporary politics and the rise of sentimentalism. Philips is usually remembered for the nickname earned by his insipid poetry, 'Namby-Pamby'. Theophilus was the son of the actor–autobiographer and Poet Laureate, Colley Cibber, whose performance as the Cardinal in his son's adaptation was famous in its day. Philips's *Humfrey Duke of Gloucester* was produced at Drury Lane in 1723. As with Crowne's second play, this generally derives from the first three acts of *2 Henry VI*, though using only thirty of Shakespeare's actual lines. Possibly Philips was consciously reacting against Crowne's politics since his play is dedicated to William Pulteney, a leading Whig statesman. Common to both, however, is anti-Catholicism which, in Philips's adaptation, takes the form of anti-Jacobitism. Theophilus Cibber's *Henry VI* (1723) succeeded Philips's play at the Drury Lane Theatre, and roughly followed the adaptation of *2* and *3 Henry VI* made by Crowne. Cibber's first act uses Act 5 of *2 Henry VI* and his second and third acts are taken from scenes in *3 Henry VI*, Acts 1 and 2. Crowne was admired for his treatment of the pathos of Rutland's death, which Cibber emulated by having the body of Rutland brought on stage at the death of his father, York. But Cibber leaves out the sequence of the paper-crowning of the Duke by the avenging Margaret. Thus the pathos is deepened, uncompromised by the malicious and grotesque. Elsewhere Cibber adds to the love interest wherever he can, and at one point he has the tigerish Queen echo Henry V.

In 1817 Edmund Kean appeared at Drury Lane in the title role of a work sometimes attributed to him, though in fact adapted by J. H. Merivale, entitled *Richard Duke of York; or, the Contention of York and Lancaster*. Merivale took material from all three parts of the *Henry VI* plays, though *2 Henry VI* predominates. From *1 Henry VI* the author drew on the Temple Garden scene (2.4) and the following scene in which Mortimer outlines to Richard Plantagenet the Yorkist claim to the crown. By 1.4 of Merivale's play Suffolk brings on Henry's new Queen, and his courtiers lament the loss of Anjou and Maine (i.e. 1.1 of *2 Henry VI*).

Cibber's treatment of York's death scene is repeated here with the addition of various echoes of such Jacobean playwrights as Chapman, Webster and Marston. Elsewhere Kean as York appropriates the famous lines of Warwick describing the dead Gloucester; the famous scenes of the animosity between Gloucester and the Cardinal are amplified; Cade's rebellion makes a brief appearance; alarms, excursions and battles proliferate. All in all a star vehicle for Edmund Kean, as a contemporary reviewer celebrated: 'we thought him, in many scenes unusually great' (Salgado, 86).

York's appropriation of Warwick's lines on the dead Gloucester was repeated in a most remarkable event in the fortunes of *2 Henry VI*. On the day of Shakespeare's tercentenary, 23 April 1864, the Surrey Theatre put on the second part with James Anderson doubling as the Duke of York and Jack Cade. *The Athenaeum* spoke of the event as a 'restoration' of the play. *The Illustrated London News* similarly reported that this was 'a revival, or rather restoration to the stage, of an utterly neglected work . . . which has not been played for 270 years'. These reports suggest that the play was at last presented as Shakespeare's rather than as an adaptation by someone else (Salgado, 81–8; Odell, II, 302). Unsurprisingly, given the significance of the English histories for such figures as A.W. Schlegel and Ulrici (see pp. 35–7), there were productions of *2 Henry VI* in nineteenth-century Germany and Austria, including a version at the Burgtheater, Vienna, in 1873 (Stahl).

The prompt-book for Frank Benson's Stratford production of *2 Henry VI* in 1899 survives in the Shakespeare Centre Library. In 1906, over three successive days at the Stratford Festival, Benson put on all three parts of *Henry VI*. This was the first staging of the complete trilogy, which was produced as part of the whole cycle of Shakespeare's two tetralogies on English history. In fact *3 Henry VI* was revived for the first time since the

Tudor–Jacobean period. To honour the occasion *The Athenaeum* printed a full-page review (12 May 1906, 587–8), from which the following quotations are taken. Following the picturesque tradition of Henry Irving, Benson paid due attention to 'dresses, armour and pageantry', but the need for scene and costume changes led to 'cutting, contraction, and transposition', thus creating intervals which disrupted 'the links of thought, causation, and characterization' of the cycle as a whole and the *Henry VI* plays in particular, which, in spite of 'fine scenes and much powerful characterization', seemed 'weak in dramatic coherence'. *2 Henry VI* was praised for original scenic effects but the Cardinal's deathbed was 'strewn unaccountably with sheaves of straw, which distracted from his tragic intensity'. However, Benson successfully played the Cardinal with 'grim bitterness'. Interestingly, the reviewer notes that at the close of the *Henry VI* trilogy Benson gave a short speech explaining 'how those dramas were rather parts of Shakespeare's philosophy of history than lessons in his dramatic art'. Benson's 'Note on the production of *Henry VI*' survives and is worth quoting at length for an 'Edwardian' understanding of the trilogy. He argues

> That the wanton aggression against France, was inevitably followed by civil disruption at home. That the Wars of the Roses, were practically a punishment, for a War of Greed and spoliation, which reached its climax in the murder of Joan of Arc. That in the process, the king-man degenerated from the type of Henry IV. and Henry V. to that represented by Edward IV. and Richard III. Finally how during the death and the ruin of so many nobles and gentry, the Commons of England were growing in power and importance, and laying the foundation of the English Empire; and how clearly Shakespeare rejects that machiavellian theory of politics which proved the ruin of Florence and Italian liberties.
>
> (Sprague, 112)

For Benson feudal dynasticism, Renaissance *Realpolitik*, tyranny and anarchy are displaced by sovereignty of the Commons, ultimately fostering maritime imperialism.

Hattaway (*Theatre*) notes that *2 Henry VI* was performed in the New World for the first time at the Pasadena Community Playhouse in California, directed by Gilmour Brown, as part of the 1935 season which included productions of all ten English histories. Later American productions were at Antioch College, Ohio (1953), and the Oregon Shakespeare Festival (1954) (see Marder; Sandoe). A later production of *2 Henry VI* at the 1977 Oregon Shakespeare Festival was described by a local reviewer in terms of contemporary film as 'a fifteenth-century spaghetti western' (Dessen, 245). The director, Jerry Turner, used a truncated script – severely cut speeches, some characters omitted, some actions excluded – in order to exploit every opportunity for spectacle, violence and horror which included additional dumb shows, and severed heads 'trailing bits of oesophagus'. Like some predecessors, Turner chose to include material from the last scene of *1 Henry VI* and the first scene of *3 Henry VI* which contributed to the overall reshaping to provide 'a more clearly charted conflict between the King and Richard of York than had Shakespeare'. Alan Dessen then addresses the kind of theatrical and historiographical complexity to be found within the complete play that such editing compromises, concluding: 'I cannot help wondering if "good theatre" is really incompatible with a fuller, more faithful rendition of the text' (246). As I indicate below (p. 17), Terry Hands's production for the Royal Shakespeare Company in the same year put this to the test.

As a young man Sir Barry Jackson saw Benson's *Henry VI* trilogy in 1906 and it was 'the unknown Second Part of *King Henry VI* that made the greatest impression on my mind' (49). Eventually Jackson's own production of the *Henry VI* plays at the Birmingham Repertory Theatre and the Old Vic, London, was to be more influential than he could have possibly foreseen.

From abridgement to full text

Sir Barry Jackson wished eventually to present all of Shakespeare at the Birmingham Repertory Theatre and turned to the *Henry VI* trilogy, directed by Douglas Seale, in the early 1950s (see Fig. 2): *2 Henry VI* in 1951; *3 Henry VI* in 1952; and *1 Henry VI* in 1953. These were brought to the Old Vic, London, later in 1953 and again in 1957, though on this occasion *Parts 1* and *2* were combined into one play, with all of the Talbot–Joan of Arc sequences removed.

Douglas Seale's direction and Finlay James's set attempted to combine concepts of fixity and movement, the ineluctable structure of feudalism and the ceaseless violence that was surely undermining it. The action was played against James's fixture of triple gothic arches, symbolic both of the trilogy and of the inescapability of violence. To support his notion, Seale disciplined non-speaking actors to remain still, which 'achieved an

2 The death of Cardinal Beaufort, from Douglas Seale's production for the Birmingham Repertory Theatre at the Old Vic, 1953, with David Dodimead as Cardinal Beaufort and Paul Daneman as Henry

undisturbed concentration upon the lines', quite in keeping, one might add, with much of the formalism of the verse. By contrast the action surged to and fro, turning Plantagenet England into the 'bear garden' of Hazlitt's phrase (T. W. Kemp, 125).

Seale had omitted, as part of the cuts, the Suffolk murder scene of 4.1, which was restored at the Old Vic, much to the play's advantage, according to *The Times* (15 July 1953, 4). In the 1957 Old Vic production, apart from the Temple Garden scene and those with Suffolk and Margaret, almost nothing remained of the 'Talbot play', *1 Henry VI*. Yet, ironically, this served to emphasize something central to the trilogy – the role of Margaret. Anticipating feminist critics of today, Sir Barry Jackson asked 'why has no major actress ever discovered the tremendous character of Margaret of Anjou, surely one of the greatest roles in the whole gallery?' (50). Summarizing the severe cuts to *Part 1* and the excision of Henry's brief restoration to the throne, in the 1957 production, Mary Clarke considered that 'this treatment makes it less a play about the reign of King Henry than about the struggles of his wife . . . on behalf of the house of Lancaster' (n.p.). Barbara Jefford took full advantage of the foregrounded role in the court and in dynastic politics, at council and in battle, varying from chilling cruelty in York's death to passionate lamentation for Suffolk and her son.

Jackson left on record an observation on the scenes of Cade's rebellion that will be of some concern in the critical reading below (pp. 89–106): 'the line between the risible and the serious' in the Jack Cade scenes 'is of such infinitesimal breadth that the reaction of the audience can never be foretold' (51). In the 1957 production, according to Mary Clarke, it got out of hand: 'Too many minor members of the crowd took the bit in their teeth and turned in hugely comic performances. The result was that Cade himself was obliterated in the hurly-burly and it is doubtful if anyone in the audience had any idea of what was going on' (n.p.). Almost echoing a line of Cade, the *Times* reviewer of the 1953 Old Vic production observed that 'the cumulative disorder is the only order of the play' (15 July 1953, 4). The later *Times* review of the 1957 production went further in a most arresting way: with 'the imposter Jack Cade [and] his people's rebellion . . . the vigorous crowd action combined with abstract discussion suggests that Shakespeare may have collaborated with M. Sartre' (17 October 1957, 5). Had that recognition of the play of ideas within farce been developed it might well have turned into a major criticism of the play.

It is no coincidence that the 1950s reinstatement of the *Henry VI* plays in the theatre occurred at exactly the period when the academic interpretation by E. M. W. Tillyard had critically revised the reputation of the English histories as a whole. One further major step was production in the vastly expanded domestic medium of television in the postwar world (see Holderness & McCullough). This was *An Age of Kings*, produced by Peter Davis and directed by Michael Hayes for the BBC. Each play (apart from *1 Henry VI* which again lost Talbot) was presented in two parts: *2 Henry VI* was divided into 'The fall of a Protector' and 'The rabble from Kent'. Terry Scully as Henry VI stressed pitifulness yet managed to suggest something other than mere pathos: for one reviewer '*Henry VI* became most interesting in the scenes of Cade's rebellion' (Crane, 326). *An Age of Kings* preceded what was to become, both in theatre and on television, the most influential of all productions of the *Henry VI* trilogy – *The Wars of the Roses* by John Barton and Peter Hall, first performed by the Royal Shakespeare Company (RSC) at Stratford (see Fig. 3).

The Wars of the Roses was announced for the 1963 season. It was a three-part adaptation of the first tetralogy, comprising *Henry VI*, '*Edward IV*' and *Richard III*, and was to be presented sequentially for the first time in the morning, afternoon and evening of a single day (Addenbrooke, 60). *Henry VI* adapts *1 Henry VI* and *2 Henry VI*, yet unlike most predecessors it retains the Talbot scenes from *Part 1*, but ends at the scene of the Cardinal's death. '*Edward IV*' combined the last two acts of *2*

3 The Council table in Sir Peter Hall's production for the Royal Shakespeare
Company at Stratford, 1964, with Peggy Ashcroft as Margaret and David
Warner as Henry

Henry VI with *3 Henry VI.* John Barton writes, 'We cut down
the number of parley-cum-battle scenes by combining the battle
of St Albans sequence . . . with the sequence leading up to the
battle of Wakefield . . . and telescoped the action elsewhere wherever possible.' These observations occur in 'The making of an
adaptation' (xvii), Barton's essay which is included with Peter
Hall's introduction to *The Wars of the Roses* (Barton & Hall).
This volume prints the texts of the three plays with Barton's
additions in italics. Michael Bakewell and John Bury add, respectively, an essay on 'The Television Production' and a note on
'The Set'. There are also seventeen pages of production photographs.

Subsequently, *The Wars of the Roses* was broadcast over three
consecutive weeks on BBC 1, April–May 1965. Later it was
broadcast in Australia, Canada and the United States. *The Wars
of the Roses* was more successful than any preceding production
of the *Henry VI* plays, and came to be regarded as the crown of

the RSC's achievement in the 1960s. Bernard Levin's fulsome voice may here represent the chorus of acclaim: 'the monumental production . . . one of the mightiest stage projects of our time . . . a production to remember all our lives' (*Daily Mail*, 21 August 1963). There were, however, dissenting voices, as we shall hear, but what was it that stirred such praise?

In conception, adaptation, acting and production, the Barton–Hall *Wars of the Roses* differed from its predecessors. Several major influences determined the nature of the work and its marked difference from a production like Douglas Seale's at the Old Vic just a few years earlier. These influences were: post-war Cambridge; the mid-1950s visit to London by Bertholt Brecht's Berliner Ensemble; Antonin Artaud's theory of a 'Theatre of Cruelty'; and the impact of the English translation of Jan Kott's study *Shakespeare Our Contemporary*, which Hall read in proof before actual publication in 1964. E. M. W. Tillyard's *Shakespeare's History Plays* was first published in 1944. (Fuller critical consideration will be given to Tillyard below, pp. 41–55.) With its belief that Shakespeare's dramatization of English history was unified by its source in the Tudor historians' embodiment of a 'Tudor myth', it came to dominate at least two generations of academic thinking about the tetralogies. Though it is generally regarded now with some scepticism, the occasional volley from a pocket of conservative supporters is still heard once in a while. Hall absorbed Tillyard at Cambridge after the war, as his introduction to *The Wars of the Roses* (Barton & Hall) makes plain with its summary of Tillyard's ideas. Hall believes, following Tillyard, that Shakespeare subscribed to the commonplace ideas of an hierarchic nature and society founded on the principle of 'degree' and the doctrine of order. Tudor historians, particularly Edward Hall, following Polydore Virgil, used these ideas to support the Tudor dynasty by promoting the notion that Henry VII had, by divine providence, rescued England from the chaos of nearly a century of war brought about as retributive punishment for the usurpation and murder of a divinely appointed monarch, Richard II (see Sinfield, 184–6).

This ideological view was to be further focused by Jan Kott's conception of Shakespeare as the dramatist of bleak and bloody political power struggle – a mechanism of history symbolized for Kott by the 'staircase of power' which all ascend only to topple off as those behind clamber bloodily upwards, etc. In its day Kott's work was enormously influential though it is very difficult now to see why, since its limited ideas are no more than extremely diluted and dehistoricized versions of Boccaccio's *de casibus* representation of the rise and fall of Fortune's wheel, Machiavellian 'policy' and Hobbesian power politics. However, Kott's rhetoric of 'contemporaneity' had the cachet of 'relevance' for the changing world of the 1960s. Artaud's book *The Theatre and its Double*, containing the essay 'The Theatre of Cruelty', had been published in translation in 1958. Artaud had already influenced Peter Brook, whose *Titus Andronicus* of 1955 had, in turn, helped Jan Kott formulate his ideas. Artaud's theatre turned from a dominant psychological realism based on character to a ritualist drama that would confront suffering, pain and evil. At the same time Brecht's Berliner Ensemble, making its first visit to London in 1956 with *The Caucasian Chalk Circle*, provided a stark political idiom backed by its theory of 'epic' theatre, which promoted ensemble acting at the expense of any star performer: a theatre completely opposed to the post-Victorian traditions of the picturesque pageantry of Plantagenet history as embodied in Leslie Hurry's costumes for *Henry VI* at the Old Vic.

As a result of Artaud's influence, for John Russell Brown, *The Wars of the Roses* maintained

> a continuous emphasis of violence and of the shallow-ness of politicians' pretensions. The plays became a high-class cartoon, a relentless horror comic . . . horror and violence were presented by liberal splashes of blood,

and by inventive business that elaborated every opportunity for the exhibition of cruelty and pain that the text suggested, and more that were foisted on the text . . . its most obvious effect was a grand guignol grip on the audience . . . and it assured the verisimilitude given to certain horrible episodes in the text of *Henry VI*.

(Brown, 149)

John Bury's set was 'designed in steel – the steel of the plate armour – the steel of the shield and the steel of the broadsword'. Naturalism gave way to symbolism: 'On the flagged floor of sheet steel tables are daggers, staircases are axe-heads, and doors the traps on scaffolds. Nothing yields: stone walls have lost their seduction and now loom dangerously – steel-clad – to enclose and to imprison. The countryside offers no escape – the danger is still there in the iron foliage of the cruel trees, and, surrounding all, the great steel cage of war' (Barton & Hall, 237). Copper foil was used to simulate steel. The concept was applied even to costume: 'you must make the costumes look like they have degrees of rust, or they must be textured or hard. So one didn't introduce any "soft" elements, one had to do the job within the language of working with metals' (Addenbrooke, 212).

Bury combined the inflexibility of steel with the necessity for fluidity of scene changes by drawing on an ancient Greek theatrical device, the *periaktos*. He used two of these large, triangular revolving structures: 'the periaktos swung round to become at one moment the walls of Harfleur, at another the council-chamber in London' (Barton & Hall, 233). Though the television production was filmed in the Stratford Memorial Theatre, it deliberately employed techniques to avoid the effect of merely shooting a play (as had been the case with the *Age of Kings* (see Crane, 325; Barton & Hall, 233–5)) such as removing a section of the stalls to provide a platform for mobile cameras, and using a hand-held camera for variation of depth and perspective. The Folio texts of the *Henry VI* plays amount to over 12,000 lines. The final playing version of *The Wars of the Roses* used approximately half of this with the addition of some 1,400 pastiche pentameters from John Barton's pen. Obviously, such severe pruning of verse drama – reminiscent of the early Quartos of the play – will fundamentally alter the audience's experience: the poetry of metaphor and analogy is lessened; seemingly digressive, incidental scenes are removed; plot-line is strengthened; movement is increased – entrances, exits, violence, battles and so on. But above all the shift in emphasis has moved from the audience as listener–spectator to the audience as spectator–listener: the balance between seeing and hearing shifts to the former. An example: Barton writes that 'in the latter part of the play [*3 Henry VI*] from 3.3 to 5.3 the text seems to me Elizabethan hack-work, dry of imagery and vigour'. By contrast, 'Shakespeare's hand seems to me most apparent . . . where the dramatic potential of a particular scene excited him (the Cade rebellion, and the death of York, for instance)' (Barton & Hall, xxiv). Nevertheless, given the necessity of getting the three plays down to two, the Cade scenes had to be cut, and on turning to them we find that Cade's confrontation with Lord Saye is completely excised.

The contrast between the grim comic brutality of the rebels and the pathos of Saye's fearful senility is very good drama, but there is more to it than that. In the verbal exchanges of accusation and defence the whole raison d'être of feudalism, its basis in law, is turned upside down. The drama here is to a considerable extent the drama of ideas, and proper audience engagement involves the realization that for all the grotesque farce there is a dialectic of thought much more complex than anything Jan Kott has to offer. This is all cut, but immediately following the first Cade scene (scene 27, '*Edward IV*') is a scene of fifty-two lines between Somerset, King Lewis, Burgundy and Alençon which is entirely Barton's invention, there to develop a narrative plot-line touched on in *2 Henry VI* 3.1.84–5. The excision of Lord Saye is highly questionable, but the addition is banal.

Several criticisms of the Barton–Hall endeavour were made (see Daniell; Hodgdon, '*Wars*'), but perhaps G. K. Hunter's ('*Henry VI*') was the most fundamental. Hunter's appraisal derived from two linked points, the cycle concept and the focus on power. Considering the notion of one particular ideological theme running through the English histories, Hunter points out that in spite of apparent connections the plays appear to have been written as separate parts for individual performance. The insistence on 'unity', he argues, derives more from post-Romantic aesthetics than Elizabethan practice, which followed an episodic centrifugal tendency in attaching small scenes to the main plot. Further, the singular focus at Stratford on the circular pattern of power relationships was only part of the plays. To concentrate exclusively on this is to narrow the plot, which consists of several interacting 'trajectories', not one. Though Hunter does not use this analogy, it may be said that the movement of the *Henry VI* plays is polyphonic, not symphonic. The dominance on stage of throne and steel council table symbolized the permanent struggle between autocracy and oligarchy, yet, as Hunter points out, an equally persistent concern of the plays is the relationship between father and son. Generally, for Hunter, Barton's cuts removed a great deal of the personal and individual experience, which is as much the basis of the political in Shakespeare's representation as is any larger overriding abstraction about power and feudalism. This is seen, for example, in the full Folio version of the Gloucester–Eleanor relationship, much cut by Barton.

However, for all the criticisms, *The Wars of the Roses* seemed to respond to the way the youth of the 1960s questioned authority and the public world. In this respect the casting of David Warner as Henry VI, 'who seemed a holy idiot out of Dostoevsky' (*Sunday Telegraph*, 21 July 1963), was truly inspired. Warner went on to become 'the students' Hamlet' as he was dubbed in the RSC's 1965 production, and then in the same year appeared as the titular Marxist anti-hero in the film of

David Mercer's *Morgan – A Suitable Case For Treatment*. In retrospect, King Henry VI was a preparation for the two more famous parts – innocence and youthful idealism aghast at the hypocrisy and violence of the world.

The impact of the Barton–Hall production was so great that there was no further British production until 1977 when Terry Hands, again with the RSC, put on all three of the *Henry VI* plays in uncut versions. For the first time ever, the three texts of the first Folio could be seen, as Hands put it, 'without any reshaping, without any tailoring, without any adapting – in fact, with less than we would do with any other production' (Swander, 148). Hands and his actors were breaking new ground; there was no preceding acting tradition to measure themselves against. In many ways what they were doing was experimental, and they demonstrated that this was how they regarded it by trusting the full texts to work on their own terms.

For the *Times* reviewer they succeeded; 'the performance continuously grips attention through its mobile control of narrative' (13 July 1977). By contrast, for G. K. Hunter, the plays were 'diffuse and dull' ('*Henry VI*', 105). Similarly, comparing these with the 'clear shape' and 'powerful sense of purpose' of the 1963 *The Wars of the Roses*, Roger Warren found that 'to tell the story simply' as with Hands's approach 'is insufficient. Shape, development, and finally meaning were absent' ('Comedies', 149). However, rather than a story simply told, Hunter recognized that in 1977 character was the basic emphasis rather the stress on plot of 1963. In his appraisal of the depth of character achieved, Homer D. Swander claimed of the RSC's achievement that 'no acting company since the death of Shakespeare had performed a greater service to its art' (146).

'The actors . . . act their hearts out in giving Stanislavski-esque "depth" to the characters', G. K. Hunter recorded ('*Henry VI*', 105), and this was particularly the case with Helen Mirren's Queen Margaret and Alan Howard as Henry. At York's death, his charge against Margaret – 'But you are more inhuman, more inexorable, / O, ten times more, than tigers of Hyrcania' (*3H6* 1.4.154–5) – is often taken as a cue line for the revelation of Margaret's character: sensuality and ambition culminating in animal cruelty. This could lend itself to a one-sided vicious caricature, but in the RSC production Helen Mirren created greater depth. At first the amorous and erotic were immediately apparent in the opening meeting with Henry. They fall in love at first sight, in spite of Margaret's association with Suffolk. Indeed, taking a cue from the end of *1 Henry VI*, Margaret agrees to the murder of Gloucester in compliance with Suffolk's machinations. Helen Mirren kept up a youthful innocence in the midst of the Machiavellian English nobles.

For example, when Gloucester is forced to resign his staff and leave the royal presence, Margaret's first line 'Why, now is Henry King and Margaret Queen' (2.3.39) was notably rendered by Barbara Jefford (at the Old Vic in 1958) in victorious exultation (which was to be repeated by Julia Foster in the BBC TV production of 1983). By contrast, Helen Mirren downplayed it, as if loving togetherness, rather than political supremacy, had been achieved. Again, when Henry reproves Margaret for her grief while cradling Suffolk's severed head – 'Thou wouldst not have mourned so much for me' (4.4.23) – Mirren's reply, 'No, my love, I should not mourn but die for thee', was genuinely meant, unlike for example the thinly veiled contempt of Julia Foster (BBC TV, 1983). Mirren explained her interpretation to Swander:

> Margaret is of course sexually involved with Suffolk, but she is utterly loyal to Henry. He is the King, and she has a deep belief in hierarchy. She would leave Suffolk in a minute for the King. Henry isn't what she expected, isn't what she wanted – she had wanted him to be her hero – but she has no doubt about his right to the throne. He is King, she is Queen, and that's that.

Not quite, as it turned out, since she went on to reveal the 'sub-text' she and Howard had worked out for their relationship –

'flagellation in the chapel' (Swander, 153), a remark which supports Hunter's observation about Stanislavsky above. To play Margaret in such a way means that it is not possible to play Henry as a 'holy fool'. There must be some depth corresponding to the nature of this Margaret's passion. The impression made by Alan Howard's achievement in this respect was quite remarkable (see Fig. 4).

This Henry was a man whose faith was not a politically incapacitating religiosity, but a visionary spirituality which set him apart from the evil scheming all around him. In the midst of violent madness Henry was the only sane man.

His sanity was emphasized by portraying the Yorks as demented sadists (drawing out the significance of York's own comment: 'You put sharp weapons in a madman's hands' (3.1.346), as the actor Emrys James explained (Swander, 154)).

4. Helen Mirren as Margaret and Alan Howard as Henry, with Ron Cooke as Suffolk, in Terry Hands's production with the Royal Shakespeare Company at Stratford, 1977

David Daniell noted the duplication of this madness in the scenes of the Mortimer *manqué*, Jack Cade, which were 'backed by a sort of mindless banner, the vacant grin of a silly turnip-lantern face with blood running down it. Emrys James makes York's claim wear an equally silly face, it being the mischievous whim of a black opportunist' (266). By contrast Alan Howard gave us 'a Henry who grows in inner power as he yields political power'. Terry Hands's more positive view of Henry in part derived from his experience of directing the same actor in the role of Henry V: 'the boy who develops has all his father's vision finally, and perception of what should be done, but lacks his father's physicality and the ability to carry it out by war, by the system that exists' (159, 162). For many this view might seem rather strained, but with the expulsion of Suffolk after Gloucester's murder Howard's full-voiced strength rose in a majestic, towering command which gave a glimpse of another Henry, and all that might have been. But the next major portrayal of Henry, on television, in what is known as the 'BBC Shakespeare', reverted to the conventional, yet in a powerfully unconventional production.

In the late 1970s BBC Television embarked on a project to produce the complete dramatic works of Shakespeare. For the most part conventional realism was the determining mode with a growing tendency for individual directors to try to outdo each other by suggestive compositional reference in set and scene to the style of famous Renaissance painters. Jane Howell's direction of the three parts of *Henry VI* and *Richard III* turned completely against this, and with her individual vision she created one of the finest versions ever of the first tetralogy.

Howell's first response to the trilogy was in terms of past theatre:

> You can see a development from very primitive, almost pageant wagon stuff up to the forerunners of the great tragedies. The verse changes; in the second play you feel as though Shakespeare's got in touch with Greek

5 The 'combat' scene (2.3), from Terry Hands' production with the Royal Shakespeare Company at Stratford, 1977

tragedy suddenly and is starting to understand those sorts of mechanisms.

(Schafer, 170)

For Howell the past enters into critical dialogue with the present: 'We felt it shouldn't be too medieval . . . we talked about Northern Ireland and Beirut and South America, about Warlords and factions' (Holderness, 'Radical', 221). To a considerable extent the approach was Brechtian. For example, in the death of Talbot and his son in *Part 1* (4.7), Howell saw not the fulfilment of heroic sacrifice but the inner contradiction of chivalric values – for 'sacrifice' read 'unnecessary slaughter' – given the political rivalry between York and Somerset which led to the failure to supply reinforcements. What is important about the death scene, for Howell, is not the pathos but the critical recognition provoked by the situation. We see this kind of Brechtian critique more subtly in the careful doubling of Howell's *2 Henry VI*, discussed below

(p. 24). The most striking and, indeed, most discussed aspect of the production was the set, which critics immediately identified as Brechtian anti-naturalism.

Oliver Bayldon, the set-designer, had pondered the idea of fairgrounds, circus rings and mystery plays, but was finally inspired by the sight of a children's adventure playground, in Fulham, West London: 'the wooden structure of palisades, steps, platforms, alcoves, walkways, gates, and swinging doors on, around and within which the actors work has been described as "a medieval adventure playground", and the director . . . remarked that it accidentally resembled "an Elizabethan theatre-in-the-round"' (S. Wells, 293). Critics were reminded of the fundamental principle of Brecht's epic theatre: 'defamiliarization', 'making strange', or the 'alienation' effect (*Verfremdungseffekt*) (see Bingham, 221–9). Fifteenth-century courtiers and soldiers were placed not against a naturalistic representation of castle chamber or battlefield, but against this strange assemblage of crude wooden structures. A major aspect of the set was the subliminal suggestion of childlike anarchy, role-playing, rivalry, game and vandalism, as if all culture were precariously balanced on the shaky foundations of atavistic aggression and power-mad possession. Ironically, the literal foundation of the set suggested a hallmark of modern middle-class domesticity – parquet flooring.

Parquet flooring (polished wooden blocks laid in a diagonal pattern) was the only one available. Bayldon thought 'Why not? It stops the set from literally representing a play-park – it reminds us we are in a modern television studio' (Fenwick, 20). Another Brechtian feature was the deliberate avoidance of stars, thereby furthering ensemble acting, and the encouragement of an acting style opposed to Stanislavsky's psychological naturalism. As Howell put it: 'A lot of the work is to say, "Look, what is the line, what is the intellectual sense, *play* the intellectual sense, stop mucking about with emotions, let the emotions follow the intellect". You have to go that way round rather than doing all this method nonsense' (Fenwick, 24). But the text was respected, as in Terry Hands's production, and given virtually uncut (only 5 per cent was omitted, as indicated in the published version).

Jane Howell saw the dominant pattern of the tetralogy as a descent from chivalric values to bleak slaughter. Accordingly, close attention was paid to increasingly sombre colour (in this respect Barton–Hall and Hands had set a precedent). For example, by *2 Henry VI* all the bright plumes have gone and the colourful tabards have been darkened by a grey spray; costume gives way to practical clothing as the almost inflated, American football-type armour of *Part 1* becomes closer-fitting metal (Fenwick, 18–19). To represent this decline careful attention was paid to the battle sequences. In *Part 1* almost cartoon-like use was made of the swing doors designed by Oliver Bayldon, by means of which defeat following triumph was almost comically instantaneous (Manheim, 'Plays', 295). In *2 Henry VI* the fighting gets dirtier with kneeing, and shields being used for aggressive attack rather than defence (use of Q's version of York and Old Clifford's deadly encounter at St Albans – TLN 2153–60 – would have supported this, but Howell retained the magnanimous exchanges of F, 5.2.20–4). Howell was probably aware of the occasional criticism that had been voiced against some of her predecessors for the indiscriminate monotony of battle scenes. Here in *2 Henry VI* the film technique of montage was used, particularly at the close of battle to represent with great effect the mangled bodies of the slain. G. K. Hunter noted that one of the patterns of the first tetralogy is that of the 'pack', the animal-like hunting of a group to bring down an individual – Gloucester, Lord Saye and eventually Henry ('*Henry VI*', 105–6). This idea of the irresistible pack was brought out very powerfully in Howell's Cade scenes: 'We had killings where Cade's followers don't fight man-to-man like soldiers; they just go in a pack and pull people down and kill them' (Fenwick, 22).

Howell's genius was to recognize that the television medium could be used actually to complement the metadramatic. Her conception of Jack Cade was of a medieval Lord of Misrule, which was fully realized not just by Trevor Peacock's brilliant acting, but by the camerawork: 'in the burning of "all the records of the realm", with Cade's exultant grimaces superimposed upon shots of slaughter, torture, and the pages of books torn up, cast into the air, and floating down onto a bonfire, [these scenes] have so timeless an impetus and vitality that they might belong to a modern play conceived entirely in televisual terms' (S. Wells, 294). Yet Howell boldly followed the Elizabethan theatre convention of the aside, here spoken directly to the camera, to add to the overall Brechtian technique (Bingham, 225).

Equally Brechtian, and Elizabethan, but much more subtle, was the doubling. The *dramatis personae* of the BBC publication gives details of the doubling, which is of particular importance for the Jack Cade scenes. Trevor Peacock played both Talbot and Jack Cade, while David Burke played Gloucester in *Parts 1* and *2*, Dick the Butcher in *Part 2*, and Catesby in *Richard III*: 'a careful doubling: all three parts are in a sense aides-de-camp to a ruler – Gloucester is Henry VI's Lord Protector, Dick is the rebel Cade's lieutenant, Catesby is Richard's right-hand man' (Fenwick, 23, 28–9). Differences in character give way to the burlesque possibilities of travesty and inversion in seeming likeness of role.

In great contrast to Terry Hands's work with Alan Howard and Helen Mirren as Henry and Margaret, which owed more to the New York Actors' Studio than to history, Jane Howell was true to her Brechtian inspiration in putting situation before character. Peter Benson, as Henry, with his gaunt sensitive features framed by lank hair, seemed like a figure straight from the monastic Middle Ages rather than the twentieth century: innocently pious, gently saintlike, childishly trusting, but hopelessly inept at the business of kingship. This portrayal closely followed the consistent implications of Henry's dialogue – there is hardly an utterance that is without some religious reference. Drama derives not from depth of characterization but from the political vulnerability of Henry's accession and marriage at a crucial phase of the Hundred Years War with the inherited problems of the Plantagenet dynasty. Comparably, Howell's Margaret, Julia Foster, was directed with a powerful singularity, though what now appears obvious went unremarked by the reviewers and critics, as far as I am aware. Julia Foster is of short stature. Her character, Margaret, is the daughter of a petty princeling, Reignier, who tries to make up for his lack of a kingdom with a string of empty titles. All her life this Margaret has been literally looked down on and her family laughed at, but through the combination of chance, politics and diplomacy, she finds herself Queen of England. Yet no sooner does she ascend the throne than she finds that she is looked down on once again and laughed at by her English courtiers, with a husband incapable of insisting on her status. Consequently, apart from the love relation with Suffolk, Julia Foster's Margaret was completely driven by the compulsion to realize her self-worth as first lady, if not first person, of the realm, which was to be passed on to, and shared with, her son. This inner anger emerged in a particular way, with Julia Foster's enunciation. Speech for

6 Julia Foster as Queen Margaret in Jane Howell's BBC production

Margaret was something systematically masticated to be either consumed or spat out, as if she were ritualistically cannibalizing the addressee. Jane Howell's completion of the tetralogy at the end of *Richard III* with Margaret cackling uncontrollably atop a huge pile of corpses, cradling the bloody deformity of Richard's body, was true to this conception, if not to the text.

'The National Front is a very Cade-like thing', said Trevor Peacock, looking back on the social unrest in Britain of the early 1980s (Fenwick, 27). Just a few years later Michael Bogdanov explored precisely this analogue in his production of *The Wars of the Roses* (1987–9) with the English Shakespeare Company. Bogdanov came to the *Henry VI* plays after successfully producing *The Henries* (1986), the Prince Hal plays. *Richard II* was added and the whole version of the two tetralogies went on tour. Fortunately, a video recording was made at the Grand Theatre, Swansea. The three *Henry VI* plays were cut and adapted to two: *Henry VI: House of Lancaster* and *Henry VI: House of York*. Bridging parts were written in for clarification. The *House of Lancaster* ends with the death of the Cardinal, and Suffolk lynched by the commons, while the Cade rebellion is carried over to the *House of York*. MacD. P. Jackson generalized: 'The episodic ups and downs of the trilogy's power struggles . . . lack dramatic shape – or the kind of dramatic shape that might fully engage a modern audience, even one reconciled to Brecht' (212). Versions of this kind of thinking, well supported by some critics, are regularly voiced, and attention drawn to the practical difficulties of staging complete texts. But note how, when (for example) Terry Hands in 1977 allowed the 'plays' to speak for themselves (and the audiences to make their own judgement), a structure emerged: 'There are three "inner plays", one in each part (Talbot, Jack Cade, and the three York brothers), and a "superplay" of all three parts and four main characters (Henry, Margaret, Warwick, and York) that is led by such others as Suffolk, Gloucester, and Winchester' (Swander, 149–50).

Michael Bogdanov, however, not only adapted plots by the

usual cutting, but engaged the audience at a level of visual presentation that once again reinforced his credentials as a radical director of the Left. The primary signifiers were the various costumes, civil and military, chosen from the pre- and post-World War I eras: 'Henry VI and his council looked like figures from pre-1914 photographs. Edward IV hinted variously at both Edward VIII and George VI . . . The war in France and the Wars of the Roses represented a merging of the first and second World Wars' (Potter, 'Recycling', 173). In my view Paul Brennen as the very boyish Henry, almost permanently got up in ceremonial military dress, with his neatly flattened hair, looked like the Duke of Windsor before his abdication. Presumably this was the point – as we see in *3 Henry VI*, Henry longs for pastoral retirement. The variety of hinted historical comparisons meant that the audience re-read the fifteenth century in terms of the twentieth (and vice versa). In Bogdanov's *Henry V*, reinterpreted in the decade of the Falklands War, as the English soldiers march off for the battlefields of France they unfold a banner inscribed 'Fuck the Frogs'. In the *House of Lancaster*, given Suffolk's love language, it comes as something of a shock to find that an actress rather far from the attractive bloom of youth has been cast as Margaret. The actress, June Watson, has sharp features matched by an equally sharp voice, and here as Margaret she had a puzzlingly contemporary kind of matronly coiffure: a Margaret for a Margaret, Margaret of Anjou as Margaret Thatcher, both bringers of misery and suffering to England, according to Bogdanov's politics (see I. Armstrong). 'Bogdanov's direction is everywhere infected by a contemporary skepticism about all political action and by a profound pessimism about Thatcher's Britain.' His view of the *Henry VI* plays is of an 'unrelievedly bleak, corrupt, and predatory Britain . . . with its culmination in the monstrous, comic-grotesque world of *Richard III*' (MacD. P. Jackson, 210).

The comic-grotesque was certainly anticipated by the Jack Cade scenes of the *House of York*. Michael Pennington first appears as Suffolk but doubles as Jack Cade and appears garbed in Union Jack vest with the white rose of York at its centre. After the slaughter of the Staffords he dons a gleaming cavalry helmet and enters beneath heads aloft on poles with his supporters bearing Union Jacks (see Fig. 7). Intermittently, they all give way to football-hooligan chanting. As Lois Potter noted, a particularly nasty aspect of the conflation of Cade and National Front demagoguery is the slaughter of the Clerk of Chartham. Here he is a middle-class flag-waving *supporter* of the mob suddenly plucked from its midst ('Recycling', 180). As Isobel Armstrong suggested, 'the brutalization which is the result of oppression can actually appear to justify the ruthless power exercised to control it' (11).

Some twenty-five years after Peter Hall's *The Wars of the Roses*, a successor at the Royal Shakespeare Company turned

7 Jack Cade and the rebels, with Michael Pennington as Cade in Michael Bogdanov's production with the English Shakespeare Company, 1987–9

again to the first tetralogy when Adrian Noble directed *The Plantagenets* at Stratford in 1988. This consisted of *Henry VI*, *The Rise of Edward IV* and *Richard III, His Death* (*The Plantagenets*). Charles Wood, a British dramatist who has specialized in writing war plays, collaborated with Noble on the adaptation. Noble and Wood regarded their work on the texts as similar to the practice and principles that Shakespeare applied to his historical sources: 'the clear narrative convenience of reducing the number of protagonists the audience is asked to follow . . . the dramatic advantages of shape and focus achieved by running several events into one . . . the need to simplify the actuality of politics both to enhance and illuminate the dramatic stature of an individual and also to marshall the events in order to achieve a particular dramatic effect' (*The Plantagenets*, viii). An example of the last-named effect is given citing Act 2, scene 7 of *Henry VI* (*The Plantagenets*) in which Eleanor is sentenced to banishment, the conjurors are executed and York completes his long soliloquy (begun at the end of scene 6) describing his plans for Cade's rebellion (i.e. running together 2.3.1–15 and 3.1.333–83 of *2 Henry VI* – everything in between, including the armourer combat scene and Eleanor and Gloucester's leave-taking scene, is cut). In what has become standard for adaptations, *Henry VI* ends with the Cardinal's death – but with an added visual grotesquery here, he is covered with leeches – and *The Rise of Edward IV* begins with Cade's rebellion. Just occasionally material written into productions can satisfyingly answer niggling questions. Why is it that in *2 Henry VI* Eleanor does not ask the witch what is to be the fate or fortune of her husband, Gloucester? But Bogdanov and Noble satisfied our curiosity. Here is Noble's equivocating version:

> ELEANOR: What dost thou prophesy of Gloucester's house?
> MARGERY JOURDAIN: Why, Gloucester shall be king, Gloucester king.

> (*The Plantagenets*, 63)

Sometimes the smallest cut or addition can alter the critical response to a scene, which in turn can add to the interpretation of the play as a whole. For example, one of Jane Howell's very small cuts was Iden's anticipation of 'the honour' he will receive for killing Cade (4.10.59–63), though her version goes on to include Iden's delivering Cade's head to the court and Henry's knighting him. Critics ponder whether Shakespeare's scenes show Iden's seeming capitulation to ambition and power in forsaking modest pastoral retirement, or whether rather his action is emblematic of loyalty and duty. Noble, however, cut both Iden's lines and all of Act 5, including Iden's knighthood.

Adrian Noble had no particular innovatory vision, but strongly resisted the notion of Shakespeare as a spokesman for Tudor orthodoxy. For him, Shakespeare's humanitarian impulse was moralistic, and at times didactic, in abhorrence of war and anarchy. Lois Potter, in contrasting *The Plantagenets* with the English Shakespeare Company production, noted the 'constantly stressed . . . power of the irrational', as if there were some inhuman process like Jan Kott's 'Grand Mechanism' at work, and seemingly hinted at in Bob Crowley's sets as the huge sun of York gives way to the great black serrated cog or saw of Richard III's reign ('Recycling', 176). Noble's view of the plays was not simply confined to the moral or political. There is a metaphysical and poetic aspect to Shakespeare's play which often leads critics to compare *2 Henry VI* with *Macbeth*. Unquestionably, Noble and Charles Wood 'were intrigued by . . . Shakespeare's universe, a cosmos with an active and real demonology where this earth was an active battleground in the fight between good and evil' (*The Plantagenets*, xii. Cf. Hibbard, *Making*, 24–32).

In his introduction Noble speaks of the Cade insurrection as 'a Peronist rebellion' which Shakespeare contemptuously satirized; he feels that the rebels want 'strong government and a revival of national pride' (*The Plantagenets*, 9). Yet at crucial moments the stage imagery could, in a sense, contravene this view. In rehearsal Noble fully developed the stage positioning of his actors before involving Bob Crowley as designer: 'The emphasis was continually on how to use the acting company as a tool of narrative, how to create vivid, poetic images with human bodies, rather than scenery. Only at a later stage, after the whole production had been "blocked", did Bob Crowley design the sets as eventually seen' (*The Plantagenets*, xiii). Accordingly, Noble created one particularly horrendous image. In the full text the heads of Lord Saye and Crowmer are carried aloft on poles by the rebels (4.7). Saye and the references to Crowmer are cut in Noble's text but on stage he had Oliver Cotton as Cade and followers enter with as many as *twelve* heads waving above the gloating rebels (see Fig. 8). The symbolic justification for this derives from the texts of *2* and *3 Henry VI* in which the severed head (Suffolk, Saye, Crowmer, York, Somerset) is just part of the bloody violence throughout. But does that violence derive from the human or the metaphysical?

Alan Sinfield's programme note for the RSC production argued for a radical interpretation: the power system was 'man-made, historically rooted rather than timeless, and capable of change', and Cade offered a parody of the power-hunger and ambition of the nobles (see Potter, 'Recycling', 178). It will be argued below (pp. 101–5) that the function of humour is crucial to any radical reading, just as Lois Potter notes of the Brechtian quality of the Simpcox episode in both Bogdanov's and Noble's versions: 'it balances Gloucester's "judgement" on Simpcox against the judgement soon to be pronounced on him, shows that the couple perpetrated their fraud for "pure need", and, by making Queen Margaret laugh when Simpcox is whipped, ensures that we will be uncomfortable if we have just done so ourselves' ('Recycling', 179).

A touchstone for the characters and the relationship of Henry and Margaret is the scene where the distressed Queen cradles the head of Suffolk (4.4), as we have seen with the 1977 (RSC) and 1983 (BBC) productions. Robert Smallwood caught this very well

8 Jack Cade and the trophies of slaughter, in Adrian Noble's production with
the Royal Shakespeare Company at Stratford, 1988

in Noble's production. Of Ralph Fiennes as Henry, he writes, 'he
conveys precisely the right suggestion of inner strength in his
political ineptitude, and a strange tenderness, too, for his volatile
queen'. Fiennes is neither the holy fool nor moral visionary of
his predecessors. Smallwood sensitively preserves the moment –
and its implications – when Fiennes's Henry is tested by the
behaviour of the Queen (Penny Downie) with the head.

The look of reproof, mixed with pity and understanding, that he gives her as she sobs her grief over the head
of Suffolk, and her surprised, uncertain recognition of
this, give some possibility of substance to her claim that
she would die for Henry while she only mourns for
Suffolk and suggests also that her motives for fighting
the Lancastrian cause may not all be based on material
obsession with her son's inheritance.

(Smallwood, 90)

The enhanced understanding of the Quartos and the subsequent
textual advance in understanding the Folio *Henry VI*s (see pp.
121–25), along with revived critical interest in the postwar years,
led to productions of further adaptations and performance of the
full text in both the old and new media – theatre and television. At
last the *Henry VI* plays proved themselves in modern revival as
great drama of the Renaissance period.

CRITICISM

Augustans to German Romantics

Though, as we have seen, John Crowne's adaptations gave evidence of a performance tradition, nothing remains from the
seventeenth century which could be considered as criticism of *2
Henry VI*. Indeed, when we turn to the eighteenth century we
find that in the burgeoning world of literary criticism discussion
of the English history plays is taken up almost entirely with the
question of Falstaff (see Knowles, *Henry IV*, 15–29). Of the few
surviving comments on *2 Henry VI*, the following two on the
death of the Cardinal indicate what the play was chiefly celebrated
for then, and anticipate the continuing response in the Romantic
period. In *Some Account of the Life of Mr William Shakespeare* pre-
fixed to his six-volume edition of the works (1709), Nicholas
Rowe observes: 'There is a short Scene [3.3] in the *Second Part of
Henry VI* which I cannot but think admirable in its kind. Cardinal

Beaufort, who had murder'd the Duke of *Gloucester*, is shown in the last Agonies on his Death-Bed with the good king praying over him. There is so much Terror in one, so much Tenderness and moving Piety in the other as must touch anyone who is capable either of Fear or Pity' (B. Vickers, 2, 199). Edward Capell put it more succinctly: 'The scene has never been equal'd on any theatre, never will be' (B. Vickers, 6, 221). The death of the Cardinal was a favourite subject for eighteenth-century printers and illustrators – Reynolds and Fuseli (see Fig. 9) for example – and was caricatured by Gillray (see Bate, *Constitutions*, 51–3). Elsewhere in the eighteenth century Dr Johnson comments on Warwick's description of the murdered Gloucester, 'I cannot but stop a moment to observe that this horrible description is scarcely the work of any pen but Shakespeare's' (B. Vickers, 5, 130), and Francis Gentleman raises an objection to the rebels on behalf of a polite bourgeois audience: 'We more cordially wish the whole of

9 *The Death of Cardinal Beaufort*, by Henry Fuseli

this crew suppressed than any character or passages we have met in our author; for though *Jack Cade* and his associates are essential to history, and might have created a real tragedy, they are miserable members to compose parts of one for representation' (B. Vickers, 6, 104).

One of the most influential of nineteenth-century critics, A.W. Schlegel, repeated the acclaim of Rowe and Capell for the Cardinal's death scene: 'it is sublime beyond all praise' (419). Schlegel's teminology points to the neoclassical aesthetics of Longinus in the late eighteenth century which provided a foundation for both English and German Romanticism, the latter represented by Schlegel in his famous lectures of 1808. Like a number of early German critics, Schlegel had no doubt about Shakespeare's sole authorship of all the English history plays, including the three parts of *Henry VI* and *Henry VIII*. What other author, he asks, 'was capable of inventing, among many others, the noble death-scenes of Talbot, Suffolk, Beaufort and York?' (442).

Belief in the unity of the plays enables Schlegel to see in them an epic accomplishment: 'I say advisedly *one* of his works, for that poet evidently intended them to form one great whole. It is, as it were, an historical heroic poem in the dramatic form, of which the separate plays constitute the rhapsodies' (419). Schlegel places *2 Henry VI* within the overall cyclic pattern of a curse, beginning with the usurpation of Richard II, and ending with the expiation of Richard III's death, thus initiating 'the Tudor myth' which came to be most often associated with the name of E. M. W. Tillyard.

Hermann Ulrici voices a similar view: England and the Lancastrians lay under a curse of usurpation which was finally lifted and redeemed by God's judgement and guidance in the pattern of history (2, 185–6, 291–2). These ideas, however, are just part of the Kantian aesthetics and Hegelian historicism which shape Ulrici's view of *2 Henry VI* and, indeed, all the histories. For Ulrici, following his philosophical mentors, history is

shaped by a teleological purpose of ethical and aesthetic realization which works through the 'tragic pathos' of such deaths as
Gloucester's, and the 'comic paralysis' of the Cade insurrection,
to ideal truth and beauty. The inner significance of historical
events, the true nature and meaning of history, is partly embodied in characters and actions. Thus though Henry's spirituality
appears pathetically at odds with the prevailing brutality, in fact
it furthers the organic inner movement of history by which the
Wars of the Roses weakened the barons and contributed to the
decay of feudalism and thus to the triumph of a nation-state.

For Ulrici 'energy' is the dynamic of historicism apparent in
both good and evil, though the latter is ultimately self-
destructive, thereby enabling the success of the good. Therefore
every event in *2 Henry VI* – plots, assassinations, battles, con-
frontations – is shaped by this Manichean conflict which is
subjected to a higher theodicy. This historicist vision enables
Ulrici to place Queen Margaret within a larger framework:

> this energy and enormity [of Margaret], this shameful dis-
> play of evil [was required by the poet as] an embodiment
> of the prevailing vices and crimes, a character in which was
> concentrated the whole demoralisation of the age . . . to
> unfold the meaning and significance of his drama.
>
> (2, 269)

This significance attached to even such minor comic scenes as
those of Horner and Peter, Simpcox the fraud, and Jack Cade and
his followers: these scenes are 'full of significance', Ulrici writes,
they 'form a parody on the substance of the historical action, and
exhibit – much in the same manner as the Falstaff episode in
"Henry IV." – evil as irrational, stupid and ridiculous, which, in
reality, it always is, in spite of its deep serious significance' (2, 268).

Unfortunately Ulrici does not elaborate on this point since it
is fully developed in his account of Falstaff (2, 241–4; Knowles,
Henry IV, 37–40). In brief the multifaceted creation of Falstaff
parodies feudal chivalry and Machiavellian policy rolled into one,

the ideal and the real of the late medieval–Renaissance world. Ulrici's remarks on comedy and parody in *2 Henry VI* are a hundred years ahead of their time and will be developed in the reading given below (pp. 80–106). Again, just in passing, Ulrici anticipates the influential developments of feminist theory in his aside on gender and role reversal in *2 Henry VI*: 'the character of the king, which had become effeminate and unmanly, required, as an organic contrast, a woman who had become masculine and depraved in character' (2, 269). In our own age, though the validity of historicist thought has been vigorously attacked, it still nevertheless survives as an element in modern theory, in a degree of hypostatization found in Cultural Materialism and New Historicism (see Popper). The measure of Ulrici's accomplishment in arguing for the towering significance of *2 Henry VI* and the first tetralogy can be seen if we turn to Hazlitt's comments on the plays: 'During the time of the civil wars of York and Lancaster, England was a perfect bear garden . . . The three parts of *Henry VI*. convey a picture of very little else' (Howe, 4, 292).

In Ulrici's principal successor as commentator on Shakespeare, Georg Gervinus, voluminous as his work is, we find a narrower approach in the nineteenth-century preoccupation with character which also tends to typify English criticism of the period. Yet Gervinus's overall sense of a national historical drama, typical of German criticism, goes beyond the limited moralism of Victorian and Edwardian commentators. Gervinus rejects both the unique claim by Johann Tieck, Shakespeare editor, leading Romantic poet, novelist and critic, that the *Henry VI* plays surpass in conception *all* Shakespeare's other works, and Ulrici's admiration for the design of the trilogy. Whereas Ulrici had made profound suggestions about seemingly minor scenes, like that of the Simpcox fraud, Gervinus dismisses their importance as having 'very slight connection with the great course of the whole' (119). Gervinus simply asserts that Shakespeare followed the narratives of Hall's and Holinshed's histories, without paying any attention to

Shakespeare's additions, omissions and conflations of character, scene and dialogue. The fact that the Simpcox story derived from Sir Thomas More by way of Grafton or Foxe (see 2.1, headnote) should have given food for thought. Yet in examining Shakespeare's reliance on his sources for the Cade scenes, Gervinus is most observant. He points out Stowe's acknowledged debt to the fourteenth-century chronicler Thomas Walsingham for details of the Wat Tyler insurrection of 1381 (120), which duly reappeared in the second edition of Holinshed, and which Shakespeare used in his presentation of Cade. Yet Gervinus, having noted the source, doesn't see the larger critical implications of Shakespeare's leaving out mitigating details of Cade's agenda for rebellion to stress more emphatically the damning identification with 1381.

In contrast to Ulrici's historicism, Gervinus partly sees the Cade rebellion as reflecting the larger pattern of divine retributive justice begun by the usurpation and death of Richard II. In *2 Henry VI* Gervinus instances the fall of Eleanor and the death of Gloucester, but it is rather unclear how the latter's perishing through 'weakness' can be part of this pattern, just as Ulrici admits that Margaret 'passes unscathed', which some might think leaves the notion of retributive justice open to question. Again Gervinus equivocates when the Cade rebellion is seen as a 'retributive judgement' on the aristocracy for the 'suffering' and 'oppression' to which the rebels have been subjected by their betters. Since God appears to side with the rebellion here, Gervinus quickly shifts his ground by implying the rebels' failure was brought on them by their own 'fury and folly' (120–1).

The rest of Gervinus's comments on *2 Henry VI* take an unusual direction by comparing the Q and F versions. Gervinus works on the revisionist assumption that *The Contention* was probably written by Greene and F represents Shakespeare's 'improving hand' (see pp. 106–10). Gervinus does not concern himself with bibliographical or ethical questions, but simply studies the two versions in terms of character. In doing so he indirectly reflects on the problems of what is lost in reductive adaptation, past and present. For example, in Q he sees Gloucester as only 'sketched' and Henry as merely a background figure. Gervinus invites the reader to compare the farewell scene between Gloucester and Eleanor for the greater subtlety of psychology and emotion in F. He draws attention to the F additions to the scene of the attack on Gloucester (1.3) in the Duke's passion and tragic confidence in the integrity of his innocence. Shakespeare's addition to the scene of Henry's defence of the Protector and yet his failure to save him is arrestingly praised by Gervinus in the following way: 'Greene placed the King as a cypher silently into the background, but Shakespeare drew him forth and delineated his nothingness' (127). It is to Gervinus's credit that he never totally removes character from scenic context, but draws attention to the dramatic function of additional F dialogue. In the course of his discussion he gets close to an illuminating paradox. At the outset he had stressed Shakespeare's dependence on chronicle narrative, but later in a comparison with Greene he recognizes that Shakespeare 'generally appears greatest just where the chronicle leaves him' (122).

Victorians and Edwardians

The reverence with which Shakespeare was regarded in Germany in the nineteenth century encouraged publishers to allow critics like Schlegel, Ulrici and Gervinus to write their voluminous commentaries. By contrast, in England comments on *2 Henry VI* and the trilogy, until the watershed of Peter Alexander's and Madeleine Doran's studies, are found only sparsely in surveys which, at times, mention them almost grudgingly.

W. J. Courthope is an exception since, within the space allowed to the *Henry VI* plays in his *A History of English Poetry* (1903), he adds suggestively to earlier critical commentary, and he also provides an appendix in which he challenges the disintegrationist view of the Quartos in Malone's *Dissertation* (see pp. 108–9). In *3 Henry VI* Richard of Gloucester undertakes to 'set the murtherous Machevil to school' (3.2.193). The 'Machevil' is most often associated with the Marlovian anti-hero, but here we have one of only three references in Shakespeare (see also *MW* 3.1.92 and *1H6* 5.4.74). Courthope summarizes, 'The whole tetralogy . . . forms a study of Machiavellism on a large scale, a dramatic comment on the theory "Might is Right" ' (65). Crime and evil, however, are punished by suffering and death at the hand of justice. Retribution by providence is not directly stressed, but Courthope suggests the metaphysical by glancing at the sources: 'his study of the chronicles may have revealed to him the profounder sense animating the arid personifications of Conscience and Justice in the old Moralities' (68). This kind of comment is a world away from such simple-minded denigration of the play for its formal artlessness, particularly in relation to the minor scenes, as that of C. F. Tucker Brooke. Similarly, in contrast to Courthope, Tucker Brooke's overall response derives from the shortcomings of King Henry: 'the essential inconvertibility of the politic and moral virtues, and the futility of attempting to pay off the great debt which the governor owes the governed with the small coin of personal piety or occasional generosity' (313, 317). As late as 1929 the charge of 'formlessness' appears once again, as H. B. Charlton reduces the Cade scenes to mere 'comic' interest in a lecture supposedly concerned with 'Shakespeare, politics and politicians', which gestures vaguely in the direction of 'pageantry', 'panorama' and 'patriotism' (8).

The minor scenes often draw the greatest variety and uncertainty of comment. For Schelling, the Simpcox and armourer combat scenes show 'promise' (without saying precisely of what), yet the Cade scenes could be dropped without impairing the epic quality of the play (83). By contrast, for Georg Brandes (24) the Cade scenes are what provide sure evidence of Shakespeare's hand (J. Dover Wilson claims they are by Nashe), whereas he feels that Greene supplied the Simpcox scene. We find such contrary views, not only between authorities but even

within the individual commentator. John Masefield seems confused to the point of self-contradiction. At first he states that the
action is interrupted and lightened by the Simpcox and Cade
scenes, and then he claims that the same scenes give rise to 'more
sadness and horror than humour' (55, 59). Perhaps Masefield
was struggling to find words for a dramatic experience that has
become so familiar by the end of the twentieth century in the
Theatre of the Absurd? Once again, Courthope provides some
illuminating and suggestive comparisons.

> Indicative above all of Shakespeare's wonderful growth
> in imaginative power are the admirable scenes represent-
> ing Cade's insurrection. Here, for the first time, the
> dramatist manifests his unequalled insight into the char-
> acter of the crowd. With something of the resolute force
> of Tamburlaine, Cade combines the absurd self-
> sufficiency and ignorance of Dogberry and Bottom, and,
> like those masterful personages, he is able to impose his
> will on his still more ignorant followers, some of whom
> are quite capable of measuring his pretensions.
>
> (Courthope, 69)

Courthope goes on to point out the comic and tragic elements in
the murder of Lord Saye. He is attempting to do some justice to
the Cade scenes by recognizing a level of generic complexity which
will be addressed in the critical discussion below (pp. 101–6).

Tillyard and the Tudor myth

The arguments of Peter Alexander and Madeleine Doran for seeing the Quartos of *2* and *3 Henry VI* as memorial reports of
Shakespeare's plays largely won the day (see pp. 122–5) and as a
consequence critics could pick up where the nineteenth-century
German commentators had left off and reconsider the English
histories in terms of holistic interrelationship and development.
In the Preface of what was to be by far the most influential study
of the subject, *Shakespeare's History Plays* (1944), E. M. W.

Tillyard acknowledged that Alexander's book 'has given me warrant for an opinion long entertained: that Shakespeare wrote all three parts of *Henry VI*' (vii). Later, after Sir Barry Jackson's presentation of the *Henry VI* trilogy at the Old Vic in 1953, Tillyard added that 'This production greatly confirmed my opinion that Shakespeare was the author and that he constructed massively and with thought' ('Cycle', 39; see Law, 'Links') – a somewhat curious claim, given the cut of eleven scenes that the Birmingham Repertory Company had made (Daniell, 250).

Tillyard hardly analyses Shakespeare's English history plays. Rather, he provides a kind of bifocal theory which, if accepted, determines how the plays are seen. He first provides a general framework of ideas and then he sets up a particular perspective. The year before *Shakespeare's History Plays*, Tillyard published *The Elizabethan World Picture* (1943). The latter is a small handbook of the cultural commonplaces of western Europe deriving from a synthesis of classical and Christian civilization. Cosmology (Ptolemaic) and biology, God and man – nature, society and history – are all linked together by correspondences in a great 'chain of being' regulated by the all-embracing providential principle of order and degree which is sustained by graduated hierarchies throughout earth and heaven. Essentially, this 'picture' of order and hierarchy as the divinely ordained nature of things provides a legitimating ideology for monarchism, autocracy and conservatism. The assemblage of conventional orthodoxies completely disregards the concrete particularity of sixteenth-century political, social, economic and intellectual history: namely, the Reformation and Counter-reformation; the rise of the centralized nation-state; the consolidation of the bourgeoisie in the movement from feudalism to capitalism; the resurgence of classical scepticism and the onset of scientific empiricism. Ironically, Tillyard's seeming all-inclusiveness is arrived at through a process of occlusion, as Hiram Haydn's alternative 'picture', *The Counter Reformation* (1950), was soon to show, with its examination of the conflicting forces of conservation and radicalism in religion, science, philosophy and politics.

Tillyard's general framework of ideas was given a specific ideological focus by linking 'providence' and 'order' with Shakespeare's primary sources for the English histories, Hall and Holinshed. From Edward Hall, particularly, Tillyard gleaned what has ever since been contentiously debated as 'the Tudor myth': this was the belief that, in the marriage of Henry Tudor and Elizabeth of York and their accession to the throne after Bosworth, the union of the houses of Lancaster and York bore witness to God's providential pattern in history's finally redeeming the land from the curse brought about by the usurpation, deposition and murder of Richard II. Tillyard had been preceded in these ideas by the work of Lily B. Campbell which was republished in book form as *Shakespeare's Histories: Mirrors of Elizabethan Policy* (1947). An equally important predecessor was Alfred Hart's *Shakespeare and the Homilies* (1934). The *Homilies* is the short title by which historians and critics usually refer to the two collections of Elizabethan sermons, subsequently published together and appointed to be read in churches. The tenth homily of the first collection, entitled 'An exhortation concerning good order and obedience to rulers and magistrates', contained the kernel of Tudor church and state orthodoxy, preaching the doctrines of the divine right of kings, non-resistance, passive obedience and the wickedness of rebellion. In 1573, following a rebellion in 1569, Pope Pius V's Bull of Deposition against Elizabeth I and rumours of an invasion of England, a lengthy new homily was added – 'Against disobedience and wilful rebellion'. The sanctity of order and degree espoused in these homilies was repeated in Shakespeare's English histories, so Hart believed, and Tillyard followed suit, frequently citing Ulysses' 'degree' speech in *Troilus and Cressida* (1.3.85–124) as an epitome of such doctrines.

Tillyard's *Shakespeare's History Plays* has remained very influential, since even many who consider its scholarship and criticism blinkered and tendentious nevertheless define their own ideas against it. Robin Headlam Wells provides a valuable summary in his essay 'The fortunes of Tillyard: twentieth-century critical debate on Shakespeare's history plays'. As an example of Tillyard's manifest shortcomings, Wells points out how, inexplicably, Tillyard completely ignored the leading commentators of his day – J. W. Allen's *A History of Political Thought in the Sixteenth Century* (1928) and George Sabine's *A History of Political Theory* (1937), which show the heterogeneity of Tudor political thought, including discussion of the all-important issue of the right of resistance against a despotic monarch.

Tillyard's method is to validate his *a priori* assumptions by turning to those parts of the text that appear to suit his hypothesis rather than empirically analysing the text as a whole to find just how much of the original hypothesis holds up. The extraordinary aspect of Tillyard's criticism is that upon examination his assessment of the first and second tetralogy, apart from some remarks on *Richard III*, is largely unfounded. Let us turn to the remarks on *2 Henry VI*. Apart from plot summary we learn that Jack Cade and his vanquisher Iden represent, respectively, anarchy and disorder, order and degree (153, 159). The micro–macro cosmic correspondence is illustrated by Henry's comment on the altercation between Gloucester and the Cardinal:

> How irksome is this music to my heart!
> When such strings jar what hope of harmony?
> I pray, my lords, let me compound this strife.
>   (2.1.55–7)

For Tillyard, this evokes 'the whole cosmic context . . . Here we have the duplication of uproar in macrocosm and microcosm, and the cosmos as a harmonious dance or a piece of music' (175). If Shakespeare's work is said to embody the imposing commonplaces of culture it seems surprising that this rather inconsequential instance is chosen to illustrate 'the Elizabethan world picture'. Elsewhere, as illustration of 'the curse incurred by the family of Henry IV from the murder of Richard II' (182), two deaths are cited. 'The judgement of God, invoked by Henry, is quick in striking two of Gloucester's murderers. Cardinal Beaufort dies in an agony of evil conscience, Suffolk is captured by a warship off the coast of Kent and put to death after the ship's captain has recited a list of his crimes' (183). It is by no means certain that the Cardinal dies as a result of contrition or remorse of conscience. He dies in physical pain after protesting that he would stand trial and seems to protest further that Gloucester died a natural death in bed. However, further pain makes him plead 'O, torture me no more! I will confess' (3.3.11). He certainly dies and such a death could, indeed, be seen as following upon Henry's invocation of divine judgement. Similarly, from a theological point of view it could be said that in Suffolk's death God works through second causes of human agency. But whether these deaths have anything to do with the usurpation of Richard II seems very dubious. Richard is mentioned only three times in *2 Henry VI*, by York in Act 2 (2.18, 26, 30), as he outlines his claim to the throne (see French, '*Henry VI*', xxxvii).

If the providentially-minded Tillyardian were to insist here on an all-encompassing chain of cause and effect, then one would have to say that in terms of the tetralogies as a whole King Richard's part in the murder of Thomas of Woodstock, Duke of Gloucester, was the original sin which began the cycle of death and retribution (see *Richard II*, 1.2.37–9). And this raises the prickly question of what a subject may or may not do when he sees his divinely appointed monarch, God's anointed deputy, acting as a murderous tyrant. Theological orthodoxy dictated that in no circumstances should a monarch be challenged, since God can act through a scourge, an instrument of his will (like Tamburlaine or Richard III) who is then in turn scourged. But sixteenth-century political history had raised awkward problems – what do Protestants do when persecuted by a Catholic king, and vice versa? And, at a simpler level, how should subjects act when rulers completely overturn the laws they are supposed to uphold? Furthermore, critics have argued that the catalogue of crime and murder in *2* and *3 Henry VI* calls into doubt God's providence and judgement, as much as, if not more than, affirming them. This is a convoluted and involved issue to which we shall return, since it remains a leading question in many discussions of the *Henry VI* plays. Whatever the limitations of Tillyard's interpretation, the issues that his approach raises remain important because they are so large and all-embracing: is there a discernible philosophy of history in the plays? Is there an ultimate providential order in the world, or how far is the so-called orthodoxy of the plays a Marlovian front for Shakespeare's Machiavellian vision of expediency as a necessary evil? One of Tillyard's gravest omissions is his bland dismissal of this last aspect – 'we do not need to give much heed to Machiavelli' (*History Plays*, 23) – even though the *Henry VI* trilogy contains Richard of Gloucester's promise to 'set the murtherous Machevil to school' (*3H6*, 3.2.194); cf. pp. 39–40.

Tillyard has had many followers, notably M. M. Reese, Irving Ribner, H. M. Richmond and Robert Rentoul Reed. And though in the 1960s and 1970s, criticism which severely qualified Tillyard's position was on the increase, as late as 1979 Robert P. Merrix mounted a defence in 'Shakespeare's histories and the new bardolaters'. Unfortunately Merrix shows no awareness of the critical and scholarly deficiences which prompted such criticism of Tillyard in the first place. Others at least gestured at a more complex vision. In his Preface M. M. Reese writes that 'Shakespeare was a poet, not a writer of political tracts, and no interpretation of his work can ignore the many-sidedness of his vision, that two-eyed scrutiny in which ideas of good and bad are called to no single account' (viii). In this Reese is probably influenced by one of the most important essays on Shakespeare's English histories, A. P. Rossiter's 'Ambivalence: the dialectic of the histories'. In his critique of Tillyard, Rossiter argued for an ambivalence in Shakespeare which 'causes an exact juxtaposition of opposites in the mind of the audience' (51), and may be seen most potently in 'the use of comic parallelism of phrase or incident.

That is, of parody, critically used; or of travesty-by-parallel' (46). Such an approach, in large part deriving from the concentration on ambiguity and irony of the New Criticism, seems to be echoed in Reese's 'many-sidedness' but what follows – particularly in 'The speciality of rule' (89–143) and 'The Shakespearean order' (111–20) – repeats the pieties of Tudor orthodoxy as spelt out by Tillyard. However, the date of Reese's book, 1961, is of interest since it just precedes the Barton–Hall production of *The Wars of the Roses*. This was in large part based on Tillyard's principles, which at the same time had been made cheaply available to the large and growing numbers of students in British universities in the 1960s when Penguin republished *Shakespeare's History Plays* under their newly inaugurated academic imprint, Peregrine Books, in 1962. It was reprinted in 1964, the year that *The Wars of the Roses* was produced on television and Jan Kott's *Shakespeare Our Contemporary* was published in translation.

For the academic world Irving Ribner provided the first specialist book-length study of *The English History Play in the Age of Shakespeare* (first edition, 1957), which was revised and reprinted in 1965. Looking at the *Henry VI* plays, Ribner, like Tillyard, stresses the background of miracle and morality drama, particularly the role of Respublica – England – as the suffering morality hero. Ribner accepts that 'Implicit in the *Henry VI* plays is a philosophy of history' (103), namely the providentially ordered scheme of retributive justice reflected in Tudor historians and the hierarchic structure of degree as reflected by Squire Iden (both found in Tillyard). Yet Ribner's reading of the *Henry VI* trilogy leads him into a paradoxical acceptance of Tillyard's promulgation of the 'Tudor myth': on the one hand Ribner believes that 'this myth Shakespeare incorporated into his *Henry VI* plays' (104), but within a page we read 'It is in part because Shakespeare emphasizes the sins committed during the reign of Henry VI rather than the initial crime against Richard II that I cannot share Tillyard's view that the

Henry VI plays and *Richard III* form one vast epic unit with the second tetralogy' (105). Presumably we are supposed to accept this intervening statement: 'although [Shakespeare] does not emphasize the deposition and murder of Richard II, that initial crime is nevertheless in the background' (105). This view might possibly be asserted following a historically chronological reading of the two tetralogies which begin with *Richard II*, but it is no more than an imposition which is in any case quite irrelevant to the *Henry VI* plays, whatever the order of their composition. The 'background' to *1 Henry VI* is primarily the legacy of the chivalric and territorial achievement of Henry V; the 'background' to *2 Henry VI* is largely the surrender of Anjou and Maine as part of Henry VI's disastrous marriage; by *3 Henry VI* background and foreground have merged in the strong Yorkist claim against Henry's Lancastrian genealogy and the total weakness of the King's grasp on the reins of power. I put it that what the *Henry VI* plays make us aware of is not in the least Richard's murder, but rather that under the conditions of feudal kingship the ramifications of genealogy and law in relation to inheritance and territory are impossible to control, given the individual's will-to-power (compare the topical readings of Erskine-Hill and Simpson). The aristocratic cohesion of chivalry was bound to fail since its ideals of loyalty, service and self-sacrifice did not reflect the harsh reality of human motives which were at least as likely to use, distort and rationalize, as well as betray, those same ideals as attempt to live up to them. However, Ribner joins Tillyard in a simplified reading and Jack Cade, for example, is seen as 'a perversion of all that Elizabethans held sacred', namely 'the divinity of kingship and the doctrine of passive obedience' (109).

A production of the two tetralogies helped to confirm another follower of Tillyard in a correspondingly holistic, organic overview of the eight plays. Robert Rentoul Reed saw the first television production of *An Age of Kings* (1961) and when writing his *Crime and God's Judgement in Shakespeare* (1984) he recalled the experience: 'To the recurring emphasis in *Richard II*, upon the theme of inherited guilt and, in consequence, upon the much later reign of Henry VI, in which that guilt is to be called into account, Shakespeare's eight-part historical epic, crystallized for us in *An Age of Kings*, owes both the basic unity and much of the structure that binds its parts into a sequence of coordinated events' (27). Again, it has to be said that this production involved 'drastic cutting' generally, including most of Talbot from *1 Henry VI* (see Crane, 324), and thus 'basic unity' here might seem more a contribution of the director than of Shakespeare.

Reed particularly builds on Tillyard's notion of retribution for the original 'crime' of Richard's deposition and murder. Rather than repeating an Elizabethan picture or Tudor homiletic orthodoxy, he spends considerable time in outlining the biblical sources for the conception of the retributive providence of God as revenge in the Tudor period. Once again we have a unilateral, homogenous sense of prevailing belief or orthodoxy. The religious and didactic materials Reed looks at are impeccably chosen, and that is precisely the point. For example, although Reed spends a few pages on *King Lear*, the work of W. R. Elton is not cited. Elton's masterly study *King Lear and the Gods* (1966) gathers together the voluminous evidence for the Renaissance revival of Epicurean thought in which the pagan philosopher espoused the complete indifference of the Gods to man, who was totally at the mercy of capricious Fortune without any comfort of divine providence.

For Reed the prophetic pronouncements of Richard and the bishop of Carlisle are sufficient: everything which follows derives from that first cause of usurpation; the *post hoc ergo propter hoc* fallacy ('after this, therefore because of this'), which every Renaissance schoolboy was taught to recognize. Pressing his thesis, Reed thus sees Gloucester in *2 Henry VI* not as defending the King from the malice and ambition of those around him, but as 'the final bulwark against God's inevitable retribution on behalf of King Richard' (106). In addition, as the son of the usurper Henry IV, the innocent Protector must suffer on that account, though not quite of the third generation of biblical retribution (Numbers 14.18) – a conceptual reinforcement Reed also draws on when faced by the deaths of the completely innocent, such as the princes in the Tower. Furthermore, to support his case in *2 Henry VI* Reed sees York's action as 'avenging the wrongs done another Plantagenet, Richard II' (110). At every step York makes plain that he acts to establish his right to the throne as legitimate heir, and the fact that Richard was its former occupant is irrelevant. Reed ignores the question of God's retributive justice seemingly overlooking Queen Margaret and the relatively painless death of Edward IV. However, many have argued that in *2 Henry VI* the Cardinal and Suffolk suffer the justice of God's immediate vengeance, as Reed notes: 'God's vengeance upon the evil doer himself . . . and not upon the heir, is an equally frequent and a much more supportable phenomenon than is the metaphysical justice by which God requires a later generation to pay for an ancestor's crime' (30). Much is implied by that word 'supportable'. Later Reed reminds us that 'it was God's traditional duty to avenge the unjustly slain' (126), such as Gloucester, Rutland or the princes in the Tower. Unwittingly, by subjecting providence to the logic of theological debate rather than appealing to the unquestioning acceptance of faith when faced with the Almighty's inscrutability, Reed opens up a deconstructive black hole. How can such murders be considered 'unjust' when they are part of divinely ordained justice? What justice is there in using evil to slay the good for a past crime for which the innocent could not possibly have any responsibility? St Augustine provided an answer to this, as we shall see, but whether the answer is acceptable is another thing. In arguing his case Reed has to refute those who in principle are ranged against him, the anti-providentialists like David L. Frey and A. L. French. Frey's book is dismissed without any examination of the *detail* of its arguments, and the key article by French is not even referred to. Both are discussed below (pp. 56–7).

Brockbank and the anti-Tillyardians

Like Tillyard, J. P. Brockbank saw the production of the *Henry VI* plays by Sir Barry Jackson at the Old Vic in 1953. But whereas Tillyard, writing his study during the war, affirmed an ultimate providential order ensuring the survival of this England (see Holderness, 'Agincourt'), Brockbank found an altogether more sombre reflection of the immediate past: 'here, it seemed, was yet another historical instance of anarchy owed to innocence and order won by atrocity' ('Frame', 73). This judgement opens the most influential single essay on the trilogy, 'The frame of disorder – *Henry VI*'. From the outset Brockbank, like Hermann Ulrici, discerns a causative agency in the relationship between historical process and the individual, a process revealed by the shape of the drama – the mould of man and monster, martyr and Machiavel, King Henry and Richard of Gloucester. Immediately the terms of Brockbank's critical approach supply the great omission of Tillyard's work, the all-important figure of Machiavelli.

Brockbank entitles the section of his essay on *2 Henry VI* 'The sacrifice of Gloucester and the dissolution of law', which anticipates the later critical focus of Edward Berry and Ralph Berry. There is the law of God, and the lawlessness of man: theology and history. Once more Brockbank anticipates the major developments in criticism by arguing that Shakespeare dramatizes the potential conflict between the opposing ideologies found within Tudor chronicle (a view which Phyllis Rackin was to develop later). On the one hand *Vindicta Dei*, the vengeance of an Old Testament God demanding retribution; on the other the Tudor historians writing

> in a tradition which had quietly assimilated the mundane, realistic attitude for which Machiavelli was to become the most persuasive apologist; and whenever they write with an eye on the prospect of Tudor security, they show themselves sympathetic to the 'machiavellian' solution – stability imposed by strong authority.
>
> (Brockbank, 82)

Brockbank does not write polemically, and up to a point his view evidently incorporates aspects of Tillyard, but then he can open up a completely different perspective with the cogent observation: 'In *Henry VI* the sacrificial idea, which makes catastrophe a consequence of sin, is sharply challenged by the "machiavellian" idea that makes it a consequence of weakness' (83), an irony particularly germane to *2 Henry VI* in which Gloucester's murder occurs largely because of Henry's timorousness. Though that murder appears to be avenged in Suffolk's death, the atrocity bears witness as much to the barbarism of men as to the providence of God, Brockbank argues, in circumstances of war and violence deriving not from the absent ghost of Richard II or Henry Bolingbroke's past usurpation, but from the actions of the men and women we see before us on stage. Brockbank thereby works round to a position somewhat complementary to that of Tillyard: rather than Shakespeare as apologist for the tenets of Tudor orthodoxy, he is seen as aghast at the fearful anarchy that proceeds from the 'dissolution of law'.

Brockbank draws attention to the dualistic aspect of Tudor chronicles, and much subsequent criticism has reinvestigated this area in relation to Tillyard's reading of a Tudor myth. Critics like H. A. Kelly and Robert Ornstein have gone back to Hall and Holinshed specifically to analyse Tillyard's claims, while many commentators have wished to reassess the whole idea of providence at work in history and in Shakespeare's plays. In a sense this movement culminates in David L. Frey's study, the only single book on the subject, the full title of which indicates his thesis, *The First Tetralogy: Shakespeare's Scrutiny of the Tudor Myth* (1976).

In *Divine Providence in the England of Shakespeare's Histories* (1970) H. A. Kelly undertook a complete re-reading of fifteenth- and sixteenth-century chronicles. Robert Ornstein published his *A Kingdom for a Stage* in 1972 and in his early chapter 'The artist as historian' closely considered the Tudor myth of Tillyard in relation to Hall and Holinshed. Ornstein's book must have gone to press as Kelly's was published since it does not include any reference to the latter. Broadly speaking, Kelly identifies three primary 'myths': the Lancastrian, the Yorkist and the Tudor. Put simply, writers of chronicles tended to favour whatever dynasty was in power at the time. The Lancaster myth regarded Henry IV's 'usurpation' as a providential blessing fully realized in the victories of Henry V. The York myth, conversely, saw providence bringing down the Lancastrians in favour of Edward IV. The Tudor myth could have different emphases depending on the consistency of the chroniclers and those who revised their work, Abraham Fleming for example, who revised the second edition (1587) of Holinshed, which Shakespeare used.

In one respect Kelly's detailed, assiduous study supports Tillyard. He finds that the deaths of Suffolk and the Cardinal in *2 Henry VI* do indeed appear to be punishments in retribution for Gloucester's death. But he cannot agree with the place of this in the larger framework of Tillyard's all-determining thesis. In this his findings are supported by Ornstein's independent research. Both note that Hall alludes to, or reports, the providential belief of 'others', for example the idea that Henry VI was punished by God for the offence of Henry IV, a view deriving from the biblical notion of sins being visited on the third generation (Numbers, 14.18) which Lily B. Campbell had found in Sir Walter Raleigh's Preface to his *History of the World* – an opportunistic rationalization, some might say, for the suffering of the completely innocent. But elsewhere Hall shows a distinctly sceptical attitude towards any claim to discern the divine at work in history, for example in his remark discerning 'man's fantasies' rather than 'divine revelation' (Kelly, 126). In Hall there is no pattern of retribution, and England is not cursed as a consequence of Richard's deposition: Hall is certainly against civil war and anarchy, but he does not appeal to doctrines of obedience, the sanctity of kingship or the sin of rebellion (Ornstein, 17). Neither Polydore Virgil nor Holinshed regards the Wars of the Roses as divine punishment (Kelly, 160). Hall actually shows admiration for Henry IV and is hostile to the rebels against him; yet later he

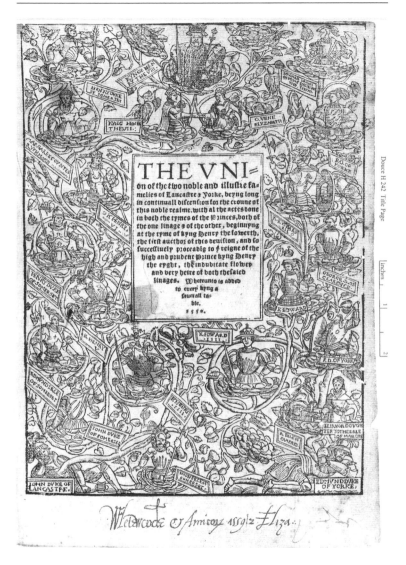

10 The houses of York and Lancaster, as shown on the title page of Edward Hall's *Union of the Two Noble and Illustre Families of York and Lancaster* (1550)

admits a providential significance in Henry VII's accession after Bosworth (Kelly, 112, 133–4).

Ironically, the Tudor myth as Tillyard conceives it can be traced back to one major source, the speech by the Duke of York to the House of Lords in 1460, reported by Hall (245–8). Hall invented this speech, in which York traces the pattern of God's punishment for Henry IV's original usurpation through the Lancastrian line in all the ensuing wars and rebellions until the Lords decided to restore the noble Duke to his rightful inheritance. However, Hall added his own deconstructive note when he made it readily apparent that the Cade rebellion came about not by God's providence but by the plots of the said Duke (Kelly, 121–5). Hall's version of history was taken up by Holinshed who thereby adopted the York myth which, in fact, conflicts with the Tudor myth in so far as Henry Tudor claimed the crown primarily through his Lancastrian inheritance while marriage to Elizabeth of York brought about the union of the red and white roses (Ornstein, 18–19). What Tillyard appears to have done is to turn to the chronicles after immersing himself in the orthodoxy of the *Homilies*, working backwards from the generally agreed Tudor condemnation of Richard III, ignoring any ironies or inconsistencies, and reimposing the Yorkist providential interpretation of history as his version of the Tudor myth. By contrast, according to Kelly, 'Shakespeare's great contribution was to unsynthesize the syntheses of his contemporaries' and to redistribute the Yorkist and Lancastrian myths between spokesmen of the two families, with Henry Tudor at the end of *Richard III* as the avowed Tudor mythologist (304–5).

Providence on trial

Though we may reject the Tudor myth reading of Shakespeare's histories as quite unsustainable, this does not make redundant the larger general question of God's providence, sin and justice in the first tetralogy generally, and in *2 Henry VI* in particular, since the Christian language of the King keeps it constantly echoing in our ears as our eyes witness crime after crime, murder after murder. It is far too limited to claim simply that 'God's intercession is repeatedly invoked, but only for the sake of dramatic irony' (Hamilton, 39). An alternative is to sidestep the Christian theological implications of Henry's appeal to God after Gloucester's death and to offer instead a pagan argument: 'the characters still exist in an ultimately ordered universe – although by no means as wholly subject to Providence as Henry imagines, or as the old morality plays had shown. Virtue may be destroyed often in the world of *Henry VI*, but Nemesis always overtakes the guilty' (Richmond, 46). But what of the sufferings of the innocent – of Henry, of the child Rutland in *3 Henry VI*, of the princes in the Tower in *Richard III* – and what of the question of divine *justice* when orthodox answers seem incommensurate with the more complex experience of the plays?

In a forthright article A. L. French ('Mills') bluntly assesses the providentialists' claims for the first tetralogy and finds that instances of unmerited suffering and death of the innocent, and the seeming lack of punishment meted out to some of the evil and guilty, amount to an arbitrary breakdown of justice and meaning which anticipates the great tragedies. Once again the death of Gloucester in *2 Henry VI* is adduced as evidence. For French, the disparity between the idea of providence and the manifest injustices we see before us on stage makes the plays 'devastatingly subversive' (323). Taking this approach a step further, David L. Frey provides unquestionably the most detailed comment to date. At the outset of his investigation Frey is very unusual since he goes against his contemporaries' general acceptance of Shakespeare's authorship of the quarto texts, after Alexander's and Doran's work, instead following C. T. Prouty's belief that *2 Henry VI* is Shakespeare's revision and expansion of *The Contention*, which is by another hand. (Frey ignores both Prouty's critics and Doran's argument for *The Contention* as an abridgement of F.)

The core of Frey's argument (2–3) is that a saintly Christian and God's anointed representative, King Henry, as well as many other innocents, suffer and die at the hands of evildoers without any sign of divine intervention. King Henry is the particular focus for Frey as he works through the differences between Q and F. The pattern he discovers is the consistent intention, particularly in 2.1 of *2 Henry VI*, to sharpen the opposition between 'Henry's innocence and his growing awareness of evil' (38). Like Edward Berry and Ralph Berry, Frey is drawn to the idea of the trial in *2 Henry VI*, but with a difference: 'Submerged in a myriad of pseudo-judicial proceedings, the real trial is Henry's,' namely, the 'serious trials of Henry's faith' (38). Which is another way of saying that it is God who is on trial. Henry, Gloucester and Lord Saye all believe in the self-defence of their own innocence. In the 3.2 variants between Q and F Frey notes the increasingly legalistic language of Henry in the latter, when he insists that Gloucester will clear himself of all charges. With report of the death of the Protector comes 'the central moment of the play, the turning point in Henry's fortune and faith' (43), as the eyes of the messenger, Suffolk, reflect 'murderous tyranny . . . in grim majesty' (3.2.49–50). A little later Henry acknowledges his suspicions of murder in arrestingly conditional phrasing: 'If my suspect be false, forgive me, God, / For judgement only doth belong to thee' (3.2.139–40). 'But what if he is right?' Frey asks, 'Is it then God who stands in need of pardon?' (44). Exactly at the time when Terry Hands was working with Alan Howard on the 1977 RSC reinterpretation of Henry's character to explore something rather more profound than the conventional saintly fool, Frey argued for a compassionate, not a cowardly king, attempting to sustain faith as all the ground on which it rests – the belief in divine providence – collapses beneath him.

Both A. L. French and David L. Frey argue with a conviction that derives from a modern humanist sensibility which refuses to countenance the logic of the death of innocents as part of a divine ordering of history. What both critics lack is the necessary recognition of the basic theological and ontological principles beneath early modern belief systems – above all, the implications of the Fall for God and man. Yet two critics, Michael Quinn and John Wilders, who do re-examine the basis of providential ideas in theology rather than their application in chronicle history, nevertheless arrive at different conclusions concerning *2 Henry VI* and the first tetralogy.

Both commentators quote Calvin's *Institutes*, I.xvi.9: 'the order, method, end, and necessity of events, are, for the most part, hidden in the counsel of God' (Quinn, 46; Wilders, 74). In a fallen world God's inscrutable wisdom is not available to man, but what appears from an earthly perspective to be capricious, arbitrary or even malign, by an article of faith is held to be not blind Fortune, but the all-seeing Almighty. God, as first cause, may intervene in the fallen world by way of evident miracles (Henry believes this of the Simpcox imposture, *2H6* 2.1.65–6); or he may use, as second cause, an evil person to scourge evil (like Richard III), who is then scourged himself. Most important for this conception of providence, which was handed down by the most influential of church fathers, St Augustine, is the recognition that retributive and distributive justice is not necessarily satisfied on earth but is fulfilled in heaven at the Last Judgement. H. A. Kelly, quoting Augustine, explains:

> 'Often, even in the present disposition of temporal things, does God plainly evince his own interference. For if every sin were now visited with manifest punishment, nothing would seem to be reserved for the final judgment; on the other hand, if no sin received now a plainly divine punishment, it would be concluded that there is no divine providence at all'. [St Augustine] draws the conclusion that when manifestly wicked persons suffer great afflictions, they are being punished by God; but when virtuous men suffer similarly, they are being benefitted by God. 'For even in the likeness of the

sufferings, there remains an unlikeness in the sufferers; and though exposed to the same anguish, virtue and vice are not the same thing. For as the same fire causes gold to glow brightly, and chaff to smoke; and under the same flail the straw is beaten small, while the grain is cleansed; and as the lees are not mixed with the oil, though squeezed out of the vat by the same pressure, so the same violence of affliction proves, purges, clarifies the good, but damns, ruins, exterminates the wicked'.

(Kelly, 3–4)

Quinn shows that in these circumstances men, and above all rulers, should not passively wait on God's intervention, and he cites William Thomas, sometime tutor to Edward VI, who 'warned his royal pupil that trust in God should not lead him to neglect "foresight" or "policie", for "miracles arr rare"' (46) – a view which Quinn applies to Henry in *2 Henry VI*. Quinn believes that Shakespeare's conception followed the distinction between a general and a particular providence. The eventual accession of Henry VII, from this point of view, represents the fulfilment of general providence overseeing the final providential outcome, whereas the deaths of the Cardinal and Suffolk are examples of particular providence – small details within the larger, general pattern (St Matthew's insistence, 10.29, that not a sparrow falls to the ground without the will of the Father is the best-known text on particular providence; see Calvin, *Institutes*, I.xvi.5). Quinn acknowledges that 'The good and innocent', like Gloucester and Lord Saye, 'can and do suffer', but 'The purpose and meaning of such apparently unmerited suffering, it would seem, remains "for the most part hidden in the counsel of God"' (51), for the greater good of general providence. Unwittingly, by admitting the sacrifice of the innocent as a means towards an end, Quinn has turned God into a Machiavel.

'[W]e are sinners all' (*2H6* 3.3.31) is the King's response to the Cardinal's death, testifying to perhaps the greatest commonplace of them all – inheritors of original sin, we are born into the fallen world. John Wilders's title, *The Lost Garden*, signals the all-pervasive, post-Edenic nostalgia found in Shakespeare for the lost innocence of a *locus amoenus*, be it Paradise or the Golden Age. At the end of his discussion of providence, in which, like Quinn, he considers thinkers from Boethius to Calvin, Wilders quotes the nineteenth-century German philosopher Schopenhauer, for whom the final nothingness of existence is inherently tragic in itself. Wilders is concerned with the continuity and development of Shakespeare, and thus in his view, 'The role of God in the history plays is comparable to that of the gods in *King Lear*: men hold conflicting views of Him and He remains inscrutable' (63). Wilders's God is a *deus absconditus*, a hidden God, certainly not to be found in *2 Henry VI*: 'for the world of the history plays like those of *Lear* and *Titus* is one from which the gods appear to be absent' (55). Wilders examines structural ironies, for example Henry's thanksgiving for the arrival of his bride – 'A world of earthly blessings to my soul' (1.1.22) – who is to be a curse on England, from a secular point of view (or a scourging agent of evil, if we accept the providential view, which in turn is challenged by a further scourge, Richard III). Wilders shows how sometimes Shakespeare juxtaposes King Henry's total incompetence with the notion of providence in such a way that the sardonic effect makes us reject any such appeal, as with the news of the total loss of French territories: 'Cold news, Lord Somerset; but God's will be done' (3.1.86). Like A. C. Hamilton and Moody E. Prior, Wilders claims that invocations of providence create dramatic irony, but his demonstration is the more impressive for taking into serious account sixteenth-century beliefs in providence.

If at this point we try to summarize what may have been the audience response to *The Contention* and *The True Tragedy* we have immediately to recognize the unacceptability of any singular unilateral reading which that word 'audience' implies. To an orthodox Christian the spectacle of evil largely extinguishing the good could have strengthened rather than called into doubt the need for redemption in a fallen world and the inscrutability of an unquestioned providence. St Augustine's extended discussion in *The City of God* (20.2) is possibly the greatest statement and needs to be read in full, though brief quotation must suffice here:

> But now, seeing that not only the good are afflicted, and the bad exalted (which seems injustice), but the good also often enjoy good, and the wicked, evil; this proves God's judgments more inscrutable, and His ways more unsearchable . . . [yet] when we come to that great judgment . . . there we shall not only see all things clearly, but acknowledge all the judgments of God, from the first to the last, to be firmly grounded upon justice.

A believer could take comfort from the apparent providence and fulfilment of prophecy in the deaths of the Cardinal and Suffolk. But for the sceptic in the audience, particularly any intellectual aware of Machiavelli and the Renaissance revival of Epicureanism and Pyrrhonism, much of *2 Henry VI* could be taken as a burlesque on the idea of providence, particularly in the expressed beliefs and language of King Henry (Champion). Possibly Shakespeare had the security of knowing that Marlowe had pushed such polarized possibilities to an extreme in *Tamburlaine 1* and *2* without, apparently, incurring censorship.

An almost wholly secular approach to *2 Henry VI*, which J. P. Brockbank anticipated with his subheading 'The dissolution of the law', is taken in the complementary chapters of Edward Berry ('*2 Henry VI*: justice and law') and Ralph Berry ('*2 Henry VI*: trial by combat'). Edward Berry notes how at the outset the pervasive legalism of *2 Henry VI* begins with the interrupted reading of the royal marriage contract by Gloucester, who becomes, as the personification of the humanist idea of the good governor, Berry's central figure, in antithesis to Jack Cade. Gloucester's unwillingness to bend to Machiavellian compromise and expediency leads to his murder but both before and after that, in the trumped-up charges and the subsequent inquest, we find a mockery of justice which leads to 'the banishment of Suffolk, a haphazard judgment at best . . . the first of a series of acts in which law and justice are turned on end' (4). Berry's interpretation of Cade's insurrection fits well into his overall approach since much of Act 4 displays grotesque travesties of legal proceedings, above all the centrepiece of the trial of Lord Saye, whose plea of innocence parallels that of Gloucester and whose fate, determined by the burlesque trial, parodies that of the Protector.

Ralph Berry sees 'The processes of a Trial – charges, investigation, arraignment, defence, verdict, sentence, and execution' as composing 'the pattern that orders *2 Henry VI*'. The number of trials is extraordinary – Eleanor, Simpcox, Gloucester, the Cardinal (of a kind), Suffolk, Horner and Peter, the Clerk of Chartham, Lord Saye and in a sense Cade's trial by combat with Iden. Trial by combat, both literal and metaphorical, is a paradigm for the larger action of the ensuing Wars of the Roses as a whole, and the battle of St Albans in particular, when 'What is at stake is a Trial, for both sides claim to be the keepers of right and justice . . . we can regard the battle of St Albans, and the entire play, as a Trial-by-Combat' (10, 11). If Berry's metaphorical approach is extended to the wider recognition that in *2* and *3 Henry VI* the 'trial' beneath the overt 'trial' is the contest between the conflicting ideologies of medieval providentialism and Renaissance Machiavellianism, then the basic imbalance of Tillyard's thesis may be redressed, and this, indeed, is what has taken place in recent years.

As we have seen, seemingly alone in the Edwardian period, Courthope had laid down the challenge that the first tetralogy 'forms a study of Machiavellism on a large scale, a dramatic comment on the theory "Might is Right"'. J. P. Brockbank elaborated on this in two crucial pages of his essay ('Frame', 82–3). Whereas he feels that in *Richard III* Margaret, as ahistorical prophetess of doom, and Clarence, as 'humane' protester against his assassins' theological self-justification, exemplify Shakespeare's ironic questioning of chronicle providence, 'In the *Henry VI* plays the chronicle theology is exposed to a different kind of test – that of the chronicle's own political ideology,' namely the creeping Machiavellianism of 'stability imposed by strong authority' (82). Brockbank's invitation here is complex and challenging and was taken up, in effect, by Frey, but only in part (the histories as 'scrutinizing' and rejecting chronicle providentialism). Michael Manheim (*Weak King*), in turn, takes up the Machiavellian issue. After discussing Brockbank's position, Manheim draws on Felix Raab's discrimination of a double standard in sixteenth-century political life: on the one hand the profession and observance of religious faith, on the other the ready compliance with the exigencies of *Realpolitik* – a dualism easily recognized throughout history. Indeed, Manheim goes one step further than Simpson's nineteenth-century topical reading and suggests that Shakespeare may have even modelled his characters on Machiavellian political contemporaries (80). Margaret, Suffolk and Cardinal Beaufort are the readily identifiable stage Machiavels for Manheim and though less obtrusive most of those around them have the mark of 'policy' on them in 'a court . . . dominated openly by sixteenth-century Machiavellian standards' (13), namely ruthlessness, deceit, violence and distrust. The rationalizations of 'law' and 'right' are merely 'veneers of crude power-rivalry' (82) in which the humanist service to the state of a Gloucester is sacrificed by rapacious Machiavellian self-serving (92). Margaret Scott singles out Suffolk's advice to murder Gloucester (*2H6* 3.1.257–9, 264–5) as 'thoroughly Machiavellian' (165).

In a study that is a major contribution to our understanding of the subject, Phyllis Rackin avidly picks up the various gauntlets of her predecessors. With comprehensive clarity she recognizes that the providentialism *v.* Machiavellianism debate of post-Tillyard criticism in fact replicated that of sixteenth-century historiography, as Brockbank had indicated, with conservatives challenged by radicals. Furthermore, she sees this to be at the heart of Shakespeare's English histories, since 'The ideological conflict between providential and Machiavellian notions of historical causation was built into the plays from the beginning' (Rackin, 46):

> Exploring the dramatic implications and exploiting the theatrical potential of rival theories of historical causation, the plays project into dramatic conflict an important ideological conflict that existed in their own time, not only by having dramatic characters speak and act from opposing ideological vantage points but also by inciting these conflicts among their audiences.
>
> (Rackin, 44–5)

Echoing Ralph Berry's approach, Rackin suggests that *all* Shakespeare's English histories can be seen 'as versions of trial by combat' (46). Again, Rackin in effect builds on Edward Berry's approach to the legalism of *2 Henry VI* by applying the concept of art as 'interrogation'. Thus 'The series of plays that begins with *Henry VI* and ends with *Henry V* replaces the teleological, providential narrative of Tudor propaganda with a self-referential cycle that ends by interrogating the entire project of historical mythmaking' (60–1). For Rackin, the greater the theatricality, the greater the interrogation since 'the growing rift between historical fact and fictional artifact [emphasizes] the constructed character of all historical representation' (71). Further, as dramatic literature gives voice to those commonly marginalized and suppressed by historiography, so vitality of performance opposes the fixity of the historians' page (203). Rackin's appraisal of *2 Henry VI* uses this approach to focus on the Cade scenes. New Historicist method often finds that the subversive power of Cade is contained by the comic mode, a containment that Falstaff bursts out of in *1* and *2 Henry IV* (221). The body politic is exorcised by laughter, it seems, a view which will be challenged in the following critical discussion (pp. 101–6), by considering what Rackin leaves out – the function of parody and burlesque in the dialectics of the carnivalesque.

Carnivalesque history

Nearly all commentators on *2 Henry VI* feel compelled to come to terms with the scenes of Jack Cade's insurrection which dominate Act 4. I say 'compelled' since the anarchic power of the rebellion is quite unparalleled in early modern dramatic literature and has an almost mesmeric stage power. Richard Helgerson is concerned with the historical significance of the theatre as an institution and what its development can tell us about society as a whole, namely what he characterizes as a shift from a 'players'' theatre to an 'author's' theatre in the 1590s. For Helgerson, the early Shakespeare of *The Contention* belongs to the players' theatre of collaborative playmaking.

The players' theatre was anarchic and populist, featuring the likes of Will Kemp playing down stage, often extempore, to the audience. Performances were rounded off by the popular jig, a combination of dance and song, mostly around a bawdy comic theme. After the departure of Kemp from the Chamberlain's Men, in spite of his triumph as Falstaff, with the transfer to the Globe, Shakespeare completed the social transformation from 'player' to 'author'. At the beginning of the 1590s, in *The Contention*, Helgerson sees Kemp performing Cade as clown–rebel and Shakespeare's attitude as derisive and satirical: 'In *The Contention* Shakespeare sets to the work of exorcism with savage zeal. His mockery of Jack Cade, in particular, is open and unmistakable' (212), a view shared by Richard Wilson. Though Helgerson argues with subtlety and insight, his conclusion here is far too crude to leave unchallenged, and I will return to it in my critical discussion (pp. 101–6). What Shakespeare may or may not have thought of Jack Cade cannot be known, but a simplistic moral judgement certainly cannot do justice to the sheer dramatic power of Shakespeare's creative ambivalence in an innovatory performance. A more nuanced approach is that of Annabel Patterson who attempts to accommodate the complexity of a work like *2 Henry VI* by applying the concept of 'ventriloquism' (47–51). The ventriloquial voice is that of an author who, in representing a class to which he or she may feel antipathetic, nevertheless gives it a voice, at least by report. Thus, in *2 Henry VI* we both hear the voice of the commons (1.3) and hear its allegiances reported (3.2). In Cade's confrontation with Lord Saye we find 'a double ventriloquilism: the voice of popular protest speaking through Cade (despite his insincerity) speaking through Shakespeare's playtext' (50), a process more complex than the influence of the rhetorical *controversia* (see Altman, 28–9). For the added complication of this ventriloquism subjected to a comic mode we need the more ramified concept of Bakhtin's dialogism and the carnivalesque to which I will turn below (pp. 103–6).

However, the critic who has come closest to assessing the nature of the comic in performance of the Jack Cade scenes is E. W. Talbert, in a chapter that is essential reading – 'Aspects of the comic' – in his *Elizabethan Drama and Shakespeare's Early Plays: An Essay in Historical Criticism* (1963). Like Helgerson, Talbert draws on the work of C. R. Baskervill on the Elizabethan jig, looking at the world of popular merriment – mummings, tavern revelry, antic clowning and the like – and the manner in which it was absorbed into Elizabethan theatre by way of the principal comedians, men like Richard Tarlton or Will Kemp. Kemp succeeded Tarlton as the most famous clown of the day and inheritor of a repertoire of comic business, particularly the mockery of such things as knighthood, gentility, learning and law. Talbert accepts the unproven hypothesis that 'Cavaliero' Kemp, as he was known, acted Cade and attempts to re-evoke the performance impact of Kemp's Lord of Misrule and retinue entry as he turns the world upside down with chop-logic and inverted situations. Parody, burlesque and grotesque are mentioned only in passing whereas further analysis of these topics might have forced Talbert to confront the thing he denies – that the Cade scenes offer a significant travesty of what takes place in the main plot. However, Talbert is alert to the interplay of clown and character in Shakespeare's allegedly most daring innovation of giving a historical role to the principal comedian, and as a consequence he recognizes the reversion to conventional comic gluttony and mock-heroism in Cade/Kemp's final encounter with Iden. (I will reinterpret these scenes when in the following discussion (pp. 103–6) I build on Talbert's propositions with the theories of Bakhtin.) Elsewhere in his study Talbert considers the interrelationship of morality–play structure, Machiavellian characterization and what he terms 'titanism' – the heritage of the Marlovian overreacher, the larger-than-life hero. The blend of these last characteristics, in his discussion of York, who in *2 Henry VI* just retains a degree of genuinely heroic chivalry, provides the subtlest account available – quite the opposite to something like the strained claim that in the hounding and death of Gloucester we see a parallel to the persecution of Christ in the miracle plays (see Jones, 35–54). Talbert's critical discrimination finely balances the informing contributions of the morality tradition, *de casibus* commonplace and Renaissance Senecanism, both as to details of character and in regard to the design of *2 Henry VI* as a whole.

Seneca, rhetoric and poetry

Commentators on the language and style of *2 Henry VI* have regularly drawn attention to the influence of Seneca. This figure has been the subject of a considerable debate which is expertly summarized by Robert S. Miola in his *Shakespeare and Classical Tragedy: The Influence of Seneca* (1–10). Scholars have argued over the extent and nature of Senecan influence, whether it was direct, by way of Seneca's actual writings, or indirect, by way of anthologies, florilegia and so on. It has been demonstrated that so-called 'Senecanism' is also characteristic of Ovid, medieval *de casibus* traditions, and the Italian novella. With the absorption of stoicism into Christian culture a major aspect of Senecanism was assimilated into western thought, and with the neoclassical revival of the Renaissance Seneca's actual tragedies were made readily available for imitation in Latin and vernacular translations of printed texts. In short, the influence of Seneca was unavoidable. It would be difficult to find any discussion of *Titus Andronicus* without some reference to Senecanism (for a judicious assessment of Seneca and Ovid in the play, see Bate, *Titus*, 29–31).

Hardin Craig feels that Shakespeare approached the history play not by way of Marlowe's *Edward II* but by way of the Senecan tragedy of *Titus Andronicus*, which he believed predated *2 Henry VI*: Shakespeare 'seems, like Seneca himself, to cultivate turbulent emotion, spectacular passion, and even violence of action' (57). Craig is a little incautious here since Seneca's was always *reported* action, whereas gory action takes place both on and off stage in Shakespeare, as we see, for example, in the Jack Cade scenes (and notoriously in *Titus*). The hallmark of Senecan drama is declamation and, as Craig points out, this is found throughout *2 Henry VI*, in Duke Humphrey's outburst over the loss of Anjou and Maine (1.1.72–100); Margaret's denunciation of Duke Humphrey and his Duchess (1.3.43–65, 76–88; 3.1.4–41); the Duchess of Gloucester's lamentation (2.4.27–57); the deliberative oratory of Duke Humphrey (3.1.142–71); and King Henry's abandonment of Humphrey (3.1.198–222). The whole scene of Suffolk's capture and death (4.1) is the most commonly cited in the context of Seneca's influence. In its opening lines this scene exemplifies a favourite device of Senecanism – sensational description. The set-piece description or declamation exploited the figures of *amplification* in the Renaissance pursuit of eloquence as copiousness. Hardin Craig lists some of the tropes and *schemata* by which this is achieved, including sententiae, hyperbole, anaphora, apostrophe and exclamation. Commonplace examples of Senecan gore drawing on classical history and mythology, which derive horror from the combination of butchery and family, can be seen in the following (see Willcock, 111–12):

> And, like ambitious Sylla, overgorged
> With gobbets of thy mother's bleeding heart.
> (*2H6* 4.1.84–5)

> Henceforth I will not have to do with pity.
> Meet I an infant of the house of York,
> Into as many gobbets will I cut it
> As wild Medea young Absyrtus did.
>   (*2H6* 5.2.56–9)

This Senecanism is used for moments of emotional heightening when such elevated language is thought to be appropriate; elsewhere, as in the Jack Cade scenes, Shakespeare exploits low-life colloquialism. Perhaps the idiom commonest to the play as a whole is the mode which permeates Elizabethan culture – the proverbial.

However, Wolfgang Clemen, in examining Eleanor's Senecan lament when she appears as a prisoner, shamed and penitentially robed (2.4.27–57), analyses Shakespeare's movement beyond classical precedent ('Aspects'). The speech is not just a detachable rhetorical address. It is closely linked to action, stage-business and setting by agonizingly describing a concrete situation rather than converting it to an abstract catalogue. As Clemen points out, it is in the second part of the speech 'that the only rhetorical formulae (double paradox enforced by alliteration and rhyme) are to be found: "No: dark shall be my light, and night my day"' ('Aspects', 11). Rhetorical questions addressed to those absent were part of the Senecan mode, but here they are addressed to Eleanor's husband who is present. The audience itself becomes equivocally related to the spectacle of shame since it has to decide whether it shares the rabble's gloating scorn or whether it finds a degree of compassion. The formalism of the verse is summarized valuably by Clemen, as follows:

> The wish to illustrate, to demonstrate, to exemplify (rather than to create characters or events) is also a major incentive in the shaping of scenes as well as language. The characters view their own doings and the events of the drama from a distance, from outside,

stepping aside, as it were, and thus becoming their own spectators, acting as their own chorus.

(Clemen, 'Aspects', 18)

This might serve as an accurate description of Bertolt Brecht's theory of acting for an 'epic' theatre (see Brecht); cf. p. 13. Clemen sees the proverbial mode as contributing to this effect: 'The frequent insertion of *sententiae* and proverbs serves as a means of objectifying and, as it were, depersonalising . . . utterances' ('Aspects', 18). In the contrast of the low-life scenes Clemen finds an element of parody but overall, in considering the emphatic clarity of such formalized language, he comes to a disturbing and subversive conclusion:

> the extraordinary clarity of utterance and character in this somewhat two-dimensional world serves in the end only to accentuate the nightmare absurdity of it all. This intolerable sequence of a century of senseless war in which the successive characters comment in an apparently convincing manner makes us all the more aware of the ultimate futility of it all.
>
> (Clemen, 'Aspects', 22)

The Senecan influence on Elizabethan drama has been called into question by G. K. Hunter ('Seneca'), who points out that the source of such gothic gore and horror is rather Ovid, who was intimately absorbed into medieval and early modern culture and education. A strong case in point would be the tragic tale of Tereus and Philomena (*Metamorphoses*, 6) which informs *Titus Andronicus* more than any particular tragedy of Seneca – such as *Thyestes*, which is usually mentioned. While the overwhelming importance of Ovid cannot be denied, Hunter's case against Senecanism is overstated: not every long speech in Shakespeare is Senecan, but the style and content of something like Suffolk's final speech in *2 Henry VI* cannot be discussed without reference to the defiant self-assertion of Senecan stoicism in the face of death.

Consider the opening of the Suffolk death scene, the Lieutenant's foreboding description:

> The gaudy, blabbing and remorseful day
> Is crept into the bosom of the sea;
> And now loud-howling wolves arouse the jades
> That drag the tragic melancholy night,
> Who with their drowsy, slow and flagging wings
> Clip dead men's graves and from their misty jaws
> Breathe foul contagious darkness in the air.
>
> (4.1.1–7)

Presumably Hardin Craig includes this in his observation that 'almost the whole of the scene of Suffolk's murder' (61) exemplifies Senecan sensationalist description. Yet G.B. Hibbard, in contrasting the comparable but maturer poetry of *Macbeth*, cites Ovid's *Metamorphoses*, 7 (ll. 218–19) as source (*Making*, 24–33). Further, Douglas Bush has shown how the apparent allusion to the dragons of Hecate here possibly refers to several other goddesses, given the syncretistic imagination of Renaissance mythographers (see 4.1.3n.). For Hibbard these lines, in direct contrast to the imagery of *Macbeth*, have no organic integration with character or action, but are 'static and pictorial', 'something applied to the scene', rather than 'an essential part of it' (compare 4.1, headnote). This organicist criticism, deriving from the formalism of post-Coleridge aesthetic theory adopted by New Criticism, provides the basis for Wolfgang Clemen's critique in his early and very influential *The Development of Shakespeare's Imagery* (1951).

Clemen quotes the above lines of the Lieutenant as an example of externalized atmospherics quite unrelated to the character of the actual speaker, who is merely a vehicle for rhetorical picture-painting. By contrast, Clemen draws attention to the unobtrusive, organically integrated imagery of the opening of *Hamlet*. Generally he characterizes the style of the *Henry VI* plays as conceited and digressive, decorative 'embroidery' ('Aspects',

40), artificial and impersonal. That is to say, to anyone hostile to this kind of mannered verse it appears 'superfluous, mere padding' ('Aspects', 41).

Yet another analysis, by James L. Calderwood, finds in *2 Henry VI* patterns of imagery which are 'active and functional' rather than 'static and ornamental', and which suggest 'that subtle, inner collusion between word and both deed and character', anticipating the so-called maturer Shakespeare. Calderwood discerns four patterns of imagery which 'are especially noteworthy, those having to do with trapping, sight, elevation, and hands' (483). Trappers and the trapped are reflected by the imagery of hunting in the natural world – snares, traps, gins and the liming of branches to entrap birds. (In addition Calderwood refers to Caroline Spurgeon's listing of five instances of butchering in the play.) 'Watchfulness, keenness of sight, a predilection for seeing into or through: these are the characteristics of the conspirators in general' (485), as well as the necessity of 'watchfulness' urged upon the innocent. By 'elevation' Calderwood refers to the opposites of high and low, above and beneath, that respectively structure the perspectives of the ambitious and the humble. Finally, in a feudal society, fighting ability depended on weapons borne by the hand, and hands also symbolize both trust and conspiracy, allegiance and betrayal. Calderwood does not claim the integrated interrelationship of imagistic cross-patterning found in the great tragedies, but the groups he looks at in *2 Henry VI* 'reveal correspondences and interrelationships rather than merely haphazard recurrence' (494). And in view of the later studies by Edward Berry and Ralph Berry the language of trial, legalism and combat might well satisfy the criteria of organic unity.

Feminism

Critical advances are made not solely by evolving theoretical models, but most radically by paradigm displacement – when a critic offers a new approach to a work. Feminist approaches to *2 Henry VI* have revitalized the play so that we are made to consider afresh what had always been before us, yet had been largely passed over. As Sir Barry Jackson observed, Queen Margaret offers one of the greatest female roles in the whole of Shakespeare. Jean E. Howard and Phyllis Rackin consider Margaret and the whole array of major and minor feminine roles in the *Henry VI* plays in the second part ('weak kings, warrior women, and the assault on dynastic authority') of their feminist reinterpretation of all the English histories, *Engendering a Nation* (1997). For Howard and Rackin, chronicle history is the preserver of male fame which the subversive female may destroy. This is seen very clearly in Joan La Pucelle's contemptuous dismissal of Sir William Lucy's roll-call of titles over the dead Lord Talbot (*1H6* 4.7.60–76). In *2 Henry VI* Eleanor is demonized by association with Joan's witchcraft and brings disgrace upon her husband, the Protector. King Henry falls into the gendered role of the effeminate or womanish man, which is brought out by his excessive uxoriousness on first meeting his wife. According to Renaissance thought, such men were unable to control their naturally disorderly counterparts. Conversely, Margaret becomes the mannish woman who, in turn, 'infantilizes' her lover Suffolk (73). This fascinating discussion of the house of York shows how masculine decline comes about only after female association, as seen in Edward IV's politically debilitating infatuation with Lady Elizabeth Grey in *Part 3*. Hitherto, untainted by the feminine, York's aggressive ambition had embodied chivalric prowess. His death at Margaret's hand inaugurates what becomes 'the cultural fantasy of the monstrous Amazonian women' (94).

As this survey has shown, with the ramifications of modern theory, the critic, scholar and student are now more than ever in a position to evaluate *2 Henry VI* and indeed the whole trilogy for their contribution to Renaissance theatre and culture.

History, justice, drama

In the preceding survey of the criticism of *2 Henry VI* from the postwar period two issues recur and dominate debate: the providential pattern of God in history and the insurrectionary eruption of the rebels in society. A divinely ordained order is threatened by the low. Such matters have been the major concern of a movement in critical and theoretical thought about early modern history and literature in the second half of the twentieth century: the dialectical movement from high to low, aristocrats to artisans; from the centre to the margins, the court to the dispossessed. This section of the Introduction (expanding on earlier work; see Knowles, 'Farce') will re-examine both aspects in relation to the main plot of *2 Henry VI* and to the minor scenes of travesty and burlesque which culminate in 'the World Turned Upside Down' of the Jack Cade mob in Act 4.

Two complementary processes took place in religion and historiography in the sixteenth century with specific relevance to England. As part of the Reformation and Renaissance various currents of Christian and non-Christian belief emphasized the separateness of God from man, and in the writing of history we discern a pattern of increasing secularization as the motives and action of man become the focus of historians. Psychology and morality offered explanations of causality without recourse to metaphysics and teleology and the invocation of providence.

Tudor England witnessed a series of social and political rebellions, such as the Pilgrimage of Grace (1536–7) and Kett's Rebellion (1549) (see Fletcher), which struck at the heart of the body politic, as the often quoted *Homily against Disobedience and Wilful Rebellion* demonstrates. Wat Tyler and Jack Cade became symbolic figures in both polemic and theatre. In the confrontation of religion and society, providence and rebellion, drama investigates the nature of justice. In the London of the 1590s a number of plays, such as *Jack Straw*, *Sir Thomas More* and Thomas Heywood's *Edward IV*, featured riot scenes, but the dramatic power of lower-class rebellion in *2 Henry VI* was to remain unsurpassed, even in comparison with Shakespeare's later representation of plebeian disorder in *Julius Caesar* and *Coriolanus*. But, before proceeding to the issue of travesty, culminating in the Jack Cade scenes, I will return to the question of providence and justice, to the arguments of the church father with which such discussions often begin.

St Augustine had provided an explanation for why the good sometimes suffer and the evil prosper: final justice is in heaven, the good who have suffered find bliss, the evil fall into hell's torment. But then, as a sign of an actively engaged providence, the faith of the virtuous is occasionally tried or rewarded and the evil punished on earth. Yet even the so-called good must remember that we are all born in sin and that God may sometimes choose to visit us with either an evil scourge (like a tyrant) or a natural disaster for the sins inherited from ancestry or the collective sins of society (1.7, 20.2; see Hutchinson, ch. 15). One response to such beliefs, emphasizing the iniquity of this world, was that which found its most potent voice in Martin Luther's promulgation, drawing on Isaiah, 45.15, of *deus absconditus*, a hidden god distantly separate from man: 'Verily thou, O God, hidest thy selfe' (see Dillenberger). Though Puritanism emphasized the hand of God in human affairs the difficulty of accepting suffering as part of justice led, in Calvinism, to a stress on the inscrutability of God's judgements (see Thomas, 78–112). Though the pagan philosophy of Epicurus at first appears to be the antithesis of Christian providentialism – the Gods were simply indifferent to all human conduct, either good or bad – both systems of belief coincided in the idea of the separation and remoteness of the divine. W. R. Elton has shown exhaustively the developing interest in the Epicurean revival of the second half of the sixteenth century, and the near-hysterical Christian response to such 'atheism'. To a certain degree, the emphases found in religious belief and practice had parallels in the beliefs and practice of history and historiography.

The common motive of the medieval chroniclers was that of Christian providentialism, demonstrating in history the unfolding plan of the divine will (the first cause) working through the actions of men (the second cause) (see Collingwood, 52–6; Dean,

3–4; Fussner, 10–11; Ribner, 20). Renaissance historiography largely secularized history by limiting the focus to secondary causes; that is, causation was seen in human terms. Thus for Francesco Patrizzi history would record the hard facts of human action; Jean Bodin insisted on turning from what man 'ought' to be, to what he 'is'; Paolo Sarpi saw the writing of history as the unmasking of self-interest, while Arrigo Caterina Davila took this scepticism a stage further in seeing the historian's task as revealing the 'pretexts' of apparent human motivation; Johann Sleidan turned against the humanist inheritance of the rhetorical invention of classical historians, to write what Peter Burke in his helpful study, *The Renaissance Sense of the Past*, from which these details are taken, calls 'pragmatic' history (see also Riggs, 34–61).

I do not wish to suggest here some kind of clear evolutionary development by which historiography freed itself from theological discourse. Nor should the converse be automatically considered the case. In Lord Berners's translation of *The Chronicle of Froissart* (1523–5) the later sixteenth century could find an initially avowed intention to record the valour and renown of chivalric deeds, and yet the closing chapters on the end of Richard II are given without reference to God or providence, sanctity or chivalry, but with the objective awareness of the final struggle between three power groups: the courtiers in disarray, the Londoners feeling their strength, Bolingbroke awaiting the most opportune moment. In *The Waning of the Middle Ages* Huizinga characterized Froissart's complete detachment from theological judgement or personal moral feeling as 'the mechanical exactitude of a cinematograph' (296; cited by Iser, 34). For a time secular historiography and providentialism co-existed, as we find in Thomas Blundeville, Holinshed and Sir Walter Raleigh, and, indeed, as some have claimed, in Shakespeare's histories. Thomas Blundeville is fascinating for the hybrid work he produced on the nature of historical writing, *The true order and Method of writing and reading Histories, according to the precepts of Francisco Patricio, and Accontio Tridentino* (1574)

(Dick). (The 'Patricio' of the title is the above-mentioned Francesco Patrizzi, and Accontio is Giacomo Concio, also known as Jacobus Acontius.) Blundeville's work is an adaptation and abridgement of Patrizzi's *Della historia diece dialoghi* (Venice, 1560) and Concio's unpublished manuscript, 'Delle osservationi, et avvertimenti che haver si debbono nel legger delle historie'.

Patrizzi sees history as the secular record of the inner and outer causes of human action – passion and will, circumstance and environment. This emphasis on what we would call the psychological, behavioural and sociological makes him sound very modern, but in fact the infrastructure of Patrizzi's method derives from converting epideictic *topoi* to naturalistic, rather than oratorical, ends (compare Dick 160, 164, with *Rhetorica*, III, IV, 10–11). However, by contrast, when Blundeville turns to Concio we find in the opening statement that the purpose of history is, first, 'that we may learne thereby to acknowledge the providence of God, whereby all things are governed and directed' (Dick, 165).

Sacred and secular co-exist in much Renaissance history writing. A few years before Bacon's separation of 'Civil history' and the 'History of Providence' in *De augmentis* (see 438; and Fussner, 253–74), we find both medieval providentialism and Mac hiavellian 'policy' in Sir Walter Raleigh's *The History of the World* (1614). Raleigh's unfinished *History* begins, like its medieval universalist predecessors, with the creation, acknowledging the first cause of all in God's will, which thereafter works through the second cause of human agency. Yet when Raleigh gets down to the particulars of political history he is reminiscent of Polybius and Machiavelli. Perhaps the best example, for the argument here, is that cited by Dean, the digression on tyranny (V, 91–102). Whereas Raleigh usually follows the providential-ists' view of tyrants as scourges of God on human evil, when he considers the examples of Francesco Sforza and his father, tyranny is discussed in Machiavellian terms of *Realpolitik*, prag-matism and 'policy' (see Orsini). Dean summarizes: 'In

Raleigh's attitude toward historical causation is to be observed the same combination of the providential and the rationalistic. Sometimes he explains events by purely human causes, more often by divine, and occasionally by both' (18–19; see Raab, 56–74).

With the above details in mind we are able to see the partiality of Tillyard and the Tillyardians more clearly (see pp. 41–50) as well as that of the opposing camp, as in Frey and French (pp. 56–7). Further, Brockbank's judicious perception of what I term the dualistic aspect of Tudor chronicles (p. 52) may now be appreciated as characteristic, with varying emphases, of Renaissance historiography on the whole. Thus Phyllis Rackin's assessment, 'The ideological conflict between providential and Machiavellian notions of historical causation was built into the plays from the beginning' (46), needs to be modified by the recognition that this was true also of the chronicles themselves.

In *2 Henry VI*, as we have seen, justice is put on trial. The Renaissance understanding of rule linked the sacred and the secular, and thus justice should reflect both the divine and human. However inscrutable, it was believed or hoped by most people that there was some kind of providence working at some level, even if beyond the awareness of man (see Elton, 9–33). The design of *2 Henry VI* has a deeply religious but politically inept monarch constantly giving voice to providential pieties in the midst of Machiavellian plots. In this respect the play reflects the mixed mode of Renaissance historiography outlined above. Further, Shakespeare added a number of small scenes which are all concerned with the nature of justice: Eleanor's witchcraft, the trial of Horner, Simpcox's fraud, Cade's insurrection. In what follows it will be argued that an unambiguous recognition of providence is not to be found in the play. On the contrary, it mostly appears to be called into question. Several critics, however, have pointed to the deaths of the Cardinal and Suffolk as making manifest the retribution of providence. There is indeed a suggestion of this, but on closer inspection it is ambivalent: the Cardinal certainly dies, but the significance of his death is rather ambiguous, as I have discussed above (pp. 44–5), and though Suffolk dies in fulfilment of the prophecies, these appear to be more infernal than divine. Yet, by whatever agency, *lex talionis* may be conceded: they die after their part in Gloucester's death.

As Elton has shown, there were many in the 1590s ready to seize on any seeming expression of anti-providentialism by 'atheists', such as Marlowe (see 23–4). However, like Marlowe, Shakespeare could rely on the Protestant bias of much of his audience when depicting Catholic 'superstition' by way of various forms of comedy such as travesty, burlesque and grotesque. In those minor scenes where justice appears to be done either laughter, irony or evident political machinations compromise, if not undermine, any sense of human judgement as reflecting providential justice. In the following analyses I shall show how the language and action of the earlier minor scenes call in question the efficacy of providence by repeatedly emphasizing human causation. This secularism is paramount in the Cade rebellion scenes where human justice is burlesqued in the carnivalesque mêlée of Misrule. But when the world is turned upside down, Cade and his followers are revealed as inversions of their betters and 'justice' is revealed as its own opposite: it is either used by the feudal aristocracy for the Machiavellian ends of power politics, or blatantly subverted as might determines right, and Cade's insurrection becomes a prelude to the larger chaos brought about by the Wars of the Roses, as chivalry descends into anarchy.

In the scene of Eleanor's conjuration the demonic burlesques the divine. Here the plot derives from the human machinations of Suffolk and the Cardinal to discredit Eleanor and thus to help bring down the Protector, Gloucester. The conjuration of Hume, Jourdain, Bolingbroke and Southwell appears to be part of an imposture until, that is, the devil himself ('Asnath') puts in an appearance and offers riddling prophecies, one of which includes the death of Suffolk, that are eventually fulfilled. The demonic and the divine might be seen as coming together, as Suffolk's death could be seen as a manifestation of God's providence; but the plot of Suffolk and the Cardinal is only part of the larger plot of the play itself, which is enacted before an audience ready to thrill to a counterfeit devil. Again, when Eleanor is judged Henry declares 'In sight of God and us, your guilt is great' (2.3.2), which in terms of theology and justice is right, but when these words are put against Henry's reaction on first hearing of the witchcraft – 'O God, what mischiefs work the wicked ones' (2.1.177) – a powerful irony emerges. In sight of the theatre audience the 'mischiefs' of the 'wicked ones', Suffolk and the Cardinal, include using justice for political ends. Preceding and following the judgement of Eleanor are scenes in which divine miracle and providence are subjected to the comic grotesque.

In the long first scene of the second act of *2 Henry VI*, the miracle episode is flanked by the hawking and the arrest of the Duchess of Gloucester. It has not been difficult to assign dramatic function to the scene itself. Hereward T. Price, for example, sees in it a dramatic 'touchstone' for the chief characters: 'We see Henry's simple faith based on an unquestioning mind, Gloucester's scepticism and quiet penetration, the Queen's cruel laughter at the horrible punishments inflicted.' To Price, 'Shakespeare steps outside his plot in order to show the deeper undercurrents in the society he is depicting' ('Mirror', 104). If, however, we also bear in mind comic parallelism the 'miracle' reveals a level of ironic integration within the main action of the *Henry VI* plays.

To a certain extent a metaphorical reading of the miracle scene of *2 Henry VI* is encouraged by the way Shakespeare opens and closes it: the characters themselves allegorize the hawking at the beginning, and then, towards the end, use the 'miracle' to mock each other:

CARDINAL
> Duke Humphrey has done a miracle today.

SUFFOLK
> True, made the lame to leap and fly away.

GLOUCESTER
> But you have done more miracles than I –
> You made in a day, my lord, whole towns to fly.
>
> (2.1.152–5)

This technique of deriving ironical metaphors from actual circumstances occurs later also when the accused Gloucester, about to be led off as a prisoner, warns the King, 'Ah, thus King Henry throws away his crutch / Before his legs be firm to bear his body' (3.1.189–90). Seeing the 'honour, truth and loyalty' (3.1.203) of Gloucester, the King is nevertheless blinded by his tears and sees only 'with dimmed eyes' (3.1.218). Shakespeare added Simpcox's lameness to the historical sources, and presumably a crutch was carried on stage with his chair, since he is said to be 'not able to stand' (2.1.145). Simpcox's wife's parting words are: 'Alas, sir, we did it for pure need' (2.1.149), the plangency of which is somewhat modulated by the comic flight of Simpcox and the ironic echo of his earlier answer to the Queen's question as to whether he came 'here by chance, / Or of devotion to this holy shrine?' 'God knows', he says, 'of pure devotion' (2.1.84–6). His 'pure devotion' is somewhat impure, his blindness and lameness are fake, and the miracle bogus. By contrast, the unremitting, single-minded purity of Henry's devotion has rendered him politically blind and lame, as Gloucester's image makes plain.

In Foxe's account of the miracle it is not initially the King who responds to the wonderous healing, but Gloucester: 'having great joy to see such a miracle, [he] called the poor man unto him, and first showing himself joyous of God's glory so showed in the getting of his sight, and exhorting him to meekness and to no ascribing of any part of the worship to himself, nor to be proud of the people's praise' (III, 713). Then in his examination of Simpcox the falseness of the miracle is exposed. In *2 Henry VI* it is the credulity of the King which is exposed in his, not Gloucester's, voicing of providential affirmation, in the doubling of the miracle by the addition of lameness, and in the further addition as Simpcox flees. The St Albans townspeople, presumably unaware of the disclosure down stage, acclaim the imposter's flight as *another* 'miracle' (2.1.145.2), while the King laments in dismay, 'O God, seest thou this, and bearest so long?' (l. 146). The worldly mockery of Margaret ('It made me laugh to see the villain run', l. 147), Suffolk and the Cardinal follows. The farcical exposure of what Foxe sees as 'the crafty working of the false miracles of the clergy' (III, 713) might indeed make a post-Reformation audience laugh at Simpcox's discomfiture and Henry's credulity brought about by Catholic piety. Shakespeare was under no obligation to use the St Albans material for his design. In choosing to do so he gave the scene ironic point in the significance of blindness, imposture and providence.

Something similar is seen in his inclusion of the combat scene of Horner and Peter. Here Shakespeare also employed the mode of travesty with more concentration and force, albeit with broader comedy. The trial by combat in Act 2, scene 3 has of course attracted some attention. Many years ago Clifford Leech saw in it something like ironic counterpoint, considering that 'the formal combat between the armourer and his man is a parody of chivalric encounter: in a way remarkably sophisticated for this early drama, it implies a critical attitude towards the warring nobles whose quarrels are grotesquely mirrored in this fight between two simple men, one terrified, one drunk' (17). More recently Ralph Berry has discussed the trial as a unifying image for the whole play (see above, p. 62). Of the combat won by the apprentice, and celebrated by the King for the revelation of 'God in justice' (l. 103), Berry concludes 'I put it that the play does not invite us to share the view of Divine Providence advanced by Peter and King Henry' (6). That conviction needs to be developed here.

From his manner of introducing the action – 'the appellant and defendant . . . to enter the lists' (ll. 49–50) – it is evident that Shakespeare knew that the combat was under the auspices of the courts of chivalry. Recognition of this helps us to gauge more precisely the burlesque nature of the scene.

Richard II had fostered the power and scope of the civil court of chivalry, thereby incurring the criticism of Parliament, which feared encroachment on the courts of common law. The articles of deposition against him included specific details of this abuse. It eventually became possible for any treason appeal to come before this court, although there were conditions which had to be fulfilled. In cases of treason, trial by combat was used when there were no witnesses and no evidence, so that one man's word simply stood against another's, provided that both parties were of good repute and not felons (see Tuck, 124, 198; Bellamy, 143; Squibb, 22–9). The practice reached its height under Henry VI. Thus Cater and Davy, the originals of Shakespeare's Horner and Peter, appeared in historical fact in the chivalric setting of the lists at Smithfield.

They may seem an incongruous pair to have done so, but there were other cases concerning parties of less than knightly standing. A few years earlier, in 1441, for example, two thieves fought in combat 'at Totehill' according to Stow (*Annals*, 381), on what appeal he does not say, and in 1426 'a gentleman, Henry Knokkis' defended himself against an appeal of treason made by 'a certain plebeian tailor' beneath the walls of Edinburgh castle (Neilson, 275). Even more strangely, an elderly friar was ordered under Henry IV to fight a woman, who had accused him of treason, with one arm tied behind his back. (The charge was then withdrawn.) The *Brut* chronicle, also, records a fight to the death between a 'Welsh clerk' and a knight (Bellamy, 145–6).

By the Tudor period, such socially inclusive combat was considered a violation of the law of arms. Spenser makes this clear by showing Calidore at first dismayed to see Tristram, who is 'no knight', slay a knight, 'which armes impugneth plaine' (VI.ii.7). In Shakespeare's day, in a work which the playwright may have consulted for the combat scene of *Richard II*, Sir William Segar spelled out 'What sorts of men ought not bee admitted to triall of Armes'. Generally, 'the triall of Armes apperteineth onelie to Gentlemen, and that Gentilitie is a degree honourable, it were not fit that anie persons of meaner condition, should thereunto be admitted' (30–1). In this judgement, amongst the ineligible, beside 'Theeves, Beggers, Bawdes, Victuallers, persons excommunicate, Usurers, persons banished the Armie', is ranked 'everie other man exercising an occupation or trade, unfit and unworthie a Gentleman or Soldier'. To sum up, then, Richard II had promoted a situation in which history itself would furnish burlesques of chivalric practice, whilst Tudor aristocratic exclusivity had heightened awareness of decorum. Thus when Horner and Peter appeared on stage in the 1590s, one drunk, the other terrified, and both carrying less than knightly weapons, the resulting burlesque confirmed the comic tenor of Peter's petition:

> PETER   Against my master Thomas Horner, for saying that the Duke of York was rightful heir to the crown.
> QUEEN   What sayst thou? Did the Duke of York say he was rightful heir to the crown?

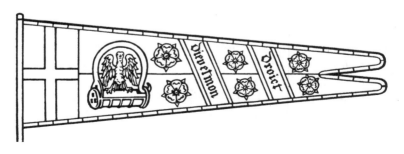

11 The Yorkist standard

> PETER   That my master was? No, forsooth, my master
>   said that he was, and that the King was an usurer.
>
> (1.3.25–31)

Yet that exaggeration of the comic will prove to have its serious point.

Details of the dramatization of the combat deserve investigation. It is removed from the traditional Smithfield venue to a 'Hall of Justice'. Gregory's *Chronicle* mentions that Cater (like Davy, it is assumed) was in 'harnys' (harness), that is, a suit of armour (see Nichols, 217, 220, for the writ and costs). Shakespeare's SD mentions a curious weapon, a '*staff with a sand-bag fastened to it*' (2.3.58.3), but no armour. The treason-duel of chivalry, usually on horseback, was never fought without a sword and spear. Shakespeare's weapon, in fact, is closer to the weapon of the duel-of-law, the baton (Neilson, 188–9). Sir Samuel Rush Meyrick, the Victorian antiquarian, was somewhat baffled by the weapons of Horner and Peter: 'Shakespeare arms his combatants with batons and sand-bags at the end of them, yet this is the only authority I have met with for the use of this latter appendage.' He then proceeded to speculate that 'probably such were the weapons of the lower class of people, and were therefore considered by him as appropriate to the parties' (2, 125). He quotes Samuel Butler's *Hudibras* in support – 'Engaged with money-bags, as bold / As men with sand-bags did of old' – and suggests a comparison with the fool's baton and bladder. The weapons are in fact combat flails, as distinct from the metal military flail or the agricultural wooden variety. Reference to them seems to be rare, but an excellent illustration (see Fig. 12) survives in one of the most detailed examples of a Renaissance festival book, *The Triumph of Maximilian I* (1526), with woodcuts by Hans Burgkmair and others. Plate 33 shows 'Five men with (leather) flails' preceding similar numbers of men 'with quarterstaves, lances, halberds, battleaxes, and various swords and shields' (Appelbaum, 7).

12 Combat flails

By choosing flails with sand-filled leather bags Shakespeare placed a weapon associated with the lower orders into the aristocratic milieu of chivalric combat, bringing on his combatants without the expected arms and armour. He also made other significant alterations to the chronicle material. As has always been recognized, Shakespeare links the armourer's treason with York, although it was not so linked in the chronicles. In the sources the armourer is the innocent party and his servant the guilty. Holinshed, for example, following Fabyan (618), found Davy a 'false servant' and Cater 'without guilt' (210), while Grafton, following Hall (207–8), saw Davy as 'a coward and a wretche' (1, 628). That wretchedness could follow from his cowardice, or it might be that Davy is called wretch for falsely accusing his master – presumably the latter, since the chroniclers see ultimate justice in his execution at Tyburn.

In assessing these alterations, we should not miss the question of drink. All sources except Gregory record the drunkenness of the armourer, but Shakespeare makes a significant change in the liquors consumed. Grafton, following Hall again, records 'Malmsey and Aqua vite'; Holinshed 'wine and strong drinke'; Fabyan 'wyne and good ale', whilst Shakespeare has 'sack' 'charneco' and 'good double beer' (2.3.60–4). The last item is the telling detail. By the sixteenth century there had developed an association between festive wassail, that is to say, extra-strong ale ('double beer' or 'double ale'), and riot and sedition. In John Bale's *King Johan* (1584), for example, Sedition enters, crying

> No noyse amonge ye? Where is the mery chere
> That was wont to be, with quaffing of double bere?
> The worlde is not yet as some men woulde it have.
>
> (2. 2460–2)

Charles Hobday (68) has noted the subversive meanings of 'merry' as egalitarian freedom in the sixteenth century generally and in Shakespeare in particular, quoting the declaration of one of Cade's followers that 'it was never merry world in England since gentlemen came up' (4.2.7–8). Again, in *The Life and Death of Jack Straw* (1593) Tom Miller, the comic rebel-clown, says of the notorious John Ball, 'You . . . / Find him in a pulpit but twice in the yeare, / And Ile find him fortie times in the ale-house tasting strong beare', and in a ludicrous self-indictment Miller promotes himself as 'a customer to helpe away . . . strong ale' (ll. 70–3, 829–30). From this we can understand the import of Cade's 'reformation' when he 'will make it felony to drink small beer' (4.2.62–3). Double beer only for the rebels! In other words, the armourer's 'treason' is further damned by association with drunken insurrectionaries.

Hall introduced the notion of Horner's height and strength: 'he beying a tall and a hardye personage' (207–8). Shakespeare changes this subtly to Horner's superior technique: Peter knows that 'I am never able to deal with my master, he hath learnt so much fence already' (2.3.78–80). Advantage is all on the side of the master, except for his overconfidence encouraged by drink. It could therefore seem that when the armourer is struck and confesses treason before dying, Peter has 'prevailed in right' (2.3.100); right seems to have defeated might, so that the combat could be seen as divinely ordered. As Segar puts it:

> all Nations . . . have (among many other trials) permit-
> ted that such questions as could not be civilie prooved
> by confession, witnesse, or other circumstances, should
> receive judgement by fight and combat, supposing that
> GOD (who onelie knoweth the secret thoughts of all
> men) would give victorie to him that justlie adventured
> his life, for truth, Honor, and Justice.
>
> (sig. A2^{v-r})

Hence the King's pious response to what has taken place: 'And God in justice hath revealed to us / The truth and innocence of this poor fellow' (2.3.103–4).

The burlesque circumstances of the combat imply more than a travesty of chivalric ritual. Perhaps an audience would be more inclined to share York's irony: 'Fellow, thank God and the good wine in thy master's way' (ll. 97–8). First cause, God's will, and second cause, man's action, coincide by default as drunkenness becomes the warranty of providence.

The effects produced in this episode show the kinds of complexity so often celebrated in the *Henry IV* plays (see Rossiter, 'Ambivalence'). In reshaping this historical material, Shakespeare created comic matter in a burlesquing of the chivalric code, in such a way as to create an ironic inversion of the main lines of action of the play, perhaps even of the action in all three *Henry VI* plays. The combat scene lies in the middle of these plays, in which an overall pattern can be discerned of a falling into a world of brute force, in the demise of chivalry in Talbot's death, in the ineffectuality of Christian piety in Henry VI, and the rise of Machiavellian *virtù* in Richard of Gloucester. Everywhere Might seems to be overcoming Right, both in the small instance –

PLANTAGENET
>   Now, Somerset, where is your argument?

SOMERSET
>   Here in my scabbard, meditating that
>   Shall dye your white rose in a bloody red.

>> *(1H6* 2.4.59–61)

– and in the large confrontation:

WARWICK
>   Do right unto this princely Duke of York,
>   Or I will fill the house with armed men . . .
>>   *He stamps with his foot, and the Soldiers show*
>>   *themselves.*

>> *(3H6* 1.1.166–9)

Momentarily the comic outcome of the combat scene in *2 Henry VI* seems to militate against this general tendency, and to affirm that Right may conquer Might. But such is the travesty of the combat that we seem to have instead an ironic pointing up of the issues, a demonstration of the arbitrariness of justice and human action. To turn the chronicles around in such a way is to invoke and then to call in question any sense of divine ordinance in human affairs.

The most developed instance of this technique is, however, in the rebellion of Jack Cade in Act 4, for which the comic scenes of the St Albans miracle and the treason combat seem a kind of preparation, from travesty of divine will to travesty of human action in the World Turned Upside Down. Jack Cade is arguably the most complex figure of the *Henry VI* plays. The complexity of his case derives from three compounded categories, the historiographical, the cultural and the artistic. Shakespeare follows his contemporaries' propagandist conflation of Cade's 1450 rebellion with that of Jack Straw and Wat Tyler of 1381. From a cultural point of view the presentation of Cade shows an affinity with the topsy-turveydom of the Lord of Misrule and the World

Upside Down, while in artistic terms it is related to the Vice and the clown. Yet, ultimately, Cade is an inverted image of authority, both its distorted representative and its grotesque critic.

The historical Jack Cade was rather different from the rebels of 1381. Though Brents Stirling points out Cade's execution of Saye and Crowmer and the freeing of prisoners, he concludes that 'most of the violence and outrage in Shakespeare's version of the Cade uprising came from the chronicle story of the earlier Peasants' Revolt', from which were taken the anti-literacy of the rebels, the wish to kill all lawyers, the destruction of the Savoy and the Inns of Court, the destruction of state documents and the ascription to Cade of Wat Tyler's belief that 'all the laws of England should come forth of his mouth' (22–3). Cade, on the contrary, was impressively personable and articulate, in the words of Holinshed 'a young man of goodly stature and right pregnant wit', 'sober in talk, wise in reasoning, arrogant in heart, and stiff in opinion' (220). Hall considered that Cade, far from being illiterate, was 'not only suborned by techers, but also enforced by pryvye scholemasters' (220). Initially Cade's forces were in fact relatively disciplined, and on behalf of his supporters he presented the fully documented 'Complaints of the Commons of Kent' (see Appendix 5).

The earlier, mid–Tudor depiction of Cade in the *Mirror for Magistrates* (1559) is moral and theological. He is heard insisting on the principle of non-resistance to divinely appointed rulers and on individuals' responsibility to 'follow reason' and 'subdue their wylles' and 'lust', rather than allow the vagaries of Fortune to rule over them. In the prose discussion following Cade's speech his insurrection is seen as an example of God's use of rebels to chastise irresponsible rulers and overmighty subjects (*Mirror*, 170–80).

By the 1590s Cade's rebellion was generally seen more in political than theological terms. Brents Stirling has shown how a conflation of the rebellions of 1381 and 1450 was further linked by conservative propagandists to English nonconformity and to the German Peasant War, by way of the Anabaptists and John of

Leiden. John of Leiden was decried for the lowness of his trade, tailoring, and Jack Cade was turned by Shakespeare, without any indication in the sources, into a 'clothier' and a 'shearman' (4.2.4, 124), that is, one who sheared the nap in the finishing stages of cloth production. Both declared themselves kings, both were opposed to learning, both proclaimed that all would be held in common and that money was to be banned. Given these parallels, it is unlikely that Shakespeare's presentation of Cade as a clothier could be made without some of the audience seeing such parallels implied in a richly compounded stage figure. Shakespeare pointedly concentrates on the anti-literacy of the 1381 rebels and adds a theme of his own, the critique of a culture that would make legible its social distinctions through the clothing of its citizens.

We hear from Medvedev and Bakhtin that 'ideological reality', that is, the 'philosophical views, beliefs or even shifting ideological moods', are 'realized in words, actions, *clothing*, manners, and organizations of people and things' (20; my italics). Consider, for example, the sack of the Savoy, John of Gaunt's house, in 1381: the rebels 'seized one of his most precious vestments, which we call a "jakke", and placed it on a lance to be used for their arrows. And since they were unable to damage it sufficiently with their arrows, they took it down and tore it apart with their axes and swords' (Pettitt, 12). Pettitt has suggested, somewhat fancifully, that this represents 'an effigy for ritual slaying, *sparagmos*, the tearing apart of the sacrificial victims in many ancient renewal ceremonies' (Pettitt, 13). More soberly, Pettitt draws a parallel with the rough treatment of the festival dummy figure of Jack o' Lent. However, if we note Sir Samuel Rush Meyrick's observations on the 'Jakke' – it was a strengthened tunic used as armour yet lined with silk (2.68) – we can see the symbolic provocation of such a thing. The Latin of Walsingham's chronicle, 'vestimentum preciosissimus ipsius' (I, 459), indicates that such a garment was uniquely noble, combining the martial and the gentle. This the rebels singled out amidst the general havoc. John Ball spoke for them: the nobles, he said, 'ar clothed in velvet and chamlet [fine fabric] furred with grise [grey fur], while we be vestured with pore clothe' (Froissart, III, 1381). In fact, Shakespeare did not need to be prompted by a specific incident, for such occurrences derived from the system of class distinction by dress enforced by law in his own day.

Although they seem often to have been more honoured in the breach than the observance, sumptuary laws persisted with various amendments in statutes and proclamations from the reign of Edward III until their final repeal by James I in 1604, even appearing in hortatory form as an Elizabethan homily. They attempted to impose the quality, colour, kind, cost and length of material worn by everybody, from monarch to serf, in order to distinguish their degree (see E. Baldwin *Legislation*; Hooper; Harte). Summarizing the period 1400–1600, Harte found that 'the sixteenth-century Acts contained a vision of society that was more complex and hierarchical' than in some earlier periods (136). Elizabeth punctiliously followed the strictures of the statute of 1533, which had reversed the relative liberality of former law. The 1533 statute contained 'exceptionally minute provisions limiting the use of silk and silk-wrought materials, according to the rank or income of wearer, between those kinds that could be used in different garments of external wear' (Hooper, 435). All materials, in varying combinations, were graded according to social standing. At the top end, 'none . . . except earls and all superior degrees, and viscounts and barons in their doublets and sleeveless coats . . . shall wear . . . cloth of gold, silver, or tinsel; satin, silk, or cloth mixed with gold or silver, nor any sables'. At the lower end, 'no servingman in husbandry or journeyman in handicrafts taking wages shall wear in his doublet any other thing than fustian, canvas, leather, or wool cloth' (Hughes & Larkin, 2, 280).

Prompted by Elizabeth in 1559, the Privy Council inaugurated a system of surveillance by suggesting to the City corporation 'that two watches should be appointed for every parish, armed with a schedule of all persons assessed to the late subsidy . . . in order to see that the prohibition against silk trimmings was being obeyed' (Hooper, 437). The dividing line between gentleman and plebeian was that between those whose annual income, after all taxes, was above or below five pounds. The sartorial manifestation of this in the gentleman was 'silk in his doublet or jackets', whereas the man below gentry rank could not wear silk at all, not even as decoration on 'any shirt, or shirtband, under or upper cap, bonnet, or hat' (Hughes & Larkin, 3, 5–6). Class-consciousness would have been most acute at this dividing line, and at least a century of discrimination, which the whole audience would have recognized, informs Jack Cade's contemptuous remark, 'As for these silken-coated slaves, I pass not' (4.2.119).

George's play on words at the opening of the Cade scenes – 'I tell thee, Jack Cade the clothier means to dress the commonwealth, and turn it, and set a new nap upon it . . . for 'tis threadbare' (4.2.4–7) – alludes to Cade's particular occupation, but in this topsy-turvy world he would indeed act the king and he has his own sumptuary proclamation: 'I will apparel them all in one livery' (4.2.68–9) (cf. R. Wilson; Bristol, 89). According to Stubbes in the *Anatomy of Abuses* (1583), the Lord of Misrule invests 'everie one of these his men . . . with his liveries, of green, yellow or some light wanton colour' (147), and it has been conjectured that 'Jack Cade may have used the Whitsun festivities of 1450 to forward or cover his enterprise' (Pettitt, 9). Cade's 'livery' as part of his visionary utterances recalls 'the simple gray cloth in which all Utopians dress' (More, *Utopia*, xli). On the other hand, Pettitt records of the 1381 revolt that, 'according to the presentments of the York jurors, the leaders of the disturbances there "gave caps and other liveries of one colour to various members of their confederacy"' (10). (Ironically, for all the messianic fervour of the German Peasant Revolt, 'one of the demands of the insurgents was that they should be allowed to wear red clothes like their betters' (Laver, 86).) Cade's 'livery', like his 'regality' and the Lord of Misrule burlesque, apes that of the great households with their liveried retainers who were overlooked in earlier sumptuary laws and granted special dispensation by Elizabeth in 1588: 'the servants of noblemen and gentlemen may wear such livery coats as their masters shall allow them, with their badges or other ornaments of any velvet or silk to be laid or added to their said livery coats' (Hughes & Larkin, 3, 7).

At one point Shakespeare may have had a sumptuary proclamation in mind. The word 'sumptuous', found only four times in his plays and only in the histories, is used in Lord Saye's protest of probity, innocence and moderation: 'Is my apparel sumptuous to behold?' (4.7.93). This may be an ironic echo of the proclamation in which Elizabeth authorized temporary detention to prove the correctness of dress and degree, 'because there are many persons that percase shall be found in outward appearance more sumptuous in their apparel than by common intendment' (Hughes & Larkin, 2, 457). The phrase 'sumptuous apparel' occurs three times in the homily 'Against excess of apparel'.

However that may be, it is certain that Cade plays sharply with words when first confronting Lord Saye: 'Ah, thou say, thou serge – nay, thou buckram lord!' (4.7.21–2). Punning on the name, Cade sees Saye's reduced circumstances in terms of a coarsening, from 'say' (silk) to 'serge' (wool) to 'buckram' (a rough linen). Materials correspond to their reversed positions, but beyond the cruelty of the wit there may be a finer dramatic point. Cade's first line had been, 'Well, he shall be beheaded for it ten times' (4.7.21). As this sentence sinks in, he seems to be prompted by the change visible in Lord Saye's face to add 'thou buckram lord!' In the sixteenth century 'buckram' had, beyond the literal meaning of the 'kind of coarse linen or cloth stiffened with gum or paste' (*OED* 2), a figurative meaning of 'stiff', 'starched', 'stuck-up'; or 'that has false appearance of stress' (*OED* 4b). Not wishing to provoke the rebels, perhaps, Lord Saye had appeared modestly dressed before them, without the distinction of his degree. Here 'buckram' may also capture Cade's perception of

Saye's sudden realization of vulnerability, a superiority of bearing stiffening in shock before the judgement of Cade. And the latter does not let class-based invective drop, as is seen in the following charge of printing books and promoting literacy, and in his rounding on the modest lord, 'Thou dost ride on a foot-cloth, dost thou not?' (4.7.42–3), pointing to the undeniable luxury of trappings which give his remarks justification: 'Marry, thou ought'st not to let thy horse wear a cloak when honester men than thou go in their hose and doublets' (4.7.45–7).

Symbolic of the 'honester men' are the 'leather apron' (4.2.11) and 'clouted shoon' (4.2.174). Drawing on the work of Keith Thomas and including the example from this play – 'Spare none but such as go in clouted shoon' – Charles Hobday notes of the clouted shoe, the peasant's hobnailed boot, that ' "clubs and clouted shoon" was a proverbial phrase for a peasant revolt which crops up in Norfolk in 1537, and again in 1549 in connection with Kett's rebellion, and in Leicester in a recusant prophecy of 1586' (69). Class contempt is echoed in George's 'The nobility think scorn to go in leather aprons' (4.2.11). Unlike aristocratic dress, peasant wear changed relatively little during the Middle Ages. The one common innovation, particularly for smiths and tanners, was the leather apron. This remained an emblem of the lower orders right into the twentieth century (Cunnington & Cunnington, 178–9), a sign of difference as clear as that of spoken language.

From symbolism of clothing we may move to the crucial question of literacy. 'We are all branded on the tongue', said Dr Johnson, but in the earlier period the crucial difference was between those who were branded on the thumb and those who were executed instead, because of their inability to read. At the heart of Cade's assault on literacy is his accusation addressed to Lord Saye: 'Thou hast appointed justices of peace, to call poor men before them, about matters they were not able to answer. Moreover, thou hast put them in prison, and because they could not read, thou hast hanged them' (4.7.37–41). As in the matter of treason combat, history itself furnishes grotesque examples, seeming travesties, in the matter of the law of benefit of clergy. In the Middle Ages benefit of clergy was the privilege, available to ordained clerks, monks and nuns accused of felony, of being tried and punished by an ecclesiastical court. As a consequence of the statute *Pro Clero* (1350), which extended the privilege to secular clerks who helped the clergy in church services, it was later extended to all who could demonstrate the ability to read in Latin their 'neck verse', Psalm 51.1. By the sixteenth century royal courts had taken control, as benefit of clergy had become an involved law which could exempt those found guilty of certain felonies from the severity of the heavily used death penalty (see Holdsworth, 294–302). But what of those unable to read who faced the death penalty? Consider the case of one John Trotter, who claimed benefit of clergy when accused of murder during the reign of Edward III. Though illiterate he seemed able to 'read' the Psalter. He could still 'read' the verse even when a suspicious judge turned the book upside down. It transpired that a kind-hearted gaoler had allowed two boys to coach him. He was found guilty as a layman, but if the boys had succeeded in teaching him to read more convincingly, his claim to clergy would have been upheld, though the gaoler would have been punished (Gabel, 73).

Cade's charge to Lord Saye applies a logic of inversion and reversal. Instead of being sentenced to death in effect for not being able to read Latin, Lord Saye is condemned for his words on Kent, '*bona terra, mala gens*'. 'Away with him, away with him! He speaks Latin' (4.7.52–3). Because of Cade's logic, in reciprocating authoritarian self-justification in kind, it is impossible to reject his judgement without recognizing the preposterousness of such law in the actual world: this manifest injustice serves to call into question the whole justice of a system maintained to ensure the 'right' of a property-owning class to oppress the propertyless. Similarly, Cade's appeal to 'ancient freedom' in scene 8 and further parts of his speech (4.8.25) echo the 'Oracion of the duke of

Alaunson' before the battle of Vernoile in 1424 (Caldwell, 62). Alençon appeals to an immemorial liberty against the tyranny of the foreigner, the English: Cade appeals against the internal enemy, the Anglo–Norman, whose yoke of a foreign aristocracy bore heavily over an indigenous Saxon yeomanry (see 4.8.25n.).

By adding the Clerk of Chartham episode to the historical confrontation with Lord Saye, Shakespeare furthered Cade's comprehensive rejection of authority and law made manifest in writing. The evidence of anti-literacy in the 1381 revolt includes nothing as systematic as the allusions in Act 4, which include: materials – 'parchment', 'wax . . . seal', 'pen and inkhorn'; production – 'paper-mill', 'printing'; education – 'grammar school', 'noun', 'verb'; and law – 'justices of the peace', 'clerk', 'court-hand', 'obligations', 'letters'.

However, as in the previous episodes discussed, it is impossible to rest securely in the sense of a radical affirmation of anti–authoritarianism. As if to surrender subversion to inconsistency, to surrender the social critic to the anarchic clown, Shakespeare also shows Cade as feudal monarch *manqué*: 'there shall not a maid be married, but she shall pay to me her maidenhead ere they have it; men shall hold of me *in capite*' (4.7.113–16). Rather than 'reformation' here, Jack will insist on his proprietary right, his *droit de seigneur*.

To this may be added further parallels. Shakespeare created 'travesty-by-parallel' with history itself, by having Cade burlesque the royal entry of the King. The real King Henry VI, returning to London from his coronation in Paris, first assembled his entourage on Blackheath before the entry, during which, as Fabyan records (605), the conduits of Cheapside ran with wine, a festive tradition. In the play Cade and the rebels assemble on Blackheath, then, after his violent entry and his declaring himself 'lord of this city', he gives orders that 'the Pissing Conduit run nothing but claret wine the first year of our reign' (4.6.3–4), 'King' Jack even has his royal rhetoric, not echoing King Henry, but echoed by King Henry. His followers deserting him, 'Was ever feather so lightly blown to and fro as this multitude' (4.8.54–5), asks Cade; his subjects deserting him, 'Look, as I blow this feather from my face . . . such is the lightness of you common men' (*3H6* 3.1.84–9), observes Henry, the failed king echoing the mock king. Cade uses the royal 'we' (compare 2.2.64, 4.2.29) and one of his favourite words is 'command'. As 'king' and subject Cade knights himself (4.2.110–11), and also Dick the Butcher in Q (TLN 1631–2) with an abruptness that is ironically reflected in Henry's knighting of Iden (5.1.78). Less glamorously, Cade shares the royal 'beggary' (compare 4.1.101, 4.2.50). This grotesque likeness in difference by which one reflects the other is perhaps seen at its most pointed when Dick the Butcher declares, 'the laws of England may come out of your mouth' (4.7.5–6). Holinshed records that Wat Tyler 'putting his hands to his lips' declared 'that within foure daies all the lawes of England should come foorth of his mouth' (2, 740). Once more it appears that Shakespeare is emphasizing the parallel with the Peasants' Revolt, but article 14 of the deposition against Richard II stated: 'he said, that the lawes of the realme were in his head and sometimes in his brest' (see 4.7.5–6n.). The arbitrary anarchy of one sphere reflects the absolutist aspirations of another – *mundus alter et idem*, the World Turned Upside Down.

A further dimension of burlesque can be seen in the way that Shakespeare carefully made Cade not merely claim the throne but also imitate York himself. More than any other critic, David Riggs (124) assembles a persuasive catalogue, showing that Cade imitates his patron York's 'claims to royal ancestry [4.2.35–45], his intention to purge Henry's court of "false caterpillars" [4.4.36; 4.7.27–9], his detestation of all things French [4.2.156–61], his admiring recollection of Henry V [4.2.146–8], his distaste for "bookish rule" [4.2.80–101], his insistence on martial eminence as requisite for aristocratic station [4.2.49], and his easy association of martial bravery and material prosperity [4.2.59–70]'. Furthermore, as has always been recognized, Cade parodies aristocratic genealogy (4.2.35–45), reflecting on a major concern through the *Henry VI* plays in general, and refer-ring to York's claims in particular. It has also been claimed, more provocatively, that 'Cade's ramshackle army is the antimasque to York's rebellion' (Ornstein, 51).

Shakespeare drives the point home by actually having Cade and York echo each other. York first refers to 'caterpillars' (3.1.90) and is echoed by Cade (4.4.36); York speaks of 'resolution' and abjures 'fear' (3.1.331, 335), Cade disowns 'fear' (4.2.54) and protests his 'resolution' (4.8.61); Warwick and York punningly lament the loss of Maine (1.1.205–10) as do Dick the Butcher and Cade (4.2.150–3); Suffolk reports that the armourer was supposed to have claimed that York was 'rightful heir' (1.3.185), which Cade repeats (4.2.122), and is then echoed by Salisbury on behalf of York (5.1.178); Iden calls Cade 'that monstrous traitor' (4.10.57), which is then hurled at York by Somerset (5.1.106). Cade's mock genealogy as a Mortimer usually receives critical attention for its obvious parody, but Stephen Longstaffe (20–1) adds to our knowledge of this sequence by re-examining the claim 'My wife descended of the Lacies' (4.2.40). Longstaffe shows that this may allude to a Polish aristocrat, Count Laski, who, during his visit to England and courtship of the high and mighty in 1583, tried to establish that his family was descended from the English Lacies who, it turned out, had died out some two centuries earlier. After cutting a figure in royal circles, incur-ring many debts, and seemingly giving offence here and there, this rather suspect figure returned home in failure. Cade's refer-ence to the Lacies plausibly draws on what had become a topical London joke, particularly as Laski had stayed on the South Bank just two hundred yards from where the Rose Theatre was shortly to be built, and where Cade delivers his gag. By associa-tion, the noble claim of the house of York, and all feudal genealogy, is subjected to carnivalesque ridicule.

A final correspondence between Cade and York, which is symbolic for the *Henry VI* trilogy when considered as a whole, is that of 'butchery'. The word butchery does not appear in

1 Henry VI, the world of Talbot's chivalric valour and renown, but by the middle of *2 Henry VI* it develops as the symbol of barbarism as the country becomes the slaughterhouse of rebellion and the Wars of the Roses, which continue into *3 Henry VI*. With Gloucester's fall and death the King and Warwick invoke the imagery of the butcher and the slaughterhouse (3.1.210–13; 3.2.189), while the Queen disingenuously asks, 'Are you the butcher, Suffolk?' (3.2.195). The metaphorical and literal are confounded as the slaughter by Dick the Butcher is anticipated (4.2.24–5) and then realized in Cade's praise of him after the death of the Staffords, 'They fell before thee like sheep and oxen, and thou behaved'st thyself as if thou hadst been in thine own slaughterhouse' (4.3.3–5). York echoes this butchery as his words – 'On sheep or oxen could I spend my fury' (5.1.27) – anticipate the butchery of *3 Henry VI*, and an irony of history itself. As Sir William Dugdale records in *The Baronage of England* (1675), after the slaughter of young Richard and others at the battle of Wakefield, Clifford was known as 'the butcher' (I, 343).

The correspondence between the butchery of the lower orders and that of the nobles finds its emblem in the severed head. The chronicles express uniform horror at the execution of Lord Saye and Sir James Crowmer, Cade having their heads hoist aloft 'and at every corner have them kiss' (4.7.127–8). In fact the historical Cade's action, repeated by Shakespeare, duplicated at least one earlier atrocity. In 1381 Suffolk rebels bore the heads of Lord Chief Justice, Sir John Cavendish, and the prior of Bury St Edmunds, 'making them sometimes as it were to kisse' (Holinshed, II, 744). Cade's protracted, cruelly delayed sentence and execution of Lord Saye stresses a barbarity which, though less apparent, is not less real in more summary execution elsewhere in the plays. The depiction of Cade and his followers here is not simply the expression of anti–egalitarianism, the anarchic many–headed monster run wild, but rather the recognition that such rebellions become a grotesque mimicry of the barbarism of feudal hierarchy. In *3 Henry VI* Shakespeare has

Warwick order that York's head be replaced by Clifford's on York gate (1.4.180; 2.6.85–6), an echo of the Cade scene, which is not in the sources. As Palmer comments, it is strange 'that those who find in Cade's barbarity an indication of Shakespeare's horror of the mob should neglect to find in the barbarity of Queen Margaret or of my lords Clifford and York an indication of his horror of the nobility' (318–19).

The historical Jack Cade and the rebellion of 1450, discussed so far, are conflated with that of the historical Wat Tyler and the insurrection of 1381, but another kind of possible conflation is of equal importance. Shakespeare may have synthesized traditions of morality play and carnival, clown and fool, in having Cade played by the leading comedian of the company.

At the beginning of Act 4, scene 2, a carefully placed qualification initiates a particular expectation. 'Come and get thee a sword,' says George, 'though made of a lath.' Editors point out that this was the weapon carried by the Vice in the old morality plays. (Feste's song in *Twelfth Night*, 4.2.120–7, puts it plain enough: 'Like to the old Vice . . . / Who with dagger of lath, in his rage and his wrath, / Cries "ah, ha!" to the devil'.) But no sooner has the audience been invited to measure the historical Cade against a Vice figure such as Sedition, than it finds George and Nick invoking the World Upside Down. Deriving from classical Greek *adunata* (or Latin *impossibilia*) and the medieval *drolerie*, the carnivalesque and pictorial tradition of the World Upside Down found on sixteenth-century broadsheets depicted a range of social and natural inversion. The social aspect concerns us here – such images as: the peasant rides, the king walks; the servant arrests his master; 'the peasant judges the judge and teaches or refuses the advice of the learned'; and 'the thief (or poor man) takes the judge or policemen to jail' (Kunzle, 51). Following Nick's observation on the nobility's scorn for leather aprons, George adds: 'Nay, more, the King's Council are no good workmen' (4.2.12–13). On which Nick muses: 'True; and yet it is said, "Labour in thy vocation"; which is as much to say

101

as "Let the magistrates be labouring men"; and therefore should we be magistrates' (4.2.14–16). Nick specifically travesties 'An homily against idleness', restricting the meaning of 'labour' to what the homily distinguishes as 'handy labour', while elaborating on 'divers sorts of labours, some of the mind, and some of the body' including the 'vocation' of 'governing the commonweal publicly' (*Homilies*, 460) and so on. The world is turned upside down first by turning language upside down: the King's magistrates are considered poor 'workmen' who should therefore carry out manual labour in a revised vocation, thereby taking the place of the regular workmen, like George and Nick, who would assume their office. The judges will be judged, and the judged will become judges, as we see in the scenes with the Clerk of Chartham and Lord Saye (4.2 and 4.4).

The opening of 4.2 prepares for the entry of the clown as the mock king, Jack Cade – just as a clown, Tom Miller, appeared in the midst of the rebels of *The Life and Death of Jack Straw* (1593). Such figures could also symbolize the collective nature of an insurrectionary mob, reminding us that the rustic buffoon provided the early model for the stage clown (see Hill, 298; Wiles, *Clown*, 61–72). Shakespeare's portrayal of Cade incorporates both cultural and theatrical traditions.

Enid Welsford points out the process whereby the court fool and the public fool 'came to be reunited in the person of "the Lord of Misrule", "the Abbot of Unreason", "the Prince of Fools" who is none other than the traditional mock-king and clown, who has adopted the appearance and behaviour of the court-jester' (197–8). Furthermore, Morris dancing was associated with the Lord of Misrule and his train. With the decline of folk custom and ceremony the spirit of misrule survived in 'the "immoderate and inordinate joye" of the Elizabethan clown, jig dancer, and "jeaster", who was accustomed, as Thomas Lodge wrote, "to coin bitter jests, or to show antique motions, or to sing baudie sonnets and ballads", and who indulged in "all the feats of misrule in the countrie" ' (Weimann, 23–4). The 'jig', as C. R.

Baskervill has shown, included 'legal parody', 'satire on the ills of society' and allusion to the Utopian Land of Cockaygne – all features of the Cade scenes. In the theatrical tradition the clown as comic actor aped his betters, yet scoffed at ranks or classes, made mock prophecies, indulged in chop-logic not without some pointed wisdom, yet scorned learning (see Talbert, 56–60). Again, these characteristics appear in the Cade scenes but in a compounded form incomparably more dynamic than in their theatrical predecessors, especially when it is recalled that the actor is not performing as a clown accompanying Cade, but is both impersonating Cade acting clownishly, and derisively evaluating such action as from without: the clown ridicules Cade the historical personage. The dialectic between the ideology of propagandist history and the conventions of art as modified by carnival inversion give the Cade scenes their uniquely ambivalent power.

In the defeat of the historical Cade, the carnival king's saturnalia comes to an end as he is offered as a sacrifice to and for laughter. By surrendering the *character* to ridicule – the perception of anarchistic folly by the powers that be – the *comedian* performer triumphs: 'King Cade is dead, long live the clown.' The containment of subversive laughter spoken of by Phyllis Rackin cannot be sustained if one recognizes the dialogism between comedian and character, art and history. Similarly, the simple claim by Helgerson that Shakespeare mocks Cade overlooks the dynamics of performance, even though Helgerson is concerned with a players' theatre (see above, p. 65). The established comedian has an unwritten compact with the audience to make them laugh to the best of his ability (as discussed by Welsford and Baskervill). On the other hand, as actor the comedian has a contract with the playwright to fulfil the role. The two meet in the presentation of Cade as a clown, acted by a clown.

As Baskervill indicates, the clown was what Bakhtin would call a deeply dialogized figure. In the commentary on Act 4, I discuss the possibility that Will Kemp played Cade. Applying

Kemps nine daies vvonder.

Performed in a daunce from
London to Norwich.

Containing the pleasure, paines and kinde entertainment
of *William Kemp* betweene *London* and that Citty
in his late Morrice.

Wherein is somewhat set downe worth note; to reprooue
the slaunders spred of him: many things merry,
nothing hurtfull.

Written by himselfe to satisfie his friends.

LONDON
Printed by *E. A.* for *Nicholas Ling*, and are to be
solde at his shop at the west doore of Saint
Paules Church. 1600.

13 Title page of *Kemp's Nine Days' Wonder*

Bakhtin's concept, Stephen Longstaffe considers that 'The figure Kemp/Cade is thus an internally dialogized one, doubling in one person the two senses of "clown"' (25). A pointed possible instance may be the use of a single word 'honest', which Cade uses three times (4.2.94, 175; 4.7.46) and which David Wiles considers Kemp's 'favourite term of approbation' on the evidence of *Kemp's Nine Days' Wonder* (8, 9, 13, 19, 21, 22) (Wiles, *Clown*, 25). The dialogism lies in Cade's usage actually pointing up the character's populist duplicity while Kemp's irony confirms his own integrity as clown revealing folly. Whoever acted Cade, in performance the principal comedian exploits the compounded comic gradations between contemporary clown and historical personage, neither ever *completely* collapsed into the other. During, before or after any sequence the comedian can either exercise carnival free play between performance and audience or signal historical distancing by allowing the role to predominate. But since the role itself is cast in the mould of character-clown there is a ceaseless dialogic dynamism between the extremes of audience participation in carnival transgression, through shared laughter, and the perceived mockery of self-contradictory folly. Where at one moment we respond to inversion, distortion and burlesque, at another we find that they have become a version, reflection and duplication.

The 'double-voicedness' of Bakhtin's dialogism (see Vice, 45–111) finds perfect expression in the parallelism of the clown and Cade, who are both obliged to noble patrons yet enthroned by populism. Comedian and character aspire to, yet reject, aristocracy; proclaim communism, yet enact tyranny; scorn learning and law, yet apply the logic of oppression and barbarism which underpins so-called order, degree and hierarchy. With the collapse into the carnage of the Wars of the Roses and the butchery of and by the nobles, given the correspondences outlined above, we are obliged to ask – who is mimicking whom?

The ideological certainties of chronicle history have gone.

History is dynamically reconstituted by the relativistic freedom of art. We confront not the farce of subplot but the possible farce of history in which self-interest, dishonour and barbarism invert, distort and burlesque fealty, honour and love, while protesting their integrity. But this sense of travesty is critical, not dogmatic, and we are made both participants in, and spectators of, the historical process, by the transformation of foreshortened dramatic time. Performance perpetuates the confederacy of laughter and the actor lives to 'personate' another day. As Moody E. Prior said: 'the three parts of *Henry VI* are the rich ore out of which the later plays are refined' (9).

TEXT

The 'upstart Crow'

The customary form of the title of this play, which is adopted here, *King Henry VI, Part 2*, derives from the title in the first Folio (F) of Shakespeare's plays assembled by the actors John Heminge and Henry Condell in 1623: *The second Part of Henry the Sixt*, to which was added, *with the death of the Good Duke* HVMFREY. Of the three parts of *Henry VI* in F two were preceded in date of printing by versions now usually referred to as *The Contention* (the Quarto, Q, of *2 Henry VI*) and *The True Tragedy* (the Octavo, O, of *3 Henry VI*). The full title of *The Contention* reads (with spelling modernized):

> The First part of the Contention betwixt the two famous Houses of York and Lancaster, with the death of the good Duke Humphrey: And the banishment and death of the Duke of *Suffolk*, and the Tragical end of the proud Cardinal of *Winchester*, with the notable Rebellion of *Jack Cade*: *And the Duke of York's first claim unto the Crown.*

Printed by Thomas Creede for Thomas Millington in London, 1594, this play was entered by Millington on the Stationers'

Register on 12 March of that year. *The True Tragedy*, with a similarly elaborate title, was published in octavo, in 1595, also by Millington. Both plays were published again by Millington in quarto format (Q2) in 1600. In 1619 the two plays were published together by Thomas Pavier as a two-part play, *The Whole Contention betweene the two Famous Houses, Lancaster and Yorke. With the Tragical ends of the good Duke Humfrey, Richard Duke of York, and King Henry the sixt*. This edition is known as Q3.

2 Henry VI is approximately a third longer than *The Contention* and this is just one feature of the texts that has contributed to a long-standing debate in the textual and bibliographic scholarship on Shakespeare. An outline of the debate is offered here. Those wishing to pursue this in greater detail may consult the scholarly works referred to in the commentary notes and bibliography. All editors take F as the control text for *2 Henry VI*, but the existence of the Quartos (Qq) raises the question of their relationship to F, and consequently how far they may be consulted and used for a modern edition. By the later nineteenth century academic opinion was divided into three camps: (1) Shakespeare was the author of *The Contention*, *The True Tragedy*, and *2* and *3 Henry VI*; (2) Shakespeare wrote *2* and *3 Henry VI* but only contributed to *The Contention* and *The True Tragedy*; (3) Shakespeare wrote *2* and *3 Henry VI* and made no contribution to *The Contention* and *The True Tragedy* (Lee). Someone like F. G. Fleay, who believed that Shakespeare played no part in any of the four plays, was completely out on a limb.

In the eighteenth century Nicholas Rowe, in his edition of Shakespeare's works, had made use of the second Quartos of *Hamlet* and *Romeo and Juliet*, but not the *Henry VI* Quartos (i.e. *The Contention* and *The True Tragedy*) (see Walton; McKerrow, 'Treatment'). Pope and Theobald believed that Shakespeare had written and then revised the earlier two-part play to produce *2* and *3 Henry VI*. With great percipience, Dr Johnson speculated that the Quartos, though published earlier than F, were in fact memorial reports deriving from the Folio versions. Of great importance in the eighteenth-century editorial tradition, however, was Edward Capell who divided his personal collection of Shakespeare Quartos into the sheep and the goats with *The Contention* and *The True Tragedy*, regarded as corrupt and unreliable, included in the latter. Johnson and Capell were not alone in their view since arguably the greatest Shakespeare editor of the time, Edmond Malone, shared their belief. Malone followed Capell in his recognition of the importance of the early Quartos, but the *Henry VI* Quartos gave him particular concern (see Walton, 1–9). In his *Dissertation on the Three Parts of King Henry VI*, which was added to his ten-volume edition of the *Plays and Poems* (1790), he reverted from his belief in the quartos as memorial reports to follow that of the revisionists: the inconsistencies, inferiorities, discrepancy in length and further arguments suggested that Robert Greene and George Peele were either joint or respective authors of the earlier plays. The 'revisionist' camp appeared to have won the day along with the 'collaborationists' who believed Shakespeare worked with others, such was the influence of Malone whose final edition of Shakespeare, brought out after his death by James Boswell in 1821 (known as the Third Variorum), included the *Dissertation*. Nineteenth-century 'revisionist' editors like Charles Knight and Alexander Dyce, following Malone, pondered on *The Contention* and *The True Tragedy* as early dramatic sketches revised either by Shakespeare himself, or by Christopher Marlowe – or by such variously combined figures as Greene and Peele, Thomas Nashe and Thomas Lodge.

At the heart of Malone's *Dissertation*, the 'central hinge' of the argument as he called it, was an interpretation of what has become one of the best-known, most controversial and unavoidably provoking texts associated with the Quarto and Octavo of *2* and *3 Henry VI*, Robert Greene's *Greene's Groatsworth of Wit* (1592) (see D. A. Carroll, *Groatsworth*). In Malone's lifetime Thomas Tyrwhitt, a classical scholar and fellow Shakespearean, first recognized a significant allusion in Greene's text and published it in the 1778 Johnson–Steevens edition of Shakespeare's works. The passage follows, with its notorious reference to Shakespeare as 'an upstart Crow':

> Base minded men all three of you, if by my miserie you be not warned: for unto none of you (like me) sought those burres to cleave: those Puppets (I meane) that spake from our mouths, those Anticks garnisht in our colours. Is it not strange, that I, to whom they all have beene beholding, is it not like that you, to whome they all have beene beholding, shall (were yee in that case as I am now) bee both at once of them forsaken? Yes trust them not: for there is an upstart Crow, beautified with our feathers, that with his *Tygers hart wrapt in a Players hyde*, supposes he is as well able to bombast out a blanke verse as the best of you: and being an absolute *Johannes fac totum*, is in his owne conceit the onely Shake-scene in a country.
>
> (D. A. Carroll, *Groatsworth*, 83–5)

It is accepted that Greene is addressing his fellow playwrights and 'University Wits' – Christopher Marlowe, George Peele and Thomas Nashe – from the poverty and misery of his deathbed. The difficulty arises in attempting to ascertain the role in which Greene is accusing Shakespeare: is it Shakespeare as actor, as aspiring playwright, or as plagiarist? Malone believed the last disparaging label to be true and was followed this century by J. Dover Wilson (Cambridge 1, xiv–xviii). But the majority view has supported Peter Alexander's interpretation in favour of the first two positions ('*Henry VI*').

The fable of Aesop's crow impudently dressing up in the colourful plumes of another bird is a familiar one which Greene himself had applied satirically elsewhere to the actor who grows rich by declaiming an author's lines. In *Never Too Late* (1590) Greene alludes to the celebrated Roman prototype of the actor: 'Why *Roscius*, art thou proud with Esop's Crow, being pranct [i.e. pranked] with the glorie of others feathers? of thy selfe thou canst say nothing' (see Alexander, '*Henry VI*', 43). Malone and Wilson, however, argue that the crow allusion here also refers to Horace's *Epistle* (I.iii) in which Horace warns Celsus against stealing from other writers, 'lest, if it chance that the flock of birds should some time or other come to demand their feathers, he, like the daw [*cornix*] stripped of his stolen colours, be exposed to ridicule' (Horace, 163). The first part of Greene's charge – 'those Puppets . . . that spake from our mouths, those Anticks garnisht in our colours' – certainly seems to allude to the actors, but the latter part of the quotation complicates the issue. From Tyrwhitt on, everyone has recognized the italicized line as one parodied by Greene from Shakespeare: '*Tygers hart wrapt in a Players hyde*'. In *3 Henry VI* the captive Duke of York stands humiliated in a paper crown on a molehill as Queen Margaret torments him with a napkin stained by the blood of his slaughtered son, Rutland; 'O tiger's heart wrapp'd in a woman's hide!' (1.4.137) is part of York's agonized reply. As Greene concludes of Shakespeare, 'he is as well able to bombast out a blanke verse as the best of you'. This would seem to point to Shakespeare more as writer than actor.

It is worth looking more closely at Greene's parody. He moves from the Aesopic feathers and crow to another beast allusion and a further analogy concerning concealment, which inverts the preceding fable. The crow had concealed its plainness with the splendours of a better-endowed bird whereas Shakespeare the (undistinguished?) actor had all along concealed the gift for the colours of rhetoric, so to speak, that shone forth in the *Henry VI* plays. Greene aptly parodies the line which refers to the destructive tiger since such powerful verse would destroy all their reputations and incomes. If read this way, the charge against Shakespeare is in fact the reverse of plagiarism: 'this fellow is as good if not better than the best of you (i.e. Marlowe)!' Further, for all the sardonic intention of 'supposes he is as well able', Greene's passage can be read as a tribute in spite of himself: 'this Shakespeare with his *Henry VI* plays has surpassed us all'.

Date, sequence and authorship

Whatever the debated interpretations of Greene's attack on Shakespeare may be, the parody of the *3 Henry VI* verse indicates that Greene, who died on 3 September 1592, had heard or read the line. This information gives us one of the few pieces of external evidence regarding the date of *The Contention* if we accept, as all commentators do, that *The True Tragedy* was written as a continuation of *The Contention*, the plays forming the two-part play that Pavier published in 1619, entitled *The Whole Contention*. Apart from this, we have the Stationers' Register entry and publication date for *The Contention*, 1594, and we know that the plague closed London theatres intermittently from 25 June 1592 to January 1594.

Thus composition and performance of *The Contention* took place by 1592, or earlier, depending on how far conjecture is allowed to influence judgement. Verbal echoes of other plays, *Tamburlaine* for example, point to the possibility of earlier dating, since there is evidence to show performance of Marlowe's two-part play some three years before its publication in 1590 (Fuller, xvii). Cairncross notes the converging dates in the Stationers' Register of publications believed to have influenced the writing of *2 Henry VI*: these are Greene's *Penelope's Web* (26 June 1587) and *Menaphon* (23 August 1589); Spenser's *Faerie Queene*, Books 1–3 (January 1590); possibly Lyly's *Pap with a Hatchet* (October 1589); and commentators always point to the date of the second edition of Holinshed's *Chronicle*, 1587. Honigmann (*Impact*, 70ff.), believing it highly unlikely that Shakespeare would not have begun a writing career before his late twenties, has explored this possibility of earlier composition in an attempt to reverse E. K. Chambers's 'late start' dating of about 1592 (II, 130). But with no hard evidence to support his case, Honigmann's argument has gained little support.

Discussion of the date of *The Contention* inevitably involves the question of the date of *1 Henry VI* and the problem of sequence of composition. There is no early quarto of *1 Henry VI*, but again we have two crucial dates which seem to offer hard evidence. First, there is Henslowe's diary reference to a play performed by Lord Strange's men at the Rose Theatre on 3 March 1592, entitled 'harey the vj'. This is designated as 'ne', which could indicate either a 'new' play or one newly licensed, or relicensed after rechecking, by the Master of the Revels. Knutson shows that when registering two-part plays Henslowe referred to the first part of a play by its main title only, whereas the second part was duly recorded as such along with the main title. Therefore it is considered that 'harey the vj' is unlikely to have referred to the second or third part of *Henry VI* and thus is believed to refer to *1 Henry VI*. Bate's observation supports this: 'All the plays so marked ['ne' in Henslowe's diary] between 1591 and 1594 seem to have been genuinely new; it was only from late 1595 onwards that the 'ne' was occasionally written beside an older play that was either newly revised or new to the company performing it' (*Titus*, 70).

The second piece of evidence, which adds credence to this, is from Thomas Nashe's *Piers Penniless His Supplication to the Devil*. Nashe's work was entered in the Stationers' Register on 8 August 1592. Here, portraying heroism on the stage, he invokes a great historical exemplar:

> How would it have ioyed brave *Talbot* (the terror of the French) to thinke that after he had lyne two hundred yeares in his Tombe, hee should triumphe againe on the Stage, and have his bones newe embalmed with the teares of ten thousand spectators at least (at severall times), who, in the Tragedian that represents his person, imagine they behold him fresh bleeding.
>
> (I, 212)

Since, as Hattaway points out (Cambridge 2, 60), another work of Nashe's, *The Terrors of the Night* (1593), echoes the language of *1 Henry VI*, then it is reasonable to conclude that the Talbot reference indicates *1 Henry VI*. Hanspeter Born (324) points out that *Piers Penniless* is dedicated to Lord Strange and that within its pages

Edward Alleyn, who was Strange's leading actor in 1592, is fulsomely praised. It is hardly likely that Nashe could be celebrating another Talbot play by a rival company. Born (325–6) offers further arguments for the Henslowe date as identifying *1 Henry VI* as a new play: the exceptional profits suggest a new, not revived, play; the play closely reflects the military adventures of the Earl of Essex in France in late 1591 and early 1592; details of the staging indicate performance in the Rose Theatre after building alterations during 1591–2.

Arguing for consecutive composition of the trilogy against those who believe that the period between March and September 1592 (when it was at first anticipated that the theatres would reopen) was simply too short for the writing of *2* and *3 Henry VI*, Born believes Shakespeare did, indeed, complete the sequence. He does not consider the concomitant of his belief; that such dating would include *2* and *3 Henry VI*, *Titus Andronicus*, perhaps *The Comedy of Errors* or work on *The Taming of the Shrew*, as well as *Venus and Adonis* and *The Rape of Lucrece* – as all written between 1592 and 1594 (see George, 320). Ironically, though Born's arguments for dating *1 Henry VI* are strong, his arguments for the composition and date of *2* and *3 Henry VI* are weak, since they rely not on hard facts but on his belief in their relative maturity of character, style and design. Further, these arguments are put forward without any reference to the huge question of mixed authorship of the three plays. Moreover, Born downplays the issue of discrepancies and inconsistencies between the first and second parts of *Henry VI*, as do Cairncross and Hattaway, in order to maintain an argument for sequential composition. In contrast, commentators like Smidt and J. Dover Wilson find such problems insurmountable, and thus see them as evidence for the reverse argument, for *2* and *3 Henry VI* preceding *1 Henry VI*, whether the date of *Part 1* is accepted as 1592, or earlier.

Born summarizes Wilson's main points and then attempts refutation. In his Introduction to *1 Henry VI* (Cambridge 1, xii), Wilson notes that *2* and *3 Henry VI* mention three times that

Henry was only nine months old when he ascended the throne, as in 1.1 of *1 Henry VI*, yet at the end of the play he is old enough for love and courtship. Addressing the anachronism here, Born appeals to T. W. Baldwin's distinction (*Genetics*, 335) between fictive convenience for dramatic representation and historical accuracy in the chronicles, which seems more like evasive rationalization than convincing refutation. Second, the character of Gloucester differs markedly between *Parts 1* and *2* of *Henry VI*: almost a ruffian in the first, he is the statesmanlike Lord Protector in the second. Born sees character development, whereas Wilson finds inconsistency. Third, Wilson finds it incomprehensible that Talbot, the hero of *Part 1*, is never mentioned in *Part 2*, even when in the first scene Gloucester recounts the glorious dead who have given their lives to preserve Henry V's victories in France. Born's response to this important, puzzling point is entirely inadequate: 'because the character is dead and mentioning it would be dramatically distractive' (327). What would Born say to the repeated mention of Henry V in *2 Henry VI*? The issue of Talbot's absence is of some significance and I will return to it. Clearly Born's response to Wilson's points is unconvincing, to put it mildly. Kristian Smidt has found a number of additional inconsistencies between the two parts which appear to strengthen the position of those inclined towards Wilson's position.

Smidt points out that the surrender of Anjou and Maine as part of the Henry–Margaret marriage treaty, a condition which is bitterly resented throughout *2 Henry VI*, is not mentioned as part of the treaty in *1 Henry VI*: conversely, in *1 Henry VI* we are reminded that Henry is already betrothed to the Earl of Armagnac's daughter, a detail seemingly forgotten in *2 Henry VI*. Further, there are details such as Suffolk's being addressed by the King as an earl at the end of *1 Henry VI*, yet he has the title of marquess at the beginning of *2 Henry VI*. Another kind of oddity, for Smidt, is the fact that though the Duke of York is given extensive opportunity to outline his dynastic claim to the crown in *2 Henry VI*, he does not once refer to the equally protracted genealogy spelt out to him by Edmund Mortimer in the Tower of London in *1 Henry VI*.

Smidt has written a number of books all devoted to demonstrating 'unconformities' in Shakespeare, applying a metaphor from the geological term for breaches in continuity. A deep irony arises here. Since Smidt's extensive studies inadvertently show that various kinds of inconsistency are actually characteristic of Shakespeare's plays, it seems rather paradoxical that he here uses such a feature to argue a case assuming that had Shakespeare followed *1 Henry VI* with the next two parts he would have either been consistent or corrected irregularities. Therefore, he argues, *2* and *3 Henry VI* came first. Furthermore, Smidt considers Shakespeare as sole author with a free hand to write and correct as he wished, which is always the assumption of those like Tillyard, Cairncross and Hattaway who argue for consecutive composition and continuity of development.

Before proceeding to the controversial issue of authorship, I wish to return to one problem from all these points concerning inconsistency, the absence of any mention of Talbot in *The Contention* or *2 Henry VI*, particularly in Gloucester's early speech (2.2.75–100). As we have seen, this is a major issue in spite of the complication, which Wilson indicates, that though Talbot dies in the first play, he was still alive and fighting in France at the historical time of Gloucester's speech. I believe that Wilson's larger point cannot be discounted. It is very hard to believe that if *1 Henry VI* preceded *2 Henry VI* Shakespeare would not, at some point, have capitalized on its success, particularly by having Gloucester recall such patriotic self-sacrifice, in spite of any anachronism. Furthermore, it is possible that, in places, the language of Cade is echoed by that of Talbot. That is, when Shakespeare was called in to assist with the composition of *1 Henry VI* he deliberately worked in an allusive contrast between hero and anti-hero (unless the alternative argument is pursued, that with subsequent revision of

1 Henry VI for what became the Folio text, Shakespeare introduced such echoes). Thus I support the view of the composition and performance of *2 Henry VI* (but with the title of *The Contention*) before the performance date of *1 Henry VI*. Before examining these matters further, the question of authorship must be looked at.

In their Introductions to the *Henry VI* plays Hart and Wilson argue extensively for the variously combined authorship of Greene, Peele, Nashe, Marlowe, Kyd and Shakespeare. As Hinchcliffe records, other scholars have suggested further contributors such as Thomas Lodge (Norman) and even the author of the *Anatomy of Melancholy*, Robert Burton (Brownlee). Such an array indicates a fundamental problem. Though collaboration is an acknowledged fact of Renaissance dramatic writing (see McMullan), how could five, or more, playwrights actually collaborate on a text? One answer to this question is often taken to be the play *Sir Thomas More* attributed by Gabrieli and Melchiori to 'Anthony Munday and others, revised by Henry Chettle, Thomas Dekker, Thomas Heywood and William Shakespeare'. We must recognize, however, that such multiple authorship as this was the exception in collaborative enterprises, not the rule. Therefore to invoke *Sir Thomas More* as some kind of evidence by example for the composite authorship of the *Henry VI* plays is highly dubious. (For a discussion of the principles of establishing authorship from external and internal evidence, and a consideration of the problem of collaboration, see Schoenbaum, 147–222, 223–30.)

The procedure of the revisionists is to identify echoes of, and allusions to, the work of the various assumed contributors, or, more ambitiously, to attribute substantial sections of a play to particular authors. Thus Wilson confidently assigns the Jack Cade scenes of *2 Henry VI* to Thomas Nashe. Again, a problem of assessing argument and evidence arises when others, with equal conviction, attribute these scenes to Shakespeare. R.W. Chambers for example (215–21) uses them to argue for

Shakespeare's authorship of what is known as the Hand D three-page manuscript of the mob scenes of *Sir Thomas More*, which is indeed now generally accepted as the only surviving holograph of Shakespeare. Arguments using the same evidence for contrary conclusions rather undermine any consensus. Hart supports Peele as the leading writer of *2 Henry VI*, with Greene in the background, while Wilson reverses this and feels that Greene is the principal contributor. Yet, as he acknowledges, Greene was a well-known plagiarist, and when it comes to comparisons with Peele, 'these two dramatists [are] often indistinguishable, the more so that Greene never hesitates to borrow from Peele' (Cambridge 1, xxvii). The issue is further complicated by the belief that at the outset of his writing career Shakespeare is highly likely to have imitated the leading figures of the day. For the majority today who, with whatever modification, accept the concept of reported texts, 'echoes' of other plays are often explained as imported recollections of the reporters inadvertently including lines remembered as actors or audience (see Appendix 3). At one time this was thought to be the case with the 'echoes' of *The Troublesome Reign of King John* in *3 Henry VI*, until scholars suggested the reverse to be the case (see Honigmann, *Impact*, 78–88). Today editors will cite verbal analogues frequently, but they are reluctant to press these as evidence of mixed authorship. What on first examination may seem to be a possible indication of another author, on closer inspection can seem quite arbitrary. Unfortunately, this experience can be felt when reading through the examples provided by Hart and Wilson. Essentially, Hart and Wilson lacked any diagnostic methodology which could adequately deal with the literature of a culture drawing on the commonplace storehouses of Roman, Greek and proverbial wisdom embodied in humanist education. Wilson's position is the most exposed because its logic is to claim that, since Shakespeare could not have written inferior verse, someone else must have written it.

There is, however, something deeply unsatisfactory in the

opposed views on authorship of leading editors of the *Henry VI* plays. Cairncross and Hattaway argue from a position of accepting that *The Contention* and *The True Tragedy* are memorial reports of *2* and *3 Henry VI*, which means for them that Shakespeare must have been sole author, since they do not believe that he began his career by revising others' work. Cairncross dismisses the question of inconsistencies as proving nothing. Hattaway, in a line, turns away from the whole debate concerning mixed authorship and reverse sequence and coolly declares that his 'account' is 'based on the premise that Shakespeare wrote the whole of the trilogy, and in the order of the events it portrays' (Cambridge 2, 61). The critically enabling assumptions of Cairncross and Hattaway certainly simplify matters, and are now more or less the norm. Dismissing argument is one thing, point by point refutation quite another. I believe that the question of mixed authorship remains open and I have included examples of Hart's and Wilson's analogues from Greene, Peele and Nashe in the commentary.

In their attempts to find a more objective and scientific method, scholars have turned to various modes of statistical analysis. Many years ago Hart (*Copies*, 25) showed most strikingly that whereas the proportion of words common to two authentic Shakespeare plays is much the same as the proportion of words common to a Shakespeare drama and its source play, approximately 50 per cent, the figure when *The Contention* and *2 Henry VI* are compared is 86.6 per cent. For developments in recent years, the Oxford editors offer an excellent introduction to stylometry and the analysis of 'function' words (*TxC*, 80–106). This contemporary mathematical approach replaces older 'metrical test' analysis, which has proved to be unreliable (see E. K. Chambers, II, 397–409), in spite of the later sophistication of it by Wentersdorf. The statistical analysis of 'function' words takes very common words and mathematically tabulates their frequency in a given body of material to establish patterns of consistency according to variation between the average and the standard statistical deviation. The accepted plays of Shakespeare are analysed to establish the norm against which a play like *2 Henry VI* can be measured. Pertinent here is Oxford's application of this method to *2 Henry VI*. The findings (*TxC*, 86) indicate that collaborative composition by two authors cannot be ruled out.

Naturally enough, those claiming Shakespeare's sole authorship of the *Henry VI* trilogy always look to the fact of Heminge and Condell's inclusion of the plays in the first Folio. By contrast there is its puzzling omission from Frances Meres's famous list of plays in his *Palladis Tamia: Wit's Treasury* (1598). Meres mentions twelve plays written by this date, not including the *Henry VI* plays (or *The Taming of the Shrew*). In fact the titles *2 Henry VI* and *3 Henry VI*, as against *The Contention* and *The True Tragedy*, are first found in 1602. The titles 'The firste and second parte of Henry the vj' were entered by Thomas Pavier in the Stationers' Register for 19 April 1602, after *The Contention* and *The True Tragedy* were handed over to him by Millington, the first publisher of the plays. In turn, as we have seen, Pavier published these in 1619 as *The Whole Contention betweene the two Famous Houses, Lancaster and Yorke*. *1 Henry VI* was registered on its first appearance in the Folio as 'The thirde parte of Henry ye Sixt', because *2* and *3 Henry VI* had been registered in 1602 as the first and second parts.

So here we have, in outline, leading facts and conjectures concerning this labyrinthine question of date, sequence and authorship. What is to be made of it? Until further documentary evidence comes to light only a general surmise can be made. I think that we have to accept that by 1623 the legal, financial and proprietorial issues concerning *1 Henry VI* had been settled and the play was placed before the other parts in the Folio as substantially Shakespeare's work. This does not mean that Shakespeare must be considered as sole author of the trilogy. Conversely, if Shakespeare was not sole author, this does not mean that we have to exclude the possibility that his contribution, plus subsequent revision, eventually provided the overall

shaping spirit, in spite of competing authors, dividing companies, opportunistic publishers and the plague. By shaping spirit
is meant that quality which has been variously described as
ambiguity, ambivalence, doubleness of vision, antithetical sense
or carnivalesque inversion, and is usefully summarized by Paola
Pugliatti (42–59) as 'perspectivism'. The following briefly offers
a particular illustration of this.

There is some critical consensus that Shakespeare wrote the
Talbot scene, 4.2, *1 Henry VI*. Malone (VI, 382), E. K. Chambers
(II, 291), Hart (Arden 1, xviii) and Wilson (Cambridge 1, xliii),
although all 'disintegrators', believed Shakespeare to be the
author of this scene. Before Bordeaux the French are threatened
with 'Lean famine' (4.2.11) and so on. The General of the town
declares that 'Ten thousand French' (4.2.8) have sworn to fight
against Talbot, a 'valiant man' of 'an invincible unconquered
spirit' (4.2.31–2). They hope finally to see Talbot's dead body
'withered' (4.2.8). As noted in the commentary and touched on
above (p. 115), in Jack Cade's confrontation with Iden (*2H6*
4.2.10ff.), within a few lines the above words are seemingly
echoed. Cade declares that 'Famine' has slain him, and but for
hunger he would otherwise defeat 'ten thousand devils'.
However, in death his 'unconquered soul' flees, leaving Iden's
garden to 'wither' (4.10.59–64). Cade's last word is 'valour'
(4.10.74) to which he had testified earlier, 'Valiant I am' (4.2.49).
The ironic parallels can hardly be accidental, whether
Shakespeare wrote them for Talbot after writing *2 Henry VI*,
or whether they were added in a later revision of *1 Henry VI*
(see p. 115). The critical point remains that Shakespeare thought
in terms of structural contrast, parallel and inversion from
play to play. Values such as heroism, valour and patriotism are
problematized and deepened by exploiting the boundaries of
social class and literary propriety in the clash of chivalric ideal
and artisan reality. Dramatic conversion of history generates
ambivalence, above all in the *Henry IV* plays and *Henry V*. The
Henry VI plays demonstrate Shakespeare's almost mock-

Hegelian grasp on how emergent figures such as Talbot, Cade and Richard of Gloucester could embody the conflicting values of society, history and art. This essential drama is fully realized in *1* and *2 Henry IV*, but it began with Shakespeare's first confrontation with the meaning of history in the *Henry VI* trilogy.

To return to the beginning: it seems probable that, by 1591, *2* and *3 Henry VI* had been performed successfully, presumably by Lord Strange's company, since 'Pembroke's Men' appears on the title-page of *The True Tragedy* and this company is generally considered as an offshoot of Strange's (see George). Though Greene and others may have had a hand in developing plot and contributing dialogue, the great surprise of the plays was the success of Shakespeare, a mere actor, in surpassing them all in writing plays. To capitalize on this success, with the contemporary political events of Essex in France and the attraction of the Talbot materials in the chronicles, collaboration began on *1 Henry VI* with Shakespeare once again being called in and repeating his success, to the great annoyance of Greene. With the outbreak of plague the chance to profit from London audiences with the Talbot play rivalling the others was dashed, and furthermore, with the break-up of Strange's large company, ownership of the plays was divided. A remnant of the older company hung on to the money-making *1 Henry VI*, while Shakespeare, perhaps because his contribution was the major part, claimed the earlier two-part sequence which was to become *2* and *3 Henry VI*. To accommodate the theatrical limitations of provincial touring, Pembroke's men made the decision to offer abridged versions of the original two-part play, possibly for consecutive performance at each showing. Returning to London after the plague, the company, facing bankruptcy, sold these versions to Millington who published them as *The Contention* and *The True Tragedy* in, respectively, 1594 and 1595. As we have seen, *The Whole Contention* appeared in 1619, and the trilogy was united for publication in the Folio in 1623.

From revision to report

Malone's legacy dominated textual history so much that a nineteenth-century follower of Dr Johnson's memorial speculation, Thomas Kenny (in *The Life and Genius of Shakespeare*, 1864), remained unknown to Peter Alexander when in 1929 he published his developed theoretical reappraisal of the memorialist position in *Shakespeare's 'Henry VI' and 'Richard III'*. There were exceptions to Malone's view, however. The German critical tradition deriving from Schlegel's belief in the organic interrelationship of the English histories as Shakespeare's national epic influenced Charles Knight in his 1842 edition which assigned all three *Henry VI* plays, as well as *The Contention* and *The True Tragedy*, to Shakespeare. But ironically, although the multivolume Cambridge Shakespeare reproduced the Quarto and Octavo of the last two, A. W. Pollard evidently considered them beyond the pale, since they receive no sustained discussion in his groundbreaking study of 1909, *Shakespeare's Folios and Quartos*, which inaugurated the New Bibliography. It was here that, following Capell, he devised the formulation of 'Good' and 'Bad' Quartos. The 'Bad' Quartos alone, he believed, were those referred to in Heminge and Condell's preface as 'stolne, and surreptitious copies, maimed, and deformed by frauds and stealthes of iniurious imposters'. 'Bad' indicated the corruption which came about through faulty shorthand or memory, which produced such texts as the first Quartos of *Romeo and Juliet*, *Henry V*, *The Merry Wives of Windsor* and *Hamlet*.

In the same year as Pollard's study Hart published the first Arden edition of *2 Henry VI*. This edition very much reflects the post-Malone revisionist or collaborationist view of the relationship of Q to F. The whole Introduction and much of the commentary are devoted to a painstaking study of the influence of, and analogues from, Greene's participation, Peele, Marlowe and all the usual suspects, discussed above (pp. 116–17).

In 1942, looking back on this inheritance of Malone, W.W. Greg remarked that '[f]rom this original misconception of Malone's sprang a whole jungle of critical and biographical error' (*Problem*, 51). The two textual scholars who eventually reversed the trend started by Malone were Peter Alexander and Madeleine Doran. Working independently they published their findings in successive years, Doran's *'Henry VI, Parts II and III': Their Relation to the 'Contention' and the 'True Tragedy'* in 1928, and Alexander's *Shakespeare's 'Henry VI' and 'Richard III'* in 1929. I will consider Alexander first because his arguments are less involved than Doran's. Alexander somewhat laboriously argues against Malone on Greene's participation, but it is when he reconsiders the reporter–memorial theory that he makes his greatest contribution. One passage in particular provided Alexander with his clinching evidence, the scene in which the Duke of York argues his claim to the crown, 2.2.9–27 (Q, TLN 736–68; F, TLN 960–86).

There is no need to quote the passage fully – the crucial detail occurs in the opening lines:

> *Yorke*. Then thus my Lords.
> Edward the third had seuen sonnes,
> The first was Edward the blacke Prince,
> Prince of Wales.
> The second was Edmund of Langly,
> Duke of Yorke.
> The third was Lyonell Duke of Clarence.
> The fourth was Iohn of Gaunt,
> The Duke of Lancaster.
> The fifth was Roger Mortemor, Earle of March.
> The sixt was sir Thomas of Woodstocke.
> William of Winsore was the seuenth and last.
>
> (Q, TLN 742–53)

> *Yorke*. Then thus:
> *Edward* the third, my Lords, had seuen Sonnes:
> The first, *Edward* the Black-Prince, Prince of Wales;
> The second, *William* of Hatfield; and the third,
> *Lionel*, Duke of Clarence; next to whom,

Was Iohn of Gaunt, the Duke of Lancaster;
The fift, was *Edmond Langley*, Duke of Yorke;
The sixt, was *Thomas* of Woodstock, Duke of Gloster;
William of Windsor was the seuenth, and last.

(F, TLN 968–76)

Alexander shows that the passage in Q is full of genealogical errors, but the chief blunder is the mistaken placing of York's ancestor as the second son of Edward III instead of the fifth, as in F. Alexander summarizes:

> We cannot say that the Quarto was written by a dramatist who had studied the chronicles, but who trusted to his memory when he came to composition and in his impatience confused the details: it is not merely the details that are incorrect; the argument in the Quarto taken as a whole has no point whatever. York had to prove that, although descended from the fifth son of Edward III, he was, because of his father's marriage with a descendant of the third son, more in the direct line of succession than the heirs of the fourth son. The Quarto writer by making him declare his ancestor the Duke of York to be second son to Edward III renders further argument superfluous; he had now no need to claim the throne through a daughter of the third son as he proceeds to do.

('*Henry VI*', 62)

Alexander proceeds to demolish the revisionists' position, and Malone's in particular, by demonstrating how the irregularities of Q – verse as prose, incoherence, echoes of other plays, phonetic spelling and suchlike – could be accounted for by the faulty memory of a reporter, or reporters, whom he identified as the actor of Warwick and the actor doubling as Suffolk and Clifford (a view which, as we shall see, was to be challenged).

In her study of the relationship of Q to F, Madeleine Doran came up with a convincing diagnostic technique: if, upon analysis, F reveals revisions on the copy given the printer, and these revisions are found in Q, then Q must be based on F. Doran located eight revisional areas, including part of the petitioners' scene (1.3), the conjuring scene (1.4), the hawking scene (2.1) and the Simpcox miracle scene (2.1) – all characterized by a questionable mixture of prose and verse. This characteristic was the focus of Doran's analysis, which concludes:

> The Folio text could not have come from the Quarto texts themselves because the traces of older verse showing through prose in the Folio are not in the Quartos; the Folio and Quartos could not have come from a common original, because the revisional prose in the Folio, half obliterating the older verse, is found likewise in the Quartos; the Quartos must have come from the Folio because of the presence in them of the revised material in the Folio, both of the upper stratum of prose and of the verse which appears printed with faulty line-divisions.
>
> (Doran, 50)

Though the extended list of memorial characteristics Doran finds is very convincing, it must be remembered that the hypothesis that Q is a reported text remains only a premiss, and her method as well as her confidence have thus a weakness (76).

The second half of Doran's thesis has proved to be somewhat prescient since it anticipated the critical and theoretical revival of interest today in the 'Bad' Quartos as deriving from performance. Rather than showing the inconsistent vagaries of faulty memory, Doran shows that Q consistently cuts non-dramatic matter, which she categorizes as dialogue describing an action implied by other speeches, parts merely heightening a character or mood, repetitions of an action, dialogue and action not necessary to the sequence of events, messengers' speeches (52). Consequently, Doran concludes that Q represents an abridgement and adaptation of F for provincial touring. This latter judgement is atypical of Doran's usual astuteness, as a scene such as the conjuring episode (1.4), with its requirement of trap door and balcony, is most likely to reflect the staging facilities of a London theatre (see Montgomery, 'Staging').

Acceptance and reaction

The studies of Peter Alexander and Madeleine Doran were met with general, if not complete, acceptance, and the *Henry VI* Quartos were effectively reinstated as shorter versions, essentially Shakespearean. The editorial problem was shifted from the discrimination of the various collaborators to the serious study of the Quartos, since there was the possibility that as memorial versions of whatever copy lay behind F – 'foul papers' or prompt-copy – they might incorporate Shakespeare's revisions of his original.

One line of scholarly research pursued the possible identity of the actor–reporters, which in turn drew close attention to the nature of the performance text reported. Alexander (*'Henry VI'*) had worked out that the actor of Warwick and the actor doubling as Clifford and Suffolk must have been responsible for reporting, and Doran had suggested an abridged text (see Appendix 4 for a doubling chart). Other actors were suggested, as John E. Jordan notes, and he applied a statistical method which indicated a single actor, doubling as Horner the armourer, the Spirit, the Mayor, Vaux and Scales (1112). As Kathleen O. Irace points out, however, Jordan did not take into account the possibility of the reporter's recalling an already abridged script, and so the weighted percentage-scoring system he devised was bound to be misleading instead of revealing. Irace's study of *The Contention* as an abridged text strengthened Alexander's case for Warwick but his case for Clifford/Suffolk was undermined by, as Scott McMillin recognized, his confusion of 'Old' and 'Young' Clifford, requiring one actor to play two parts simultaneously.

Not everyone followed the lead of Alexander and Doran. Though he nominally endorsed the memorialist approach, J. Dover Wilson argued in his editions of *2 Henry VI* (1952) and *3 Henry VI* (1952) that Malone's reading of Greene's 'upstart

Crow' passage as a charge of plagiarism remained valid, though long since dismissed by other editors and critics. Nowhere in his edition does Dover Wilson look at the theoretical demonstration of Alexander and Doran. He simply carries on where the first Arden editor of the *Henry VI* plays, Hart, left off – isolated in an echo chamber of Shakespeare, Greene, Peele, Marlowe and Nashe. Dover Wilson does not even stress the significant condition that his editorial position implies – belief in reporters does not necessarily make Shakespeare the sole author of what is reported. Within two years of Dover Wilson's editions appeared the first major attempt to reject the memorialist approach, C.T. Prouty's *'The Contention' and Shakespeare's '2 Henry VI'* (1954). Though T. W. Baldwin (*Genetics*, 298), concluding his demonstration that *The Contention* derives from *2 Henry VI* by consistently contracting the latter, dismissed Prouty in a footnote, more serious consideration was given elsewhere.

James G. McManaway (145–6) drew attention to the old-fashioned approach of Prouty, who ignored the development of bibliographical and textual studies which posited the general features of prompt-books and foul papers to understand the derivation of printed copy. For example, the fact that the forms of speech prefixes in *The Contention* are unvaried while those in F do vary suggests that the latter was set from a manuscript that had not yet undergone the assumed regularization into a prompt-book (see Urkowitz, 'All things'). Scholars agree that stage directions can be most revealing, and the two complex examples from Q, cited by McManaway, which almost narrate stage business, may well, as he argued, indicate the agency of reporters (see facsimile, TLN 1312–16, 1463–67).

In Prouty we have a familiar phenomenon: what does not suit an argument is left to one side or silently passed over. For example, Prouty ignores the whole issue of accidentals like phonetic spelling as evidence for reporting, as adduced by Hereward T. Price ('Review'): instances are 'Bewford' (Beauford), 'Eyden' (Iden), 'Vawse' (Vaux), 'sypris tree' (Cypresse tree), 'cearies'

(Ceres). McManaway goes on to show, following Doran, how features of Q suggest a report of a text cut for performance, whereas analysis of F shows derivation from an author's manuscript which had been partly annotated by a prompter. G. Blakemore Evans, having shown how all Prouty's arguments for F as an expanded revision of Q can be reversed to argue the opposite, namely for Q as a cut version of F, adds that the complex issue of Q3's being consulted in setting up F is ignored. However, Evans also acknowledged that Prouty had contributed a finding of some importance – 'revision' of a text can produce the same characteristics as a 'report'. In recent years Laurie Maguire has published a whole study, using this and other ideas to reassess severely the memorialist theory. Generally, the work of Maguire and others has challenged the assumptions of McManaway's generation, (see Irace; Cloud; Urkowitz, 'Good news'; Werstine).

Maguire represents part of the present-day reaction against the division of the Quartos into 'Good' and 'Bad' which was such a major contribution to the founding of twentieth-century New Bibliography. In a nutshell Maguire summarizes thus: 'the textual disturbance caused by faulty memory is very difficult to identify because it is identical to the textual disturbance caused by scribes, compositors, forgetful authors, revising authors, adapters, or other playhouse personnel adding to a MS' (155). Another contemporary textual critic who has recently attempted a direct critique of Alexander is Steven Urkowitz ('Mistake'). As Prouty had attempted to explain away *The Contention*'s bungled genealogy of the Duke of York by tenuous hypothetical reference to English chronicles, so Urkowitz takes on this central passage, which had provided primary evidence for Alexander. Urkowitz points out that in both Q and F the Duke of York claims his right to the throne by way of his *matrilineal* inheritance from Philippa, daughter of Lionel, Duke of Clarence, the third son of Edward III, and thus one place in front of the fourth son, John of Gaunt, the Duke of Lancaster and progenitor of the Lancastrian dynasty. This is quite true, but it does not in any way affect Alexander's demonstration of the ludicrousness of the Q genealogy and so cannot affect his argument for reporting. The logical redundancy of the whole genealogical speech after the placing of 'Edmund of [*sic*] Langly, / Duke of Yorke' as the second son remains, though Urkowitz seems to believe that his observation renders it insignificant.

Again, Urkowitz believes that the close correspondence in stage directions between Q and F seriously undermines the claim for actor–reporters and 'ought to have proven terminally embarrassing to Alexander's case' ('Mistake', 253). However, Kathleen O. Irace argues that this is an example of contamination, of the compositors of F having consulted and used Q. Urkowitz believes that those stage directions were copied into the script underlying F when Shakespeare revised the shorter Q version. He does not consider the possibility of contamination. Alexander had briefly entertained the idea but settled instead for the belief that the actor–reporters had fragments of manuscript for reference. The problem was taken up by R. B. McKerrow ('Bad Quartos'), who offered the then challenging hypothesis that rather than this correspondence indicating, as at first might be thought, part of the 'Good' Folio being found in a 'Bad' Quarto, the contrary is the case. McKerrow conjectures that where the original manuscript of *2 Henry VI* was partially illegible, the F typesetter would have recourse to the Quarto. Thus where these passages occur in Q and F, modern editors should be aware that such contamination could mean that the F passages might be suspect.

In his edition of *2 Henry VI* Cairncross subsequently developed a particular hypothesis for the use of Q2 and Q3 which involved expanding McKerrow's brief note to explain approximately a quarter of the text. Cairncross believed that the printing-house editor supplying the compositors with the copy for F had at hand a manuscript of Shakespeare's which had been used as a prompt-book, with a few prompter's notes. Given

Heminge and Condell's accolade – 'wee have scarse received from him a blot in his papers' – this is taken to be 'fair' rather than 'foul' and quite legible. Yet analysis of F shows Quarto contamination, as McKerrow suggested. Cairncross develops this further, believing that printed copy was preferred for (greater) legibility and speed. The deficiencies of Q (inaccurate reporting and missing passages) were supplied by slips of paper, inserted or pasted onto the printed page, in addition to marginal corrections and additions (though here Cairncross adds in a footnote that these could have been printed in F directly from the manuscript). Cairncross's complex hypothesis begins to get rather confusing at this stage, since he notes that those passages not in Q are 'therefore taken by F direct from the manuscript' (xxxiii). Why then bother to copy them out on slips of paper and attach or insert them in Q, as he has just surmised? Further complications arise. On pages xxxvii–xxxviii Cairncross now proposes that both Q2 and Q3 were used in a scissors-and-paste operation, cutting out one page and presumably sticking it on the manuscript and having recourse to the other text when material on the other side of the page was needed. As Hattaway points out, the pagination of Q2 and Q3 is not identical, which calls in question this part of the theory. But Cairncross's imagination leads him into an absurd position: we now have not one but two heavily modified sources of copy for F, the printed Quarto with additions on the borders plus slips stuck on or inserted, and the authorial MS with sections of the printed quarto page stuck on, presumably not obscuring the prompter's notes on the MS. At the outset Cairncross has assumed the legibility of the original MS and all this heavily time-consuming business was done, we are told, for the sake of speed. It simply does not make sense. If the authorial MS was legible why use anything else, especially as all the various corrections and additions would have come from the MS anyway? If the MS was damaged in places, as McKerrow speculates, then the Quarto text (copies of Q2 and Q3, as Cairncross claims, but without evidence for the former) could be consulted, or even cut out and pasted in. But Cairncross's theory appears to postulate a quarto page amended from the MS which is then stuck over the passage used for amendment (see xxxviii).

The edition of *2 Henry VI* in the Oxford *Complete Works* – there entitled *The First Part of the Contention* – is by William Montgomery, who in a sense curbs the excesses of Cairncross. In reassessing Cairncross's editorial principles and practice in his original research work ('Critical Edition') and for the Oxford edition (see *TxC*) Montgomery re-examined the question of the relationship of Q1 and Q3 to F (the Q2 variants are negligible, deriving from the printer's errors, corrections and sophistica-tion). The following discussion is indebted to his work.

One of the difficulties with Q1 is that it appears to derive from a report of a London production and bears no marks of alteration for touring during the plague, which we have to assume took place, given the coincidence of the publication date of *The Contention* and the end of the plague in 1594. Perhaps the answer lies with stage directions like those referred to above. Many years ago McManaway suggested that the graphic, descriptive element of such directions seems to be elaborated for readers of the play, rather than reflecting any prompt-copy. Thus it would seem possible that, whatever alterations might have been made for provincial touring, the report of the London production with developed stage directions was sold to a sta-tioner for publication. Montgomery speculates that perhaps the original foul papers of the report of the London production might have been sold to Millington. There is a further possibil-ity that some differences between Q and F do not reflect abridgement for the stage, but are of another kind, and may have come about for political reasons.

Barbara Hodgdon (*End*, 62) suggests that the elimination of Buckingham from F in 1623 might reflect on the sensitivity of echoing the name of James I's favourite on the public stage. Again, in Q Margaret is more forward in the plot against

Gloucester whereas in F the Cardinal is prime mover. Perhaps, Hodgdon conjectures, Q in 1594 was meant here to reflect on the recent arch-manipulator Mary, Queen of Scots (*End*, 62). Generally, in terms of usurpation, monarchy and subversion, Hodgdon discerns a Yorkist stress in Q in contrast to a Lancastrian emphasis in F (*End*, 65–8); yet it is also acknowledged that 'neither Quarto nor Folio is without contradictions' and 'those particulars of representational politics' in specifics of performance emphasis 'remain unknown' (*End*, 68). A celebrated 'particular' which Honigmann considers (*Lost Years*, 153–4) is Young Clifford's speech on discovering the body of his father (5.2.31–56). All commentators, from F. P. Wilson (*Marlowe*, 117–18), accept that this must be a later revision since the verse and diction are strongly reminiscent of Shakespeare's mature, tragic period. The oddity is that only this passage appears to be revised in this way. When this was done why did Shakespeare not revise other parts of the play, those 'unconformities' for example? Honigmann explores the possibility of Shakespeare's 'exalting' Young Clifford as an ancestor, through his wife's forebears, of the company's patron, Lord Strange. I suggest that, in view of the terrible soubriquet conferred on Young Clifford by history – 'the butcher' (see 5.2.52n.) – Shakespeare took the opportunity to attempt to mollify the reputation with the tragic austerity of the poetry.

Revisions of a textual kind, however, between Q1 and Q3, have to be confronted by editors of *2 Henry VI*. Montgomery isolated 176 substantive variants in Q3, nearly all of which could be explained as printing errors, corrections or sophistications: that is, all but six. One of these is the notoriously bungled genealogy of York which, as we have seen, gave Alexander his key to reveal the practice of memorial report. In Q3 York's genealogy is fully corrected. In fact each of these six examples is closely followed in F (see Appendix 2 for the five variants, excluding York's genealogy). Alternatively, the Q3 corrections could derive from the source of the F text. The issue is important since it leads to the question of contamination of F, and appropriate editorial response. However, Montgomery goes on to recognize that the five variants (excluding York's genealogy) could be accounted for by problems of casting off copy, or as Q1 press variants which have not survived in any extant copy. This leaves open the possibility, which Montgomery cautiously refrains from drawing out, that the revised York genealogy could conceivably be the only substantial variant. If this hypothesis is entertained then the revision could have been made by referring to a chronicle, without any reference to foul papers, or by someone who knew the F text of the play. If we stay with the six variants we have to ask what was Pavier's source when he came to print Q3?

Montgomery applies two principal hypotheses, but they both develop from, and return to, the same assumption: that Pavier possessed an annotated exemplar of Q1. The first hypothesis develops from the assumed possibility of a revival of 'some version of *2 Henry VI*' ('Critical Edition', xxxiii) which included the variants. 'Someone' heard the differences and subsequently noted them in a copy of Q1 which came into Pavier's possession. The second hypothesis proposes that either Pavier got hold of such a prompt-book which had served as a basis for Q1 (and noticed the difference), or Pavier's copy of Q1 had already been corrected by reference to that prompt-book. Surprisingly, Montgomery, whose research is characterized by an exacting combination of theory, evidence and caution, prefers the first hypothesis as more probable, when it seems rather glaringly improbable. Consider the fourth variant, found at 2.1.10–14, the hawking scene at St Albans:

> My Lord Protectors Hawke done towre so well,
> He knows his maister loues to be aloft.
>   *Humphrey*. Faith my Lord, it is but a base minde
> That can sore no higher than a Falkons pitch.
> (Q1, TLN 561–4)

My Lord Protectors hawkes do towre so well.
They know their master sores a Faulcons pitch.
    Hum. Faith my Lord, it's but a base minde,
That sores no higher than a bird can sore.

(Q3, 18)

Could it be possible that someone, unbriefed, having heard a performance containing the very slight transposition and variation of half-lines to different speakers found in Q3, could precisely remember this and the other variants? Further, could that person then subsequently emend a copy of Q1 confident of accuracy? Surely this could only be done with the assurance of corroboration by consulting documentary evidence, i.e. the foul papers of the report or, possibly, a prompt-book made from them. Therefore Montgomery's second hypothesis seems much more acceptable, but I would like to modify it by taking one simple logical step: the annotator of Q1, recognizing the absurdity of the report of York's genealogy, which persists in Q2, took the opportunity of a third printing to correct this and a few other details with reference to the original foul papers of the report, or the prompt-copy. This may have been negotiated by Pavier as part of the enterprise of bringing out the two-part *Whole Contention* for the first time. In due course, it is agreed, the Folio editors had recourse to Q3 for *2 Henry VI*.

Cairncross developed a hypothesis of large-scale contamination of F by Q3. I have above criticized Cairncross's theory in terms of practicality; Montgomery goes directly to the conceptual core. He points out that to accept an F reading as correct, as Cairncross does, is in effect to affirm that that reading stood in the manuscript behind F. How, then, can it be claimed that this reading demonstrates a reliance on one or other of the Quartos? However, much of Cairncross's case for the contamination of F by Q rested on the category of agreement in error. Believing that a few demonstrable instances of contamination indicated large-scale corruption, Cairncross confounded inductive and deductive approaches and duly discovered a large number of instances only a few of which had been observed by other editors. Reassessing Cairncross's work, Montgomery found that he could agree on a small number of instances of mislineation which showed F's dependence on Q. As we have seen, Alexander had originally explained some close QF correspondences by conjecturing the reporters' use of fragments of manuscript to supplement memory (it is remarkable how just the right fragments are found at just the right time). However, McKerrow's alternative explanation ('Bad Quartos') won the day: where the manuscript behind F was faulty, Q was consulted. In effect Montgomery's critique of Cairncross's excesses scales down the contamination to something approaching McKerrow's speculations on limited instances.

An important category overlooked by Cairncross, though mentioned by Alexander, was the evidence of transcription of parallel stage directions. For example, consider the following:

> After the Beadle hath hit him one girke, he leapes
> ouer the stoole and runnes away, and they run after
> him, crying, A miracle, a miracle.
>
> (Q1, TLN 681–3)

> *After the Beadle hath hit him once, he leapes ouer*
> *the Stoole, and runnes away: and they follow,*
> *and cry, A Miracle.*
>
> (F, TLN 902–4)

The dialogue of Q1 and F does not include the actions referred to here, Simon's flight and the crowd following him. Moreover, though Q1 has Gloucester repeat 'A miracle, a miracle' (TLN 684), there is no such echo in F. Yet the directions agree. Presumably the reporter of Q1 records in detail what he saw; with slight emendation F copies this. Therefore, as editors recognize, there is a solid case for contamination, most probably through the use of Q3, but hardly on the scale envisaged by Cairncross.

> **Cap.** Yes Poull.
> **Suffolke.** Poull.
> **Cap.** I Poull, puddle, kennell, finke and durt,

Q1 (TLN 1509–11)

> **Suff.** Thou dar'ft not for thine owne.
> **Cap.** Yes *Pole*.
> **Suffolke.** *Pole*.
> **Cap.** I *Pole*, puddle, kennell, finke and durt,

Q3 (page 44)

> **Lieu.** Conuey him hence, and on our long boats fide,
> Strike off his head.   **Suf.** Thou dar'ft not for thy owne.
>   **Lieu.** *Poole*, Sir *Poole?* Lord,
> I kennell, puddle, finke, whofe filth and dirt
> Troubles the filuer Spring, where England drinkes:

F (TLN 2236–40)

14 The Lieutenant–Suffolk exchange at 4.1.68–72 in Q1, Q3 and F

As an example of the editing problems arising from Q/F differences I will turn to the exchange between the Lieutenant and
Suffolk in Act 4, scene 1 (see Fig. 14). To avoid misrepresenta-
tion the example from Q1 reproduces just three lines which are
from the top of a page. The Q3 section is included because,
though varying only in accidentals, it becomes important when
considering spelling and the function of the pun here. A further

minor difference is the altered speech prefix, from Captain to Lieutenant, but of greater significance is the question of the extra line in F: '*Poole*, Sir *Poole*? Lord,'. An editor of a modern-spelling edition has to weigh the arguable accuracy of the Q report against the possible inaccuracy of F, which is usually considered corrupt here. That is, are there grounds for considering that the compositor for this passage of F misread the extra line in the manuscript which had been dropped, by misreport or abridgement, from Q?

Capell set a precedent by conflating the two readings, which is followed in this edition, but with the first 'Pole' changed to 'poll' (agreeing with Wilson) and adopting the F speech prefix, thus:

LIEUTENANT
    Yes, poll!
SUFFOLK   Pole!
LIEUTENANT   Pool! Sir Pool! Lord!

Hattaway also follows Capell's precedent, but Cairncross leaves out the extra F line quoted above, which Wilson emends to 'Sir Pool! Lord Pool!' In this Cairncross follows the recommendation of Alexander ('Restoring Shakespeare', 7–8) who believes that the line derives from misreading the speech prefixes *Suf.* and *Lieu.* as 'Sir' and 'Lord'. Wells and Taylor follow Alexander and Cairncross but prefer Q's speech prefix 'Captain' (a preference shared by Hart, who otherwise adopts Capell's conflated reading). 'Captain' may have been a guess by the reporters, or it may have been the result of a revision between foul papers and prompt-book, as Wells and Taylor speculate. 'Lieutenant' is followed in this edition, as there seems to me no doubt that that is what it was on the manuscript behind F. Sisson took up this passage and supported Kittredge, who followed Capell, against Alexander who, he believed, subordinated the more authoritative F text to Q. In passing, Sisson rejected Wilson's emendation 'poll', as Suffolk's family name Pole was pronounced 'pool', and he believed that the pun, following 'Strike off his head', would not be perceived. Capell recognized the disrespect of the Lieutenant's 'Pole' and presumably felt that F's extra lines developed the punning possibilities, just as Wilson's emendation ensures that the punning sequence begins from the outset. I believe that Wilson was justified and, further, that F's '*Poole*, Sir *Poole*? Lord,' is an integral part of this sequence, though Alexander found it 'hardly intelligible'.

There is evidence to support the punning recognized by Wilson, and thus appropriate for a modern-spelling edition: Hart quotes *Jack Straw*, 'I puld you out of Rochester Castell by the powle! / And in recompence I will help to set your head on a pole. / Pray you, let's be powlde first' (1133–7). Suffolk's surname attracted such word-play in fifteenth-century political verse. Scattergood quotes a poem on the rumour that Suffolk and others had drowned Gloucester, 'Hit is a shrewde pole, pounde or a welle, / That drownythe the dowghty' (158). Sisson criticizes Wilson, but the variant spellings of 'poll' recorded by the *OED* suggest a range of possibilities in orthographic likeness to Pole: 'polle, powle, poulle, poolle, poil, powl, pool, poole'. In *Hamlet* one of Ophelia's songs includes the line, '[All] flaxen was his pole' (F spelling, 4.5.196). The Riverside editor adopts the spelling of the Quartos and Folios, which Hanmer changed to 'poll' (and was subsequently followed by most editors).

The punning sequence begins, therefore, with the Lieutenant's rejoinder to Suffolk's defiance, 'poll'. The variance in the *OED* forms suggests that pronunciation may have been more elastic than Sisson and Cercignani (221, 222, 225) allow for, particularly when it comes to spoken distortion on stage for sardonic effect. The double insult of the Lieutenant is answered by further defiance, with Suffolk's aristocratic insistence on his correctly pronounced name (Pole as pool) which the Lieutenant immediately takes up by literalizing as 'Pool'. The following expression 'Sir Pool' is presumably what puzzled Alexander. If we notice it as placed between 'Pool' and 'sink' a phonetic play on a long-obsolete term can be recognized: this is on the word 'sus-prall', a variant of 'suspiral'. The susprall was the vent or pipe in the London conduit system of water supply which also meant, in the sixteenth century, cesspool (see *OED* Suspiral 4). The Lieutenant is debasing Suffolk's rank and name by calling him a cesspool. The insult is spelt out in the following lines, 'Ay, ken-nel, puddle, sink, whose filth and dirt / Troubles the silver spring where England drinks'. The common word for cesspool in the sixteenth century was 'sink'. Cesspool appears in the following century probably deriving, in part, from 'suspiral/susprall' (see *OED* Cesspool). To give this sequence plosive force on the page I have chosen to space it as an irregular verse line, to avoid the somewhat deadening effect that prose arrangement would have.

The Arden 3 text inevitably takes the first Folio as its control text. Editors recognize that the manuscript behind the Folio is Shakespeare's, or derives from Shakespeare's papers, but there is a range of opinion on precisely the status of the document. That is to say, characteristics of F lend themselves to different inter-pretative emphases, which might suggest either an authorial manuscript or a scribal copy used in the theatre.

Aspects of the text, such as the number of indefinite stage directions (e.g. '*Enter Cade … with infinite numbers*', 4.2.28.1–2; '*Enter multitudes with halters about their necks*', 4.9.9) suggested authorial foul papers to W. W. Greg (*Folio*, 182–3), with whom most modern editors agree. In addition he cites uncertainty of designation in variable speech prefixes, unmarked entrances, uncertain directions and vague staging. Wells and Taylor (*TxC*, 176) add unmarked necessary exits. Hattaway points out that the confusion of names between Margaret, the Queen, and Eleanor, Duchess of Gloucester, would have been sorted out in a prompt-copy (Cambridge 2, 218). On the other hand, other tex-tual characteristics, for example, the attention paid to sound effects in the text, indicated the prompter. Yet textual scholars past and present differ absolutely on some of the same evidence – like F's '*Enter Beuis, and Iohn Holland*' at 4.2 (Holland was one of Lord Strange's men and George Bevis is accepted as another actor). Arguing against Dover Wilson, Greg thought that these could not possibly be authorial, while Wells and Taylor find no objection to attributing these and the sound effects to Shakespeare. In retrospect, it is difficult to see how Greg could be so confident.

Greg ultimately concluded that F was printed from an annotated fair-copy manuscript, which had at some time been used as a prompt-book, since it was unlikely that original foul papers would survive so long, although it is believed that where possible the acting companies retained these as a prudential measure. Since McKerrow's closer investigation into Q and F, after Alexander's work, editors have accepted that the F compositors had recourse to the Quartos where the manuscript was, presumably, illegible or damaged. Initial collation of Q and F suggests that in at least two passages the manuscript for F was amended because of censorship (see 2.1.38n.; 3.1.281–3n.). Because Q, as a performance text, probably represents a stage later than the manuscript behind F, its stage directions have a particular importance and are frequently adopted in this edition. (For the major Q1/F and Q3/F variants, see Appendix 2.) The adoption of readings from the Quartos in this edition is recorded in the textual notes with further discussion in the commentary where necessary (see, for example, 1.3.25–6, 28–33; 2.3.66–7; 4.1.70). All critics agree that the maturity of the verse in Young Clifford's speech at 5.2.31–49 indicates a revision of the manuscript later than Q, in which case there is simply no way of knowing what might have been added or emended after 1594 elsewhere in the manuscript behind F.

The foregoing outline of textual hypotheses uses the terminology and follows the conclusions of the New Bibliographers. A recent and radical redirection of textual scholarship suggests that the theories and practice of the New Bibliography, and the editorial principles derived from them, may be less scientifically based than was once supposed. Citing the doubts of

Orgel, Goldberg and Honigmann (*Stability*), Paul Werstine has re-examined the development from Pollard to Greg to McKerrow of the concept of printed texts as deriving from foul papers and finds that it has next to no foundation in empirical evidence. Furthermore, there is evidence to show that the distinctions usually made between foul papers and prompt-books are frequently unsustainable since, for example, 'scribal transcripts often contain the variety and ambiguity in naming characters – some of it introduced by the scribes themselves – that McKerrow ['Bad Quartos', 71] said was the unique mark of the "author's original MS" ' (71). The implications of Werstine's full argument, which he refrains from spelling out, are that if we can no longer feel assured of foul papers behind a printed text, but instead have to posit a transcript of some description, then the reliance on detail of the printed text as likely to derive directly from the author can no longer have so firm a theoretical basis. In the light of Werstine's scrutiny we have to acknowledge that there can be no certainty in discriminating among the possible various agents whose interventions may stand between authorial manuscripts and the printed texts of Q and F.

KING HENRY VI
PART TWO

LANCASTRIANS

KING Henry the Sixth		
QUEEN Margaret		
Humphrey, Duke of GLOUCESTER	*uncle of the King*	
ELEANOR, Duchess of Gloucester		5
CARDINAL Beaufort, Bishop of Winchester	*great-uncle of the King*	
Marquess of SUFFOLK		
Duke of SOMERSET		
Duke of BUCKINGHAM		
OLD CLIFFORD		10
YOUNG CLIFFORD	*his son*	
VAUX		

YORKISTS

Richard, Duke of YORK		
EDWARD	} *his sons*	15
RICHARD		
Earl of SALISBURY		
Earl of WARWICK	*his son*	

PETITION AND COMBAT 1.3, 2.3

Thomas HORNER	*armourer*	20
PETER Thump	*his apprentice*	
PETITIONERS, APPRENTICES, NEIGHBOURS		

CONJURATION 1.4

John HUME		25
John SOUTHWELL		
Margery JOURDAIN	*a witch*	
Roger BOLINGBROKE	*a conjuror*	
SPIRIT		

THE FALSE MIRACLE 2.1 30

Simon SIMPCOX		
Simpcox's WIFE		
MAYOR of St Albans		
BEADLE		
TOWNSMEN		35

ELEANOR'S PENANCE 2.4

Sir John STANLEY
SHERIFF of London
HERALD, GUARDS
SERVANTS, OFFICERS, COMMONERS   40

GLOUCESTER'S MURDER 3.2

Two MURDERERS
COMMONS

SUFFOLK'S MURDER 4.1

LIEUTENANT   45
MASTER
Master's MATE
Walter WHITMORE
Two GENTLEMEN

CADE'S REBELLION 4.2-10   50

GEORGE
NICK
Jack CADE
Dick the BUTCHER
Smith the WEAVER   55
SAWYER
Rebels
Emmanuel the CLERK of Chartham
MICHAEL
Sir Humphrey STAFFORD   60
Stafford's BROTHER
Lord SAYE
Lord SCALES
Matthew GOUGH
Alexander IDEN   65
Drummers, Soldiers
Trumpeter, Citizens

OTHERS

Attendants, Falconers
Post, Messengers   70

LIST OF ROLES First given imperfectly by Rowe. For the doubling chart see Appendix 4. The following notes were compiled with reference to Boyce's and W. H. Thomson's dictionaries.

1 LANCASTRIANS The royal dynasty, like the Yorkists, ultimately deriving from the house of Plantagenet founded by the counts of Anjou: its name is said to originate from the habit of Geoffrey (1113–51), who was said to bear a sprig of broom (*plante genêt*) in his cap. Edmund, the second son of Henry III, was created first Earl of Lancaster in 1267. By marriage John of Gaunt, the fourth son of Edward III, gained the Lancastrian titles and possessions which, on his death, were denied his son Henry Bolingbroke by Richard II. Bolingbroke returned from exile, defeated and deposed the King, claimed his right, and then ascended the throne as Henry IV.

2 KING Henry VI (1421–71), the only son of Henry V and Catherine of Valois, was King of England 1422–61 and 1470–1.

3 QUEEN Margaret of Anjou (1430–82), daughter of Reignier, Duke of Lorraine and Anjou, married Henry VI by proxy at Nancy in 1445.

4 GLOUCESTER The Duke of Gloucester (1391–1447), known as the Good Duke Humphrey, was the youngest son of Henry IV and brother to Henry V. Shakespeare particularly stresses the title 'Protector of England' which he actually held until 1429, when Henry VI was crowned.

5 ELEANOR Eleanor Cobham (d. 1454) was from the lesser gentry, but became the Duke of Gloucester's mistress, then wife, after his first marriage was annulled.

6 CARDINAL Henry Beaufort (1374–1447), Bishop of Winchester, was made a cardinal in 1426. He was the son of John of Gaunt and Catherine Swinford, and a great-uncle to the King. A guardian of the young Henry, he had been Chancellor under Henry V.

7 SUFFOLK William de la Pole (1396–1450), Earl, Marquess and first Duke of Suffolk, acted as proxy in the King's marriage to Margaret in France.

8 SOMERSET Edmund Beaufort (1406–55), Duke of Somerset, was the younger brother of John Beaufort (1403–44), the first Duke of Somerset. John Beaufort appears in *1H6*. During this earlier part of the King's reign Hall and Holinshed at one point mistakenly refer to him as Edmund, the Duke of *2H6*. Shakespeare himself confused the sons of Edmund – Henry (1436–64) and Edmund (*c*. 1438–1471) – in *3H6*, where events from both their lives are conflated in a single 'Duke of Somerset', the title which in fact passed from one to the other.

9 BUCKINGHAM Sir Humphrey Stafford, Duke of Buckingham (1402–60). His death is reported at the beginning of *3H6*, though he was actually killed at the battle of Northampton in 1460, not at St Albans in 1455.

10 OLD CLIFFORD Lord Thomas Clifford (1414–55), a devoted Lancastrian who fell at St Albans (though *3H6* 1.1 and 1.3 give two varying accounts of his death)

11 YOUNG CLIFFORD Lord John Clifford (*c*. 1435–61), son and avenger of Thomas, who slaughters Rutland in *3H6* (1.3) and then, in turn, is killed at the battle of Towton (2.6)

12 VAUX Sir William Vaux, a member of the Cardinal's household who later died fighting for the Lancastrian cause at Tewkesbury in 1471

14 YORK Richard Plantagenet, Duke of York (1411–60). Descended through his father from Edmund of Langley, the fifth son of Edward III and first Duke of York, and, by way of his mother's Mortimer line, from Lionel, Duke of Clarence, the third son of Edward III. His father had been executed for conspiracy against Henry V in 1415, but his title was restored, as we see in *1H6* (3.1). York claims that his mother's genealogy gives him a right to the throne

superior to that of Henry VI, who is descended from John of Gaunt, the fourth son of Edward III.

15 EDWARD The eldest son of York, Edward, Earl of March (1442–83), becomes king as Edward IV in *3H6*.

16 RICHARD Another son of York, the notorious Richard 'Crookback' (1452–85) was Duke of Gloucester and then King Richard III.

17 SALISBURY Richard Neville (1400–60), was the son of the Earl of Westmoreland, who appears in *1* and *2H4*, and son-in-law of the Earl of Salisbury, who died at the siege of Orléans in *1H6* (1.4) and whose title he inherited. Warwick 'the kingmaker' was the son of the Earl of Salisbury, who was executed in Pomfret (Pontefract) Castle after capture at the battle of Wakefield, fighting in the Yorkist cause.

18 WARWICK Richard Neville, Earl of Warwick (1428–71), remembered in history as 'the kingmaker', is a leading supporter of York in *2H6* and of his son, Edward IV, in *3H6*, before reverting to Henry VI and Queen Margaret's side. Shakespeare slightly confused this Warwick with his father-in-law, Richard de Beauchamp, Earl of Warwick (1382–1439) of *1H6*, some of whose military triumphs are claimed by 'the kingmaker' (*2H6* 1.1.116–19).

20 HORNER Horner the armourer, though not named by Hall or Holinshed, appears in earlier records like that of Gregory's *Chronicle*, from whom Fabyan probably took the name of Robert Horne, who was actually one of the presiding sheriffs at the combat. Stow's *Survey* records the armourer's name as William Cater, which Stow took from the original warrant (reprinted by Nichols).

21 PETER Stow's *Survey* names the armourer's man as John David, from the warrant which reads 'Johes Davey' (reprinted by Nichols).

25 HUME Though this mysterious figure appears in sixteenth-century chronicles, where he is in fact pardoned, he is absent from Harvey's account (270–80), which draws on contemporary records of Eleanor's disgrace.

26 SOUTHWELL Hall tells us that Southwell (d. 1441) was a priest and canon of St Stephen's, Westminster, where he, his associates and Eleanor were eventually tried. Southwell, however, died before his sentence was given.

27 JOURDAIN a witch who was finally burned at the stake for her part in Eleanor's conjuration (1.4.23–40)

28 BOLINGBROKE Reputedly 'a cunning necromancer' (Holinshed, 204), he was executed at Tyburn.

29 SPIRIT addressed as 'Asnath' by Jourdain

31 SIMPCOX anonymous in the source but perhaps thus named by Shakespeare from 'Sim subtle' (OED Sim¹) and 'coxcomb', to combine the ideas of craftiness and folly. Wiles (*Clown*, 51) draws attention to the jig of *Singing Simpkin* (1595) featuring 'Sim the clown' (predating OED's 'Simpkin' entry by over a hundred years). Probably played by Alexander Cooke of Pembroke's Men, thus Q and Fs '*Saunder*'. For the adoption of 'Simon' here, see 2.1.120n.

37 STANLEY Sir John in Hall and Holinshed, but corrected by Boswell-Stone to Sir Thomas. Another John Stanley was one of the two officials who escorted Eleanor to Leeds Castle in Kent upon her initial arrest (see 2.3.13n.).

48 WHITMORE Walter, pronounced 'Water' in Elizabethan English, is used ironically in relation to the prophecy concerning Suffolk's death (1.4.65), but Whitmore – not found in the sources – appears to be Shakespeare's invention.

51–2 GEORGE, NICK These rebels' names are adopted from Q. For F's [George] Bevis and John Holland see 4.2.0.1n.

53 CADE Holinshed (226–7) reprints the writ for Cade's arrest, which includes details of his association with the household of Sir Thomas Dacre, an

association confirmed by modern historians (see 4.2.29n.).

60 STAFFORD Sir Humphrey Stafford (d. 1450) had been Sheriff of the County of Gloucester and Governor of Calais.

61 BROTHER Sir William Stafford (d. 1450)

62 SAYE James Fiennes, Lord Saye and Sele (d. 1450), attained the positions of Lord Chamberlain and Lord Treasurer to the King.

63 SCALES Thomas de Scales (d. 1460), a veteran of the French wars who survived combat, imprisonment and Cade's rebellion, only to die at the hands of London boatmen while seeking sanctuary after the surrender of the Tower to Salisbury's forces

64 GOUGH Gough was another veteran of the French wars who had fought with Scales and Talbot. Hattaway notes that he was appointed commissioner by Henry to hand over Anjou and Maine to Charles VI.

65 IDEN historically Sheriff of Kent following the death of William Crowmer, his predecessor, whose widow (daughter of Lord Saye) he married

KING HENRY VI,
PART TWO

1.1 *Flourish of trumpets; then hautboys. Enter the* KING,
GLOUCESTER, SALISBURY, WARWICK *and* [CARDINAL]
Beaufort, *on the one side; the* QUEEN, SUFFOLK, YORK,
SOMERSET *and* BUCKINGHAM, *on the other* [; *with attendants*].

SUFFOLK

As by your high imperial majesty
I had in charge at my depart for France,
As procurator to your excellence,
To marry Princess Margaret for your grace;
So, in the famous ancient city Tours,   5

1.1 location: the royal palace, London
(Theobald). The action of *2H6* follows
directly upon that of *1H6* (for the debate
about sequence, see Introduction, pp.
111–15). Suffolk's opening words here
contrast ironically with his lines at the
close of *1H6*. There he had, in soliloquy,
acknowledged his covert intention by
means of the royal marriage to rule
Queen Margaret, King Henry and the
realm. Here in public he formally
describes the completion of his mission
as ambassadorial proxy for the royal
union. Suffolk's duplicity is perhaps
overshadowed by the public fact, known
to all present, that to fulfil this marriage
King Henry has broken his agreement
to marry the Earl of Armagnac's daughter (see *1H6* 5.1.15–20, 5.5.26–45).
Oaths and allegiance are central to
Shakespeare's representation of the
medieval world as a whole (see 5.1.20,
179–90). For Suffolk and the marriage
see Hall, 203–4, and Holinshed, 205–7.

1   **imperial** referring to the empire of
England, France and Ireland, part of
which Suffolk has just given away.
Before his death Suffolk's arrogance
provokes the murderers with his *imperial tongue* (4.1.123).

2   **had in charge** was commissioned
(*OED* Charge *sb.* 12)
     depart departure (Abbott, 451)

3–8   closely based on Hall (205)

3   **procurator** deputy, proxy: Hall's
word (205)

TITLE] *this edn;* The second Part of Henry the Sixt, with the death of the Good Duke HVMFREY.
F; THE First part of the Contention betwixt the two famous Houses of Yorke and Lancaster, with
the death of the good Duke Humphrey: And the banishment and death of the Duke of *Suffolke*, and
the Tragicall end of the proud Cardinall of *Winchester*, with the notable Rebellion of *Iacke Cade*: And
the Duke of Yorkes first claime vnto the Crowne Q (see p. 376)   1.1] *(Actus Primus. Scoena Prima.); not
in Q*   0.1–4] *F subst.; Enter at one doore, King* Henry *the sixt, and* Humphrey *Duke of* Gloster, *the
Duke of* Sommerset, *the Duke of* Buckingham, *Cardinall* Bewford, *and others. Enter at the other doore,
the Duke of* Yorke, *and the Marquesse of* Suffolke, *and Queene* Margaret, *and the Earle of* Salisbury *and*
Warwicke. *Q, Oxf*

In presence of the Kings of France and Sicil,
The Dukes of Orleans, Calaber, Bretagne and Alençon,
Seven earls, twelve barons and twenty reverend bishops,
I have performed my task and was espoused,
And humbly now upon my bended knee,   [*Kneels.*]   10
In sight of England and her lordly peers,
Deliver up my title in the Queen
To your most gracious hands, that are the substance
Of that great shadow I did represent;
The happiest gift that ever marquess gave,   15
The fairest queen that ever king received.

KING

Suffolk arise.   [*Suffolk rises.*]
                – Welcome, Queen Margaret:
I can express no kinder sign of love
Than this kind kiss.   [*Kisses her.*]
                – O Lord, that lends me life,

6   **Kings** Charles VII of France, and
Margaret's father Reignier, titular
monarch of Sicily
7   **Dukes** respectively Charles of Orleans,
the Duke of Calabria; Francis I, the
Duke of Brittany; John, Duke of
Alençon
9   **espoused** betrothed. The initial ceremony of betrothal (engagement in
contract of marriage) at Tours in 1444
was followed by marriage, again with
Suffolk as proxy, at Nancy in 1445.
Shakespeare follows Hall (205) in having Suffolk's language conflate the two
meanings (see *OED* Espouse *v.* 1 and
2) and occasions. (Cf. *OED* Betroth *v.*
1 and 2.) The marriage ceremony with
Henry himself present took place later
at Tichfield Abbey on 22 April 1445
(Griffiths, 485–7).
11 **England** King Henry
lordly occurs in *1* and *2H6* and *Luc*
only, in Shakespeare. See Hart, *1H6*

3.1.43.
12 **title** rights as proxy spouse: doubly
ironic in view of the adulterous liaison
between Margaret and Suffolk which
Shakespeare added to the sources, and
the fact that, as is shortly revealed, it is
Henry who has delivered up his title to
Anjou and Maine (see 49–50).
13–14 **substance . . . shadow** a common
Shakespearean antithesis. See *1H6*
2.3.35–65.
15 **happiest** most fortunate
18–19 **kinder . . . kind** a punning pro-
gression in meaning from 'more natural' to 'loving'
19–22 **O . . . soul** Here begins the
pietistic tenor of Henry's speech in all
situations which proves to be his most
disabling political weakness.
19–20 **lends . . . Lend** punning on the
two meanings of 'lend' as to loan and
to give (cf. *OED v.*² 1 and 2)

7] Orleans . . . Alençon *(Orleance, Calaber, Britaigne,* and *Alanson)*   8 twenty] *Q3, F;* then the *Q*
10 SD] *this edn*   17 SD] *this edn*   19 SD] *Oxf*

Lend me a heart replete with thankfulness!   20
For thou hast given me in this beauteous face
A world of earthly blessings to my soul,
If sympathy of love unite our thoughts.

QUEEN

Great King of England, and my gracious lord,
The mutual conference that my mind hath had   25
By day, by night, waking and in my dreams,
In courtly company, or at my beads,
With you mine alderliefest sovereign,
Makes me the bolder to salute my King
With ruder terms, such as my wit affords   30
And overjoy of heart doth minister.

KING

Her sight did ravish, but her grace in speech,
Her words y-clad with wisdom's majesty,
Makes me from wondering fall to weeping joys,
Such is the fulness of my heart's content.   35
Lords, with one cheerful voice welcome my love.

ALL [*Kneel.*]

Long live Queen Margaret, England's happiness!

QUEEN

We thank you all.   *Flourish.*

24–31 For the Q version see Appendix 2.
25 **mutual conference** intimate communing, or 'private thoughts'
27 **beads** prayers with a rosary. Contrast Margaret's contempt for precisely this a little later: 'But all his mind is bent to holiness, / To number Ave-Maries on his beads' (1.3.56–7).
28 **alderliefest** dearest of all: an archaism for 'alder', the older genitive plural of 'all', and 'lief', dear (*OED* All *adj.* D3); not found elsewhere in Shakespeare
30 **ruder** less mannered: a rhetorical dis-

claimer
wit mind, intellect
31 **minister** provide
32–3 **grace . . . majesty** a fitting response to the formal decorousness of Margaret's speech but quite incongruous with Q's reading, which is cursory to the point of bluntness: 'Lest I should speak more than beseems a woman. Let this suffice' (TLN 53–4).
33 **y-clad** clad: a Spenserian archaism substituting the Middle English prefix 'y' for the Old English 'ge'; seemingly in response to Margaret's 'alderliefest'

---

33 y-clad] (yclad)   34 wondering] (wondring)   37 SP, SD] *Cam; All kneel. F*   38 SD] *Sound Trumpets. Q*

SUFFOLK

My Lord Protector, so it please your grace,
Here are the articles of contracted peace   40
Between our sovereign and the French King Charles,
For eighteen months concluded by consent.

GLOUCESTER *(Reads.)*   Imprimis, *it is agreed between the*
French King Charles and William de la Pole, Marquess of
Suffolk, ambassador for Henry, King of England, that the   45
said Henry shall espouse the Lady Margaret, daughter unto
Reignier, King of Naples, Sicilia and Jerusalem, and crown
her Queen of England, ere the thirtieth of May next ensuing.
Item, *that the duchy of Anjou and the county of Maine shall*
be released and delivered to the King her father.   50
[*Lets the paper fall.*]

KING

Uncle, how now?

GLOUCESTER   Pardon me, gracious lord.
Some sudden qualm hath struck me at the heart
And dimmed mine eyes, that I can read no further.

KING

Uncle of Winchester, I pray read on.

CARDINAL [*Reads.*]   Item, *it is further agreed between them*   55

39 **Protector** On the death of Henry V, Prince Henry was only 8 months old. Gloucester claimed the position of regency according to an ambiguous codicil of Henry's will. The lords resisted this and conferred the title of 'Protector and Defender of the Realm and Chief Councillor', a title which was relinquished when Henry VI was crowned in London in 1429 (Griffiths, 20–4; Lander, 63).
40–1 See Hall, 203.
43 **Imprimis** first
46 *espouse* See 9n.
47 *King . . . Jerusalem* 'hauyng only the

name and stile of the same, without any peny profite, or fote of possessio*n*' (Hall, 204)
50 SD In the chronicles Gloucester's dismay derives in large part from the fact of the King's prior betrothal to the daughter of the Earl of Armagnac. Gloucester's protest below, 72–100, is put in more fundamental terms of chivalric nobility, honour and conquest defamed.
53 **dimmed mine eyes** Cf. 3.1.218.
54 **Uncle** The Cardinal was Henry IV's half-brother and thus great-uncle to the King. See List of Roles.

43 Imprimis] *Q;* Inprimis *F*   47 *Reignier*] *Raynard Qq;* René *Oxf*   49 Item, *that*] *Item.* It is further agreed betwene them, that *Q*, *Ard²*, *Oxf*   50 SD] *Cam;* Duke *Humphrey* lets it fall. *Q*

that the duchy of Anjou and the county of Maine shall be
released and delivered to the King her father, and she sent
over of the King of England's own proper cost and charges,
without having any dowry.

KING

They please us well. – Lord Marquess, kneel down.   60
 [*Suffolk kneels.*]
We here create thee the first Duke of Suffolk,
 [*Suffolk rises.*]
And girt thee with the sword. – Cousin of York,
We here discharge your grace from being regent
I'th' parts of France, till term of eighteen months
Be full expired. – Thanks, uncle Winchester,   65
Gloucester, York, Buckingham, Somerset,
Salisbury and Warwick.
We thank you all for this great favour done,
In entertainment to my princely Queen.
Come, let us in, and with all speed provide   70
To see her coronation be performed.
        Exeunt King, Queen and Suffolk [*with attendants*].
            [*Gloucester stays all*] *the rest.*

---

58 ¹*of* at (Abbott, 168)
59 *without . . . dowry* In Hall, Gloucester
  protests 'that it was more conveniente
  for a Prince, to marie a wife with riches
  and frendes, than to take a make with
  nothying, and disinherite himself and
  his realme of olde rightes and auncient
  seigniories' (204).
61 **Duke of Suffolk** This elevation in
  fact occurred three years later in 1448.
  The Earl of Suffolk had been made a
  marquess during negotiations for the
  royal marriage (Hall, 204–5, 207).
62 **girt** gird, in the sense of formally invest
  Cousin York was Henry's third

cousin, once removed; also the form of
address used by a monarch to a noble-
man (*OED sb.* 5a).
62–4 **Cousin . . . France** In the chronicles York is replaced by Somerset as
  regent in 1446, the year after the
  King's marriage (Hall, 206).
63 **regent** See *1H6* 4.1.162–3.
64 **parts** regions (*OED* Part *sb.* 13)
64–5 **till . . . expired** The office of regent
  will be kept vacant for eighteen months.
  Henry thereby inadvertently creates further rivalry between York and Somerset
  and their adherents. See 1.3.102–9.
69 **entertainment** courtly reception

---

56 *duchy*] *Ard²*; Dutchesse *Q3*, F *Anjou . . . Maine*] *Ard²*; *Aniou and Maine* F; *Anioy* and of *Mayne Q*
57 *delivered to*] *Ard²*; *delivered over to QF* 60–7] *Ard² lines* well. / thee / sword. / Grace / France,
/ expir'd / York, / Warwick; / 60 SD] *Oxf* 61 SD] *Oxf* 71 SD] *Ard² subst.*; *Exit . . . Manet the*
rest. F; *Exet . . . and Duke Humphrey staies all the rest. Q*

GLOUCESTER

> Brave peers of England, pillars of the state,
> To you Duke Humphrey must unload his grief,
> Your grief, the common grief of all the land.
> What! Did my brother Henry spend his youth,   75
> His valour, coin and people, in the wars?
> Did he so often lodge in open field,
> In winter's cold and summer's parching heat,
> To conquer France, his true inheritance?
> And did my brother Bedford toil his wits   80
> To keep by policy what Henry got?
> Have you yourselves, Somerset, Buckingham,
> Brave York, Salisbury and victorious Warwick,
> Received deep scars in France and Normandy?
> Or hath mine uncle Beaufort and myself,   85
> With all the learned council of the realm,
> Studied so long, sat in the council house

72 **peers** probably a pun on 'piers', a support. See Sledd, 10 (Cairncross).
   pillars . . . state proverbial (Dent, PP10)
75 **Henry** Henry V. Possibly trisyllabic pronunciation here.
   spend employ, occupy (*OED v.*4). See *TGV* 1.3.5.
77 **lodge** camp. Cf. *LLL* 2.1.85, 'He rather means to lodge you in the field', and *3H6* 1.1.32.
78 **summer's parching heat** Hart cites Peele's *Eclogue* for the same expression. Cf. *1H6* 1.2.77, 'sun's parching heat'.
79 **his true inheritance** Henry V secured his title to the French throne by the Treaty of Troyes (1420), a claim deriving from Edward III's marriage to Isabelle, daughter of Philip IV of France.
80 **Bedford** Created Duke of Bedford in 1415, John of Lancaster (1389–1435), the third son of Henry IV, was an ear-

lier regent of France and protector of England. Shakespeare dramatizes his death in *1H6* 3.2.
   toil his wits use his acumen: 'the duke of Bedforde, Regent of Fraunce, no lesse studied then toke payne, to kepe and ordre the countrees and regions by Kyng Henry late conquered and gained' (Hall, 115).
81 **policy** political shrewdness
81–4 **Henry . . . Normandy** Unfortunately this roll-call, following upon the evocation of military hardihood and political astuteness, is rather ironic since the enmity between York and Somerset, in particular, specifically led to the chivalric sacrifice of Talbot and his son and therefore contributed to the loss of France (see *1H6* 4.7).
85 **Beaufort** the Cardinal
86 **learned** learnèd
   council the King's Privy Council

86 council] *F3;* Counsell *F*

Early and late, debating to and fro
How France and Frenchmen might be kept in awe,
And had his highness in his infancy   90
Crowned in Paris in despite of foes?
And shall these labours and these honours die?
Shall Henry's conquest, Bedford's vigilance,
Your deeds of war and all our counsel die?
O peers of England, shameful is this league;   95
Fatal this marriage, cancelling your fame,
Blotting your names from books of memory,
Razing the characters of your renown,
Defacing monuments of conquered France,
Undoing all, as all had never been!   100

CARDINAL

Nephew, what means this passionate discourse,
This peroration with such circumstance?
For France 'tis ours; and we will keep it still.

GLOUCESTER

Ay, uncle, we will keep it if we can,

---

88 **to and fro** for and against: the proce-
    dures of deliberative rhetoric
89 **awe** submission: 'brought to dewe
    obeysance' (Hall, 115)
91 **Crowned** crownèd: in 1431, aged 10.
    See *1H6* 4.1.
    despite defiance (*OED sb.* 2b)
95 **shameful . . . league** See headnote
    and 59n.
96 **Fatal** a hint here of aligning Margaret
    by gender with the Parcae or Fates, as
    if she were the means and end of des-
    tiny, as well as a historical personage
96–100 **fame . . . been** These lines evoke
    the great humanist commonplace by
    which past fame achieved in action is
    made eternal in the written record of
    history, and thus a timeless model for
    emulation.
97 **books of memory** chronicles. Cf.
    'the book of fame' (Hall, 15) and *1H6*

2.4.101.
98 **Razing the characters** erasing the
    written record. Cf. *R2* 2.3.75, 'To raze
    one title of your honour out'.
99 **monuments** extending the metaphor
    to (1) defacing stone monuments; and
    (2) memory preserved as a written
    record. Cf. *1H6* 3.2.118–20, 'Bur-
    gundy / Enshrines thee in his heart,
    and there erects / Thy noble deeds as
    valour's monument'.
100 **as** as though (also at 184)
102 **peroration . . . circumstance**
    rhetorical speech . . . illustration. *OED*
    Peroration 2 records this as the first
    instance, as against the earlier meaning
    of a concluding part of a speech, dis-
    course etc. (*OED* 1). Only here in
    Shakespeare.
103 **For** as for
    still forever

90 had] *White;* hath *F*   98 Razing] *(Racing)*   102 peroration] *F2;* preroration *F*   104+ Ay,] *(I)*

But now it is impossible we should.   105
Suffolk, the new-made duke that rules the roast,
Hath given the duchy of Anjou and Maine
Unto the poor King Reignier, whose large style
Agrees not with the leanness of his purse.

SALISBURY

Now by the death of Him that died for all,   110
These counties were the keys of Normandy.
But wherefore weeps Warwick, my valiant son?

WARWICK

For grief that they are past recovery.
For were there hope to conquer them again
My sword should shed hot blood, mine eyes no tears.   115
Anjou and Maine! Myself did win them both;
Those provinces these arms of mine did conquer;
And are the cities that I got with wounds
Delivered up again with peaceful words?
Mort Dieu!   120

YORK

For Suffolk's Duke, may he be suffocate,
That dims the honour of this warlike isle!

106 **new-made** See 61n.
  rules the roast proverbial (Dent, R144): to dominate proceedings, as a master at table. Hall (232) has 'the Quene, which then ruled the rost and bare the whole rule'.
108–9 **whose . . . purse** 'For kyng Reyner her father, for al his long stile, had to short a purse, to sende his doughter honorably, to the kyng her spouse' (Hall, 205).
108 **large style** grandiose title
109 **Agrees** accords
110 **the . . . all** Cf. 2 Corinthians, 5.15, 'And he dyed for all' (Shaheen, 44).
111 **keys of Normandy** Fabyan's phrase (617); also found in *Brut*: 'the Duchie of Angeo & therldome of Mayn, which

was the key of Normandy' (510)
116 **Myself . . . both** The speaker, Richard Neville, is credited here with the deeds of his father-in-law, Richard de Beauchamp (d. 1439), who appears in *1H6*. See 2.2.78–9n. and List of Roles. He actually became Earl of Warwick ('the kingmaker') in 1449.
118–19 **wounds . . . words** Cf. *3H6* 2.1.99, 'The words would add more anguish than the wounds'.
120 *Mort Dieu!* a common French oath ('by the death of God'). See *H5* F 4.5.3.
121 **Suffolk's . . . suffocate** Cf. the puns on 'main . . . Maine', 205–9 below, and 'poll', 'Pole', 'Pool', 4.1.70.
  suffocate suffocated
122 **warlike isle** Cf. *Oth* 2.3.53.

106 roast] *(rost)*

France should have torn and rent my very heart
Before I would have yielded to this league.
I never read but England's kings have had   125
Large sums of gold and dowries with their wives;
And our King Henry gives away his own,
To match with her that brings no vantages.

GLOUCESTER

A proper jest, and never heard before,
That Suffolk should demand a whole fifteenth   130
For costs and charges in transporting her!
She should have stayed in France, and starved in France
Before –

CARDINAL

My Lord of Gloucester, now ye grow too hot:
It was the pleasure of my lord the King.   135

GLOUCESTER

My Lord of Winchester, I know your mind.
'Tis not my speeches that you do mislike,
But 'tis my presence that doth trouble ye.
Rancour will out: proud prelate, in thy face
I see thy fury. If I longer stay   140

---

124 **yielded** consented
125 **I . . . but** I have always read that
126 **dowries** See 59n.
128 **match with** to ally himself in marriage (*OED* Match *v.* 1c). Cf. *1H6*
5.5.66–7, 'Whom should we match
with Henry, being a King, / But
Margaret, that is daughter to a King?'
vantages advantages
129 **proper** real, true, as an intensifier (cf.
3.1.115); but also a witty ironic play on
'proper' as 'of real value': i.e. Margaret
not only brings nothing but that nothing costs money to bring over.
130 **fifteenth** a tax of one-fifteenth on
property and money: 'the Kyng with
her had not one peny, and for the

fetchyng of her, the Marques of
Suffolke, demaunded a whole fiftene,
in open parliament' (Hall, 205). In
1H6 5.5.92–3 Suffolk was licensed to
gather a tenth. Jack Cade's rebels
inflate the demand to 'one-and-twenty
fifteens' (4.7.19).
132 **starved** died of hunger, referring to
Margaret's relative lack of means
134 **hot** choleric. See Appendix 2 for Q
variant.
139 **proud prelate** This expression is
found twice in the Gloucester section
of *Mirror* (155, 205). Cf. 'haughty
prelate', *1H6* 1.3.23, *R3* 4.4.502.

132 starved] *(steru'd)*

157

We shall begin our ancient bickerings. –
Lordings, farewell; and say when I am gone,
I prophesied France will be lost ere long.   *Exit.*

CARDINAL

So, there goes our Protector in a rage.
'Tis known to you he is mine enemy,   145
Nay more, an enemy unto you all,
And no great friend, I fear me, to the King.
Consider, lords, he is the next of blood
And heir apparent to the English crown.
Had Henry got an empire by his marriage   150
And all the wealthy kingdoms of the west,
There's reason he should be displeased at it.
Look to it, lords; let not his smoothing words
Bewitch your hearts; be wise and circumspect.
What though the common people favour him,   155

---

141 **bickerings** in the two senses of words ('wrangling') and actions ('skirmishes'): see *OED* Bickering *sb.* 1 and 2. Editors refer to *1H6* 3.1, but if *1H6* 1.3 is also considered, in both we find not only arguments between Gloucester and the Cardinal but also 'skirmishes' – i.e. 'a petty fight or encounter' (*OED* Skirmish *sb.* 1) – between their men. Gloucester's line 'I will not answer thee with words, but blows' (*1H6* 1.3.69) is followed by the stage direction '*Here they skirmish again*' (cf. *1H6* 3.1.85.1 and 91.1).

142 **Lordings** an early form of 'my lords': not necessarily contemptuous

148 **next of blood** As yet childless, Henry VI has no heir; thus Gloucester, Henry V's only surviving brother, is next in line. See Appendix 6, Table 1.

149 **heir apparent** incorrect. Gloucester is only 'heir presumptive'. Only a son born to Henry VI would have the closer claim of 'heir apparent'. (See *OED* Apparent *a.* 4.) Perhaps the

Cardinal is being facetious?

151 an anachronistic reference to the Spanish conquests of South America. Cairncross quotes 'all the wealthy kingdoms I subdu'd' (*1 Tamburlaine*, 1.4.19).

152 'He would have reason to be displeased' (since an heir is likely to be born).
he Gloucester

153 **Look to it** beware
smoothing plausible; blandishing; flattering (*OED a.* 2). Cf. *R3* 1.2.168, 'My tongue could never learn sweet smoothing word'.

154 **wise and circumspect** an echo of Ephesians, 5.15, 'Take heed therefore that ye walke circumspectly, not as fools, but as wise'.

155–9 Both Hall and Holinshed fostered the exemplary image of the Protector ('the good duke of Gloucester', Hall, 209; 'a prince so well beloued of the people', Holinshed, 211), but the latter in offering a brief eulogy recommends the reader to 'maister Foxe's booke of

143 SD] *Exit Humfrey. F*

Calling him 'Humphrey, the good Duke of Gloucester',
Clapping their hands and crying with loud voice,
'Jesu maintain your royal excellence!',
With 'God preserve the good Duke Humphrey!',
I fear me, lords, for all this flattering gloss,   160
He will be found a dangerous Protector.

BUCKINGHAM

Why should he then protect our sovereign,
He being of age to govern of himself?
Cousin of Somerset, join you with me,
And all together, with the Duke of Suffolk,   165
We'll quickly hoist Duke Humphrey from his seat.

CARDINAL

This weighty business will not brook delay;
I'll to the Duke of Suffolk presently.   *Exit.*

SOMERSET

Cousin of Buckingham, though Humphrey's pride
And greatness of his place be grief to us,   170
Yet let us watch the haughty Cardinal;
His insolence is more intolerable

Acts and Monuments' (212). Foxe's epitome, copied virtually word for word by Grafton, probably suggested this passage: 'And thus much, hitherto, for the noble prowess and virtues, joined with the like ornaments of knowledge and literature, shining in this princely duke: for which he was both loved of the poor commons, and well spoken of, of all men, and no less deserving the same, being called the "good" duke of Gloucester; so neither wanted he the enemies and privy enviers' (713).

160 **I fear me** For Shakespeare's use of reflexive verbs now used intransitively, see Abbott, 296.
   gloss combines the two meanings of 'comment' and 'fair semblance' (*OED sb.*[1] 1 and *sb.*[2] 1b)

161–3 **Protector . . . himself** Henry was 24 at the time of his marriage and Gloucester no longer Protector, but Shakespeare retains the title to add to the gravity of his fall.
166 **hoist** lift. Cf. Eleanor's lines in *Mirror*, 'Thus hoysted high vpon the rollinge wheele / I sate so sure' (48–9).
167 **brook** allow
168 **presently** immediately
170 **place** position
   grief harm (*OED sb.* 2)
171 **haughty Cardinal** See 139n.
172–4 **His . . . Protector** In fact the Cardinal had been Chancellor several times and his immense wealth made him virtually Henry's private banker. See Harriss, 'Beaufort'.
172 **insolence** overbearing pride

165 all together] *Rowe;* altogether *F*   166 hoist] *Oxf;* (hoyse) *F*

Than all the princes' in the land beside.
If Gloucester be displaced, he'll be Protector.

BUCKINGHAM

Or thou or I, Somerset, will be Protectors,　　　175
Despite Duke Humphrey, or the Cardinal.

Exeunt Buckingham and Somerset.

SALISBURY

Pride went before; Ambition follows him.
While these do labour for their own preferment,
Behoves it us to labour for the realm.
I never saw but Humphrey, Duke of Gloucester,　　　180
Did bear him like a noble gentleman.
Oft have I seen the haughty Cardinal,
More like a soldier than a man o'th' church,
As stout and proud as he were lord of all,

---

173 **beside** over and above (*OED adv.* and *prep.* 2). Cf. *1H6* 4.1.25.

175 **Or . . . or** either . . . or

177 Salisbury is ostensibly adapting the proverb 'Pride goes before, and Shame comes after' (Dent, P576), with the Cardinal as the former and Somerset and Buckingham as Ambition. However, perhaps the overreaching commonplace is that from Scripture, 'Pride goeth before destruction, and an high minde before the fall' (Proverbs, 16.18), encapsulated as 'Pride will have a fall' (Dent, P581), particularly in view of *haughty*, 182.

178 **preferment** advancement

179 **Behoves it us** it is necessary for us
realm *OED* records that this spelling, following upon such older forms as 'reame' and 'reume', became standard by 1600.

180–1 I have always seen that . . . conducted himself like a noble gentleman.

182 **haughty Cardinal** See 139n. and 177n.

183 **More . . . soldier** In 1426–7, on behalf of Pope Martin V, the Cardinal had campaigned with German armies against the Hussites in Bohemia.

184 **stout** If this reflects on *Swear* and *demean* in the next line, then *OED adj.* 4c, 'Of utterance or demeanour: Resolute, defiant', would be appropriate rather than *stout* as a synonym for pride, or the alternatives of 'brave', 'hardy', 'strong' etc. Cf. *Cor* 3.2.78–9, 'correcting thy stout heart, / Now humble'.
proud Sixteenth-century chronicles perpetuated the view held by such Reformation divines as Latimer and Tyndale of the Cardinal as the stereotypical proud prelate of the Roman church. Some of Hall's general comments on Beaufort are quite close to those on Cardinal Wolsey (cf. 210 and 214), and his overall assessment is considerably influenced by the denunciatory petition of the 'good' Duke Humphrey (Hall, 197–202).

---

173 princes'] Princes *F*　176 SD *Exeunt*] Cam; *Exit F*

Swear like a ruffian, and demean himself   185
Unlike the ruler of a commonweal. –
Warwick, my son, the comfort of my age,
Thy deeds, thy plainness and thy housekeeping
Hath won thee greatest favour of the commons,
Excepting none but good Duke Humphrey. –   190
And, brother York, thy acts in Ireland
In bringing them to civil discipline;
Thy late exploits done in the heart of France

185 **Swear . . . ruffian** Shakespeare particularly associated a ruffian with this behaviour. See *TS* 2.1.288; *2H4* 4.5.124. The most common association is with physical violence (see *OED sb.* 1). **demean** behave. 'Demean' as 'debase' (*OED v.*²) develops in the seventeenth century, but Dr Johnson, in his *Dictionary*, took this as the meaning of *CE* 4.3.82.

186 **commonweal** the realm or body politic composed of the estates and degrees of men within the feudal system

187–9 **Warwick . . . commons** See Hall: '[Warwick] was . . . a man of marvelous qualities . . . from his youth . . . so set them forward, with wittie and gentle demeanour, to all persones of high and of lowe degre, that emong all sortes of people, he obteined greate love, muche favor, and more credence: / whiche thynges daily more encreased, by his abundant liberalitie, and plentifull house kepynge, then by his riches, aucthoritie, or high parentage: by reason of whiche doynges, he was in suche favor and estimacion, emongest the common people, that thei judged hym able to do all thynges, and that without hym, nothyng to be well done' (231–2).

188 **plainness** unostentatiousness: all the more remarkable in a society characterized by the pomp and magnificence of hierarchic display
housekeeping hospitality, from the

extremes of supporting an entire entourage on a royal progress, to sustaining the beggar or pilgrim at the door (see 4.10.23)

190 **Excepting none but** except only that shown to Gloucester, whose 'honourable houshold & lybertie . . . passyd all other before his tyme' (Fabyan, 619) (Wilson)
Humphrey probably trisyllabic pronunciation here

191 **brother** brother-in-law, having married Salisbury's sister Cecily Neville

191–2 **acts . . . discipline** an anachronistic reference to what took place four years later, in 1449, when it was claimed that York's 'pollitique governau*n*ce, his gentle behavior, to all the Iryshe nacion . . . had brought that rude and savage nacion, to civile fashion, and Englishe urbanitie' (Hall, 219). See 3.1.

193 **late exploits** See Holinshed's account (194–6) of Talbot and York's relief of Pontoise, but note Griffiths's less than heroic comment on Talbot's recovery of the same town in 1437: 'The duke [of York] seems to have played little part in these military operations and stayed comfortably at Rouen' (455). Moreover, in *1H6*, in great contrast to the chivalric heroism of Talbot, we see an emphasis on faction and the 'jarring discord of nobility' (4.1.188), particularly between York and Somerset.

189 thee] *Q, Oxf;* the *F*

When thou wert regent for our sovereign,
Have made thee feared and honoured of the people. –   195
Join we together for the public good,
In what we can to bridle and suppress
The pride of Suffolk and the Cardinal,
With Somerset's and Buckingham's ambition;
And, as we may, cherish Duke Humphrey's deeds,   200
While they do tend the profit of the land.

WARWICK

So God help Warwick, as he loves the land
And common profit of his country!

YORK

And so says York, [*aside*] for he hath greatest cause.

SALISBURY

Then let's make haste and look unto the main.   205

WARWICK

Unto the main! O father, Maine is lost,
That Maine which by main force Warwick did win,
And would have kept so long as breath did last!

---

194 **regent** the chroniclers' designation followed by Shakespeare. York was twice made Lieutenant-General of France and Normandy in 1436 and 1440 for, respectively, a one-year and then a five-year period (Griffiths, 455, 459).

196 **public good** (as against private self-interest) a concept inherited from classical antiquity and absorbed into the political thought of medieval and modern Europe

200 **cherish** to hold dear; to make much of (*OED v.* 1). Cf. *1H4* 5.4.30.

201 **tend the profit** further the welfare

204 **cause** the Yorkist claim to the throne

205–9 **main . . . chance** a series of puns,

referring to the lost duchy of Maine (206–7, 209); the proverb 'look to the main chance' (205, 209) (Tilley, E235); and the adjective meaning 'sheer' (207) (*OED* 1b). The proverb derives from the dice game of hazard and means 'to look for the best opportunity in a course of action' (*OED* Main chance 1). In the game the player chooses a 'main' number (between 5 and 9). If the number is cast he wins; if aces or deuces he loses; if another number it becomes the player's 'chance'. Casting continues until either the 'main' or 'chance' numbers are thrown. If the former the banker wins, if the latter

---

197 can] can, F   198] *Ard² (following Q) inserts between 198 and 199* The reuerence of mine age, and *Neuels* name, / Is of no little force if I command,   204–6] *Pope; F lines* Yorke, / cause. / away, / maine. / maine? / lost, /   204 SD] *Theobald*   205 haste] *Pope;* hast away, F

162

Main chance, father, you meant, but I meant Maine,
Which I will win from France, or else be slain.   210
                    Exeunt Warwick and Salisbury.

YORK

Anjou and Maine are given to the French;
Paris is lost; the state of Normandy
Stands on a tickle point now they are gone.
Suffolk concluded on the articles,
The peers agreed, and Henry was well pleased   215
To change two dukedoms for a duke's fair daughter.
I cannot blame them all – what is't to them?
'Tis thine they give away, and not their own.
Pirates may make cheap pennyworths of their pillage
And purchase friends, and give to courtesans,   220
Still revelling like lords till all be gone;
While as the silly owner of the goods
Weeps over them, and wrings his hapless hands,
And shakes his head, and trembling stands aloof,
While all is shared and all is borne away,   225
Ready to starve and dare not touch his own.
So York must sit and fret and bite his tongue,
While his own lands are bargained for and sold.

the player (*OED* Main *sb.*³ 1). Cf. *1H4*
4.1.47–8, 'To set so rich a main / On
the nice hazard of one doubtful hour'.
213 **on . . . point** unbalanced, precarious
(Dent, TT14; *OED* Tickle *a.* 6)
214 **concluded on** agreed on (*OED*
Conclude *v.* 13a). Cf. *Ham* 3.4.201;
and Hall: 'When those thynges wer
concluded, the Erle of Suffolke with
his company . . . departed from Toures
. . . to the Kyng to Westminster . . .
openly . . . declared . . . that Godly
affinitie, which he had concluded'
(204).

218 **thine** my rightful inheritance
219 **cheap pennyworths** This looks like
a variant on 'Robin Hood's penny-
worth' (*OED* 2d), 'a thing or quantity
sold at a robber's price, i.e. far below
the real value'.
222 **While as** while (Abbott, 116)
silly helpless, pitiful
223 **hapless** unfortunate
224 **aloof** at a distance
226 **starve** perish. See 132n.
227 **bite his tongue** keep silent (Dent,
T400.1). See *3H6* 1.4.47.

210 SD] *Cam; Exit Warwicke, and Salisbury. Manet Yorke.* F

Methinks the realms of England, France and Ireland
Bear that proportion to my flesh and blood   230
As did the fatal brand Althaea burnt
Unto the prince's heart of Calydon.
Anjou and Maine both given unto the French!
Cold news for me, for I had hope of France
Even as I have of fertile England's soil.   235
A day will come when York shall claim his own;
And therefore I will take the Nevilles' parts
And make a show of love to proud Duke Humphrey,
And when I spy advantage, claim the crown,
For that's the golden mark I seek to hit.   240
Nor shall proud Lancaster usurp my right,
Nor hold the sceptre in his childish fist,
Nor wear the diadem upon his head,
Whose church-like humours fits not for a crown.

230 **that proportion** the same relation (*OED sb.* 3)

231–2 The Fates deemed that the newly born Meleager, prince of Calydon, should live only as long as a burning brand. Althaea, his mother, extinguished the fire and preserved the wood until years later, when, in revenge for her brothers, slain by her son, she returned the brand to the flames (Ovid, 8. 593–687).

231 **fatal brand** 'Brand' and 'firebrand' are Golding's preferred words, occurring respectively four and three times in the story, for Ovid's *stirpes* (log, trunk), *ramus* (branch, bough), and *lignum* (firewood, timber). 'Fatal brand' echoes Ovid's *lignum fatale* (479), which Golding translates as 'deathfull brand' (665).

232 **the . . . Calydon** Latinate construction: the heart of the prince of Calydon

234–5 See 3.1.87–8 for almost a repetition of these lines by the same speaker.

234 **Cold** unwelcome: common Shakespearean usage

237 **take . . . parts** ally with the Nevilles, i.e.

Salisbury and Warwick. But as 2.2 shows, it is the Nevilles who ally with York.

240 **golden mark** Three ideas are superimposed here. The *mark* is the white centre of the archery target (*OED sb.*[2] 7); the substance (gold) and shape (circular) of the *crown* (239) are metaphorically imposed on this; and lastly 'mark' is a denominated weight for gold (*OED sb.*[2] 1). All suggest violence, power and wealth.

241 **Lancaster** Henry VI

242–3 **sceptre . . . diadem** The sceptre and the crown were part of the regalia of kingly office conferred in the sanctity of the coronation ceremony and vividly recalled in *H5* 4.1.260ff., ''Tis not the balm, the sceptre, and the ball, / The sword, the mace, the crown imperial'. Cf. *3H6* 2.1.153–4.

244 **church-like humours** pious disposition: 'kyng Henry . . . was a man of meke spirite . . . there could be none, more chaste, more meke, more holy' (Hall, 208). See 19–22n.
  fits For the usage of plural subject with singular verb, see Abbott, 333.

Then, York, be still awhile, till time do serve.   245
Watch thou and wake, when others be asleep,
To pry into the secrets of the state;
Till Henry, surfeiting in joys of love
With his new bride and England's dear-bought Queen,
And Humphrey with the peers be fallen at jars.   250
Then will I raise aloft the milk-white rose,
With whose sweet smell the air shall be perfumed,
And in my standard bear the arms of York,
To grapple with the house of Lancaster;
And force perforce I'll make him yield the crown,   255
Whose bookish rule hath pulled fair England down.   *Exit.*

245 **still . . . serve** restrained until occasion arises
248 **Till** while (*OED* Till B *conj.* 2)
    surfeiting indulging to excess, usually to the point of sickness in Shakespeare (e.g. *2H4* 4.1.55–6)
250 **at jars** into dissension. The analogical relationship between the well-ordered state and harmony, and civil dissension and discord, is best brought out by *1H6* 4.1.188, 'This jarring discord of nobility'.
251 **milk-white rose** the Yorkist emblem (see *1H6* 2.4): 'milk-white' is proverbial (see Dent, M931, M931.1). Taken from the insignia of Edmund Mortimer, Earl of March. See Scott-Giles, 136–41. In the 'Temple Garden' scene (1.4) of *1H6*, invented by Shakespeare, York – then Richard Plantagenet – had plucked the white rose, while the Lancastrian supporters opposed to his claim to the throne by prior descent had plucked the red rose.
253 **standard . . . arms** Accuracy is set aside to introduce the verbal play on

arms . . . grapple with. The *standard* was the pennon-shaped battle ensign. Scott-Giles provides two illustrations of Yorkist standards which incorporate the white rose (129–30) (see Fig. 11). York bore the royal arms and crest with the label of York added (Scott-Giles, 126).
254 **grapple with** 'to encounter hand to hand: to battle or struggle with' (*OED* Grapple *v.* 8c): first recorded usage of this idiom (Hattaway)
255 **force perforce** by violence (with a tautology as intensifier). Common in Shakespeare: see *2H4* 4.1.114, 4.4.46.
256 **bookish rule** specifically Henry's devotion to religious texts, generally contemplation at the expense of active engagement in the practice of ruler-ship. Compare 'fitter is my study and my books / Than wanton dalliance with a paramour' (*1H6* 5.1.22–3). RP points out the association between this and the anti-literacy motivation of Cade and the rebels.

248 surfeiting in] surfeit in the *Hanmer, Oxf*   253 in] *F2;* in in *F*

[1.2]   *Enter* GLOUCESTER *and his wife* ELEANOR.

ELEANOR
    Why droops my lord, like over-ripened corn
    Hanging the head at Ceres' plenteous load?
    Why doth the great Duke Humphrey knit his brows,
    As frowning at the favours of the world?
    Why are thine eyes fixed to the sullen earth,   5
    Gazing on that which seems to dim thy sight?
    What seest thou there? King Henry's diadem
    Enchased with all the honours of the world?
    If so, gaze on, and grovel on thy face,
    Until thy head be circled with the same.   10
    Put forth thy hand, reach at the glorious gold.
    What, is't too short? I'll lengthen it with mine;
    And having both together heaved it up,
    We'll both together lift our heads to heaven,
    And never more abase our sight so low   15
    As to vouchsafe one glance unto the ground.

1.2 location: Gloucester's house
(Theobald). This scene and 1.4 enact
the historical record of Eleanor's
dabbling in witchcraft, but her fall
occurred in 1441, four years before the
arrival of Margaret. To interrelate historical materials for dramatic effect
Shakespeare invented the enmity of
the Queen and the Duchess, as well as
Hume's agency for the Cardinal–
Suffolk faction. Hall records: 'dame
Elyanour . . . was accused of treason,
for that she, by sorcery and enchaunt-
ment, entended to destroy the kyng, to
thentent to aduau*n*ce and to promote
her husbande to the croune' (202).
1   **over-ripened** the only example given
    in *OED*
2   **Ceres'** Ceres was the Roman goddess
    of agriculture deriving from the Greek
    Demeter. Sometimes depicted wearing

a garland of corn-ears round her head,
which might be part of the allusion
here.
3   **knit his brows** proverbial (Dent,
    KK4). Cf. 3.1.15; *3H6* 2.2.20, 3.2.82.
    Hart on *3H6* 2.2.20 notes from
    Grafton, *Continuation*, 'The protec-
    toure . . . came in agayn . . . with a
    sowre angry countenaunce, knittynge
    the brows, frownynge, and frettyng'
    (493).
4   **favours** high regards; good will
5   **sullen** dull
8   **Enchased** 'set' as in *OED* Set *v.* 63, to
    fix a gem on a metal surface: only here
    in Shakespeare
9   **grovel** to lie face downward. For an
    association with supernatural invoca-
    tion see 1.4.11 and n.
13 **heaved** raised. Cf. 4.10.50.

1.2] *Capell*   0.1] *F subst.*   0.1+ ELEANOR] *(Elianor)*

GLOUCESTER

O Nell, sweet Nell, if thou dost love thy lord,
Banish the canker of ambitious thoughts.
And may that hour, when I imagine ill
Against my King and nephew, virtuous Henry,   20
Be my last breathing in this mortal world!
My troublous dreams this night doth make me sad.

ELEANOR

What dreamed my lord? Tell me, and I'll requite it
With sweet rehearsal of my morning's dream.

GLOUCESTER

Methought this staff, mine office-badge in court,   25
Was broke in twain; by whom I have forgot
But, as I think, it was by th' Cardinal;
And on the pieces of the broken wand
Were placed the heads of Edmund, Duke of Somerset,

---

18 **canker** corruption, the figurative meaning deriving from a gangrenous disease of the body or plants. Most commonly the latter in Shakespeare: cf. 'Hath not thy rose a canker, Somerset?' (*1H6* 2.4.68). A good example is found in the Duke of York's oration before parliament in 1460: 'this noble realme . . . shall neuer be vnbukeled from her quotidia*n* feuer, exept I (as the principall Physician & you, as trew and trusty Appotecaries) consult together, in makyng of the pocion, and trye out the clene and pure stuffe, fro*m* the old, corrupt, and putrefied dreggs. For vndoutedly, the rote & botome of this long festured ca*n*kar, is not yet extirpat' (Hall, 245–6).

19 **imagine ill** form harmful designs (*OED* Imagine *v.* 7) (Hattaway)

21 **last . . . world** final breath. Cf. 'To prove it on thee to the extremest point / Of mortal breathing' (*R2* 4.1.47–8).

22 **this night** last night

23 **requite** give a return for (*OED v.* 4)

24 **rehearsal** recounting
   morning's dream Dreams in the morning are said to tell the truth (Hart).

25–30 See Appendix 2 for Q1/Q3 variants.

25–6 **staff . . . broke** Part of the nightmarish aspect here is that the staff is broken by *others*, not the holder of office. Cf. Worcester's resignation of office and breaking of his staff in *R2* 2.2.59 and *1H4* 5.1.34.

28 **wand** staff of office (*OED sb.* 7)

29 **Edmund, Duke of Somerset** John, Edmund's older brother (d. 1444), held the title at the time (1441). Hall (233) records Edmund's death at the first battle of St Albans (1455). In Shakespeare's presentation (5.2.65.1–2; *3H6* 1.1.16.1) Edmund is killed and decapitated by Richard Plantagenet (later Richard III).

---

19 hour] *Ard² (Vaughan);* thought *F*

And William de la Pole, first Duke of Suffolk.   30
This was my dream; what it doth bode, God knows.

ELEANOR

Tut! This was nothing but an argument
That he that breaks a stick of Gloucester's grove
Shall lose his head for his presumption.
But list to me, my Humphrey, my sweet Duke: 35
Methought I sat in seat of majesty
In the cathedral church of Westminster,
And in that chair where kings and queens are crowned,
Where Henry and Dame Margaret kneeled to me,
And on my head did set the diadem.   40

GLOUCESTER

Nay, Eleanor, then must I chide outright:
Presumptuous dame, ill-nurtured Eleanor!
Art thou not second woman in the realm,
And the Protector's wife, beloved of him?
Hast thou not worldly pleasure at command,   45

---

30 **Suffolk** Again, decapitation is emphasized in Shakespeare's dramatization;
see 4.4. Thus Gloucester's dream is
doubly ominous, for himself and for
his unsuspecting enemies.

32 **argument** manifestation as evidence
or proof (*OED sb.* 1). Cf. 'In argument
and proof of which contract, / Bear
her this jewel' (*1H6* 5.1.46–7).

33 **a . . . grove** as if Gloucester's many
honours multiplied his staff into a
grove, defacement of the least part of
which would merit such punishment

34 **presumption** For the class of words in
which the penultimate, prevocalic 'i' is
sounded, see Cercignani, 308.

36–40 For Eleanor's dream as the *somni-
um animale* – dream deriving from pre-
occupations of the waking mind –
rather than the prophecy she believes,
see Presson.

36 **in seat** For omission of the definite
article (cf. 79) see Abbott, 89.

38 are] *Q;* wer *F*

38 **chair** the coronation throne

39 **Dame** Semantics and status were
sufficiently flexible by the end of the
sixteenth century for such a word to
acquire contemptuous possibilities.
Consider the following: 'Every poor
woman that hath either maid, or
apprentise is called *Dame*: and yet
Dame is as much *Domina* and used to
Ladies of greatest account' (Bishop
Thomas Bilson, *The Perpetual
Government of Christ's Church* (1593),
58, quoted *OED* 2). Contempt is surely implied by Margaret imagined as
'kneeling'?

42 **dame** Gloucester is echoing Eleanor's
contemptuous language of 39.
ill-nurtured poorly bred. Responding to the above contempt,
Gloucester reminds his wife that she
came from a family considerably lower
than his own royal lineage.

Above the reach or compass of thy thought?
And wilt thou still be hammering treachery
To tumble down thy husband and thyself
From top of honour to disgrace's feet?
Away from me and let me hear no more!   50

ELEANOR

What, what, my lord! Are you so choleric
With Eleanor, for telling but her dream?
Next time I'll keep my dreams unto myself,
And not be checked.

GLOUCESTER

Nay, be not angry, I am pleased again.   55

Enter Messenger.

MESSENGER

My Lord Protector, 'tis his highness' pleasure
You do prepare to ride unto Saint Albans,
Whereas the King and Queen do mean to hawk.

GLOUCESTER

I go. Come, Nell, thou wilt ride with us?

ELEANOR

Yes, my good lord, I'll follow presently.   60
                          [*Exeunt Gloucester and Messenger.*]

---

46 beyond the bounds of your imagination. Cf. 'they did perform / Beyond thought's compass' (*H8* 1.1.35–6).

47 **hammering** contriving insistently (*OED* Hammer *v.* 2 and 4)

49 **top of honour** Cairncross cites 'From top of honors hye' from *Mirror*'s account of Suffolk's fall. See 1.2.67 LN.

51 **choleric** enraged. Cf. 'Boiling choler chokes / The hollow passage of my poison'd voice' (*1H6* 5.4.120–1). Deriving from the physiology of the

four 'humours', or fluids: yellow bile (choleric), black bile (melancholy), blood (sanguine), phlegm (phlegmatic). Temperament depended on balance among them; a predominance of one 'humour' led to a dangerous psychological strain. Jonson's Induction to *Every Man out of his Humour* (1600) is the most-quoted exposition of the subject (3.431–2).

54 **checked** rebuked (*OED* Check *v.* 10)

58 **Whereas** where (Abbott, 116)

60–7 See Appendix 2 for Q1/Q3 variants.

57+ Saint Albans] *(S. Albons)*   58 Whereas] *(Where as)*   59 with us?] With us, I'm sure? *Dyce subst.;* Come *Nell,* thou wilt go with vs vs I am sure *Q*   60 SD] *Capell; Ex. Hum opp. 59 F*

Follow I must; I cannot go before
While Gloucester bears this base and humble mind.
Were I a man, a duke and next of blood,
I would remove these tedious stumbling-blocks
And smooth my way upon their headless necks.   65
And, being a woman, I will not be slack
To play my part in Fortune's pageant. –
Where are you there? Sir John!

Enter HUME.

                              Nay, fear not, man,
We are alone; here's none but thee and I.

HUME

Jesus preserve your royal majesty!   70

---

61 **I . . . before** proverbial (Dent, G156),
and acknowledging Margaret's prece-
dence

64 **stumbling-blocks** *OED* 4d instances
this as the simple meaning of 'obstacle'.
However, since Tyndale's coinage of
the phrase in his translation of New
Testament Greek (1526) the figurative
meaning is also moral and spiritual, 'an
occasion of moral stumbling . . . scandal . . . of falling into calamity or ruin'
(see *OED* 4a and b). Clearly, given
what ensues, it is Eleanor who has provided the 'stumbling-block' which
results in her own 'ruin'. In the context, Shakespeare may well have
picked up the phrase from Foxe's later
defence of his original inclusion of
discussion of Eleanor and Bolingbroke, in his second edition of *Acts and
Monuments*, the corrections of which
consider the 'stumbling blocks in . . .
men's walks' (3.709).

67 **pageant** Sanders gives 'play, spectacle'; Cairncross 'scene or act in a mystery play' (see *OED sb.* 1). Hart quotes
Hall (279), 'The Erle of Warwickes

doynges, which must need play a
pageaunt in this enterlude' (the figurative meaning of *OED sb.* 1b). See
LN.

68 **Sir John** 'A common early designation
for a clerk in holy orders. See Grafton
I. 241, "Till the King had payde all
which their Clergie had demaunded
. . . yea every sawcy *Sir Ihon* for his
part"' (Hart). John was Hume's first
name in the chronicles, which spell the
surname either 'Hum' or 'Hun'. Only
Foxe uses the form found here.

68.1 Editors usually follow F and place
this after 69. As Honigmann argues,
this is a characteristic instance of F
placing the SD two or three lines after
the actual entry ('Re-enter', 117–18).

69 **thee** See Abbott, 213, for the use of
'thee' for 'thou' after the verb 'to be',
and cf. 4.1.119.

70 **your royal majesty** 'Henry VIII was
the first English sovereign who was
styled "His Majesty". Henry IV was
"His Grace"; Henry VI, "His
Excellent Grace"' (Brewer, 796).

68.1] *Q subst.; opp. 69 F*

ELEANOR

What sayst thou? Majesty! I am but grace.

HUME

But by the grace of God, and Hume's advice,
Your grace's title shall be multiplied.

ELEANOR

What sayst thou, man? Hast thou as yet conferred
With Margery Jourdain, the cunning witch,   75
With Roger Bolingbroke, the conjuror?
And will they undertake to do me good?

HUME

This they have promised, to show your highness
A spirit, raised from depth of underground,
That shall make answer to such questions   80
As by your grace shall be propounded him.

ELEANOR

It is enough, I'll think upon the questions.
When from Saint Albans we do make return
We'll see these things effected to the full.
Here, Hume, take this reward; make merry, man,   85
With thy confederates in this weighty cause.   *Exit.*

HUME

Hume must make merry with the Duchess' gold;

71–3 **grace . . . multiplied** Hume is corrected by Eleanor and responds by punning on 1 Peter, 1.2, 'Grace and peace be multiplied vnto you' (Shaheen, 44).
75 **Margery Jourdain** 'Old mother Madge her neyghbours did hir name' (*Mirror*, 435). If Hall's designation 'the Witche of Eye' (202) is that of the Eye near Bury St Edmunds, rather than of those near Peterborough and Worcester, then this Suffolk connec-

tion ties in with Hume's revelation (95, 101) that he is in part working on the Duke of Suffolk's behalf.
cunning skilful. Cf. 2.1.128 and 4.1.34.
76 **conjuror** one who conjures spirits, a magician (*OED* 1)
78 **promised** promisèd
79 **spirit** See 1.4.22.1–3, 1.4.24n.
81 **propounded** put to: not elsewhere in Shakespeare

---

75 the cunning witch] the cunning Witch of *Ely Q*, *Q2*; the cunning witch of *Rye Q3*; the cunning witch of Eie *Alexander, Ard²*

171

Marry, and shall. But how now, Sir John Hume!
Seal up your lips and give no words but mum;
The business asketh silent secrecy.   90
Dame Eleanor gives gold to bring the witch:
Gold cannot come amiss, were she a devil.
Yet have I gold flies from another coast:
I dare not say from the rich Cardinal
And from the great and new-made Duke of Suffolk,   95
Yet I do find it so. For, to be plain,
They, knowing Dame Eleanor's aspiring humour,
Have hired me to undermine the Duchess
And buzz these conjurations in her brain.
They say 'A crafty knave does need no broker',   100
Yet am I Suffolk and the Cardinal's broker.
Hume, if you take not heed, you shall go near
To call them both a pair of crafty knaves.
Well, so it stands; and thus, I fear, at last
Hume's knavery will be the Duchess' wrack,   105

---

88 **Marry** a mild oath, 'by the Virgin Mary'. 'Marry, and shall' was proverbial (Dent, M699.1).

88–9 **Hume . . . mum** Since 'No word but mum' was proverbial (Dent, W767), Hume might be playing on the alternative form of his name, 'Hum', for the purposes of comic rhyme.

90 **asketh** requires, demands (*OED* Ask *v.* 23). Cf. *TS* 2.1.114.

90–1 **silent secrecy . . . gold** following the proverbs (88–9), and in view of the proverb quoted by Hume (100), a sardonic metadramatic irony here in the speaker revealing in soliloquy his subornation, since it is also proverbial that 'Gold speaks' (Dent, G285a). Cf. *R3* 4.2.38.

93 **flies . . . coast** comes from another quarter: possibly alluding to Spain's plunder of South America

94 **rich** See 1.1.172–4n.

97 **They, knowing** not historically true;

part of Shakespeare's technique of linking major dramatic concerns with subplot or episode, as with York and Jack Cade (see 3.1.355–8)

98 **hired** For the disyllabic possibilities of 'hi-erd' and 'hirèd' see Cercignani, 25, 357.

99 **buzz** whisper (*OED v.*[1] 4). But *OED v.*[1] 7, 'incite by suggestion' (first entry 1637), is very much an emphasis here. **conjurations** incantations

100–3 Hume plays on the currency of two related proverbs: 'A crafty knave needs no broker' (Dent, K122), and 'Two false knaves need no broker' (Tilley, 147). See 88–9n. and 90–1n.

100 **broker** go-between, middleman, usually of a dubious kind. Cf. 'that sly divel, / That broker, that still breaks the pate of faith' (*KJ* 2.1.567–8).

105 **wrack** ruin. Possibly proverbial: 'All wrong comes to wrack' (Tilley, W942).

96 so.] *this edn;* so: *F* 97 They... humour,] They (...humor) *F*

And her attainture will be Humphrey's fall.
Sort how it will, I shall have gold for all.   *Exit.*

[1.3]   *Enter three or four* Petitioners, [PETER] *the
armourer's man being one.*

1 PETITIONER   My masters, let's stand close. My Lord
Protector will come this way by and by, and then we
may deliver our supplications in the quill.

2 PETITIONER   Marry, the Lord protect him, for he's a
good man, Jesu bless him.   5

Enter SUFFOLK *and* QUEEN.

---

106 **attainture** The meaning here is much stronger than 'dishonour' (*OED* 2). As Hall relates, Eleanor 'was accused of treason' (202). To be attainted for treason (*OED* Attaint *v.* 6) was to run the risk of losing not just life, but title and property denied to one's heirs by a bill of attainder. From this point of view Eleanor gets off rather lightly. For a crucial legal distinction concerning 'attachment' and 'attainder' and the right of Richard Plantagenet to inherit the title Duke of York, see *1H6* 2.4.90–7. Richard, Earl of Cambridge, Richard's father, was arrested for treason ('attached') and executed, but his conviction and sentence were carried out without a bill of attainder having been issued.

107 **Sort . . . will** come what may. Cf. *MND* 3.2.352.

1.3 location: the royal palace, London (Hanmer). The story of the armourer and his servant is found, briefly, in Hall (207–8), Holinshed (210), Grafton (628) and Fabyan (168). The allegation concerning the Duke of York is Shakespeare's invention, once again serving to link main plot and

episode (see 1.2.97n.). For the larger implications of chivalric burlesque see Knowles, 'Farce', and Introduction, pp. 82–8. Margaret now takes centre stage: Hall's statements 'The Quene . . . entierly loued the Duke' (218) and 'the Quenes dearlynge . . . Suffolke' (219) hint at a major dramatic development which may have been introduced after revision at the end of *1H6*. For sequence, see Introduction pp. 111–15.

1 **close** together as a group (*OED adv.* 1), and presumably close to where they expect their superiors to pass

2 **by and by** immediately, just as one sense of Elizabethan 'presently' has changed its meaning from 'immediately' to 'in a while'

3 **supplications** petitions
in the quill *OED* Quill *sb.²* gives this instance for 'In a body; in combination or concert'. Perhaps a later-recorded proverb (1640), 'To piss in the same quill' (Tilley, Q177), throws some retroactive light on this as a comic image of exigent mutuality?

4 **protect** another pun on Gloucester's title. See 38–9.

4–5 See Appendix 2 for Q variant.

1.3] *Capell*   0.1 PETER] *Theobald*

1 PETITIONER   Here 'a comes, methinks, and the Queen
    with him. I'll be the first, sure.

2 PETITIONER   Come back, fool! This is the Duke of
    Suffolk, and not my Lord Protector.

SUFFOLK   How now, fellow; wouldst anything with me?   10

1 PETITIONER   I pray, my lord, pardon me, I took ye for
    my Lord Protector.

QUEEN   'For my Lord Protector'? Are your supplications to
    his lordship? Let me see them. [*Takes First Petitioner's
    supplication.*] What is thine?   15

1 PETITIONER   Mine is, an't please your grace, against
    John Goodman, my Lord Cardinal's man, for keeping
    my house and lands and wife and all from me.

SUFFOLK   Thy wife too! That's some wrong indeed. –
    What's yours? What's here! [*Reads.*] *Against the Duke*   20
    of Suffolk, for enclosing the commons of Melford. How
    now, sir knave!

2 PETITIONER   Alas, sir, I am but a poor petitioner of our
    whole township.

6   SP Original MS designation of '*Pet.*'
    may have led to compositorial confusion.
    '*a* he. For colloquial ellipsis of the
    nominative see Abbott, 402.
10 **fellow** not necessarily haughty, the
    customary title of address by a supe-
    rior (*OED sb.* 10a)
13 *Hattaway follows Capell's and
    Sisson's (2.75) substitution of 'For' for
    F's 'To', thereby making the Queen
    sarcastically repeat the First Pe-
    titioner's phrase, rather than following
    Rowe's addition of an SD which has
    the Queen read from something she
    then goes on to ask for.
17 **man** obviously more powerful than a
    manservant, one of the Cardinal's
    executive staff
17–18 for all the comic element, empha-
    sized by Suffolk (19), an indication of
    commoners as ultimately victims of

the high and mighty, as the following
lines elaborate
19 **Thy . . . indeed.** Suffolk's comic
    indictment ironically reveals his own
    culpability in relation to the King and
    Margaret.
21 *enclosing the commons* aristocratic
    enclosure of the lower orders' common
    arable land for purposes of sheep pas-
    ture. This charge against Suffolk is not
    found in Hall or Holinshed but, as Hart
    points out, Grafton reprints grievances
    including 'enrychyng hymselfe with the
    King's goods, and landes' (639), which
    he takes to signify enclosure. See Siemon
    and W.C. Carroll, 'Nurse', for modern
    re-examination of the whole problem of
    sixteenth–century enclosures.
    Melford Long Melford, Suffolk
22 **sir knave** a contemptuous oxymoron
24 **township** only here in Shakespeare

6 SP] *F4 subst., Oxf;* Peter F   13 For] *Capell;* To F   14–15 SD] *Oxf subst.*   20 SD] *Rowe*

PETER [*Offers his petition.*] Against my master Thomas   25
Horner, for saying that the Duke of York was rightful
heir to the crown.

QUEEN What sayst thou? Did the Duke of York say he
was rightful heir to the crown?

PETER That my master was? No, forsooth, my master   30
said that he was, and that the King was an usurer.

QUEEN An usurper thou wouldst say.

PETER Ay, forsooth, an usurper.

SUFFOLK Who is there? [*Snatches Peter's supplication.*]

Enter Servant.

Take this fellow in, and send for his master with a   35
pursuivant presently. – We'll hear more of your matter
before the King.   *Exit* [*Servant with Peter*].

QUEEN

And as for you, that love to be protected
Under the wings of our Protector's grace,

25–6 **Thomas Horner** Fabyan draws on
Gregory for the name of Robert Horne,
one of the sheriffs in charge of the combat. Presumably the cuckold surname
seemed appropriate, given Suffolk's role
and his remarks at 19. Peter's comic surname is Thump (following Q), as we
find at 2.3.85. Stow records the real
names of the servant and master as John
David and William Catur, which he
must have taken from the original warrant ('Johes Davy . . . Willm Catour'),
reprinted in Nichols, 217.

28–33 *To complete the comic sequence
of malapropism (*usurer . . . usurper*)
following misconstruction of *he*, the
'gag' material from Q is adopted. Wells
& Taylor adopt Q on the technical
supposition of eyeskip from 'an vſurer'
to 'an vſurper', but it is included here

rather as a significant contribution to
the carnivalesque parody in the play as
a whole. See Introduction, pp. 102–3.

31 *usurer Ironically, Henry's foreign policy was sustained by continual borrowing, primarily from London and Calais
merchants, and from the Cardinal
(Griffiths, 390–4). See 1.1.172–4n.

35 **with** by (Abbott, 193)

36 **pursuivant** a royal official authorized
to deliver warrants

39 **Under the wings** Hart suggests
verbal allusion to Ruth, 2.12, which
can be supported in view of the
ironic context in which a landowner,
Boaz, sympathetically welcomes the
stranger, Ruth, into his domain: 'a full
reward be giuen thee of the Lord God
of Israel, vnder whose wing thou art
come to trust'.

25 SD] *Sanders* 30 ¹master] *Warburton;* Mistresse *F* 31 usurer] *Q;* Vsurper *F* 32–33] *Q; not
in F* 34 SD] *Oxf subst.*

Begin your suits anew, and sue to him.   40
   Tears the supplication.
Away, base cullions! Suffolk, let them go.
ALL PETITIONERS   Come, let's be gone.   *Exeunt.*
QUEEN
  My Lord of Suffolk, say, is this the guise,
  Is this the fashions in the court of England?
  Is this the government of Britain's isle,   45
  And this the royalty of Albion's king?
  What, shall King Henry be a pupil still
  Under the surly Gloucester's governance?
  Am I a queen in title and in style
  And must be made a subject to a duke?   50
  I tell thee, Pole, when in the city Tours
  Thou ran'st a-tilt in honour of my love
  And stol'st away the ladies' hearts of France,
  I thought King Henry had resembled thee
  In courage, courtship and proportion.   55

41 **cullions** low wretches (Italian *coglioni*, testicles)
43–4 **guise . . . fashions** customs, practices
44 **Is** with plural object see Abbott, 335. Cf. 3.2.11.
46 **Albion's** 'Albion' was a mythic name for England with several historical sources, the oldest being an originally Greek treatise, *De mundo*, describing England and Ireland three hundred years before Julius Caesar's supposed etymology of *albus* (white) in allusion to the cliffs of Dover (Brewer, 27).
48 **governance** As Hart noted, though found only here in Shakespeare, this word is common in Hall and a particular passage of the chronicler seems to be recalled here: 'the aucthoritie and gouernaunce of the realme' was mostly in Gloucester's hands while Henry was 'like a yong scholer or innocent pupille' (208).
51 **Pole** de la Pole, Suffolk's family name. See 1.1.44, 4.1.70 and n.
52 **ran'st a-tilt** charged on horseback with a lance in a joust. The earliest recorded occurrences of this rare expression are attributed to Shakespeare here and in *1H6* 3.2.51 (see *OED* A-tilt 2). The verbal and substantive forms of 'tilt' are more familiar. Hall refers to the 'triumphaunt Justes' (205) on the occasion in 1444. Monstrelet's mention of the tilt at Dijon in 1443 is one of the earliest. See Young.
53 Cf. the Latinate construction of 1.1.232.
54 **had** would have. For the subjunctive form absorbed by the past indicative, see Abbott, 361.
55 **courtship . . . proportion** courtliness . . . figure

40 SD *Tears*] *Rowe; Teare F*   42 SP] *Oxf; All. F*   SD] *Rowe; Exit. F*

But all his mind is bent to holiness,
To number Ave-Maries on his beads.
His champions are the prophets and apostles,
His weapons, holy saws of sacred writ;
His study is his tilt-yard, and his loves   60
Are brazen images of canonized saints.
I would the college of the cardinals
Would choose him Pope, and carry him to Rome
And set the triple crown upon his head:
That were a state fit for his Holiness.   65

SUFFOLK

Madam, be patient. As I was cause
Your highness came to England, so will I
In England work your grace's full content.

QUEEN

Beside the haughty Protector have we Beaufort,
The imperious churchman, Somerset, Buckingham   70
And grumbling York; and not the least of these
But can do more in England than the King.

56–61 an elaboration on York's phrase *church-like humours* (see 1.1.244n.)
56 **bent to holiness** Cf. Richard III 'Divinely bent to meditation' (*R3* 3.7.62).
  bent inclined (*OED pp.*[1] *a.* 3). Cf. 2.1.158.
57 **beads** rosary. Cf. 1.1.27.
58 **champions** as Sanders points out, Christian spiritual champions described metaphorically by St Paul in Ephesians, 6. The King's personal champion was a hereditary office. See 4.10.54n.
59 **saws** sayings. Cf. 'Full of wise saws and modern instances' (*AYL* 2.7.156).
60 **tilt-yard** The royal tilt-yard, at Westminster, was on land now occupied by the Houses of Parliament. This yard in Whitehall had recently superseded the one at Greenwich as

the scene for tournaments. (See Young, 106–10, and 52n. above.)
61 **brazen images** bronze statues
  canonized For the stress on the second syllable see Abbott, 491.
62 **college . . . cardinals** formal elective body
64 **triple crown** the Pope's triple diadem
65 **state** status
66 **patient** trisyllabic. See Cercignani, 309.
68 **work . . . content** act to fulfil all your aspirations
69 **haughty** proud and arrogant. Cf. *3H6* 2.1.169 and *R2* 4.1.254.
71 **grumbling** discontented
71–2 **not . . . can** even the least of them can
72 **But** This usage combines the meaning of 'without exception' and the function of displacing a relative pronoun for greater emphasis. See Abbott, 123.

---

69 haughty] *(haughtie)*

SUFFOLK

And he of these that can do most of all
Cannot do more in England than the Nevilles:
Salisbury and Warwick are no simple peers.   75

QUEEN

Not all these lords do vex me half so much
As that proud dame, the Lord Protector's wife.
She sweeps it through the court with troops of ladies,
More like an empress than Duke Humphrey's wife.
Strangers in court do take her for the Queen.   80
She bears a duke's revenues on her back
And in her heart she scorns our poverty.
Shall I not live to be avenged on her?
Contemptuous base-born callet as she is,
She vaunted 'mongst her minions t'other day   85
The very train of her worst wearing gown

---

74 **Nevilles** After the misfortunes of the Percies under Henry IV, the Nevilles rose to become arguably the most powerful northern aristocratic family. Of Lancastrian descent from John of Gaunt, they were affiliated with the Yorkists through Salisbury's sister's marriage to the Duke of York. See 1.1.237 and n.

75 **no simple peers** no ordinary peers (see *OED* Simple *a*. 5)

78 **it** For this indefinite use see Abbott, 226.

80 **Strangers** foreigners

81 Cf. 'He wears a whole Lordship on his back' (Dent, L452). Hart cites Marlowe, *Edward II*, 'He wears a lord's revenue on his back' (1.4.409). In the anonymous 'The Lament of the Duchess of Gloucester' (1441) Eleanor's luxurious dress is particularly singled out: 'ffarewell, damaske and clothys of gold, / ffarewell, velwette and clothys in grayne [dyed], / ffarewell, my clothys so manyfold' (Robbins, 179).

   revenues stressed on the second syllable (Cercignani, 42)

84 **Contemptuous** contemptible (*OED a*. 3)

   base-born See 1.2.42n. and 4.8.46n.

   callet strumpet. Gloucester's illicit relationship with Eleanor, before his first marriage to Jacqueline of Bavaria had been annulled, provoked some public abuse. Part of Eleanor's final punishment, dramatized in 2.4, was that normally meted out to prostitutes.

85 **vaunted** boasted

   minions favourites. Hall has 'the Quene with her minions' (217).

86 **train** extended length of gown trailing behind or carried by servants, indicating the aristocratic status of the wearer. Cf. 'Dignified with this high honour – / To bear my lady's train' (*TGV* 2.4.158–9).

   worst wearing gown Hattaway and Sanders assume 'least fashionable'. The tautologous *wearing* (*OED vbl sb.*[1] 2b) seems to be added for alliterative contempt. Perhaps it means the gown that Eleanor least esteemed herself? At the other extreme to her *worst wearing gown*,

---

81] *not in Q; She beares a Dukes whole reuennewes on her backe Q3*

Was better worth than all my father's lands,
Till Suffolk gave two dukedoms for his daughter.

SUFFOLK

Madam, myself have limed a bush for her
And placed a choir of such enticing birds   90
That she will light to listen to the lays
And never mount to trouble you again.
So let her rest; and, madam, list to me –
For I am bold to counsel you in this –
Although we fancy not the Cardinal,   95
Yet must we join with him and with the lords
Till we have brought Duke Humphrey in disgrace.
As for the Duke of York, this late complaint
Will make but little for his benefit.
So one by one we'll weed them all at last,   100
And you yourself shall steer the happy helm.

Sound a sennet. Enter the KING, GLOUCESTER, CARDINAL
Beaufort, BUCKINGHAM, YORK, SALISBURY, WARWICK
and ELEANOR.

Eleanor had been permitted to wear the robes of the Garter (K. H. Vickers, 277).

88 Cf. 1.1.211–16.

89 **limed a bush** a metaphor from the fowler's practice of smearing branches and twigs with birdlime to ensnare prey. See 2.4.54 and 3.3.16. Birdlime was a sticky substance taken from holly.

90 **enticing birds** decoys (Sanders). The 'coy duck' or 'decoy duck' appears later in the seventeenth century (*OED* Coy *sb.* 1 and 4); the sixteenth-century word was 'stale' (*OED sb.*³ 1). See *Shakespeare's England*, 2.372.

91 **lays** songs: 'The Fowler . . . allureth Birds, by the chirping of lure-birds' (Comenius, 107).

95 **fancy** love (*OED v.* 8)

98 **late** recent: that of the armourer's servant, 25–7

99 will do him little good

100 **weed** a common horticultural metaphor for getting rid of (uprooting) political dissidents, malcontents, favourites and the like (see 3.1.31–3). Perhaps the best-known example is from *R2*: 'The caterpillars of the commonwealth / Which I have sworn to weed' (2.3.166–7).

101 **steer . . . helm** deriving from the common ship-of-state metaphor. Cf. King Henry's 'Thus stands my state . . . Like to a ship' (4.9.31–2).

101.1 *sennet* a sequence of cornet or trumpet notes made upon an entrance

90 choir] *(Quier)* 101 helm.] *Rowe; Helme. Exit. F* 101.1–3 GLOUCESTER, CARDINAL Beaufort, . . . ELEANOR] *this edn; Duke Humfrey, Cardinall, . . . the Duchesse F*

KING

> For my part, noble lords, I care not which;
> Or Somerset, or York, all's one to me.

YORK

> If York have ill demeaned himself in France,
> Then let him be denied the regentship.   105

SOMERSET

> If Somerset be unworthy of the place,
> Let York be regent; I will yield to him.

WARWICK

> Whether your Grace be worthy, yea or no,
> Dispute not that; York is the worthier.

CARDINAL

> Ambitious Warwick, let thy betters speak.   110

WARWICK

> The Cardinal's not my better in the field.

BUCKINGHAM

> All in this presence are thy betters, Warwick.

WARWICK

> Warwick may live to be the best of all.

SALISBURY

> Peace, son! – And show some reason, Buckingham,
> Why Somerset should be preferred in this.   115

QUEEN

> Because the King, forsooth, will have it so.

---

or exit. The word is found only in SDs (*OED*). As Cairncross suggests, part of Q's SD anticipates the dialogue: 'Enter King *Henry*, and the Duke of *Yorke* and the Duke of *Somerset* on both sides of the King, whispering with him'.

102 **I . . . which** a rare occasion on which Henry's political disability derives not from religious inclination but from fatal diffidence

103 **Or** either
Somerset, or York The rivalry, which began in *1H6* 2.4 and which

continues here and in 3.1 and 5.1, is both personal and a reflection of dynastic faction: York will challenge the Lancastrians, while Somerset is a Beaufort and thus connected with the Cardinal.

104 **demeaned** behaved. See 1.1.185n.
112 **presence** the presence chamber, or royal reception room; or the presence of the king
116 **forsooth** from Old English 'for sooth (truth)': in truth, truly. *OED* notes derisive parenthetical usage, as here.

GLOUCESTER

Madam, the King is old enough himself

To give his censure. These are no women's matters.

QUEEN

If he be old enough, what needs your grace

To be Protector of his excellence?   120

GLOUCESTER

Madam, I am Protector of the realm,

And at his pleasure will resign my place.

SUFFOLK

Resign it then, and leave thine insolence.

Since thou wert king – as who is king but thou? –

The commonwealth hath daily run to wrack,   125

The Dauphin hath prevailed beyond the seas,

And all the peers and nobles of the realm

Have been as bondmen to thy sovereignty.

CARDINAL

The commons hast thou racked; the clergy's bags

Are lank and lean with thy extortions.   130

SOMERSET

Thy sumptuous buildings and thy wife's attire

---

117 **old enough** From one point of view this had been true for several years, since, following the examples of Henry III and Richard II, the king was considered to attain majority at the age of 14. Henry had confirmed this by authorizing a warrant with his own sign manual in 1436 (Griffiths, 231–2).

118 **censure** judgement

120, 121 **Protector** See 1.1.39n.

123 **insolence** haughty arrogant bearing, rather than speech, at this date (*OED sb.* 1): encapsulated in Hamlet's phrase, 'The insolence of office' (*Ham* 3.1.72)

125–6 Editors point out that these charges appear to be based on those brought against Suffolk himself in

1449. See Hall, 217–18. But the brief generality of these two lines, set against the extensive specificity of the chronicle, rather blunts any possible irony. In contrast see 136n. No record of the actual treason charges brought against Gloucester has survived.

126 **Dauphin** pronounced 'dolphin' (and so spelled throughout in F)

128 **bondmen** slaves

129 **racked** demanded extortionate levies from

bags purses

131 **sumptuous buildings** pre-eminently 'the manor of Pleasaunce', as it was known, at Greenwich, inherited by Gloucester from his brother

126+ Dauphin] *(Dolphin)*

181

Have cost a mass of public treasury.

BUCKINGHAM

Thy cruelty in execution

Upon offenders hath exceeded law,

And left thee to the mercy of the law.　　　　　　　　135

QUEEN

Thy sale of offices and towns in France,

If they were known, as the suspect is great,

Would make thee quickly hop without thy head.

　　　　　　　　　　　　　　　　　　　Exit Gloucester.

[*The Queen drops her fan.*]

Give me my fan. What, minion! Can ye not?

She gives Eleanor a box on the ear.

I cry you mercy, madam; was it you?　　　　　　　　140

ELEANOR

Was't I! Yea, I it was, proud Frenchwoman.

Could I come near your beauty with my nails

Henry V. See K. H. Vickers, 444–6. The word *sumptuous* may have been picked up from Holinshed's account of Jack Straw's rebellion and the sacking of the Savoy, 'the dukes house [of Lancaster], all the iewels, plate, and other rich and sumptuous furniture which they there found' (2.738). See 4.7.93n.

thy wife's attire This charge adds a dimension to Margaret's line, 86.

132 **treasury** wealth

133–4 Hall particularly draws attention to this charge, 'in especiall one, that he had caused men adiudged to dye, to be put to other execucion, then the law of the land had ordered or assigned' (209).

136 The extensive charges recorded by Hall against Suffolk include: 'the saied duke, beyng in Fraunce in the kynges seruice, and one of the priuiest of his

counsaill there, traiterously, declared and opened to the capitaines and conduyters of warre, apperteinyng to the kynges enemies, the kynges counsaill, purueiaunce of his armes, furniture of his tounes, and all other ordinaunces, wherby the kynges enemies . . . haue gotten tounes and fortresses' (218).

137 **suspect** ground of suspicion (*OED* sb^1 1f)

138 **hop . . . head** be beheaded: proverbial (Dent, HH11)

139 **minion** here the derogatory sense of 'hussy'. See 85n.

140 **I . . . mercy** I beg your pardon (sarcasm).

142–3 **with . . . face** 'I'd scratch your face': proverbial (Tilley, C553); deriving from the notion that God scratched the Ten Commandments with his fingernails – 'written with the finger of God', Exodus, 31.18

---

138 SD *Gloucester*] *Humfrey F*　SD 2] *Johnson*; The Queene lets fall her gloue, *Q*　139 SD *Eleanor*] *this edn; the Duchesse F*

I'd set my ten commandments in your face.

KING

Sweet aunt, be quiet; 'twas against her will.

ELEANOR

Against her will! Good King, look to't in time;   145
She'll pamper thee, and dandle thee like a baby.
Though in this place most master wear no breeches,
She shall not strike Dame Eleanor unrevenged.   *Exit.*

BUCKINGHAM

Lord Cardinal, I will follow Eleanor,
And listen after Humphrey, how he proceeds.   150
She's tickled now, her fury needs no spurs,
She'll gallop far enough to her destruction.   *Exit.*

(Shaheen, 44–5). In addition to this example Tilley (C553) quotes from *Taming of a Shrew*, 'Hands off I say, and get you from this place; / Or I will set my ten commandments in your face' (TLN 330–1).

144 **quiet** calm (*OED sb.* 3)
against her will unintentional

146 ***pamper** over-indulge, spoil (*OED v.* b). The mothering, or nursing, image of 'dandle thee like a baby' (cf. the Duchess of York's 'I am your sorrow's nurse, / And I will pamper it with lamentation', *R3* 2.2.87–8) supports McKerrow's conjectural emendation, especially as 'hamper' is not found elsewhere in Shakespeare.

147 **most . . . breeches** The master of the house isn't wearing breeches; that is, the mistress lords it over the master (proverbial: Dent, M727). Cf. 'She wears the breeches' (Dent, B645). See *3H6* 5.5.24.
most master the greatest master (*OED adj.* 1h): the Queen, ironically. Greene uses the phrase in *Pandosto*: see Tilley, M727.

150 **listen after** keep an ear out for (*OED* Listen *v.* 2c). Cf. *2H4* 1.1.29.

151 **tickled** easily provoked (combining *OED* Tickle *v.* 7 and *a.*³). If Buckingham is aware of the Somerset–Cardinal plot to entrap Eleanor, *tickled* here, as Sanders suggests, probably also means 'nearly caught', from the practice of trout fishing (*OED* Tickle *v.* 4c). See *TN* 2.5.22.
*fury F's 'fume', as 'rage', is appropriate but might well be a misreading of 'furie', as Sisson argues (2,76), which better fits the metre as well as the proverb in the following line, 'Do not spur a free (willing) horse' (pointed out by Hattaway). Blake defends 'fume' as 'fuddled' reflecting on the implied metaphor of 'tickle' as 'tickle-brain' (strong drink as in *1H4* 2.4.386). Unfortunately *OED* does not support this and 'tickle-brain' is used by Falstaff to shut up Mistress Quickly's 'tickle-tongue', her garrulity ('Peace good pint pot'), which is presumably a result of strong drink (see *OED* Tickle *a.* 9a).

143 I'd] *Ide Q;* I could *F*   145 will! Good King,] *Ard¹ following Johnson;* will, good King? *F*   146 pamper] *Oxf (McKerrow);* hamper *F*   151 fury] *Dyce subst.;* Fume *F*

Enter GLOUCESTER.

GLOUCESTER

> Now, lords, my choler being overblown
> With walking once about the quadrangle,
> I come to talk of commonwealth affairs.   155
> As for your spiteful false objections,
> Prove them, and I lie open to the law.
> But God in mercy so deal with my soul
> As I in duty love my king and country.
> But to the matter that we have in hand. –   160
> I say, my sovereign, York is meetest man
> To be your regent in the realm of France.

SUFFOLK

> Before we make election, give me leave
> To show some reason, of no little force,
> That York is most unmeet of any man.   165

YORK

> I'll tell thee, Suffolk, why I am unmeet:
> First, for I cannot flatter thee in pride;
> Next, if I be appointed for the place

---

153 **being overblown** now blown over (see *Tem* 2.2.110)

154 **quadrangle** rectangular courtyard of the palace: sole usage in Shakespeare, earliest in *OED*

155 **commonwealth** See 1.1.186n. Only elsewhere as an adjective, in the same phrase, in *H5* 1.1.41.

156 **spiteful . . . objections** malicious . . . accusations

158 Cf. Psalms, 119.124, 'O deal with thy servant according unto thy louing mercy' (Cairncross). The context is ironic, 'that the proude doe me no wrong' (122), which is to be Gloucester's fate.

161 **meetest** most suitable

163 **election** choice

165 See Abbott, 409, on confusion of two constructions in superlatives (i.e. 'York is the most unfitting man' and 'amongst unmeet men York is the most unfitting').
unmeet unfitting. Hattaway suggests an echo of lines peculiar to Holinshed, 'York . . . a man most meet . . . appointed as Regent of France' (208).

167 **for . . . pride** because flattery would be beneath my dignity

168 **if . . . appointed** See Hall (179) and Holinshed (208–9) for the rivalry of York and Somerset for the regency of France.

152.1 GLOUCESTER] *Pope; Humfrey F*

My Lord of Somerset will keep me here
Without discharge, money or furniture,   170
Till France be won into the Dauphin's hands.
Last time I danced attendance on his will
Till Paris was besieged, famished and lost.

WARWICK

That can I witness, and a fouler fact
Did never traitor in the land commit.   175

SUFFOLK

Peace, headstrong Warwick!

WARWICK

Image of pride, why should I hold my peace?

---

170 **discharge** exoneration (see *OED sb.*
4b). For the accusations implicit in
Somerset's malignity, see 172–3n.
  furniture payment; military equipment
172–3 **Last . . . lost.** This would seem to
refer to *1H6* 4.3, as Hart and Hattaway
note, where York execrates Somerset's
failure to supply horsemen for Talbot's
relief. But if historical rather than dramatic sequence is followed this is an
anachronism, as Cairncross points out,
since this incident refers to the siege of
Bordeaux in 1453. Paris fell in 1436,
the year of York's first appointment as
Lieutenant-General. Holinshed refers
to this in his later account of York's
attempt to renew his office in 1446, a
passage that Shakespeare seems to
have used, as it is not in Hall: 'But the
duke of Summerset still maligning the
duke of Yorkes aduancement, as he
had sought to hinder his dispatch at
the first when he was sent over to be
regent, as before yee haue heard: he
likewise now wrought so, that the king
reuoked his grant . . . and with helpe of
William marquesse of Suffolke
obteined that grant for himselfe'
(208–9). See Boswell-Stone, 252.
172 **danced attendance on** wasted time
waiting on: proverbial (Dent, A392).

Cf. *R3* 3.7.56.
173 **famished** dramatic licence here; no
sign of this in the chronicles. Paris fell
because of the shifting allegiance of
the citizens and the superior numbers
of the besiegers, combined with mistaken English tactics. (See Holinshed,
185–6.)
174–5 See 1.1.116n. for Shakespeare's
confusion between Richard Neville
and his father-in-law.
174 **fact** evil deed, crime: the commonest
sixteenth- and seventeenth-century
meaning (*OED* Fact 1c). Cf. *Mac*
3.6.10, 'To kill their gracious father?
Damned fact!'
177 **Image** embodiment, type. Cf. *KL*,
'Behold the great image of authority'
(4.6.158). A more complex interpretation is of *Image of pride* meaning
'reflection of pride' as in *TC* 2.3.155,
'pride is his own glass', and 3.3.47–8,
'Pride hath no other glass / To show
itself but pride'. Cf. *OED* Image *sb.* 2,
'appearance . . . reflected as from a
mirror'. Consider this exchange
between Clifford, 'Why, what a brood
of traitors have we here!', and York,
'Look in a glass, and call thy image so'
(5.1.141–2). Pride is self-revealing and
self-reflecting.

177.1] *Theobald;* Enter the Armourer and his man. *Q, F subst.*

Enter [HORNER *the*] *armourer and his man* [PETER, *guarded*].

SUFFOLK

    Because here is a man accused of treason:

    Pray God the Duke of York excuse himself!

YORK

    Doth anyone accuse York for a traitor?   180

KING

    What mean'st thou, Suffolk? Tell me, what are these?

SUFFOLK

    Please it your majesty, this is the man

    That doth accuse his master of high treason.

    His words were these: that Richard, Duke of York,

    Was rightful heir unto the English crown,   185

    And that your majesty was an usurper.

KING

    Say, man, were these thy words?

HORNER   An't shall please your majesty, I never said nor

    thought any such matter. God is my witness, I am

    falsely accused by the villain.   190

PETER   By these ten bones, my lords, he did speak them to

    me in the garret one night as we were scouring my Lord

    of York's armour.

YORK

    Base dunghill villain and mechanical,

178–9 **accused . . . excuse** Cf. Romans, 2.15, 'accusing one another, or excusing' (Cairncross).

180 **for** for being. Cf. *CE* 5.1.32.

185 **rightful heir** 2.2 is largely taken up with York's claim as *heir* but it is Jack Cade who repeats the precise phrase (4.2.122), which is then echoed by Salisbury (5.1.178). Cf. York's claim in Hall: 'I am the very trew and lineall heyre' (246).

189 **God . . . witness** Romans, 1.9.

Shaheen points out that this commonplace utterance is found in the seeming reconciliation of Gloucester and Winchester in Holinshed (595).

191 **ten bones** fingers: proverbial (Dent, TT7)

192 **garret** a turret watchtower (*OED sb.* 1) (Hattaway): only here in Shakespeare
scouring cleaning or polishing by abrasion

194 **dunghill** a figurative intensifier of the vileness of villain status, plus the

188+ SP] *Rowe; Armorer. F*

I'll have thy head for this thy traitor's speech! –   195
I do beseech your royal majesty,
Let him have all the rigour of the law.

HORNER   Alas, my lord, hang me if ever I spake the words.
My accuser is my prentice, and when I did correct him
for his fault the other day, he did vow upon his knees he   200
would be even with me. I have good witness of this,
therefore I beseech your majesty, do not cast away an
honest man for a villain's accusation.

KING
Uncle, what shall we say to this in law?

GLOUCESTER
This doom, my lord, if I may judge by case: 205
Let Somerset be regent o'er the French,
Because in York this breeds suspicion;
And let these have a day appointed them
For single combat in convenient place,

---

suggestion of cowardice associated
with the combinatory usage which
derives from the craven dunghill cock
as opposed to the fighting game cock
(see *OED* Dunghill 2b and c, 3d)
mechanical servile manual labourer.
OED's illustration (*a*. and *sb*. 2) seems
pertinent: 'Wherein mechanicall and
men of base condition doo dare to censure the dooings of them, of whose
acts they be not worthie to talke'
(1589). Cf. *MND* 3.2.9.
195 **traitor's** RP suggests that F's
'Traytors' might be a variant form of
the adjective 'traitorous'.
197 **rigour . . . law** Cf. *RJ*, 'the rigour of
severest law' (5.3.269).
199 **correct** Given Horner's character,
physical chastisement seems more
likely than verbal rebuke (*OED v.* 4).
202 **cast away** a common biblical usage.
Possibly echoing Job, 8.20, 'God will
not cast away an upright man, neither
will he take the wicked by the hand'.

203 **for** because of (Abbott, 150)
205 **doom** judgement
   *by case** by case-law (precedent).
   Cairncross is followed here in his
   adoption of Q on the grounds that the
   phrase restores the metre. Wells &
   Taylor agree, adding the argument
   that it is difficult to think of a reporter
   inventing this phrase and comparative-
   ly easy to suppose a compositor overlooking it. Hattaway, however, following F, points out that Shakespeare
   often begins a declarative speech with
   a metrically irregular line.
207 because this suggests doubts about
   York's loyalty. See *H8* 3.1.51–3.
209 **single combat** Q specifies details of
   weaponry and place: 'With *Eben
   staues*, and *Standbags* combatting /
   In Smythfield' (TLN 432–3). For the
   nature of these weapons see 2.3.58.3n.,
   and Introduction, pp. 85–6.
   convenient appropriate

195 traitor's] (Traytors)   205 by case] *Q, Ard²; not in F*

For he hath witness of his servant's malice.   210
This is the law, and this Duke Humphrey's doom.

SOMERSET

I humbly thank your royal majesty.

HORNER   And I accept the combat willingly.

PETER   Alas, my lord, I cannot fight. For God's sake
pity my case! The spite of man prevaileth against me.   215
O Lord, have mercy upon me! I shall never be able to
fight a blow. O Lord, my heart!

GLOUCESTER

Sirrah, or you must fight, or else be hanged.

KING

Away with them to prison, and the day
Of combat shall be the last of the next month.   220
Come, Somerset, we'll see thee sent away.   *Flourish.*
                                                                Exeunt.

---

210 This repeats Horner's statement
(200–1), but grammatically – taking
For as 'because' (Abbott, 150) –
suggests that the legal procedure of
single combat is determined by it
particularly. None of the chronicles
contains Horner's claim. In fact treason trial by combat was used when
there were no witnesses and no
evidence (see Introduction, p. 83;
Knowles, 'Farce', 171; and Bellamy,
143). Shakespeare seems to have
reversed the situation and unnecessar-
ily invented this justification.
211 Cairncross gives this line to the King
to make Somerset's next line seemingly consistent. But the Protector
speaks for the King and Somerset's
reply acknowledges this formality.

Theobald inserts Q's lines between
211 and 212, 'Then be it so my Lord of
Somerset. / We make your grace
Regent ouer the French' (TLN
468–9). Wells & Taylor adopt this.
Hattaway follows Sanders's suggestion
and adds the SD '*King Henry nods
assent*'.
215 **The . . . me.** Various biblical reso-
nances are suggested: Hattaway cites
Psalms, 65.3; Shaheen points to
Jeremiah, 1.19, 15.20; 2 Chronicles,
14.11; Psalms, 13.4.
218 **Sirrah** contemptuously addressing
an inferior
   or you either you
220 **last . . . month** 31 January 1446. See
2.3.48n.

219–21] *Capell; prose F*

188

[1.4]   *Enter* [Margery JOURDAIN,] *a witch, the two priests,*
         [HUME *and* SOUTHWELL,] *and* BOLINGBROKE.

HUME   Come, my masters! The Duchess, I tell you, expects
    performance of your promises.
BOLINGBROKE   Master Hume, we are therefor provided.
    Will her ladyship behold and hear our exorcisms?
HUME   Ay, what else? Fear you not her courage.   5
BOLINGBROKE   I have heard her reported to be a woman
    of an invincible spirit; but it shall be convenient,
    Master Hume, that you be by her aloft, while we be
    busy below; and so, I pray you, go in God's name, and   9
    leave us.   *Exit Hume.*
    Mother Jourdain, be you prostrate and grovel on the
    earth; John Southwell, read you; and let us to our work.

         Enter ELEANOR *aloft* [, HUME *following*].

ELEANOR   Well said, my masters, and welcome all. To this

1.4 Neither Hall (202) nor Holinshed
(203–4), the main sources for this
scene, indicates a specific location.
Editors since Capell have assumed that
the action takes place in Gloucester's
house or garden since Q has Eleanor
specify the place earlier, 'on the backside of my Orchard heere' (TLN 272),
and in this scene Q includes the stage
direction 'She goes vp to the Tower'
(TLN 488), which is replaced by F's
'aloft' (8, 12.1), referring to the tiring-
house gallery. For Q variations see
Appendix 2.
    Shakespeare alters considerably the
original 'sorcery' of making a wax
image of the King to waste away his
life, by substituting satanic and criminal acts of conjuration and prophecy
(see 2.1.166n.), thereby increasing the

association of femininity and witchcraft.
3 **provided** equipped. See LN.
5 Certainly. Don't doubt her determina-
   tion.
8, 12.1 **aloft** See headnote.
11 **Mother** For the significance of this
    title as connoting malevolence, manip-
    ulation and persecution in sixteenth-
    century witchcraft see Willis.
    prostrate and grovel Cf. Q: '*Witch.*
    Then *Roger Bullinbrooke* about thy
    taske, / And frame a Cirkle here vpon
    the earth, / Whilst I thereon all
    prostrate on my face, / Do talke and
    whisper with the diuels be low, / And
    coniure them for to obey my will'
    (TLN 492–6).
13 **Well said** Well done. For praise of an
    action, see *2H4* 3.2.275. Cf. 28n.

1.4] *Capell*   0.1–2] *Ard² subst.; Enter the Witch, the two Priests, and Bullingbrooke.* F   12.1 HUME *fol-*
lowing] *Dyce subst.*

gear, the sooner the better.

BOLINGBROKE

Patience, good lady; wizards know their times.　　　　15
Deep night, dark night, the silent of the night,
The time of night when Troy was set on fire,
The time when screech-owls cry and ban-dogs howl,
And spirits walk, and ghosts break up their graves;
That time best fits the work we have in hand.　　　　20
Madam, sit you, and fear not. Whom we raise
We will make fast within a hallowed verge.

Here do the ceremonies belonging, and make the circle; Bolingbroke
or Southwell reads, 'Conjuro te', etc. It thunders and lightens
terribly; then the Spirit *riseth.*

SPIRIT

Adsum.

JOURDAIN

Asnath,

14　**gear** business (*OED sb.* 11c). See *Tit* 4.3.53.
　the . . . better See Dent, S641.
15–20 Cf. the proverb found in *Luc*, ' "For day", quoth she, "night's scapes doth open lay" ' (747). See Dent, N179.
16　**silent** For adjectives as nouns see Abbott, 5.
17　**Troy . . . fire** As every grammar-school boy knew, this came about by deceit and self-delusion. See Virgil, *Aeneid*, Bk 2.
18–19 Editors refer to Ovid, 'The Screeche owle sent from hell . . . The doggs did howle' (15.887–95), describing the omens before the death of Julius Caesar.
18　**screech-owls** further ominous association with death. See *3H6* 2.6.56.
　ban-dogs fierce guard dogs tied by a band
19　**ghosts . . . graves** Cf. *MM* 3.1.85–6.
　up open

22　**verge** circle, usually of metal (*OED sb.* 13b), as in *R3* 4.1.59–60, but here the *circle* of 22.1
22.1–3 characteristic supernatural machinery, as editors note, citing plays such as Marlowe's *Dr Faustus*, Peele's *The Old Wife's Tale* and Greene's *Friar Bacon and Friar Bungay*
22.2　SD *Southwell* named in the sources
　'Conjuro te' I conjure thee.
22.3　*the* Spirit *riseth* conventional entrance through stage trap (Hattaway, *Theatre*, 115)
23　*Adsum.* I am here.
24　*Asnath* Cairncross's emendation of F's 'Asmath' is accepted. With the minim misprint adjusted we have an anagram for 'Satan', or 'Sathan' as it appears in *Prayer Book* (Noble, 280). Other editors have suggested that 'Asmath' is a corruption of or derivation from Asmenoth, Astmeroth, Asteroth and Asmodeus.

24–7] *Capell; F lines* God, / at, / speake, / hence. /　24 Asnath] *Ard²; Asmath* F

By the eternal God whose name and power   25
Thou tremblest at, answer that I shall ask;
For till thou speak thou shalt not pass from hence.

SPIRIT

Ask what thou wilt – that I had said and done!

BOLINGBROKE [*Reads.*]

First of the King: what shall of him become?

SPIRIT

The duke yet lives that Henry shall depose,   30
But him outlive, and die a violent death.

[*As the Spirit speaks, Southwell writes the answer.*]

BOLINGBROKE

Tell me, what fate awaits the Duke of Suffolk?

SPIRIT

By water shall he die and take his end.

BOLINGBROKE

What shall betide the Duke of Somerset?

---

26 **Thou tremblest at** If, as Cairncross suggests, this refers to James, 2.19, 'Thou beleeuest that there is one God . . . the deuils also beleeue it, and tremble', his case for Asnath–Sathan seems very strong, particularly in view of ample evidence of the role of anagrams in conjuration.
 that that which

28 **that . . . done** Considerable dramatic tension is gained from the tradition of spirits' unspecified reluctance to speak. Malone refers to *Mac* 4.1.70.
 that would that

30–1 referring to the Duke of York, murdered by Margaret and others in *3H6* 1.4, at the battle of Wakefield. Ambiguous syntax is characteristic of such prophecies; is it the Duke or Henry who is the subject of *depose*, *outlive* and *die*? As we see in *3H6*, Henry is deposed by York yet outlives him, but both die a violent death.
 Hume's earlier admission of fabri-

cated *conjurations* (1.2.99) brings this and the following prophecies (33, 35–7) into doubt which may be qualified by the hint of satanic authenticity in 26n., and the eventual fulfilment of the predictions. Kelly points up the larger cultural ambivalence of the issue: 'it was universally accepted by Christians in Shakespeare's day that only God had certain knowledge of the future, and that evil spirits could only conjecture future events from already existing causes. But we must no doubt admit that this doctrine was often contradicted in practice, and that men ascribed more knowledge to spirits than theologians could justify' (254).

32 *Tell me added by Pope in view of 64. Cairncross assumes uncorrected Q copy, but both could derive from the MS tradition behind F.

33 See 4.1.31–5.

34 *betide F's 'befall' looks like contamination from 'shall' (33, 34). Cf. 66.

---

29 SD] *Capell* 31 SD] *Capell* 32 *Tell me*] *Pope; not in F (cf. 64)* fate awaits] *Capell;* fates await F 34 betide] *Q;* befall F *(cf. 66)*

SPIRIT

> Let him shun castles: 35
> Safer shall he be upon the sandy plains
> Than where castles mounted stand.
> Have done, for more I hardly can endure.

BOLINGBROKE

> Descend to darkness and the burning lake!   39
> False fiend, avoid!   *Thunder and lightning.*

Exit Spirit.

Enter the Duke of YORK *and the* Duke of BUCKINGHAM
with their guard, [Sir Humphrey STAFFORD,] *and break in.*
[*Guards rush in above.*]

YORK

> Lay hands upon these traitors and their trash!
> Beldam, I think we watched you at an inch. –
> What, madam, are you there? The King and
>   commonweal
> Are deeply indebted for this piece of pains.

---

35 See 5.2.67–9.

38 See 28n.

39 **the burning lake** both classical (*Tit* 4.3.43–4) and biblical (Revelation, 19.20, 20.10). Shaheen (46) suggests that as no associated classical terms are used, and in view of the satanic reference in the next line, a scriptural allusion is intended. See Appendix 2 for Q variant.

40 Shaheen (46) gives references to Matthew, 4.10, the *Prayer Book* reading for the first Sunday in Lent. Curiously the revised Bishops' Bible, post-1572, differs from all other versions, which have 'Auoide Satan' (cf. *CE* 4.3.43), with 'Get thee hence behind me, Satan'.

40.1 **Duke of** YORK as Wilson comments, a surprising appearance when Hume's machinations were on behalf

of the Cardinal and Suffolk, who was York's avowed enemy

40.2* **Sir Humphrey** STAFFORD added here on the evidence of 52

41 **trash** a word of varied meaning; but Hattaway's 'doxy' or 'worthless woman' (Margery) is supported by the usage in *Oth* 5.1.85, though elsewhere in that play it is used of a male (2.1.303). Sanders opts for 'conjuring paraphernalia'.

42 **Beldam** hag, witch. See *Mac* 3.5.2.
     at an inch close at hand (*OED* Inch *sb.*[1] 3; Dent, I12): not elsewhere in Shakespeare though twice in Greene, as Hart points out

44 **piece of pains** trouble (you have taken): only here in this phrase, otherwise 'pains' alone, as 'trouble', in Shakespeare

---

40.2 Sir Humphrey STAFFORD] *Oxf*   40.3 *this edn*

My Lord Protector will, I doubt it not,   45
See you well guerdoned for these good deserts.

ELEANOR

Not half so bad as thine to England's king,
Injurious duke, that threatest where's no cause.

BUCKINGHAM

True, madam, none at all.   [*Shows papers.*]
                    What call you this? –
Away with them, let them be clapped up close   50
And kept asunder. – You, madam, shall with us. –
Stafford, take her to thee.   [*Exit Stafford.*]
                    [*Exeunt Eleanor, Hume and guard, above.*]
We'll see your trinkets here all forthcoming.
All away!

                    Exeunt [*Jourdain, Southwell, Bolingbroke and guard.*]

YORK

Lord Buckingham, methinks you watched her well. –   55
A pretty plot, well chosen to build upon. –
Now, pray, my lord, let's see the devil's writ.
What have we here?   (*Reads.*)
The duke yet lives that Henry shall depose,
But him outlive, and die a violent death.   60
Why, this is just

---

46 **guerdoned** rewarded
48 **Injurious** insulting
50 **clapped up close** locked up securely.
    Cf. *Tem* 5.1.231.
51 **shall** must go (Abbott, 315). Cf. 'Mark
    you his absolute "shall" ' (*Cor* 3.1.90).
53 **trinkets** tools, implements. *OED*
    (Trinket *sb.*[1] 1) quotes 'A conjuror . . .
    had all his trynkettes and furniture
    concerning suche matters in a redi-
    nesse', John Daus (transl.), *Sleidan's
    Commentaries* (1560).
    forthcoming a technical legal term

for court appearance, usually found in
the context of someone undertaking
responsibility for such, or charging
someone with that responsibility, as in
TS 5.1.93
55–6 For alternative staging see LN.
57 **devil's writ** as against Holy Writ, or
    Scripture. Cf. *R3* 1.3.334–7.
58 Cf. Dent, W280.2
59–69 In Q these lines appear in 2.1,
    where they are read out by Henry
    (TLN 706–15) at approximately 168ff.
61 **just** exactly

49 SD] *Capell subst.*   52 SD1] *this edn*   SD2] *Dyce subst.*   54 SD] *Rowe subst.; Exit.* F
61–2] *one line* F

Aio te, Aeacida, Romanos vincere posse.
Well, to the rest:
'Tell me, what fate awaits the Duke of Suffolk?'
By water shall he die, and take his end.   65
'What shall betide the Duke of Somerset?'
Let him shun castles.
Safer shall he be upon the sandy plains
Than where castles mounted stand.
Come, come, my lords, these oracles   70
Are hardly attained, and hardly understood.
The King is now in progress towards Saint Albans,
With him the husband of this lovely lady.
Thither goes these news as fast as horse can carry them:
A sorry breakfast for my Lord Protector.   75

62 *Aio . . . posse* 'I proclaim that you, the descendant of Aeacus, can conquer the Romans'; or 'I proclaim that the Romans can conquer you, the descendant of Aeacus'. This was the ambiguous oracle given by the Pythian Apollo to the Greek Pyrrhus when he asked whether he would defeat Rome (recorded in Ennius' *Annals* and quoted by Cicero, *De divinatione*, 2.56). Puttenham (267) deals with the subject under *Amphibologia*. Hart gives full documentation, including the most famous instance in English Renaissance drama, Marlowe's *Edward II*: 'Edwardum occidere nolite timere bonum est, / Fear not to kill the king, 'tis good he die . . . kill not the king, 'tis good to fear the worst' (5.4.8–11).

70–1 Hibbard conjectures, 'Come, come, my lords, these oracles are hard, / Hardly attain'd and hardly understood' ('Emendation'), assuming that F here is a compositorial error from Shakespeare's foul papers rather than use of Q copy. 'These oracles are hardly attained / And hardly understood' (Wells & Taylor).

71 are obtained with difficulty and barely understood

72 **in progress** both travel and display of the royal entourage. 'The progress was an important and traditional instrument of royal propaganda. The King, with an impressive retinue, could show himself at various keypoints of the realm, and thereby impress the populace with the reality of an authority which must, frequently, have seemed very remote' (Anglo, 21). Perhaps Shakespeare is anticipating the next act with his historical materials in mind: 'King Henry the sixt . . . as he roade in Progresse there came to the towne of Saint Albons a certaine beggar with hys wyfe' (Grafton, 1.630).

73 **this lovely lady** See 1.4.55–6 LN.

74 **goes** For singular verb with plural predicate, see Abbott, 335.

75 **A sorry breakfast** Hattaway suggests a comparison with the proverb 'To give a hot breakfast' (Dent, B636). Perhaps, ironically, 'Laugh before breakfast, you'll cry before supper' (Tilley, M1176) is relevant? Cf. *H8* 3.2.202–3.

62 *te*] *Rowe; not in F*   70–1] *Capell, Ard²; F lines* Lords, / attain'd, / vnderstood. /   74] *Pope; F lines* Newes, / them: /

BUCKINGHAM

Your grace shall give me leave, my Lord of York,

To be the post, in hope of his reward.

YORK

At your pleasure, my good lord.   [*Exit Buckingham.*]

Who's within there, ho?

Enter a servingman.

Invite my Lords of Salisbury and Warwick   79

To sup with me tomorrow night. Away!   *Exeunt.*

[2.1]   *Enter the* KING, QUEEN, GLOUCESTER, CARDINAL

and SUFFOLK, *with Falconers hallooing.*

QUEEN

Believe me, lords, for flying at the brook

---

77 **post** messenger
78 *SD If Buckingham and York leave together at the end of the act, then York apparently risks revealing his conspiratorial orders given to the servingman. Here, York accedes to the request and calls his servant as Buckingham leaves. **Who's** Cairncross assumes Q corruption and deletes.
80 **sup** See 2.2.2.
2.1 location: St Albans (Pope, following 1.2.57–8). For 1–57 of this scene Shakespeare probably used a brief passage from Hall (236), where Margaret 'caused the kyng to make a progresse into Warwyckeshyre, for his health & recreacion and so with Hawkyng and Huntyng came to the citie of Couentrey, where were diuers wayes studied priuely, to bryng the quene to her hartes ease, and long expectate desire: which was the death & destruccion of the duke of Yorke, the erles of Salisbury and Warwycke'. In this scene

the hawking is used to further the conflict between Gloucester and the Cardinal, principally. The St Albans miracle section (58–155) is not found in Hall or Holinshed but is in Grafton (1.630), where the source, Sir Thomas More, is acknowledged. In his *Dialogue* (Bk 1, ch. 14, leaf 25), More repeats the story of the bogus miracle told him by his father. Foxe prints the story, which is then told again by Grafton. Boswell-Stone reprints More as source; Wilson insists on Grafton; Cairncross chooses Foxe. For the miracle in relation to the play as a whole see Knowles, 'Farce', and Introduction, pp. 80–2.
0.2 *Falconers hallooing* directing the hounds to rouse the waterfowl from cover
1   **at the brook** at the waterfowl driven from bankside cover. Such hawking was considered the most royal of sports. Cf. Drayton, 'of a Flight at brook' (*Polyolbion*, XX, 203).

78] *Capell; F lines* Lord. / hoe? /   78 SD] *Q subst.*   2.1] *Pope*   0.1–2] *F subst.;* Enter the King and Queene with her Hawke on her fist, and Duke *Humphrey* and *Suffolke*, and the *Cardinall*, as if they came from hawking. *Q*

I saw not better sport these seven years' day;
Yet, by your leave, the wind was very high
And, ten to one, old Joan had not gone out.

KING [*to Gloucester*]

But what a point, my lord, your falcon made   5
And what a pitch she flew above the rest!
To see how God in all his creatures works!
Yea, man and birds are fain of climbing high.

SUFFOLK

No marvel, an it like your majesty,
My Lord Protector's hawks do tower so well,   10
They know their master loves to be aloft,
And bears his thoughts above his falcon's pitch.

GLOUCESTER

My lord, 'tis but a base ignoble mind
That mounts no higher than a bird can soar.

---

2 **these . . . day** for the last seven years up to this day: very common in Shakespeare; proverbial (see Dent, Y25)

4 **gone out** Though seemingly not a hawking term, 'to go out' does appear to have been used in the military sense of entering the field to engage the enemy (*OED* Go *v*. 85c). For example, upon false recruitment Mouldy protests to Falstaff, 'there are other men fitter to go out than I' (*2H4* 3.2.115). Q is helpful here: 'My Lord, how did your grace like this last flight? / But as I cast her off the winde did rise, / And twas ten to one, old Ione had not gone out' (TLN 551–3). So the sense seems to be, given Margaret's implied boast, and adapting the verb metaphorically, 'with the wind rising [immediately after I cast her off] the odds were against old Joan engaging with the prey [but returning to me, yet she did]'.

5 **point** position to windward from which to swoop on the fowl (Hart)

6 **pitch** the highest point. Cf. the figurative use in *R2* 1.1.109, 'How high a pitch his resolution soars'.

8 **fain** fond

9 **an it like** if it please

10 **tower** soar: hawking terminology (cf. *Mac* 2.4.12). Editors speculate on the possible significance of the falcon as a heraldic device of such figures as Suffolk and Gloucester, as well as the Duke of York, but it appears to be so common that perhaps over-determined allusion should be resisted (see Hattaway and Sanders). Both Shakespeare and his patron the Earl of Southampton included the falcon in their armorial bearings (Scott-Giles, 30–1). In fact the falcon, according to Fox-Davies (243), is the most frequently found bird in heraldry.

10–14 See Appendix 2 for Q1/Q3 variants.

CARDINAL

I thought as much: he would be above the clouds.   15

GLOUCESTER

Ay, my Lord Cardinal, how think you by that?

Were it not good your grace could fly to heaven?

KING

The treasury of everlasting joy.

CARDINAL

Thy heaven is on earth, thine eyes and thoughts

Beat on a crown, the treasure of thy heart,   20

Pernicious Protector, dangerous peer

That smooth'st it so with king and commonweal!

GLOUCESTER

What, Cardinal? Is your priesthood grown

   peremptory?

Tantaene animis coelestibus irae?

16 **how . . . that** What are you implying?

17–20 **heaven . . . treasury . . . heart** echoing Matthew, 6.19–21: 'Lay not up treasures for your selues upon earth . . . But lay up treasures for your selues in heauen . . . For where your treasure is, there will your heart be also' (Cairncross).

20 **Beat . . . crown** As the falcon, having dived on its prey, beats its wings to carry it off, so, metaphorically, the Cardinal imagines Gloucester seizing the crown. The image arises naturally from the dramatic situation, but Pope's emendation, 'Bent', remains attractive. Though Johnson initially followed Pope, in the later edition with Steevens 'Bate' is suggested as an alternative, a term from hawking meaning 'to beat wings impatiently', which Hattaway considers might well be right. Alternatively, 'eyes and thoughts / Bent on a crown' is entirely characteristic of Shakespeare. For 'bent' in the sense of *OED* Bend *v.*, 'to

direct, turn, incline . . . the eyes', see *R2* 5.2.25 and *1H4* 3.2.79. The figurative application to mind as here (*thoughts*) is found in this play, 1.3.56, and *JC* 2.3.6.

crown In the religious context of 17–20 (see n.), the Cardinal is playing on the biblical notion of an earthly and a heavenly crown. See particularly Isaiah, 28.1 and 5, and 1 Corinthians, 9.25. Cf. Marlowe's 'The sweet fruition of an earthly crown' (*1 Tamburlaine*, 2.7.29).

22 **smooth'st . . . with** thus mollify, flatter. See 1.1.153n.

23 **peremptory** incontrovertible, in the legalistic sense of a charge being unanswerable (*OED a.* 1 and 1a): 'has your priestly status made you unchallengeable?' Stressed on the second syllable here, but for varying stresses elsewhere in Shakespeare see Cercignani, 43.

24 *Tantaene . . . irae?* 'Is there so much anger in heavenly minds?' (Virgil, *Aeneid*, 1.11).

24–5] *Theobald; F lines* hot? / mallice: /

Churchmen so hot? Good uncle, hide such malice: 25
With such holiness can you do it?
SUFFOLK
No malice, sir; no more than well becomes
So good a quarrel and so bad a peer.
GLOUCESTER
As who, my lord?
SUFFOLK   Why, as you, my lord.
An't like your lordly Lord Protectorship.   30
GLOUCESTER
Why, Suffolk, England knows thine insolence.
QUEEN
And thy ambition, Gloucester.
KING   I prithee, peace,
Good Queen, and whet not on these furious peers;
For blessed are the peacemakers on earth.
CARDINAL [*aside to Suffolk*]
Let me be blessed for the peace I make   35
Against this proud Protector with my sword!
GLOUCESTER [*aside to Cardinal*]
Faith, holy uncle, would 'twere come to that!
CARDINAL [*aside to Gloucester*]
Marry, when thou dar'st.

25–6 **Good . . . it** F's unsatisfactory lineation has prompted various suggestions, but the sense is apparent.
26 **such** Wells & Taylor suggest 'some'.
   can . . . it RP suggests 'can you not do it?'
33 **whet not on** do not urge on (cf. *3H6* 1.2.37)
34 **blessed . . . peacemakers** See Matthew, 5.9. One of the beatitudes (Tilley, P155).

35–6 **peace . . . sword** Matthew, 10.34, 'I came not to send peace, but the sword' (Cairncross).
38 Q has lines here in which Gloucester taunts Winchester with bastardy. Wells & Taylor include these, as does Cairncross, assuming censorship. Hattaway points out that the same charge is made in *1H6* 3.1.42 and Q's lines could be actor's gag material. F is followed here. See Appendix 2.

25–6 Good . . . it] Good uncle, can you dote, / To hide such malice with such holiness? *Ard*² hide
. . . holiness] *not in Q*   26 do it?] doet? F; doate Q; dote? *Q2*; do't. *Q3*; dote, *Ard*²   30 Lord] *F4*;
Lords F   32–3 I . . . peers] *Malone, Ard*²; F lines Queene, / Peeres, /   35 SD] *this edn*   37–52 SDs]
Rowe

198

GLOUCESTER [*aside to Cardinal*]

Make up no factious numbers for the matter,

In thine own person answer thy abuse.   40

CARDINAL [*aside to Gloucester*]

Ay, where thou dar'st not peep; and if thou dar'st,

This evening on the east side of the grove.

KING

How now, my lords?

CARDINAL

     Believe me, cousin Gloucester,

Had not your man put up the fowl so suddenly,

We had had more sport. [*aside to Gloucester*]

      Come with thy two-hand sword.   45

GLOUCESTER

True uncle. [*aside to Cardinal*]

Are ye advised? The east side of the grove.

CARDINAL [*aside to Gloucester*]

I am with you.

KING   Why, how now, uncle Gloucester?

GLOUCESTER

Talking of hawking, nothing else, my lord.

39–40 **Make . . . person** Come alone, without your rebellious gang.

40 **answer thy abuse** defend your slander

44 **your man** the falconer
put . . . fowl make the game rise from cover (*OED* Put 53b *put up*)

45 **two-hand sword** 'swoord and buckler' in Q. In the course of the sixteenth century, the 'two-hand' or 'long' sword was superseded by the fashion and practice of the sword and buckler and the rapier and dagger, but not entirely so. Giacomo di Grassi's *True Art of Defence* (1594) includes a chapter on 'the manner how to handle the Two-hand sword in single combat', and it was available in fencing schools

(*Shakespeare's England*, 2.393–4). For a comic association between old age and the weighty long sword, see *MW* 2.1.228 and *RJ* 1.1.75. Cf. Jonson's *Epicoene* (1609), 'He has got somebody's old *two-hand sword* to mow you off at the knees' (Hart). Shakespeare's reference here has a hint of chivalric burlesque which is developed in Act 4.

47 **Are ye advis'd?** You understand?

48 *Cairncross's recognition that F's 'Cardinall' should be an SP is the neatest emendation and is accepted here.
I . . . you. I'll be even with you (Dent, WW22); but the senses 'I'll be with you' or 'I understand you' seem more appropriate.

41–2] *Theobald; F lines* peepe: / Euening, / Groue. /   43] *Cam¹; F lines* Lords? / *Gloster*, / 45] *Rowe; F lines* sport. / Sword. /   47 *this edn; F lines* aduis'd? / Groue: /   47 Are . . . groue] *Theobald gives line to Cardinal*   48] *Ard¹; Glost. . . .* Cardinall, I am with you. F

[*aside to Cardinal*] Now, by God's mother, priest, I'll
    shave your crown for this,   50
Or all my fence shall fail.

CARDINAL [*aside to Gloucester*]
    Medice teipsum. –
    Protector, see to't well, protect yourself.

KING
    The winds grow high; so do your stomachs, lords.
    How irksome is this music to my heart!   55
    When such strings jar what hope of harmony?
    I pray, my lords, let me compound this strife.

Enter Townsman *crying,* 'A miracle!'

GLOUCESTER
    What means this noise?
    Fellow, what miracle dost thou proclaim?

TOWNSMAN
    A miracle! A miracle!   60

SUFFOLK
    Come to the King and tell him what miracle.

---

50 **God's mother** F and Q3; Q's 'Faith'
probably reflects censorship.
crown the tonsure
51 unless my fencing skills let me down
52 *Medice teipsum.* 'Physician heal
thyself'. Shakespeare's only use of the
Vulgate, Luke, 4.23, 'Medice cura
teipsum' (Noble, 121). Proverbial
(Dent, P267). The incomplete utterance is given separate lineation.
54 **stomachs** tempers. Cf. *1H6* 1.3.89.
55–6 drawing on the commonplace
analogy between political and musical
concord, which in turn derives from
religious and cosmological notions of
creation itself as harmony (and chaos

as discord). The most famous allusion
in Shakespeare is found in what is
known as Ulysses' 'degree speech' (*TC*
1.3.85–124): 'Take but degree away,
untune that string, / And hark what
discord follows' (109–10).
57 **compound** settle. Cf. *TS* 2.1.341.
59–155 See headnote. Cairncross points
out how the account of Simpcox
regaining his sight follows John, 9.
Hattaway stresses the parodic aspect,
which can be compared with the issues
of human motives and supernatural
significance in the Eleanor–witchcraft
scene (1.4) and the armourer–servant
combat (2.3).

50] *Ard²* *subst.*; F lines Priest, / this, / by . . . priest] Faith Priest *Q*, *Q2;* Gods mother Priest *Q3*
52–3] *Medice . . .* yourself] *Theobald; prose F* 54] *Theobald; F lines* high, / Lords: / 57.1] *F subst.;*
Qq repeat 'A miracle!' 58–60] *Ard² lines* miracle / proclaim? / miracle! /

TOWNSMAN

Forsooth, a blind man at Saint Alban's shrine
Within this half-hour hath received his sight –
A man that ne'er saw in his life before.

KING

Now God be praised, that to believing souls   65
Gives light in darkness, comfort in despair!

Enter the Mayor of Saint Albans *and his brethren,*
with music, bearing the man [SIMPCOX] *between two in a*
chair[, *his* Wife *and Townsmen following*].

CARDINAL

Here comes the townsmen, on procession,
To present your highness with the man.

KING

Great is his comfort in this earthly vale,

62 **Saint Alban's shrine** St Alban is considered the first English martyr. Alban was a Romano-Briton living at Verulamium (now the city of St Albans) who gave shelter to fleeing Christians during Diocletian's persecution. The Venerable Bede records his execution by beheading *c*. 287.

65 **Now . . . praised** All three sources record that it is Gloucester who is overjoyed at the miracle, 'having great ioy to see suche a miracle . . . shewying himselfe ioyous of Gods glorie' (Grafton, 1.630). Shakespeare transfers it to Henry's pious credulity and contrasts Gloucester's worldly astuteness here.

66 **light in darkness** Editors suggest a number of biblical allusions, including Luke, 1.79; Psalms, 112.4 and 18.28; Isaiah, 42.16; Micah, 7.8. Shaheen (48) considers the similar recitation of morning and evening prayer (Luke, 1.79, 'To giue light to them that sit in darknesse') as the primary source. But if the spiritual symbolism of blindness is added to that of light and darkness, a considerable part of the Old and New Testaments could be adduced in this respect.

66.1 **Mayor** a bailiff in Henry VI's time. Saint Albans was not incorporated until Edward IV's reign (Sanders). **brethren** members of the town corporation

66.2 *with music* The sources note that a *Te Deum* was sung after the miracle. The effect of such in production would add considerably to the ensuing travesty.

67 **comes** For this third person plural form see Abbott, 333. **on** in (Abbott, 180)

69 **earthly vale** Cf. 'this wretched earth and vale of all misery' (*Homily*, 490) (Cairncross).

62+ Alban's] *(Albones)*   66.1–3] *F subst.*   66.1–2 *brethren . . . man*] brethren with Musicke, bearing the man that had bene blind *Qq*   66.2 SIMPCOX] *Rowe*   66.3 *his . . . following*] *Ard¹ subst.*

Although by sight his sin be multiplied.   70

GLOUCESTER

Stand by, my masters, bring him near the King.

His highness' pleasure is to talk with him.

KING

Good fellow, tell us here the circumstance,

That we for thee may glorify the Lord.

What, hast thou been long blind and now restored?   75

SIMPCOX

Born blind, an't please your grace.

WIFE   Ay, indeed, was he.

SUFFOLK

What woman is this?

WIFE   His wife, an't like your worship.

GLOUCESTER

Hadst thou been his mother, thou couldst have better

    told.

KING

Where wert thou born?

SIMPCOX

At Berwick in the north, an't like your grace.   80

KING

Poor soul, God's goodness hath been great to thee.

Let never day nor night unhallowed pass,

But still remember what the Lord hath done.

---

70 Cf. John, 9.41, 'If ye were blind, ye
should not haue sinne, but nowe ye
say, We see: therefore your sinne
remaineth' (Noble, 122).

74 Noble (122) suggests the sentence
most frequently read at the Com-
munion Offertory, 'and glorifie
your Father which is in heaven'
(Matthew, 5.16).

80 **Berwick** Berwick-upon-Tweed, on
the Northumberland–Scotland border

82–3 In the sources it is Gloucester who
counsels humility. See 65–6nn. and
headnote.

82 **unhallowed** unholy, since at night evil
spirits walk abroad, such as Bolingbroke
invokes at 1.4.16–19

83 **still** always

70 sight] *Wilson (Lloyd);* his sight *F*   76] *this edn; F lines* Grace. / he. / an't] *(*and't*)*   80 Berwick]
*Rowe; (*Barwick*) F*   81] *Pope; F lines* Soule, / thee: /

QUEEN

    Tell me, good fellow, cam'st thou here by chance,

    Or of devotion to this holy shrine?   85

SIMPCOX

    God knows, of pure devotion; being called

    A hundred times and oft'ner, in my sleep,

    By good Saint Alban, who said, 'Simon, come;

    Come offer at my shrine, and I will help thee.'

WIFE

    Most true, forsooth; and many time and oft   90

    Myself have heard a voice to call him so.

CARDINAL

    What, art thou lame?

SIMPCOX   Ay, God Almighty help me!

SUFFOLK

    How cam'st thou so?

SIMPCOX   A fall off of a tree.

WIFE

    A plum-tree, master.

GLOUCESTER   How long hast thou been blind?

SIMPCOX

    O, born so, master.

GLOUCESTER   What, and wouldst climb a tree?   95

SIMPCOX

    But that in all my life, when I was a youth.

---

85 **of** for (Abbott, 168)
88 **Simon** See 120n.
89 **offer** make an offering
92–3 Shakespeare added lameness to the source. The blind and the lame are linked several times in Scripture and – given Simon's origin in Berwick – Jeremiah, 31.8, seems most apposite:

'Behold I will bring them from ye North country, and gather them from the coastes of the worlde, with the blind and the lame among them'. Combining both disabilities in one person compounds the comic grotesque.
96 **But** only (Abbott, 128)

84–5] *Capell subst.; F lines* good-fellow, / Deuotion, / Shrine? /   86–9] *Cam; F lines* Deuotion, / oftner, / *Albon:* / Shrine, / thee. /   88 Simon] *(Symon);* Simpcox *Pope;* Saunder *Capell*

WIFE

Too true, and bought his climbing very dear.

GLOUCESTER

'Mass, thou lov'dst plums well, that wouldst venture so.

SIMPCOX

Alas, good master, my wife desired some damsons,

And made me climb, with danger of my life.   100

GLOUCESTER

A subtle knave! But yet it shall not serve. –

Let me see thine eyes; wink now – now open them.

In my opinion yet thou seest not well.

SIMPCOX

Yes, master, clear as day, I thank God and Saint Alban.

GLOUCESTER

Sayst thou me so? What colour is this cloak of?   105

SIMPCOX

Red, master, red as blood.

GLOUCESTER

Why, that's well said. What colour is my gown of?

SIMPCOX

Black, forsooth, coal-black as jet.

---

97 **bought . . . dear** 'Dear bought and far
fetched are dainties for ladies' (Tilley,
D12) seems to be behind this.

98 **'Mass** by the mass

98–9 **plums . . . damsons** may connote
testicles (Partridge, 163–4). The
earthy bawdiness here is in contrast to
the spiritual antecedents of the
Gospels.

101 **subtle** crafty. Throughout the
English histories this word is used
pejoratively.
But . . . serve. But it will hardly hold
good (*OED* Serve *v.* 29, 'to be valid, to
hold good'). R. Berry provides a critical framework for the investigation
which follows: 'The processes of a

Trial – charges, investigation, arraignment, defence, verdict, sentence, and
execution – compose the pattern that
orders *2 Henry VI*' (2).

102 **wink** close your eyes

103 **yet** still

104 **clear as day** proverbial (Tilley,
D56). Cf. *H5* 1.2.86, 'as clear as is the
summer's sun' (Dent, S969).

105 **Sayst . . . so?** Is that so?

106 **red as blood** proverbial (Dent,
B455). See *LC* 198.

108 **coal-black as jet** proverbial (Dent,
J49). Cf. *Tit* 5.2.50. Jet is a natural
hard substance, lignite or brown coal,
which can be polished to a glossy black
to make ornaments, toys or buttons.

98–100] *prose F*   104 Alban] *F3, F4*; Albon *F2*; *Albones F1*   106 Red] *Q3, F*; Why red *Q*

KING

    Why then, thou knowst what colour jet is of?

SUFFOLK

    And yet, I think, jet did he never see.   110

GLOUCESTER

    But cloaks and gowns before this day a many.

WIFE

    Never before this day, in all his life.

GLOUCESTER

    Tell me, sirrah, what's my name?

SIMPCOX   Alas, master, I know not.

GLOUCESTER   What's his name?   115

SIMPCOX   I know not.

GLOUCESTER   Nor his?

SIMPCOX   No, indeed, master.

GLOUCESTER   What's thine own name?

SIMPCOX

    Simon Simpcox, an if it please you, master.   120

GLOUCESTER

    Then, Simon, sit there the lying'st knave

    In Christendom. If thou hadst been born blind

    Thou mightst as well have known all our names as thus

    To name the several colours we do wear.

    Sight may distinguish of colours, but suddenly   125

    To nominate them all, it is impossible.

    My lords, Saint Alban here hath done a miracle.

---

111 **a many** See Abbott, 87.

120 ***Simon** McMillin (159) argues that Q's '*Sander*' is probably Alexander Cooke, an actor in Pembroke's Men, the company responsible for Q. F's '*Saunder*' at this point probably derives from Q, therefore Simon, as identified at 88, is restored.

121–2 **lying'st . . . Christendom** Cf. *TS* Induction.2.24

122–6 Cf. Tilley, M80, 'Blind men can judge no colours'.

126 **nominate** name

120, 121 Simon] *Oxf; Saunder* F; *Sander* Q   121 sit] sit thou *Ard²*   121–9] *Ard² subst.; prose Q;* F lines there, / Christendome. / blinde, / Names, / weare. / Colours: / all, / impossible. / Miracle. / great, / againe. /

And would ye not think that cunning to be great
That could restore this cripple to his legs again?

SIMPCOX

O master, that you could!   130

GLOUCESTER

My masters of Saint Albans, have you not
Beadles in your town, and things called whips?

MAYOR

Yes, my lord, if it please your grace.

GLOUCESTER

Then send for one presently.

MAYOR

Sirrah, go fetch the beadle hither straight.   135

Exit [a Townsman].

GLOUCESTER

Now fetch me a stool hither by and by. –
Now, sirrah, if you mean to save yourself from
      whipping,
Leap me over this stool, and run away.

SIMPCOX

Alas, master, I am not able to stand alone.

---

128 *that Rowe's emendation is accepted on the assumption that the F compositor misread MS 'y' with a superscript 't'.
cunning skill
129 **cripple** See 153n.
132 **Beadles** constables appointed by the parish to keep order in church and punish offenders. Cf. *Per* 2.1.91–2, 'if all your beggars were whipp'd, I would wish no better office than to be a beadle'.
things called whips a phrase which gained proverbial status (Dent, W306.1). One of the 1602 additions to *The Spanish Tragedy*, sometimes attributed to Ben Jonson, reads 'And there is Nemesis and Furies, / And things

called whips' (Kyd, *Tragedy*, p. 129). In *A Nest of Ninnies* (1608) Robert Armin possibly indicates that this line occurred in the Ur-*Hamlet* in which he acted: 'There are as Hamlet says, *things called whips* in store' (G3ᵛ). Cairncross points out the earlier phrase, 'of *whips* such wondrous *store*', in Thomas Deloney's 'A New Ballet' (1588).
134 **presently** immediately
136 **by and by** immediately. See 1.3.2n.
138 **Leap . . . stool** on the evidence of Jonson's *Epicoene* (1609) a popular game: 'and lift as many join'd stools and leap over 'em' (5.1.39)
139 **alone** without support

128 that] *Rowe; his Q; it, F*   131–2] *Ard²; F lines Albones, / Towne, / Whippes? /*   132 Beadles] A beadle *Ard²*   135 SD *a Townsman] this edn*   137–8] *Ard²; prose F*

You go about to torture me in vain.   140

Enter a Beadle *with whips.*

GLOUCESTER   Well, sir, we must have you find your legs.
Sirrah beadle, whip him till he leap over that same stool.
BEADLE   I will, my lord. –
Come on, sirrah, off with your doublet quickly.
SIMPCOX
Alas, master, what shall I do? I am not able to stand.   145
After the Beadle hath hit him once, he leaps over the stool
and runs away; and they follow and cry, 'A miracle!'
KING
O God, seest thou this, and bearest so long?
QUEEN
It made me laugh to see the villain run.
GLOUCESTER
Follow the knave, and take this drab away.
WIFE
Alas, sir, we did it for pure need.
GLOUCESTER
Let them be whipped through every market town   150

---

140 **go . . . me** set about torturing me
(*OED* Go *v.* 49b)
144 **doublet** precursor of the modern
jacket, but sometimes sleeveless, of
varying fashion adapted to all classes.
See *Shakespeare's England*, 2.98–113.
146 **bearest** 'Bear' is frequently used in
the Bible to mean to endure or to suffer.
148 **drab** slut, whore. Cf. *MM* 2.1.223,
'If your worship will take order for the
drabs and knaves'.
149 **pure need** Margaret herself recognizes 'deceit bred by necessity' (*3H6*
3.3.68) in the actions of the great.
150–1 Gloucester is echoing the statutory

amendment of 1576 to an earlier Act of
1572 (14 Eliz. c. 5) concerning 'impo-
tent', as against 'sturdy', beggars and
vagabonds: 'everye suche person shall
for his or her suche firste offence bee
whipped and so retourned Home
againe unto his her or their Parishe'
(18 Eliz. c. 3: *The Statutes of the Realm*,
4.613). In fact the good Duke
Humphrey is being very lenient by
seemingly overlooking the crime of the
imposture and desisting from the sev-
erer penalties of the law – execution,
branding or mutilation (see 4.2.53n.).
Beier (107–23) discusses the legal and
social contexts.

140.1] *F subst.; after 138 Q*   141–2] *Ard² omits* Sirrah beadle *and lines* legs. / stool. /   145 SD *once*]
one girke *Q*

Till they come to Berwick, from whence they came.

Exeunt [Wife, Beadle, Mayor and others].

CARDINAL

Duke Humphrey has done a miracle today.

SUFFOLK

True, made the lame to leap and fly away.

GLOUCESTER

But you have done more miracles than I –

You made in a day, my lord, whole towns to fly.   155

Enter BUCKINGHAM.

KING

What tidings with our cousin Buckingham?

BUCKINGHAM

Such as my heart doth tremble to unfold.

A sort of naughty persons, lewdly bent,

Under the countenance and confederacy

---

153 All commentators cite Isaiah, 35.6, 'Then shall the lame man leape as an harte'. However, Acts, 14.8–9, is worth some consideration in this regard: there was 'a certain man . . . a creeple from his mother's womb, who had never walked'. Then on St Paul's command 'Stand upright on thy feete . . . he leaped up, and walked'. Simpcox is described as a *cripple* (129), a word rarely used in Shakespeare. The possibility of an Isaiah allusion is strengthened by the preceding verse's reference to sight restored (see 70n. and 92–3n.). Typological interpretation of the Bible encouraged the linking of the Old and New Testaments. W. C. Carroll (*Fat King*, 153–4) suggests an analogy from Thomas Harman's *A Caveat or Warning for Common Cursitors* (1567), in which those pretending dumbness ('Dommerars') are made to speak.

155 as editors note, probably referring to the towns in Anjou and Maine given away as part of Margaret's dowry. But there may be an anachronistic reference here to the fifth of the articles of treason presented by the commons against Suffolk in 1450: Suffolk is charged with traitorously betraying details of defence in Normandy, whereby 'the kynges enemies . . . haue gotten tounes and fortresses, and the Kyng by that meane, depriued of his inheritaunce' (Hall, 218).

158–60 A . . . Eleanor a kind of villainous band, bent on evil, aided and abetted by Lady Eleanor

158 **lewdly** wickedly (*OED adv.* 2). Cairncross quotes A. F. Pollard, 492, 'For the punishment of persons that are *lewd* or badly *bent*'.

bent inclined. See 1.3.56 and n.

159 **countenance** patronage, favour (*OED sb.* 8). Cf. *1H4* 1.2.29.

151 SD] *Capell; Exit. F*

Of Lady Eleanor, the Protector's wife,   160
The ringleader and head of all this rout,
Have practised dangerously against your state,
Dealing with witches and with conjurors,
Whom we have apprehended in the fact,
Raising up wicked spirits from under ground,   165
Demanding of King Henry's life and death,
And other of your highness' Privy Council,
As more at large your grace shall understand.

CARDINAL

And so, my Lord Protector, by this means
Your lady is forthcoming yet at London.   170
This news, I think, hath turned your weapon's edge.
'Tis like, my lord, you will not keep your hour.

GLOUCESTER

Ambitious churchman, leave to afflict my heart.
Sorrow and grief have vanquished all my powers,
And, vanquished as I am, I yield to thee   175
Or to the meanest groom.

---

confederacy criminal league; conspiracy

160 **Eleanor** pronounced 'El'nor'

161 **rout** criminal gang

162 **practised** conspired (*OED* Practise *v.* 9). Cf. *AC* 2.2.38–9, 'if you there / Did practise on my state'.

164 **in the fact** in the act, 'red-handed'

166 **Demanding of** inquiring about (*OED* Demand *v.* 12). Cf. *R2* 1.3.7. Hall records that at her request the Duchess's cohorts 'had deuised an image of waxe, representyng the kynge, whiche by their sorcery, a litle and litle consumed, entendyng thereby in conclusion to waist, and destroy the kynges person, and so to bryng hym death' (202). Elizabeth kept in the statute 33 Hen. 8 c. 8 'It shall be felony to practise, or cause to be practised

conjuration, witchcraft, enchantment or sorcery . . . or to consume any person in his body' (*Statutes*, 208).

167 Q prints the prophecies of 1.4.59ff. after this line.

168 **at large** at length

170 **forthcoming** in custody; due for trial. See 1.4.53n.

171 **turned** blunted (*OED* Turn *v.* 9b)

172 **like** likely

hour an appointed time (*OED* 4), taken to refer to the duel arrangements (39–42) though they only refer to 'This evening' (42)

173 **leave to afflict** cease afflicting

174 **vanquished** Hattaway suggests that the compositor's eye might have caught this from the next line. (See t.n.) However, the word occurs twice with one speaker in *3H6* 2.1.72–3.

---

175 vanquished] (vanquisht); languish'd (*Walker*); banish'd (*Vaughan*)

KING

    O God, what mischiefs work the wicked ones,
    Heaping confusion on their own heads thereby!

QUEEN

    Gloucester, see here the tainture of thy nest,
    And look thyself be faultless, thou wert best.   180

GLOUCESTER

    Madam, for myself, to heaven I do appeal
    How I have loved my king and commonweal;
    And for my wife I know not how it stands.
    Sorry I am to hear what I have heard.
    Noble she is, but if she have forgot   185
    Honour and virtue, and conversed with such
    As, like to pitch, defile nobility,
    I banish her my bed and company
    And give her as a prey to law and shame
    That hath dishonoured Gloucester's honest name.   190

KING

    Well, for this night we will repose us here;
    Tomorrow toward London back again,
    To look into this business thoroughly
    And call these foul offenders to their answers,
    And poise the cause in Justice' equal scales,   195

'Usurped' would fit the sense but not the metre: cf. 'sorrow is an enemy, / And would usurp upon my wat'ry eyes' (*Tit* 3.1.267–8).

177 **wicked ones** Cairncross draws attention to Matthew, 13.38, for 'wicked one', which is also in 13.19 and is found again four times in 1 John (2.13, 14; 3.12; 5.18).

178 **confusion** destruction; damnation. Cf. 5.2.31.

179 **tainture** defilement. Only here in Shakespeare. Cf. the proverb 'It is a foul bird that defiles his own nest' (Dent, B377). Cf. *AYL* 4.1.183.

180 You are best advised to make sure you are faultless.

183 **how it stands** the full circumstances

187 **pitch, defile** a proverb deriving from the apocryphal book of Ecclesiasticus: 'He that toucheth pitche, shalbe defiled with it' (13.1). See Dent, P358, where several other uses in Shakespeare are given.

191 **repose us** For this reflexive usage see Abbott, 296.

179 tainture] *(*Taincture*)*

Whose beam stands sure, whose rightful cause
   prevails.

                                              Flourish.
                                              Exeunt.

[**2.2**]   *Enter* YORK, SALISBURY *and* WARWICK.

YORK

   Now, my good Lords of Salisbury and Warwick,
   Our simple supper ended, give me leave
   In this close walk to satisfy myself
   In craving your opinion of my title,
   Which is infallible, to England's crown.   5

SALISBURY

   My lord, I long to hear it out at full.

WARWICK

   Sweet York, begin; an if thy claim be good,
   The Nevilles are thy subjects to command.

YORK   Then thus:

---

196 **beam stands sure** crossbar is even-
   ly balanced. The image is classical
   (Virgil, *Aeneid*, 12.725–7, following
   Homer, *Iliad*, 8.68–77). Surprisingly,
   in the Bible scales appear in relation to
   God's creation of the world.
2.2 location: the Duke of York's garden,
   London (Capell). Hall records that in
   1448, 'Rychard duke of Yorke . . .
   perceiuyng the kyng to be a ruler not
   Ruling, & the whole burden of the
   Realme, to depend in the ordinaunces
   of the Quene & the duke of Suffolke,
   began secretly to allure to him frendes
   of the nobilitie, and priuatly declared
   to them, his title and right to the
   Crowne' (210).
2 **supper** See the closing reference to
   the invitation, 1.4.
3 **close** private, secluded

5 **infallible** York refers to Edward III
   as 'trew and infallible heyre' (Hall,
   246) in his 1460 oration before parliament.
9–52 A longer version of the genealogical
   exposition of *1H6* 2.5 from the ailing
   Mortimer in response to the young
   York's (Richard Plantagenet's) request
   (59–92). The sources are Stow,
   Holinshed and Hall. Boswell-Stone
   (256) prints the articles between
   Henry and York (Stow, *Annals*,
   679–80) which Holinshed (265–6)
   incorporates sequentially after the
   Duke's oration before parliament in
   1460. Hall (2–3) substantially includes
   these materials at the opening of his
   chronicle beginning with the reign of
   Henry IV. Salisbury's details (39–42)
   are found in Hall (23) and York's

2.2] *Capell*   6 it out] *Oxf (McKerrow); it F*   at full] thus at full *F3, F4;* at the full *Capell*   9] *om. Ard²*

Edward the Third, my lords, had seven sons: 10
The first, Edward the Black Prince, Prince of Wales;
The second, William of Hatfield; and the third,
Lionel, Duke of Clarence; next to whom
Was John of Gaunt, the Duke of Lancaster;
The fifth was Edmund Langley, Duke of York;   15
The sixth was Thomas of Woodstock, Duke of
    Gloucester;
William of Windsor was the seventh and last.
Edward the Black Prince died before his father,
And left behind him Richard, his only son,
Who after Edward the Third's death reigned as king,   20
Till Henry Bolingbroke, Duke of Lancaster,
The eldest son and heir of John of Gaunt,
Crowned by the name of Henry the Fourth,
Seized on the realm, deposed the rightful king,
Sent his poor queen to France, from whence she came,   25
And him to Pomfret; where, as all you know,
Harmless Richard was murdered traitorously.

WARWICK

Father, the Duke of York hath told the truth;
Thus got the house of Lancaster the crown.

---

concluding genealogy (43–52) in the oration before parliament (246). See Appendix 6, Genealogical Table 2.

12 **second . . . Hatfield** Q reads 'The second was Edmund of Langly, / Duke of Yorke', an error which makes the rest of the argument redundant since if he is directly descended from the second son there can be no debate. Edmund Langley was the fifth son, as F records, and thus York has to argue his claim by way of his father's marriage with a descendant of the third son. It was study of this error by Alexander and Doran which led to the

revised view of Q as a memorial reconstruction of F, a 'bad quarto', and not a source for F or otherwise an early version. See Introduction, pp. 122–5.

26 **Pomfret** Pontefract, near York
all you know The phrase is found in York's 1460 oration (Hall, 246); but elsewhere in Shakespeare it is used when addressing two people, as here (see *2H4* 3.1.35).

28 *****Duke of York** Obvious eyeskip, as Cairncross points out: *of York* fills out the metre and balances *Lancaster* in the next line.

---

26 Pomfret] (Pumfret)   28 Duke of York] *Ard²* *subst.;* Duke F

YORK

> Which now they hold by force and not by right;   30
> For Richard, the first son's heir being dead,
> The issue of the next son should have reigned.

SALISBURY

> But William of Hatfield died without an heir.

YORK

> The third son, Duke of Clarence, from whose line
> I claim the crown, had issue Philippe, a daughter,   35
> Who married Edmund Mortimer, Earl of March;
> Edmund had issue, Roger, Earl of March;
> Roger had issue, Edmund, Anne and Eleanor.

SALISBURY

> This Edmund in the reign of Bolingbroke,
> As I have read, laid claim unto the crown   40
> And, but for Owen Glendower, had been king,
> Who kept him in captivity till he died.

30 **force . . . right** proverbial (Dent, M922). See *2H4* 5.4.24–5, 'that right should thus overcome might' (Mistress Quickly reverses the terms of the proverb). Cf. *3H6* 1.1.37, 'By words or blows here let us win our right'. The exigency of 'might' and the ambivalence of 'right' constitute the dialectic of Shakespeare's English histories. See Introduction, pp. 87–9.

38 **Edmund** fifth Earl of March, declared heir presumptive by Richard II in 1398

39 **This Edmund** The several Edmund Mortimers of the fourteenth and fifteenth centuries led to a confusion in the chronicles which reappeared in Shakespeare's *1H4* (1.3, 3.1), *1H6* (2.5) and here. Salisbury confuses the fifth Earl of March (1391–1425) with his uncle Sir Edmund Mortimer (1376–1409), the brother of Roger Mortimer, the fourth Earl of March.

Sir Edmund Mortimer was captured by Glendower, eventually marrying his daughter and fighting on his side. The Mortimer depicted in *1H6* is the fifth Earl of March, though it was his cousin Sir John Mortimer who died as prisoner in the Tower of London. See West.

41 **Owen Glendower** (1359?–1416?), Owain ab Gruffydd, Lord of Glyndwr. Originally of Lancastrian connection, after the death of Richard II, accession of Henry IV and declaration of Prince Henry as Prince of Wales, he began a nationalist rebellion the memory of which has sustained Welsh nationalism ever since. *Glendower* is disyllabic, rhyming with 'slender', or pronounced as 'Glendour' (see Cercignani, 229, and *1H4* 1.3.100–1).

42 **kept . . . died** Boswell-Stone (258) points out that Hall (23) says this of Lord Grey of Ruthin, a fellow prisoner with Mortimer of Glendower. None of

34–5] *Pope; F lines* Clarence, / Crowne, / Daughter, /

But to the rest.

YORK   His eldest sister, Anne,
My mother, being heir unto the crown,
Married Richard, Earl of Cambridge, who was son   45
To Edmund Langley, Edward the Third's fifth son.
By her I claim the kingdom; she was heir
To Roger, Earl of March, who was the son
Of Edmund Mortimer, who married Philippe,
Sole daughter unto Lionel, Duke of Clarence.   50
So, if the issue of the elder son
Succeed before the younger, I am king.

WARWICK

What plain proceeding is more plain than this?
Henry doth claim the crown from John of Gaunt,
The fourth son; York claims it from the third.   55
Till Lionel's issue fails, Gaunt's should not reign;
It fails not yet, but flourishes in thee
And in thy sons, fair slips of such a stock.
Then, father Salisbury, kneel we together,
     [*They kneel.*]
And, in this private plot, be we the first   60
That shall salute our rightful sovereign
With honour of his birthright to the crown.

---

the Mortimers died in the Tower.

53 After the extensive exposition by York this seems almost a music-hall riposte. The plainness is in the next two-line redaction.
    proceeding line of descent: the genealogy

56 *Gaunt's* added for clarity

57–8 **flourishes . . . slips . . . stock** alluding to the genealogical family

tree: *slips* are cuttings, *stock* the trunk. Cf. 3.2.213–14. For explicit reference to family 'tree' see *3H6* 5.7.31–2, *R2* 1.2.13–21 and *R3* 3.7.167.

60 **plot** ground. Along with the adjective *close* (3), an inescapable sense of conspiracy?

62 **birthright** of the first-born, not of all births, according to the law of primogeniture. Cf. *3H6* 1.1.219.

45–50] *Theobald; F lines* Cambridge, / *Langley,* / Sonne; / Kingdome: / March, / *Mortimer,* / Daughter / Clarence. /   45 son] *Rowe; not in F*   46 fifth son] *Theobald;* fift Sonnes Sonne *F*   53 proceeding] *F2–4;* proceedings *QF*   56 Gaunt's] *this edn;* his *QF;* John's *Oxf*   59 SD] *this edn*

BOTH

Long live our sovereign, Richard, England's king!

YORK

We thank you, lords.　　[*They rise.*]
　　　　　　　　　　But I am not your king
Till I be crowned and that my sword be stained　　　65
With heart-blood of the house of Lancaster;
And that's not suddenly to be performed
But with advice and silent secrecy.
Do you as I do in these dangerous days –
Wink at the Duke of Suffolk's insolence,　　　　70
At Beaufort's pride, at Somerset's ambition,
At Buckingham, and all the crew of them,
Till they have snared the shepherd of the flock,
That virtuous prince, the good Duke Humphrey.
'Tis that they seek; and they, in seeking that,　　　75
Shall find their deaths, if York can prophesy.

SALISBURY

My lord, break we off; we know your mind at full.

WARWICK

My heart assures me that the Earl of Warwick

---

64 **We** the royal use of a plural pronoun, immediately taken up by York. Cf. the first words of York's insurrectionary *doppelgänger*, 'We, John Cade' (4.2.29).
65 **that** until the time that
67–76 For the Q variant here see Appendix 2.
67 **suddenly** without preparation (*OED adv.* 1)
68 **with advice** advisedly, with prudence (see *OED* Advice 2)
silent secrecy Cf. 1.2.90.
70 **Wink at** close the eyes to. Shakespeare almost always uses this older sense, though modern usage makes 'wink' and 'blink' synonymous. Cf. Hall (202), 'so what for feare, and what for fauour the mater was wynked at'.

71 echoing 1.1.177
73 **shepherd . . . flock** reapplying a phrase of Hall's (112) describing Henry V. Shaheen (50) draws attention to Matthew's (26.31) quotation of Zechariah (13.7), 'I will smite the shepherd, and the sheepe of the flocke shalbe scattered'.
75–6 **seek . . . find** This collocation is found many times in the Bible: see particularly Jeremiah, 29.13; Matthew, 7.1; and Luke, 11.9.
78–9 This anticipates Warwick's sobriquet, 'the kingmaker', which was coined by Daniel: 'That great King-maker Warwick, so far growne / In grace with Fortune, that he gouerns it, / And Monarchs makes' (V.xvi). John

64–5] *Pope; F lines* Lords: / Crown'd, / stayn'd /　　64 SD] *this edn*

215

Shall one day make the Duke of York a king.

YORK

And, Neville, this I do assure myself: 80
Richard shall live to make the Earl of Warwick
The greatest man in England but the king.   *Exeunt.*

[**2.3**]   *Sound trumpets. Enter the* KING[, *the* QUEEN,
GLOUCESTER, YORK, SUFFOLK, SALISBURY;] *and* ELEANOR[,
Margery JOURDAIN, SOUTHWELL, HUME *and* BOLINGBROKE,]
under guard.

KING

Stand forth, Dame Eleanor Cobham, Gloucester's wife.
In sight of God and us, your guilt is great;
Receive the sentence of the law for sin

Major's sixteenth-century Latin history, *De gestis Scotorum* (1521), calls Warwick '*regum creator*' (330).

82 **but** except for

2.3 location: since the Horner–Peter combat (59–106) took place in Smithfield, an open space, as Sanders suggests, might be more appropriate than Capell's 'hall of justice'. Hall (202) mentions that Eleanor was tried in St Stephen's Chapel, whereas Fabyan (615) says that the others were 'arreygned' at Guildhall. The sequence of events concerning Eleanor's arrest and trial is most fully given by the *Brut* chronicle. On Sunday 23 July Bolingbroke and his instruments of necromancy were displayed in St Paul's churchyard while a sermon was preached. On the 25th Eleanor took sanctuary in Westminster. Bolingbroke implicated Eleanor before the King's Council and Eleanor pleaded not guilty before the senior ecclesiasts in St Stephen's Chapel. On the 26th Bolingbroke testified against her. Between 26 July and 11 August a com-

mission gathered evidence. Eleanor was found guilty of treason and felony at Westminster, and on 11 August she was taken to Leeds Castle in Kent for safe custody following suspicions of a planned flight from sanctuary. The others were kept in the Tower. In late October Eleanor was brought to St Stephen's Chapel and all the evidence re-examined before sentence. Southwell died in the Tower before his sentence; Margery Jourdain was burnt at Smithfield. Eleanor was sentenced to penance (see 2.4) and banishment on 6 November. On the 17th Bolingbroke was hanged, drawn and quartered at Tyburn. Hume is not mentioned in *Brut*, but Holinshed (204) and Hall (202) record that he received a pardon.

0.1–4 Q includes Buckingham, the Cardinal and Warwick, though they say nothing and are not addressed.

3–4 See Deuteronomy, 18.10–12, 'Let none be founde among you that . . . vseth witchcraft, or a regarder of times, or a marker of flying of foules, or a sorcerer,

2.3] *Capell*   0.1–4] *Capell subst.*; *Sound Trumpets. Enter the King and State, with Guard, to banish the Duchesse. F*   1] *Rowe¹; F lines Cobham, / Wife: /*

Such as by God's book are adjudged to death.
You four, from hence to prison back again;   5
From thence unto the place of execution.
The witch in Smithfield shall be burnt to ashes
And you three shall be strangled on the gallows.
You, madam, for you are more nobly born,
Despoiled of your honour in your life,   10
Shall, after three days' open penance done,
Live in your country here, in banishment
With Sir John Stanley in the Isle of Man.

ELEANOR

Welcome is banishment; welcome were my death.

GLOUCESTER

Eleanor, the law, thou seest, hath judged thee: 15

/ Or a charmer, or that counselleth with spirites, or a soothsayer, or that asketh counsell at the dead. For all that doe such things are abomination unto the Lord'. Cf. Exodus, 22.18, 'Thou shalt not suffer a witch to liue' (Shaheen, 51).

4   **adjudged** judged by predetermined decree (*OED* Adjudge *v.* 2). Hall (202) uses the word: see next note. Cf. *3H6* 4.6.34.

5–8 As the dramatic focus is on Eleanor the sentences are put cursorily. Cf. Hall (202), 'for the which treison, they wer adiudged to dye, & so Margery Iordayne was brent in smithfelde, & Roger Bolynbroke was drawen & quartered at tiborne, takyng vpon his death, that there was neuer no suche thyng by theim ymagined, Ihon Hum had his pardon, & Southwel died in the toure before execution'.

7   **Smithfield** from 'Smoothfield', west of Aldgate and north of Newgate; used for combat, sale of horses (see *2H4* 1.2.46) and the execution of heretics

8   **strangled** hanged

9   **for** because (Abbott, 151)

10 **Despoiled** despoilèd: deprived, stripped (*OED* Despoil *v.* 2). The only

occurrence in Shakespeare, but particularly apt in both literal and figurative meanings since part of Eleanor's immediate punishment, according to *Mirror*, was, by implication, to be stripped of her fine clothes (see 1.3.86–7) and covered by a white sheet (see the following scene). Cf. 1.4 headnote.

11 **open penance** See Hall (202), 'iudged, to do open penaunce'. Cairncross notes the phrase 'done open penance' in *Homilies* (154).

13 **With** in the custody of
    Sir John Stanley thus in Hall and Holinshed, but correctly Sir Thomas Stanley (d. 1456) in Fabyan and Stow. See LN.

14 ²**welcome** Perhaps 'more welcome' is implicit (cf. 2.4.88) since banishment is elsewhere considered worse than death in Shakespeare: cf. e.g. Queen Margaret's words in *R3*, 'I do find more pain in banishment / Than death can yield me here' (1.3.167–8).
    were would be

15–16 Hattaway compares Romans, 2.12–13, 'As many as have sinned in the law shall be judged by the law . . . but the doers of the law shall be justified'.

15 **judged** judgèd

217

I cannot justify whom the law condemns.
Mine eyes are full of tears, my heart of grief.

              [Exeunt Eleanor and other prisoners, guarded.]

Ah, Humphrey, this dishonour in thine age
Will bring thy head with sorrow to the ground! –
I beseech your majesty, give me leave to go;   20
Sorrow would solace, and mine age would ease.

KING

Stay, Humphrey, Duke of Gloucester. Ere thou go,
Give up thy staff. Henry will to himself
Protector be; and God shall be my hope,
My stay, my guide and lantern to my feet.   25
And go in peace, Humphrey, no less beloved
Than when thou wert Protector to thy king.

QUEEN

I see no reason why a king of years
Should be to be protected like a child.

---

17 SD *Sanders is followed here, as such an emotional farewell as 17 brings out the full dramatic tension between public and private spheres. Cf. 2.4.86.

19 **ground** Cairncross emended F's 'ground' in view of the head–sorrow–grave association elsewhere (5.1.162–70; *TGV* 3.1.19–21) and the Q1 and F reading of 'grave' at *Ham* 4.5.39 for Q2's 'ground'. Cf. 'Ye shall bring my grey head with sorowe vnto the graue' (Noble, 123).

21 **would** requires, needs (Abbott, 329) **ease** relief from office

23 **staff** See 1.2.25–6 and n.

24 **hope** found throughout Scripture, meaning variously God, the Messiah, the Gospels, resurrection and salvation. St Paul's epistles are particularly insistent on the word.

25 **My . . . guide** Cf. Sternhold & Hopkins, Psalms, 42.9, 'O Lord thou art my guide and stay'.

stay support. Shaheen (51) assembles several quotations showing how the Geneva Bible favoured the word, e.g. Psalms, 18.18, 'The Lord was my stay'.

lantern . . . feet See Psalms, 119.105, 'Thy worde is a lanterne unto my feete' (Shaheen, 52).

26 **go in peace** Hattaway suggests Luke, 2.29, 'Lord, now lettest thou thy servant depart in peace'.

27–9 Yet again the title of Protector is harped upon. See 1.1.39 and n., 1.1.159–61 and n.; and cf. 1.3.119–21, 2.1.21ff.

28 **of years** of age, beyond minority. See 1.3.117n.

29 **Should be** For 'be' as subjunctive, see Abbott, 298. Margaret is repeating 1.3.119–20. Cf. *RJ* 2.5.42.

---

17 SD] *Theobald subst. after 16; Exit some with Elnor. Q; after 17 Sanders*   19 ground] grave *Ard²*
22–5] *Pope; F lines* Gloster, / Staffe, / Protector be, / guide, / feete: /   25 lantern] *(Lanthorne)*

God and King Henry govern England's realm!   30
Give up your staff, sir, and the King his realm.
GLOUCESTER
My staff? Here, noble Henry, is my staff:
As willingly do I the same resign
As e'er thy father Henry made it mine;
And even as willing at thy feet I leave it   35
As others would ambitiously receive it.
    [*Lays down staff.*]
Farewell, good King. When I am dead and gone
May honourable peace attend thy throne.   *Exit.*
QUEEN
Why, now is Henry King and Margaret Queen,
And Humphrey Duke of Gloucester scarce himself,   40
That bears so shrewd a maim: two pulls at once;
His lady banished, and a limb lopped off.
This staff of honour raught,   [*Picks up staff.*]
                    there let it stand
Where it best fits to be, in Henry's hand.
SUFFOLK
Thus droops this lofty pine and hangs his sprays;   45

---

31 **King his** King's (Abbott, 217). Give up your power over the King's realm, symbolized by your staff.

34 **Henry . . . mine** For Henry V's will see 1.1.39n.

37 **dead and gone** Cf. *1H6* 1.4.93. Included by Dent (DD9) as a proverbial phrase.

41 **bears . . . maim** suffers such a severe mutilation (amputation)
shrewd severe (*OED a.* 8). Cf. *KJ* 5.5.14.
pulls pluckings. The proverb 'To pull (pluck) one's plumes' (Dent, P441.1) is implicit. See *1H6* 3.3.7, where Joan la Pucelle says of Talbot, 'We'll pull his plumes and take away his train'.

43 **raught** seized: past participle of 'reach' (see *OED* Reach *v.* 4c); a cue word for the SD

45 **lofty pine** Cairncross refers to the 'loftie Pine' in Whitney, known to Shakespeare: as the mountainous, far-seen pine is brought down by 'rageinge windes', so 'they, that truste to muche in fortunes smiles . . . are often snar'de with wyles, / And from alofte, doo hedlonge fall to grounde' (59). Cf. *Cym* 4.2.174–6. This seems more appropriate as an allusion than the heraldic suggestion adopted by Cairncross, and followed by editors, of the stock of a tree on a badge borne by Henry IV, adapted from Thomas of Woodstock, Duke of Gloucester, in honour of his birthplace (Rothery, 47).
sprays branches (dependants)

---

30 realm] helm *Steevens (Johnson)*   34 e'er] *Cam;* ere F; erst *Q*   35 willing] *Q;* willingly F
36 SD] *this edn*   43 SD] *this edn*

Thus Eleanor's pride dies in her youngest days.

YORK

Lords, let him go. Please it your majesty,
This is the day appointed for the combat,
And ready are the appellant and defendant,
The armourer and his man, to enter the lists,   50
So please your highness to behold the fight.

QUEEN

Ay, good my lord; for purposely therefore
Left I the court to see this quarrel tried.

KING

I'God's name, see the lists and all things fit;
Here let them end it, and God defend the right!   55

YORK

I never saw a fellow worse bested,
Or more afraid to fight, than is the appellant,
The servant of this armourer, my lords.

Enter at one door [HORNER] *the armourer and his* Neighbours,
drinking to him so much that he is drunk; and he enters with a drum

---

46 **her** its (Abbott, 229). Pride like a 'spray' is young, not Eleanor.
47 **Please it** if it please
48 **day** 'an armyrer and hys owne man fought whythe yn the lystys in Smethefylde the laste day of Januer', 1446 (Gregory, 187)
   combat See Neilson. Nichols prints the writ for the combat. See Introduction, pp. 82–9, for the significance of the combat for the play as a whole.
49 **appellant and defendant** Having first impeached another for treason the *appellant* becomes the challenger when, under the auspices of the Courts of Chivalry, trial by combat is decided on.
50 **lists** the double barriers or palisades

customarily used in trials by combat; also the word denoting the space thus enclosed (see Young, 194). In *R2* the barriers are specifically referred to: 'On pain of death, no person be so bold / Or daring-hardy as to touch the lists' (1.3.42–3).
52 **purposely therefore** for that specific reason
53 **quarrel** accusation (*OED sb.³*). In the more general sense, by *3H6* 'quarrel' comes to signify the 'Whole Contention' between the houses of York and Lancaster (see *3H6* 3.2.6).
55 **God . . . right!** See 100–6 n.
56 **bested** bestèd: circumstanced, placed (*OED pa. pple.* 5): only occurrence in Shakespeare

54 I'God's] *this edn;* A Gods *F*   56 bested] *(bestead)*

*before him, and his staff with a sandbag fastened to it; and at the
other door* [PETER,] *his man, with a drum and sandbag, and*
Prentices *drinking to him.*

1 NEIGHBOUR   Here, neighbour Horner, I drink to you in
a cup of sack; and fear not neighbour, you shall do well   60
enough.

2 NEIGHBOUR   And here, neighbour, here's a cup of
charneco.

3 NEIGHBOUR   And here's a pot of good double beer,
neighbour: drink, and fear not your man.   65

HORNER   Let it come, i'faith, and I'll pledge you all; and a
fig for Peter!

1 PRENTICE   Here, Peter, I drink to thee, and be not afraid.

2 PRENTICE   Here, Peter, here's a pint of claret wine for
thee.   70

3 PRENTICE   And here's a quart for me; and be merry,
Peter, and fear not thy master. Fight for credit of the

58.3 *staff . . . sandbag* combat flails with
long, thin leather 'bags', as distin-
guished from the wooden agricultural
flail or the metal military flail. See Fig.
12 and Introduction, p. 85. Cf. the
fight between the Friar and the disguised Mortimer in Peele's *Edward I*:
'*They take the Flailes* . . . "And thrash
this Potter with thy flaile"' (120).
60 **sack** a general term for white wines
imported from Spain and the Canaries
63 **charneco** a kind of port
(*Shakespeare's England*, 2.136): only
occurrence in Shakespeare. Halliwell
quotes 'charnoco' in a list of wines
from *The Discovery of a London
Monster Called the Black Dog of
Newgate* (1612), and observes that it
was named after a village near Lisbon.
64 **double beer** extra-strong ale. None of
the sources mentions this drink. For
the association of festive wassail,

strong ale and political insurrection
see Bale, in which Sedition enters crying, 'No noyse amonge ye? Where is
the mery chere / That was wont to be,
with quaffing of double bere?' (ll.
2460–2). In *Jack Straw* we hear of
John Ball, 'You . . . / Find him in a
pulpit but twice in the yeare, / And Ile
find him fortie times in the ale-house
tasting strong beare' (ll. 70–3).
66–7 **a fig for** proverbial (Dent, F210). In
glossing Pistol's 'The fig of Spain'
(*Henry V*, Cam², 3.7.50), Andrew Gurr
draws attention to the addition in Q
which reads 'the figge of *Spaine* within
thy jawe'. The saying was usually
accompanied by an obscene gesture of
the thumb, thrust through the fingers or
into the mouth. See G. Williams, 'fig'.
69–73 *See LN.
72–3 **Fight . . . prentices.** a line calcu-

64 And here's] Here's *Q*   66+ SP] *Armorer. F*   68 afraid] afeard *Q*   69–71 Here . . . me; and] *Q,
Oxf; not in F*

prentices.

PETER   I thank you all. Drink and pray for me, I pray you,
for I think I have taken my last draught in this world.   75
Here, Robin, an if I die, I give thee my apron; and Will,
thou shalt have my hammer; and here, Tom, take all the
money that I have. O Lord bless me, I pray God, for I
am never able to deal with my master, he hath learnt so
much fence already.   80

SALISBURY   Come, leave your drinking, and fall to blows.
Sirrah, what's thy name?

PETER   Peter, forsooth.

SALISBURY   Peter! What more?

PETER   Thump.   85

SALISBURY   Thump! Then see thou thump thy master
well.

HORNER   Masters, I am come hither, as it were, upon my
man's instigation, to prove him a knave and myself an
honest man; and touching the Duke of York, I will take   90
my death I never meant him any ill, nor the King, nor
the Queen; and therefore, Peter, have at thee with a
downright blow!

---

lated to rouse a volatile section of the amphitheatre audience. See Gurr, *Playgoing*, 65–6.

80 **fence** fencing skill: parodically recalling Gloucester at 2.1.51, the only other occurrence in the play

88–93 Q reads 'Heres to thee neighbour, fill all the pots again, for before we fight, looke you, I will tell you my minde, for I am come hither as it were of my mans instigation, to proue my selfe an honest man, and Peter a knaue, and so haue at you Peter with down-right blowes, as Beuys of South-hampton fell vpon Askapart'. Jordan calcu-

lates that the actor playing Horner was the reporter here, and it appears that the actor's name was Bevis (see 4.2.0.1 and n.). The allusion to the hero of popular romance, probably gag material, would be inappropriate for a later cast. But as Freeman argues, the F version of the whole speech from drunken slapstick to something more 'sober and dignified' detracts from the dramatic force of the scene. See 94n., on *double*.

90–1 **take my death** 'take my oath on pain of death' (Sanders)

93 **downright** straight down (*OED adv.* 1). Cf. *3H6* 1.1.12.

76 apron] *(Aporne); aperne Q*   92–3 a . . . blow] down-right blowes, as Beuys of South-hampton fell vpon Askapart *Q*

YORK Dispatch! This knave's tongue begins to double.   94
 Sound trumpets!   *Alarum to the combatants.*
   They fight, and Peter strikes Horner down.

HORNER Hold, Peter, hold! I confess, I confess treason.
   [*Dies.*]

YORK Take away his weapon. – Fellow, thank God and
 the good wine in thy master's way.

PETER [*Kneels.*] O God! Have I overcome mine enemies
 in this presence? O Peter, thou hast prevailed in right!   100

KING

 Go, take hence that traitor from our sight,

 For by his death we do perceive his guilt.

 And God in justice hath revealed to us

 The truth and innocence of this poor fellow,

 Which he had thought to have murdered wrongfully.   105

 Come, fellow,   [*Peter rises.*]

        follow us for thy reward.   *Sound a flourish.*
                        Exeunt.

94 **Dispatch!** Get this over with! (*OED v.* 5).
double stammer, splutter. Not in Q,
yet the preceding speech there (see
88–93n.) is much more suited to
drunken spluttering than the relative
formality of F. The name of the giant
'Askapart' defeated but spared by Sir
Bevis, who becomes his page, seems
almost designed for the drunken
tongue to *double* on.
95 SD1 *Alarum* the call to arms
96 SD See LN.
98 **in . . . way** hindering your master.

Wells & Taylor adopt the northern
dialect 'wame' (belly) for *way* as appropriate to the speaker, York.
99–100 See 1.3.215n. With the word
enemies here, Psalms, 13.4, and Isaiah,
42.13, are possibly evoked.
100 **in this presence** before the King
100–6 **O . . . reward.** See 2.2.30n. and
2.3.55. Is human drunkenness a mockery or a vindication of divine justice?
For the multiple ironies of the combat
see Introduction, p. 89.
105 **Which** whom

95 SD1] *Oxf; as dialogue in F*   SD2] *F subst.*   96 SD] *Q*   98 way] wame *Oxf*   99 SD] He kneeles
downe. *Q*   106 SD1] *this edn*

223

[2.4] *Enter* GLOUCESTER *and his Servants in mourning cloaks.*

GLOUCESTER

    Thus sometimes hath the brightest day a cloud;

    And after summer evermore succeeds

    Barren winter, with his wrathful nipping cold;

    So cares and joys abound, as seasons fleet.

    Sirs, what's o'clock?

SERVANT   Ten, my lord.   5

GLOUCESTER

    Ten is the hour that was appointed me

    To watch the coming of my punished duchess;

    Uneath may she endure the flinty streets,

    To tread them with her tender-feeling feet.

    Sweet Nell, ill can thy noble mind abrook   10

    The abject people gazing on thy face

2.4 location: a street (Theobald). Eleanor's act of penance is given in greatest detail by the *Brut* chronicler: 'And so Dam Alianore Cobham, by ordynaunce and charge of the Archebisshop of Canterbury and his brethern, was Joyned to hir penaunce for *th*e grete offence and trespasse *that* she had doon ayenst God and holy Chirche, and for the fals sorcery and wicchecraft *that* she vsed and longe tyme had wrought, *that* she shuld go from Westm*inster* to London .iij. market dayes in the weke, Monday, Wednesday, and Friday, wi*th* a taper brennyng in her hande: oon to Seint Paules, an other to Cristchirch, and *th*e thridde to Seint Michell*es* in Cornhill. And the Monday, the xiij*th* day of Nouembr*e*, Dame Alianore Cobh*a*m come by water from Westm*inster* to the Temple brigge, forto do hir charge of penaunce, on fote thurgh Fletestrete to Seint Paules; and *there* she offred hir first taper. And the Wednesday next she come from Westm*inster* by Water to the Swanne in Tamystrete, and come on fote wi*th* a taper in hir hande, and com vp Tamystrete to Seint Magnus corn*er*, and vp Briggestrete, and Eschepe and Graschirch, and so to the Corn*er* of Leden-Hall, and so to Cristchirch; and there offred the secund taper. And the Friday next, she come from Westm*inster* by water to the Quene-Hithe, and so vp *th*urgh Bredstrete into Chepe; and thu*r*gh Chepe into Cornhill, to Seint Michell*es* chirch, and *there* offred a tap*er* of a pound wex*e*; And then was she brought ageyn to Westm*inster*, into the Constable ward' (481).

0.1 *mourning cloaks* long black hooded cloaks (see *3H6* 2.1.161)

1 **sometimes . . . cloud** proverbial (Dent, D92)

4 **fleet** pass by quickly

8 **Uneath** with difficulty: only here in Shakespeare

10 **abrook** brook, endure: not again in Shakespeare. See Abbott, 24, for the common prefix.

2.4] *Capell* 0.1 GLOUCESTER] *Pope; Duke Humfrey* F   servants] *this edn* 4 abound] rebound *Oxf*
5 Ten] Almost ten *Q*

With envious looks, laughing at thy shame,
That erst did follow thy proud chariot wheels
When thou didst ride in triumph through the streets.
But soft, I think she comes; and I'll prepare   15
My tear-stained eyes, to see her miseries.

Enter ELEANOR *[barefoot, and] a white sheet [about her, with a wax
candle] in her hand, [and verses written on her back and pinned on,
and accompanied with] the* Sheriff *[of London, and* Sir John
STANLEY *and Officers with bills and halberds and commoners].*

SERVANT
So please your grace, we'll take her from the sheriff.
GLOUCESTER
No, stir not for your lives; let her pass by.
ELEANOR
Come you, my lord, to see my open shame?
Now thou dost penance too. Look how they gaze!   20
See how the giddy multitude do point

12 **envious** malicious, spiteful (*OED a.* 2)
13–14 inevitably recalling Marlowe, *2
Tamburlaine*: 'And, as thou rid'st in
triumph through the streets, / The
pavement underneath thy chariot
wheels / With Turkey carpets will be
covered' (1.3.41–3).
13 **erst** formerly
15 **soft** stay
16.1–4 The greater specificity of Q (cf.
31, 34, 105) suggests performance; *and
Commoners* is added in view of 20–3.
16.1 *barefoot . . . sheet* 'shrouded in a
sheete . . . bare foote' (*Mirror*, 436); 'on
fote' (*Brut*, 481)
16.1–2 *wax candle* See headnote.
16.3–4 **Sir John** STANLEY See 2.3.13n.
16.4 *bills* long-handled weapons, 'having
at one end a blade or axe-shaped head'
(Onions)

halberds similar to bills, but up to
seven feet long (Onions)
17 **take** rescue
19 **open shame** public disgrace.
Eleanor's phrase in *Mirror*, 436.
Probably taken directly from this
source, though Hart shows its occurrence in Ovid (328, 329). It recurs in
CE 4.4.67 and *Luc* 890.
20 **they** the *Commoners* (see 16.4), and the
theatre audience
21 **giddy** Several meanings are implied
here: 'fickle', the crowd turning from
former respect; 'excited' to the point of
being maddened by her demonic criminality; 'dizzy' literally and metaphorically in the sense of unstable, an incipi-
ent crowd hysteria, and thus ultimately
dangerous. All these meanings are realized in the Jack Cade scenes of Act 4.

12 looks] looks still *F2*   16.1–4] *Q subst.; Enter the Duchesse in a white Sheet, and a Taper burning in
her hand, with the Sherife and Officers. F*   16.1 ELEANOR] *this edn; Dame Elnor Cobham Q*   16.4 *and
commoners*] *this edn*   17 sheriff] Sheriffes *Q*

And nod their heads and throw their eyes on thee.
Ah, Gloucester, hide thee from their hateful looks
And, in thy closet pent up, rue my shame
And ban thine enemies, both mine and thine.   25
GLOUCESTER
Be patient, gentle Nell, forget this grief.
ELEANOR
Ah, Gloucester, teach me to forget myself;
For whilst I think I am thy married wife
And thou a prince, Protector of this land,
Methinks I should not thus be led along,   30
Mailed up in shame, with papers on my back,
And followed with a rabble that rejoice
To see my tears and hear my deep-fet groans.
The ruthless flint doth cut my tender feet,
And when I start, the envious people laugh   35

---

multitude Perhaps unsurprisingly, in view of the later rebellion scenes, the word occurs more times in this than any other play. Cf. 'The Multitude, a Beast of many heads', *Jack Straw*, 188.

22 **throw** *OED* Throw *v.* 16, '*To throw one's eye or eyes*'. The early English sense of 'throw' as 'turn' in this phrase means to 'turn urgently' with expectation. This usage is found three times in *3H6* (1.4.37, 2.3.36, 2.5.85).

23 **hateful** full of hate in the sense of 'eager to see him suffer'

24 **closet** private chamber
   pent up close-confined, shut in
   rue pity

25 **ban** curse (see 3.2.319 and n.)

27 **forget myself** lose remembrance of my own station (Dent, FF9). See *KJ* 3.1.134.

31 **Mailed up** enveloped, wrapped up (*OED* Mail *v.*³ 1). 'Mailed' was also a term in falconry indicating breast feathers, 'some pure white maylde' (*OED* Mailed *a.* 4). Given the hawking language found elsewhere (particularly

2.1), Dyce's quotation of Randle Holmes's *Academy of Armory* (1688) seems relevant: '"Mail a hawk" is to wrap her up in a handkerchief or other cloth, that she may not be able to stir her wings or struggle'. Cf. *OED* Mail *v.*³ 2 and Eleanor's *white sheet*, 16.1.

papers . . . back See 16.2–3. This seems to be an innovation for performance since the detail is not found in the chronicles or *Mirror*. More common was a mock paper crown as worn by Roger Bolingbroke (see 1.4.3 LN). In *LLL* we find 'Why, he comes in like a perjure, wearing papers' (4.3.46), which Hart glosses with reference to papers worn or otherwise placed on the head as part of public punishment.

32 **with** by (Abbott, 193)

33 **deep-fet** fetched from deep within: only here in Shakespeare. Cf. *far-fet* (3.1.292).

34 Cf. Kyd, *Tragedy*, 'Wearing the flints with these my withered feet' (3.7.71).
   ruthless unpitying (*OED a.*)

35 **start** flinch with pain (*OED v.* 1e)
   envious malicious

And bid me be advised how I tread.
Ah, Humphrey, can I bear this shameful yoke?
Trowest thou that e'er I'll look upon the world,
Or count them happy that enjoys the sun?
No: dark shall be my light and night my day;   40
To think upon my pomp shall be my hell.
Sometime I'll say, 'I am Duke Humphrey's wife,
And he a prince and ruler of the land;
Yet so he ruled, and such a prince he was,
As he stood by whilst I, his forlorn duchess,   45
Was made a wonder and a pointing-stock
To every idle rascal follower.'
But be thou mild and blush not at my shame,
Nor stir at nothing, till the axe of death
Hang over thee, as sure it shortly will.   50
For Suffolk, he that can do all in all
With her that hateth thee and hates us all,
And York and impious Beaufort, that false priest,
Have all limed bushes to betray thy wings;

36 **be advised** advisèd: be counselled (*OED* Advised *ppl. a.*). Common in this sense throughout Shakespeare: see particularly *2H4* 1.2.134–5, 'As I was then advised by my learned counsel in the laws'. The rabble's mockery here is to poke fun at the wife of the chief counsellor of the realm.
38 **Trowest** dost thou believe
39 **enjoys** For the singular inflection see Abbott, 247.
45 **As** that (Abbott, 109)
   forlorn wretched and forsaken. The stress here is on the first syllable (cf. 4.1.65), as in *TGV* 5.4.12. See Cercignani, 33.
46 **wonder** spectacle arousing derisive astonishment. Cf. *MA* 4.1.239, 'the wonder of her infamy'.
   pointing-stock 'a laughing stocke' in Q: a person pointed at, as object of ridicule. Only here in Shakespeare. In modern English we still have the

phrase 'laughing stock' and the word 'butt' as in 'butt of the joke'. 'Stock' and 'butt' here derive from meaning the trunk of a tree. Figuratively this developed as the type of what is void of sensation, hence a stupid or senseless person (*OED* Stock *sb.*[1] 1c). The idea of stolidity and stupidity as unfeelingness encouraged the play on stoics and stocks, as in *TS* 1.1.31. Stupidity extends to folly as in 'laughing stock' and its parallel 'flouting stock', which are both found in the Welshisms of Evans in *MW* 3.1.86 and 117–18.
47 **rascal** low-born (*OED sb.* and *a.* 2). Cf. 4.4.50.
48 **mild** not easily provoked (*OED a.* 1d)
49 **stir** take action
52 **her** Queen Margaret
   hateth thee 'loues him so' in Q. The 'him' of Q refers to the *Suffolk* of 51.
54 **limed** smeared with birdlime. See 1.3.89n.

And fly thou how thou canst, they'll tangle thee.   55
But fear not thou until thy foot be snared,
Nor never seek prevention of thy foes.

GLOUCESTER

Ah, Nell, forbear! Thou aimest all awry.
I must offend before I be attainted.
And had I twenty times so many foes,   60
And each of them had twenty times their power,
All these could not procure me any scathe
So long as I am loyal, true and crimeless.
Wouldst have me rescue thee from this reproach?
Why yet thy scandal were not wiped away,   65
But I in danger for the breach of law.
Thy greatest help is quiet, gentle Nell:
I pray thee, sort thy heart to patience;
These few days' wonder will be quickly worn.

Enter a Herald.

HERALD

I summon your grace to his majesty's parliament,   70

---

55 **fly . . . canst** flee as best you may
tangle entangle in a net (*OED v.*[1] 3)
56 **snared** Cf. Gloucester's 'As I my selfe,
which caught was in the snare'
(*Mirror*, 459).
57 **seek prevention of** seek means of
forestalling
58–63 These lines reflect Hall's account of
a politically naive aspect of Gloucester's
character even after his enemies had laid
charges against him: 'Although the duke
(not without great laude and praise) sufficiently answered to all thynges to him
obiected, yet because his death was
determined, his wisedome litle helped,
nor his truth smally auailed: but of this
vnquietnes of mynde, he deliuered
hymself, because he thought neither of
death, nor of condempnacion to dye:
suche affiaunce had he in his strong

truthe, and suche confidence had he in
indifferent iustice' (209).
58 **aimest** guess, conjecture (*OED* Aim *v.* 3)
awry twistedly; wide of the mark
59 **attainted** condemned for treason or
felony. See 1.2.106n.
62 **procure** 'to endeavour to cause or
bring about (mostly something evil) *to*
or *for* a person' (*OED v.* 3)
scathe harm
65 **yet . . . were not** still . . . would not be
67 **quiet** acceptance
68 **sort** dispose (*OED v.*[1] 1b)
patience For the secondary accented
syllable see Cercignani, 294.
69 **days' wonder** Cf. 'a wonder lasts but
nine days' (Dent, W728). See *AYL*
3.2.173.
worn worn out; forgotten
70–1 See 3.1 headnote.

Holden at Bury the first of this next month.

GLOUCESTER

And my consent ne'er asked herein before?

This is close dealing. Well, I will be there.   [*Exit Herald.*]

My Nell, I take my leave; and, master sheriff,

Let not her penance exceed the King's commission.   75

SHERIFF

An't please your grace, here my commission stays,

And Sir John Stanley is appointed now

To take her with him to the Isle of Man.

GLOUCESTER

Must you, Sir John, protect my lady here?

STANLEY

So am I given in charge, may't please your grace.   80

GLOUCESTER

Entreat her not the worse, in that I pray

You use her well. The world may laugh again,

And I may live to do you kindness if

You do it her. And so, Sir John, farewell.

          [*Gloucester begins to leave.*]

ELEANOR   What, gone, my lord, and bid me not farewell?   85

GLOUCESTER

Witness my tears, I cannot stay to speak.

          Exeunt Gloucester [*and Servants*].

ELEANOR

Art thou gone too? All comfort go with thee,

For none abides with me; my joy is death;

---

71 **Holden** To be held
  Bury Bury St Edmunds, Suffolk
73 **close dealing** secret plotting
75 **the King's commission** what is
  authorised by royal warrant
77 **Sir John Stanley** See 2.3.13n.
81 **Entreat** treat
82 **world may laugh** Johnson considered

the phrase proverbial, though it is not
recorded by Tilley or F. P. Wilson,
ODEP. The verses from a Whitney
emblem, cited 2.3.45n., include the line
'Thoughe worlde do laughe, and wealthe
doe moste abounde'. Cf. 'Fortune . . .
smile once more' (*KL* 2.2.172).
85–6 cf. *TGV* 2.2.16–18

73 SD] *Theobald*   83–4] *Pope; F lines* her. / farewell. /   84 SD] *Oxf*   86 SD *and Servants*] *Capell*

229

Death, at whose name I oft have been afeared,
Because I wished this world's eternity.   90
Stanley, I prithee go, and take me hence,
I care not whither, for I beg no favour;
Only convey me where thou art commanded.

STANLEY

Why, madam, that is to the Isle of Man,
There to be used according to your state.   95

ELEANOR

That's bad enough, for I am but reproach;
And shall I then be used reproachfully?

STANLEY

Like to a duchess, and Duke Humphrey's lady,
According to that state you shall be used.

ELEANOR

Sheriff, farewell, and better than I fare,   100
Although thou hast been conduct of my shame.

SHERIFF

It is my office, and, madam, pardon me.

ELEANOR

Ay, ay, farewell; thy office is discharged.
          [Exit Sheriff with Officers and Commoners.]
Come, Stanley, shall we go?

STANLEY

Madam, your penance done, throw off this sheet,   105
And go we to attire you for our journey.

90 **wished . . . eternity** wished to live for
   ever
95 **state** rank, standing. In late medieval/
   early modern England punishment
   and imprisonment were hierarchically
   graded, in effect. Note above the different kinds of punishment meted out
   to Eleanor and her accomplices: see
   2.3.5–13. Perhaps *Justice' equal scales*
   (2.1.195) aren't so equal after all, a

concern at the heart of Jack Cade's
rebellion.
96 **reproach** disgrace. Eleanor echoes
   Gloucester (64) as she bitterly allego-
   rizes her *state.*
100 **better . . . fare** fare better than I do
101 **conduct** conductor; guard
102 **office** duty
103 **is discharged** has been carried out

103 SD] *this edn*   105] *Pope; F lines* done, / Sheet, /

ELEANOR   My shame will not be shifted with my sheet:
No, it will hang upon my richest robes
And show itself, attire me how I can.   109
Go, lead the way, I long to see my prison.   *Exeunt.*

[**3.1**] *Sound a sennet. Enter [two Heralds before,] the* KING,
QUEEN, CARDINAL, SUFFOLK, YORK, BUCKINGHAM,
SALISBURY *and* WARWICK *to the parliament[, with attendants].*

KING
I muse my Lord of Gloucester is not come.
'Tis not his wont to be the hindmost man,
Whate'er occasion keeps him from us now.
QUEEN
Can you not see, or will ye not observe
The strangeness of his altered countenance?   5
With what a majesty he bears himself,
How insolent of late he is become, how proud,
How peremptory, and unlike himself.
We know the time since he was mild and affable;
An if we did but glance a far-off look,   10

107 **shifted** punning on the general sense
of 'removed', and the highly specific
meaning of 'changed clothes, or
undergarments' (*OED* Shift *v.* 9a, 9b).
Cf. *MA* 3.3.142.
3.1 location: the Abbey at Bury St
Edmunds. Shakespeare telescopes 1441
and 1447, respectively the years of
Eleanor's arrest and the summoning of
the parliament at Bury. Hall (208–9)
and Holinshed (210–11) record the culmination of the plots against
Gloucester. Initially the parliament was
to have met at Cambridge, but then at
short notice it was shifted to Bury St
Edmunds. This was a power base of the
Duke of Suffolk far from Gloucester's
support in London or his landed power

in Wales. Gloucester was ordered to
attend with only a small retinue while
the King packed the countryside
around the quiet town with soldiers
(Griffiths, 496). The unsuspecting
Duke walked straight into the trap,
'snared' as Eleanor predicted.
1 **muse** wonder. Cf. *3H6* 1.1.1, 2.1.1.
2 It isn't his habit to be the last to arrive.
4–5 Hart quotes Hardyng: 'He waxed
then straunge eche day unto ye kyng, /
For cause she [Eleanor] was foriudged
for sossery, . . . / And to the kyng had
great heuynesse' (400).
5 **strangeness** aloofness (*OED* 2)
7 **insolent** proud, disdainful (*OED a.* 1)
9 **since** when (Abbott, 132)
10 **far-off** distant

3.1] *Pope*   0.1–3] *F subst.*   0.1 *two Heralds before*] *Q*   0.3 *with attendants*] *Oxf*   4 ye] you *Qq,*
Theobald

Immediately he was upon his knee,
That all the court admired him for submission.
But meet him now, and be it in the morn,
When everyone will give the time of day,
He knits his brow and shows an angry eye   15
And passeth by with stiff unbowed knee,
Disdaining duty that to us belongs.
Small curs are not regarded when they grin,
But great men tremble when the lion roars;
And Humphrey is no little man in England.   20
First note that he is near you in descent,
And should you fall, he is the next will mount.
Meseemeth then it is no policy,
Respecting what a rancorous mind he bears
And his advantage following your decease,   25
That he should come about your royal person
Or be admitted to your highness' Council.
By flattery hath he won the commons' hearts;
And when he please to make commotion,
'Tis to be feared they all will follow him.   30
Now 'tis the spring, and weeds are shallow-rooted;
Suffer them now and they'll o'ergrow the garden
And choke the herbs for want of husbandry.

---

12 **That** so that
   admired wondered at (*OED* Admire
   v. 1)
14 **give . . . day** greet each other
16 **unbowed** unbowèd
17 **Disdaining duty** without kneeling in
   respect
18 **grin** bare the teeth (*OED v.*² 1). Cf.
   3H6 1.4.56.
19 **lion** the heraldic symbol of England,
   'a lion passant guardant or' (Fox-
   Davies, 181)
23 **Meseemeth** it seems to me
23–4 **no policy, / Respecting** not prudent, considering
29 **commotion** rebellion (*OED sb.* 4). See
   3.1.357 and n. Hattaway draws attention

to Hall here: 'his capitall enemies and
mortal foes, fearyng that some tumulte
or commocion might arise, if a prince so
well beloued of the people, should bee
openly executed, and put to death,
determined to trappe & vndoo hym, or
he thereof should haue knowledge or
warnyng' (209). For discussion of the
class of words retaining the prevocalic 'i'
before a metrically stressed syllable, see
Cercignani, 308–9. Cf. *submission*, 12.
31 **weeds** See 1.3.100n.
   shallow-rooted not elsewhere in
   Shakespeare
32 **Suffer them now** allow them to take
   root and grow now
33 **herbs** plants generally

The reverent care I bear unto my lord
Made me collect these dangers in the Duke.   35
If it be fond, call it a woman's fear;
Which fear if better reasons can supplant,
I will subscribe and say I wronged the Duke.
My Lord of Suffolk, Buckingham and York,
Reprove my allegation if you can,   40
Or else conclude my words effectual.

SUFFOLK

Well hath your highness seen into this Duke;
And had I first been put to speak my mind,
I think I should have told your grace's tale.
The Duchess by his subornation,   45
Upon my life, began her devilish practices;
Or if he were not privy to those faults,
Yet by reputing of his high descent,
As next the King he was successive heir –
And such high vaunts of his nobility –   50

35 **collect** *OED v.* 5 uses this instance to illustrate the now obsolete meaning of 'conclude, deduce, infer'. Hart considers that the sense of 'gather' derives from association with the preceding gardening imagery, as in *Ham* 3.2.257 and 4.7.144.

36 **fond** foolish

37 **supplant** The two ideas of 'uproot' and 'replace' (*OED v.* 4 and 5) are combined here. See 35n.

38 **subscribe** usually the legalistic meaning of signing a document agreeing to something; but given the following reference to speech, 'to confess oneself in the wrong' (*OED v.* 8c) is meant.

40 **Reprove** disprove (*OED v.* 5). Cf. *MA* 2.3.232.
     allegation used here in the legal sense of a charge before a tribunal of the noble Lords (*OED* 1): only here and 181

41 **effectual** Editors follow *OED a.* 6, which uses this occurrence as illustration for the meaning ' "To the point", pertinent, conclusive'. But given the legal implications of the preceding diction, possibly *OED a.* 1 is also hinted at – 'Of legal documents or covenants: Valid, binding'. Exactly the same combination of meaning occurs in *Tit* 5.3.43–4.

43 **put** obliged, called upon (*OED v.*[1] 28b)

45 **subornation** procuring (magicians etc.). Cf. 180. For scansion see 29n.

46 **practices** plots (*OED* 5c). Cf. the 'devilish plots' of *R3* 3.4.60. See 3.2.22n.

47 **privy to** privately aware of; informed about

48 **reputing** thinking (*OED* Repute *v.* 5): only here in this participial form

49 See 1.1.149n.

50 **vaunts** boasts

40 Reprove] Disproue *Q*

Did instigate the bedlam brainsick Duchess
By wicked means to frame our sovereign's fall.
Smooth runs the water where the brook is deep,
And in his simple show he harbours treason.
The fox barks not when he would steal the lamb.   55
No, no, my sovereign, Gloucester is a man
Unsounded yet and full of deep deceit.

CARDINAL

Did he not, contrary to form of law,
Devise strange deaths for small offences done?

YORK

And did he not, in his Protectorship,   60
Levy great sums of money through the realm
For soldiers' pay in France, and never sent it?
By means whereof the towns each day revolted.

BUCKINGHAM

Tut, these are petty faults to faults unknown
Which time will bring to light in smooth Duke
  Humphrey.   65

---

51 **instigate** an equivocation confounding direct and indirect causes. Lines 45–6 insist on Gloucester's active initiative, while 47–52 acknowledge Eleanor's role but imply that Gloucester is still responsible, however indirectly, since the Duchess is mad. Suffolk's argument is seen to be doubly disingenuous because we have been shown the opposite in 1.2.
  bedlam mad. 'Bedlam' is usually found as a noun; it derives from the Hospital of St Mary of Bethlehem, which became a lunatic asylum after 1402.
52 **frame** contrive (*OED v.* 8a)
53 proverbial (Dent, W123). Cairncross demonstrates how Shakespeare would have come across the proverb as part of Camerarius' schoolbook version of Aesop.
54 **simple show** innocent demeanour
55 proverbial in tone, but not found in Dent or Tilley. Hart quotes the nearest he could find from Greene's *Mamillia*:

'The *Foxe* wins the favour of the *lambes* by play, and then deuoures them'.
57 **Unsounded** unfathomed. Cf. *TGV* 3.2.80.
58–9 a charge brought earlier (see 1.3.133–4n.), and by York (121–2)
60–2 In fact Hall records the rumour that 'the duke of Somerset, for his awne peculier profite, kept not halfe his nombre of souldiors, and put their wages in his purse' (216). A not uncommon allegation wherever there are commanders and soldiers: see *R2* 1.1.88–90.
63 **By means whereof** because of which
64 **to** compared with
65 **time . . . light** Cf. the proverbs 'Time brings truth to light' (Dent, T324) and 'Time discloses all things' (Tilley, T333). This great commonplace of time as revealer, particularly the notion of *veritas filia temporis*, 'truth daughter of time', plays a considerable part in the history of iconography: see Saxl.
  smooth plausible; bland (*OED a.* 6b)

KING

My lords, at once: the care you have of us
To mow down thorns that would annoy our foot
Is worthy praise; but, shall I speak my conscience,
Our kinsman Gloucester is as innocent
From meaning treason to our royal person   70
As is the sucking lamb or harmless dove.
The Duke is virtuous, mild and too well given
To dream on evil or to work my downfall.

QUEEN

Ah, what's more dangerous than this fond affiance?
Seems he a dove? His feathers are but borrowed,   75
For he's disposed as the hateful raven.
Is he a lamb? His skin is surely lent him,
For he's inclined as is the ravenous wolves.

66 **at once** found elsewhere in Shakespeare usually as part of a hasty farewell, but here Sanders suggests three possibilities: (1) answering you all together; (2) without further discussion; (3) once and for all
67 **annoy** injure (*OED v.* 4)
68 **shall . . . conscience** if I speak truly. Cf. *H5* 4.1.80.
69–71 **innocent . . . lamb** Cf. the proverb 'As innocent as a lamb' (Dent, L34.1). See 4.2.73.
71 **sucking lamb** See 1 Samuel, 7.9 (Shaheen, 52).
    harmless dove proverbial (Dent, D572) from Matthew, 10.16, Bishops' Bible: 'Be ye therefore wise as the serpents, and harmelesse as the Doues' (Shaheen, 52).
72 **given** disposed. Cf. *JC* 1.2.197.
73 **dream on** have any conception of (*OED v.*² 5)
    work evilly bring about (combining *OED v.* 1b and 10)
74 **fond affiance** foolish trust. Cf. *H5* 2.2.127.
75 The animal imagery draws on the Bible, fable and proverb. Margaret turns

Henry's biblical allusion to Matthew (see *harmless dove*, 71n.) to the proverbial 'As white as a dove' (Dent, D573.2). T. W. Baldwin (*Small Latine*, 1,609–40) established that Shakespeare alludes to Camerarius, which Cairncross applies and develops extensively in his commentary here, and at 53–7 and 77–9. *Feathers . . . borrowed* refers to Aesop's crow (a jackdaw in some versions) dressing up in borrowed plumes, sometimes a peacock's (cf. *JC* 1.1.72). Greene is alluding to this fable, if not this passage, in his famous accusation of Shakespeare as an 'vpstart Crow, beautified with our feathers' (*Groatsworth*, 84). See Introduction pp. 108–10.
76 **he's disposed** disposèd: he has the disposition of
77–8 **lamb . . . skin . . . wolves** biblical: Matthew, 7.15, 'Beware of false Prophets, which come to you in sheepes clothing, but inwardly they are rauening wolues' (Shaheen, 52). Proverbial (Dent, W614). Aesop includes the fable of a wolf in a sheep's skin hanged by a farmer.

78 wolves] wolf *Rowe*

Who cannot steal a shape, that means deceit?
Take heed, my lord; the welfare of us all　　　　　80
Hangs on the cutting short that fraudful man.

Enter SOMERSET.

SOMERSET

All health unto my gracious sovereign!

KING

Welcome, Lord Somerset. What news from France?

SOMERSET

That all your interest in those territories
Is utterly bereft you; all is lost.　　　　　85

KING

Cold news, Lord Somerset; but God's will be done.

YORK [*aside*]

Cold news for me; for I had hope of France
As firmly as I hope for fertile England.
Thus are my blossoms blasted in the bud,
And caterpillars eat my leaves away;　　　　　90
But I will remedy this gear ere long,

79 **steal a shape** adopt a guise
   means intends
81 **Hangs** depends (*OED v.* 13)
   cutting short a grim play on forestalling as beheading, echoing the
   proverbial 'shorten by the head' (Dent,
   SS10)
   fraudful treacherous: only here in
   Shakespeare
84–5 This reference to the loss of
   Normandy is an anachronism. The
   conquest and surrender took place in
   1448–9, two years later. See Hall
   (215–16) and Griffiths (504–22) for a
   full account.
84 **interest** claim by legal title (*OED sb.*
   1). Cf. *KJ* 5.2.89, 'Acquainted me with
   interest to this land'.
85 **utterly bereft** completely seized from

all is lost Holinshed's marginal note
here is 'The English loose all in
France' (215).
87–8 almost a precise repetition of York's
words at 1.1.234–5
89 proverbial: 'To nip (blast) in the bud
(blossom)' (Dent, B702). See *TGV*
1.1.48.
   blasted blighted (*OED* Blast *v.* 6 and 7)
90 **caterpillars** See 4.4.36n.
91 **gear** Editors gloss this as 'matter,
business' (*OED sb.* 11c; see 1.4.14); but
following the primary medical meaning of 'remedy' in the context of disease (*blasted*), perhaps the more specific meaning of corruption or poison is
intended (*OED sb.* 10b), as in *RJ*
5.1.60, 'A dram of poison, such soon-
speeding gear'.

87 SD] *Rowe*

Or sell my title for a glorious grave.

Enter GLOUCESTER.

GLOUCESTER
All happiness unto my lord the King!
Pardon, my liege, that I have stayed so long.

SUFFOLK
Nay, Gloucester, know that thou art come too soon,   95
Unless thou wert more loyal than thou art.
I do arrest thee of high treason here.

GLOUCESTER
Well, Suffolk's Duke, thou shalt not see me blush,
Nor change my countenance for this arrest.
A heart unspotted is not easily daunted.   100
The purest spring is not so free from mud
As I am clear from treason to my sovereign.
Who can accuse me? Wherein am I guilty?

YORK
'Tis thought, my lord, that you took bribes of France,
And, being Protector, stayed the soldiers' pay,   105
By means whereof his highness hath lost France.

GLOUCESTER
Is it but thought so? What are they that think it?
I never robbed the soldiers of their pay,
Nor ever had one penny bribe from France.
So help me God, as I have watched the night,   110
Ay, night by night, in studying good for England!

---

92 **sell** the biblical sense of 'exchange'
   (*OED v.* 6b). See Genesis, 29.31.
   title claim to the crown
94 **stayed** tarried (*OED v.*[1] 7)
98 **Suffolk's Duke** See 1.1.61n.
99 **for** because of (Abbott, 150)
100 **unspotted** untainted. Cf.   *1H6*

5.3.182–3.
104 **of** from
105–6 See 60–2n.
105 **stayed** held back (*OED* Stay *v.*[1] 20)
107 **What** who (Abbott, 254)
110 **watched the night** kept awake
   (*OED* Watch *v.* 1)

98 Suffolk's Duke] *Q; Suffolke F*   104] *Pope; F lines* Lord, / France, /   107] *Pope; F lines* so? / it? /

That doit that e'er I wrested from the King,
Or any groat I hoarded to my use,
Be brought against me at my trial day!
No: many a pound of mine own proper store, 115
Because I would not tax the needy commons,
Have I dispursed to the garrisons
And never asked for restitution.

CARDINAL

It serves you well, my lord, to say so much.

GLOUCESTER

I say no more than truth, so help me God! 120

YORK

In your Protectorship you did devise
Strange tortures for offenders, never heard of,
That England was defamed by tyranny.

GLOUCESTER

Why, 'tis well known that whiles I was Protector
Pity was all the fault that was in me, 125
For I should melt at an offender's tears,
And lowly words were ransom for their fault.

---

112 **That** may that
　　doit *OED* records 'a small Dutch coin [worth] half of an English farthing'. Brewer gives as follows: 'a Scotch silver coin [worth] one third of a farthing. In England the doit was a base coin of small value prohibited by [the statute] 3 Henry V. c. 1' (369). Used contemptuously several times by Shakespeare.
113 **groat** the great silver coin of Edward III, equal to four penny pieces (Brewer, 556)
　　to for
114 **trial** Q's 'iudgement' perhaps suggests the biblical Day of Judgement, but F's 'trial' in relation to money creates the possibility of dramatic irony found in the Cardinal's death, 3.3.8.

115 **proper store** personal wealth
117 **dispursed** dispursèd; 'disbursed' in F4: defrayed costs or expenses. Only here in Shakespeare and only two entries in *OED* with this the first.
119 **serves you well** is very opportune (*OED* Serve *v.*[1] 25)
121–2 See 58–9 and 1.3.133–4n.
123 **was defamed by** became infamous for: *defamed* only here in Shakespeare
124 **whiles** while. For the obsolescent genitive see Abbott, 137.
125 **Pity** a word which gains tragic impetus in *3H6* and gives the last soliloquy of Richard III a dimension beyond the demise of a Machiavellian villain. See *R3* 5.3.201–3, and cf. 5.2.56n. below.
127 and humble contrite words paid for the offence

114 my trial] the iudgement *Qq*　117 dispursed] disbursed *F4*

Unless it were a bloody murderer,
Or foul felonious thief that fleeced poor passengers,
I never gave them condign punishment.   130
Murder indeed, that bloody sin, I tortured
Above the felon or what trespass else.

SUFFOLK

My lord, these faults are easy, quickly answered,
But mightier crimes are laid unto your charge
Whereof you cannot easily purge yourself.   135
I do arrest you in his highness' name
And here commit you to my Lord Cardinal
To keep until your further time of trial.

KING

My Lord of Gloucester, 'tis my special hope
That you will clear yourself from all suspense.   140
My conscience tells me you are innocent.

GLOUCESTER

Ah, gracious lord, these days are dangerous.
Virtue is choked with foul ambition,

---

129 **felonious** wicked: not elsewhere in
Shakespeare
fleeced stripped: Shakespeare's only
use
poor passengers travellers on foot
(*OED* 1b)
130 **condign** well-deserved. Cairncross
refers to Foxe: 'And thus have you
heard the full story and discourse of
duke Humphrey, and of all his
adversaries: also of God's condign
punishment upon them for their
bloody cruelty' (3.717).
132 more than other crimes or offences
felon possibly the rare and obsolescent
form of 'felony' (*OED sb.*¹): if so, only
here in Shakespeare
133 **easy** insignificant, slight (*OED a.* 15)
135 **purge** clear, in the legal sense of

taking an oath and clearing one's name
with compurgation (*OED v.*¹ 5). Cf.
1H4 3.2.20.
138 **keep** guard
further later
140 **suspense** 'Doubt as to a person's
character or conduct' (*OED sb.* 3d), a
meaning seemingly created for this,
the only instance in Shakespeare, and
once elsewhere in Nashe: 'Bring you
me a princoks beardlesse boy . . . to call
my name in suspense?' (*Traveller*, 77).
143 **choked** literally 'strangled' here.
Gloucester accurately anticipates his
end. Cf. 'Go forward, and be choked
with thy ambition!' (*1H6* 2.4.112), and
'Here dies the dusky torch of
Mortimer, / Chok'd with ambition of
the meaner sort' (*1H6* 2.5.122–3).

136 you] thee *Q*   137 commit you] commit thee *Q; commit Capell*   my] my good *Q*   140 suspense] *F subst.;* suspect *Capell*

And charity chased hence by rancour's hand;
Foul subornation is predominant,   145
And equity exiled your highness' land.
I know their complot is to have my life;
And if my death might make this island happy
And prove the period of their tyranny,
I would expend it with all willingness.   150
But mine is made the prologue to their play;
For thousands more that yet suspect no peril
Will not conclude their plotted tragedy.
Beaufort's red sparkling eyes blab his heart's malice,
And Suffolk's cloudy brow his stormy hate;   155
Sharp Buckingham unburdens with his tongue
The envious load that lies upon his heart;
And dogged York, that reaches at the moon,
Whose overweening arm I have plucked back,
By false accuse doth level at my life.   160

144 **rancour's hand** Cf. 1.1.139–40.
145 **subornation** See 168 LN.
    predominant in the ascendant, powerful (from astrology). Cf. *AW* 1.1.197.
146 **equity exiled** Cf. Hall, 'justice and equitie was clerely exiled' (231). See Holinshed, 237.
    equity justice, the goddess Astraea, who fled from the earth at the onset of the iron age in Ovid (1.150). The myth is explicitly invoked in *Tit* 4.3.4. In jurisprudence, 'the recourse to general principles of justice . . . to correct or supplement the provisions of the law' (*OED* 3). In the 1593 parliament Nicholas Fuller denounced a proposed bill as making 'schisms to be equal with seditions and treasons, which is against the equity of the former law' of 1581 (Neale, 288).
    exiled stressed on the second syllable (Cercignani, 38)
147 **complot** conspiracy. Cf. *R2* 1.1.96.
149 **prove the period** mark the end. See *1H6* 4.2.17.
150 **expend it** pay the price of death

151 **mine** the tragedy of my death. See 3.2.194 and n.
    prologue . . . play Cf. *Ham* 5.2.30–1.
152–3 The metadramatic irony here derives from Gloucester's unwitting anticipation of the violent deaths of those who are plotting his own *tragedy*, all within the encompassing *de casibus* tragedy of the drama itself.
157 **envious** malicious
158 **dogged** doggèd; stubborn
    reaches . . . moon Cf. 'He casts beyond the moon' (Dent, M1114). See *Tit* 4.3.66. Cf. Whitney, 213, which depicts a dog baying at the moon, and Hotspur in *1H4* 1.3.201–2.
159 **overweening** overreaching; presumptuous. The association of this and *dogged* is found later: see 5.1.151–2.
160 **accuse** accusation (Abbott, 451)
    level aim, as with a weapon. See *2H4* 3.2.266–7, 'the foeman may with as great aim level at the edge of a penknife'.

And you, my sovereign lady, with the rest,
Causeless have laid disgraces on my head
And with your best endeavour have stirred up
My liefest liege to be mine enemy.
Ay, all of you have laid your heads together –   165
Myself had notice of your conventicles –
And all to make away my guiltless life.
I shall not want false witness to condemn me,
Nor store of treasons to augment my guilt.
The ancient proverb will be well effected: 170
A staff is quickly found to beat a dog.

CARDINAL

My liege, his railing is intolerable.
If those that care to keep your royal person
From treason's secret knife and traitor's rage
Be thus upbraided, chid, and rated at,   175
And the offender granted scope of speech,
'Twill make them cool in zeal unto your grace.

SUFFOLK

Hath he not twit our sovereign lady here
With ignominious words, though clerkly couched,
As if she had suborned some to swear   180

---

162 **Causeless** without cause. For adjectives as adverbs see Abbott, 1.
164 **liefest** dearest: only here in the superlative form; but otherwise, in the expression 'I had as lief' (I would rather), common throughout Shakespeare. Cf *alderliefest* 1.1.28.
165 **laid . . . together** proverbial (Dent, H280). Cf. 4.8.57.
166 **conventicles** clandestine meetings (*OED* 3): stress on the first and third syllables (Cercignani, 43). Only here in Shakespeare. See LN.
167 **make away** put an end to (*OED v.*[1] 84)
168 **want** lack
false witness a common biblical phrase deriving from the Ten Commandments: 'Thou shalt not bear false witness against thy neighbour' (Exodus, 20.16). Not found elsewhere in Shakespeare. See LN.
169 **store** abundance (*OED sb.* 4)
170 **effected** fulfilled (*OED v.* 2)
171 'It is an easy thing to find a staff to beat a dog' (Dent, T38).
175 **rated at** berated
176 **scope** licence (*OED sb.*[2] 7b, but with only *MM* 1.2.127 as illustration). Cf. *MM* 1.1.64.
178 **twit** twitted (Abbott, 342). See *1H6* 3.2.55.
179 **clerkly couched** learnedly put (*OED* Couch *v.*[1] 15)
180–1 **suborned . . . allegations** subornèd. See 168LN.

241

False allegations to o'erthrow his state?

QUEEN

But I can give the loser leave to chide.

GLOUCESTER

Far truer spoke than meant: I lose indeed –

Beshrew the winners, for they played me false!

And well such losers may have leave to speak.   185

BUCKINGHAM

He'll wrest the sense and hold us here all day.

Lord Cardinal, he is your prisoner.

CARDINAL

Sirs, take away the Duke and guard him sure.

GLOUCESTER

Ah, thus King Henry throws away his crutch

Before his legs be firm to bear his body.   190

Thus is the shepherd beaten from thy side,

And wolves are gnarling who shall gnaw thee first.

Ah, that my fear were false; ah, that it were!

For, good King Henry, thy decay I fear.

Exit Gloucester [with attendants].

---

181 **state** high position
182 proverbial: 'Give losers leave to speak' (Dent, L458). Cf. *Tit* 3.1.232–3. Margaret's sarcasm rebounds against her, since the terms of her marriage meant that the English throne was the *loser*.
183 **truer . . . meant** See 182n. and 186.
184 **Beshrew** curse: *be* + *shrew*, the obsolete Old English verb 'to curse'
185 **losers . . . speak** See 182 and n.
186 **wrest the sense** twist the meaning. See 183. Cf. *MA* 3.4.33–4.
189–90 in contrast to the pseudo-pious Simpcox, who presumably abandoned his crutch and ran off stage in 2.1 (see Introduction, p. 81)
191–2 Several biblical passages could be cited (see Shaheen, 53). Editors usual-

ly select Matthew, 26.31, 'I will smite the shepherd, and the sheepe of the flocke shalbe scattered', and Ezekiel, 34.8, 'my sheep were devoured of all the beasts of ye field, having no shep-heard'. Cf. *3H6* 5.6.7–8, where Henry laments, 'So flies the reckless shepherd from the wolf', in contrast to his pastoral idealization of *3H6* 2.5.21–54.
191 **shepherd** as York anticipated, 2.2.73
192 **gnarling** 'snarring' in Q: snarling (*OED* Gnarl $v.^1$ 1). Sole occurrence in this sense. *R2*'s 'gnarling sorrow' (1.3.292), the only other usage, has the sense of 'self-revealing', like conscience gnawing (*OED* Gnarl $v.^1$ 2).
194 **decay** to decline from prosperity or fortune (*OED* v. 1b). Cf. *KJ* 4.3.154.

192 gnarling] snarring *Q*   194 SD *with attendants*] *this edn;* with the *Cardinals* men *Q*

KING

My lords, what to your wisdoms seemeth best   195
Do, or undo, as if ourself were here.

QUEEN

What, will your highness leave the parliament?

KING

Ay, Margaret; my heart is drowned with grief,
Whose flood begins to flow within mine eyes,
My body round engirt with misery;   200
For what's more miserable than discontent?
Ah, uncle Humphrey, in thy face I see
The map of honour, truth and loyalty;
And yet, good Humphrey, is the hour to come
That e'er I proved thee false or feared thy faith.   205
What louring star now envies thy estate
That these great lords and Margaret our Queen
Do seek subversion of thy harmless life?
Thou never didst them wrong, nor no man wrong.
And as the butcher takes away the calf   210
And binds the wretch and beats it when it strains,
Bearing it to the bloody slaughterhouse,

195–6 Cf. the Duke's questionable dele-
    gation of power in *MM* 1.1.
200 **engirt** encircled
203 **map** embodiment, image (*OED sb.*[1]
    2b). Hart suggests that this common-
    place of the 1590s might be one of the
    borrowed plumes (see 75n.) and quotes
    several instances from Greene before
    2H6. In *TN* 3.2.79 Maria pokes fun at
    what had become a cliché.
    loyalty Scott-Giles (131) suggests an echo
    of Gloucester's motto, *Loyalle et belle*.
205 **proved** found (*OED v.* 3)
    feared thy faith doubted your loyalty
    (cf. 5.1.166)
206 **louring** threatening. Cf. *R2*'s 'lour-
    ing tempest' (1.3.187).
    envies thy estate maliciously resents

your position
208 **subversion** overthrow (*OED* 4b):
    though found in the chronicles, only
    here in Shakespeare
    harmless guiltless, innocent. Cf.
    2.2.27.
210–13 See 3.2.188–90 and 3.2.195. In the
    Jack Cade scenes this imagery becomes
    literal in the figure of Dick the butch-
    er. But finally Henry is to learn that he
    is the 'harmless sheep' and Richard his
    'butcher' (see *3H6* 5.6.8–9).
211 *****strains** Cairncross's emendation,
    following Vaughan, is supported by
    recognizing the same compositor's
    error in *H5* 3.1.32 (misreading the
    probable MS 'stra̅ying'). Similarly, *KL*
    Q's 'straied' (1.1.69) is 'strain'd' in F.

211 strains] *Ard*[2] *(Vaughan)*; strayes *F*; strives *Theobald*

243

Even so remorseless have they borne him hence;
And as the dam runs lowing up and down,
Looking the way her harmless young one went,   215
And can do naught but wail her darling's loss,
Even so myself bewails good Gloucester's case
With sad unhelpful tears, and with dimmed eyes
Look after him, and cannot do him good,
So mighty are his vowed enemies.   220
His fortunes I will weep, and 'twixt each groan
Say, 'Who's a traitor, Gloucester he is none.'
                    Exit [*with Buckingham, Salisbury and Warwick*].

QUEEN

Free lords, cold snow melts with the sun's hot beams.
Henry my lord is cold in great affairs,
Too full of foolish pity; and Gloucester's show   225
Beguiles him, as the mournful crocodile
With sorrow snares relenting passengers,
Or as the snake, rolled in a flowering bank,
With shining checkered slough doth sting a child

---

214 **dam** mother
217 **myself bewails** See Abbott, 296.
219 **do him good** help him
220 **vowed** vowèd
222 **Who's** whoever is
223 **Free** noble, honourable (*OED a.* 3)
    snow . . . beams proverbial (Dent, S593.1)
224 **cold** passive and indecisive
225 **pity** See 125n. Cf. 'Foolish pity mars a city' (Dent, P366).
    show outward appearance. See 54n.
226 **mournful crocodile** i.e. 'crocodile tears' (Dent, 831): a widespread Renaissance commonplace. In the context of political dissimulation Hall refers to 'thys cancard crocodryle' (239). In the medieval bestiaries the crocodile was said to weep while, or after, devouring a victim. It was also believed to weep in order to lure its

prey. Greene often refers to the crocodile, but the best-known texts of the century are in Hakluyt's account of Sir John Hawkins's second voyage (1565) and Spenser, 1.v.18. Cf. *Oth* 4.1.242.
227 **relenting** pitying (*OED* Relent *v.*[1] 5c)
228 **snake . . . bank** proverbial (Dent, S585). Cf. *R2* 3.2.19–20 and *Tit* 2.3.13.
229 **checkered** of variegated colour (*OED* Chequered, checkered *ppl. a.* 2). Cf. 'check'ring the eastern clouds with streaks of light' (*RJ* 2.3.2).
    slough skin (*OED sb.*[2] 1), with the suggestion of a skin that has been cast off
    sting Though received wisdom included several ways by which the snake might harm its victim, Renaissance writers, Shakespeare particularly, were drawn by the notion of the tongue's poisonous sting: 'such addres greue*th* most, now wi*th* bytyng and wi*th* blowyng and

---

222 SD *with . . . Warwick*] *Riv*   223] *Pope; F lines* Lords: / Beames: /   228 flowering] (flowring)

That for the beauty thinks it excellent. 230
Believe me, lords, were none more wise than I –
And yet herein I judge mine own wit good –
This Gloucester should be quickly rid the world,
To rid us from the fear we have of him.

CARDINAL

That he should die is worthy policy; 235
But yet we want a colour for his death.
'Tis meet he be condemned by course of law.

SUFFOLK

But in my mind that were no policy.
The King will labour still to save his life,
The commons haply rise to save his life; 240
And yet we have but trivial argument,
More than mistrust, that shows him worthy death.

YORK

So that, by this, you would not have him die?

SUFFOLK

Ah, York, no man alive so fain as I.

YORK [*aside*]

'Tis York that hath more reason for his death. – 245

---

wi*th* smytyng wi*th* *th*e taile, now wi*th*
styngynge, now wi*th* lokynge and si*g*ht
. . . The serpent . . . cesse*th* nou*gh*t to
turne and wynde *th*e tonge for he
moeue*th* it alwey and *th*at by 'streng*th*e
of venyme' (Bartholomeus, 1125, 1245).
Cf. 3.1.343, 3.2.47, 3.2.267, 3.2.325.
233 **rid** removed from
235 **worthy policy** a prudent expedient.
  'Policy' in the devious sense is always
  associated with the Renaissance
  Machiavel. See Scott.
236–7 **colour . . . law** The Cardinal has in
  mind here not just the usual sense of
  'colour' as pretext, but the particular
  legal meaning, 'an apparent or *prima facie*
  right' (*OED sb.* 12c) such as by 'colour of
  title' or 'colour of office'. *1H4* 1.3.108–9

has a sophisticated pun, 'Never did bare
and rotten policy / Colour her working
with such deadly wounds', while *2H4*
5.5.87–8 has the recognized puns on
'colour'/'collar' (noose) and 'die'/'dye'.
237 **meet** fitting
238 **were** would be (Abbott, 301)
239 **labour still** always endeavour
240 See 28–30 and 29n.
  haply rise perhaps rebel
241 **trivial argument** slight grounds
242 **mistrust** suspicion, distrust. Perhaps Rosalind's reply to Duke Fred-
  erick provides the aptest gloss: 'Yet
  your mistrust cannot make me a
  traitor' (*AYL* 1.3.56).
243 **by this** by this reasoning
244 **fain** glad

245 SD] *Oxf.* (*Walker*)

But, my Lord Cardinal, and you, my Lord of Suffolk,
Say as you think, and speak it from your souls:
Were't not all one an empty eagle were set
To guard the chicken from a hungry kite,
As place Duke Humphrey for the King's Protector?   250

QUEEN

So the poor chicken should be sure of death.

SUFFOLK

Madam, 'tis true; and were't not madness then
To make the fox surveyor of the fold,
Who being accused a crafty murderer,
His guilt should be but idly posted over   255
Because his purpose is not executed?
No – let him die in that he is a fox,
By nature proved an enemy to the flock,
Before his chaps be stained with crimson blood,
As Humphrey proved, by reasons, to my liege.   260
And do not stand on quillets how to slay him;

---

247 proverbial: 'To speak as one thinks' (Dent, S725). Cf. *1H6* 5.3.141.

248 **Were't ... one** wouldn't it be just the same as if
empty hungry. Cf. *TS* 4.1.190, 'My falcon now is sharp and passing empty'. In *3H6* 1.1.268–9 Henry sees York 'like an empty eagle / Tire on the flesh of me and of my son'.

249 **kite** normally a familiar scavenger for carrion over Elizabethan London (cf. 5.2.11), but 'When pressed by hunger [it] becomes more fearless; and instances have occurred in which a bird of this species has entered the farmyard and boldly carried off a chicken' (Harting, 44). Cf. 3.2.193.

253 'Give not the wolf (fox) the wether (sheep) to keep' (Dent, W602).
surveyor overseer (*OED* 1)

254–9 What might seem glaring sophistry in such tendentious analogy would in some measure be received otherwise by

a Renaissance audience, the educated members of which would be familiar with the rhetorical and logical procedures of drawing on commonplaces from fable and natural history to provide 'artistic proof', as it was called.

254–5 **Who ... His** For this use of the supplementary pronoun see Abbott, 249.

255 **His guilt** the verdict of guilty on him
posted over postponed (*OED* Post *v.*[1] 7)

256 because his intention to murder has not yet been carried out

257 Man by nature is sinful as the fox by nature is murderous. Both are 'guilty'. Suffolk by implication thus confounds the distinction between actual and potential murder, and actual and potential treason. Cf. *MM* 5.1.450–3.

260 **reasons** See LN.

261 **stand on** base arguments on (*OED v.* 74b)
quillets verbal niceties. Cf. *1H6* 2.4.17.

---

260 Humphrey] *(Humfrey)*; Humphrey's *Hanmer*   reasons] treasons *Hudson*

Be it by gins, by snares, by subtlety,
Sleeping or waking, 'tis no matter how,
So he be dead; for that is good deceit
Which mates him first that first intends deceit.   265

QUEEN

Thrice-noble Suffolk, 'tis resolutely spoke.

SUFFOLK

Not resolute, except so much were done;
For things are often spoke and seldom meant.
But that my heart accordeth with my tongue –
Seeing the deed is meritorious,   270
And to preserve my sovereign from his foe –
Say but the word, and I will be his priest.

CARDINAL

But I would have him dead, my Lord of Suffolk,
Ere you can take due orders for a priest.
Say you consent and censure well the deed,   275
And I'll provide his executioner;
I tender so the safety of my liege.

---

262 **gins** bird or animal traps of varying kinds from the handmade springe, or *snare*, to the steel device for larger creatures

264 **So** provided that

264–5 **for . . . deceit** Cf. 'To deceive the deceiver is no deceit' (Dent, D182). Scott singles out Suffolk's advice as 'thoroughly Machiavellian'. See *MM* 3.2.280–1.

265 **mates** checkmates; kills (*OED v.*[1] 1 and 2b)

266 **Thrice-noble** This superlative, popular with Shakespeare, Peele and others, is thought by Hart to derive from Spenser's 'thrice-happy' (1.x.51 etc.). See Hart, *1H6*, xxxiii–xxxvi. Cf., 3.2.157, *this thrice-famed duke.*

267 **except** unless (*OED prep.* 2a)

268 Cf. Tilley, S720, 'speak fair and think what you will'.

269 See Dent, H334, 'What the heart thinks the tongue speaks'.
that to show that

270 **meritorious** a deeply cynical remark, especially provocative for a post-Reformation audience, particularly in the link with *priest* (272). See LN.

272 **I . . . priest** proverbial: 'To be one's priest' (Dent, P587), i.e. to say the last rites over, to kill. Cf. Kyd, 'Who first lays hands on me, I'll be his priest' (*Tragedy*, 3.3.37).

274 **take due orders** take holy orders, be ordained (*OED Order sb.* 6b)

275 **censure well** approve of (see *OED Censure v.* 1, 2 and 3)

276 See 3.2.1–2n.

277 **tender so** am so much concerned for (*OED Tender v.*[2] 3a). Cf. *CE* 5.1.132.
safety For one man's *safety* is another's murder.

---

264 deceit] conceit *Delius, Oxf*

247

SUFFOLK

Here is my hand, the deed is worthy doing.

QUEEN

And so say I.

YORK   And I: and now we three have spoke it,

It skills not greatly who impugns our doom.   280

Enter a Post.

POST

Great lords, from Ireland am I come amain

To signify that rebels there are up

And put the Englishmen unto the sword.

Send succours, lords, and stop the rage betime,

Before the wound do grow uncurable;   285

For, being green, there is great hope of help.

CARDINAL

A breach that craves a quick expedient stop! –

What counsel give you in this weighty cause?

YORK

That Somerset be sent as regent thither.

---

278 **worthy** See LN.
279 **spoke** spoken (see Abbott, 343)
280 **skills not** doesn't matter (*OED v.*[1] 2b). Cf. *TS* 3.2.128.
   impugns our doom calls our judgement into question (*OED* Impugn *v.* 2)
281–3 Cf. Q: 'Madame I bring you newes from Ireland, / The wilde Onele my Lords, is vp in Armes, / With troupes of Irish Kernes that vncontrold, / Doth plant themselues within the English pale' (TLN 1125–6). For the echoes of Marlowe see Appendix 2. Owen O'Neill (1380–1456) for decades had intermittently attacked the English in Ireland, but in the course of the 1590s Hugh O'Neill, the Earl of Tyrone, adopting the forbidden title of 'the O'Neill', came to be Queen Elizabeth's most dangerous enemy in Ireland. Obviously, as Cairncross sur-

mises, this passage in Q had to be censored.
281 **amain** at full speed
282 **To signify** to inform, notify (King and Council) (*OED v.* 6). This meaning, slightly different in emphasis from 'announce' (*OED v.* 3), appears to be limited to political or diplomatic messengers. Cf. 3.2.368.
   up up in arms, risen in rebellion (*OED adv.*[2] 10)
284 **succours** help
   rage violent action (*OED sb.* 2)
   betime in good time
285–6 proverbial: 'a green wound is soon healed' (Dent, W927)
285 **uncurable** incurable (see Abbott, 442)
286 **green** fresh. Cf. *H5* 5.1.42.
287 **expedient** hasty, expeditious (*OED adj.* 1). See *KJ* 2.1.60.
289–91 bitterly sarcastic. See 1.3.103n.

'Tis meet that lucky ruler be employed; 290
Witness the fortune he hath had in France.

SOMERSET

If York, with all his far-fet policy,
Had been the regent there instead of me,
He never would have stayed in France so long.

YORK

No, not to lose it all, as thou hast done. 295
I rather would have lost my life betimes
Than bring a burden of dishonour home
By staying there so long till all were lost.
Show me one scar charactered on thy skin;
Men's flesh preserved so whole do seldom win. 300

QUEEN

Nay, then, this spark will prove a raging fire
If wind and fuel be brought to feed it with.
No more, good York. Sweet Somerset, be still.
Thy fortune, York, hadst thou been regent there,
Might happily have proved far worse than his. 305

YORK

What, worse than naught? Nay, then a shame take all!

SOMERSET

And in the number thee, that wishest shame.

CARDINAL

My Lord of York, try what your fortune is.

---

290 **meet** appropriate
292 **far-fet** far-fetched; devious: nowhere else in Shakespeare
296 **betimes** early
299 **charactered** inscribed (*OED ppl. a.*). Cf. 'character'd and engrav'd', *TGV* 2.7.4. For the stress on the second and last syllable see Cercignani, 41.
300 For the implied nominative plural 'men' taking 'do', see Abbott, 337.
301 **this . . . fire** proverbial: 'Of a little

spark a great fire' (Dent, S714). Cf. *3H6* 4.8.7–8.
303 **still** quiet
305 **happily** perhaps
306 **naught** nothing (*OED sb.* 1)
307 Editors quote the motto of the Order of the Garter, *Honi soit qui mal y pense* – 'Evil be to him that evil thinks' (Cf. *MW* 5.5.69). In Q, Somerset is blunt: 'he might haue lost as much as I' (TLN 1135).

Th'uncivil kerns of Ireland are in arms
And temper clay with blood of Englishmen.   310
To Ireland will you lead a band of men
Collected choicely, from each county some,
And try your hap against the Irishmen?

YORK

I will, my lord, so please his majesty.

SUFFOLK

Why, our authority is his consent,   315
And what we do establish he confirms.
Then, noble York, take thou this task in hand.

YORK

I am content. Provide me soldiers, lords,
Whiles I take order for mine own affairs.

SUFFOLK

A charge, Lord York, that I will see performed.   320
But now return we to the false Duke Humphrey.

CARDINAL

No more of him; for I will deal with him
That henceforth he shall trouble us no more.
And so break off, the day is almost spent.

---

309 **uncivil** uncivilized
kerns light-armed Irish foot soldiers (*OED sb.*[1] 1). Stanyhurst's contemporary account gives a more colourful picture: 'the kerne . . . is an ordinarie souldior, vsing for weapon his sword and target, and sometimes his peece, being commonlie so good markemen as they will come within a score of a great castell. Kerne signifieth (as noble men of deepe iudgement informed me) a shower of hell, because they are taken for no better than for rakehels, or the diuels blacke gard, by reason of the stinking sturre they kéepe, wheresoeuer they be' (68).
310 **temper** moisten (as with mortar etc.) (*OED v.* 10). Cf. 'Grind their bones to

powder small / And with this hateful liquor temper it' (*Tit* 5.2.199–200). 'To temper clay' appears in *KL* 1.4.304.
313 **hap** fortune
316 **establish** ratify (*OED v.* 1b)
319 **take order for** make arrangements (*OED* Order *sb.* 14). See *MM* 2.1.234.
321–5 See facsimile TLN 1158–61 for Q variant.
324 **break off** This appears to be an early imperative form of what survives in modern usage only in the past tense, i.e. 'stopped talking'. Perhaps we should read it as the more polite 'let us break off'? *LLL*, however, has a plain example of the former: 'Not one word more, my maids; break off, break off' (5.2.262).

[*aside*] Lord Suffolk, you and I must talk of that event.   325

YORK

My Lord of Suffolk, within fourteen days

At Bristol I expect my soldiers;

For there I'll ship them all for Ireland.

SUFFOLK

I'll see it truly done, my Lord of York.   *Exeunt* [*all but York*].

YORK

Now, York, or never, steel thy fearful thoughts,   330

And change misdoubt to resolution.

Be that thou hop'st to be, or what thou art

Resign to death; it is not worth th'enjoying.

Let pale-faced fear keep with the mean-born man

And find no harbour in a royal heart.   335

Faster than springtime showers comes thought on

  thought,

And not a thought but thinks on dignity.

My brain, more busy than the labouring spider,

Weaves tedious snares to trap mine enemies.

---

325 Most editors follow F and give this line to the Cardinal. The rhyme of 324–5 would support this (RP). Hattaway's addition of '*aside*', followed here, provides a precisely devious touch.
328 **Ireland** probably trisyllabic (see Cercignani, 356)
330 **Now . . . never** proverbial (Dent, N351)
  steel harden. Cf. *R2* 3.2.111.
  fearful apprehensive (*OED a.* 3)
331 **misdoubt** mistrust (*OED sb.*), but in context 'uncertainty' seems more appropriate: elsewhere in Shakespeare, mostly as a verb
  resolution For the stress on the first, third and fifth syllable, see Cercignani, 296.

333 **Resign to death** in fighting for 'that thou hop'st to be'
334 **pale-faced** Cf. *R2* 2.3.94.
  keep dwell, live (*OED v.* 37)
  mean-born low-born. The only other occurrence is Q *R3* 4.2.55.
336 **comes** For this common third person plural inflection see Abbott, 333.
337 **not . . . but** every thought without exception. See Abbott, 123.
  dignity high estate (of kingship)
339 **tedious** *OED* is not directly helpful and editors' 'intricate' is not convincing. *Tedious* here feels like a transposed adverb for 'wearily weaving' or weaving in the wearisome circumstances of night (the commonest association in Shakespeare). Thus the final meaning might be 'tirelessly weaves'.

---

325 SD] *Cam²* Lord Suffolk] *SP in Ard²*; QUEEN Lord Suffolk *TxC (Taylor)*   327 Bristol] (Bristow)   329 SD] *Cam subst.*; *Manet Yorke.* F   332 art] *F4*; art; F

Well, nobles, well; 'tis politicly done,   340
To send me packing with an host of men;
I fear me you but warm the starved snake
Who, cherished in your breasts, will sting your hearts.
'Twas men I lacked, and you will give them me;
I take it kindly, yet be well assured   345
You put sharp weapons in a madman's hands.
Whiles I in Ireland nurse a mighty band
I will stir up in England some black storm
Shall blow ten thousand souls to heaven or hell;
And this fell tempest shall not cease to rage   350
Until the golden circuit on my head,
Like to the glorious sun's transparent beams,
Do calm the fury of this mad-bred flaw.
And for a minister of my intent

341 **send me packing** summarily dismiss; get rid of (see *OED* Pack *v.*[1] 10 and Send *v.*[1] 1g). Cf. *1H4* 2.4.297.

342–3 The cautionary fable about the frozen snake which, when revived by the warmth of its rescuer's breast, then wakes to sting him, is included in Camerarius' Aesop and is cited by Cairncross here (cf. 53n., 55n., 75n., 77–8n.). The tale duly found its way into proverb collections: 'To nourish a viper (snake) in one's bosom' (Dent, V68). Cf. *R2* 3.2.131.

342 **starved** starvèd: perished with cold (*OED ppl. a.*). See *Tit* 3.1.251.

343 **sting** See 229n.

346 proverbial: 'Ill putting (put not) a naked sword in a madman's hand' (Tilley, P669).

347 **Whiles** while

348 **stir up** an expression which came to be particularly associated with revolt (see *OED v.* 13c). Cf. 'so stirring them up to rebellion' (*Homily*, 524). See *3H6* 4.8.12, and 377n. below.

350 **fell** destructive (*OED a.* and *adv.* 2)

351 **circuit** crown. Cf. *3H6* 1.2.30.

353 **mad-bred** The *storm, tempest* and

flaw (squall) of rebellion will be bred from the irrational and impulsive 'madness' of the lower orders. Only occurrence in Shakespeare; unrecorded by *OED*. Possibly a misreading of MS 'madde-brād' (RP)? Cf. *Tim* 5.1.174, 'mad-brain'd war'.

flaw sudden squall (*OED sb.*[2] 1). Cf. 'It chanced another time, Diagoras sailing upon the sea, that a great flawe of wind arose' (Hutchinson, 76).

354–8 Tudor historians associated the Yorkist faction with Jack Cade's rebellion. Holinshed puts it most plainly: 'Those that fauored the duke of Yorke, and wished the crowne vpon his head, for that (as they iudged) he had more right thereto than he that ware it, procured a commotion in Kent' (220). Hall goes so far as to suggest that the Yorkist instigators chose the county of Kent to draw attention away from themselves (see 219–20). Shakespeare here takes the final step of York's confession, albeit in soliloquy. Modern historians still debate the precise nature of York's involvement; see Harvey, 147–8.

354 **minister** agent (*OED sb.* 2). Cf. 5.2.34.

347 nurse] *Oxf;* nourish *F*   353 mad-bred] mad-brain'd *Rowe*

I have seduced a headstrong Kentishman,   355
John Cade of Ashford,
To make commotion, as full well he can,
Under the title of John Mortimer.
In Ireland have I seen this stubborn Cade
Oppose himself against a troop of kerns,   360
And fought so long till that his thighs with darts
Were almost like a sharp-quilled porpentine;
And in the end, being rescued, I have seen
Him caper upright like a wild Morisco,
Shaking the bloody darts as he his bells.   365
Full often, like a shag-haired crafty kern,
Hath he conversed with the enemy

355 **Kentishman** Cade's provenance remains problematic. *Brut* (517) and *An English Chronicle* (64) describe him as an Irishman, as does Holinshed (220) following *Polychronicon*. See 4.2.29n.

356 **Ashford** a mid-Kent town where rebels were reported to be assembling in 1450 and probably chose Cade as their leader (Griffiths, 610). For Bury St Edmunds as an alternative claim, see 3.2.240n. Dick the butcher comes from Ashford (see 4.3.1).

357 **commotion** Cf. Hall: 'it was thought necessary [by York's supporters] to cause some great commocion and rysyng of people to be made against the King' (219). Cf. 29n.

358 **John Mortimer** See 4.2.35, 126–36. Sir John Mortimer, attainted of treason and executed in 1424, was the cousin of Edmund Mortimer, whom Richard II declared heir presumptive to the crown (Hall, 128; Holinshed, 144). See 2.2.39n. Cf. *1H4* 1.3.144–6. See Appendix 2 for Q1/Q3 variants.

360 **kerns** See 309n.

361 **till that** until

darts arrows (*OED sb.* 1)

362 **porpentine** porcupine. See *Ham* 1.5.20.

364 **caper** dance spiritedly with great leaps

upright without reeling. Cf. *R3* 3.2.38–9.

Morisco morris dancer. Will Kemp was the leading comic performer of Lord Strange's Men, a company from which grew Pembroke's Men, who are referred to in the Q title-pages of *3H6*. Kemp was also the best-known morris dancer of his day. If, as has been suggested in the Introduction (pp. 104–5), Kemp played Cade, then this allusion appears to be designed to heighten the anticipation of an audience eager to see the celebrated entertainer. For Kemp and morris-dance capering see Wiles, *Clown*, 44–5. See also 4.10.56LN.

365 **he** the morris dancer

bells shaken by the dancer's movements

366 **shag-haired** having thick matted hair. Cf. *R2* 2.1.156, 'rug-headed kerns'.

367 **conversed** conversèd

358 Mortimer] *QF;* Mortimer, / (For he is like him every kinde of way) *Q3*

And, undiscovered, come to me again
And given me notice of their villainies.
This devil here shall be my substitute;   370
For that John Mortimer, which now is dead,
In face, in gait, in speech, he doth resemble.
By this I shall perceive the commons' mind,
How they affect the house and claim of York.
Say he be taken, racked and tortured,   375
I know no pain they can inflict upon him
Will make him say I moved him to those arms.
Say that he thrive, as 'tis great like he will,
Why then from Ireland come I with my strength
And reap the harvest which that rascal sowed.   380
For Humphrey being dead, as he shall be,
And Henry put apart, the next for me.   *Exit.*

374 **affect** favour; incline to. Cf. *KL*
1.1.1.
375 **taken** captured
  racked tortured on a frame by the
  stretching of joints
  tortured torturèd
377 **moved . . . arms** stirred him up to
  rebellion (see *OED v.* 8, citing 27 Eliz.
  c. 2.1 (1585), 'Seminarie Priestes . . .
  stire up and move Sedition, Rebellion
  and open Hostilitie'). Cf. 'all such . . .
  most ready to move rebellion' (*Homily*,
  517).
378 **great like** very likely
380 **reap . . . sowed** proverbial: 'One
  sows, another reaps' (Dent, S691). See
  Matthew, 25.26; Luke, 19.22; and
  John, 4.38.
  rascal low-born knave. *An English
  Chronicle* (64) calls Cade a 'ribaud',

which can mean a worthless low rascal
(*OED sb.* and *a.* 2) but also an irregular
retainer in French royal households
used in warfare (*OED sb.* and *a.* 1): a
meaning which probably derives from
the imputation, contained in the
proclamation for his arrest, that
Cade had served under Charles VII
(Holinshed, 226). Q's 'coystrill' is
accepted by Wells & Taylor. (Cf. *TN*
1.3.40.) Marina in *Per* (4.6.166, 190)
evokes the opprobrious meanings
attached to 'coystrill' as groom or
knave. 'Groom' is an aristocratic term
of abuse used several times in *2H6* and
it is specifically directed against Cade
at 4.2.115.
382 **apart** aside: a euphemism
  the . . . me I will seize the next opportunity to claim the throne.

380 rascal] coystrill *Q*

[3.2]   *Enter two or three* [Murderers] *running over the stage,*
from the murder of Duke Humphrey.

1 MURDERER
    Run to my Lord of Suffolk; let him know
    We have dispatched the Duke as he commanded.
2 MURDERER
    O that it were to do! What have we done?
    Didst ever hear a man so penitent?

Enter SUFFOLK.

3.2 location: a room in the Cardinal's house, Bury St Edmunds. The sub-titles of both F and Q indicate that the death of the good Duke Humphrey was presented as a leading feature of the play. Hall recounts that 'The duke the night after his emprisonement, was found dedde in his bed, and his body shewed to the lordes and commons, as though he had died of a palsey or empostome: but all indifferent persons well knewe, that he died of no natural death but of some violent force: some iudged hym to be strangled: some affirme, that a hote spitte was put in at his foundement: other write, that he was stiffeled or smoldered betwene twoo fetherbeddes' (209). See Holinshed, 211.

0.1–2 See t.n. for Q's version of the mur-der. Saunders argues that F 'stands as Shakespeare's intended staging' while Q 'is understood as the record of pop-ular adaptation' (25).

1–2 The Cardinal dies in 3.3 as if he, not Suffolk, was responsible for Gloucester's murder. But the inconsis-tency which Wilson implied in the murderer's claim here is difficult to see. The association of Suffolk and the Cardinal as the Duke's enemies is well testified, 'Of the which', Holinshed summarizes, 'diuerse writers affirme the marquesse of Suffolke, and the duke of Buckingham to be the cheefe, not vnprocured by the cardinall of Winchester, and the archbishop of Yorke' (230). Of the 'diuerse writers' it is Foxe who forcefully stresses 'the contention' between the Cardinal and the Duke, and explicitly identifies him along with Suffolk and Margaret as 'principal enemies and mortal foes' who instigated his murder (3.709–16). Q bears out the joint complicity (TLN 1120–1). Cairncross points out the association between Suffolk and the Cardinal in *2H6*. Earlier, at 3.1.325, 'Lord Suffolk, you and I must talk of that event', the Cardinal gives suffi-cient indication of the plot. He will supply the murderers, who are subse-quently given instructions by Suffolk. For Foxe on the Cardinal's death see 3.3 headnote.

3–4 The conscience of the relenting mur-derer, not in Q, became part of the stock repertoire of stage assassins. See Wiggins, 115–17.

3 **to do** yet to be done (so that we might not carry it out). See Abbott, 405.

3.2] *Capell*   0.1–2] *F subst.;* Then the Curtaines being drawne, Duke *Humphrey* is discouered in his bed, and two men lying on his brest and smothering him in his bed. And then enter the Duke of *Suffolke* to them. *Q*

1 MURDERER

> Here comes my lord.   5

SUFFOLK

> Now, sirs, have you dispatched this thing?

1 MURDERER

> Ay, my good lord, he's dead.

SUFFOLK

> Why, that's well said. Go, get you to my house,
> I will reward you for this venturous deed.
> The King and all the peers are here at hand.   10
> Have you laid fair the bed? Is all things well,
> According as I gave directions?

1 MURDERER

> 'Tis, my good lord.

SUFFOLK

> Away, be gone!   *Exeunt [Murderers].*

Sound trumpets. Enter the KING, *the* QUEEN, CARDINAL,
SOMERSET, *with attendants.*

KING

> Go, call our uncle to our presence straight;   15
> Say we intend to try his grace today
> If he be guilty, as 'tis published.

SUFFOLK

> I'll call him presently, my noble lord.   *Exit.*

---

9 **venturous** risky (*OED a.* 2)
11 **laid fair** tidied, straightened up
   Is all things For singular verb and
   plural noun see Abbott, 335.
14.1–2 *F's SD includes Suffolk, which
   must be an error as he has just been left
   on stage by the murderers and is
   shortly to leave, following the King's

command.
15 **straight** immediately
17 **If** whether
   published publishèd: proclaimed
   (*OED ppl. a.* 1). Cf. 'publish'd and
   proclaim'd' (*TS* 4.2.85).
18 **presently** at once

13] All things is hansome now my Lord. *Q*; 'Tis handsome, my good lord. *Ard²*   14] Then draw the
Curtaines againe and get you gone, And you shall haue your firme reward anon. *Q*; Then draw the curtains
close; away, begone. *Oxf*   14 SD *Murderers*] *Q subst.*   14.1–2 CARDINAL, *Q subst.*; *Cardinall, Suffolke, F*

KING

Lords, take your places; and, I pray you all,
Proceed no straiter 'gainst our uncle Gloucester   20
Than from true evidence, of good esteem,
He be approved in practice culpable.

QUEEN

God forbid any malice should prevail
That faultless may condemn a noble man!
Pray God he may acquit him of suspicion!   25

KING

I thank thee, Meg; these words content me much.

Enter SUFFOLK.

How now? Why look'st thou pale? Why tremblest
  thou?
Where is our uncle? What's the matter, Suffolk?

SUFFOLK

Dead in his bed, my lord; Gloucester is dead.

QUEEN

Marry, God forfend!   30

CARDINAL

God's secret judgement. I did dream tonight

---

20 **straiter** more strictly, more rigorously.
This form of the comparative occurs
only here in Shakespeare.

21 **good esteem** creditable worth

22 **approved in** proved guilty of. Cf. *Oth*
2.3.211.
practice a word with a range of meanings in the early modern period from
'practices / Pleasant' to 'foul practice'
(respectively, *Ham* 2.2.38–9, 5.2.317),
the latter dividing into the evil or
demonic (as at *2H6* 3.1.46 and *Oth*
1.3.102) and, as here, the political,
connoting conspiracy and plotting (cf.
1H6 4.1.7). See *OED* 6, 6b, 6c.

25 **acquit him** clear himself. See Abbott,
296, for reflexive verbs.

26 *Meg 'Nell' F*: cf. '*Elianor*' or '*Elinor*'
for Margaret in F and at 79, 100 and
120. An error, presumably in
Shakespeare's foul papers, which
would have been corrected in the
theatre prompt-book.

30 **forfend** forbid

31 **God's secret judgement** Hattaway
suggests the effectiveness of this as an
aside showing compunction. Much
better the reverse showing the irony of
such hypocrisy and the ultimate vindication in his own fate. The Cardinal's

26 Meg] *Capell; Nell F*

The Duke was dumb and could not speak a word.
The King swoons.

QUEEN

How fares my lord? Help, lords, the King is dead!

SOMERSET

Rear up his body; wring him by the nose.

QUEEN

Run, go, help, help! O, Henry, ope thine eyes! 35

SUFFOLK

He doth revive again; madam, be patient.

KING

O heavenly God!

QUEEN How fares my gracious lord?

SUFFOLK

Comfort, my sovereign! Gracious Henry, comfort!

KING

What, doth my Lord of Suffolk comfort me?
Came he right now to sing a raven's note, 40
Whose dismal tune bereft my vital powers;
And thinks he that the chirping of a wren,

---

words encapsulate Foxe's summary: 'In this cruel fact of these persons, who did so conspire and consent to the death of this noble man, and who thought thereby to work their own safety, the marvellous works of God's judgment appear herein to be noted.' In the margin here is found 'judgement of God upon those who persecuted the duke' (3.715).

tonight last night (Abbott, 190)

34 **Rear up** support; raise
wring . . . nose twist (and/or squeeze) the nose to restore circulation and thus revive the person, as in *VA* 475. Even if practically effective, neither word nor action can evade some ignominy?

35–7 **Henry . . . gracious lord?** At a moment of genuine emotional crisis, formal address is dropped and then restored. It would almost be atypically touching were it not for Margaret's later self-conscious usage for ulterior motives, 289. See Replogle, 183.

40 **raven's note** proverbially ominous (Dent, R33) and found throughout Shakespeare. The raven's fatal 'croak' (*Mac* 1.5.38–9) might well have come from the bittern, otherwise known as the 'night-raven' (*MA* 2.3.82) or 'night-crow' (*3H6* 5.6.45). See Harting, 101–2.

41 **dismal** fatal (*OED a.* 2)
bereft deprived me of
vital powers the fundamental inspiriting energy of life

32 SD] *F4 subst.; King sounds. F*

By crying comfort from a hollow breast,
Can chase away the first-conceived sound?
Hide not thy poison with such sugared words; 45
Lay not thy hands on me – forbear, I say!
Their touch affrights me as a serpent's sting.
Thou baleful messenger, out of my sight!
Upon thy eyeballs murderous tyranny
Sits in grim majesty to fright the world. 50
Look not upon me, for thine eyes are wounding.
Yet do not go away; come, basilisk,
And kill the innocent gazer with thy sight.
For in the shade of death I shall find joy,
In life but double death, now Gloucester's dead. 55

QUEEN

Why do you rate my Lord of Suffolk thus?
Although the Duke was enemy to him,
Yet he most Christian-like laments his death.
And for myself, foe as he was to me,

43 **hollow** a pun on 'deceitful' and the fact that the wren's song resonates loudly for such a small bird (see Harting, 142)

44 **chase away** as the wren was believed to chase away large marauding birds (Harting, 143). See *Mac* 4.2.9–10.
first-conceived conceivèd: first-perceived (*OED* Conceive *v.* 10). This meaning is rare in the *OED* and the hyphenated expression is found only here in Shakespeare. Hart cites Marlowe's *1 Tamburlaine*, 3.2.12 (Zenocrate's 'first-conceiv'd disdain').

45 **poison . . . sugared words** Cf. *R3* 3.1.13–14. Dent has 'poison under sugar' (P458.1) and 'sugared words' (SS27).

47 **serpent's sting** Cf. Hall: 'the serpent lurked vnder the grasse, & under sugered speache, was hide pestiferous poyson' (236). See 3.1.229n.

48 **baleful** deadly. Cf. 'Baleful news' (*3H6* 2.1.97).

52 **basilisk** the king of serpents in mythology (from Greek *basileus*, a king), supposedly having the power to kill with its glance. Also known as the cockatrice (see *R3* 4.1.54), and alleged to be hatched from a cock's egg by a serpent. One of the many myths perpetuated by Mandeville: 'An other yle is there northward where are many evill and fell women and they haue precious stones in their eies, & they haue suche kinde yᵗ if they beholde any man with wrath, they sley them of the beholding as the Basalysk doeth' (207). Browne provides a compendious review of the topic. See 324n.

54 **shade of death** proverbial: 'shadow of death' (Dent, SS5). Cf. *1H6* 5.4.89. Cf. Psalm 23.4.

56 **rate** berate, chide

45 sugared] *(sugred)*

Might liquid tears, or heart-offending groans,   60
Or blood-consuming sighs recall his life,
I would be blind with weeping, sick with groans,
Look pale as primrose with blood-drinking sighs,
And all to have the noble Duke alive.
What know I how the world may deem of me?   65
For it is known we were but hollow friends.
It may be judged I made the Duke away.
So shall my name with slander's tongue be wounded,
And princes' courts be filled with my reproach.
This get I by his death. Ay me, unhappy!   70
To be a queen, and crowned with infamy.

KING

Ah, woe is me for Gloucester, wretched man!

QUEEN

Be woe for me, more wretched than he is.
What, dost thou turn away and hide thy face?
I am no loathsome leper – look on me!   75
What? Art thou, like the adder, waxen deaf?
Be poisonous too and kill thy forlorn Queen.
Is all thy comfort shut in Gloucester's tomb?
Why then Queen Margaret was ne'er thy joy.

60–3 **tears . . . primrose** E. A.
Armstrong (80) notes the recurrent
image cluster of the primrose, liquid
tears, pearl or dew, and death.
Cairncross compares *Ham* 1.3.40–1.

60 **heart-offending** heart-wounding:
only here in Shakespeare

61 **blood-consuming** from the belief
that each sigh drew a drop of blood
from the heart. Cf. 'blood-sucking
sighs' (*3H6* 4.4.22). Only here in
Shakespeare.

63 **blood-drinking** See 61n. and *1H6*
2.4.108.

65 **deem** judge

69 **reproach** shame (*OED sb.* 2b)

72 **woe is me** I grieve

73 **woe** sorry

76 **like . . . deaf** proverbial (Dent, A32)
from Psalms, 58.4–5, 'like the deafe
adder that stoppeth his eare. Which
heareth not the voyce of the inchanter'
(Shaheen, 53). Many times in Greene
(Hart). Cf. *TC* 2.2.172.
waxen grown (*DED* wax *v*!)

77 **poisonous** the more customary
attribution, found throughout
Shakespeare, e.g. *3H6* 1.4.112. See
3.1.229n.

79 Queen] *Oxf;* Dame *F*   Margaret] *Rowe; Elianor F*

Erect his statue and worship it,   80
And make my image but an alehouse sign.
Was I for this nigh wrecked upon the sea
And twice by awkward wind from England's bank
Drove back again unto my native clime?
What boded this, but well-forewarning wind   85
Did seem to say, 'Seek not a scorpion's nest,
Nor set no footing on this unkind shore'?
What did I then, but cursed the gentle gusts
And he that loosed them forth their brazen caves
And bid them blow towards England's blessed shore   90
Or turn our stern upon a dreadful rock.
Yet Aeolus would not be a murderer,
But left that hateful office unto thee.
The pretty vaulting sea refused to drown me,

80 **statue** The trisyllabic pronunciation preserves the metre. Cf. *JC* 2.2.76.

81 **alehouse sign** The alehouse was the socially humblest institution beneath the tavern and the inn. In the course of Shakespeare's lifetime the traditional stake and bush put out when ale was available began to give way to painted signs in imitation of taverns and inns (see Clark, 67–8). The quality of such signs is indicated at 5.2.67 – 'an ale-house' paltry sign' – and *Tit* 4.2.98.

82–113 Cf. Margaret's extensive speech on military shipwreck, *3H6* 5.4.1–38.

83 **awkward** adverse (*OED a.* 3): only here with this meaning
bank coast (*OED sb.* 9). Cf. *1H4* 3.1.44.

84 **Drove** For past participle form see Abbott, 343.

85 **but** unless (Abbott, 120)
well-forewarning justly warning

86 **scorpion's nest** According to received wisdom, the scorpion's young when hatched in the nest immediately kill the mother. Second, the scorpion

was considered more dangerous to women than to men (see headnote, Cruden). Perhaps this antifeminist mythology is hinted at here?

88 **gentle** kindly, in *well-forewarning* and presumably, in view of what follows, 92–100, because for all their power they would not drown her

89 **he** Aeolus (see 92), granted dominion by Zeus over the winds
loosed them forth released them from. For prepositional use of 'forth', see Abbott, 156.
brazen caves Editors take *brazen* to mean 'strong' (*OED a.* 1b) and consider the possible derivation from Homer, Virgil or Ovid. See LN.

94 **pretty** clever, skilful (*OED a.* 1b); pleasing (*OED a.* 3b). As with *gentle* (88), the waves can be characterized as such because they did not drown the Queen.
vaulting the rapid rising and falling of overarching waves

80 statue] statua *Dyce*   82 wrecked] *(*wrack'd*)*   85 well-forewarning] *this edn;* well fore-warning *F*
wind] winds *Q*

Knowing that thou wouldst have me drowned on shore   95
With tears as salt as sea through thy unkindness.
The splitting rocks cowered in the sinking sands
And would not dash me with their ragged sides,
Because thy flinty heart, more hard than they,
Might in thy palace perish Margaret.   100
As far as I could ken thy chalky cliffs,
When from thy shore the tempest beat us back,
I stood upon the hatches in the storm,
And when the dusky sky began to rob
My earnest-gaping sight of thy land's view,   105
I took a costly jewel from my neck –
A heart it was, bound in with diamonds –
And threw it towards thy land. The sea received it,
And so I wished thy body might my heart;
And even with this I lost fair England's view,   110
And bid mine eyes be packing with my heart,
And called them blind and dusky spectacles
For losing ken of Albion's wished coast.
How often have I tempted Suffolk's tongue –
The agent of thy foul inconstancy –   115

96 **salt as sea** proverbial (Dent, S170.1)
97 **splitting** capable of splitting ships. Cf. *3H6* 5.4.10.
   sinking able to sink vessels. See *3H6* 5.4.30.
99 **Because** in order that, referring to the future (see Abbott, 117)
   flinty heart proverbial (Dent, H311)
100 **perish** For this transitive use see Abbott, 291.
101 **ken** descry (*OED v.*[1] 6)
   chalky cliffs found in Peele, *Tale*: 'these chalkie Cliffs of Albion' (l. 132)
103 **hatches** deck (*OED sb.*[1] 3); only later the covering for the hatchway. Cf. *R3* 1.4.13, 17.
104 **dusky sky** 'Dusky night' occurs in

Golding (15.35) as well as 'hatches' (11.538) (Hart).
105 **earnest-gaping** eagerly peering (Sanders): only here in Shakespeare
107 **bound in** enclosed (*OED v.*[1] 2b). Cf. *R2* 2.1.61, 63, and *LLL* 5.2.3.
111 **be packing** be gone. Cf. 3.1.341.
   heart the *jewel*
112 **spectacles** a means of seeing (*OED sb.* 5)
113 **Albion's** See 101n: 1.3.46 and n.
   wished wishèd; longed for. Cf. *TS*, 'wished haven' (5.1.128).
114–15 Such heavy irony subverts the romantic passion of the whole speech.
114 **tempted** enticed (*OED v.* 5)
115 **agent** as Henry's proxy

100 Margaret] *Rowe; Elianor F*

To sit and witch me, as Ascanius did
When he to madding Dido would unfold
His father's acts, commenced in burning Troy!
Am I not witched like her? Or thou not false like him?
Ay me, I can no more! Die, Margaret,   120
For Henry weeps that thou dost live so long!

Noise within. Enter WARWICK, [SALISBURY]
and many Commons.

WARWICK

It is reported, mighty sovereign,
That good Duke Humphrey traitorously is murdered
By Suffolk and the Cardinal Beaufort's means.
The commons, like an angry hive of bees   125
That want their leader, scatter up and down
And care not who they sting in his revenge.
Myself have calmed their spleenful mutiny,
Until they hear the order of his death.

KING

That he is dead, good Warwick, 'tis too true;   130
But how he died, God knows, not Henry.
Enter his chamber, view his breathless corpse,

116–18 See LN.
116 *witch bewitch
117 **madding** driven frantic by love: 'A favourite word with Peele, Kyd etc.' (Hart)
119 an alexandrine. For this feature of Shakespeare's versification, see Wright, 143–8.
   witched bewitched
120 **I . . . more!** I cannot continue (my strength fails me).
125 **hive of bees** a commonplace analogy for the commonweal deriving in large part from Virgil's *Fourth Georgic*, but found in many classical sources, and appearing in Whitney (200). The image is considerably developed in *H5*

1.2.187–204.
126 **want** lack
127 **his revenge** revenge for him
128 **spleenful mutiny** aggrieved revolt
129 **order** nature; circumstances
131 **God knows** Cf. 'God he knows, not I' (Dent, G189.1).
   Henry Cercignani (357–8) challenges Kökeritz's claim (292–3) that 'Hen[e]ry' is trisyllabic as 'not attested'.
132 **breathless** lifeless. *OED* (*a*. 1b) gives *KJ* 4.3.66 as the earliest occurrence; but though the word recurs in Shakespeare Hart points out its appearance in Greene and Peele, and in view of similar coinages in the latter considers it might derive from Peele.

116 witch] *Theobald;* watch *F*   120 Margaret] *Rowe; Elinor F*   121.1 SALISBURY] *Q*

And comment then upon his sudden death.

WARWICK

 That shall I do, my liege. Stay, Salisbury,

 With the rude multitude till I return.   135

  [*Exeunt severally Warwick, and Salisbury with the Commons.*]

KING

 O thou that judgest all things, stay my thoughts:

 My thoughts that labour to persuade my soul

 Some violent hands were laid on Humphrey's life.

 If my suspect be false, forgive me, God,

 For judgement only doth belong to thee.   140

 Fain would I go to chafe his paly lips

 With twenty thousand kisses, and to drain

 Upon his face an ocean of salt tears,

 To tell my love unto his dumb deaf trunk,

 And with my fingers feel his hand unfeeling; 145

 But all in vain are these mean obsequies.

 And to survey his dead and earthy image,

---

133 **comment then upon** 'To make comments or remarks . . . Often implying unfavourable remarks.' *OED v.* 4 gives *TGV* 2.1.40–1 as the earliest example: 'a Physician to comment on your malady'. This seems even stronger here as evidently, from the following dialogue, Henry fears the worst. Cf. *R3*'s 'fearful commenting' (4.3.51).

135 **rude multitude** ignorant and violent crowd (see *OED* Rude *a.* 1 and 5d). Cf. *Homily*, 'great multitudes of the rude and rascal commons' (515). This homily particularly associates 'ignorance' and the 'multitude' (see 520–1): similarly Bishop Jewel, 'the rash inconstant people and unlearned multitude . . . the rude multitude' (54). Cf. *LLL* 5.1.89.

136 **judgest all things** Genesis, 18.25, 'the judge of all the world'
 stay restrain

139 **suspect** suspicion. See Abbott, 451,

for the use of verbs as nouns.

140 Cairncross quotes Sternhold & Hopkins, Psalms, 3.8, 'Salvation onely doth belong / to thee O Lord aboue'.

141 **Fain** gladly
 chafe warm (*OED v.* 1). See *VA* 477.
 paly pale. Cf. *RJ* 4.1.100.

142 **drain** let fall (*OED v.* 2b): unique in this meaning in the *OED* and Shakespeare

143 **ocean . . . tears** proverbial (Dent, T82.2)

144 **trunk** This word could refer either to a headless body or to the whole corpse (*OED sb.* 2 and 3).

147 **earthy** With the separation of the soul at death, man's body is no more than the dust or earth of its creation and to which it is returned in the grave: 'As is the earthy, suche are they that are earthy' ('The Order for the Burial of the Dead', *Prayer Book*, 426, commenting on 1 Corinthians, 15.47). See 152n.

---

135 SD] *Ard² subst.; Exet Salbury. Q*

What were it but to make my sorrow greater?

Bed put forth. [Enter WARWICK.]

WARWICK
Come hither, gracious sovereign, view this body.
[*Draws the curtains, and shows Gloucester in his bed.*]
KING
That is to see how deep my grave is made,   150
For with his soul fled all my worldly solace;
For, seeing him, I see my life in death.
WARWICK
As surely as my soul intends to live
With that dread King that took our state upon Him
To free us from his Father's wrathful curse,   155
I do believe that violent hands were laid
Upon the life of this thrice-famed duke.
SUFFOLK
A dreadful oath, sworn with a solemn tongue!
What instance gives Lord Warwick for his vow?
WARWICK
See how the blood is settled in his face.   160

148 SD **Bed put forth** is accepted here, and Q's SD adopted at 149, to further the dramatic relationship between the verbal and the visual, as the audience's experience is made to parallel that of Henry and the others on stage, from *to survey* to *seeing him.* Warwick completes the picture at 160–76.
149 SD **curtains* Cf. Q: '*Suffolke* Then draw the Curtaines againe and get you gone, / And you shall haue your firme reward anon' (TLN 1197–8), at 3.2.14 above.
152 Cf. 'In the mideste of lyfe we bee in death' ('The Order for the Burial of the Dead', *Prayer Book*, 424).
154 **King** Christ

155 Editors cite Galatians, 3.13, 'Christ hath redeemed vs from the curse of the Lawe, when he was made a curse for us'; but the *curse* here is wider than the doctrinal divide between law and faith in St Paul's epistle, and refers to the general 'curse' of Genesis, 3.17.
157 **thrice-famed** famèd: very famous. See 3.1.266n.
158 **solemn tongue** Cf. *Tit* 5.3.81.
159 **instance** proof; evidence; fact. For the more specific meanings within scholastic logic see *OED sb.* 5 and 6, which are arguably at play in *TC* 5.2.153–5.
160 **settled** coagulated (*OED ppl. a.* 6). Cf. *RJ* 4.5.26.

148.1 *Enter* WARWICK] *this edn*   149 SD] *Q subst.*

Oft have I seen a timely-parted ghost
Of ashy semblance, meagre, pale and bloodless,
Being all descended to the labouring heart
Who, in the conflict that it holds with death,
Attracts the same for aidance 'gainst the enemy,   165
Which with the heart there cools and ne'er returneth
To blush and beautify the cheek again.
But see, his face is black and full of blood,
His eyeballs further out than when he lived,
Staring full ghastly like a strangled man;   170
His hair upreared, his nostrils stretched with
     struggling;
His hands abroad displayed, as one that grasped
And tugged for life and was by strength subdued.
Look, on the sheets his hair, you see, is sticking;
His well-proportioned beard made rough and rugged,   175
Like to the summer's corn by tempest lodged.
It cannot be but he was murdered here;
The least of all these signs were probable.

161 **timely-parted ghost** body of a dead
person who has died in a timely or natural manner (for 'ghost' as 'corpse', see
OED sb. 9). 'Untimely' death is found
several times in Shakespeare, but this
expression is unique.
162 **meagre** emaciated. Cf. *RJ*, 'Meagre
were his looks, / Sharp misery had
worn him to the bones' (5.1.40–1).
163 **Being** (the blood) having
  labouring throbbing
165 **aidance** assistance: the only instance
in Shakespeare's plays. See *VA* 330.
166 **Which** (the blood)
170 **full** an intensifier, 'very', yet combining adjectival and adverbial usage in
that the exposed fullness of the eyeballs creates the ghastly staring. Cf.
3H6 2.1.123, 'Who look'd full gently'.
171 **upreared** standing on end: only here

with this meaning
172 **abroad displayed** spread widely
apart (*OED* Abroad *adv.* 1c)
175 **well-proportioned** well-shaped:
only here in Shakespeare's plays. See
VA 290.
  rugged shaggy
176 **lodged** beaten flat (*OED v.* 5). See
R2 3.3.162 and *Mac* 4.1.55.
178 **probable** capable of giving proof
(*OED a.* 1)
178 SD *The actor of the dead
Gloucester, as described by Warwick,
could not sustain that expression for
long. From this point argument takes
over, and to continue to expose the
actor thus would divide and weaken
the attention of that part of an audience to whom he was visible. See
148.1n.

177 murdered] *(murdred)*

[*He closes the curtains.*]

SUFFOLK

    Why, Warwick, who should do the Duke to death?

    Myself and Beaufort had him in protection,   180

    And we, I hope, sir, are no murderers.

WARWICK

    But both of you were vowed Duke Humphrey's foes,

    And you, forsooth, had the good Duke to keep.

    'Tis like you would not feast him like a friend,

    And 'tis well seen he found an enemy.   185

QUEEN

    Then you, belike, suspect these noblemen

    As guilty of Duke Humphrey's timeless death?

WARWICK

    Who finds the heifer dead and bleeding fresh

    And sees fast by a butcher with an axe,

    But will suspect 'twas he that made the slaughter?   190

    Who finds the partridge in the puttock's nest

    But may imagine how the bird was dead,

    Although the kite soar with unbloodied beak?

    Even so suspicious is this tragedy.

QUEEN

    Are you the butcher, Suffolk? Where's your knife?   195

    Is Beaufort termed a kite? Where are his talons?

---

183 **keep** guard, protect

184 **'Tis like** it is likely

186 **belike** perhaps

187 **timeless** untimely. Cf. *1H6* 5.4.5.

188–90 duly to be realized on stage with Dick the butcher in Act 4. See 3.1.210–13n.

191 **puttock's** kite's. See 3.1.249n.

193 For the image association of 'kite', 'blood' and 'sheet' (174) see E. A. Armstrong, 11–17.

194 **tragedy** in the simple sense of lamentable death. Cf. *1H6* 1.4.77. As Shakespeare's tragic sense grew more complex, the less he used the word. See Rossiter, 'Tragedy'.

178 SD] *this edn*   179, 182 Duke] *F3; D. F*

[*The bed is withdrawn.*]

[*Exeunt Cardinal, Somerset and others.*]

SUFFOLK

I wear no knife to slaughter sleeping men,
But here's a vengeful sword, rusted with ease,
That shall be scoured in his rancorous heart
That slanders me with murder's crimson badge.   200
Say, if thou dar'st, proud Lord of Warwickshire,
That I am faulty in Duke Humphrey's death.

WARWICK

What dares not Warwick, if false Suffolk dare him?

QUEEN

He dares not calm his contumelious spirit,
Nor cease to be an arrogant controller,   205
Though Suffolk dare him twenty thousand times.

WARWICK

Madam, be still, with reverence may I say;
For every word you speak in his behalf
Is slander to your royal dignity.

196 *SDs Having accepted *Bed put forth*
  (148.1), apart from Turner &
  Williams, editors usually neglect to
  take it off. Editors mostly follow Capell
  by having the Cardinal and
  others exit at 202, which completely
  upstages the dramatic challenges
  exchanged by Suffolk and Warwick at
  201–3. Warwick's indirect accusations
  against Suffolk and the Cardinal
  culminate at 196 in response to the
  Queen's direct challenge of 195–6.
  This provides an appropriate opportunity to clear the stage of the bed and
  those not engaged in the following
  arguments, and is consistent with
  whatever feelings of guilt and rage the
  Cardinal may have.
198 **with ease** with lack of use
199 **scoured** scourèd: cleaned or polished

with the action of a ramrod cleaning a
gun barrel. Cf. 1.3.192 and *H5* 2.1.56.
200 **badge** insignia of allegiance. See
  5.1.201–3.
202 **faulty** guilty (*OED a.* 3a)
204 **contumelious** insolent (*OED a.* 1b).
  Cf. *1H6* 1.4.39.
205 **controller** Editors adopt *OED* 3,
  'censorious critic', a less than convincing entry given the variable, limited
  quotations it derives from. Perhaps the
  Queen is facetiously cutting Warwick
  down to size by addressing the noble
  lord as a household servant, a steward
  or comptroller? (See *OED* 1 and 2.)
  This interpretation agrees with Bate's
  gloss on *Tit* 2.2.60, 'saucy controller of
  my private steps'.
207 **still** silent

196 SD1] *this edn*   SD2] *this edn; usually placed by eds after 202, following Capell*   202 faulty]
guiltie *Q*

SUFFOLK

Blunt-witted lord, ignoble in demeanour!   210
If ever lady wronged her lord so much,
Thy mother took into her blameful bed
Some stern untutored churl, and noble stock
Was graft with crab-tree slip, whose fruit thou art,
And never of the Nevilles' noble race.   215

WARWICK

But that the guilt of murder bucklers thee,
And I should rob the deathsman of his fee,
Quitting thee thereby of ten thousand shames,
And that my sovereign's presence makes me mild,
I would, false murderous coward, on thy knee   220
Make thee beg pardon for thy passed speech,
And say it was thy mother that thou meant'st,
That thou thyself wast born in bastardy;
And after all this fearful homage done,
Give thee thy hire and send thy soul to hell,   225
Pernicious blood-sucker of sleeping men!

SUFFOLK

Thou shalt be waking while I shed thy blood,

---

210 **Blunt-witted** only here in Shakespeare
212 **blameful** guilty: an epithet transferred from *mother*
213 **stern untutored** bold ignorant. Cf. 'stern ungentle' (*Tit* 2.4.16).
   churl base peasant (*OED sb.* 5)
   stock the genealogical trunk of the family tree. See 2.2.57–8n.
214 **graft** grafted (Abbott, 342)
   crab-tree Cuttings were usually grafted onto crab-trees, not the other way round. The crab-tree, or wild apple-tree, was notedly crooked and gnarled, thus the ignominy of the slander. Cf. *Cor* 2.1.188.
   slip cutting, and a pun on sexual misdemeanour

216 **bucklers** shields. See *3H6* 3.3.99.
217 **deathsman** executioner. *OED*'s first entry is from Greene's *Menaphon*.
218 **Quitting** ridding: this form only here in Shakespeare
219 **makes me mild** restrains me from such provocation
221 **passed** passèd: uttered (*OED v.* 9). See *LLL* 1.1.19.
224 **fearful homage** timorous obeisance
225 **hire** payment (death). Cf. Dent, H474.1, 'To quit (give) one his hire', i.e. to kill him.
226 **Pernicious** destructive
   blood-sucker In Hall the Duke of York protests against 'the bludsuckers of the nobilitie' (226). See Holinshed, 230.

220 murdered] *(murd'rous)*

If from this presence thou dar'st go with me.

WARWICK

Away even now, or I will drag thee hence.
Unworthy though thou art, I'll cope with thee   230
And do some service to Duke Humphrey's ghost.

Exeunt [Suffolk and Warwick].

KING

What stronger breastplate than a heart untainted?
Thrice is he armed that hath his quarrel just,
And he but naked, though locked up in steel,
Whose conscience with injustice is corrupted.   235

A noise within. [The Commons cry, 'Down with Suffolk!']

QUEEN

What noise is this?

Enter SUFFOLK *and* WARWICK *with their weapons drawn.*

KING

Why, how now, lords? Your wrathful weapons drawn
Here in our presence? Dare you be so bold?
Why, what tumultuous clamour have we here?

SUFFOLK

The traitorous Warwick with the men of Bury   240

228 **presence** royal presence
230 **cope with** fight with and outmatch, or overcome (see *OED v.²* 2 and 3). Cf. *TC* 2.3.264.
232 **breastplate** Cf. Ephesians, 6.14, 'hauing on the brestplate of righteousnesse', and Wisdom, 5.18–20 (Shaheen, 54). Only here in Shakespeare.
233 **quarrel just** Cf. *R3* 1.2.136.
234 **locked . . . steel** buckled in armour

(see *OED* Buckle *v.* 2)
237–8 **weapons . . . presence** Such an action was a punishable offence. See *1H6* 1.3.46.
240 **men of Bury** In the post-rebellion hearings of 1453 it was alleged that a plot was hatched at Bury St Edmunds to overthrow the King and install the Duke of York; that Jack Cade was elected 'Captain' there before joining the assembly at

231 SD *Suffolk and Warwick*] Hanmer; Warwick puls him out. *Exet Warwicke and Suffolke*, and then all the Commons within cries, downe with *Suffolke*, downe with *Suffolke*. And then enter againe, the Duke of *Suffolke* and *Warwicke*, with their weapons drawne. *Q*   235 SD *The . . . Suffolk*] *Cam² subst.*
237] *Pope; F lines* Lords? / drawne, /

Set all upon me, mighty sovereign.

Enter SALISBURY [*from the Commons, again crying,*
'Down with Suffolk! Down with Suffolk!']

SALISBURY [*to the Commons, who try to enter*]
Sirs, stand apart; the King shall know your mind. –
Dread lord, the commons send you word by me,
Unless Lord Suffolk straight be done to death,
Or banished fair England's territories,   245
They will by violence tear him from your palace
And torture him with grievous lingering death.
They say, by him the good Duke Humphrey died;
They say, in him they fear your highness' death;
And mere instinct of love and loyalty,   250
Free from a stubborn opposite intent,
As being thought to contradict your liking,
Makes them thus forward in his banishment.
They say, in care of your most royal person,
That if your highness should intend to sleep   255
And charge that no man should disturb your rest,
In pain of your dislike, or pain of death,
Yet notwithstanding such a strait edict,
Were there a serpent seen, with forked tongue,
That slyly glided towards your majesty,   260

Blackheath; that letters were sent from
Bury inciting the men of Kent to rise
(Harvey, 116–18). See 3.1.356n.
244 **straight** immediately
245 **banished** banishèd
250 **mere** unalloyed
   instinct accented on the second syllable (Cercignani, 37)
251 **opposite** antagonistic (*OED a.* 4)
252 which might be thought opposed to
   your wishes
253 **forward in** zealous for (*OED adj.*

6c). Cf. *Tit* 1.1.56.
256 **charge** order (*OED v.* 14)
257 **In pain of** on penalty of (see Abbott,
   160; *OED* Pain *sb.* 1b)
258 **strait** strict
   edict accent on second syllable
   (Cercignani, 38). See Abbott, 490, for
   Ben Jonson on accentuation.
259–60 **serpent . . . majesty** See *Ham*
   1.5.39–40.
259 **forked** forkèd

241.1–2 *from . . .* Suffolk] Q *subst.*   242 SD] *Capell subst.*   247 lingering] *(*lingring*)*

It were but necessary you were waked,
Lest, being suffered in that harmful slumber,
The mortal worm might make the sleep eternal.
And therefore do they cry, though you forbid,
That they will guard you, whe'er you will or no,   265
From such fell serpents as false Suffolk is,
With whose envenomed and fatal sting
Your loving uncle, twenty times his worth,
They say is shamefully bereft of life.

COMMONS (*within*)

An answer from the King, my Lord of Salisbury!   270

SUFFOLK

'Tis like the commons, rude unpolished hinds,
Could send such message to their sovereign.
But you, my lord, were glad to be employed
To show how quaint an orator you are.
But all the honour Salisbury hath won   275
Is that he was the lord ambassador
Sent from a sort of tinkers to the King.

COMMONS [*within*]

An answer from the King or we will all break in!

---

262 **suffered** allowed to remain
  harmful another transferred epithet;
  cf. *blameful*, 212.
263 **mortal worm** deadly snake
265 **whe'er** whether
266 **fell** deadly poisonous (*OED a.* 2)
267 **With** by
  envenomed envenomèd
  sting See 3.1.229n.
269 **bereft** deprived
271 **like** likely. For adverbial use of adjectives see Abbott, 23. Suffolk implies
  Salisbury's duplicity.
  rude See 135n.
  unpolished unrefined, inelegant:
  Suffolk's aristocratic superciliousness
  again

hinds rural labourers. Cf. 4.2.113 and
  4.4.32.
274 **quaint** clever and cunning (combining *OED adj.* 1 and 1b), as in *1H6*
  4.1.102–3, 'with forged quaint conceit
  / To set a gloss upon his bold intent'
277 **tinkers** itinerant repairers of kettles
  and the like, infamous for swearing,
  thus suitably *unpolished* for Suffolk's
  opprobrium. In the course of the sixteenth century the increasing number
  of vagrants (ex-soldiers, masterless
  men) became a source of apprehension
  for law-abiding communities. Tinkers
  became loosely associated with these
  (*OED sb.* 1 and 1b). See Beier.

265 whe'er] *Oxf;* where *F;* whe'r *F4*   278 SP] *not in F;* The Commons cries, an answer from the
King, my Lord of *Salsbury. Q*

KING

    Go, Salisbury, and tell them all from me

    I thank them for their tender loving care;   280

    And had I not been cited so by them,

    Yet did I purpose as they do entreat.

    For sure, my thoughts do hourly prophesy

    Mischance unto my state by Suffolk's means.

    And therefore by His majesty I swear,   285

    Whose far unworthy deputy I am,

    He shall not breathe infection in this air

    But three days longer, on the pain of death.   [*Exit Salisbury.*]

QUEEN

    O Henry, let me plead for gentle Suffolk!

KING

    Ungentle Queen, to call him gentle Suffolk!   290

    No more, I say; if thou dost plead for him

    Thou wilt but add increase unto my wrath.

    Had I but said, I would have kept my word;

    But when I swear, it is irrevocable.

    If after three days' space thou here be'st found   295

    On any ground that I am ruler of,

    The world shall not be ransom for thy life.

    Come, Warwick, come; good Warwick, go with me;

281 **cited** aphetic form of 'incited': urged

284 **Mischance** disaster, calamity (*OED sb.* 1)

285 **His** God's

286 **far** very (Abbott, 40)
    deputy a post-Henrician stress on the king as God's vicegerent which often drew on Proverbs, 8.15, and Romans, 13, thus to surpass the Pope as Christ's vicar. See LN.

287–8 **He . . . But** he shall contaminate the air of England only

289 **gentle** noble

290 **Ungentle** discourteous (*OED a.* 2).

Perhaps Henry's bitter play on words and uncharacteristic decisiveness here derive from the recognition found in Hall: 'kyng Henry perceiued, that the commons wer thus stomacked and bent, against the Quenes dearlynge' (219).

294 **irrevocable** Cf. *Jack Straw*, 440–1, 'And when a King doth set downe his decree, / His sentence should be irreuocable' (Cairncross).

295 **be'st** For indicative used subjunctively, see Abbott, 298.

286 far unworthy] *(*farre-vnworthie*)*   288 SD] *Q subst.*

I have great matters to impart to thee.

       Exeunt [all but Queen and Suffolk].

QUEEN

Mischance and sorrow go along with you!   300

Heart's discontent and sour affliction

Be playfellows to keep you company!

There's two of you, the devil make a third,

And threefold vengeance tend upon your steps.

SUFFOLK

Cease, gentle Queen, these execrations,   305

And let thy Suffolk take his heavy leave.

QUEEN

Fie, coward woman and soft-hearted wretch!

Hast thou not spirit to curse thine enemies?

SUFFOLK

A plague upon them! Wherefore should I curse them?

Could curses kill, as doth the mandrake's groan, 310

I would invent as bitter searching terms,

As curst, as harsh and horrible to hear,

Delivered strongly through my fixed teeth,

With full as many signs of deadly hate,

---

299 SD Does absence of a *Flourish* indicate Henry's loss of authority, or, like
the omission of removing or curtain-
ing the bed, an oversight?

303 proverbial: 'There cannot lightly come
a worse except the devil come himself'
(Dent, W910). See *MV* 3.1.78.

306 **heavy** sorrowful (*OED a.* 27). Cf.
3H6 2.6.42.

310 **mandrake's groan** 'The root of the
mandragora often divides itself into
two, and presents a rude appearance of a
man . . . Some mandrakes cannot be
pulled from the earth without producing fatal effects, so a cord used to be
fixed to the root, and round a dog's

neck, and the dog being chased drew out
the mandrake and died. Another superstition is that when the mandrake is
uprooted it utters a scream, in explanation of which Thomas Newton, in his
Herball to the Bible, says, "It is supposed
to be a creature having life, engendered
under the earth of the seed of some
dead person put to death for murder"'
(Brewer, 802). Cf. *RJ* 4.3.47–8.

311 **searching** probing; piercing (in
examining a wound). See *OED* Search
v. 8. Cf. *AYL* 2.4.44.

313 **fixed** fixèd: presumably 'clenched'
(Hattaway) or 'gritted' (Sanders). In
this sense only here in Shakespeare.

299 SD] *Cam; Exit. F* 307 soft-hearted] *(*soft harted*)* 308 enemies] *Q;* enemy *F* 310 Could]
Q; Would *F*

As lean-faced Envy in her loathsome cave.   315
My tongue should stumble in mine earnest words,
Mine eyes should sparkle like the beaten flint,
My hair be fixed on end, as one distract;
Ay, every joint should seem to curse and ban.
And even now my burdened heart would break   320
Should I not curse them. Poison be their drink!
Gall, worse than gall, the daintiest that they taste!
Their sweetest shade a grove of cypress trees;
Their chiefest prospect murdering basilisks;
Their softest touch as smart as lizards' stings;   325

315 **lean-faced Envy** As Hart points out, the linking of *envy* and *cave* points to Ovid's *Metamorphoses*. Minerva (Pallas) approaches, 'She goes me straight to Envies house, a foule and irksome cave, / Replete with blacke and lothly filth and stinking like a grave . . . There saw she Envie sit within fast gnawing on the flesh / Of snakes and Todes . . . Hir lippes were pale, hir cheekes were wan, and all her face was swart: / Hir bodie leane as any Rake' (2.949–67). 'Pale' envy reappears in a play deeply influenced by Ovid: see *Tit* 1.1.153.

316 **stumble** falter (*OED v.* 2b). Cf. *LLL* 2.1.239.
    earnest intense (*OED a.* 1)

318 **distract** distracted, mad (Abbott, 342)

319 **curse and ban** Cf. Bishop Latimer, 'They will curse and ban . . . even into the deep pit of hell' (*Remains*, 302).
    ban invoke damnation on (*OED v.* 2)

322 **Gall** bile
    daintiest choicest (*OED* Dainty *a.* 3). Cf. *R2* 1.3.68.

323 **cypress trees** The 'funereal cypresses' of Virgil (*Aeneid*, 6.216) and Horace (*Epodes*, 5.18) bequeathed a commonplace to Renaissance verse and customs. Cypresses were planted in graveyards and 'Cypresse garlands are of great account at funeralls amongst the gentiller sort' (William Coles, *The Art of Simpling* (1656), cited Brewer, 323).

Hart quotes Peele, *The Battle of Alcazar* (1594), 'deadly yew and dismal cypress tree'. Cf. *TN* 2.4.52.

324 **prospect** sight, view
    basilisks Suffolk's curse works through the categories of taste, sight, touch and hearing, drawing on the properties of nature, as it was understood, which would mean that *basilisks* indicates the fabulous beast (see 52n.). However, the association between *prospect* and *basilisks* in Suffolk's language suggests the large cannon named after the creature (cf. *1H4* 2.3.54): consider, 'Before the eye and prospect of your town . . . The cannons have their bowels full of wrath' (*KJ* 2.1.208–10). That is, Suffolk's curse also possibly evokes his besieged enemies staring into the mouth of a cannon. The Queen's reply immediately seizes on this implication to warn her lover (331–2).

325 **smart** painful, sharp (*OED a.* 1)
    lizards' stings John of Trevisa's late fourteenth-century translation of Bartholomeus further transmitted classical and medieval encyclopaedists into the printed book of the Renaissance: 'Plinius sei*th* *th*at *th*e lusard liue*th* most by dewe and *th*ough he be a fayr beste and faire ypented, *y*it he is right venemous' (1244). Snakes and lizards were often confused. See *3H6* 2.2.138, and 3.1.229n. above.

324 murdering] (murd'ring)

Their music frightful as the serpent's hiss,
And boding screech-owls make the consort full!
All the foul terrors in dark-seated hell –

QUEEN

Enough, sweet Suffolk; thou torment'st thyself,
And these dread curses, like the sun 'gainst glass,   330
Or like an overcharged gun, recoil
And turns the force of them upon thyself.

SUFFOLK

You bade me ban, and will you bid me leave?
Now, by the ground that I am banished from,
Well could I curse away a winter's night   335
Though standing naked on a mountain top,
Where biting cold would never let grass grow,
And think it but a minute spent in sport.

QUEEN

O, let me entreat thee cease. Give me thy hand,
That I may dew it with my mournful tears;   340
[*Kisses his hand.*]

---

326 **serpent's hiss** Cf. Bartholomeus:
'*th*e serpent . . . hisse or he byte and
slee*th* alle *th*at he byte*th*' (1245–6; see
325n. above). Hart quotes from Peele's
Alcazar again (see 323n.). 'Hiss' as a
noun occurs only here in Shakespeare.
327 **screech-owls** Horace juxtaposes
'funereal cypresses' and 'nocturnal
screech-owl' (*Epodes*, 5.18, 20). See
323n. and 1.4.18–19n.
    consort group of musicians. Cf. *RJ*
3.1.46.
328 **dark-seated** situated in darkness:
only here in Shakespeare. Cf. 'Some
dark deep desert seated from the way'
(*Luc* 1144). See *OED* Seated *ppl. a.* 2.
330 **dread curses** Heavily ironic given that
Queen Margaret's curses on Richard
will be probably the most protracted in
Shakespeare: see *R3* 1.3.194–232.
    sun 'gainst glass the sun reflected,

dazzlingly, in a mirror. Cf. *Cym*
1.2.31–3.
331 **overcharged** overchargèd: over-
loaded (cf. *Mac* 1.2.37)
333 **leave** stop, leave off
335–7 **winter's . . . grow** Cf. *WT*
3.2.210–13.
338 **sport** a diversion (*OED sb.* 2a). Cf.
AYL 1.2.28.
339–56 Bate relates this passage in general
terms to the classical and medieval tradition of lamenting women (*Ovid*, 66–7).
Cairncross specifically compares the
detail of Ovid's *Tristia*, 1.3. Perhaps the
irony is of equal importance here. Ovid
evokes his wife's distress at his exile by
Caesar, while Margaret, the wife of the
King, bemoans her exiled lover.
340 **dew . . . tears** proverbial (Dent,
DD13). Hart compares Kyd's *Spanish
Tragedy* and Marlowe's *1 Tamburlaine*.

340 SD] *Cam²*

Nor let the rain of heaven wet this place
To wash away my woeful monuments.
O, could this kiss be printed in thy hand,
That thou mightst think upon these by the seal,
Through whom a thousand sighs are breathed for thee.   345
So, get thee gone that I may know my grief;
'Tis but surmised whiles thou art standing by,
As one that surfeits thinking on a want.
I will repeal thee or, be well assured,
Adventure to be banished myself.   350
And banished I am, if but from thee.
Go; speak not to me; even now be gone!
O, go not yet. Even thus, two friends condemned
Embrace, and kiss, and take ten thousand leaves,
Loather a hundred times to part than die.   355
Yet now farewell, and farewell life with thee.

SUFFOLK

Thus is poor Suffolk ten times banished,
Once by the King, and three times thrice by thee.
'Tis not the land I care for, wert thou thence:
A wilderness is populous enough,   360
So Suffolk had thy heavenly company.
For where thou art, there is the world itself,
With every several pleasure in the world;

---

342 **woeful monuments** tears as memorials of grief. Cf. *Luc* 797–8.
344 **these . . . seal** these lips by the sealed imprint
346 **know** confront; fully realise
348 as one that surfeits in your presence now while thinking on your future absence
349 **repeal** to recall from exile (*OED v.*[1] 3b)
350 **Adventure** dare, venture, risk (*OED v.* 1–5). Cf. *R3* 1.3.115.

350–7 **banished** banishèd
350–1 **banished . . . thee** Cf. *RJ* 3.3.40–50; 'banish'd from her / Is self from self' (*TGV* 2.1.172–3).
358 **three times thrice** proverbial (Dent, TT11); several times in Shakespeare
361 **So** on condition that. For 'so' used with the future and subjunctive, see Abbott, 133.
363 **several** separate (*OED a.* 1)

---

359 wert] *(wer't)*

And where thou art not, desolation.
I can no more. Live thou to joy thy life,   365
Myself no joy in naught but that thou liv'st.

Enter VAUX.

QUEEN

Whither goes Vaux so fast? What news, I prithee?

VAUX

To signify unto his majesty
That Cardinal Beaufort is at point of death;
For suddenly a grievous sickness took him,   370
That makes him gasp, and stare, and catch the air,
Blaspheming God and cursing men on earth.
Sometime he talks as if Duke Humphrey's ghost
Were by his side; sometime he calls the King
And whispers to his pillow, as to him,   375
The secrets of his overcharged soul.
And I am sent to tell his majesty
That even now he cries aloud for him.

QUEEN

Go, tell this heavy message to the King. –   *Exit* [*Vaux*].

---

365 **I . . . more.** See 120n.
366 **no . . . naught** The double negative gains an emotional intensity which annuls any sense of contradiction (see Abbott, 406).

joy enjoy (Abbott, 460)
366.1 VAUX Sir William Vaux (Q's '*Vawse*' indicates pronunciation), see List of Roles. Attainted by Edward IV's first parliament in 1461 and his estates confiscated, he probably fled abroad, but returned from Normandy with Margaret in 1471. See John Warkworth's *Chronicle of the First Thirteen Years of the Reign of King Edward the Fourth* (1839).
368 **signify unto** announce to (*OED v.* 3b)

371 Saunders (see 3.2 headnote) stresses the irony of parallelism with Gloucester's death in verbal and stage image. Cf. 170–3.
372 **Blaspheming . . . cursing** Cf. 'By his own interdiction stands accurs'd / And does blaspheme his breed' (*Mac* 4.3.107–8).
375–6 Cf. 'infected minds / To their deaf pillows will discharge their secrets' (*Mac* 5.1.72–3).
375 **as** as if (he were whispering). For the implied subjunctive see Abbott, 107.
376 **overcharged** overchargèd: overburdened (with guilt). Cf. *3H6* 2.5.78.
379 **heavy** grievous, sorrowful (*OED a.* 25). Cf. 'heavy news', *1H4* 1.1.37.

366 no] to *Singer*   373 Sometime] Sometimes *Q*   379 SD *Vaux*] *Q* (*Vawse*)

Ay me! What is this world? What news are these?   380
But wherefore grieve I at an hour's poor loss,
Omitting Suffolk's exile, my soul's treasure?
Why only, Suffolk, mourn I not for thee
And with the southern clouds contend in tears,
Theirs for the earth's increase, mine for my sorrow's?   385
Now get thee hence; the King, thou knowst, is coming.
If thou be found by me thou art but dead.

SUFFOLK

If I depart from thee I cannot live,
And in thy sight to die, what were it else
But like a pleasant slumber in thy lap?   390
Here could I breathe my soul into the air,
As mild and gentle as the cradle-babe
Dying with mother's dug between its lips;
Where, from thy sight, I should be raging mad
And cry out for thee to close up mine eyes,   395
To have thee with thy lips to stop my mouth;
So shouldst thou either turn my flying soul,
Or I should breathe it so into thy body,
And then it lived in sweet Elysium.

---

380 **What . . . world?** proverbial (Dent, W889.1, 'What a world is this')
381 **hour's poor loss** the otherwise natural span of life left to the Cardinal
382 **Omitting** disregarding (*OED v.* 2c)
384 **southern clouds** Cf. Bartholomeus: '*th*is sou*th*erne wynde . . . bryng*ith* for*th* moche reyne' (575). A phenomenon touched on by Ovid, 1.313–20, and Spenser, 3.iv.13, perhaps finding most expressive comment in Milton's *Paradise Lost*, 11.738–45. For the place of this in early modern cosmology, see Svendson, 96–7.
385 **earth's increase** Cf. Psalms, 67.6, 'earth bring foorth her increase', and several other places in the Old Testament. See *Tem* 4.1.110.

387 **by me** at my side
   but dead as good as dead
388–402 Again, Cairncross demonstrates how this speech derives from Ovid's *Tristia*, 3.3, particularly 43–4 and 61–2. See 339–56n. above.
391 Not just a periphrasis for 'death', but the commonplace separation of soul from body through the lips (unless the dying person was wounded). Middleton's *Women Beware Women* gives a very plain example: 'My soul stands ready at my lips' (5.2.194).
393 **dug** nipple
394 **Where** whereas
   from out from
397 **turn** return; restore
399 **lived** would live (Abbott, 361)

385 sorrow's] *(sorrowes)*   393 its] *F4;* it's *F;* his *Q*

To die by thee were but to die in jest;   400
From thee to die were torture more than death.
O let me stay, befall what may befall!

QUEEN

Though parting be a fretful corrosive
It is applied to a deathful wound.
To France, sweet Suffolk! Let me hear from thee;   405
For wheresoe'er thou art in this world's globe,
I'll have an Iris that shall find thee out.
Away!

SUFFOLK

    I go.

QUEEN   And take my heart with thee.   [*She kisses him.*]

SUFFOLK

A jewel locked into the woefullest cask
That ever did contain a thing of worth.   410

Elysium In Homer a paradisal land of immortal heroes on the western seaboard, whereas in Hesiod and Pindar it becomes the Islands of the Blessed. Alternatively, in Virgil Elysium is part of the lower world of Hades where reside the shades of the blessed. Cf. *TGV* 2.7.38.

400 but . . . jest merely to counterfeit a death. Cf. *3H6* 2.3.28, 'As if the tragedy / Were played in jest by counterfeiting actors'. RP suggests Ralegh's line 'Only we die in earnest, that's no jest' ('On the Life of Man', 10).

401 From absent from (see Abbott, 158)
    were would be

402 befall . . . befall proverbial: 'Come (Hap, Befall) what come (hap, befall) may' (Dent, C529). Cf. *LLL* 5.2.870 and *Tit* 5.1.57.

403 an apparent alexandrine in F which is made into a pentameter by eliding the unstressed middle syllable of *corrosive* (Abbott, 492, 497; Cercignani, 39)
    fretful irritating, corrosive (see *OED*

a. 1a, and Fret *v.*[1] 3 and 6)
    corrosive caustic medication, or plaster (*OED sb.* 2b): used by Shakespeare only here and in *1H6* 3.3.3. The variant 'corsive' indicates pronunciation. See *OED* (Corrosive *a.* and *sb.*).

404 applied appli'èd: in the medical sense (*OED v.* 3 *trans.*), to apply a plaster or unguent
    deathful mortal: only here in Shakespeare

407 Iris In Homer's *Iliad* Iris is the messenger of the gods, especially of Zeus and Hera. In her swiftness she was made a personification of the rainbow, though sometimes the rainbow is depicted as her path to earth. Iris plays a considerable part in the wedding masque of *Tem* (4.1.60–138).

409–12 a speech as coda in reprise of Margaret's language at 94–113, in which are found *splitting rocks* (97), *jewel* (106), *heart* (107)

409 cask casket

---

403 Though] *Ard²*; Away; Though *F*   408 Away!] *Ard²: not in F* SD] *Q*   409 woefullest] *(wofulst)*

Even as a splitted bark, so sunder we:
This way fall I to death.   *Exit [by one door].*
QUEEN   This way for me. *Exit [by another].*

[**3.3**]   *Enter the* KING, SALISBURY *and* WARWICK, *to the*
        CARDINAL *in bed[, raving and staring as if he were mad].*

KING

How fares my lord? Speak, Beaufort, to thy sovereign.

CARDINAL

If thou be'st Death I'll give thee England's treasure,
Enough to purchase such another island,
So thou wilt let me live and feel no pain.

KING

Ah, what a sign it is of evil life   5
Where death's approach is seen so terrible!

WARWICK

Beaufort, it is thy sovereign speaks to thee.

---

4 11 **splitted bark** vessel split in two
   so sunder we The literal and figurative meanings combine to signify 'we
   are torn apart'.
3.3 location: the bedchamber of the
   Cardinal's house. As we have seen
   (3.2.31n.), it was Foxe who directly
   accused the Cardinal of complicity in
   Gloucester's murder and saw his
   death, although a year later, as God's
   judgement: 'The next year following,
   it followed also that the cardinal, who
   was the principal artificer and ringleader of all this mischief, was suffered
   of God no longer to live' (3.716). For
   an alternative minor chronicle account
   of the Cardinal dying 'with the same
   business-like dignity in which for so
   long he had lived and ruled', see

McFarlane, and Harriss, *Cardinal*,
376–98. Harriss goes into some detail
on the Cardinal's repeated amendments to the codicils of his will: these
indicate a mental state quite different
from Shakespeare's portrayal of a
guilt-wracked villain, which subsequently inspired many paintings (see
Fig. 9 and Bate, *Constitutions*, 45–58).
2–4 For all his innovation, Shakespeare
   seems here to take his cue from Hall:
   'Fye, will not death be hyered, nor will
   money do nothyng?' (210).
2 **England's treasure** This implies ille-
   gal appropriation. For the Cardinal's
   wealth see 1.1.172–4n.
4 **So** provided that. For 'so' used with
   the future and subjunctive, see Abbott,
   133.

---

4 12 SDs] *Q subst.*   3.3.0.1–2] *F subst.*; Enter King and *Salsbury*, and then the Curtaines be drawne,
and the Cardinall is discouered in his bed, rauing and staring as if he were madde. *Q*

CARDINAL

    Bring me unto my trial when you will.

    Died he not in his bed? Where should he die?

    Can I make men live whe'er they will or no?   10

    O, torture me no more! I will confess.

    Alive again? Then show me where he is.

    I'll give a thousand pound to look upon him.

    He hath no eyes, the dust hath blinded them.

    Comb down his hair; look, look, it stands upright   15

    Like lime twigs set to catch my winged soul!

    Give me some drink, and bid the apothecary

    Bring the strong poison that I bought of him.

KING [*Kneels.*]

    O Thou eternal mover of the heavens,

    Look with a gentle eye upon this wretch.   20

    O beat away the busy meddling fiend

    That lays strong siege unto this wretch's soul,

    And from his bosom purge this black despair.

WARWICK

    See how the pangs of death do make him grin.

---

8 **trial** once more a reference to legal process; see Berry and 2.1.101n.

9 **he** Gloucester
  Where . . . die? Where else would you expect him to die?

10 **whe'er** whether

13 **thousand pound** proverbial hyperbole (Dent, T248.1)

14 **dust** Cairncross has an extensive note from Vaughan on 'dust-beds' (no entry in *OED*), apparently made up with very fine chopped straw which if used to smother Gloucester, as Hall suggests, might well have left this *dust*. Hattaway suggests the biblical dust-earth to which all must return at death.

15 **hair . . . upright** Cf. 3.2.171 and 3.2.371n.

16 **lime twigs** See 1.3.89n. and cf. 'O limed soul . . . struggling to be free' (*Ham* 3.3.68).

  winged wingèd

17 **apothecary** The apothecary made and 'stored' drugs and is thus the historical predecessor of the pharmacist. Cf. *RJ* 5.1.37–52.

18 **of** from (Abbott, 170)

19 **mover** St Thomas's scholastic synthesis of classical thought and Christian doctrine identified God with Aristotle's Unmoved Prime Mover, beyond the *primum mobile*, 'First mover of those tenfold crystal orbs' (Hart quoting *Selimus* (anon., 1594)). This sense only here in Shakespeare.

24 **pangs of death** 2 Samuel, 22.5, 'The pangs of death hath compassed mee'; and Psalms, 18.3, has 'panges of death' (Bishops' Bible), 'sorowes of death' (Geneva Bible) (Shaheen, 55).
  grin bare the teeth

---

10 whe'er] *(where)* 16 lime twigs] *(Lime-twigs)* 19 SD] *this edn*

SALISBURY

    Disturb him not; let him pass peaceably.   25

KING

    Peace to his soul, if God's good pleasure be.

    Lord Cardinal, if thou thinkst on heaven's bliss,

    Hold up thy hand, make signal of thy hope.

      [*Cardinal dies.*]

    He dies and makes no sign. O God, forgive him!

WARWICK

    So bad a death argues a monstrous life.   30

KING [*Rises.*]

    Forbear to judge, for we are sinners all.

    Close up his eyes, and draw the curtain close,

    And let us all to meditation.   *Exeunt.*

[**4.1**]   *Alarum. Fight at sea. Ordnance goes off. Enter*
Lieutenant, SUFFOLK [*disguised, a prisoner, the* Master *and*
Master's *Mate, and* Walter WHITMORE, *with two*
Gentlemen *as prisoners*] *and others.*

25 **pass** pass on, die

28 **hope** Throughout the New Testament 'hope' signifies faith in the Gospels' record of Christ's death, resurrection and promise of salvation. See particularly St Paul's epistles.

30 **argues** evinces, indicates (*OED v.* 3)

31 See Matthew, 7.1, 'Iudge not, that ye be not iudged', and Romans, 3.23, 'For all haue sinned'.

33 **meditation** Of a specifically religious kind as recommended by Erasmus: 'This meditation of death is the meditation of true life, And it causeth not only that the philosopher promiseth, which is that the soul should depart from the bodye with lesse heavynysse,

but also that with cheerfullness of hart it should lepe merily, as it were out of a darke and painful prison, into blessed liberty, and into that light so lovely, which is void of any nyght or darkenesse' (*Preparation*, Aiv^r). For the class of words in which the penultimate, prevocalic 'i' is sounded, see Cercignani, 308.

4.1 location: the coast of Kent (Pope). Hall (219) provides the basic narrative source and is followed by Holinshed. Hall's ambiguous reference to the Duke of Exeter in relation to the ship *Nicholas of the Tower* (see 9n.) is a false surmise which assumes some sort of relationship since the Duke was Constable of the Tower of London.

28 SD] *Q* 31 SD] *this edn* **4.1**] *Pope* 0.1–4] Alarmes within, and the chambers be discharged, like as it were a fight at sea. And then enter the Captaine of the ship and the Maister, and the Maister's Mate & the Duke of Suffolke disguised, and others with him, and Water Whickmore. *Q* 0.2–4 *disguised . . . prisoners*] *this edn*

283

LIEUTENANT
> The gaudy, blabbing and remorseful day
> Is crept into the bosom of the sea;
> And now loud-howling wolves arouse the jades
> That drag the tragic melancholy night,
> Who with their drowsy, slow and flagging wings   5
> Clip dead men's graves and from their misty jaws

Modern scholars have not been able to ascertain precisely the ownership of the vessel in 1450. Virgoe, however, offers a fascinating conjecture deriving from a 1453 grand jury indictment in Suffolk of followers of the Duke of York for seditious conspiracy and plotting to murder the Duke of Suffolk. The conspiracy originated from Bury St Edmunds, which, as we have seen, can also be linked to Jack Cade and the Kent rising (see 3.2.240n.). The Duke of Suffolk first left England from the coast of Suffolk and it is possible that the *Nicholas of the Tower* was in the right place at the right time because of informants working with the anti-Suffolk, pro-York faction from Bury. See Virgoe, 'Death'.

1–7 Hart felt that these lines were 'inartistically joined to the scene by the word "therefore"'. On the contrary, Shakespeare's poetic design is evident in the careful transition from scene to scene. King Henry unsuccessfully invokes the *gentle eye* of God to *purge . . . black despair* from the Cardinal's *bosom* (3.3.20, 23). The Cardinal's eyes are closed and the curtains of his bed are drawn. Here the light has disappeared over the horizon into the *bosom* of the sea. The Cardinal's *black despair* is now externalized into the all-engulfing blackness of *melancholy night*, and contagion spreads uncontained by purgation.

1 **gaudy** bright. Cf. the proverbs 'A

gaudy morning bodes a wet afternoon' and 'Too bright a morning breeds a lowring daie' (Wilson, *ODEP* 297).
    blabbing revealing, divulging (in speech analogous to light here). Cf. 3.1.154. This form occurs only here in Shakespeare.

2 **crept . . . bosom** proverbial (Dent, B546)

3 **loud-howling** only here in Shakespeare
    jades worn-out draught horses: given the *flagging wings* (5), a pejorative reference to the dragons of the night associated with Ceres and Hecate, in contrast to the commonplace horses of Phoebus' chariot. For the process by which something like the 'horses of the night' of Ovid's *Amores*, 1.13.40 (invoked by Marlowe's Faustus, 5.1.152), were transformed by Renaissance mythographers into 'dragons', see Bush. Cf. *Cym* 2.2.48.

4–5 For the 'That . . . Who' construction see Abbott, 260.

4 **tragic melancholy night** a triple association of blackness here – black bile, the blackness of night and the tragic blackness of despair and death – all associated with *melancholy*. See Babb.

5 **flagging** drooping. Cf. Spenser, 1.xi.10, 'flaggy wings'.

6 **Clip** embrace (*OED v.*[1] 1): reflects the melancholic compulsion to resort to graveyards (see Babb, 112, n. 4). F's 'Cleape' has led to speculation on 'clepe' as 'call' or 'summon' (*OED v.* 1).

6 Clip] *(Cleape)*

Breathe foul contagious darkness in the air.
Therefore bring forth the soldiers of our prize,
For whilst our pinnace anchors in the Downs,
Here shall they make their ransom on the sand,   10
Or with their blood stain this discoloured shore.
Master, this prisoner   [*Indicates First Gentleman.*]
                                        freely give I thee,
And thou that art his mate, make boot of this;
    [*Indicates Second Gentleman.*]
The other,   [*Indicates Suffolk.*]
            Walter Whitmore, is thy share.

1 GENTLEMAN
What is my ransom, master? Let me know.   15
MASTER
A thousand crowns, or else lay down your head.
MATE
And so much shall you give, or off goes yours.
LIEUTENANT
What, think you much to pay two thousand crowns,
And bear the name and port of gentlemen?
WHITMORE
Cut both the villains' throats! [*to Suffolk*] For die you   20
shall.

---

7 **contagious darkness** Cf. *Ham*
3.2.389–90, 'When churchyards yawn,
and hell itself breathes out /
Contagion to this world'.
9 **pinnace** the *Nicholas of the Tower*
(Hall, 219). The square-rigged pinnace was small and light in comparison
with the full-scale man-of-war, varying
from forty to a hundred tons. Though
carrying ordnance it was primarily
used for scouting (*Shakespeare's
England*, 1.145, 151).
Downs in the 'Douere Rode' (Hall,
219), an anchorage sheltered by the
Goodwin Sands (Cairncross)

11 **discoloured** prolepsis: 'which will be
discoloured'
13 **boot** profit (*OED sb.*[1] 1). Cf. *H5* 1.2.194.
18 **much** too much
19 **port** social position or station (*OED
sb.*[4] 2). See *TS* 1.1.203.
20 SP *Both Oxf and Cam[2] follow this
conjecture by Malone and add the
Whitmore prefix. Otherwise the
speech would be quite inconsistent
with the later 'Be not so rash' (28) of
the Lieutenant. The Master and Mate
have made their demands with their
prisoners and this bloodthirstiness is
consistent with Whitmore.

12–14 SDs] *this edn*   20 SP] *Oxf (Malone²)*   20 SD] *Oxf*

LIEUTENANT

   The lives of those which we have lost in fight

   Be counterpoised with such a petty sum.

1 GENTLEMAN

   I'll give it, sir, and therefore spare my life.

2 GENTLEMAN

   And so will I, and write home for it straight.

WHITMORE [*to Suffolk*]

   I lost mine eye in laying the prize aboard,   25

   And therefore to revenge it shalt thou die,

   And so should these, if I might have my will.

LIEUTENANT

   Be not so rash; take ransom, let him live.

SUFFOLK

   Look on my George; I am a gentleman.

   [*Reveals his badge.*]

   Rate me at what thou wilt, thou shalt be paid.   30

WHITMORE

   And so am I; my name is Walter Whitmore.

   How now! Why starts thou? What, doth death affright?

21–2 Hattaway and Wells & Taylor give these lines to Whitmore. They are, however, quite uncharacteristic of his language but consistent with that of the Lieutenant.

22 **counterpoised** compensated (*OED v.* 2)

24 **straight** at once

25 **laying . . . aboard** positioning my ship alongside the prize (*OED* Aboard 2c). Cf. *RJ* 2.4.202.

29 **George** a badge of St George mounted slaying the dragon worn on a blue ribband as part of the insignia of the Order of the Garter, added by Henry VII (see Scott-Giles, 169). Q has 'ring', which seems more appropriate with a disguise, but the flourish of the *George* provides a strong piece of stage business. Cf. *R3* 4.4.366.

30 However high you set my ransom, it will be paid.

   Rate estimate, set the value (of the ransom). Cf. *2H4* 1.3.44.

31 **Walter Whitmore** Walter (pronounced with a silent 'l') was needed for the ironic fulfilment of the prophecy but 'Whitmore' appears to be unprecedented. According to a letter written to John Paston on 5 May 1450 by William Lomner, one Richard Lenard, a sailor, 'oon of the lewedest of the shippe', was Suffolk's executioner. See Virgoe, 'Death', 494.

32 **starts** instead of 'startest': see Abbott, 340

   thou Suffolk has revealed his knightly

SUFFOLK

Thy name affrights me, in whose sound is death.
A cunning man did calculate my birth
And told me that by water I should die.   35
Yet let not this make thee be bloody-minded,
Thy name is Gualtier, being rightly sounded.

WHITMORE

Gualtier or Walter, which it is I care not.
Never yet did base dishonour blur our name
But with our sword we wiped away the blot.   40
Therefore, when merchant-like I sell revenge,
Broke be my sword, my arms torn and defaced
And I proclaimed a coward through the world.

SUFFOLK

Stay, Whitmore, for thy prisoner is a prince,
The Duke of Suffolk, William de la Pole.   45
    [*Removes his cloak.*]

WHITMORE

The Duke of Suffolk, muffled up in rags?

status, both with his *George* and the
two *thou*s (30) of his address, as
superior to a social inferior. Whitmore,
instead of responding deferentially,
shows that nothing has changed with
his continuing familiarity. Cf. *TN*
3.2.45–6, 'if thou thou'st him some
thrice, it shall not be amiss'.
death Vaughan's conjecture, 'thee', is
attractive. However, Suffolk's confidence at 29–30 indicates that the
threat of 26 has not shaken him.
Evidently Suffolk did not clearly hear
14, and 33 seems to be directly answering Whitmore's assumption.
34 **cunning man** a man with knowledge
of the occult (*OED* Cunning *sb.* 4),
referring here to the conjured spirit
and prophecy of 1.4.32–3. See *Tem*
3.2.43. Q has 'cunning Wyssard'.

calculate my birth cast my horo-
scope: not evident in 1.4 but very
effective here for the sense of fate's
inevitability
37 **Gualtier** the French version
sounded pronounced (*OED v.* 8). Cf.
TS 2.1.191.
39 **blur** *OED v.* 2 gives this as the first figurative instance for 'stain, sully, blem-
ish'. As a substantive, and in literal
verbal usage, it appears in the middle
of the sixteenth century. Only elsewhere in *Ham* 3.4.41 and *Cym* 4.2.104.
41 **merchant-like**   not   again   in
Shakespeare
sell revenge (for ransom)
42 **arms . . . defaced** See *R2* 3.1.25.
arms heraldic coat of arms
45–6 Cf. *Cor* 4.5.54–7 (RP).

34 man] Wyssard *Q*   45 SD] *this edn*

SUFFOLK

Ay, but these rags are no part of the Duke.

Jove sometime went disguised, and why not I?

LIEUTENANT

But Jove was never slain as thou shalt be.

SUFFOLK

Obscure and lousy swain, King Henry's blood,   50

The honourable blood of Lancaster,

Must not be shed by such a jaded groom.

Hast thou not kissed thy hand and held my stirrup?

And bare-head plodded by my foot-cloth mule,

---

48 *Pope inserted this line from Q to make sense of the following rejoinder. **Jove . . . disguised** In Ovid, 6.126–41, the disguises of Jove include the lowly appearance as a 'sheepeherd to Mnemosyne', which presumably gave Marlowe the line 'Jove sometimes masked in a shepherd's weed' (*1 Tamburlaine*, 1.2.199).

49 The bluntness sounds more like Whitmore but the reference to Jove sounds more like the Lieutenant, to whom the line is given. However, in view of F's attribution of both 49 and 50 to the Lieutenant, a doubt remains.

50 **lousy** scurvy, vile (*OED a.* 2). Pope adopted Q's 'lowly' and is followed by Cairncross. Editors point out Hall's description of Jack Cade's 'lousy lynage' (221), but 'lousy knave' occurs several times elsewhere in Shakespeare. **King Henry's blood** Suffolk claims more than he could justify since his mother was only a distant cousin of the King.

52 **jaded** The context of contempt confers a meaning, but the *OED* (*ppl. a.* 3) separates this as a unique instance apart from 'jaded' as 'worn out'. See 3n. on *jades*.
groom The exclusive association with horses is post-seventeenth century.

Generally 'groom' meant a socially inferior male, of the servant class (*OED sb.* 3). Sometimes the context indicates something more specific as in *R2* 5.5.72, 'I was a poor groom of thy stable'.

53–64 I can find no explanation for the apparent recognition of a former household servant here. The Lieutenant's reply (70–103), which gives voice to the specific charges of widespead complaint, simply ignores this, as does Whitmore's at 65. Perhaps what is more important is the dramatic function in the pathos of recollected greatness? It is possible that Shakespeare's invented relationship fortuitously anticipates the rumours of 1453 concerning the relationship of the *Nicholas* to Bury. See headnote.

53 **kissed thy hand** Cf. *LLL* 5.2.323–4, 'this is he / That kiss'd his hand away in courtesy'.

54 *bare-head Servants were bareheaded in deference to their masters, who always wore hats (see *Shakespeare's England*, 2.108–9).
foot-cloth mule mule used to carry the conspicuously sumptuous covering for a horse. As a sign of status and dignity it becomes a focus for the rebels in 4.7.42–3.

48] *Q, Pope; not in F*   50 SP] *Q, Pope; not in F*   lousy] lowly *Q*   51 The] *Suf. The F*   54 And bare-head] *Q (*barehead*); Bare-headed F*

And thought thee happy when I shook my head?   55
How often hast thou waited at my cup,
Fed from my trencher, kneeled down at the board
When I have feasted with Queen Margaret?
Remember it, and let it make thee crestfallen,
Ay, and allay this thy abortive pride.   60
How in our voiding lobby hast thou stood
And duly waited for my coming forth?
This hand of mine hath writ in thy behalf
And therefore shall it charm thy riotous tongue.
WHITMORE
Speak, captain, shall I stab the forlorn swain?   65
LIEUTENANT
First let my words stab him, as he hath me.
SUFFOLK
Base slave, thy words are blunt, and so art thou.
LIEUTENANT
Convey him hence, and on our longboat's side
Strike off his head.   Thou dar'st not for thy own.
SUFFOLK

55 and were happy just to be noticed. Q
seems apposite: 'And thought thee
happie when I smilde on thee'.
57 **trencher** a dinner plate; in an aristocratic household, made of silver (of
earthenware, wood or bread, lower in
the social scale)
kneeled . . . board served deferentially at table
60 **abortive** *OED*'s (*a.* and *sb.* 2) 'Failing
of the intended effect . . . fruitless . . .
unsuccessful', citing this as first
instance, is unsatisfactory. Suffolk
means that whatever pride has plans
for, it will miscarry. Cf. 4.8.46.
61 **voiding lobby** an ante-room or reception area for those discharged from the
main presence chamber
voiding sending away, discharging (*OED*

vbl. sb. 2): nowhere else in Shakespeare
63 presumably alluding to legal testimo-
nials
64 **shall** Following the force of *therefore*,
shall means 'must' here (see Abbott,
315).
charm . . . tongue proverbial (Dent,
CC9)
charm silence (*OED v.*[1] 4). Cf. *TS*
1.1.209.
riotous unrestrained (*OED a.* 3b)
65 **forlorn swain** wretched lover. In view
of *TGV* 5.4.12, 'Thou gentle nymph,
cherish thy forlorn swain', this can be
read as Whitmore turning Suffolk's
class usage – *lousy swain* (50) – towards
the romantic (*OED sb.* 5) to sneer at
the Suffolk–Margaret liaison, which is
duly taken up by the Lieutenant at 75.

69 thy] thine *Q*

LIEUTENANT
   Yes, poll!

SUFFOLK   Pole!

LIEUTENANT   Pool! Sir Pool! Lord!   70
   Ay, kennel, puddle, sink, whose filth and dirt
   Troubles the silver spring where England drinks;
   Now will I dam up this thy yawning mouth
   For swallowing the treasure of the realm.
   Thy lips that kissed the Queen shall sweep the ground;   75
   And thou that smiledst at good Duke Humphrey's
      death
   Against the senseless winds shall grin in vain
   Who in contempt shall hiss at thee again.
   And wedded be thou to the hags of hell
   For daring to affy a mighty lord   80
   Unto the daughter of a worthless king,

---

70 The passage turns on the punning possibilities of Suffolk's family name, de la Pole, in the grotesque circumstances of comic insolence and the threat of death by decapitation. The primary puns are *poll* (decapitated head), *pool* (filthy water) and *pole* (which will hoist the head aloft). See Introduction, p.138, for the pun on 'susprall', the Elizabethan cesspool.

71 **kennel** gutter. Cf. *TS* 4.3.98, the only other instance in Shakespeare.
puddle, sink Cf. 'For he that nameth rebellion . . . nameth the whole puddle and sink of all sins against God and man' (*Homily*, 507) (Cairncross).
sink cesspool, see 70n.

72 **Troubles** stirs up and muddies (*OED v.* 1). Cf. 'like a fountain troubled, muddy, ill seeming, thick' (*TS* 5.2.142–3).

73–4 **dam . . . swallowing** stop up your devouring mouth to prevent it swallowing

73 **yawning** not in tiredness but in order to devour (see *OED ppl. a.* 1): only here in this sense in Shakespeare

74 **For** to prevent it (Abbott, 154)

75 **lips . . . ground** The image is a grisly one – either of the head lowered to the ground for execution, or the decapitated head picked up by the hair, the lips thus 'sweeping' the ground.

77 **Against** exposed to (*OED prep. conj.* 1b)
senseless unfeeling
grin grimace, bare the teeth

78 **again** in reply (*OED adv.* 2)

79 **hags of hell** the Furies, known as the Furiae or Dirae to the Romans, the Eumenides or Erinyes to the Greeks: namely, Tisiphone, Alecto and Megaera. Cf. *R3* 1.4.57.

80 **affy** a variant of the now obsolete 'affiance': betroth (*OED* Affy *v.* 6). See *affiance*, 3.1.74; also *TS* 4.4.49, and 1.1.9n. above.

81 **worthless king** Reignier, Margaret's father. See 1.1.108–9n.

---

70 Yes, poll!] *Cam¹; not in F*   SUFFOLK Pole!] *Q subst.; not in F*   ¹Pool! . . . Lord!] *(Poole, Sir Poole?* Lord,*)*   76 smiledst] *(smil'dst)*   77 shall] shalt *F2*

Having neither subject, wealth nor diadem.
By devilish policy art thou grown great
And, like ambitious Sulla, overgorged
With gobbets of thy mother's bleeding heart.   85
By thee Anjou and Maine were sold to France,
The false revolting Normans thorough thee
Disdain to call us lord, and Picardy
Hath slain their governors, surprised our forts
And sent the ragged soldiers wounded home.   90
The princely Warwick, and the Nevilles all,
Whose dreadful swords were never drawn in vain,
As hating thee, are rising up in arms.
And now the house of York, thrust from the crown
By shameful murder of a guiltless king   95
And lofty, proud, encroaching tyranny,
Burns with revenging fire, whose hopeful colours
Advance our half-faced sun, striving to shine,

83 **devilish policy** Thus qualified, Machiavellian *policy* takes on a hellish aura. See 3.1.235n. The word 'policy' occurs six times in *2H6*, more than in any other play of Shakespeare.

84 **Sulla** Lucius Cornelius Sulla (138–78 BC). As elected Dictator of Rome, having defeated foreign enemies and opposing factions in civil war, Sulla devised an ongoing *Proscriptio*, or proscription list, by which all surviving enemies could 'legally' be slaughtered at sight by anyone (slaves included), thus introducing a singular reign of terror with such unprecedented measures. **overgorged** not elsewhere in Shakespeare; no other entries between 1575 and 1641 in *OED*. Hart notes an instance in Golding's Ovid, 4.353.

85 **gobbets** pieces of raw flesh (*OED sb.* 1b): only here and 5.2.58 in Shakespeare
*mother's Abbott (338) suggests that F's 'Mother-bleeding' prints a hyphen

which indicated an 's' in the MS. Sulla's Rome, Suffolk's England.

87 **thorough** through (Abbott, 478; Cercignani, 357)

88–90 **Picardy . . . home** See LN.

92 **dreadful** to be dreaded (*OED a.* 2)

93 **As hating** in hate of

95 **guiltless king** Richard II, whose deposition established the House of Lancaster over that of York

97 **hopeful colours** (House of York's) standards raised in hope of the crown (see Fig. 11)

98 **Advance** raise aloft

98–9 **half-faced . . . *nubibus*** The passage is confusing, not least for the unidentified Latin, 'Despite the clouds'. Drayton describes the ensign of the county of Suffolk at Agincourt as 'a Sunne halfe risen from the brack' (14) (Hart). Referring to Camden's *Remains* (1623, 183), editors point out that the sunburst emblem over a cloud was a device of Edward III, as it was of Richard II (see

84 Sulla] Sylla *F*   85 mother's bleeding] *Rowe;* Mother-bleeding *F*   93 are] *Rowe;* and *F*

Under which is writ '*Invitis nubibus*'.
The commons here in Kent are up in arms;   100
And, to conclude, reproach and beggary
Is crept into the palace of our King,
And all by thee. Away! Convey him hence.

SUFFOLK

O, that I were a god, to shoot forth thunder
Upon these paltry, servile, abject drudges!   105
Small things make base men proud: this villain here,
Being captain of a pinnace, threatens more
Than Bargulus, the strong Illyrian pirate.
Drones suck not eagles' blood, but rob beehives.
It is impossible that I should die   110
By such a lowly vassal as thyself.
Thy words move rage and not remorse in me.

LIEUTENANT

Ay, but my deeds shall stay thy fury soon.

SUFFOLK

I go of message from the Queen to France;

Scott-Giles, 65). But this emblem was not associated with Richard Plantagenet, Duke of York. The speaker here aligns himself with a supporting Yorkist group; perhaps Shakespeare, needing a bit of *ad hoc* heraldry, just made it up? See Wilson's comparison with an example from Greene's *James IV*.

100 looking back to 3.1.355–6 and anticipating 4.2

101 **reproach** disgrace, shame (*OED sb.* 2)
beggary For Henry's borrowing see 1.3.31n., and note again the ironic verbal parallelism of *beggary* at 4.2.50.

102 **Is crept** For singular verb see Abbott, 336.

104 **god . . . thunder** Jupiter was worshipped as the god of lightning and thunder and was often depicted holding a thunderbolt. See *KL* 2.4.227. In

JC we find a plurality of 'gods, with all your thunderbolts' (4.3.81).

107 **pinnace** See 9n.

108 **Bargulus** See LN.

109 **Drones . . . beehives.** See LN.

111 **vassal** base or abject person. See LN.

112 **Remorse** remorse of conscience; compunction and regret (*OED sb.* 1 and 2). Cf. Tyrrel in the murders of the princes in the Tower, 'Hence, both are gone with conscience and remorse. / They could not speak' (*R3* 4.3.20–1).

114 As Sanders points out, in response to Q's line (TLN 1500), Suffolk introduces his diplomatic status. In fact what added to the gravity of Suffolk's execution was that he was formally under the King's safe conduct (see Virgoe, 'Death', 493).
of on (see Abbott, 175)

113] *Q; not in F*

I charge thee waft me safely 'cross the Channel.   115
LIEUTENANT
    Walter!
WHITMORE
    Come, Suffolk, I must waft thee to thy death.
SUFFOLK
    Pene gelidus timor occupat artus:
    It is thee I fear.
WHITMORE
    Thou shalt have cause to fear before I leave thee.   120
    What, are ye daunted now? Now will ye stoop?
1 GENTLEMAN
    My gracious lord, entreat him, speak him fair.
SUFFOLK
    Suffolk's imperial tongue is stern and rough,
    Used to command, untaught to plead for favour.
    Far be it we should honour such as these   125
    With humble suit: no, rather let my head

---

115 **charge** order, command
   waft *OED* Waft *v.*[1] 2 gives this as the
   first instance with the meaning spelt
   out by Suffolk, combining conveyance
   with safety. Hence the pointed sarcasm
   of Whitmore's reversal of meaning at
   117. Cf. *3H6* 5.7.41.
116 *Cairncross argues that F's 'Water:
   W' is in fact an SP, '*Lieu.*' having
   dropped from a missing line, which
   Sanders feels might be the case, given
   the type arrangement of F. Adoption
   of the reading here gives a vivid
   emphasis to the fulfilment of the
   prophecy.
118 *Pene . . . artus* 'Cold fear almost
   completely seizes my limbs.' Editors
   agree that this seeming quotation is a
   confused recollection of *Aeneid*,
   7.446, 'subitus tremor occupat artus'
   ('a sudden trembling seized his

limbs'), and Lucan's *Pharsalia*, 1.246,
'gelidos pavor occupat artus' ('terror
seizes their chilly limbs') (Loeb edn,
21). Again, Steevens suggested *Aeneid*,
11.424, 'cur ante tubam tremor
occupat artus' ('Why, before even the
trumpet sounds, does trembling seize
our limbs?'). In view of the puzzling
variant on Ascanius (see 3.2.116–18
LN) and the irony of the Bargulus
allusion (4.1.108 LN), it is difficult to
know whether this is a simple misre-
membering or a subtle indication of
Suffolk's psychological state as he recognizes his end. F's '*Pine*' makes no
sense.
122 **fair** civilly, courteously (*OED adv.* 2).
   See 'To speak (one) fair', Dent, SS16.
123 **imperial** commanding (*OED adj.* 5)
125 Note the royal 'we'.
126 **suit** petition

116–17] *Rowe³ subst.*; *Lieu.* Water: W. Come Suffolke, I must waft thee to thy death. *F as prose*
118 *Pene*] *Malone*; *Pine F*; *not in F2–4*; *Paenae / Theobald*; Pro! *Cam¹*

Stoop to the block than these knees bow to any
Save to the God of heaven and to my King;
And sooner dance upon a bloody pole
Than stand uncovered to the vulgar groom.   130
True nobility is exempt from fear;
More can I bear than you dare execute.

LIEUTENANT
Hale him away, and let him talk no more.

SUFFOLK
Come, soldiers, show what cruelty ye can,
That this my death may never be forgot.   135
Great men oft die by vile Bezonians.
A Roman sworder and banditto slave
Murdered sweet Tully; Brutus' bastard hand

129 **bloody pole** The decapitated heads
and quartered bodies of traitors were
thus displayed at the entrance to
London Bridge and other towns, as
designated.
130 **uncovered** hat in hand, respectfully.
See 54n. This line inverts the imagery
of 54–5.
   vulgar groom See 52n. Q has 'Iadie
[jadie] groome', and 'jadie' for F's
'jaded' at 52. Oxf accepts the Q reading on the grounds that it is a rare
word otherwise unrecorded until 1873.
131 And yet Suffolk had jeered at
Gloucester's 'such high vaunts of his
nobility' (3.1.50). Cf. *H8* 2.4.143. For
similar high-minded Senecan self-
dramatization Hart cites Kyd's
Cornelia (2.1.297), 'true noblesse never
doth the thing it should not'.
133 **Hale** haul
136 **Bezonians** needy beggars; base fel-
lows. See LN.
137–8 **Roman . . . Tully** In North's
Plutarch 'Herennius a Centurion, and
Pompilius Laenas, Tribune of the soldiers', were the murderers of Cicero

on the orders of Mark Antony.
Herennius was of high rank and *banditto slave* probably refers to
Philologus, Cicero's young enfran-
chised slave who betrayed his master's
whereabouts.
137 **sworder** *OED* gives this and *AC*
3.13.31, the only instances before
1828, as 'assassin, cutthroat' and 'glad-
iator'. For the 'er' suffix signifying an
agent see Abbott, 443.
   *banditto Bandetto in F: bandit. This
is the first instance in *OED*, immediately followed by Nashe; not elsewhere
in Shakespeare.
138 **sweet** In a double sense as 'dear', a
form of address (*OED adj.* 8c), and as
'pleasing' and 'persuasive' (*OED adj.*
5c), since Cicero was a model of the
Renaissance ideal of eloquence. Cf.
'sweet discourse', *TGV* 1.3.31, *R3*
5.3.99, *RJ* 3.5.53.
   bastard North's Plutarch perpetuates
this story: 'For when [Caesar] was a
young man, he had been acquainted
with Servilia [Brutus' mother], who
was extremely in love with him. And

134 SP] *Hanmer; not in F*   135 That] *Suf.* That *F*   137 banditto] *(Bandetto)*

Stabbed Julius Caesar; savage islanders
Pompey the Great; and Suffolk dies by pirates.   140
Exit Whitmore with Suffolk [and others].

LIEUTENANT

And as for these whose ransom we have set,
It is our pleasure one of them depart:
Therefore come you with us, and let him go.
Exeunt all but First Gentleman.

Enter WHITMORE *with Suffolk's body and head.*

WHITMORE

There let his head and lifeless body lie,   144
Until the Queen his mistress bury it.   *Exit.*

1 GENTLEMAN

O barbarous and bloody spectacle!
His body will I bear unto the King.
If he revenge it not, yet will his friends;
So will the Queen, that living held him dear.
[Exit with the body and head.]

because Brutus was born at that time when their love was hottest, he persuaded himself that he begat him' (*Brutus*, 106). In his life of Julius Caesar, Suetonius records the popular belief that Caesar cried out to Brutus (in Greek), 'What! art thou, too, one of them? Thou, my son!' (51). Servilia became Caesar's mistress after her lawful husband's death. See *JC* (Ard³) 3.1.77 and n.

139–40 **savage . . . Great** North's Plutarch relates that Pompey was killed off the coast of Egypt by three of his centurions. Editors note that the assassins were advised by Theodotus of Chios, an island, which may account for the *savage islanders*. In Chapman, Pompey is killed on the island of Lesbos, perhaps deriving from Theophanes of Lesbos advising Pompey. Like Suffolk's, Pompey's head is struck off on a vessel and his body abandoned on the strand.

146 **bloody spectacle** Cf. *3H6* 2.5.73, 'O piteous spectacle! O bloody times!'

149 **held him dear** See 1.3 headnote.

140 SD *and others*] Capell   143 SD, 143.1] *Capell subst.; Exit Lieutenant, and the rest. Manet the first Gent. Enter Walter with the body.* F   143.1 *and head*] *this edn*   149 SD] *Capell subst.   and head*] *this edn*

[4.2]   [*Enter two of the Rebels*[, GEORGE *and* NICK,]
               with long staves.]

GEORGE   Come and get thee a sword, though made of a
     lath; they have been up these two days.
NICK   They have the more need to sleep now, then.
GEORGE   I tell thee, Jack Cade the clothier means to dress

4.2 location: Blackheath (Capell). To suppress the rebellion the King assembled a great army whereupon Cade and his forces withdrew to Sevenoaks. The seeming retreat was taken as a sign of weakness. Sir Humphrey Stafford and his brother William mistakenly believed they were routing the rebels.

Wilson discerns the hand of Nashe throughout this scene.

For a critical account of the multi-cultural perspectives involved in the presentation of Jack Cade's rebellion, see Introduction, pp. 89–106. Here, at the outset, it is important to grasp how Cade's insurrection of 1450 is superimposed on that of Jack Straw, Wat Tyler and others, in the Peasants' Revolt of 1381 under Richard II. The account of Jack Straw's rebellion is found principally in Holinshed, 2.735–51. Cade's insurrection is found in Hall (219–22) and in Holinshed (220–7), who reprints 'The complaint of the commons of Kent' (222–3; see Appendix 5) which was presented to the King's Council.

0.1 *F's [George] Bevis and John Holland are known actors of the day. Holland is named in the plot of *The Seven Deadly Sins*, played by Strange's or the Admiral's or the Alleyn company about 1590. From the gag about Bevis of Southampton in Q, in the armourer combat scene, it is usually accepted by editors that F's SP

'George' is the same actor who had been one of Pembroke's Men, according to the title-page of *3H6* O. Holland is named in *3H6* 3.1. F names Holland along with 'Sinklo'/Sincler (see 4.10.56n. on *clown*) as the keepers (see E. K. Chambers, 1, 288). Here, the names 'George' and 'Nick' are taken from Q.

1–2 **sword . . . lath** a mock weapon made from a thin strip of wood, the stock property of the Vice in morality plays and interludes. Cf. *TN* 4.2.124–6, 'like to the old Vice . . . with dagger of lath', and see Humphreys' extended note on *2H4* 2.4.130. In an important study Wiles shows that a practice wooden sword was used by London apprentices and was known as a 'waster' (*Clown*, 121–2). Thus in the first line of the scene the possibilities of comic grotesque and burlesque mockery are registered.

2 **up** in rebellion (*OED adv.*[2] 10). Taken comically by Nick (3) as 'out of bed'.

4 **clothier** a cloth worker. See LN.

4–7 **dress . . . threadbare** England is like a garment worn *threadbare*. Jack will reverse it, and turn it inside out to provide a *new nap* (see *OED* Dress *v.* 13g). The analogy suggests implicit social criticism of *gentlemen* exploiters and a radical political programme of inversion, the 'world turned upside down', the reverse of *OED* Dress *v.* 2 and 2b – to set in order, to redress.

4.2] *Pope*   0.1–2] *Q subst.; Enter Beuis, and Iohn Holland. F*   1+ SP GEORGE] *Q; Beuis. F*   3+ SP NICK] *Q; Hol. F*

the commonwealth, and turn it, and set a new nap   5
upon it.

NICK   So he had need, for 'tis threadbare. Well, I say it was
never merry world in England since gentlemen came up.

GEORGE   O miserable age! Virtue is not regarded in
handicraftsmen.   10

NICK   The nobility think scorn to go in leather aprons.

GEORGE   Nay, more, the King's Council are no good
workmen.

---

5   **commonwealth** Cf. Hall: 'Ihon Cade
. . . assuring them, that their attempt
was both honorable to God and the
King, and also profitable to the common wealth' (220). Holinshed (224)
recounts that at one point the King's
soldiers were unwilling to attack the
rebels as 'they would not fight against
them that laboured to amend the com-
monweale'. (A sobriquet of Cade's was
'John Amendall'.) The language of
Hall's chronicle parallels that of
Salisbury echoed by Warwick (1.1.201,
203) in a speech concerned with 'the
ruler of a commonweal' (1.1.186).
Meanings of 'commonwealth' could
vary between the feudal obligations
towards and from lordship, and the
humanistic concept of an abstract
obligation of all to an underpinning
prior law. Thus rebels could appropriate the term as landowner and tanner
Robert Kett's Norfolk followers did;
Cheke protested, 'ye pretend a commonwealth. How amend ye it? By
killing of gentlemen, by spoiling of
gentlemen, by imprisoning of gentlemen. A marvellous tanned commonwealth' (989).

8   **merry world** Hobday notes the
subversive meanings of 'merry' as
egalitarian freedom: e.g. 'Robert Kett's
followers, looking back on the Norfolk
rebellion of 1549 after its suppression,
remembered that " 'twas a merry
world when we were yonder, eating of
mutton" ' (68). Cf. John Ball in *Jack
Straw*, 'But merrily with the world it
went, / When men eat berries of the

hauthorne tree' (89–90). For generally
more neutral usage of the proverbial
phrase 'It was never merry world since
. . .', see Dent, W878.1. *AYL*
1.1.115–16 recalls 'Robin Hood' and
his 'merry men'. For the legendary
epithet and associations of egalitarian
freedom versus authority, see Wiles,
Robin Hood, 1.72.
   came up came into fashion (*OED*
Came 69e)

10   **handicraftsmen** artisans, artificers.
The first instance of 'handicraftes
man' in *OED* is that of Raphe
Robynson's translation of Sir Thomas
More's *Utopia* (1551). In *Utopia*, 2.4,
we find discussion of the virtuous
handicraftsmen working for the good
of the 'common wealthe' in contrast to
the wastrel 'gentlemen' elsewhere, a
contrast exemplified in the simple
leather clothing of the Utopians
against the luxurious silk of others
(see 11n., 119n.). See Harvey, 124,
for the artisan class in fifteenth-
century rebellion. Not elsewhere in
Shakespeare.

11   **leather aprons** worn by smiths,
tanners and some masons whereas
most fifteenth-century working dress
reflected guild or company affiliation
(Cunnington and Cunnington, 178–9).
See Hobday (8n.), who examines this
as both a synecdoche of scorn and an
emblem of radical class solidarity. Cf.
2.3.76 and *Cor* 4.6.95–6, 'You have
made good work, you and your apron
men'.

NICK   True; and yet it is said, 'Labour in thy vocation';
    which is as much to say as, 'Let the magistrates be   15
    labouring men'; and therefore should we be magistrates.

GEORGE   Thou hast hit it; for there's no better sign of a
    brave mind than a hard hand.

NICK   I see them! I see them! There's Best's son, the
    tanner of Wingham.   20

GEORGE   He shall have the skins of our enemies to make
    dog's leather of.

14–16 Nick's comic chop-logic begins by misreading the injunction of the homily (see 14n.) as 'thy vocation is labouring', thus magistrates (rulers) should labour in this sense. He then reverses his own syntax into 'let labouring men be magistrates'. Further, Nick specifically goes against the careful distinctions of the homily: 'But when it is said, all men should labour, it is not so straitly meant, that all men should use handy labour . . . there be divers sorts of labours, some of the mind, and some of the body, and some of both . . . whosoever doth good to the common-weal . . . with his industry and labour . . . by governing the commonweal publicly . . . the same person is not to be accounted idle . . . though he work no bodily labour' (460). Thus Nick anticipates the World Upside Down of the following scenes, where hierarchy and office are inverted, the judges will be judged, the thief hangs the magistrate, and so on (see Kunzle).

14 'Labour . . . vocation' biblical, proverbial, and found as such in *Homilies*: 'Everyone must walk (labor) in his own calling (vocation)' (Dent, C23); 1 Corinthians, 7.20, 'Let euery man abide in the same vocation wherein he was called' (Shaheen, 56); 'everyone ought, in his lawful vocation and calling, to give himself to labour'

('An Homily Against Idleness'; see the whole sequence, 459–60). The patriotic Earl of Salisbury has perhaps anticipated this in his words on members of the King's Council: 'While these [Buckingham and Somerset] do labour for their own preferment, / Behoves it us to labour for the realm' (1.1.178–9). Cf. *1H4* 1.2.102.

17 **hit it** 'hit the nail on the head'

19–20 **Best's . . . Wingham** the son of Best, the tanner of Wingham (see Maxwell). Wingham is a village east of Canterbury. The commission of inquiry into the rebels' complaints showed that officials patronized by Lord Saye, in a whole circle of corruption and oppression, had seized tenants of the Archbishop of Canterbury at Wingham and criminally extorted money in 1449 (Virgoe, 'Indictments', 240). Robert Kett, leader of the 1549 Norfolk uprising, though a landowner, is described as a tanner.

22 **dog's leather** for glove-making. *OED* has only this and an entry from Randle Cotgrave's French–English dictionary of 1611, 'Dogs leather gloues oyled in the inside to keepe the hands moist, and coole'. Shakespeare's father was a glover. Cf. *TNK* 3.5.45, of which Potter notes, 'Gloves, often worn in dancing, were a common gift on festive occasions, dogskin being the cheapest kind.'

NICK   And Dick the butcher.

GEORGE   Then is sin struck down like an ox, and
   iniquity's throat cut like a calf.   25

NICK   And Smith the weaver.

GEORGE   Argo, their thread of life is spun.

NICK   Come, come, let's fall in with them.

Drum. Enter CADE, *Dick [the] Butcher, Smith the Weaver,
and a Sawyer, with infinite numbers [carrying long staves].*

CADE   We, John Cade, so termed of our supposed father –

---

23 **Dick the butcher** One of Cade's followers was known as 'the Captain's
bucher' (Harvey, 98). Robert Kett's
brother, William, was described as a
butcher (see 19–20n.), and one Fulke
the butcher killed Lord Sheffield in
the 1549 rebellion (see Fletcher, 58).
For the reputation of Young Clifford
after the battle of Wakefield as 'the
butcher', see 5.2.52n. See also
28.1–2n. Q adds a whole company here
(see TLN 1560–5).

24–5 reminiscent of Old Testament ritu-
als of atonement for 'sin' and 'iniquity'
using various beasts, including the calf
and bullock. See Leviticus, 9 and 16.
Cf. 4.3.3n.

26 **weaver** See 4.2.4LN. Weavers were
accused of plotting rebellion in Essex
in 1566 (see Pettitt, 7).

27 **Argo** contemporary unlearned pronunciation for *ergo*, 'therefore'
(Cercignani, 66)
thread . . . spun proverbial (Dent,
T249). Alluding to the three Parcae or
Fates. Clotho is usually represented as
spinning man's fate on a distaff or
spindle; Lachesis assigns each his fate;
and Atropos cuts the thread of life.
Often associated or confused with the
Furies (see *hags of hell*, 4.1.79 and n.),

as in *MND* 5.1.284–6. At the close of
Jack Straw a plea is made for the lives
of the rebels who believe they are
about to be executed, 'When thrid of
life is almost fret in twaine' (1024).

28.1–2 The artisan background of the
rebels can be checked with great accuracy since the statute of 1 Hen. 5 c. 5
insisted that the name, condition and
habitation of the accused be recorded.
If not, or if there was any inaccuracy,
indictments were not acceptable in law.
We can therefore rely on the transcrip-
tions made by Virgoe ('Indictments';
see 19–20n. above), including the
recurring occupations of weaver,
tanner, carpenter, shipman, smith,
butcher – and the occasional 'sawyer'.

29 **We** At the outset Cade adopts royal
address.
John   Cade   Holinshed   (226–7)
reprints the writ issued for Jack Cade
at the defeat of the rebels. It includes
details of Cade's association with Sir
Thomas Dacre and the story that he
killed a pregnant woman. Modern
historians confirm that John Cade, a
yeoman of Hurstpierpoint, mid-
Sussex, did flee the country and that
the manor of Hurstpierpoint was held
by Dacre (Harvey, 78–9).

28.2 *carrying long staves*] *Q subst.*

BUTCHER [*aside*]   Or rather of stealing a cade of herrings.   30
CADE   For our enemies shall fall before us, inspired
 with the spirit of putting down kings and princes.
 Command silence.
BUTCHER   Silence!
CADE   My father was a Mortimer –   35
BUTCHER [*aside*]   He was an honest man, and a good
 bricklayer.
CADE   My mother a Plantagenet –
BUTCHER [*aside*]   I knew her well, she was a midwife.
CADE   My wife descended of the Lacies –   40
BUTCHER [*aside*]   She was indeed a pedlar's daughter and
 sold many laces.
WEAVER [*aside*]   But now of late, not able to travel with her

---

30 SD Arguing against the customary use of asides here (30–57), Longstaffe proposes a carnivalesque free speech which cancels the SD in a Bakhtinian reading of all-inclusive laughter, not divisive and derisive mockery.
 of as a consequence of (Abbott, 168)
 cade a barrel of herrings (*OED sb.*[1] 2)
31–2 Cf. Leviticus, 26.8, 'and your enemies shall fall before you upon the sword' (Hattaway). Texts like Ezekiel, 21.26, 'Remove the diadem, and take off the crown . . . exalt him that is low, and abase him that is high', and Luke, 1.52, 'He hath put down the mighty from their seats, and exalted them of low degree', provided a revolutionary agenda for the Anabaptist leaders, as in Thomas Müntzer's 'Special Exposure of False Faith' (1524). See 63n. Holinshed records Jack Straw's final confession: 'our purpose was to haue slaine all such knights, esquiers, and gentlemen . . . Finally . . . we would haue slaine all such noble men . . . and lastlie we would haue killed the king' (2.751).
31 **fall** possibly a pun on Latin *cado*, 'I fall'

35 Thus begins Cade's mock genealogy, a parody of York's claim. For John Mortimer see 3.1.358 and n., 2.2.39n.
37 **bricklayer** punning on 'Mort'mer', 'mortar'
38 **Plantagenet** from *planta genista*, the 'broom cod' or 'broom plant', the badge of the dynasty first used by Henry II (Fox-Davies, 468). Richard, Duke of York, adopted the surname Plantagenet, reviving it for the first time in three hundred years (Lander, 73).
40 **Lacies** possibly in comic contemporary allusion to the Polish noble Albrecht Laski, who, upon arrival in London in 1583, sought to establish a family relationship with the English Lacies, whose line had died out in 1348, as John Ferne showed in *Lacy's Nobility*, published with *The Glory of Generosity* as *The Blazon of Gentry* (1586). I am indebted to Stephen Longstaffe for this information (see 30 SD n.).
42 **laces** punning on 'Lacies'
43–4 Editors assume bawdy *double entendre* on *furred pack* as female genitalia, from the recognized 'fur' as pubic hair (G. Williams, 1.567), and as the

---

30, 36, 39, 41, 43, 46, 50, 52, 55, 57 SDs] *Capell*   31 fall] *F4;* faile *F*   40 Lacies] Brases *Q*
43 now] not *Ard*[2]

furred pack, she washes bucks here at home.

CADE　Therefore am I of an honourable house.　　45

BUTCHER　[*aside*]　Ay, by my faith, the field is honourable, and there was he born, under a hedge; for his father had never a house but the cage.

CADE　Valiant I am.

WEAVER　[*aside*]　'A must needs, for beggary is valiant.　　50

CADE　I am able to endure much.

BUTCHER　[*aside*]　No question of that, for I have seen him whipped three market days together.

CADE　I fear neither sword nor fire.

pedlar's pack, either made or trimmed with fur outside (though no actual example is given). The phrase *washes bucks* refers literally to washing linen and metaphorically to bucks as cuckolds (see G. Williams, 2.161, and *MW* 3.3.157–9), i.e. provides cuckolds with the opportunity of revenge in kind. By the early seventeenth century laundering was reputedly a guise for whores (see G. Williams, 2.787–8); and in Stubbes, 'starching houses' for ruffs are considered 'brothel houses' (35).

46 **field is honourable** The butcher plays on the notion of an ordinary field as against the field of battle (almost always used as such in Shakespeare) in which 'honour' may be found (see *KJ* 1.1.53–4), and as an associative extension of 'field', the background colour of the coat of arms (Fox-Davies, 69). In the context of burlesque the language alludes to the heroic asceticism of Henry V as evoked by Gloucester, 'Did he so often lodge in open field . . . To conquer France . . . ?' (1.1.77–9), and it is in *H5* that the honourable field is both travestied (3.2.8–11) and vividly celebrated (4.6.18–19).

47 **born . . . hedge** the proverbial provenance of the humble (Dent, 361.1). Lord Talbot's encomium on the Order of the Garter as an 'honourable order' compares him who degrades 'the

sacred name of knight' with 'a hedge-born swain / That doth presume to boast of gentle blood' (*1H6* 4.1.40, 42–3).

48 **cage** a prison for petty criminals and vagabonds (*OED sb.* 2)

49 **Valiant** an epithet particularly associated with Lord Talbot, the embodiment of chivalric heroism, in *1H6* (see 1.1.121 and 4.7.61)

50 **'A must needs** he must be (Abbott, 402)

　　beggary is valiant Since 1531 the phrase 'valiant beggar' (*OED* Valiant *a.* 1b) paralleled that of 'sturdy beggar', to whom alms should not be given as they are fit enough to work. Juvenal had bequeathed the proverb 'The beggar may sing before the thief' (Dent, B229): the lowest can go no lower, there is nothing to lose. Yet note the ironic parallelism with the *beggary* of King Henry himself (4.1.101).

53 **whipped** Elizabeth had repealed a statute of Henry VIII by which, as well as whipping, vagabonds were 'burned through the gristle of the right ear with a hot iron of the compass of an inch' (14 Eliz. c. 5), but in 1593 an act confirmed that 'whipping . . . shall henceforth stand and be revived, and remain in full force and strength' (34 Eliz. c. 7. xxv). See 2.1.150–1 and n.

WEAVER [*aside*]   He need not fear the sword, for his coat   55
    is of proof.

BUTCHER [*aside*]   But methinks he should stand in fear of
    fire, being burnt i'th' hand for stealing of sheep.

CADE   Be brave, then, for your captain is brave, and vows
    reformation. There shall be in England seven half-   60
    penny loaves sold for a penny; the three-hooped pot
    shall have ten hoops, and I will make it felony to drink

55–6 **coat . . . proof** humorously playing on *coat* as assumed coat of arms deriving from Cade's claimed fore-bears, and as coat of mail, or coat-armour. To be *proof* is to be tested as impenetrable and strong enough to withstand attack (see *R2* 1.3.73 and *R3* 5.3.219). Perhaps the humour derives from the immediate spectacle of Cade's actual linen or leather tunic being encrusted with mud. But Wilson draws attention to a passage in Nashe which indicates a peasant prac-tice; John of Leiden's peasant Anabaptist army at Münster is described: 'as sailors do pitch their apparel to make it storm-proof, so had most of them pitched their patched clothes to make them impierceable: a nearer way than to be at the charges of armour by half' (*Traveller*, 279).

58 **burnt . . . hand** branded with a 'T' for 'Thief'. Hart gives several examples, including *Two Angry Women of Abington*: 'Nor that same hisse that by a fier doth stand / And hisseth T. or F. vpon the hand' (see Porter, 3022–3).

59 **captain** the regular title conferred by rebels on their leaders (see 23n.)

60 **reformation** Social and political rebels often claimed to be about the work of 'reformation', as when Kett and his followers in 1549 established a court beneath what was called the Oak of Reformation, upon which several were eventually hanged. (For Puritan and radical references in the sixteenth century see Hampton, 114–33.) Perhaps Holinshed provides the most

categorical comment in his marginal gloss on the 1381 insurrectionaries, 'All rebels pretend reformatio*n* but indeed purpose destruction both of king and countrie' (2.738).

There shall be 5 Eliz. c. 15 had re-enacted earlier statutes of Henry VIII and Edward VI punishing such utopi-an fantasies: 'any person . . . by writ-ing, printing, signing or any other open speech or deed, to any other person . . . any fond, fantastical or false prophecy . . . to the interest thereby to make any rebellion, insurrection, dis-sension, loss of life, or other distur-bance with this realm' (*Statutes*, 207).

60–1 **halfpenny . . . penny** Cade's an-archic plenty by decree makes no reference to the price of wheat, by which the local authorities' Assize of Bread and Ale determined the weight of the loaf (*Shakespeare's England*, 1.317). Poor harvests, scarcity and inflated prices were a frequent cause of riot: see Walter & Wrightson.

62 **ten hoops** Cairncross points out that the wooden drinking vessel holding a quart was bound by three equidistant hoops. As with bread, the Assize regu-lated the amount of beer purchased for a penny according to the price of bar-ley (*Shakespeare's England*, 1.317). Again, Cade's tripling of quantity and value makes no reference to cause and perhaps seems as arbitrary as the reversals of inflation in the actual world of the 1590s?

62–3 **felony . . . beer** Small beer was very weak ale. Cade's logical inver-

small beer. All the realm shall be in common, and in
Cheapside shall my palfrey go to grass. And when I am
king, as king I will be – 65

ALL God save your majesty!

CADE I thank you, good people. – There shall be no
money, all shall eat and drink on my score, and I will
apparel them all in one livery, that they may agree like

sion here is elliptical. Drunkenness
was punishable by law but it would be
rather difficult to get drunk on such a
low-alcohol beverage, thus Cade's law
would enforce the consumption of
festive double beer or strong ale.
That is to say, drunkenness would
be legalized and compulsory (see
2.3.64n.).

63 **All . . . common** See LN. Not recorded as part of Cade's agenda in the
chronicles, but in 1381 Jack Straw
'craued of the king that all warrens,
waters, parks and woods should be
common' (Holinshed, 2.742). Most
notorious in the Peasants' Revolt was
John Ball the revolutionary preacher's
communist message: 'Ah, ye good people, the matters goeth not well to pass
in England, nor shall not do till everything be common, and that there be no
villains or gentlemen, but that we be all
united together' (Froissart, 3,251). In
Jack of Leiden's Anabaptist tyranny at
Münster, in the German peasants'
uprising, 'all things were to be in common' (see Cohn, 287–9). Such was the
fear set up by this doctrine, echoed
here by Jack Cade, who came to be
identified with the Anabaptists (see
4.2.4 LN), that it found its way into
the Thirty-Nine Articles of the
Elizabethan church (1563): 'The
Riches and Goods of Christians are
not common, as touching the right,
title, and possession of the same, as
certain Anabaptists do falsely boast'
(Article 38).

63–4 ²**in . . . grass** inversion again. The
commercial centre of the city will
revert to commons grazing land as
token symbolism against the widespread enclosure of commons for
sheep-rearing, as we see in the petition
against Suffolk in 1.3 (see 1.3.21n.).

64 **palfrey** the saddle-horse for ordinary
riding, as against the war-horse

65 **king** Jack of Leiden proclaimed himself king at Münster, in spite of the
avowed communism (see 63n.; Cohn,
295). Cade appears to wish to put
down the mighty and exalt himself: see
31–2n. and 154n. Cf. *Tem* 2.1.146–69.

67–8 **no money** as in More's *Utopia* and
Jack of Leiden's Münster

68 **all . . . score** Cf. the distribution of
free food in More's *Utopia*.
score account (*OED sb.* 10). See
4.7.31–2 and n.

69 **one livery** See LN. Pettitt conjectures
that Cade may have used the Whitsun
festivities of 1450 'to forward or cover
his enterprise' (9), while Stubbes
records that the Lord of Misrule
invests 'euerie one of these his men
. . . with his liueries, of green, yellow
or some light wanton colour' (147).
Cade's *livery*, like his regality and the
Lord of Misrule burlesque, apes that
of the great households with their
liveried retainers, those overlooked in
earlier sumptuary laws and granted
special dispensation by Elizabeth in
1588: 'the servants of noblemen and
gentlemen may wear such livery coats
as their masters shall allow them, with
their badges or other ornaments of any
velvet or silk to be laid or added to
their said livery coats' (Hughes &
Larkin, 3, no. 697, 7).

brothers and worship me their lord.   70

BUTCHER   The first thing we do, let's kill all the lawyers.

CADE   Nay, that I mean to do. Is not this a lamentable thing,
that of the skin of an innocent lamb should be made
parchment; that parchment, being scribbled o'er, should
undo a man? Some say the bee stings, but I say 'tis the   75
bee's wax; for I did but seal once to a thing and I was
never mine own man since. How now? Who's there?

Enter [some, bringing forward the] Clerk [of Chartham].

WEAVER   The clerk of Chartham: he can write and read
and cast account.

CADE   O, monstrous!   80

---

70 **worship** Taken to an apocalyptic
extreme, when Jack of Leiden was
considered to be the Messiah of the
Last Days by his followers (see 63n.;
Cohn, 295).

71 **kill . . . lawyers** Sometimes regarded
as the most famous line of the play,
this recalls two passages in Holinshed.
Wat Tyler wanted an article inserted
into a charter, 'to haue had a commission to put to death all lawiers,
escheaters, and other which by any
office had any thing to doo with the
law' (2.740). John Ball's notorious sermon, in order to 'cast off the yoke of
bondage' to gain 'equalitie in libertie'
and 'equall authoritie in all things',
recommended that the rebels 'destroie
first the great lords of the realme, and
after the iudges and lawiers' (2.749).
Cf. *Jack Straw*: 'wele not leaue a man
of lawe' (519).

73 **innocent lamb** proverbial (Dent,
L34). Cf. 3.1.69–71.

74 **parchment** from the skin of sheep,
lamb or goat. Cade is referring to legal

documents.

76 **bee's wax** used for sealing legal documents; only here in Shakespeare. Cf.
JC 3.2.128. Included in the
'Complaints of the Commons of Kent'
was the notorious 'Greene Wax' which
sealed summons and fines extortion-
ately exacted by the likes of Crowmer
(see Holinshed, 222).

76–7 **for . . . since** Given the ironies of
the context, Cade probably alludes to
signing one's name on a legal document as security for another person,
thus 'I was never mine own man [mas-
ter] since.' See *OED* Seal $v.^1$ 4 and cf.
MV 1.2.74.

77.1 **Clerk of Chartham** See LN.

78 **write and read** For the 1381 rebels
literacy was the tool of oppression,
authority and thus punishment.

79 **cast account** to sum up or reckon
accounts (*OED* Cast $v.$ 37c). F's older
form, 'accompt', derives from late
Latin *accomptare*. See *OED* Account $v.$
and cf. *H5* Prologue.17n.

77.1] *Capell subst.; Enter a Clearke. F;* Enter *Will* with the Clarke of *Chattam. Q*   79 account] *Q;*
accompt *F*

WEAVER   We took him setting of boys' copies.

CADE   Here's a villain!

WEAVER   H'as a book in his pocket with red letters in't.

CADE   Nay, then, he is a conjuror.

BUTCHER   Nay, he can make obligations and write court-   85
hand.

CADE   I am sorry for't. The man is a proper man, of mine
honour; unless I find him guilty, he shall not die. Come
hither, sirrah, I must examine thee. What is thy name?

CLERK   Emmanuel.   90

BUTCHER   They use to write that on the top of letters.
'Twill go hard with you.

CADE   Let me alone. Dost thou use to write thy name? Or
hast thou a mark to thyself, like an honest plain-dealing
man?   95

CLERK   Sir, I thank God I have been so well brought up
that I can write my name.

ALL   He hath confessed: away with him! He's a villain and
a traitor.

---

81 **setting . . . copies** providing specimen
copies for penmanship (*OED* Copy *sb.*
8b). As here, the village clerk's duties
could include the schoolmaster's work.
In 1381 the rebels compelled 'teachers
of children in grammer schools to
sweare neuer to instruct any in their
art' (Holinshed, 2.746). For 'of' following a verbal noun, see Abbott, 178.

83 **red letters** either a school primer with
red capitals or an almanac with saints'
days in red

84 **conjuror** magician. (Almanacs printed astrological information.)

85 **make obligations** draw up legal
bonds concerning payment which, if
not met, entailed penalties (*OED*
Obligation 2). Cf. *MW* 1.1.10–11.

85–6 **court-hand** the general term for
the scripts employed in drawing up
charters and other formal legal

documents (*Shakespeare's England*,
1.290–2); only here in Shakespeare.
Lawcourts are referred to, not the
royal court.

87 **proper man** fine fellow: a common
phrase in Shakespeare. Cade's repetition here seems sardonic and he may
be touching on what in 1613 was called
an 'old proverb', namely 'The proper-
er man, the worse luck' (Tilley, M360).
of by (Abbott, 169)

90 **Emmanuel** transliterated Hebrew for
'God with us': a conventionally pious
prefix on documents

94–5 **mark . . . man** like Shakespeare's
father

96–9 'The world turned upside down'.
Literacy is apparently a crime, invert-
ing the actual law by which illiteracy,
in certain circumstances, was punishable by death. See 4.7.37–42n.

83 H'as] *Rowe³;* Ha's *F*   91 that] *Q;* it *F*   94 an] a *F*   plain-dealing] *(plain dealing)*

CADE   Away with him, I say! Hang him with his pen and   100
inkhorn about his neck.   *Exit one with the Clerk.*

Enter MICHAEL.

MICHAEL   Where's our general?

CADE   Here I am, thou particular fellow.

MICHAEL   Fly, fly, fly! Sir Humphrey Stafford and his
brother are hard by, with the King's forces.   105

CADE   Stand, villain, stand, or I'll fell thee down. He shall
be encountered with a man as good as himself. He is but
a knight, is 'a?

MICHAEL   No.

CADE   To equal him I will make myself a knight presently.   110
[*Kneels.*] Rise up, Sir John Mortimer. [*Rises.*] Now
have at him!

Enter Sir Humphrey STAFFORD *and his* Brother
with Drum and Soldiers.

STAFFORD

Rebellious hinds, the filth and scum of Kent,
Marked for the gallows, lay your weapons down;

100–1 **Hang . . . neck.** Holinshed records
of the 1381 rebellion: 'For it was dangerous among them to be knowne for
one that was lerned, and more dangerous, if any men were found with a pen-
ner and inkhorne at his side: for such
seldome or neuer escaped from them
with life' (2.746). In contrast Harvey
notes that, for the fifteenth century,
'Nearly every rebel leader . . . had his
scribe or secretary and a messenger
service' (75). For Henry Wilkhous,
Cade's scrivener, see Harvey, 99, and
4.2.77.1 LN.
101.1 MICHAEL perhaps an actor's name?
103 **particular** private (*OED a.* and *sb.*

3b). The *particular–general* (102–3)
wordplay is very common in Shakespeare.
108 **'a** he (Abbott, 402)
109 **No.** nothing but that merely: presumably, as Cairncross suggests, like
the northern dialect expression 'nob-
but'
110 **presently** immediately
112.1 **Brother** Sir William Stafford
113 **hinds** See 3.2.271n.
114 **Marked . . . gallows** Cf. 'He has the
gallows in his face' (Tilley, G20), and
'his complexion is perfect gallows'
(*Tem* 1.1.32).

101.1 MICHAEL] *Tom Q; Messenger Oxf*   111 SDs] *Dyce*

Home to your cottages, forsake this groom.   115
The King is merciful, if you revolt.

BROTHER

But angry, wrathful and inclined to blood,
If you go forward: therefore yield, or die.

CADE

As for these silken-coated slaves, I pass not.
It is to you, good people, that I speak,   120
Over whom, in time to come, I hope to reign,
For I am rightful heir unto the crown.

STAFFORD

Villain, thy father was a plasterer,
And thou thyself a shearman, art thou not?

CADE

And Adam was a gardener.

BROTHER   What of that?   125

---

115 **Home . . . cottages** An act of 1589 (31
Eliz. c. 7) indicates that too many cottages were erected and then abandoned
without any maintenance of the surrounding ground, presumably because
of the mobility of rural labourers (see
Statutes, 409). The 'highly mobile
labouring community' of Kent who
supported Cade were in part reacting
against the restrictions of the Statute of
Labourers, 1351 (Griffiths, 638).
  groom See 4.1.52n.
116 **revolt** return to your allegiance
(*OED v.* 2b). Cf. *KJ* 3.1.174.
119 **silken-coated** Visual class distinction was maintained by the
Elizabethan sumptuary laws whereby
the wearing of silk was the enforced
dividing line between gentlemen and
plebeians. (See Hooper and Harte.) Cf.
Richard Tarlton's comic entry as
Derick in *Famous Victories*, who expos-
tulates 'Am I a clown? 'Zounds, masters, do clowns go in silk apparel? I am
sure all we gentlemen-clowns in Kent

scant go so well' (2.2.30–1).
  pass care (*OED v.* 23): not elsewhere
in Shakespeare; frequently in Greene
and Nashe (Wilson)
123 **plasterer** only here in Shakespeare
124 **shearman** See 4.2.4 LN.
125 **Adam . . . gardener** Froissart records
John Ball's speech of 1381: 'We be all
come from one father and one mother,
Adam and Eve: whereby can they say or
shew that they be greater lords than we,
saving by that they cause us to win and
labour for that they dispend? They are
clothed in velvet and camlet furred with
grise, and we be vestured with poor
cloth' (3,251; see 63n. above).
Holinshed quotes the 'text' of the
'common prouerbe' for John Ball's sermon on Blackheath forever afterwards
associated with his name: 'When Adam
delu'd, and Eue span, / Who was then
a gentleman?' (2.749). This is duly dramatized in *Jack Straw*, 82–3. See Dent,
A30. For the context of contemporary
egalitarianism see Hobday, 8n. above.

125 What] *Ard²*; And what *F*

CADE

 Marry, this: Edmund Mortimer, Earl of March,

 Married the Duke of Clarence' daughter, did he not?

STAFFORD

 Ay, sir.

CADE

 By her he had two children at one birth.

BROTHER

 That's false. 130

CADE

 Ay, there's the question; but I say 'tis true.

 The elder of them, being put to nurse,

 Was by a beggar-woman stolen away;

 And, ignorant of his birth and parentage,

 Became a bricklayer when he came to age. 135

 His son am I; deny it if you can.

BUTCHER

 Nay, 'tis too true, therefore he shall be King.

WEAVER Sir, he made a chimney in my father's house,

 and the bricks are alive at this day to testify it; therefore

 deny it not. 140

STAFFORD

 And will you credit this base drudge's words,

 That speaks he knows not what?

ALL

 Ay, marry, will we; therefore get ye gone.

BROTHER

 Jack Cade, the Duke of York hath taught you this.

CADE [*aside*] He lies, for I invented it myself. – Go to, 145

 sirrah, tell the King from me, that for his father's sake,

 Henry the Fifth, in whose time boys went to span-

---

131 **question** problem (*OED sb.* 3)
136 **deny . . . can** a proverbial phrase
 (Dent, 202.1)

141 **credit** believe
 drudge's slave-labourer's
147–8 **span-counter** 'A game in which

126 Edmund] Roger *Q* 133 stolen] *(*stolne*)* 145 SD] *Capell*

counter for French crowns, I am content he shall reign,
but I'll be Protector over him.

BUTCHER   And furthermore, we'll have the Lord Saye's   150
head for selling the dukedom of Maine.

CADE   And good reason, for thereby is England mained
and fain to go with a staff, but that my puissance holds
it up. Fellow kings, I tell you that that Lord Saye hath
gelded the commonwealth and made it an eunuch; and   155
more than that, he can speak French, and therefore he
is a traitor.

STAFFORD
O gross and miserable ignorance!

CADE   Nay, answer if you can: the Frenchmen are our
enemies; go to then, I ask but this – can he that speaks   160
with the tongue of an enemy be a good counsellor or no?

---

the object of one player was to throw
his counters so close to those of his
opponent that the distance between
them could be spanned with the hand'
(*OED*) (cf. 'span-farthing'): only here
in Shakespeare

148 **French crowns** punning on coins,
écus; baldness caused by venereal disease; the monarch's diadem

148–9 **I . . . him** a proleptic parody of
what takes place in *3H6* 1.1.237–48

150–1 **Lord Saye's . . . Maine** See Hall,
219, and 4.4.0.3n.

152 **mained** an archaic form of
'maimed', punning on Maine. Again
Cade mimics the nobles; cf. Warwick,
1.1.206–9.

153–4 **fain . . . up** Cade's language ironically reflects on the way in which
Gloucester's protectorship, symbolized by his staff, propped up the country. See 2.3.31–2 and 3.1.189–90.

153 **fain to go** obliged to walk
puissance power

154 **Fellow kings** In Q Cade knights
Dick the butcher as well as himself

(TLN 1630–2), and we hear elsewhere
that 'we must all be Lords or squires,
assoone as Jacke Cade is King' (TLN
1564–5). See 4.8.36 and n. This paradoxical egalitarianism is found repeatedly in *Jack Straw* (123, 516, 719). On
his entry Cade immediately spoke of
'the spirit of putting down kings and
princes' (32; see 65n.). Cairncross suggests Marlowe's *2 Tamburlaine*, 1.6.24.

155 **gelded   the   commonwealth**
metaphorical unseemliness specifically
decried by Cicero: 'Nolo dici morte
Africani "castratam" esse rempubli-
cam' ('I deprecate the expression that
the death of Africanus "left the state
gelt"') (*De oratore* (Loeb edn, 1942),
3.41.164). Wilson points out that this
is   quoted   by   Talaeus   in   his
Renaissance schoolbook *Rhetorica*.

156–61 ¹**he . . . no** The falsity of Cade's
syllogism is transparent even without
the evident equivocation on *tongue*.

158 **miserable** contemptible; pitiable
(*OED a.* and *sb.* 5)

154 Fellow kings] (Fellow-Kings)

ALL

No, no, and therefore we'll have his head.

BROTHER

Well, seeing gentle words will not prevail,

Assail them with the army of the King.

STAFFORD

Herald, away, and throughout every town   165

Proclaim them traitors that are up with Cade;

That those which fly before the battle ends

May, even in their wives' and children's sight,

Be hanged up for example at their doors.

And you that be the King's friends, follow me.   170

Exeunt [the two Staffords and Soldiers].

CADE

And you that love the commons, follow me.

Now show yourselves men; 'tis for liberty.

We will not leave one lord, one gentleman:

Spare none but such as go in clouted shoon,

For they are thrifty honest men, and such   175

As would, but that they dare not, take our parts.

BUTCHER

They are all in order and march toward us.

CADE   But then are we in order when we are most out of

order. Come, march forward.   *[Exeunt.]*

162–4 See Appendix 2 for Q variant.

163 **gentle words** hardly appropriate to 113–14

166 **up** up in arms

172–3 John Ball 'exhorted them to consider . . . to . . . cast off the yoke of bondage, & recouer libertie . . . they might destroie first the great lords of the realme . . . and all other . . . against the commons . . . there should be an equalitie in libertie, no difference in degrees of nobilitie, but a like dignitie and equall authoritie in all things' (Holinshed, 2.749).

174 **clouted shoon** either patched shoes or shoes studded with clout nails otherwise known as hobnailed boots (see *OED* Clout shoe). For the proverbial phrase for peasant revolt in sixteenth-century England, 'clubs and clouted shoon', see Hobday, 8n. above.

178–9 **But . . . order.** the underlying topos of the *mundus inversus* theme, perhaps best commented upon by applying Nicholas Sotherton's sharp remark on Robert Kett, 'his preposterous authoritie' (Beer, 82)

170 SD] *Theobald subst.; Exit. F*   179 SD] *Theobald*

[4.3]   *Alarums to the fight, wherein both the Staffords*
are slain. Enter CADE *and the rest.*

CADE   Where's Dick, the butcher of Ashford?

BUTCHER   Here, sir.

CADE   They fell before thee like sheep and oxen, and thou
behaved'st thyself as if thou hadst been in thine own
slaughterhouse. Therefore, thus will I reward thee: the   5
Lent shall be as long again as it is, and thou shalt have
a licence to kill for a hundred lacking one.

BUTCHER   I desire no more.

CADE   And, to speak truth, thou deserv'st no less. [*Takes
up Stafford's sword.*] This monument of the victory   10

4.3 location: editors usually number this
scene separately as 'Another part of
Blackheath', but the action continues
from 4.2. Hall (220) relates Cade's
retreat to Sevenoaks and the Staffords'
fatal pursuit.

3–5 They . . . thee Presumably Dick
carries around on stage the meat
cleaver of his trade, rather like the
West Country rebel of 1450 who
'carried an axe ready for the beheading
of appropriate victims' (Harvey, 126).

3   sheep and oxen This language and
Dick the butcher's action specifically
realize the imagery evoked by
Gloucester's fate (see 3.1.210–12;
3.2.189, 195). To make the parallelism
of aristocratic and plebeian violence
even more emphatic, in his anger York
declares, 'On sheep or oxen could I
spend my fury' (5.1.27). There is possibly an allusion here to the Israelites
fighting the Philistines: see 1 Samuel,
14.32.

6   as long again twice as long, i.e. eighty
days

7   licence to kill Slaughter of animals
during Lent was prohibited by law
though a special licence could be

obtained for exemptions. This encouraged the fishing industry and consequently strengthened the navy.

hundred lacking one the conventional figure of ninety-nine found on
leases, referring here to years, animals
or persons. Q's 'foure score & one a
week' implies the second or third.

9–10 SD Editors usually draw on details
of Stafford's armour as found in
Polychronicon (8.573), *Brut* (518) and
Fabyan (623), which give the fullest
details of sallet ('salade', a light helmet
with neck guard), brigandine (coat of
mail with steel rings or plates sewed
upon leather or linen) and gilt spurs.
Unlacing and then lacing up a brigandine would take too long for what
remains of this short scene. Cade is
anticipating his triumphal entry where
the Mayor's sword will duplicate
Stafford's.

10–13 See LN for historical accounts. For
comparison with a Roman triumphal
entry see Venezky, 185. Cf. 4.6.2–4n.

10   monument . . . victory a memorial
trophy, here probably Stafford's sword,
like those displayed as part of triumphal entries. See 10–13n.

4.3] *Capell*   **9–10 SD]** *this edn*

will I bear, and the bodies shall be dragged at my horse
heels till I do come to London, where we will have the
Mayor's sword borne before us.

BUTCHER   If we mean to thrive and do good, break open
the gaols and let out the prisoners.   15

CADE   Fear not that, I warrant thee. Come, let's march
towards London.   *Exeunt [dragging off the bodies].*

[**4.4**]   *Enter the* KING *with a supplication, and the* QUEEN *with*
Suffolk's head, the Duke of BUCKINGHAM
and the Lord SAYE.

QUEEN [*aside*]
Oft have I heard that grief softens the mind
And makes it fearful and degenerate;

14–15 **break . . . prisoners** Hall (222)
records that 'the lusty Kentishe
Capitayne, hopying on more frendes,
brake vp the gayles of the kinges
benche and Marshalsea, and set at libertie, a swarme of galantes, both mete
for his seruice and apte for his enterprise' (cf. Holinshed, 226), events paralleling 1381: 'they . . . brake vp the
prisons of the Marshalsea, & the
Kings bench, set the prisoners at libertie, & admitted them into their com-
panie' (Holinshed, 2.737).

16 **Fear . . . thee.** Don't doubt that, I
promise you.

17 **London** Q adds ', for to morrow I
meane to sit in the Kings seate at
Westminster' (TLN 1693–4). See
Appendix 2.

4.4 location: London, the royal palace

0.1 *supplication*   Cade's   petition.
Caldwell reprints as Appendices A, B
and C the three British Library
Harleian MSS in the handwriting of
John Stow. See Appendix 5, pp. 443–7.

0.2 *Suffolk's head* King Henry ordered
that the body of Suffolk be taken to

Wingfield for interment in the family
tomb.

0.3 **Lord** SAYE James Fiennes, Lord Saye
and Sele. Before attaining the high positions of Lord Chamberlain and Lord
Treasurer, Saye had been Sheriff of
Kent (1437) and then of Surrey and
Sussex (1439). In 1446–7 he was
Constable of Dover and Warden of the
Cinque Ports. Shakespeare chose to
ignore the implications of corrupt, if not
criminal, behaviour in the chronicles and
presents Saye as a vulnerable victim,
pathetic, sick and frightened of the brutality of the rebels. The 'great extortioners' named by Cade, 'Sleg, Cromer, Isle,
and Robert Est' (Holinshed, 224), were
all associates of Saye in the 1440s in various official government capacities in
Kent, such as sheriffs and members of
parliament. All levels of Kentish society
were their victims and it was believed
that Saye himself started the rumour,
which began the whole rebellion, that
Kent was to be laid waste in revenge for
Suffolk's murder (see Griffiths, 630–3;
Harvey, 38–43, 73).

17 SD *dragging . . . bodies*] *this edn*   **4.4**] *Pope*   0.1–3] *F subst.*   1, 14, 55 SDs] *Collier*

Think therefore on revenge and cease to weep.
But who can cease to weep and look on this?
Here may his head lie on my throbbing breast;   5
But where's the body that I should embrace?

BUCKINGHAM

What answer makes your grace to the rebels'
    supplication?

KING

I'll send some holy bishop to entreat,
For God forbid so many simple souls
Should perish by the sword. And I myself,   10
Rather than bloody war shall cut them short,
Will parley with Jack Cade their general.
But stay, I'll read it over once again.

QUEEN [*aside*]

Ah, barbarous villains! Hath this lovely face
Ruled like a wandering planet over me   15
And could it not enforce them to relent,
That were unworthy to behold the same?

KING

Lord Saye, Jack Cade hath sworn to have thy head.

SAYE

Ay, but I hope your highness shall have his.

---

3   **revenge** Cairncross points out that
    this is 'the first statement of the
    revenge motif which is later to domi-
    nate the part of Margaret', finally with
    full Senecan rhetoric in *R3*.

7   **rebels' supplication** Cade's petition,
    printed by Holinshed (221–4) before
    the account of the Staffords' fate

8   **holy bishop** Hall (220) and Holinshed
    (224) mention the Archbishop of
    Canterbury (and Buckingham). As we
    see in 4.8.6, Buckingham and Clifford
    are the emissaries on stage.

10 **perish . . . sword** common in the
    Authorised Version; but as Hart points

out, Matthew, 26.52, 'all that take the
sword, shall perish with the sword'
(Geneva Bible), is probably alluded to.

11 **cut them short** Cf. the pun at 3.1.81.

12 **parley . . . Cade** in imitation of
    Richard II's personal confrontation
    with the rebels. Cade would not 'be
    perswaded to dissolue his armye,
    except the kynge in person wolde come
    to him, and assent to all thynges, which
    he should requyre' (Hall, 221).

15 **Ruled . . . planet** According to early
    astrology a planet in the ascendant
    determined behaviour.

17 **That** who

313

KING

    How now, madam?   20

    Still lamenting and mourning for Suffolk's death?

    I fear me, love, if that I had been dead

    Thou wouldest not have mourned so much for me.

QUEEN

    No, my love, I should not mourn but die for thee.

Enter a Messenger.

KING

    How now? What news? Why com'st thou in such

        haste?   25

MESSENGER

    The rebels are in Southwark; fly, my lord!

    Jack Cade proclaims himself Lord Mortimer,

    Descended from the Duke of Clarence' house,

    And calls your grace usurper, openly,

    And vows to crown himself in Westminster.   30

    His army is a ragged multitude

    Of hinds and peasants, rude and merciless.

    Sir Humphrey Stafford and his brother's death

    Hath given them heart and courage to proceed.

    All scholars, lawyers, courtiers, gentlemen,   35

    They call false caterpillars and intend their death.

KING

    O, graceless men! They know not what they do.

---

26 **Southwark** south of the Thames, by way of London Bridge, the only gateway to the city. Wat Tyler crossed here.

27 See 4.6.1 and n.

29 **usurper** Cf. 1.3.33, 186.

31–2 **ragged . . . rude** See 3.2.135 and n.

36 **false caterpillars** paralleling York's charge at 3.1.90. In the course of the sixteenth century the figurative meaning of 'rapacious extortioner' (*OED* Caterpillar

2) absorbed the meaning of the earlier 'piller', a robber, despoiler, thief, and 'caterpillar of the commonwealth' became a proverbial phrase (Dent, CC7) as is found in *R2* 2.3.166. See Dodson.

37 **graceless** without divine grace
They . . . do. See Luke, 23.34, 'Father forgive them; for they knowe not what they doe'.

23 wouldest] *Theobald;* would'st *F*

BUCKINGHAM

My gracious lord, retire to Killingworth
Until a power be raised to put them down.

QUEEN

Ah, were the Duke of Suffolk now alive,   40
These Kentish rebels would be soon appeased.

KING

Lord Saye, the traitors hateth thee,
Therefore away with us to Killingworth.

SAYE

So might your grace's person be in danger.
The sight of me is odious in their eyes;   45
And therefore in this city will I stay
And live alone, as secret as I may.

Enter another Messenger.

2 MESSENGER

Jack Cade hath almost gotten London Bridge;
The citizens fly and forsake their houses;
The rascal people, thirsting after prey,   50
Join with the traitor; and they jointly swear
To spoil the city and your royal court.

BUCKINGHAM

Then linger not, my lord: away, take horse!

KING

Come, Margaret. God, our hope, will succour us.

QUEEN [*aside*]

My hope is gone, now Suffolk is deceased.   55

KING

Farewell, my lord. Trust not the Kentish rebels.

---

38 **Killingworth** Kenilworth, near Warwick
39 **power** army
41 **appeased** pacified (*OED* Appease *v.* 1a)
42 See 0.3n.

44 **So** then (Abbott, 66)
50 **rascal people** rabble (*OED* Rascal *adj.* B1): Hall's phrase (29)
52 **spoil** despoil, pillage

42 traitors] traitrous rabble *Oxf*   48 almost] *Q; not in F*

BUCKINGHAM

　Trust nobody, for fear you be betrayed.

SAYE

　The trust I have is in mine innocence,

　And therefore am I bold and resolute.　　　　　*Exeunt.*

[**4.5**]　　*Enter* Lord SCALES [*aloft*] *upon the Tower walking.*
　　　　　Then enters two or three Citizens *below.*

SCALES　How now? Is Jack Cade slain?

1 CITIZEN　No, my lord, nor likely to be slain; for they
　have won the bridge, killing all those that withstand
　them. The Lord Mayor craves aid of your honour from
　the Tower to defend the city from the rebels.　　　　　5

SCALES

　Such aid as I can spare you shall command,

　But I am troubled here with them myself;

　The rebels have assayed to win the Tower.

　But get you to Smithfield and gather head,

　And thither I will send you Matthew Gough.　　　　　10

　Fight for your king, your country and your lives!

　And so farewell, for I must hence again.　　*Exeunt [severally].*

---

58 **innocence** See 0.3n.
59 **bold** Cf. 'Innocence is bold' (Dent, I82).
4.5 location: outside the walls of the Tower of London
0.1 **Lord** SCALES Thomas de Scales, seventh Lord (1399?–1460), a veteran of the French wars and a Lancastrian supporter. He was left behind by Henry to defend the Tower of London (Hall, 221).

Tower the gallery used at 1.4
3 **bridge** London Bridge
4–5 **The . . . rebels.** In the chronicles this occurs after Cade has actually entered the city (Hall, 221).
4 **Lord Mayor** Thomas Charlton (Harvey, 92)
　craves begs (*OED v.* 2)
8 **assayed** tried
10 **Matthew Gough** See 4.7.0.1n.

57 be betrayed] *F2;* betraid *F*　**4.5**] *Pope*　0.1–2] Enter three or four citizens below. *Q*　0.1 *aloft*] *this edn*　2–5] *Prose Pope; F lines* slaine: / Bridge, / them: / Tower / Rebels. /　2 lord] lord Scales *Oxf*　they] he and his men *Oxf*　3 withstand] did withstand *Oxf*　9 But . . . and] Get you to Smithfield, there to *Oxf*　10 Gough] *Capell following Holinshed; (Goffe) F*

[**4.6**]   *Enter* Jack CADE *and the rest,*
                  and strikes his staff on London Stone.

CADE   Now is Mortimer lord of this city. And here, sitting
    upon London Stone, I charge and command that, at
    the city's cost, the Pissing Conduit run nothing but
    claret wine this first year of our reign. And now hence-
    forward it shall be treason for any that calls me other   5
    than Lord Mortimer.

                  Enter a Soldier *running.*

SOLDIER   Jack Cade! Jack Cade!
CADE   Knock him down there. *They kill him.*
BUTCHER   If this fellow be wise, he'll never call ye Jack

4.6 location: Cannon Street

0.2 *staff* 'sword' in Q, Hall (221) and
    Holinshed (224); but *staff* carries great
    visual irony given its function earlier in
    relation to Gloucester (2.3.31–2 and
    3.1.189–90) and Cade's own words
    (4.2.152–3), and later to the pious
    King (5.1.97).
London Stone 'The central milliarium
    (*milestone*) of Roman London, similar
    to that in the Forum of Rome. The
    British high roads radiated from this
    stone, and it was from this point they
    were measured' (Brewer, 770).
    Originally on the south side of Cannon
    Street, it is now built into the wall of
    St Swithun's Church.

1 **Now . . . city.** the words of Hall (221)
    and Holinshed (224)

2–4 **I . . . reign** a burlesque of the royal
    entry of King Henry VI on returning
    to London after his coronation in
    Paris. He first assembled on Black-
    heath before entering his capital,
    where, as Fabyan (605) records, the
    conduits of Cheapside ran with wine, a
    festive tradition. For royal entry con-

ventions and Cade, see Venezky, 185.
    See also 4.3.10–13 LN.

3 **Pissing Conduit** Hart quotes Stow,
    'The little Conduite called the *pissing
    Conduite*, by the Stokes Market'
    (*Survey*). Steevens notes the expres-
    sion in French historical records dat-
    ing from 1453.

4 **claret** yellowish or light red, in con-
    trast to red or white; only here in
    Shakespeare

4–6 **And now . . . Mortimer** perhaps sug-
    gested by 'He also put to execution in
    Southwarke diuers persons . . . lest they
    shoulde blase & declare his base byrthe,
    and lowsy lynage, disparagyng him from
    his vsurped surname of Mortymer'
    (Hall, 221). Similarly, executed with
    Crowmer (see 4.7.103–4n.) was one
    Bayly who, Fabyan speculates, 'was of
    the famylyer & olde acquayntaunce of
    Iak Cade, wherfore so soon as he espyed
    him commynge to hym warde, he caste
    in his mynde that he wolde dyscouer his
    lynynge & olde maners and shewe of his
    vyle kynne and lynage' (624).

9–10 **If . . . warning.** Cf. 'He is wise that

4.6] *Capell*   0.2 *staff on*] sword upon *Q*   1–6] *Prose Pope; F lines* City, / Stone, / cost / Wine /
raigne. / any, / Mortimer. /   2 at] *this edn; of F*

317

Cade more. I think he hath a very fair warning. [*Reads*   10
soldier's message.] My lord, there's an army gathered
together in Smithfield.

CADE   Come, then, let's go fight with them. But first go
and set London Bridge on fire; and, if you can, burn
down the Tower too. Come, let's away.   15

Exeunt [*with the body*].

[**4.7**]   *Alarums. Matthew Gough is slain and all the rest.*
Then enter Jack CADE *with his company.*

CADE   So, sirs: now go some and pull down the Savoy.

is ware in time' (Tilley, T291).

14 London . . . fire In the fighting 'the
multitude of the rebelles draue the
citezens from the stoulpes ['stoops' –
posts or pillars] at the bridge foote, to
the drawe bridge, and began to set fyre
in diuers houses' (Hall, 222).

14–15 burn . . . Tower There is no mention of this in the chronicles (Sanders).

4.7 location: Smithfield. The action continues from 4.6.

0.1–3 Q's 'Then enter *Iacke Cade* again'
indicates that a battle takes place
onstage.

0.1 *Matthew Gough* Gough was described
by an English contemporary as 'surpassing all the other esquires in war at that
time in bravery, hardihood, loyalty and
liberality' (Griffiths, 521). The heroic
image reappears in Hall: 'the often
named capitayne in Normandy . . . he
was both of manhode, and experience
greatly renoued and noysed . . . more
expert in marcial feates, then the other
cheuetaynes of the citie . . . a man of
great wit, much experience in feates of
chiualrie, the which in continual warres,

had valeauntly serued the kyng and his
father, in the partes beyo*n*d the sea'
(221–2). For the military reversal and
contrast with Cade see Warren,
'Contrarieties'. For the audience to be
aware of Gough's death in the course of
the *alarums* his livery may have been as
famous as his name, announced at 4.5.10.

1–2 probably from Fabyan's account of
1381, as Holinshed (738) mentions only
the Savoy: 'they . . . came vnto ye duke
of Lancasters place standyng wi*th*out ye
Temple Barre, callyd Sauoy, & spoyled
that was therin, & after set it vpo*n* fyre &
brent it . . . Tha*n* they entryd the cytie &
serchid the Temple and other innes of
court, & spolyd theyr placys & brent
theyr bokys of lawe, & slewe as many
men of lawe & questmongers as they
myght fynde' (Fabyan, 530).

1 **Savoy** the London residence of the
Duke of Lancaster, named after Peter,
Earl of Savoy, uncle of Queen Eleanor,
the wife of Henry III. It was burnt
down by Wat Tyler and the rebels in
1381 and was rebuilt by Henry VII in
1505 (Brewer, 1106).

10–11 SD] *Oxf subst.; not in QF*   **13–15**] *Prose Pope; F lines* them: / fire, / too. / away. /   **14** on fire]
a fire *Q*   **15 SD** *with the body*] *this edn; omnes F*   **4.7**] *Capell*   **0.1–3**] *F subst.* Alarmes, and then
Mathew Goffe is slaine, and all the rest with him. Then enter *Iacke Cade* again, and his company. *Q*

Others to th'Inns of Court; down with them all!

BUTCHER   I have a suit unto your lordship.

CADE   Be it a lordship, thou shalt have it for that word.

BUTCHER   Only that the laws of England may come out of   5
your mouth.

NICK [*aside*]   'Mass, 'twill be sore law then, for he was
thrust in the mouth with a spear and 'tis not whole yet.

WEAVER [*aside*]   Nay, Nick, it will be stinking law, for his
breath stinks with eating toasted cheese.   10

CADE   I have thought upon it, it shall be so. Away, burn
all the records of the realm, my mouth shall be the

---

2 **Inns of Court** the Inner Temple, Middle Temple, Lincoln's Inn and Gray's Inn, the societies and offices of practising barristers

4 **lordship** a lord's domain (*OED sb.* 2): in this sense only here in Shakespeare

5–6 **laws . . . mouth** Cf. Wat Tyler, 'putting his hands to his lips, that within foure daies all the lawes of England should come foorth of his mouth' (Holinshed, 2.740). Tyler anticipates article 14 of the articles of deposition against Richard II: 'Item, he said, that the lawes of the realme were in his head, and sometimes in his brest, by reason of which fantasticall opinion, he destroied noble men, and impouerished the poore commons' (Holinshed, 2.860). The author of *Woodstock* put these words into the mouth of Richard's favourite, Tresilian: 'It shall be law, what I shall say is law' (1.2.49). Tyler and Cade parody their autocratic betters, and anticipate King Edward's 'And for this once my will shall stand for law' (*3H6* 4.1.50).

7, 9, 14 SDs On these asides, see 4.2.30 SD n.

7 **'Mass** 'by the mass', an oath invoking the Eucharist of the Catholic church

10 **toasted cheese** In Jane Howell's BBC production, shortly after this line, Cade carries a huge block of cheese, which he waves under Lord Saye's nose. However, this is not just a personal allusion, but social and, as elsewhere in Shakespeare, ethnic. Social inferiors could not afford the beef of their superiors (as with Corporal Nym, *H5* 2.1.9). See Davies, 286–90. 'Toasted cheese' as a jestbook insult was usually directed at the Welsh (see Zall, 132), e.g. in Falstaff's remark to Sir Hugh Evans: 'Am I ridden with a Welsh goat too? . . . 'Tis time I were chok'd with a piece of toasted cheese' (*MW* 5.5.139). See LN.

12 **records . . . realm** The 1381 rebels 'purposed to burne and destroie all records, euidences, court-rolles, and other minuments, that the remembrance of ancient matters being remooued out of mind, their landlords might not haue whereby to chalenge anie right at their hands' (Holinshed, 2.737); 'so likewise did they at Westminster, where they brake open the eschequer, and destroied the ancient bookes and other records there' (Holinshed, 2.739).

1–2] *Prose Cam; F lines* Sauoy: / all. / 7 SP] *this edn; Iohn. F*   7, 9, 14 SDs] *Capell*   9 Nick] *this edn;* John *F*

parliament of England.

NICK [*aside*]   Then we are like to have biting statutes,
   unless his teeth be pulled out.   15

CADE   And henceforward all things shall be in common.

Enter a Messenger.

MESSENGER   My lord, a prize, a prize! Here's the Lord
   Saye which sold the towns in France; he that made us
   pay one-and-twenty fifteens, and one shilling to the
   pound, the last subsidy.   20

Enter GEORGE *with the* Lord SAYE.

CADE   Well, he shall be beheaded for it ten times. Ah, thou
   say, thou serge – nay, thou buckram lord! Now art thou
   within point-blank of our jurisdiction regal. What

---

14 **biting** severe (punning on *mouth* and
   teeth)
16 See 4.2.63n. and LN
18 **towns** in Anjou and Maine. See
   4.2.150–1.
19 **one-and-twenty fifteens** a tax of 140
   per cent: a comic inflation of Suffolk's
   request for a tax of one-fifteenth to
   bring Margaret to England (see
   1.1.130n.). Cade promised his
   followers 'that neither fiftenes should
   hereafter be demaunded, nor once any
   imposicions, or tax should be spoken
   of' (Hall, 220).
20 **subsidy** a parliamentary grant to aid
   the sovereign (*OED sb.* 2). See *3H6*
   4.8.45, the only other occurrence in
   Shakespeare.
20.1 **GEORGE** See 4.2.0.1n.
22 **say . . . serge . . . buckram** Cade's
   mockery begins with a sophisticated
   pun on Lord Saye's name. *Say* was
   used to describe cloth made from
   either coarse or fine silk. Sometimes it

was equated with the French *soie*
(Hart). Presumably Saye has appeared
dressed with deliberate modesty in
order not to provoke by dressing
according to his status and the sumptuary laws (93 and n., 4.2.119n.). Cade
seizes on the discrepancy between aristocratic entitlement demarcated by silk
and the relative plainness before him.
Serge, a cheap material, is added for
mockery, while *buckram* gives expression to Cade's dismissive exposure of
Saye's pretence. 'Buckram' (*OED sb.* 2)
was a coarse linen stiffened with gum
or paste for linings or, in the theatre, to
make dummy figures or costumes.
Figuratively it connoted 'stiff',
'starched', 'stuck-up', or a false
appearance of strength (*OED sb.* 3 and
4).
23 **point-blank** within direct range. To
   aim and fire arrow or gun point-blank
   was to fire horizontally straight to a
   target. Cf. *MW* 3.2.33–4.

14–15] *Prose Cam; F lines* Statutes / out. /   22 serge] *(*Surge*)*; George *Q*

canst thou answer to my majesty for giving up of
Normandy unto Mounsieur Basimecu, the Dauphin of   25
France? Be it known unto thee by these presence, even
the presence of Lord Mortimer, that I am the besom
that must sweep the court clean of such filth as thou
art. Thou hast most traitorously corrupted the youth of
the realm in erecting a grammar school; and, whereas   30
before our forefathers had no other books but the score
and the tally, thou hast caused printing to be used and,
contrary to the King his crown and dignity, thou hast
built a paper-mill. It will be proved to thy face that thou
hast men about thee that usually talk of a noun and a   35

25 **Basimecu** a Gallophobe vulgarisation
from *baise mon cul*, 'kiss my arse'
26 **Be . . . presence** a legal formula for
the opening of official documents in
which Cade confuses *per has literas
presentes* ('by these present documents') with the royal *presence*. Hart
gives other examples in drama and
cites the 'presents'/'presence' pun in
AYL 1.2.22–4. See *OED* Present *sb.*[1]
II 26.
27 **besom** broom. Proverbially 'A new
broom sweeps clean' (Tilley, B682).
Hart compares Isaiah, 14.23, 'I will
sweepe it with the besome of destruction'. Not elsewhere in Shakespeare.
29–30 **Thou . . . school** As part of their
anti-authoritarian agenda, the 1381
rebels sought 'to compell teachers of
children in grammer schooles to
sweare neuer to instruct any in their
art' (Holinshed, 2.746). In contrast,
Cade was said to be 'suborned by techers, but also enforced by pryuye
scholemasters' (Hall, 220).
30 **grammar school** Though *OED*
records a fourteenth- and a fifteenth-
century occurrence, the *grammar
school* is associated with the sixteenth-

century humanist revival of classical
Latin in the dominance of rhetoric
within the teaching of the trivium
(grammar, rhetoric, logic).
31–2 **score . . . tally** The *score* (see
4.2.68), or reckoning, was cut in the
tally (stick) which was split lengthwise
as a record of account for purchaser
and seller. 'Tally' occurs only here in
Shakespeare.
32 **printing . . . used** an anachronism.
Under the year 1459 Holinshed has a
marginal note, 'Printing first inuent-
ed', and the comment, 'William
Caxton of London mercer brought it
into England about the yeare 1471'
(250), now thought to be about 1476.
The books which the rebels destroyed
were manuscript volumes of legal
records (see Holinshed, 2.738–9).
33 **King . . . dignity** a standard legal formula
34 **paper-mill** another anachronism.
Paper was imported in the fourteenth
century; however, John Tate started
the first English paper-mill at Hertford
in 1498 (*Shakespeare's England*, 2.238).
35 **usually** habitually

25 Basimecu] bus mine cue *Q*   Dauphin] *(Dolphine)*   26 presence] presents *F4*

verb, and such abominable words as no Christian ear
can endure to hear. Thou hast appointed justices of
peace, to call poor men before them, about matters they
were not able to answer. Moreover, thou hast put them
in prison, and because they could not read thou hast   40
hanged them, when indeed only for that cause they
have been most worthy to live. Thou dost ride on a
foot-cloth, dost thou not?

SAYE   What of that?

CADE   Marry, thou ought'st not to let thy horse wear a   45
cloak when honester men than thou go in their hose
and doublets.

BUTCHER   And work in their shirts too; as myself, for
example, that am a butcher.

SAYE   You men of Kent –   50

BUTCHER   What say you of Kent?

SAYE   Nothing but this: 'tis *bona terra, mala gens.*

---

36 **abominable** 'abhominable' in F. Cf.
LLL 5.1.23–4, 'This is abhominable –
which he would call "abbominable"'.
Woudhuysen notes: 'Up to the mid-
seventeenth century "abominable" was
regularly spelled "abhominable", since
it was assumed the word came from
the Lat. *ab homine*, meaning "away
from man", hence "inhuman" or
"beastly". The correct etymology for
the word is from Lat. *abominabilis*,
meaning "deserving imprecation or
abhorrence".'

37–42 **Thou . . . live.** Cade refers to the
legal procedure known as benefit of
clergy. This was the privilege, available
to ordained clerks, monks and nuns
accused of felony, of being tried and
punished by an ecclesiastical court. As
a consequence of the statute *Pro clero*
it was later extended to all who could
read in Latin their 'neck verse', Psalm,
51.1. In effect it meant exemption

from the death penalty (see Gabel).
Cade now applies the 'prepostrous
authoritie' (see 4.2.178–9n.) not of
radical anarchy but of the actual feudal, hierarchical world, against one of
its own.

39 **answer** defend themselves by rebut-
ting (charges) (*OED v.* 1)

43 **foot-cloth** See 4.1.54n.

46–7 **hose and doublets** breeches and
short coats: inadequately dressed, that
is, in comparison with the well-
covered horse. *MW* makes it clear: 'in
your doublet and hose, this raw
rheumatic day!' (3.1.46–7).

48 **in their shirts** i.e. without any outer
garments

52 *bona . . . gens* 'a good land, a bad people' (Dent, L49.1). Dent, E146,
'England is a good country but ill people', draws on Boorde, 'The Italyen
and the Lombarde say Anglia terra,
bona terra, mala gent [*sic*]' (I.ii, C1).

---

36 abominable] *(abhominable)*   42 on] *Q;* in *F*   48 shirts] *Oxf;* shirt *F*

CADE   Away with him, away with him! He speaks Latin.

SAYE

    Hear me but speak, and bear me where you will.

    Kent, in the *Commentaries* Caesar writ,   55

    Is termed the civil'st place of all this isle;

    Sweet is the country, because full of riches,

    The people liberal, valiant, active, wealthy;

    Which makes me hope you are not void of pity.

    I sold not Maine, I lost not Normandy,   60

    Yet to recover them would lose my life.

    Justice with favour have I always done;

    Prayers and tears have moved me, gifts could never.

    When have I aught exacted at your hands,

    Kent to maintain, the King, the realm and you?   65

    Large gifts have I bestowed on learned clerks

    Because my book preferred me to the King:

    And seeing ignorance is the curse of God,

    Knowledge the wing wherewith we fly to heaven,

    Unless you be possessed with devilish spirits,   70

    You cannot but forbear to murder me.

    This tongue hath parleyed unto foreign kings

---

53 **speaks Latin** Benefit of clergy is reversed. See 37–42n.

55–6 Steevens points out Golding's translation (1564) of Caesar's book, *De bello gallico* (5.14): 'Of all the inhabitants of this isle the civillest are the kentish folke'. Malone added that Lyly's *Euphues* (1578) repeats this exactly.

56 **civil'st** most civilized

58 Cf. *3H6* 1.2.43.
    valiant Cf. 'men in Kent / Whose Valiaunt hartes refuse none enterprise' ('Jack Cade', 57–8: *Mirror*, 173).

59 **void of** without
    pity See 3.1.125n.

62 part of the idealized representation. See 4.4.0.3n.

64 **exacted** a provocatively ambiguous word to use, since it could mean enforcing the payment of fees and taxes etc. to the point of extortion

65 **Kent** With the exception of Hattaway, editors accept Johnson's emendation, 'But', which actually concedes the extortion Saye is denying and suggests legal sanction, Saye thereby doubly damning himself.

66 **learned clerks** learnèd: men of learning, scholars

67 **book preferred me** learning gained me preferment

71 **cannot but** must
    forbear refrain

72 **parleyed unto** conferred diplomatically with

54 where] *(wher'e)*   65 Kent] But *(Johnson)*

For your behoof –

CADE   Tut, when struck'st thou one blow in the field?

SAYE

> Great men have reaching hands; oft have I struck   75
> Those that I never saw, and struck them dead.

GEORGE   O monstrous coward! What, to come behind folks?

SAYE

> These cheeks are pale with watching for your good.

CADE   Give him a box o'th' ear, and that will make 'em red
again.   80

SAYE

> Long sitting to determine poor men's causes
> Hath made me full of sickness and diseases.

CADE   Ye shall have a hempen caudle then and the help of
hatchet.

BUTCHER   Why dost thou quiver, man?   85

SAYE

> The palsy and not fear provokes me.

---

73 **behoof** benefit, advantage: only here in Shakespeare
74 **field** (of battle)
75 **Great . . . hands** proverbial: 'Kings have long arms' (Dent, K87). Found in several languages; Wilson gives Ovid, *Heroides*, 17.166, while Hart demonstrates its commonplace nature in English Renaissance literature.
     reaching far-reaching
78 **watching** keeping awake through the night (*OED v.* 1b). Cf. *R2* 2.1.78.
79 **box . . . ear** from the title of Lyly's *Pap with an Hatchet. Alias, A fig for my Godson. Or, crack me this nut. Or, A Country cuff, that is, a sound box of the ear* etc., 1589 (Hart) – first occurrence of the phrase (*OED sb.*[3] 2). Several times in Shakespeare. See 83–4n.
81 **sitting** (as a judge)
     determine settle, decide (*OED v.* 4)
     causes lawsuits (*OED sb.* 7)
83 **a hempen caudle** a fortifying drink

made from rope (ironic). The hangman's rope was made from hemp, and 'caudle' was a restorative beverage of spiced gruel and wine or ale. *OED* (Hempen *a.* 1b) attributes this phrase to Shakespeare here, along with other contemporary cant terms such as 'hempen lane', 'hempen snare', 'hempen circle', 'hempen squincey'. Presumably for idiomatic force, Shakespeare was using what was current.
83–4 **help of hatchet** Cairncross prefers the proverbial 'pap with a hatchet' (rough chastisement of children); see 79n. Saye is to be hanged, and then beheaded for display of his head on a pole.
86 **palsy** the 'shaking palsy' (Parkinson's disease) in contrast to a paralytic stroke, as in *R2* 2.3.104 (*Shakespeare's England*, 1.436). Shakespeare's invention – not in the sources. See 4.4.0.3n.
     provokes me makes me tremble (*OED* Provoke *v.* 6b)

---

78 with] *F2;* for *F*   83 caudle] *F4;* candle *F*   help of] pap with a *Ard²;* health o'th' *Oxf*

CADE   Nay, he nods at us, as who should say, 'I'll be even
with you.' I'll see if his head will stand steadier on a
pole, or no. Take him away and behead him.

SAYE

Tell me, wherein have I offended most?   90
Have I affected wealth or honour? Speak.
Are my chests filled up with extorted gold?
Is my apparel sumptuous to behold?
Whom have I injured, that ye seek my death?
These hands are free from guiltless bloodshedding,   95
This breast from harbouring foul deceitful thoughts.
O, let me live!

CADE [*aside*]   I feel remorse in myself with his words, but
I'll bridle it. He shall die, an it be but for pleading so
well for his life. – Away with him! He has a familiar   100
under his tongue; he speaks not i'God's name. Go, take

---

87 **as who** like one who
91 **affected** made ostentatious display of
(*OED v.*¹ 5)
92 **extorted gold** See 64n. and 4.4.0.3n.
93 **apparel sumptuous** This may be an
ironic echo of the proclamation of 1588
in which Elizabeth authorized temporary detention to prove the correctness
of dress and degree according to the
sumptuary laws: 'because there are
many persons that percase shall be
found in outward appearance more
sumptuous in their apparel than by
common intendment'. See Hughes &
Larkin, 3, no. 697, 7, and 4.2.69n. above.
94 **injured** One Reginald Peckham, Esq.,
had particular reason to feel 'injured'
since Saye and his wife in 1448 threatened him with 'death and imprisonment, drawing and hanging', in order
to 'extort feloniously and fraudulently'
his land under the pretence that it was
being exchanged (Virgoe, 'Indictments', 234).
95 **guiltless bloodshedding** shedding

the blood of innocent victims
98 **remorse** compunction, guilt. Cf.
'melted by the windy breath / Of soft
petitions, pity, and remorse' (*KJ*
2.1.477–8).
with expressing cause and effect. See
Abbott, 193.
99 **an ... but** if only
100–1 **familiar ... tongue** The *familiar*
was the familiar spirit or devil usually
appearing as a cat, dog or toad. By
under his tongue Cade refers to Saye's
Latin speech. Cf. Elizabeth Francis in
1556, in a deposition concerning her
witchcraft, 'she said that when she
wolde wil hym [the familiar] to do any
thinge for her, she wolde say her Pater
noster in laten' (Murray, 209–10; for
what is still one of the best accounts of
'familiars', see also 205–37). A memo-
rable story of a familiar is that of the
Witch of Endor, 1 Samuel, 29.7–14.
Cf. Joan, *1H6* 3.2.122.
101 *****i'God's** For F's 'a' proceeding the
modern 'in', see Abbott, 140.

98 SD] *Capell*   100 has] *(*ha's*)*   101 i'God's] *(a God's)*   101–2 take him away] take him to the
standerd in Cheapside and chop off his head, and then go to milende-greene *Q*

him away, I say, and strike off his head presently; and
then break into his son-in-law's house, Sir James
Crowmer, and strike off his head, and bring them both
upon two poles hither.   105

ALL   It shall be done.

SAYE

Ah, countrymen, if when you make your prayers
God should be so obdurate as yourselves,
How would it fare with your departed souls?   110
And therefore yet relent and save my life!

CADE   Away with him! And do as I command ye.

         [*Exeunt one or two with the Lord Saye.*]

The proudest peer in the realm shall not wear a head on
his shoulders, unless he pay me tribute; there shall not
a maid be married, but she shall pay to me her
maidenhead ere they have it; men shall hold of me *in*   115
capite; and we charge and command that their wives be
as free as heart can wish or tongue can tell.

---

102 **presently** immediately
103–4 **break . . . head** Both Hall (221)
and Holinshed (225) say that Cade
went to Mile End and 'apprehended'
Sir James, whose correct name is
William Crowmer, a London alderman
who acquired property in Kent and
eventually served two terms as Sheriff
of that county (Griffiths, 630–3;
Harvey, 39–40). See LN.
112 **proudest peer** Cf. *1H6* 5.1.57.
113–15 **there . . . it** alluding to the notorious 'droit de seigneur', the feudal
lord's right to spend the first night (*jus
primae noctis*) with his vassal's new
bride. Cade's demand is literal, whereas historians consider the custom a
means of raising fees for non-enforce-
ment, parallel to receiving payment for
waiving the right to select a bride.
Blackstone could find no evidence that
this custom prevailed in England,

though it did in Scotland, where it was
known as 'mercheta mulierum', until
abolished by Malcolm III (83). The
plot of Beaumont and Fletcher's
Custom of the Country (1619–23) turns
on this abuse.
115–16 *in capite* in chief: a law term. A
tenant *in capite* held land direct from
the king, the feudal head. (Cade is
punning on *maidenhead*; cf. *RJ*
1.1.25–6.) As Spelman demonstrates,
such tenure would give the holders
privilege as barons to attend the king's
parliament (see Pocock, 108–9). See
4.8.36n. Cf. the charge against the
Pope, in the homily on rebellion, of
giving away others' kingdoms 'unto
strangers, to hold . . . *in capite*, and as
of the chief lords thereof' (*Homilies*,
523).
117 **free . . . tell** proverbial (Dent,
H300.1). Halliwell claims, without

107 prayers] *(*prair's*)*   111 SD] *Q subst.*

BUTCHER   My lord, when shall we go to Cheapside and
    take up commodities upon our bills?

CADE   Marry, presently.   120

ALL   O brave!

        Enter one with the heads [upon poles].

CADE   But is not this braver? Let them kiss one another,
    for they loved well when they were alive. Now part
    them again, lest they consult about the giving up of
    some more towns in France. Soldiers, defer the spoil of   125
    the city until night; for with these borne before us
    instead of maces will we ride through the streets, and
    at every corner have them kiss. Away!   *Exeunt.*

illustration, that this formula is often
found in the royal grants of land. The
irony is that Cade is granting *wives*
this liberty of sexual promiscuity. Jack
of Leiden gathered fifteen wives
(Cohn, 293). See Appendix 2 for Q
here.

119 **take . . . bills** a euphemism for raising decapitated heads on their
weapons, playing on buying goods on
credit; for the specific practice of evad-
ing usury laws by buying back goods
already sold on credit for cash (see
OED Commodity 7b); and for sex (cf.
KJ 2.1.571–3). For 'bill' as penis see
Partridge, 82. For the commercial pun
see *MA* 3.3.177–8.

120 The sexual implication of 119 is
brought out here by Q, which reads:
'*Cade*. Marry he that will lustily stand
to it, / Shall go with me, and take vp
these commodities following: / Item, a
gowne, a kirtle, a petticoate, and a
smocke' (TLN 1783–5).

121 **brave** fine

122 **kiss one another** This atrocity of
1450 (Hall, 221; Holinshed, 225)
duplicates that of 1381 when the
rebels carried the heads of Sir John
Cavendish, the Lord Chief Justice, and
the Prior of St Edmundsbury into
Bury: 'they made sport with their
heads, making them sometime as it
were to kisse' (Holinshed, 2.744). The
horror and violence of such so-called
justice arbitrarily meted out on both
sides is symbolized by the decapitated
head which is given so much prominence in this play. Harvey relates that
following the executions after the tri-
bunals of 1451, 'As villagers of northern Kent saw the shocking sight of
carts going laden from the gallows
along the wintry roads to exhibit their
cargoes on London Bridge they
dubbed the royal progress "the harvest
of heads"' (152).

125 **spoil** looting

128 For Q variants from here to 4.8.53,
see facsimile TLN 1854–87.

121.1 *upon poles*] *Q subst.*   122–8] *Prose Theobald; F lines* brauer: / well / againe, / vp / Soldiers, /
night: / Maces, / Corner / Away. /   128 SD] *Rowe; Exit. F*

[**4.8**]   *Alarum and retreat. Enter again* CADE
                    and all his rabblement.

CADE   Up Fish Street! Down Saint Magnus' Corner! Kill
and knock down! Throw them into Thames!
                                                    Sound a parley.
What noise is this I hear?

Enter BUCKINGHAM *and* OLD CLIFFORD[, *attended*].

Dare any be so bold to sound retreat or parley when I
command them kill?   5
BUCKINGHAM
Ay, here they be that dare and will disturb thee!
Know, Cade, we come ambassadors from the King
Unto the commons, whom thou hast misled,
And here pronounce free pardon to them all

4.8 location: Theobald assigned the scene to Southwark, as indicated by Hall (222), and by Holinshed: 'for some tyme the Londoners were bet back to the stulpes ['stoops' – posts or pillars] at sainct Magnes corner, and sodaynly agayne the rebelles were repulsed and driuen backe, to the stulpes in Southwarke' (225); but, as Wilson objects, the scene clearly seems to open north of London Bridge. In Hall and Holinshed the two prelates, the Archbishop of Canterbury and the Bishop of Winchester, replaced here by Buckingham and Old Clifford, cross over the bridge into Southwark to offer pardon. In his 'Preface to Shakespeare' Johnson argued for the imaginative acceptance of Rome and Alexandria on the same stage, so perhaps the breadth of the Thames hardly matters? Action is continuous with 4.7.

0.2 *rabblement* elsewhere in Shakespeare only in *JC* 1.2.245

1 **Fish Street** the Fish Street Hill of today, which 'originally led down to the approach to medieval London

Bridge which lay downstream of the present bridge', so-called because it was the route from Billingsgate fish market to the city (Fairfield, 119–20)
Saint Magnus' Corner St Magnus' Church lay at the bottom of Fish Street.
Kill See 4.7.122n.

2   SD *Sound* by a trumpet call

2SD, 5 *parley* to treat or discuss terms, especially with an opponent or enemy. (Though *OED v.*[1] 2 gives 1600 as the earliest instance there are several in Shakespeare's 1590s plays; cf. 4.4.12.)

3.1 SD Usually placed after 5 by editors, but positioned here it reflects the direct challenge and confrontation of the two 'dares'.
OLD CLIFFORD Lord Thomas Clifford (1414–55). An old hand in Normandy of the 1430s, and subsequently at the relief of Calais in the 1450s. Killed at the first battle of St Albans (5.2), thereby giving his son a major revenge motif in *3H6*.

9   **pronounce** formally declare (*OED v.* 1)
free pardon Hall and Holinshed

4.8] *Capell; not in F or Oxf* 1 Magnus'] *Warburton;* Magnes *F*   3–5] *Prose Hanmer; F lines* heare? / Parley / kill? / 3.1 *after 5 in F*   attended] *Theobald*

That will forsake thee and go home in peace.   10

OLD CLIFFORD

    What say ye, countrymen? Will ye relent,
    And yield to mercy whilst 'tis offered you?
    Or let a rebel lead you to your deaths?
    Who loves the King and will embrace his pardon,
    Fling up his cap and say, 'God save his majesty!'   15
    Who hateth him and honours not his father,
    Henry the Fifth, that made all France to quake,
    Shake he his weapon at us, and pass by.
       [*They forsake Cade.*]

ALL   God save the King! God save the King!

CADE   What, Buckingham and Clifford, are ye so brave?   20
    And you, base peasants, do ye believe him? Will you
    needs be hanged with your pardons about your necks?
    Hath my sword therefore broke through London gates,
    that you should leave me at the White Hart in
    Southwark? I thought ye would never have given o'er   25
    these arms till you had recovered your ancient freedom;
    but you are all recreants and dastards and delight to
    live in slavery to the nobility. Let them break your

---

describe it as a 'general pardon'.

11 **countrymen** men of Kent and Essex (see *OED* 1). But as Clifford's appeal develops, so the term retroactively takes on the larger inclusive meaning associated with the monarcho-nationalism of Henry V (cf. *H5* 4.0.34, 'And calls them brothers, friends, countrymen').
    relent yield, give up (*OED v.*[1] 2b)

13 ***rebel** Singer's emendation is preferred to F's misreading of 'rabble' since Clifford is reinforcing the distinction between commons and Cade just made by Buckingham.

14, 16 **Who** whoever

14 **embrace** accept gladly (*OED v.*[2] 2d). Cf. *Cym* 1.4.156.

20 **brave** audacious

24 **White Hart** Cade appears to have made this inn his headquarters. When Iden brought Cade's body back to London the mistress of the inn identified it (Harvey, 100).

25 **given o'er** surrendered. See *OED* Give 63d(b). Walker's conj. is accepted (see t.n.) as 'F's' out seems an obvious error and attempts to account for it by reference to *OED* come under strain.

26 **ancient freedom** John Ball's liberty and freedom from bondage. See LN and 4.2.172–3n.

27 **recreants** deserters (*OED sb.* 2)
    dastards cowards (*OED sb.* 2)

---

13 rebel] *Q*; rabble *F*   18 SD] *Q*   24 White Hart] *F4*; White-heart *F*   25 o'er] over *(Walker)*; out *F*

backs with burdens, take your houses over your heads,
ravish your wives and daughters before your faces. For   30
me, I will make shift for one, and so God's curse light
upon you all!

ALL   We'll follow Cade! We'll follow Cade!

[*They run to Cade again.*]

OLD CLIFFORD

Is Cade the son of Henry the Fifth
That thus you do exclaim you'll go with him?   35
Will he conduct you through the heart of France
And make the meanest of you earls and dukes?
Alas, he hath no home, no place to fly to,
Nor knows he how to live but by the spoil,
Unless by robbing of your friends and us.   40
Were't not a shame that whilst you live at jar
The fearful French, whom you late vanquished,
Should make a start o'er seas and vanquish you?
Methinks already in this civil broil
I see them lording it in London streets,   45

---

31 **I . . . one** 'I'll shift for myself': proverbial (Dent, S334.1). In *Mirror* (175)
Cade relates his followers' reaction to
the pardon: they 'shranke all awaye,
eche man to shift for one' ('Jack Cade',
124).
make shift look out

34 **Henry** trisyllabic (cf. 3.2.131 and n.)

37 The line seems to imply that Henry V
did this, a beguiling fantasy of historical romance, but presumably it refers
obliquely to the ridiculousness of Cade
knighting himself (4.2.110–11) and
Dick the butcher (in Q TLN 1630–3),
as well as Q's 'we must all be Lords or
squires, assoone as Jacke Cade is King'
(TLN 1564–5). Cf. 'Fellow kings',
4.2.154.
meanest lowliest born

39–40 This was the case with the dis-

gruntled soldiers returning from
Normandy to England, many unpaid,
who in desperation joined Cade's followers (Harvey, 88, 113, 133).

39 **the spoil** looting. Cade and his follow-
ers' spoils were seized and an inventory made of the various gold and silver
items, jewels etc., including objects
indicating pillaged churches. (See
Harvey, 100, and Palgrave, 217–20.)

41 **at jar** in discord (*OED sb.* 5c). But it is
the 'jarring discord of nobility' (*1H6*
4.1.188) which is to erupt into the
Wars of the Roses.

42 **fearful** frightened
vanquished vanquishèd

43 **start** sudden invasion (*OED sb.*[2] 2c):
with this meaning, only here in
Shakespeare

44 **broil** conflict (cf. *1H6* 1.1.53)

33] *Rowe; verse F, lined* ¹*Cade,* / ²*Cade.* /   SD] *Q*   43 o'er seas] *(ore-seas)*

Crying '*Villiago!*' unto all they meet.
Better ten thousand base-born Cades miscarry
Than you should stoop unto a Frenchman's mercy.
To France! To France! And get what you have lost!
Spare England, for it is your native coast.   50
Henry hath money, you are strong and manly;
God on our side, doubt not of victory.

ALL   A Clifford! A Clifford! We'll follow the King and
    Clifford.   [*They forsake Cade.*]

CADE [*aside*]   Was ever feather so lightly blown to and fro   55
    as this multitude? The name of Henry the Fifth hales
    them to an hundred mischiefs and makes them leave me
    desolate. I see them lay their heads together to surprise
    me. My sword make way for me, for here is no staying.
    – In despite of the devils and hell, have through the very   60
    midst of you! And heavens and honour be witness that
    no want of resolution in me, but only my followers'
    base and ignominious treasons, makes me betake me to

---

46 '*Villiago!*' from Italian *vigliacco*, 'coward'. Cairncross notes that Florio
(1598) has 'Vigliacco, a raskal, a villain,
a base, vile abiect skurvie, a
scoundrell'. Hart gives examples from
drama, and Spanish variants.

47 **base-born** 'this Cade beinge but base
borne' (*Mirror*, 170: 'Jack Cade',
15–16). Cf. 1.3.84.
miscarry perish (*OED v.* 1)

51 **Henry hath money** See 38–9n. and
1.3.31n.

53 **A Clifford!** anglicized French *à*: 'To
Clifford!', a rallying cry. Cf. 'A Talbot!
a Talbot' (*1H6* 1.1.128).

55–6 **Was . . . multitude?** Two proverbial commonplaces are run together
here: 'As light as a feather' (Dent,
F150) and 'As wavering as feathers in
the wind' (Dent, F162). In *3H6*
(3.1.84, 89) we hear from Henry,

'Look, as I blow this feather from my
face . . . such is the lightness of you
common men', the failed king echoing
the mock king.

56 **hales** drags

58 **lay . . . together** proverbial (Dent,
H280). Cf. 3.1.165.
surprise capture (*OED v.* 2b). Cf.
4.9.8.

60 **despite** spite
have through Cf. 'have at thee with a
downright blow', 2.3.92–3. For this
imperative idiom see *OED* Have *v.* 20.
Cf. Q, 'My staffe shall make way
through the midst of you . . . He runs
through them with his staffe, and flies
away' (TLN 1891–3).

62 **resolution** a wry parallel here: Cade's
subornation had been part of York's
resolution (3.1.331), lengthily rehearsed
in soliloquy.

53–4] *Prose Rowe; verse F, lined* ²Clifford, / ³Clifford. /   54 SD] *Q*   55 SD] *Dyce*

my heels.   *Exit.*

BUCKINGHAM

What, is he fled? Go some and follow him.   65
And he that brings his head unto the King
Shall have a thousand crowns for his reward.

Exeunt some of them.

Follow me, soldiers; we'll devise a mean
To reconcile you all unto the King.   *Exeunt.*

[**4.9**]   *Sound trumpets. Enter* KING, QUEEN *and*
                   SOMERSET *on the terrace* [*aloft*].

KING

Was ever king that joyed an earthly throne
And could command no more content than I?
No sooner was I crept out of my cradle
But I was made a king at nine months old.
Was never subject longed to be a king   5
As I do long and wish to be a subject.

Enter BUCKINGHAM *and* [OLD] CLIFFORD.

67 **crowns** similarly at 4.10.27 but
amended into a thousand marks, as in
the chronicles, at 5.1.79. The value of
golden marks would have amounted to
a huge figure (a crown was valued at 5*s*,
the mark at 13*s* 4*d*).

68 **mean** means

4.9 location: Kenilworth   Castle
(Theobald). The King retired to
Kenilworth at the end of 4.4 but did
not sit in judgement on the rebels until
after Cade's death, according to Hall
(222) and Holinshed (227). Though
York returned from Ireland in 1450,
the plot against Somerset and the raising of an army occurred two years

later. Q (TLN 1898–1926) completely
rewrites this scene: see Appendix 2.

0.2 **terrace** the   tiring-house   gallery.
Similarly used at 1.4.12.1 and 4.5.

1–6 For the cares-of-kingship topos, cf.
H5 4.1.230–84.

1–5 **Was ever ... Was never** Spenserian
(Hart). See Abbott, 84.

1 **joyed** enjoyed

4 **nine months old** He was born at
Windsor on 6 December 1421; Henry
V died at Vincennes on 31 August
1422, leaving Henry VI as England's
youngest monarch.

5–6 Cf. Henry's eulogy on the shepherd's
life, *3H6* 2.5.21–54.

69 SD] *Exeunt omnes. F*   **4.9**] *Capell*   0.2 *terrace*] *(Tarras)*   *aloft*] *this edn*   6.1] *F subst.*   OLD]
Capell

BUCKINGHAM

> Health and glad tidings to your majesty.

KING

> Why, Buckingham, is the traitor Cade surprised,
> Or is he but retired to make him strong?

Enter multitudes with halters about their necks.

OLD CLIFFORD

> He is fled, my lord, and all his powers do yield,   10
> And humbly thus with halters on their necks
> Expect your highness' doom of life or death.

KING

> Then, heaven, set ope thy everlasting gates
> To entertain my vows of thanks and praise.
> Soldiers, this day have you redeemed your lives   15
> And showed how well you love your prince and country.
> Continue still in this so good a mind,
> And Henry, though he be unfortunate,
> Assure yourselves will never be unkind.

---

8 **surprised** captured. Cf. 4.8.57.
9 **retired** retreated (*OED* Retire *v.* 2).
   Cf. *KJ* 2.1.326.
   him himself
9.1 usually glossed comparing the anonymous *Edward III* (1596): '*Enter six*
   CITIZENS *in their shirts, bare foot, with
   halters about their necks*'. This occurs at
   5.1.7.1 as the citizens of Calais surrender to the English and plead 'that the
   trembling multitude be saved' (5.1.18).
   However, there is a directly relevant
   incident from historical sources which
   Harvey notes (152–3). After Cade's
   death many of his followers had joined
   the uprising of a new 'captain',
   William Parmynter, late in 1450, again
   in Kent. Widespread hanging followed; but when Henry returned to

London, at Blackheath he was met by
three thousand (a 'multitude' indeed)
begging for mercy, described as 'naked
to the middle, having prostrated themselves to the ground before the king
through public streets, with cords
bound round their necks' (*Calendar*,
453).
halters nooses
10 **powers** forces
12 **Expect** await
13 **everlasting gates** Psalms, 24.7, 9
   (Sternhold & Hopkins): 'Ye princes
   ope your gates, and stand ope / the
   everlasting gate' (Cairncross).
14 **entertain** give favourable reception to
   (*OED v.* 14)
15 See 4.8.38–9n.
19 **unkind** cruel

18 unfortunate] *F3;* infortunate *F*

333

And so, with thanks and pardon to you all,   20
I do dismiss you to your several countries.
ALL   God save the King! God save the King!   [*Exeunt Rebels.*]

Enter a Messenger.

MESSENGER
Please it your grace to be advertised
The Duke of York is newly come from Ireland,
And with a puissant and a mighty power   25
Of gallowglasses and stout kerns
Is marching hitherward in proud array,
And still proclaimeth, as he comes along,
His arms are only to remove from thee
The Duke of Somerset, whom he terms a traitor.   30
KING
Thus stands my state, 'twixt Cade and York distressed,
Like to a ship that having scaped a tempest
Is straightway calmed and boarded with a pirate.
But now is Cade driven back, his men dispersed,
And now is York in arms to second him.   35
I pray thee, Buckingham, go and meet him,

---

21 **several countries** various regions.
  See 4.8.10n.
23 **advertised** advertisèd: warned (*OED
  ppl.* 1); accent on second syllable
  (Cercignani, 41)
24 **newly** recently, just
25 **puissant** powerful
  power army
26 **gallowglasses** soldiers retained by
  Irish chieftains: 'a galloglasse [uses] a
  kind of pollax for his weapon. These
  men are commonlie weieward rather by
  profession than by nature, grim of
  countenance, tall of stature, big of lim,
  burlie of bodie, well and stronglie tim-
  bered, chieflie feeding on beefe, porke &

butter' (Stanyhurst, 68; see 3.1.309n.).
  stout hardy; valorous
  kerns See 3.1.309n.
28–30 Cf. Bolingbroke's claims, *R2*
  2.3.164–7.
28 **still** repeatedly
30 **Duke of Somerset** Somerset found
  patronage and favour in Margaret after
  Suffolk's death and thus conveniently
  provided a pretext for York's action
  (Hall, 225).
31 **state** condition; situation
33 **calmed** becalmed
  with by (Abbott, 193)
34 **But** just (*OED* 6b)
35 **second** support, back up (*OED v.* 1)

---

22 SD] *Hanmer subst.*   26 stout] stout Irish *Collier (Mitford)*   33 calmed] *F4;* calme *F;* claimd *F3*
34 dispersed] *(dispierc'd)*   36 meet] meet with *Rowe*

And ask him what's the reason of these arms.
Tell him I'll send Duke Edmund to the Tower –
And, Somerset, we will commit thee thither,
Until his army be dismissed from him.   40

SOMERSET

My lord, I'll yield myself to prison willingly,
Or unto death, to do my country good.

KING

In any case, be not too rough in terms,
For he is fierce and cannot brook hard language.

BUCKINGHAM

I will, my lord, and doubt not so to deal   45
As all things shall redound unto your good.

KING

Come, wife, let's in, and learn to govern better;
For yet may England curse my wretched reign.   *Flourish.*
                                                                                Exeunt.

[**4.10**]   *Enter* CADE.

CADE   Fie on ambitions! Fie on myself that have a sword

37 **of** for
38 **Duke Edmund** Edmund Beaufort,
  Duke of Somerset
43 **rough in terms** harsh in conditions
44 **brook hard language** put up with
  (listening to) harsh words
45 **deal** negotiate
46 **redound unto** turn out for (*OED v.*
  6b)
48 **yet** so far, up to this time (Abbott, 76)
4.10 location: Iden's garden (Capell).
  Drawing on Hall 'one Alexander Iden,
  esquire of Kent found hym in a garden,
  and there in his defence, manfully slewe
  the caitife Cade' (222). Capell locates a
  Kentish garden but Holinshed (227)
  and many other chronicles refer to a
  Sussex garden (for the various sugges-

tions, see Griffiths, 653, n. 45).
Shakespeare idealizes Iden as a Horatian
country gentleman in this scene; but in
fact as a Sheriff of Kent, succeeding
Crowmer, he hunted down Cade with a
posse for the reward (Harvey, 99; see
4.2.77.1 LN) and subsequently married
his predecessor's wife (Barron, 518). Q's
SD here suggests Iden's party: 'Enter
Iacke Cade at one doore, and at the
other, maister *Alexander Eyden* and his
men'. The SD continues, 'and *Iack
Cade* lies downe picking of hearbes and
eating them' (TLN 1928–9).
1 **Fie on ambitions!** A mock addition
  to the chorus on *ambition*: see 1.1.177,
  199; 2.1.32; 2.2.71; 3.1.143. Cf. Iden's
  first words, 4.10.16–23.

41] *Oxf; F lines* Lord, / willingly, / myself] *om. Ard²*   **4.10**] *Steevens*   1 ambitions] ambition *F2*

and yet am ready to famish! These five days have I hid
me in these woods and durst not peep out, for all the
country is laid for me; but now am I so hungry that if I
might have a lease of my life for a thousand years, I   5
could stay no longer. Wherefore, o'er a brick wall have
I climbed into this garden, to see if I can eat grass, or
pick a sallet another while, which is not amiss to cool a
man's stomach this hot weather. And I think this word
'sallet' was born to do me good: for many a time, but for   10
a sallet, my brain-pan had been cleft with a brown bill;
and many a time, when I have been dry and bravely
marching, it hath served me instead of a quart pot to
drink in; and now the word 'sallet' must serve me to
feed on.   [*He lies down picking of herbs and eating them.*]   15

Enter IDEN [*and his men*].

IDEN
Lord, who would live turmoiled in the court

3–4 **all . . . me** Retreating from Kent to
Sussex, Cade hid in the country he knew
best since the 'Hothfield' (Heathfield),
Sussex, reported by Holinshed (227), is
only twenty miles east of Hurstpierpoint, with which, it appears, Cade
had strong ties (see 4.2.29n.).
4 **laid** set with traps (*OED* Lay $v.^1$ 18b)
5 **lease . . . life** Cf. 'No man has lease of
his life' (Dent, M327).
6 **stay** wait
8 **sallet** an obsolete form of 'salad', a cold
dish of herbs and/or vegetables, usually uncooked, thus the resort of the indi-
gent. Hart (8n.) gives several examples
of the pun on the soldier's headgear
stolen by Cade (see 4.3.9–10 SD n.).
another while yet again; 'another
time' (see *OED* While *sb.* II 6, where
North's Plutarch provides the only
example)

8–9 **cool . . . stomach** Culpeper specifies that a herb like sorrel 'cools the
. . . stomach' (324, 337).
9–15 **And . . . on.** If Cade removes his
helmet here, this would create a mock-
heroic touch in the disarming of the
hero at a point of danger. Cf. Hector at
TC 5.9 and the Redcrosse Knight in
Spenser, 1.vii.2–3 (RP).
11 **sallet** 'a light globular headpiece,
either with or without a vizor, and
without a crest, the lower part curving
outwards behind' (*OED* 1). See
4.3.9–10 SD n.
brain-pan skull: nowhere else in
Shakespeare
brown bill the bronzed halberd carried by watchmen and constables
15 SD, 15.1 See headnote.
16 **turmoiled** turmoilèd: disturbed,
harassed. Only here in Shakespeare.

---

6 o'er] *Hanmer;* on F   15 SD] *Q*   15.1 *and his men*] *Q*

And may enjoy such quiet walks as these?
This small inheritance my father left me
Contenteth me, and worth a monarchy.
I seek not to wax great by others' waning   20
Or gather wealth I care not with what envy;
Sufficeth that I have maintains my state,
And sends the poor well pleased from my gate.

CADE [*aside*]   Here's the lord of the soil come to seize me
for a stray for entering his fee-simple without leave. –   25
Ah, villain, thou wilt betray me and get a thousand
crowns of the King by carrying my head to him; but I'll
make thee eat iron like an ostrich, and swallow my
sword like a great pin, ere thou and I part.
            [*Draws his sword.*]

IDEN

Why, rude companion, whatsoe'er thou be,   30
I know thee not; why then should I betray thee?
Is't not enough to break into my garden
And like a thief to come to rob my grounds,

17 **And may** when he can
19 a line designed in contrast to 4.9.1–2
20 **wax** grow
21 **I . . . what** regardless of others'
22 It is enough that what I have maintains
my position. Cf. '*Satis quod sufficit*'
[That is] enough which suffices (LLL
5.1.1) and Dent E159.
Sufficeth (it). For ellipsis see Abbott,
404.
23 **well pleased** pleasèd: with generous
alms. See *TS* 4.3.4–5. Cf. *Jack Straw*,
'rich men triumph to see the poore beg
at their gate' (79).
24 **lord . . . soil** owner of the estate (*OED*
Soil *sb.*[1] 5a)
25 **stray** Stray animals could be im-
pounded.
fee-simple absolute possession,
entailed for ever
27 **crowns** See 4.8.66n.

28 **eat . . . ostrich** proverbial (Dent, 997).
The ostrich was considered to con-
sume iron for digestive or other purposes (see Bartholomeus, 640).
Browne gives the most learned summary of these beliefs (62–6). In paint-
ing and illustration the ostrich was
commonly depicted carrying a horse-
shoe in its beak. Cade is colourfully
anticipating running Iden through (cf.
3.2.198–9).
28–9 **swallow . . . pin** Cade's threat
alludes to sword-swallowing, a refine-
ment on the stereotype braggart-
soldier vaunt exemplified in Falstaff's
''zounds, I would make him eat a piece
of my sword' (*1H4* 5.4.152–3).
30 **rude companion** rough fellow. The
pejorative meaning of 'companion'
(*OED sb.*[1] 4) is often found in
Shakespeare, e.g. *R2* 5.3.7.

20 waning] *Rowe*[3] *subst.*; warning *F*   24 SD] *Dyce*   Here's] Sounes, heres *Q*; Zounds, here's *Oxf*
26 Ah] *(A)*   29 SD] this edn

Climbing my walls in spite of me the owner,
But thou wilt brave me with these saucy terms?   35
CADE   Brave thee? Ay, by the best blood that ever was
    broached, and beard thee too. Look on me well: I have
    eat no meat these five days, yet come thou and thy five
    men, an if I do not leave you all as dead as a doornail, I
    pray God I may never eat grass more.   40
IDEN

Nay, it shall ne'er be said, while England stands,
That Alexander Iden, a squire of Kent,
Took odds to combat a poor famished man.
Oppose thy steadfast-gazing eyes to mine,
See if thou canst outface me with thy looks.   45
Set limb to limb, and thou art far the lesser;
Thy hand is but a finger to my fist,
Thy leg a stick compared with this truncheon.
My foot shall fight with all the strength thou hast;
An if mine arm be heaved in the air   50

---

35 **brave** defy; insult. See *TS* 4.3.124.
    saucy terms insolent words. Cf. *KL* 2.2.97.
37 **broached** *OED* $v.^1$ 1 gives 'pierced, stabbed'; but Cade alludes to the figurative meaning (*OED* $v.^1$ 4), 'to pierce, or tap a cask to draw the liquor'. Cf. *1H6* 3.4.40.
    beard defy: from the idea of openly – in front of his face (beard) – opposing someone (see *OED* Beard *sb.* 5c). Cf. *1H6*, 'I beard thee to thy face' (1.3.44).
38 **eat** the past participle with the 'en' inflection dropped, pronounced to rhyme with 'set'; see Abbott, 343.
    meat food (*OED sb.* 1)
38–9 **five men** See headnote.
39 **dead . . . doornail** See Dent, D567. Only here in Shakespeare.
39–40 **²I . . . more** The comic element of Cade's dialogue, noted above (9–15n.,

28–9n.), is sustained.
42 ***a squire** 'A man belonging to the higher order of English gentry, ranking immediately below a knight' (*OED sb.¹* 2). Cf. *H5* 4.8.84. For the metrical adjustment of F here cf. *E3*, 4.7.51n.
43 **Took odds** accepted such an unequal wager (see *OED* Odds *sb.* 5). Cf. *1H4* 5.1.97. The unequal odds are Iden's *five men* (38–9).
45 **outface** defy. See *AYL* 1.3.122.
46 **Set . . . limb** pit limb against limb (*OED* Set *v.* 117). See 56 LN.
47 Your hand is only as wide as one of my fingers.
    to compared to
48 **compared** comparèd
    truncheon a short, thick staff (*OED sb.* 2): Iden's leg
50 **heaved** heavèd: raised (*OED* Heave *v.* 1)

---

42 a squire] *this edn;* an esquire *F;* an Esquire *Ard²*   44 steadfast-gazing] stedfast gazing *F*

Thy grave is digged already in the earth.
As for words, whose greatness answers words,
Let this my sword report what speech forbears.
        [*Draws his sword.*]

CADE   By my valour, the most complete champion that
   ever I heard! Steel, if thou turn the edge or cut not out   55
   the burly-boned clown in chines of beef ere thou sleep
   in thy sheath, I beseech God on my knees thou mayst
   be turned to hobnails. (*They fight* [*and Cade falls down*].)
   O, I am slain! Famine and no other hath slain me. Let
   ten thousand devils come against me, and give me but   60

52–3 Cf. York, 5.1.8–9.
52 **whose greatness** (ironic) the extent
   of whose power merely
   answers gives back in kind (*OED*
   Answer *v.* 25). Cf. *H5* 4.0.8.
53 Iden is rephrasing a proverbial commonplace most memorably expressed
   as 'Actions speak louder than words'
   (Wilson, *OEDP*, 3). Cf. 'Not words but
   deeds' (Dent, W820). See *1H6* 3.2.49.
   report express
   forbears desists from (*OED v.* 5)
54 **champion** martial defender of a cause
   (*OED sb.*[1] 3). See *R2* 1.3.7, and 1.3.58
   above.
55–8 **Steel . . . hobnails**. a parody of the
   biblical swords turning into plough-
   shares (Isaiah, 2.4)
55 **turn** blunt (*OED v.* 9b). Cf. 2.1.171.
56 **burly-boned** big-boned, hulking
   (Sanders): an expression found in
   Nashe, but not elsewhere in
   Shakespeare (Hart)
   clown a boorish country peasant (see
   OED sb. 1–3). Cf. Holinshed on a
   Norfolk rebel of 1381: 'Sir Robert
   Salle . . . had his braines dasht out by a
   countrie clown' (2.745). Wiles notes
   that 'The word "clown" is never found
   outside stage directions unless used *of*,
   or (for ironic effect) *by* the character
   who is designated as *the* clown of the
   play.' (*Clown*, 68.9). See LN.

chines joints (*OED sb.*[2] 3)

57 *God F's 'Ioue' was probably a correc-
   tion in response to the blasphemy law
   of 1606, 'An Act to Restrain Abuses of
   the Players'. A fine of ten pounds was
   ordered for any jesting or prophane
   use of the names of God, Jesus Christ,
   the Holy Ghost or the Trinity.
58 **turned to hobnails** proverbial (Dent,
   H480.1). Hobnails were used to stud
   the soles of the heavy boots of the
   lower classes. See *clouted shoon*, 4.2.174
   and n.
59 **Famine** possibly alluding to the
   notoriously thin actor John Sincler,
   thus externalising Cade's self-defeat
   by his hunger rather than by Iden's
   valour (with a hint of carnivalesque
   riot defeated by Lenten famine). See
   clown, 56 LN.
60–4 **ten thousand . . . unconquered
   soul** Cade parodies the inadvertent
   tribute paid by the French General at
   Bordeaux to Lord Talbot: there 'Ten
   thousand French' single out the
   'unconquer'd spirit' of the English
   hero (*1H6* 4.2.28–32). Cade continues,
   Wither, garden (61–2), whereas the
   General invokes the corpse of Talbot
   'withered' (47). See LN. For the
   hypothesis that Shakespeare revised
   the later *1H6* to make this parodic contrast, see Introduction p. 120.

---

52 answers] *Rowe;* answer's *F*   53 SD] *this edn*   57 God] *Q;* Ioue *F*   58 SD] *Q; Heere they Fight. F*

the ten meals I have lost, and I'd defy them all. Wither,
garden, and be henceforth a burying place to all that do
dwell in this house, because the unconquered soul of
Cade is fled.

IDEN

Is't Cade that I have slain, that monstrous traitor?   65
Sword, I will hallow thee for this thy deed,
And hang thee o'er my tomb when I am dead.
Ne'er shall this blood be wiped from thy point,
But thou shalt wear it as a herald's coat
To emblaze the honour that thy master got.   70

CADE   Iden, farewell, and be proud of thy victory. Tell
Kent from me she hath lost her best man, and exhort all
the world to be cowards. For I, that never feared any,
am vanquished by famine, not by valour.   *Dies.*

IDEN

How much thou wrong'st me, heaven be my judge.   75
Die, damned wretch, the curse of her that bore thee!
And as I thrust thy body in with my sword,
So wish I I might thrust thy soul to hell.
Hence will I drag thee headlong by the heels
Unto a dunghill, which shall be thy grave,   80

---

65 **monstrous traitor** unnatural traitor.
The parallel charge is brought against
York, 5.1.106.

66 **hallow** consecrate. Cf. *MW* 4.2.204.

68 **wiped** wipèd

69 **herald's coat** heraldic coat of arms

70 **emblaze** to celebrate as a heraldic
device (*OED v.*² 1a): only here in
Shakespeare; common in Greene
(Hart). There may be an allusion here
to the Lord Mayor's sword which slew
Wat Tyler being subsequently included in the city coat of arms. See
4.3.10–13 LN.

76 **damned** damnèd

77 **thrust . . . sword** thrust my sword
into thy body

78 anticipating Richard of Gloucester's
words as he kills King Henry (*3H6*
5.6.67)

79 **drag . . . heels** as Cade had dragged
Lord Saye. See 4.3.11–12 and
4.3.10–13 LN.
headlong head downmost (*OED adv.*
1)

80 Contrast those about to die at
Agincourt: 'Dying like men, though
buried in your dunghills, / They shall
be fam'd' (*H5* 4.3.99–100); also *KL*
3.7.96–7.

---

76 bore] *Oxf;* bare *F*

And there cut off thy most ungracious head,
Which I will bear in triumph to the King,
Leaving thy trunk for crows to feed upon.

Exeunt [*Iden and his men with the body*].

[**5.1**]   *Enter* YORK *and his army of Irish,*
                  with Drum and Colours.

YORK

From Ireland thus comes York to claim his right
And pluck the crown from feeble Henry's head.
Ring, bells, aloud; burn, bonfires, clear and bright,
To entertain great England's lawful king.
Ah, *sancta majestas*, who would not buy thee dear?   5
Let them obey that knows not how to rule.
This hand was made to handle nought but gold.
I cannot give due action to my words,

---

81 **ungracious** graceless, wicked (*OED a.* 1)

83 Cf. 5.2.11.

5.1 Pope divided Act 5 into seven scenes (5.2 at 5.1.56; 5.3 at 5.1.83; 5.4 at 5.1.148; 5.5 at 5.2; 5.6 at 5.2.72; 5.7 at 5.3). Capell, on the other hand, begins Act 5 at 4.10 (followed by 5.2 at 5.1 and so on).

Location: the countryside between Dartford and Blackheath (Malone). Events between York's return and the first battle of St Albans (1455) are telescoped and the war in France (which included Talbot's death in this period) set aside in order to focus on internal dissension leading to the Wars of the Roses. For the events dramatized see Hall, 226, 232, and Holinshed, 230, 233.

0.1 *army of Irish* See 4.9.25–6 and nn.

0.2 *Drum* drummer
Colours flag-bearers

1–2 Contrast 35–8 and 4.9.28–30.

2 **pluck the crown** Cf. *3H6* 2.1.153.

3 **bells . . . bonfires** 'Bonefiers' and 'belles', along with such things as 'triumphes' and 'mai-games', are included in a catalogue of town amusements in R. Wilson's *The Three Lords and Three Ladies of London* (1590) (*Shakespeare's England*, 2.172).

4 **entertain** hospitably receive (*OED v.* 13). Cf. *CE* 3.1.120.

5 *sancta majestas* sacred majesty

6 **them . . . knows** See Abbott, 247, for relative taking a singular verb following a plural antecedent.

7 **gold** the ceremonial regalia

8–9 'My words can only be made good with the authority of the royal sceptre or sword in my hand'; or 'Only as King, bearing the sword and sceptre, can my words turn into actions'. York is thinking of the regalia of the coronation, but substitutes *sword* for orb as war is on his mind (see 1.1.242–3 and *H5* 4.1.260ff.). Contrast Iden, 4.10.52–3.

83 SD] *Dyce subst.; Exit. F*   **5.1**] *Pope*   6 knows] know *Rowe*

Except a sword or sceptre balance it;
A sceptre shall it have, have I a soul,   10
On which I'll toss the fleur-de-lis of France.

Enter BUCKINGHAM.

Whom have we here? Buckingham, to disturb me?
The King hath sent him, sure. I must dissemble.
BUCKINGHAM
York, if thou meanest well, I greet thee well.
YORK
Humphrey of Buckingham, I accept thy greeting.   15
Art thou a messenger, or come of pleasure?
BUCKINGHAM
A messenger from Henry, our dread liege,
To know the reason of these arms in peace;
Or why thou, being a subject as I am,
Against thy oath and true allegiance sworn,   20
Should raise so great a power without his leave
Or dare to bring thy force so near the court?
YORK [*aside*]
Scarce can I speak, my choler is so great.

---

9 **Except** unless
   balance *Balance* here means 'weigh' if
   it refers to *hand* (see *OED* Balance *sb.*
   12), otherwise 'counterpoise' if *it*
   refers to *action*. The only place in
   Shakespeare where 'balance' functions
   as a verb rather than a noun. The verbal form of the word is found mostly
   in the seventeenth century.
10 As I have a soul! My hand shall grasp a
   sceptre (cf. 97–8, 102).
11 **fleur-de-lis** the heraldic three-leaved
   lily of the French royal coat of arms.
   'One of the royal sceptres shown on
   Henry V's seal is topped with a fleur-
   de-lis, perhaps in allusion to his claim

   to the French crown' (Scott-Giles, 136).
12 **Whom . . . here?** proverbial phrase
   (Dent, W280.2). Cf. *WT* 3.3.69.
   Buckingham In the chronicles the
   Bishops of Winchester and Ely represented the King.
16 **of** expressive of internal motive
   (Abbott, 168). Cf. 2.1.85.
17 **dread liege** respected lord (in the
   sense of a feudal superior to whom
   allegiance is owed)
18 **arms** armed retainers
23 **choler** anger: one of the four humours
   (see 1.2.51n.). York's choler has
   already appeared in *1H6* 5.4.120.

---

11 fleur-de-lis] *F (*Fleure-de-Luce*), *Oxf;* flower-de-luce *Cam*   23 SD] *Rowe*

O, I could hew up rocks and fight with flint,
I am so angry at these abject terms;   25
And now like Ajax Telamonius,
On sheep or oxen could I spend my fury.
I am far better born than is the King,
More like a king, more kingly in my thoughts.
But I must make fair weather yet awhile   30
Till Henry be more weak and I more strong. –
Buckingham, I prithee pardon me
That I have given no answer all this while;
My mind was troubled with deep melancholy.
The cause why I have brought this army hither   35
Is to remove proud Somerset from the King,
Seditious to his grace and to the state.

BUCKINGHAM

That is too much presumption on thy part;
But if thy arms be to no other end,
The King hath yielded unto thy demand: 40
The Duke of Somerset is in the Tower.

YORK

Upon thine honour, is he prisoner?

BUCKINGHAM

Upon mine honour, he is prisoner.

24 **hew up** *Hew up*, rather than 'down' is something of a rarity, *OED* giving only one twelfth-century example of hewing 'up' a tree by the roots. Otherwise 'hew' generally means to chop, carve or cut. The sense is obvious enough, but the verb remains anomalous.
   flint Cf. *E3*, 4.3.68–73, 4.6.12–16, 4.6.35–8.
25 exactly as King Henry anticipated, 4.9.43–4
   abject terms despicable words
26–7 Ajax, the son of Telamon, enraged after defeat by Ulysses in the contest for Achilles' armour, went mad and slew a flock of sheep belonging to the Greeks, before committing suicide. See LN.
27 **spend** expend; vent
28 **better born** in the sense that his claim to the throne is superior (2.2)
30 **make fair weather** 'make the best of it': proverbial (Dent, W221). Hart gives several sixteenth-century occurrences.
32 **I prithee** I pray thee: I beg you to

32 Buckingham] O Buckingham *F2*

YORK

    Then, Buckingham, I do dismiss my powers.

    Soldiers, I thank you all; disperse yourselves;   45

    Meet me tomorrow in Saint George's Field,

    You shall have pay and everything you wish.

                        [Exeunt Soldiers.]

    And let my sovereign, virtuous Henry,

    Command my eldest son, nay, all my sons,

    As pledges of my fealty and love,   50

    I'll send them all, as willing as I live.

    Lands, goods, horse, armour, anything I have

    Is his to use, so Somerset may die.

BUCKINGHAM

    York, I commend this kind submission.

    We twain will go into his highness' tent.   55

Enter KING *and Attendants.*

KING

    Buckingham, doth York intend no harm to us

    That thus he marcheth with thee arm in arm?

YORK

    In all submission and humility

---

46 **Saint George's Field** an open space, named after the church of St George the Martyr, between Southwark and Lambeth on the south side of the Thames; a well-known ground for mustering the trained bands of London and thus a natural point of assembly for York's army (see *2H4* 3.2.195)

49 **Command** demand (from me). See *OED v.* 7.

50 **pledges . . . fealty** sureties (*OED sb.* 1) . . . loyalty. In *R2* cf. York of his son Aumerle, a supporter of Richard II: 'I am in Parliament pledge for his truth /

And lasting fealty to the new-made king', Henry IV (*R2* 5.2.44–5).

53 **so** provided that (Abbott, 133)

54 **kind** proper (*OED a.* 1c)

55 Quoting Q's later SD, ·'bearing the Duke of *Buckingham* wounded to his Tent' (TLN 2191–2), Hattaway considers that tents might have been erected on stage for the battle sequences. However, at this place in Q (TLN 2000–1) we hear, 'Come York, thou shalt go speake vnto the King, / But see, his grace is comming to meete with vs', which is what happens in F.

47 SD] *Q2 subst.; Exet soldiers. Q*

York doth present himself unto your highness.

KING

Then what intends these forces thou dost bring?   60

YORK

To heave the traitor Somerset from hence
And fight against that monstrous rebel Cade,
Who since I heard to be discomfited.

Enter IDEN *with Cade's head.*

IDEN

If one so rude and of so mean condition
May pass into the presence of a king,   65
Lo, I present your grace a traitor's head,
The head of Cade, whom I in combat slew.

KING

The head of Cade! Great God, how just art Thou!
O let me view his visage, being dead,
That living wrought me such exceeding trouble.   70
Tell me, my friend, art thou the man that slew him?

IDEN

I was, an't like your majesty.

KING

How art thou called? And what is thy degree?

IDEN

Alexander Iden, that's my name;
A poor esquire of Kent, that loves his King.   75

60 **intends** For 's' inflection preceding a
   plural subject, see Abbott, 355.
62 **monstrous** unnatural
63 **discomfited** defeated (*OED* Discomfit
   v. 1). Cf. *1H4* 1.1.67. 'Warwicke . . .
   fiersly set on the kynges foreward, and
   theim shortly discomfited' (Hall, 232).
64 **rude . . . mean condition** uncourtly
   . . . low rank. Cf. Hall: 'the bodies of

the noble men, were buried in the
Monastery, and the meane people in
other places' (233).
72 **an't like** if it please
73 **degree** rank. For degree as the cor-
   nerstone of feudal society and a hierarchical cosmos, see Ulysses' celebrated
   speech, *TC* 1.3.83–124.
75 **esquire** See 4.10.42n.

63 heard] hear *Capell*   72 was] wis *Oxf*

BUCKINGHAM

> So please it you, my lord, 'twere not amiss
> He were created knight for his good service.

KING

> Iden, kneel down.   [*Iden kneels.*]
>   Rise up a knight.   [*Iden rises.*]
> We give thee for reward a thousand marks
> And will that thou henceforth attend on us.   80

IDEN

> May Iden live to merit such a bounty,
> And never live but true unto his liege.   [*Exit.*]

Enter QUEEN *and* SOMERSET.

KING [*aside to Buckingham*]

> See, Buckingham, Somerset comes with the Queen.
> Go bid her hide him quickly from the Duke.

QUEEN

> For thousand Yorks he shall not hide his head,   85
> But boldly stand and front him to his face.

YORK

> How now! Is Somerset at liberty?
> Then, York, unloose thy long-imprisoned thoughts
> And let thy tongue be equal with thy heart.

---

78 The knighting of Iden is not found in Hall or Holinshed and editors consider it to be in imitation of that of William Walworth, who killed Wat Tyler, particularly, as Hart points out, in the comparable abruptness of the ceremony dramatized in *Jack Straw* (1177–9). Yet closer is the proleptic travesty of Cade conferring knighthood in Q: 'Then kneele downe Dicke Butcher, / Rise vp sir Dicke Butcher' (TLN 1631–2). Cf. *KJ* 1.1.162–3.

79 **marks** agreeing here with the denom-ination in Hall (222) and Holinshed (227). See 4.8.66n. and 4.10.27.

80 **will** command

82.1 The Queen's and Somerset's entry coincides with the end of the ceremony of knighthood and Iden joining the ranks of attendant courtiers. In the ensuing movement and noise the King vainly hopes Somerset can be screened from York.

86 **front** confront

89 **be equal with** adequately express

---

78 SD1] *Johnson subst.*   SD2] *this edn*   82 SD] *Q*   83 SD] *this edn*   the] *(*th'*)*   88 long-imprisoned] *Cam (*long imprisoned*)*

Shall I endure the sight of Somerset?   90
False king, why hast thou broken faith with me,
Knowing how hardly I can brook abuse?
'King' did I call thee? No, thou art not king,
Not fit to govern and rule multitudes,
Which dar'st not, no, nor canst not rule a traitor.   95
That head of thine doth not become a crown;
Thy hand is made to grasp a palmer's staff
And not to grace an awful princely sceptre.
That gold must round engirt these brows of mine,
Whose smile and frown, like to Achilles' spear,   100
Is able with the change to kill and cure.
Here is a hand to hold a sceptre up
And with the same to act controlling laws.
Give place! By heaven, thou shalt rule no more
O'er him whom heaven created for thy ruler.   105

SOMERSET

O monstrous traitor! I arrest thee, York,
Of capital treason 'gainst the King and crown.
Obey, audacious traitor, kneel for grace.

---

92 **hardly** barely
   brook abuse abide lies. If *broken* (91)
   was pronounced 'brooken' (Cercignani,
   184) there may be a pun here.
95 **Which** who (Abbott, 265)
96 **doth not become** is not fit to bear
97 **palmer's staff** Though often considered the same as a pilgrim, strictly
   speaking the palmer permanently
   made pilgrimage to holy shrines,
   under vows of poverty, bearing a palm
   branch or leaf, and carrying a staff
   which indicated a visit to the Holy
   Land. Cf. *R2* 3.3.151. At key moments
   in *2H6* staffs are highly symbolic of
   character, situation and function:
   Gloucester's surrender of his staff
   (2.3.32–6); Cade's striking his staff on
   London Stone (4.6.0.2); the *ragged*

staff of the Nevilles' crest, turned to
rebellion and sedition (5.1.203).
98 **awful** awe-inspiring
99 **engirt** encircle
100 **Achilles' spear** The power of
   Achilles' spear to both wound and heal
   became proverbial (Dent, S731). See
   LN.
103 **act** bring about; enact
   controlling effective (in contrast to
   laws which are empty words)
104 **shalt** must
105 **heaven . . . ruler** a counter to
   Henry's claim at 3.2.286 (see n. and
   LN)
106 **monstrous traitor** Cf. 4.10.65.
107 **capital** punishable by death (*OED
   adj.* 2b)

YORK

Wouldst have me kneel? First let me ask of these

If they can brook I bow a knee to man.   110

Sirrah, call in my sons to be my bail.   [*Exit Attendant.*]

I know, ere they will have me go to ward

They'll pawn their swords for my enfranchisement.

QUEEN

Call hither Clifford; bid him come amain,

To say if that the bastard boys of York   115

Shall be the surety for their traitor father.

                                        [*Exit Buckingham.*]

YORK

O blood-bespotted Neapolitan,

Outcast of Naples, England's bloody scourge!

The sons of York, thy betters in their birth,

Shall be their father's bail; and bane to those   120

That for my surety will refuse the boys!

---

109 *these York's attendants
111 my sons In fact Edward and Richard were both young children at the time.
112 ward custody (*OED sb.*² 3). Cf. 'The duke . . . named Edmond duke of Somerset, whom if the kyng would commit to warde . . . he promised . . . to dissolue his armie' (Hall, 226).
113 enfranchisement release
114 amain quickly
115 if that whether
117 blood-bespotted blaming all the subsequent bloodshed in the wars on the disastrous terms of the marriage contract
Neapolitan in reference to Margaret as daughter of Reignier who had an unfulfilled claim on the crown of Naples
118 Outcast contemptuous reference to Margaret's bringing no dowry: i.e.

penniless
bloody scourge Cf. *1H6* 1.2.129, where Joan of Arc is the 'English scourge'. As Cairncross points out, this makes Margaret her successor, but there is more in it than that. 'Scourge' carried the theological implication of being a punishment on behalf of God (*flagellum dei*) as part of divine providence meting out justice on fallen human nature. Often the scourge of God was extremely evil: Marlowe's Tamburlaine is the most thoroughgoing example in English drama. Unhistorically Margaret survives into *R3*, where her cumulative evil seems part of the greater pattern of Richard Crookback's scourge on a fallen nation (see Hammond, 103).
120 bane destruction

Enter EDWARD *and* RICHARD.

See where they come. I'll warrant they'll make it
good.

Enter [OLD] CLIFFORD [*and* YOUNG CLIFFORD].

QUEEN
And here comes Clifford to deny their bail.
OLD CLIFFORD [*Kneels to Henry.*]
Health and all happiness to my lord the King.   [*Rises.*]
YORK
I thank thee, Clifford. Say, what news with thee?   125
Nay, do not fright us with an angry look.
We are thy sovereign, Clifford; kneel again.
For thy mistaking so, we pardon thee.
OLD CLIFFORD
This is my king, York, I do not mistake;
But thou mistakes me much to think I do.   130
To Bedlam with him! Is the man grown mad?
KING
Ay, Clifford; a bedlam and ambitious humour
Makes him oppose himself against his king.
OLD CLIFFORD
He is a traitor; let him to the Tower,
And chop away that factious pate of his.   135
QUEEN
He is arrested, but will not obey;

---

122 **warrant** guarantee (*OED v.* 4)
131, 132 **Bedlam** See 3.1.51n.
132 **humour** temperamental inclination.
    Cf. Henry's *church-like humours*

(1.1.244). See 1.2.51n. for the four
humours.
134 **let** let him be sent (*OED v.*[1] 10)
135 **factious pate** seditious head

122.1] *Cam subst.; Enter Clifford. F;* Enter the Duke of *Yorkes* sonnes, *Edward* the Earle of *March*, and crook-backe *Richard*, at the one doore, with Drumme and soldiers, and at the other doore, enter *Clifford* and his sonne, with Drumme and soldiers, and *Clifford* kneels to *Henry*, and speakes. *Q after 114*   124 SD1] *Q*   SD2] *Oxf*   130 mistakes] mistak'st *F2*

His sons, he says, shall give their words for him.

YORK

Will you not, sons?

EDWARD

Ay, noble father, if our words will serve.

RICHARD

And if words will not, then our weapons shall.   140

OLD CLIFFORD

Why, what a brood of traitors have we here!

YORK

Look in a glass, and call thy image so.

I am thy king, and thou a false-heart traitor.

Call hither to the stake my two brave bears,

That with the very shaking of their chains   145

They may astonish these fell-lurking curs.

Bid Salisbury and Warwick come to me.

Enter the Earls of WARWICK *and* SALISBURY.

OLD CLIFFORD

Are these thy bears? We'll bait thy bears to death

And manacle the bearherd in their chains,

If thou dar'st bring them to the baiting-place.   150

---

142 **glass** mirror
143 **false-heart** treacherous. Cf. *TC*
    5.1.88.
144–6 alluding to the Elizabethan sport
    of bear-baiting by dogs (see
    Shakespeare's England, 2.428–33) and
    to the fact that Warwick's heraldic
    device was a bear chained to a *ragged
    staff* (cf. 5.1.203)
146 **astonish** terrify (*OED v.* 3). Cf. *JC*
    1.3.56.
    fell-lurking waiting for the opportu-

nity to pounce and kill: only here in
Shakespeare
149, 210 ***bearherd** bear-keeper, handler.
F's 'Berard' indicates pronunciation
(Cercignani, 129). 'Bearward' is an
alternative modern form chosen by
some editors.
150 **baiting-place** bear pit. Since 1526
bear-baiting had taken place in the
manor of Paris Garden on the
Bankside in Southwark (*Shakespeare's
England*, 2.428).

149, 210 bearherd] *Oxf;* Berard *F;* bear-ward *Pope*   150 baiting-place] *(*bayting place*)*

RICHARD

Oft have I seen a hot o'erweening cur

Run back and bite, because he was withheld;

Who, being suffered, with the bear's fell paw

Hath clapped his tail between his legs and cried;

And such a piece of service will you do,   155

If you oppose yourselves to match Lord Warwick.

OLD CLIFFORD

Hence, heap of wrath, foul indigested lump,

As crooked in thy manners as thy shape.

YORK

Nay, we shall heat you thoroughly anon.

OLD CLIFFORD

Take heed, lest by your heat you burn yourselves.   160

KING

Why, Warwick, hath thy knee forgot to bow?

151–4 Awkwardness here is created primarily by the possible meanings of *suffered*. *OED* (Suffer *v.* 11) uses this instance to illustrate the causative meaning 'injured by', which is accepted by Wilson and Hattaway; Cairncross follows *OED v.* 13, 'allowed', in antithesis to *withheld*. However, whatever meaning is preferred, the general sense of Richard's taunt turns on the sarcastic contrast between the seeming ferocity and aggression displayed by the cur when restrained (*withheld* by a leash), as against fearfulness and flight upon actual, or imminent, encounter.

151 **o'erweening** presumptuous

152 **Run . . . bite** strain against the leash. Cf. 'A man may cause his own dog to bite him' (Dent, M258), which may suggest an additional interpretation to 151–4n.

153 **Who** For application to animals, see Abbott, 264.

suffered See 151–4n.

156 **oppose yourselves** align yourselves

in opposition

match fight (*OED v.* 3)

157 **foul indigested lump** Editors quote Ovid's *Metamorphoses*, 'Chaos, rudis indigestaque moles' (1.7), and Golding's translation, 'chaos . . . a huge rude heap . . . a heavy lump' (1.7–8). 'Indigested' as 'improperly formed' reappears in *3H6* 5.6.51. Hall's portrait perpetuated the Tudor propagandist image of Richard Crookback: 'As he was small and little of stature so was he of body greatly deformed, the one shoulder higher then the other . . . his contenaunce was cruel, and such, that a man at the first aspect would judge it to sauor and smel of malice, fraude, and deceite: when he stode musing he would byte and chaw besely his nether lippe, as who sayd, that his fyerce nature in his cruell body alwaies chaffed, sturred and was euer vnquiete' (421).

159 **heat you** make you hot with fighting

anon soon

---

153 suffered,] *Ard²*; suffer'd *F*   156 oppose] suppose *F3*   157 SP] y. C. *(Capell)*

Old Salisbury, shame to thy silver hair,
Thou mad misleader of thy brainsick son!
What, wilt thou on thy deathbed play the ruffian,
And seek for sorrow with thy spectacles?   165
O, where is faith? O, where is loyalty?
If it be banished from the frosty head,
Where shall it find a harbour in the earth?
Wilt thou go dig a grave to find out war,
And shame thine honourable age with blood?   170
Why art thou old, and want'st experience?
Or wherefore dost abuse it, if thou hast it?
For shame, in duty bend thy knee to me,
That bows unto the grave with mickle age.

SALISBURY

My lord, I have considered with myself   175
The title of this most renowned duke,
And in my conscience do repute his grace
The rightful heir to England's royal seat.

KING

Hast thou not sworn allegiance unto me?

SALISBURY

I have.   180

KING

Canst thou dispense with heaven for such an oath?

162–74 Cairncross compares Genesis, 42.38; 44.29, 31.
165 **spectacles** Cf. Jaques's pantaloon, 'With spectacles on nose' (*AYL* 2.7.159), and *KL* 1.2.35.
167 **frosty** white with age
168 **harbour** in the context of banishment, refuge or asylum (*OED sb.*[1] 2)
169–70 If we take the meaning of *to find out* as 'to discover what is hidden' (*OED v.* 20), the irony becomes apparent: 'Do you need to die dishonourably

in bloodshed to discover what civil war means?'
171 **want'st** lack
172 **abuse** ill use, misuse
174 **That bows** you who bow
   mickle much, great
176 **renowned** renownèd
177 **repute** consider (*OED v.* 1). Cf. *1H4* 5.1.54.
181 **dispense with heaven** gain dispensation from God (*OED* Dispense with)

169 dig . . . war] find out war to dig a grave *Cam (Roderick)*

SALISBURY

It is great sin to swear unto a sin,
But greater sin to keep a sinful oath.
Who can be bound by any solemn vow
To do a murderous deed, to rob a man,   185
To force a spotless virgin's chastity,
To reave the orphan of his patrimony,
To wring the widow from her customed right,
And have no other reason for this wrong
But that he was bound by a solemn oath?   190

QUEEN

A subtle traitor needs no sophister.

KING

Call Buckingham, and bid him arm himself.

YORK

Call Buckingham, and all the friends thou hast.
I am resolved for death or dignity.

OLD CLIFFORD

The first, I warrant thee, if dreams prove true.   195

WARWICK

You were best to go to bed and dream again,
To keep thee from the tempest of the field.

OLD CLIFFORD

I am resolved to bear a greater storm

182–90 Oaths and oath-breaking are central to feudal society and its depiction in the histories and to Shakespeare's work as a whole (see Shirley). Margaret immediately grasps Salisbury's obvious fallacy. He identifies his oath of allegiance with an oath to undertake murder, robbery, rape etc. Cf. the proverbial 'An unlawful oath is better broken than kept' (Dent, O7).

187 **reave** rob (*OED v.* 1)

188 **customed right** rights of inheritance by custom and law

191 **sophister** a sophist, adept at specious reasoning: not elsewhere in Shakespeare

194 **resolved for** determined on (*OED* Resolved *ppl. a.* 1). Cf. *Cor* 1.1.4–6.
dignity my due rank (as King)

196 **You . . . to go** For this construction see Abbott, 352.

193–4] Both thou and they shall curse this fatal hour; *Ard²* *(following Q) between 193 and 194*
194 or] *Rowe³; and F*   196 You] Thou *Ard²*

Than any thou canst conjure up today;
And that I'll write upon thy burgonet,   200
Might I but know thee by thy household badge.

WARWICK

Now by my father's badge, old Neville's crest,
The rampant bear chained to the ragged staff,
This day I'll wear aloft my burgonet,
As on a mountain top the cedar shows   205
That keeps his leaves in spite of any storm,
Even to affright thee with the view thereof.

OLD CLIFFORD

And from thy burgonet I'll rend thy bear
And tread it underfoot with all contempt,
Despite the bearherd that protects the bear.   210

YOUNG CLIFFORD

And so to arms, victorious father,
To quell the rebels and their complices.

RICHARD

Fie, charity for shame! Speak not in spite,
For you shall sup with Jesu Christ tonight.

YOUNG CLIFFORD

Foul stigmatic, that's more than thou canst tell.   215

200, 204 **burgonet** 'The Burgonet . . . was an open-faced head-piece with a ridged crest, and often worn in war and the tilt-yard . . . The Burgonet was the defence for mounted men' (*Shakespeare's England*, 1.131).

201 **household** possessive case

202 The second part of Whitney (105) begins with a title-page illustration of the bear and ragged staff, followed by a dedicatory poem to the contemporary Earl of Warwick.
father's father-in-law's: Richard Beauchamp, the Warwick of *1H6* (see Scott-Giles, 147)

204 **aloft** on top of, as a crest

205 **mountain . . . cedar** Cedars of Lebanon were famous enough from the Bible; and Bartholomeus, in addition to various attributes, talks of the tree from 'mont Libani' (921). In the hierarchic system of things the cedar was regarded as kingly for the majesty of its size and because the eagle was said to nest in its upper branches, as Warwick recalls at his death (*3H6* 5.2.11–15).

212 **complices** accomplices. Cf. *3H6* 4.3.44.

215 **stigmatic** literally one who was branded; figuratively having a deformity equivalent to being marked out. Cf. *3H6* 2.2.136.
that's . . . tell Cf. 'That's more than I know' (Dent, M1155.1).

---

201 household] *Q subst.*; housed *F*; house's *F2*   207 to] *Q*; io *F*; so *F2–4*

RICHARD

If not in heaven, you'll surely sup in hell. *Exeunt* [*severally*].

[**5.2**]   [*An inn-sign of the Castle is displayed.
                  Alarums to the battle.*] *Enter* WARWICK.

WARWICK

Clifford of Cumberland, 'tis Warwick calls;
An if thou dost not hide thee from the bear,
Now, when the angry trumpet sounds alarum,
And dead men's cries do fill the empty air,
Clifford, I say, come forth and fight with me!   5
Proud northern lord, Clifford of Cumberland,
Warwick is hoarse with calling thee to arms.

Enter YORK.

How now, my noble lord! What, all afoot?

216 Cf. *R3* 5.3.313 ('Richard's wheel
comes full circle' – RP).
5.2 location: St Albans (Capell). The first
battle of St Albans took place in 1455.
As York led his forces from the
Marches of Wales, Henry took his
troops northwards to St Albans, fear-
ing Yorkist sympathizers in London.
Holinshed includes the formal
exchanges between York and the King
before the battle (239). In Hall (235)
and Holinshed (240) Old Clifford is
simply reported as amongst the slain
while here he is killed by York before
us. The scene is most famous for the
speech of Young Clifford in which he
undertakes revenge, anticipating the
slaughter of the child Rutland, York's
youngest son, at Wakefield (*3H6* 1.3).
For the Q version and an encounter
with Richard of Gloucester, see

Appendix 2.
0.1 Hattaway is adopted here since 67
indicates that there must have been a
sign, as Q makes plain: 'then enter the
Duke of *Somerset* and *Richard* fighting,
and *Richard* kils him vnder the signe of
the Castle in saint *Albones*'.
1 **Clifford of Cumberland** an
anachronism, as Hattaway points out,
since the title Earl of Cumberland was
conferred on Old Clifford's great-
grandson Henry de Clifford in 1525
2–5 The antagonists of 5.1.140–60
resume confrontation but now with
weapons on the battlefield, not just
words.
2 **bear** continuing the allusions from
5.1.144–54
3 **alarum** the call to arms; mostly found
as a stage direction (see 0.2)
4 **dead** dying: a prolepsis

216 SD *severally*] *Theobald*   **5.2**] *Steevens; 5.3 Capell*   0.1 *An . . . displayed.*] *Cam²*   0.2 *Alarums
. . . battle.*] *Q*   8 How] *Rowe; War.* How *F*

YORK

The deadly-handed Clifford slew my steed;
But match to match I have encountered him   10
And made a prey for carrion kites and crows
Even of the bonny beast he loved so well.

Enter [OLD] CLIFFORD.

WARWICK

Of one or both of us the time is come.

YORK

Hold, Warwick, seek thee out some other chase,
For I myself must hunt this deer to death.   15

WARWICK

Then nobly, York; 'tis for a crown thou fight'st.
As I intend, Clifford, to thrive today,
It grieves my soul to leave thee unassailed.   *Exit.*

OLD CLIFFORD

What seest thou in me, York? Why dost thou pause?

YORK

With thy brave bearing should I be in love,   20
But that thou art so fast mine enemy.

OLD CLIFFORD

Nor should thy prowess want praise and esteem,

---

9 **deadly-handed** murderous: nowhere else in Shakespeare
10 **match to match** equal to equal, with the added sense, in the context (9–12), of equal outcome in the death of both horses
11 **kites** See 3.1.249n. Cf. *Ham* 2.2.579–80.
12 **bonny** handsome, strapping (*OED a.* 2a): a common word in Greene (Wilson). Q elaborates: 'The boniest gray that ere was bred in the North' (TLN 2144). Cf. *E3*, 1.2.57, 'saddle

my bonny black'.
13 Cf. 'One dies when his hour comes' (Dent, H741.1).
14–15 *3H6* has almost the same lines, 'single out some other chase; / For I myself will hunt this wolf to death' (2.4.12–13).
14 **chase** prey (*OED sb.*[1] 4). Cf. *H5* 2.4.68.
17 **to thrive** Cf. 'So thrive I' (*R3* 4.4.398).
21 **fast** firmly, fixedly (*OED a.* 1)
22 **want** lack

---

9 deadly-handed] *(deadly handed)*   12.1 OLD] *this edn*   19] *Pope; F lines* Yorke? / pause? /

But that 'tis shown ignobly and in treason.

YORK

So let it help me now against thy sword
As I in justice and true right express it.   25

OLD CLIFFORD

My soul and body on the action both!

YORK

A dreadful lay! Address thee instantly.
[*They fight, and Old Clifford falls.*]

OLD CLIFFORD

La fin couronne les oeuvres.   [*Dies.*]

YORK

Thus war hath given thee peace, for thou art still.   29
Peace with his soul, heaven, if it be thy will!   [*Exit.*]

Enter YOUNG CLIFFORD.

YOUNG CLIFFORD

Shame and confusion! All is on the rout,
Fear frames disorder, and disorder wounds
Where it should guard. O war, thou son of hell,
Whom angry heavens do make their minister,
Throw in the frozen bosoms of our part   35
Hot coals of vengeance! Let no soldier fly.

23 **'tis shown** it shows itself
24–5 May my valour with the justice and
    right of my cause defeat you.
26 **action** outcome of the action
27 **lay** wager
    Address prepare. Cf. *WT* 4.4.53.
28 ***'The end crowns the works' (Dent,
    E116), which appears to be a variant of
    'The end tries (proves etc.) all' (Dent,
    E116.1). Cf. 'still the fine's the crown'
    (*AW* 4.4.35) and *TC* 4.5.224. The
    chivalric encounter is brutalized in Q:
    see facsimile TLN 2153–65.

31–65 For Q variants see facsimile TLN
    2167–90.
31 **confusion** overthrow and ruin (*OED*
    1). See *1H6* 4.1.77.
    on the rout routed, put in disorderly
    flight
32 **frames** brings about (*OED v.* 8d)
34 **heavens . . . minister** See *bloody
    scourge*, 5.1.118n. Cf. *Ham* 3.4.175.
35 **part** party, side
36 **coals of vengeance** Cf. Psalms,
    140.10, 'Let burning coals fall upon
    them'.

27 lay] day *F3* SD] *Capell subst.* 28 couronne les oeuvres] *F2 (Corronne les oevres); Corrone les
eumenes F* SD] *F2* 30 SD] *Pope* 31 SP] *Q; Clif. F* confusion! All] *Pope;* Confusion all *F*

He that is truly dedicate to war
Hath no self-love; nor he that loves himself
Hath not essentially, but by circumstance,
The name of valour. [*Sees his dead father.*]
           O, let the vile world end,   40
And the premised flames of the last day
Knit earth and heaven together!
Now let the general trumpet blow his blast,
Particularities and petty sounds
To cease! Wast thou ordained, dear father,   45
To lose thy youth in peace and to achieve
The silver livery of advised age,

37 **dedicate** For the participal form without final 'd', see Abbott, 342.

38 **Hath no self-love** must be selfless

38–40 **nor . . . valour** A person concerned with self gains the name of valour only accidentally because of circumstance, rather than because of innate selflessness. Cairncross conjectures that the distinction between essence and circumstance here derives from the scholastic duality of substance and accidents.

40–5 **O . . . cease!** This passage alludes to scriptural anticipation of the end of the world as recounted in Revelation. An analogue is found in Ovid (1.299–304), but the spiritual significance of Holy Writ would have been foremost within a Christian culture.

41 **premised** premisèd. *OED ppl. a.* gives (1) 'stated or mentioned previously, aforesaid' and (2) 'sent before the time' with this as the only example. Editors take it to mean 'preordained'; and Hart was right to stress that Young Clifford himself is invoking a change in the divine plan, not acknowledging that God has brought forward the last day. Not elsewhere in Shakespeare. Given (2), George Walton Williams suggests that perhaps F's 'premised' is a mis-

reading of 'promised' as in 'Is this the promis'd end?' (*KL* 5.3.264).
    flames Cf. Revelation, 20.9, 'and fire came down from God out of heaven, and devoured them'. See 42n.
    last day See John, 11.24, 'he shall rise again in the resurrection at the last day'.

42 'And the stars of heaven fell unto the earth' (Revelation, 6.13). See 41n.

43 **general trumpet** the trumpet announcing doomsday to all. Cf. 1 Corinthians, 15.52, 'at the last trump: for the trumpet shall sound, and the dead be raised incorruptible'.

44 **Particularities** personal trifles, in antithesis to *general*
    petty sounds in contrast to *blast*

46 **lose . . . peace** poetic licence here. Old Clifford was involved in such matters as the siege of Pontoise (1437) as Holinshed notes, though he calls him John instead of Thomas (193).
    lose part with

47–9 This passage reads almost as an epitome of the death of the aged and sick Bedford at Rouen after watching the battle from his chair (*1H6* 3.2).

47 **silver livery** silver hair as emblematic of old age. Cf. *Per* 5.3.7.
    advised advisèd: cautious (*OED ppl. a.* 2). See *H5* 1.2.179.

40 SD] *Theobald subst.*

And, in thy reverence and thy chair-days, thus
To die in ruffian battle? Even at this sight
My heart is turned to stone, and while 'tis mine   50
It shall be stony. York not our old men spares;
No more will I their babes; tears virginal
Shall be to me even as the dew to fire,
And beauty, that the tyrant oft reclaims,
Shall to my flaming wrath be oil and flax.   55
Henceforth I will not have to do with pity.
Meet I an infant of the house of York,
Into as many gobbets will I cut it
As wild Medea young Absyrtus did.
In cruelty will I seek out my fame.   60
Come, thou new ruin of old Clifford's house;
[*He takes him up on his back.*]
As did Aeneas old Anchises bear,
So bear I thee upon my manly shoulders;

48 **chair-days** *1H6* makes the best comment: 'When sapless age and weak unable limbs / Should bring thy father to his drooping chair' (4.5.4–5). Not elsewhere in Shakespeare.

50–1 **My . . . stony.** 'A heart as hard as stone' (Dent, H311). Editors compare 1 Samuel, 25.37, and Ezekiel, 11.19.

52 **babes** anticipating the murder of Rutland in *3H6* 1.3. See headnote and 4.2.23n. Dugdale records that after the battle of Wakefield, Young Clifford was 'reported to have made so great a slaughter with his own hands, that he was thenceforth called *the Butcher*' (1.343). Perhaps Shakespeare's dramatization in part developed from this historical memory?

53 **as . . . fire** as drops of water to a conflagration

54 **that . . . reclaims** that often reforms the tyrant (See *OED* reclaim v.2b)

55 **oil and flax** Cf. 'Put not fire to flax' (Dent, F278) and 'To add oil to the fire' (Dent, O30).

56 **pity** Cf. Richard of Gloucester's 'I, that have neither pity, love, nor fear' (*3H6* 5.6.68), and see 3.1.125n. above.

58 **gobbets** Cf. 4.1.85 for parallel mythological usage.

59 **Absyrtus** Medea's brother. In flight from Colchos with Jason, her lover, Medea murdered her brother and cut up his body, strewing the pieces around to delay her father Aeetes' pursuit. Given the number of beheadings in *2H6* (see 4.7.122n.), it may be significant to note that in a source well known to the Renaissance (Ovid, *Tristia*, 3.9) Medea places the head and hands high up on a rock to gain her father's attention.

62 Virgil, *Aeneid*, Bk 2, tells the story of Aeneas rescuing his father from burning Troy. As Hattaway says, the event provided an emblem of *pietas*, devotion and duty to gods, country and elders – a sentiment that jars with the preceding dedication to cruelty. Cf. *JC* 1.2.112–14.

61 SD] *Q*

But then Aeneas bare a living load,
Nothing so heavy as these woes of mine. 65

[Exit with the body.]

Enter the Duke of SOMERSET *and* RICHARD *fighting.*
[Somerset is killed.]

RICHARD

So, lie thou there;
For underneath an alehouse' paltry sign,
The Castle in Saint Albans, Somerset
Hath made the wizard famous in his death.
Sword, hold thy temper; heart, be wrathful still: 70
Priests pray for enemies, but princes kill.

[Exit with the body.]

Fight. Excursions. Enter KING, QUEEN *and others.*

QUEEN

Away, my lord! You are slow, for shame, away!

KING

Can we outrun the heavens? Good Margaret, stay.

QUEEN

What are you made of? You'll nor fight nor fly.

---

67 **alehouse' paltry sign** See 3.2.81n.
69 **wizard** Roger Bolingbroke (see 1.4). By fulfilling the prophecy Somerset's death makes Bolingbroke famous (see 1.4.34–7).
70 **hold** maintain
temper . . . wrathful Richard plays on *temper* as 'temperament' and as the combination of hardness and flexibility in tempering steel (see *OED sb.* 3 and 5). His sword is to retain its tempered balance while his temperament is to be overbalanced by wrath. Cf. *RJ* 3.1.115.

still always
71 **Priests . . . enemies** This reflects Christ's Sermon on the Mount: 'Loue your enemies . . . pray for them which hurt you' (Matthew, 5.44).
71.1 *Excursions* sallies, sorties (*OED* 3): found in Holinshed
73 **outrun the heavens** escape providence. Cairncross compares Amos, 9.2, 3, and Psalms, 139.6–7, but Shaheen comments, 'At best analogies rather than references' (61).
74 ¹**nor** neither

---

65 SD *Exit*] *Rowe   with the body*] *this edn*   65.1] *Q subst.; (Enter Richard, and Somerset to fight.) F*
65.2] *Rowe*   71 SD *Exit*] *Theobald   with the body*] *this edn*

Now is it manhood, wisdom and defence   75
To give the enemy way and to secure us
By what we can, which can no more but fly.
   Alarum afar off.
If you be ta'en we then should see the bottom
Of all our fortunes; but if we haply scape –
As well we may, if not through your neglect –   80
We shall to London get, where you are loved
And where this breach now in our fortunes made
May readily be stopped.

        Enter [YOUNG] CLIFFORD.

YOUNG CLIFFORD
But that my heart's on future mischief set,
I would speak blasphemy ere bid you fly;   85
But fly you must; uncurable discomfit
Reigns in the hearts of all our present part.
Away for your relief! And we will live
To see their day and them our fortune give.   89
Away, my lord, away!   *Exeunt.*

---

75 **is it** it is
76 to give way to the enemy and gain safety
77 **what** whatever means
  which who
  no more but only
78 **ta'en** captured: pronounced 'tane'
  bottom lowest point
79 **all our fortunes** the fortunes of us all
  haply by chance
80 **if . . . neglect** unless your failure to act prevents us

81 **you are loved** This conflicts with the historical record (see headnote). Cairncross points out that in *3H6* 1.1.67 Henry says 'the city favours them'.
84 **mischief** plots to harm the enemy
85 **ere** rather than; before
86 **uncurable discomfit** irreversible defeat
87 **present part** surviving followers
88 **relief** deliverance; escape from danger
89 to see the situation reversed

83.1 YOUNG] *Dyce* 84 SP] *Capell; Clif. F* 87 part] *Dyce;* parts *F;* pow'rs *Hanmer;* party *Warburton*

[5.3]   *Alarum. Retreat. Enter* YORK, RICHARD, *[Edward,]*
       WARWICK *and Soldiers with Drum and Colours.*

YORK

Old Salisbury, who can report of him,
That winter lion, who in rage forgets
Aged contusions and all brush of time,
And, like a gallant in the brow of youth,
Repairs him with occasion? This happy day   5
Is not itself, nor have we won one foot
If Salisbury be lost.

RICHARD   My noble father,
Three times today I holp him to his horse,
Three times bestrid him; thrice I led him off,
Persuaded him from any further act;   10
But still where danger was, still there I met him,

5.3 location: St Albans. The action continues from 5.2. (Malone).

The play could have ended by simply following the chronicles' events, recording York's noble treatment of Henry at St Albans, his escorting him to London, the calling of a parliament, a truce, reconciliation and the protectorship for the House of Lancaster's former enemy. But though the flight of Henry and the Queen in 5.2 is fictitious, it maintains the tension, and keeps the action going from *2H6* to *3H6*, which opens with the Yorkists having pursued the royal party to London. The dramatist thus closes the gap between the battle of St Albans (1455) and the battle of Wakefield (1460) as action is driven by the dynastic momentum of revenge and power.

0.1 **Edward* Edward has two lines in Q (TLN 2018–19), none in F; but he is included here as part of the pattern of generations locked into an overarching cycle of struggle, just as the presence of Young Clifford in 5.1 is important

even though he says only a couple of lines at 211–12.

2 **winter** aged

3 **Aged** agèd

brush hostile encounter (*OED sb.*[3] 3). Cf. 'brushes of the war' (*TC* 5.3.34), the only other such usage in Shakespeare. Alternatively Warburton's conjecture, 'bruise', is attractive through being synonymous with contusions; cf. *MA* 5.1.65, 'And with grey hairs and bruise of many days'.

4 **brow of youth** unmarked by the wrinkles of age. Cf. *KL* 1.4.284.

5 **Repairs . . . occasion** restores himself to 'a gallant in the brow of youth', with fighting (see *OED* Repair *v.*[2] 4). Cf. *Cym* 1.1.132.

6 **one foot** (of ground)

8–9 **Three . . . Three . . . thrice** possibly Homeric formula

8 **holp** helped

9 **bestrid** stood over to protect (*OED* Bestride *v.* 2c). See *CE* 5.1.192.

11 **still . . . still** continually . . . always (*OED adv.* 3)

5.3] *Steevens*   **0.1** *Edward] Q3*   **1** Old] *Collier following Q;* Of *F*   **3** brush] bruise *Warburton*

And like rich hangings in a homely house,
So was his will in his old feeble body.
But, noble as he is, look where he comes.

Enter SALISBURY.

Now, by my sword, well hast thou fought today.   15
SALISBURY
By th' mass, so did we all. I thank you, Richard.
God knows how long it is I have to live,
And it hath pleased him that three times today
You have defended me from imminent death.
Well, lords, we have not got that which we have: 20
'Tis not enough our foes are this time fled,
Being opposites of such repairing nature.
YORK
I know our safety is to follow them,
For, as I hear, the King is fled to London
To call a present court of parliament.   25
Let us pursue him ere the writs go forth.
What says Lord Warwick? Shall we after them?
WARWICK
After them? Nay, before them if we can!
Now by my faith, lords, 'twas a glorious day.
Saint Albans' battle won by famous York   30
Shall be eternized in all age to come.

---

12 **rich hangings** wall tapestries. *Rich* probably refers to both fabric and the scene depicted.
20 **got** secured
21 **fled** See headnote.
22 being enemies able to flee (*OED* v^1 1) and yet restore (*OED* v^2 4) their position. Salisbury makes a warning pun on the two meanings of 'repair'.
23 **safety** safeguard

24 See headnote.
25 **present** immediate
29 *****faith** Q is restored as F's 'hand' probably indicates response to the Act to Restrain Abuses of Players (1606).
31 **eternized** immortalized: nowhere else in Shakespeare; first recorded instance 1580 (*OED*); 'eternest' in Q (TLN 2231)

15 Now] *Cam¹ (A. W. Pollard) Sal.* Now *F*   16 SP] *Cam¹; not in F*   29 faith] *Q;* hand *F*

Sound drum and trumpets, and to London all,
And more such days as these to us befall! *Exeunt.*

FINIS

32–3 Note that 'the kingmaker' has the
last word but the irony of the final line
will tell against him in *3H6*.

32 drum] *(*Drumme*);* drums *Q*

LONGER NOTES

1.2.67 pageant If the word is re-examined in relation to 63–7 it takes on the further meaning associated with the pageant car of actual triumphal processions (*OED sb.* 3) and as depicted in Petrarch's influential *Trionfi*. The sense of triumphal progress and pageant is found throughout the two parts of Marlowe's *Tamburlaine* ('And now themselves shall make our pageant', *2*, 4.3.90). Moreover, the god-like Tamburlaine seems allied to Fortune. Here, as a woman, Eleanor associates herself with Fortune, who was occasionally depicted as a queen (Patch, 60ff.), whose pageant car rides over the bodies of her enemies. If this is compared to the depiction of Eleanor in Baldwin's *Mirror* there is great irony, for there she is conventionally brought down by Fortune's wheel in the *De Casibus* tradition. Finally, as Shakespeare shows (2.4), following *Mirror* and the chronicles, according to her sentence Eleanor is forced to act out a last pageant in the spectacle of public shame. Venezky (198) suggests that Eleanor is thinking of a show of Fortune's favourites, as in *The Rare Triumphs of Love and Fortune* (1589). For trisyllabic pronunciation, see Cercignani (309).

1.4.3 provided Bolingbroke and his 'instruments' were eventually displayed in St Paul's churchyard as *Brut* records: 'all theire fals werkys and tresoun *th*at they ymagyned and wroght, which was openly shewed afore all peple *th*at wold com to Seint Paules Crosse on the Sonday, the xxiij. day of Iully, by Roger *th*at was hir Clerk, a Nigromancier, by the deuels crafte and ymaginacion in his worching, which was shewed openly in *th*e sermontyme, the day aboueseyd, to all peple *th*at wold come to se it, of her*e* scriptures, ymages of silu*er*, of wex*e*, and of *oth*er metall*e*s, and swerdys, w*ith* many *oth*er dyu*er*s instrument*e*s of this fals craft of Nigromancy and the devels power*e*. And *th*ere Rog*er*, this Clerk, stode vpon an high stage, w*ith* all his Instrumentes about hym, spoyling of his garment; and did vpon hym a surplyce, w*ith* a crowne of papir vpon his hede, forto forsake all his fals craft of the devell, and for the relapse all *th*at he had doon and wrought by the devyll and his power*e*' (478). *An English Chronicle* adds some details: 'the forsaid maister Roger with all his instruments of nygromancie – that is to say a chaier ypeynted, wherynne he was wont to sitte whanne he wroughte his craft, and on the iiij corners of the chaier stood iiij swerdis, and vpon euery swerd hanggyng an ymage of copir – and with meny othir instrumentis accordyng to his said craft, stood in a high stage aboue alle mennes heddis in Powlis chircheyerd befor the cros whiles the sermon endurid, holdyng a suerd in his right hand and a septre in his lift

365

hand, araid in a maruaillous aray whereynne he was wont to sitte whanne he wrougte his nygromancie' (57).

1.4.55–6 Hattaway remarks that there is 'much dramatic effect in watching the embarrassment of Eleanor and her crew'. This could indeed be staged: Buckingham appears to indicate that Eleanor be separated from the other prisoners, given her status (51), and I conjecture that Stafford exits (52) to carry out Buckingham's order. *All away!* refers to those on stage as indicated by the SD (54). If Stafford, Eleanor and a guard re-entered here, *this lovely lady* (73) would sarcastically refer to her on stage, and *A pretty plot* (56) could be addressed to her, punning on place, the conspiracy, and the papers Buckingham holds. This timing of Eleanor's leaving the gallery and re-entering below would be almost identical to that of *R2*, according to Capell's SDs at 3.3.183–6, which are followed by modern editors (compare the Countess's descent in *Edward III*, 1.2.89–93). The dramatic force in the comic deflation of the double take would provide an apt close for the act. In contrast Wells & Taylor find 'artless redundancy' in the repetition of the prophecies and adopt Q here.

2.3.13 **Sir John Stanley** Tudor chroniclers inherited the confusion found in fifteenth-century predecessors, who also mention a John Stanley, Esquire. Thomas succeeded his father John as Governor of the Isle of Man. Later, ironically, he assisted in Gloucester's arrest at Bury (K. H. Vickers, 272–3). *An English Chronicle* records that, when Eleanor was first arrested and sent to Leeds Castle (see 2.3 headnote), 'she was committid to the warde of sir Johan Stiward knyghte, and of Johan Stanley squier' (58). John Steward was the Constable of Leeds Castle and John Stanley one of his officers (see Griffiths, 360).

Sir Thomas Stanley's two sons appear elsewhere in Shakespeare's histories: Sir Thomas Stanley (1435–1504) is prominent in *R3*, and Sir William Stanley (1436–95) appears briefly in *3H6* (4.5), where he helps Edward escape from captivity.

The initial confusion of the two names was compounded by Boswell-Stone (259), who, with the additional authority of the King's warrant to Sir Thomas (*Proceedings and Ordinances of the Privy Council of England* (1837), 6.51), silently emended his text of Holinshed from 'John' to 'Thomas'. This subsequently led such commentators as Hart and McKerrow to accept 'Thomas' as the accurate record of the 1587 Holinshed (somewhat weakening McKerrow's argument for Shakespeare's use of the first, 1577 edition, which he believed differed by reading 'John': see 'Note').

2.3.69–73* In F there is no Third Prentice and the second half of the Q line, 'Be merry, Peter, and fear not thy master. Fight for credit of the prentices', is adjusted and displaces the Second Prentice's line. In Peter's speech (74–80) F includes Q's 'I thank you all', the 'all' indicating more than two (thus corresponding to Horner's 'I'll pledge you all'), but not necessarily so, as in 2.2.26. But then the three apprentices are named as

Robin, Will and Tom. Wells & Taylor adopt Q's reading here on the supposition that these lines, though absent from the foul papers used for F's
composition, were introduced to the prompt-book and reflect the
performance tradition behind Q. Much of the farcical comedy of this
scene derives from the relationship of order to disorder – ceremony and
drunkenness, law and anarchy, chivalry and burlesque. The travesty of
symmetry (three neighbours, three apprentices, parallel drinking, and the
dead-drunk/frightened-sober inversion) adds considerably to this.

2.3.96 SD **Hall** is slightly ambiguous here: the armourer 'was vanqueshed of
his seruaunte, beyng but a cowarde and a wretche, whose body was drawen
to Tiborne, & there hanged and behedded' (208). Grafton (628) repeats
this. The imprecise syntax suggests that the armourer's body was hanged
etc. Fabyan, however, whom Holinshed (210) follows, is clearer: the
armourer 'was slayne with gylt. But that false seruaunt lyued nat longe
vnpunysshed, for he was after hanged for felony at Tyborne' (618).
Shakespeare reverses guilt and innocence and links the content of
Horner's treason to York's claim to the crown. Gregory makes plain the
fate of the armourer's body: 'the master was slayne and dyspoylyde owte
of hys harnys, and lay stylle in the fylde alle that day and that nyght next
folowynge. And thenne afty[r]ward, by the kyngys commaundement, he
was d[r]awyn, hanggyde, and be-heddyde, and hys hedde sette on London
Brygge, and the body hynggyng a-bove erthe be-syde the towre' (187).
Nichols (see 2.3.48n.) prints the full costs for the combat and the dispos-
al of the body (220). I am indebted to Prof. Sydney Anglo for the last two
references.

3.1.166 **conventicles** Editors quote Hall: 'THE Erles of Marche and
Warwicke, and other beyng at Calice, had knowledge of all these doynges,
and secrete conuenticles' (242). But as *2H6* was written and performed
the word had a greater political immediacy, as became apparent in the act
of 1593 'to Retain the Queen's Majesty's Subjects in their Due
Obedience', aimed at Popish recusants, and, some argued, at separatists
and nonconformity generally. The act condemned those enticing others to
'assemblies, conventicles or meetings' (*Statutes*, 423). An anonymous
Puritan diarist, reflecting on the wording of the act, recorded that 'the
reach of this word, "conventicles", was much feared' (Neale, 293). See
Collinson.

3.1.168 **false witness** In the secular realm of law the sixteenth century saw
'the growth of the practice of proving facts by witnesses instead of rely-
ing on the statements of counsel' (Holdsworth, III, 648), so much so that
Elizabeth re-enacted the statute of 32 H8 c.9 with greater penalties as *An
act for punishment of such as shall procure or commit any wilfil perjury*, 1563
(5 Elizabeth c.9). Here the language of the Bible reappeared, '*the said
offence of subornation, and sinister procurement of false witnesses, hath . . .
greatly increased and augmented*' (*Statutes* VI, 189). Cf. Acts 6.11–13,
'Then they suborned men . . . And set foorth false witnesses'.

3.1.260 **reasons** Cairncross, following Hudson, emended to 'treasons' as consonant with the various treasons alluded to throughout this scene thus far. Furthermore, the 'treason'/'reason' misprint was also made by compositor B in *F R2* 5.3.50. Sanders rejects this: 'the whole point is that Gloucester cannot be proved to have committed treason and so the peers have to resort to giving the weak king trivial arguments as justification for their animosity'. Alternatively, Hattaway suggests that the *reasons* referred to are those given by Gloucester himself at 142ff., which is odd since they largely consist of a catalogue of *false accuse* (160) against his enemies. Suffolk's *reasons* are his own, just given in the preceding speech (see 253–9nn.), in contrast to the Cardinal's plea for legal *colour* (see 236–7n.), the *quillets* Suffolk dismisses in the following line.

3.1.270 **meritorious** The question of 'deeds' having merit echoes a central debate between the Catholic and Reformed churches, between works and merit, faith and grace. Protestantism rejected 'merit' as Papist, those 'merit-mongers' as Bishop Latimer scornfully put it (*Sermons*, 521), and the word appears in the official prayers of the English church: 'I have no merits, nor good works which I may allege before thee' (*Liturgies*, 257). The homily against rebellion accuses the Pope of encouraging all disobedience and insurrection as 'most meritorious' (*Homilies*, 525). By the 1580s the word had acquired specific opprobrium in the idea of assassination of heretics, such as Elizabeth I, as 'meritorious': 'to murther a king, a prince, or other necessarie member of the commonwealth is meritorious' (*Contre-League*, 52, cited Kocher, 160). Oliver suggests that 'the deed is meritorious', said by the assassin-Friar of Marlowe's *The Massacre at Paris* (23.28), may be a contamination from *2H6*. Cf. *KJ* 3.1.176.

3.1.278 **worthy** Given the above references to deeds, merit and the priesthood, Suffolk's reply here, reinforced by his gestures, has a parallel theological significance. 'Worthiness' is a central spiritual concept in the language of the *Prayer Book*: 'by the death and merites of . . . Jesus Christ . . . wee . . . maye wortheley receiue . . . although we be unworthy . . . not waiying our merites' (223). See *OED* Worthy 6. More specifically the meaning of 'worthy' as found in Romans, 8.18, of the Bishops' Bible was rigorously defended by William Fulke in a Reformation debate of 1583: 'We say our translation, both in word and sense, is the same in English that St Paul did write in Greek. As for the argument against "merit" or "desert" which doth follow thereof, we affirm that it is as necessarily gathered of the words "equal", or "comparable", or "correspondent", as of the word "worthy".'

3.2.89 **brazen caves** In Homer (*Iliad*, 10.3–4) Aeolus' island is surrounded by bronze walls (bronze in modern translations; but the word was coined in the eighteenth century, and Pope's translation has 'walls of brass', with which it was identified earlier). Brass does not occur in Virgil's account of Aeolus' cave (*Aeneid*, 1.52–4). Hattaway suggests familiarity with Ovid

(*Metamorphoses* 1.262–3), but here, again, there is no 'brazen'. However, re-examining Shakespeare's frequent use of the word we find that meaning is divided roughly into two: substance and sound. *OED a.* 2 registers the transferred or figurative meaning of 'brazen' as 'resembling (brass) in colour or sound' – that is, the sound associated with 'brazen' instruments like the trumpet (see *AC* 4.8.36), bell (*KJ* 3.3.38) and pipe (*TC* 4.5.7). *Brazen caves* evidently refers to the turbulent resonance of the winds' enclosure, as Virgil particularly stresses, and their sonorous release rehearsed here in a passage Cairncross notes for its phonetic expressiveness.

3.2.116–18 Shakespeare undoubtedly knew that it is Aeneas, upon Dido's invitation at the opening of Book 2 of Virgil's *Aeneid*, who tells the story of Troy, not his son Ascanius (see *Tit* 3.2.27–8). In Virgil Venus has Cupid appear as Ascanius bearing gifts from Troy to Dido, to inflame her heart with love (*Aeneid*, 1.658–756). Marlowe generally repeats this in *Dido*, but with the sequence reversed, Cupid as Ascanius appearing after Aeneas' harrowing account. Wilson mistakenly attributes Shakespeare's variant to a misreading of Chaucer's *The Legend of Good Women* (1129–55), which in fact gives the basic Virgilian details. J. A. K. Thomson notes, 'It is thought that this perversion of the *Aeneid* comes from the *Roman d'Énéas* (latter half of the twelfth century), in which it is Ascanius who excites Dido's love' (89). Presumably there must be a more mainstream source which, as yet, remains unidentified. Given the irony of Margaret's speech at this point, perhaps Shakespeare was drawn by the image of Suffolk–Cupid–Ascanius?

3.2.286 **deputy** Cf. W. Baldwin: 'Princes being by God put in authority are his vice-gerents, and should therefore require obedience' (74). The anointing of the coronation ceremony strengthened the analogy with biblical priest-kingship, as in *R2*, 'God's substitute, His deputy anointed in His sight' (1.2.37–8). In *Woodstock* (*c.* 1592–5) Richard II speaks of 'our sacred person, / The highest God's anointed deputy' (5.3.57–8). And in *Mirror* (177) Jack Cade finally acknowledges, 'God hath ordayned the power, all princes be / His Lieutenauntes, or debities in realmes' ('Jack Cade', 155–6). A comic counterpart is found in *LLL* with Don Armado's letter to the King of Navarre, who is addressed as 'Great deputy, the welkin's vicegerent' (1.1.219–20).

4.1.88–90 **Picardy . . . home** The catalogue of crimes and misdemeanours up to this point can be documented from the chronicles, particularly in the articles presented by the commons against Suffolk (Hall, 217–18; Holinshed, 218–19), but this final charge has puzzled editors, since no source can be found. Perhaps the answer lies in Holinshed's account of the loss of Pontoise (1441), in which the French 'took the capteine, and diuerse other Englishmen, and slue to the number of foure hundred' (195). The carnage stands out here since the common practice in siege warfare was for 'composition', a town's evacuation upon terms, when starvation or complete destruction otherwise appeared the only prospect. Holinshed's account follows on from the chronicle of Talbot's skirmishes in Picardy and the Normandy Marches (article 5, 193–4); and although Pontoise is in the Île de France, if the passage is read hurriedly, Pontoise could be taken to be in Picardy, which is stressed more than in Hall's record. Suffolk had nothing to do with this defeat, but the Pontoise episode reads as an extension of article 5; by Suffolk 'the kynges enemies . . . haue gotten townes and fortresses' (Hall, 218).

4.1.108 **Bargulus** Cicero's *De officiis* (2.11) has 'Bardulis Illyrius latro' ('Bardulis, the Illyrian bandit') (Cicero, 208–9). As Steevens noted, following Farmer, 'Bargulus' is the spelling found in two Tudor translations of the *Offices* by Robert Whytington (1534) and Nicholas Grimald (1533), who follow Renaissance Latin editions. Given the familiarity of Cicero's book in Renaissance education, the allusion here must be ironic since Bardulis is cited, in spite of his criminality, for his justness in dividing spoils amongst his followers. Cicero says nothing about Bardulis and threats. In Q is found 'This villain being but Captain of a Pinnais, / Threatens more plagues then mightie Abradas, / The great Masadonian Pyrate', which, as editors note, is found in two works by Greene, *Web* and *Menaphon*: '*Abradas* the great *Macedonian* Pirate, thought euerie one had a letter of Marte, that bare sayles in the Ocean' (*Menaphon*, 49). 'Abradas' is just part of a euphuistic catalogue of examples; again there are no threats. Hart suggests that this might have been one of the feathers worn by the 'upstart crow' (see 3.1.75n.). For *Menaphon* as the likely source see the note on *vassal* below (111 LN). Presumably an exotic pirate's name was needed, regardless of original context, and Shakespeare – possibly self-conscious about his borrowing – replaced Greene with Cicero?

4.1.109 **Drones . . . beehives**. The lazy drone consuming the honey others have made was an ancient commonplace (see *Per* 2.Chorus.18, 2.1.46–7) and is duly recorded by Bartholomeus, citing the fundamental sources of Pliny and Isidore of Seville (1206–7), but the fable of the drone and the eagle repudiated by Suffolk appears to be an addition of Renaissance mythographers. The anonymous *Edward III* (1596) has 'like the lazy drone / Crept up by stealth into the eagle's nest' (1.1.94–5, cited Cairncross). The context here is one of vehement defiance, yet E. A. Armstrong (25) quotes from Lyly's *Endymion* (1591) with fuller detail: 'There might I behold Drones, or Beetles, . . . creeping under the winges of a princely Eagle, who being carried into her neast, sought there to sucke that veine, that wolde have killed the Eagle.' See the note on *vassal* below (111 LN).

4.1.111 **vassal** Surprisingly, the pejorative sense of 'base or abject person' apparent here (*OED sb.* and *a.*) is not recorded before 1589 in Greene's *Menaphon* (see 108 LN), as against the earlier feudal meaning of the vassal who holds lands from a superior on condition of homage and allegiance (*OED sb.* and *a.* 1). In Greene's pastoral romance the context is a song or 'roundelay' by Menaphon and occurs a few pages before the 'Abradas' reference (37–8 and 49; see 108 LN above). Further, the roundelay is an elaboration on the proverb collected by Erasmus as *Aquila non captat muscas*, 'An eagle does not hunt flies' (*Adages*, 3.2.64: 34.249). See *AC* 2.2.185 (Dent, E1). Menaphon's song is the reverse of the Suffolk–Lieutenant relationship. The eagle at first threatens the fly, 'Vassaile auant', and then relents: 'I scorne by me the meanest creature die'.

4.1.136 Bezonians From Italian *bisognoso*, 'needy'. Hart cites several Renaissance contemporaries in this sense but also notes in William Garrard's *Art of War* (1591), 'Bisonians and fresh water soldiers', which corresponds to *OED*'s other meaning, 'a raw recruit', from Spanish *bisoño*. Though Shakespeare's military vocabulary might derive indirectly from Spanish writings on war, Ancient Pistol's predilection for terms from the Italian and his own 'Bezonian' (*2H4* 5.3.113) indicate the pejorative 'beggar' (see *Shakespeare's England*, 1.120–1).

4.2.4 clothier From line 124 it appears that Cade was known as a *shearman*. There is no hint of this in the sources. (Earlier in the century, in 'A Sermon on Rebellion', Archbishop Cranmer (196) referred to Cade as a 'Blacksmith'.) Cloth workers received cloth from weavers for the subsequent processes of dyeing, fulling etc. The shearman trimmed, or sheared, the excessive nap on cloth. R. Wilson draws attention to the topical significance of this since London shearmen of the early 1590s were opposed to the export of unfinished cloth or cloth finished in the provinces. But for at least two centuries cloth workers had been associated with riot and sedition. Sharp studies evidence of a rural wage-earning industrial proletariat susceptible to trade depression or bad harvests in the Tudor period, the cloth workers in particular (1–9). In parts of Kent near Ashford, where Cade is alleged to have originated, Harvey estimates that almost a quarter of the male population was engaged in the cloth industry in the 1440s (19). Again, Lollards thrived amid the artisan communities associated with social disturbance before and after Cade's uprising, specifically in weaving villages of Essex and south-west Kent (Harvey, 24). By the late sixteenth century, patterns of religious, political and social dissent were conflated and Jack Cade the clothier came to be associated not only with Jack Straw, but with Jack of Leiden, a tailor, 'King of Sion' and archetypal Anabaptist bogeyman (Stirling, 109–36). In sixteenth-century England Anabaptists were sneered at as 'cowherds, clothiers, and such-like mean people', and even in the following century Kentish Anabaptism was considered ineradicable (Heriot, 268).

4.2.63 All . . . common Cf. *Jack Straw*: 'But follow the counsel of Iohn Ball . . . And make diuision equally / Of each man's goods indifferently' (104–7). This was a doctrine spread by poor Franciscans and resisted by Langland (B XX, 275–7), whose first English printer, Robert Crowley, in the wake of Kett's rebellion, rehearsed the belief of the rich that contemporary sedition derived from this egalitarianism (142–3). When Cade's followers were rounded up and charged the indictments followed a common formula, the rebels 'believing and proposing as lollards and heretics that all things should be held in common (*credentes et proponentes ut lollardi et heretici omnia tenere in communi*)' (Virgoe, 'Indictments', 246; see 4.2.19–20n.). John Ball was thought to be a follower of Wycliffe, from whom the Lollards originated, but he abandoned their founder's monarchism and blended primitive Christianity, doctrines of natural law and legends of prelapsarian plenty. Acts, 4.32, says of the Apostles and their followers that 'they had all things common'. Schoolmen like William of Ockham believed that private property ensured by civil law came about through sin, whereas in the prelapsarian state natural law determined that all was in common. Legends like 'The Land of Cokaygne' perpetuated ideas of the pagan Golden Age and biblical Eden, where 'al is commune to *y*ung & old' (Robbins, 123) in utopian bliss (see Gaus). Needless to say, More's *Utopia* includes this communism, while his contemporary Elyot strongly rejects those who believe that the translation 'common weal' for *Respublica* means 'that everything should be to all men in common' (1). In post-Reformation England Wycliffe had become a proto-Protestant hero, and as a consequence authoritarian ideology transferred demonization of radicalism from the Lollards to the Anabaptists.

4.2.69 one livery Cade's *livery* as part of his visionary utterances recalls the simple grey cloth worn by the Utopians. On the other hand Pettitt notes of the 1381 revolt that 'according to the presentments of the York jurors, the leaders of the disturbances there "gave caps and other liveries of one colour to various members of their confederacy"' (10). Ironically, for all the messianic fervour of the German peasant revolt, 'one of the demands of the insurgents was that they should be allowed to wear red clothes like their betters' (Laver, 86).

4.2.77.1 Clerk of Chartham The Weaver's immediate designation at 78. The title indicates that the official was a parish clerk with secretarial responsibilities as scribe and notary. Q has '*Chattam*', which Oxf adopts as the modern 'Chatham'. Oxf's argument is twofold, typographical and topographical. Compositor B's foul case 'error' in F of setting 'r' for 't' occurs three times. But as the editors acknowledge, the reverse also occurs four times. Similarly the typesetter for Q could just as easily have mistaken a 't' for an 'r'. The assumption of the topographical argument is that Cade gathered followers on his progress through Kent and that the clerk more likely came from Chatham than Chartham. Equally, it may be argued that many sympathizers from various parts of Kent would have been drawn to join Cade, travelling from their towns and villages. Ashford and Wingham have been identified earlier so Chartham, which lies between, seems very likely. Oxf's argument concerning Cade's doubling-back on a route to get to Chartham is tendentious since we have no concrete information about routes beyond the fact that the rebels assembled at Blackheath. The Weaver, it appears, abducted the Clerk, and his trade implies that he is from the clothing areas associated with the Lollards, which were found more in the heartland of Kent, the 'Weald', than on the coast, like Chatham, which as a larger town would probably have had more than one clerkly official. Given these arguments and associations I prefer F's 'Chartham'. Further, Iden, Jack Cade's slayer, as Sheriff of Kent, after the insurrection hunted down Henry Wilkhous, Cade's scrivener, and caught him at Little Chart, near Ashford (Harvey, 99).

4.3.10–13 'the seid capitaigne cam riding w*it*h his peple on foot from Suthwerk thurgh the citee to powles in a blewe gown of velvet with sables furred and a strawe hat upon his heed and a sewerd drawen in his hand . . . And atte Standard in Chepe he hoved and thedir was the lord Say brought from the Guyldhall wher he was be diverse enquestes endited of treson and atte same Standard the capitan ded doo the said Lord Say beheded and dispoylled him of his aray boond his legges w*it*h a roop to an hors and drewe his body on the pavement thurgh a great part of the citee' (*Bale's Chronicle*, 133). This eyewitness account was unknown to the sixteenth-century chroniclers as it was left in Dublin by the author's namesake John Bale in 1553. *An English Chronicle* gives slightly varying comment and detail on Cade's entry and Saye's demise: 'as he hadde be a lord or a kny*gh*t, – and yit was he but a knaue, – and hadde his swerd born befor him . . . [Saye's] body was drawe naked at a hors taille vpon the pament so that the flesshe clivid to the stone fro Chepe in to Suthwerk' (66–7). Among the 'gentellys' whom Gregory tells us Cade compelled to rise with him was Robert Poynings, son of Lord Poynings and stepbrother of William Crowmer (see 4.7.103–4n. and LN), who became his carver and sword-bearer (Harvey, 107). In 1381 Wat Tyler was killed by the Lord Mayor's sword, which was subsequently added to the coat of arms of the city (see *Jack Straw*, 1182–3).

4.7.10 **toasted cheese** Longstaffe comments: 'Cade's toasted cheese may even be a specifically Kempian reference. Kemp's clowning is mentioned in *The Pilgrimage to Parnassus* (1598), where Dromo, speaking to a clown, says that "Clownes have been thrust into playes by head and shoulders, ever since Kempe could make a scurvey face", and advises him that "if thou canst but drawe thy mouth awrye, laye thy legge over thy staffe, saw a peece of cheese asunder with thy dagger, lape up drinke on the earth, I warrant thee, theile laughe mightilie". Cade the cheese-eater with bad breath sounds rather like a theatrical clown, if not Kemp himself' (29).

4.7.103–4 **break . . . head** Shakespeare indicates Crowmer's residence, but of all the historical records only *An English Chronicle* makes the circumstances clear: 'a squier callid Crowmer . . . be commaundement of the capteyne was broughte out of Flete, that was committed thider for certayn extorsiones that he hadde do in his office, and lad to Mile Ende, withoute

Londoun, and there withoute eny othir iugement his hed was smyte of' (67). Mile End Green was the point of assembly for the Essex rebels heading towards London. Cade was also demonstrating his 'captainship' by obligingly beheading one 'Bayly' (see 4.6.4–6n.). Though indiscriminate killing took place (see, e.g., 4.8.1–2), Barron notes of the twenty-three identifiable victims of attack that they were 'a privileged "establishment" . . . a corrupt and vicious network of privilege and position which enmeshed the King' (537).

4.8.26 ancient freedom Cade's phrase is found in the 'Oracion of the duke of Alaunson' before the battle of Vernoile (1424). The French will become 'slaues & bondmen' and their 'wiues and children' will be brought to 'extreme bondage' under the English, unless they recover their 'auncient fredome' (Hall, 123). Cade's travesty carries a sharp ironic point: the values which are called upon to unite the nation against an external enemy are the same as those which divide feudal society internally. By the 1590s and thereafter the word 'ancient' was used ideologically to reinforce the notion of immemorial prehistory which sanctioned custom and law before the Norman yoke of what developed into monarchal tyranny (see Pocock).

4.10.56 clown All three parts of *H6* were written for Lord Strange's Men, out of which grew the Pembroke's Men who staged *2H6*. The principal comedian of Lord Strange's Men was Will Kemp, who, it is commonly assumed, played Cade (T. W. Baldwin, *Organisation*, 268). If this may be conjectured, then Kemp, the famously athletic and *burly-boned clown*, would have directed these words at Iden, who has begun the sequence (46–53) of physical contrasts, presumably built around the notoriously skinny actor John Sincler, who is known to have acted in *3H6* (see 4.2.0.1 headnote and Gurr, *Companies*, 280). Extended gag provides a richly burlesque reversal in the carnivalesque defeat of Cade by Lenten *Famine* (59). For Sincler as the Apothecary in *RJ* ('Famine is in thy cheeks', 5.1.69), the First Beadle in *2H4* ('famish'd correctioner', 5.4.20) and other roles, see Gaw.

4.10.60–4 ten thousand . . . soul Q here is shorter but also rather allusive: in Q Cade summons 'ten thousand diuels' (TLN 1957–8), but any corresponding phrase is absent in F and *1H6*. However, at the opening of his speech in Q Cade celebrates himself as 'the floure of Kent for chiualrie' (TLN 1956–7), and his closing valediction is 'for Iacke Cade must die' (TLN 1959–60). Here Cade's language seems appropriate to Talbot but actually anticipates Edward's outburst on hearing of the death of his father, the Duke of York: 'thou hast slain / The flow'r of Europe for his chevalry' (*3H6* 2.1.70–1). Cade's close echoes the words of Marlowe's Tamburlaine: 'For Tamburlane, the scourge of God, must die' (*2*, 5.3.249). If the Q reporter–abridger had Cade as a mock Talbot in mind, this is rather appropriate, since Talbot, like Tamburlaine, is seen by the General in the same speech as a 'bloody scourge' bringing 'tyranny' (*1H6* 4.2.16–17). Whether the allusions to *1H6* in F were part of the copy altered by Q, or represent later revisions, it is difficult to say. For dating implications, see Introduction, p. 120.

5.1.26–7 This aspect of the Ajax legend is not found in Homer, but appears in such a well-known source as Horace, *Satires*, 2.3.193–202 (see Bush). The oddity is that none of the classical sources mentions oxen. Cade celebrates Dick the butcher's slaughter with a reference to sheep and oxen which possibly alludes to 1 Samuel, 14.32 (see 4.3.3n. for aristocratic and plebeian barbarism). Perhaps Shakespeare is deliberately compounding allusions for ironic effect, or perhaps this reflects that the Latin *pecus* (Horace, 202) could mean either 'flock' or 'herd'. Apuleius' *The Golden Ass*, in the Tudor translation of William Adlington (1566), refers to Ajax' victims as a 'whole heard of beasts' (Apuleius, 66), for example.

5.1.100 **Achilles' spear** The legend derives from post-Homeric story and folk medicine. In defending Troy, Telephus, son-in-law of King Priam, was wounded by Achilles' spear. An oracle advised that only 'Achilles' (meaning the yarrow or milfoil plant, called 'Achillea' after Achilles) could heal the wound. Telephus healed himself after applying the yarrow which grew from the rust filings of his spear. Achilles was supposed to have been taught the virtues of plants by Chiron the centaur. Yarrow became renowned for curing wounds made by metal tools (Brewer, 10). See Ovid, 12.121–2; 13.210–12.

APPENDIX 1

THE FIRST QUARTO (1594)

Reproduced in reduced photographic facsimile by courtesy of the
Folger Shakespeare Library. Call No. STC 26099.

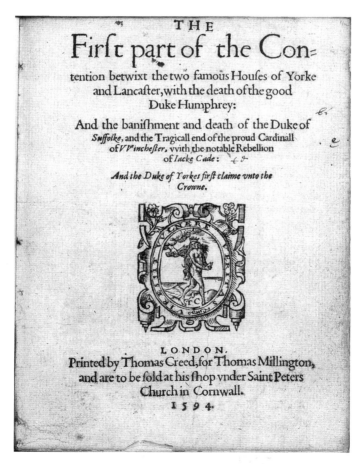

THE
First part of the Con=
tention betwixt the two famous Houses of Yorke
and Lancaster, with the death of the good
Duke Humphrey:

And the banishment and death of the Duke of
Suffolke, and the Tragicall end of the proud Cardinall
of *VVinchester*, vvith the notable Rebellion
of *Iacke Cade*:

And the Duke of Yorkes first claime vnto the
Crowne.

LONDON.
Printed by Thomas Creed, for Thomas Millington,
and are to be sold at his shop vnder Saint Peters
Church in Cornwall.
1594.

THE FIRST PART OF THE CON-
TENTION OF THE TWO FAMOVS
Houses of *Yorke* & *Lancaster*, with the death of
the good Duke *Humphrey*.

Enter at one doore, King Henry the fixt *, and* Humphrey *Duke of*
Glofter, *the Duke of* Sommerfet, *the Duke of* Buckingham, *Car-*
dinall Bewford, *and others.*

Enter at the other doore, the Duke of Yorke *, and the Marquefse of*
Suffolke, *and* Queene Margaret *, and the Earle of* Salisbury *and*
Warwicke.

Suffolke.

S by your high imperiall Maiefties command,
I haft in charge at my depart for *France*,
As Procurator for your excellence,
To marry Princes *Margaret* for your grace,
So in the auncient famous Citie Towres,
In prefence of the Kings of *France* & *Cifsile*,
The Dukes of *Orleance*, *Calaber*, *Brittaine*, and *Alanfon*.
Seuen Earles, twelue Barons, and then the reuerend Bifhops,
I did performe my taske and was efpoufde,
And now, moft humbly on my bended knees,
In fight of England and her royall Peeres,
Deliuer vp my title in the Queene.
Vnto your gratious excellence, that are the fubftance
Of that great fhadow I did reprefent:
The happieft gift that euer Marqueffe gaue,

A 2 The

The fairest Queene that euer King posselt.

King. Suffolke arise.

Welcome Queene *Margaret* to English *Henries* Court,
The greatest shew of kindnesse yet we can bestow,
Is this kinde kisse: Oh gracious God of heauen,
Lend me a heart repleat with thankfulnesse,
For in this beautious face thou hast bestowde
A world of pleasures to my perplexed soule.

Queene. Th'excessiue loue I beare vnto your grace,
Forbids me to be lauish of my tongue,
Least I should speake more then beseemes a woman:
Let this suffice, my blisse is in your liking,
And nothing can make poore *Margaret* miserable,
Vnlesse the frowne of mightie Englands King.

Kin. Her lookes did wound, but now her speech doth pierce,
Louely Queene *Margaret* sit down by my side:
And vnkle *Gloster*, and you Lordly Peeres,
With one voice welcome my beloued Queene.

All. Long liue Queene *Margaret*, Englands happinesse.

Queene. We thanke you all.   Sound Trumpets.

Suffolke. My Lord Protector, so it please your grace,
Here are the Articles confirmde of peace,
Betweene our Soueraigne and the French King *Charles*,
Till terme of eighteene months be full expirde.

Humphrey. Imprimis, It is agreed betweene the French King
Charles, and *William de la Poole*, Marquesse of *Suffolke*, Emba-
sador for *Henry* King of England, that the said *Henry* shal wed
and espouse the Ladie *Margaret*, daughter to *Raynard* King of England, ere the 30 of the next month.

Item. It is further agreed betweene them, that the Dutchies of *An-*
ioy and of *Maine*, shall be released and deliuered ouer to the
King her fa...
                   Duke Humphrey lets it fall.

Kin. How now vnkle, whats the matter that you stay so sodenly,
                                              Humphrey.

Humph. Pardon my Lord, a sodain qualme came ouer my hart,
Which dimmes mine eyes that I can reade no more.
Vnkle of *Winchester*, I pray you reade on.

Cardinall. Item, It is further agreed betweene them, that the
Duches of *Anioy* and of *Maine*, shall be released and deliuered ouer to the King her father, & the sent ouer of the King
of Englands owne proper cost and charges without dowry.

King. They pleasd vs well, Lord Marquesse kneele downe, We
here create thee first Duke of *Suffolke*, & girt thee with the
sword. Cosin of *Yorke*, We here discharge your grace from
being Regent in the parts of *France*, till terme of 8. months
be full expirde.

Thankes vnckle *Winchester*, *Gloster*, *Yorke*, and *Buckingham*, *So-*
merset, *Salsbury* and *Warwike*.
We thanke you all for this great fauour done,
In entertainment to my Princely Queene,
Come let vs in, and with all speed prouide
To see her Coronation be performde.

    Exet King, Queene, and Suffolke, and Duke
              Humphrey staies all the rest.

Humphrey. Braue Peeres of England, Pillars of the state,
To you Duke *Humphrey* must vnfold his griefe,
What did my brother *Henry* toyle himselfe,
And waste his subiects for to conquere *France*?
And did my brother *Bedford* spend his time
To keepe in awe that stout vnruly Realme?
And haue not I and mine vnckle *Beuford* here,
Done all we could to keepe that land in peace?
And is all our labours then spent in vaine,
For *Suffolke* lie, the new made Duke that rules the roast,
Hath giuen away for our King *Henries* Queene,
The Dutches of *Anioy* and *Maine* vnto her father.
Ah Lords, fatall is this marriage cancelling our states,
Reuersing Monuments of conquered *France*,
Vndoing all as none had nere bene done,

Card. Why how now cosin *Gloster*, whats needs this?

A 3   As

The first part of the contention of the two famous

As if our King were bound vnto your will,
And might not do his will without your leaue,
Proud Protector, enuy in thine eyes I see,
The big swolne venome of thy hatefull heart,
That dares presume gainst that thy Soueraigne likes.

Humphr. Nay my my Lord is not my words that troubles you,
But my pretence, proud Prelate as thou art:
But it be gone, and giue thee leaue to speake:
Farewell my Lords, and say when I am gone,
I prophesied *France* would be lost ere long.

    Exet Duke Humphrey.

Card. There goes our Protector in a rage,
My Lords you know he is my great enemy,
And though he be Protector of the land,
And thereby couers his deceitfull thoughts,
For well you see, if he but walke the streets,
The common people swarme about him straight,
Crying Iesus blesse your royall excellence,
With God preserue the good Duke *Humphrey.*
And many things besides that are not knowne,
Which time will bring to light in smooth Duke *Humphrey.*
But I will after him, and if I can
Ile laie a plot to heaue him from his seate.

    Exet Cardinall.

Buck. But let vs watch this haughtie Cardinall,
Cosen of *Somerset* be rulde by me,
Weele watch Duke *Humphrey* and the Cardinall too,
And put them from the marke they faine would hit.

Somerset. Thanks cosin *Buckingham,* ioyne thou with me,
And both of vs with the Duke of *Suffolke,*
Weele quickly heaue Duke *Humphrey* from his seate.

Buck. Content. Come then let vs about it straight,
For either thou or I will be Protector.

    Exet Buckingham and Somerset.

Salsb. Pride went before, Ambition followes after.
Whilst thefe do feeke their owne preferments thus,

        My

Houses, of Yorke and Lancaster.

My Lords let vs seeke for our Countries good,
Oft haue I seene this haughtie Cardinall
Sweare, and forsweare himselfe, and braue it out,
More like a Ruffin then a man of Church.
Cosin *Yorke,* the victories thou hast wonne,
In *Ireland, Normandie* and in *France,*
Hath wonne thee immortall praise in England.
And thou braue *VVarwicke,* my thrice valiant sonne,
Thy simple plainnesse and thy houf-keeping,
Hath wonne thee credit amongst the common sort,
The reuerence of mine age, and *Newils* name,
Is of no litle force if I command,
Then let vs ioyne all three in one for this,
That good Duke *Humphrey* may his state possesse,
But wherefore weepes *Warwicke* my noble sonne.

VVarw. For griefe that all is lost that *VVarwicke* won,
Sonnes. *Anioy* and *Maine,* both giuen away at once,
Why *VVarwick* did win them, & must that then which we wonne
    with our swords be giuen away with wordes.

Yorke. As I haue read, our Kings of England were woont to
haue large dowries with their wiues, but our King *Henry*
giues away his owne.

Salfb. Come sonnes away and looke vnto the maine,

VVar. Vnto the *Maine?* Oh father *Maine* is lost,
Which *VVarwicke* by maine force did win from *France,*
Maine chance father you meant, but I meant *Maine,*
Which I will win from *France* or elfe be flaine.

    Exet Salsbury and Warwicke.

Yorke. Anioy and *Maine,* both giuen vnto the French,
Cold newes for me, for I had hope of *France,*
Euen as I haue of fertill England.
A day will come when *Yorke* shall claime his owne,
And therefore I will take the *Newils* parts,
And make a show of loue to proud Duke *Humphrey:*
And when I spie aduantage, claime the Crowne,
For dars the golden marke I seeke to hit.

        Nor

The first part of the contention of the two famous

Nor shall proud *Lancaster* vsurpe my right,
Nor hold the scepter in his childish fist,
Nor weare the Diademe vpon his head,
Whose church-like humours fits not for a Crowne:
Then *Yorke* be still a vvhile till time do serue,
Watch thou, and vvake vvhen others be asleepe,
To prie into the secrets of the state,
Till *Henry* surfeiting in ioyes of loue,
With his newe bride, and Englands dear bought queene,
And *Humphrey* vvith the Peeres be false at iarres,
Then vvill I raise aloft the milke-white Rose,
With vvhole svveete smell the aire shall be perfumde,
And in my Standard beare the Armes of *Yorke*,
To graffle vvith the Houfe of *Lancaster*:
And force perforce, Ile make him yeeld the Crovvne,
Whose bookish rule hath puld faire England dovvne.

         Exet Yorke.

 Enter Duke Humphrey, and Dame Ellnor,
    Cobham his wife.

 Elnor. Why droopes my Lord like ouer ripend corne,
Hanging the head at *Ceares* plentious loade,
What seeft thou Duke *Humphrey* King *Henries* Crovvne?
Reach at it, and if thine arme be too short,
Mine shall lengthen it, Art not thou a Prince,
Vnckle to the King, and his Protector?
Then what shouldst thou lacke that might content thy minde.
 Humph. My lovely *Nell*, far be it from my heart,
To thinke of Treasons gainst my foueraigne Lord,
But I was troubled vvith a dreame to night,
And God I pray it do betide no ill.
 Elnor. What drempt my Lord, Good *Humphrey* tell it me,
And Ile interpret it, and vvhen thats done,
Ile tell thee then, vvhat I did dreame to night.
 Humphrey. This night vvhen I was laid in bed, I dreampt that this

Houfes, of Yorke and Lancaster.

This my staffe mine Office badge in Court,
Was broke in two, and on the ends were plac'd,
The heads of the Cardinall of *Winchester*,
And *William de la Poule* first Duke of *Suffolke*,
 Elnor. Tush my Lord, this signifies nought but this,
That he that breakes a sticke of *Glosters* groue,
Shall for th'offence, make forfeit of his head.
But now my Lord, Ile tell you what I dreampt,
Me thought I was in the Cathedrall Church
At Westminster, and seated in the chaire
Where Kings and Queenes are crownde, and at my feete
Henry and *Margaret* with a Crowne of gold
Stood readie to set it on my Princely head.
 Humphrey. Fie *Nell*, Ambitious woman as thou art,
Art thou not second woman in this land,
And the Protectors wife belou'd of him,
And wilt thou still be hammering treason thus,
Away I say, and let me heare no more.
 Elnor. How now my Lord, What angry with your *Nell*,
For telling but her dreame. The next I haue
Ile keepe to my selfe, and not be rated thus.
 Humphrey. Nay *Nell*, Ile giue no credit to a dreame,
But I would haue thee to thinke on no such things.

     Enters a Messenger.

 Messenger. And it pleafe your grace, the King and Queene to
morrow morning will ride a hawking to Saint Albones,
and craues your company along with them.
 Humphrey. With all my heart, I will attend his grace:
Come *Nell*, thou wilt go with vs vs I am fure.
            Exet Humphrey.
 Elnor. Ile come after you, for I cannot go before,
But ere it be long, Ile go before them all,
Defpight of all that feeke to croffe me thus,
Whos within there?

                Enter

B

The first part of the contention of the two famous

Enter sir *Iohn Hum.*

What sir *Iohn Hum,* what newes with you?
Sir Iohn. Iesus preserue your Maiestie.
Elnor. My Maiestie. Why man I am but grace.
Sir Iohn. I but by the grace of God & *Hums* aduise,
Your graces state shall be aduanst ere long.
Elnor. What hast thou confed with *Margery Iordaine,* the
cunning Witch of *Ely,* with *Roger Bullingbroeke* and the
rest, and will they vndertake to do me good?
Sir Iohn. I haue Madame, and they haue promised me to raise
a Spirite from depth of vnder grounde, that shall tell your
grace all questions you demaund.
Elnor. Thanks good sir *Iohn.* Some two daies hence I gesse
Will fit our time, then see that they be here:
For now the King is ryding to Saint *Albones,*
And all the Dukes and Earles along with him,
When they be gone, then safely they may come,
And on the backside of my Orchard heere,
There cast their Spelles in silence of the night,
And so resolue vs of the thing we wish,
Till when, drinke that for my sake, And so farewell. *Exet Elnor.*

Sir Iohn. Now sir *Iohn Hum,* No words but mum.
Seale vp your lips, for you must silent be,
These gifts ere long will make me mightie rich,
The Duches she thinks now that all is well,
But I haue gold comes from another place,
From one that hyred me to set her on,
To plot these Treasons gainst the King and Peeres,
And that is the mightie Duke of *Suffolke.*
For he it is, but I must not say so,
That by my meanes must worke the Duches fall,
Who now by Coniurations thinkes to rise.
But whilst sir *Iohn,* no more of that I trowe,

For

Houses of *Yorke* and *Lancaster.*
For feare you lose your head before you goe. *Exet.*

Enter two Petitioners, and *Peter* the
Armourers man.

1. *Peti.* Come firs let vs linger here abouts a while,
Vntill my Lord Protector come this way,
That we may show his grace our seuerall causes.
2. *Peti.* I pray God saue the good Duke *Humphries* life,
For but for him a many were vndone,
That cannot get no succour in the Court,
But see where he comes with the Queene.

Enter the Duke of *Suffolke* with the Queene, and they
take him for Duke *Humphrey,* and giues
him their writings.

1. *Peti.* Oh we are vndone, this is the Duke of *Suffolke.*
Queene. Now good-fellowes, whom would you speak withall?
2. *Peti.* If it please your Maiestie, with my Lord Protectors
Grace.
Queene. Are your sutes to his grace, Let vs see them first,
Looke on them my Lord of *Suffolke.*
Suffolke. A complaint againt the Cardinals man,
What hath he done?
2. *Peti.* Marry my Lord, he hath stole away my wife,
And th'are gone together, and I know not where to finde them.
Suffolke. Hath he stole thy wife, that's some iniury indeed.
But what say you?
Peter Thump. Marry fir I come to tel you that my maister said,
that the Duke of *Yorke* was true heire vnto the Crowne, and
that the King was an vsurer.
Queene. An vsurper thou wouldst say.
Peter. I forsooth an vsurper.
Queene. Didst thou say the King was an vsurper? how
Peter. No forsooth, I saide my maister said so, th'other day
when

B 2

The first part of the contention of the two famous

when we were leowring the Duke of *Yorks* Armour in our
garret,

Suffolke. I marry this is something like,
Whose within there?
    Enter one or two.
Sirra take in this fellow and keepe him close,
And send out a Pursiuant for his maister straight,
Weele here more of this before the King.
    Exet with the Armourers man.

Now sir what yours? Let me see it,
Whats here?
A complaint against the Duke of *Suffolke* for enclosing the com-
mons of long Melford.
How now sir knaue?
 1. *Peti.* I beseech your grace to pardon me, me, I am but a
Messenger for the whole town-ship.
    He teares the papers.
Suffolke. So now Ihow your petitions to Duke *Humphrey,*
Villaines get you gone and come not neare the Court,
Dare these pesants write against me thus.
    Exet Petitioners.

Queene. My Lord of *Suffolke,* you may see by this,
The Commons loues vnto that haughtie Duke,
That seekes to him more then to King *Henry:*
Whole eyes are alwaies poring on his booke,
And nere regards the honour of his name,
But still must be protected like a childe,
And gouerned by that ambitious Duke,
That scarce will moue his cap nor speake to vs,
And his proud wife, high minded *Elinor,*
That ruffles it with such a troupe of Ladies,
As strangers in the Court takes her for the Queene.
The other day she vanted to her maides,
That the very traine of her worst gowne,
Was worth more wealth then all my fathers lands,
Can any griefe of minde be like to this.

            Iell

House, of Yorke and Lancaster.

I tell thee *Poull,* when thou didst runne at Tilt,
And stolst away our Ladies hearts in *France,*
I thought King *Henry* had bene like to thee,
Or else thou hadst not brought me out of *France.*
Suffolke. Madame content your selfe a litle while,
As I was cause of your comming to England,
So will I in England worke your full content:
And as for proud Duke *Humphrey* and his wife,
I haue set lime-twigs that will intangle them,
As that your grace ere long shall vnderstand
But staie Madame, here comes the King.

Enter King *Henry,* and the Duke of *Yorke* and the Duke of *So-*
merset on both sides of the *King,* whispering with him, and enter Duke *Humphrey,* Dame *Elnor,* the Duke of *Buckingham,*
the Earle of *Salsbury,* the Earle of *Warwicke,* and the Cardinall
of *VVinchester.*

King. My Lords I care not who be Regent in *France,* or *Yorke,*
 or *Somerset,* alls wonne to me.
Yorke. My Lord, if *Yorke* haue ill demeande himselfe,
Let *Somerset* enioy his place and go to *France.*
Somerset. Then whom your grace thinke worthie, let him go,
And there be made the Regent ouer the French.
VVarwicke. VVhom soeuer you account worthie,
Yorke is the worthiest.
Cardinall. Peace *VVarwicke.* Giue thy betters leaue to speake.
VVar. The Cardinals not my better in the field.
Buc. All in this place are thy betters faire.
VVar. And *Warwicke* may liue to be the best of all.
Queene. My Lord in mine opinion, it were best that *Somerset*
 were Regent ouer *France.*
Humphrey. Madame our *King* is old inough to giue his
To giue his answere without your consent.
 Queene. If he be old inough, what needs your grace
To be Protector ouer him so long.
       B 3   *Humphrey.*

The firſt part of the contention of the two famous

Humphrey. Madame I am but Protector ouer the land,
And when it pleaſe his grace, I will reſigne my charge.
Suffolke. Reſigne it then, for ſince that thou waſt King,
As who is King but thee. The common ſtate
Doth as we ſee all wholly go to wracke,
And Millions of treaſure hath bene ſpent,
And as for the Regentſhip of France,
I ſay Somerſet is more worthie then Yorke.
Yorke. Ile tell thee Suffolke why I am not worthie,
Becauſe I cannot flatter as thou canſt.
War. And yet the worthie deeds that Yorke hath done,
Should make him worthie to be honoured here.
Suffolke. Peace headſtrong VVarwicke.
VVar. Image of pride, wherefore ſhould I peace?

Enter the Armourer and his man.

Suffolke. Becauſe here is a man accuſde of Treaſon,
Pray God the Duke of Yorke do cleare himſelfe.
Ho, bring hither the Armourer and his man.

If it pleaſe your grace, this fellow heere, hath accuſed his maiſter of
high Treaſon, And his words were theſe,
That the Duke of Yorke was lawfull heire vnto the Crowne, and
that your grace was an vſurper.
Yorke. I beſeech your grace let him haue what puniſhment the
the law will afford, for his villany.
King. Come hether fellow, didſt thou ſpeake theſe words?
Armour. Ant ſhall pleaſe your Maieſtie, I neuer ſaid any ſuch
matter, God is my witneſſe, I am falſly accuſde by this villain.
Peter. Tis no matter for that, you did ſay ſo.   (here.
Yorke. I beſeech your grace, let him haue the lavv.
Armour. Alaſſe my Lord, hang me if euer I ſpake the words,
my accuſer is my prentiſe, & when I did correct him for his
fault the other day, he did vovv vpon his knees that he vvould
be euen vvith me, I haue good vvitneſſe of this, and therefore
I beſeech your Maieſtie do not caſt avvay an honeſt man for
a villaines accuſation.
King. Vnckle Gloſter, what do you thinke of this?
                                         Humphrey.

Houſe, of Yorke and Lancaſter.

Humphrey. The lavv my Lord is this by caſe, it reſts ſuſpitious,
That a day of combat be appointed,
And there to trie each others right or vvrong,
Which ſhall be on the thirtith of this month,
With Eben ſtaues, and Standbags, combatting
In Smythfield, before your Royal Maieſtie.
                                   Exeat Humphrey.
Armour. And I accept the Combat willingly.
Peter. Alaſſe my Lord, I am not able to fight.
Suffolke. You muſt either fight firra or elſe be hangde:
Go take them hence againe to priſon.   Exeat with them.

The Queene lets fall her gloue, and hits the Duches of
Gloſter, a boxe on the eare.
Queene. Giue me my gloue, Why Minion can you not ſee?
                                   She ſtrikes her.
I cry you mercy Madame, I did miſtake,
I did not thinke it had bene you.
Elnor. Did you not proud French-vvoman,
Could I come neare your dauntie viſſage vvith my nayles,
Ide ſet my ten commandments in your face.
King. Be patient gentle Aunt.
It vvas againſt her vvill.
Elnor. Againſt her vvill? Good King ſheele dandle thee,
If thou vvilt alvvaies thus be rulde by her.
But let it reſt. As ſure as I do liue,
She ſhall not ſtrike dame Elnor vnreuengde.
                                   Exeat Elnor.
King. Beleeue me my loue, thou vvart much to blame,
I vvould not for a thouſand pounds of gold,
My noble vnckle had bene here in place.
                        Enter Duke Humphrey.
But ſee where he comes, I am glad he met her not.
Vnckle Gloſter, vvhat anſvvere makes your grace
Concerning our Regent for the Realme of France,
Whom thinks your grace is meeteſt for to ſend.
                                   Humphrey.

The first part of the contention of the two famous

Humphrey. My gratious Lord, then this is my resolue,
For that these words the Armourer should speake,
Doth breed suspition on the part of *Yorke*,
Let *Somerset* be Regent ouer the French,
Till trials made, and *Yorke* may cleare himselfe.
King. Then be it so my Lord of *Somerset*.
We make your grace Regent ouer the French,
And to defend our rights gainst forraine foes,
And so do good vnto the Realme of *France*.
Make hast my Lord, tis time that you were gone,
The time of Truse I thinke is full expirde.
Somerset. I humbly thanke your royall Maiestie,
And take my leaue to poste with speed to *France*.
Exet Somerset.

King. Come vnckle *Glofter*, now lets haue our horse,
For we will to Saint Albones presently.
Madame your Hawke they say is swift of flight,
And we will trie how the will flie to day.
Exetomnt.

Enter Elnor, with sir Iohn Ham. Roger Bullenbrooke a Coniurer,
and Margery Iourdaine a Witch.
Elnor. Here sir *Iohn*, take this scrole of paper here,
Wherein is writ the questions you shall aske,
And I will stand vpon this Tower here,
And here the spirit what it faies to you,
And to my questions, write the answeres downe,
She goes vp to the Tower.
Sir Iohn. Now firs begin and cast your fpels about,
And charme the fiendes for to obey your wils,
And tell Dame *Elnor* of the thing fhe askes.
Witch. Then *Roger Bullenbrooke* about thy taske,
And frame a Cirkle here vpon the earth,
Whilft I thereon all proftrate on my face,
Do talke and whisper with the diuels be low,
And coniure them for to obey my will.
She lies downe vpon her face.
Bullen-

Houses of Yorke and Lancaster.
Bullenbrooke makes a Cirkle.
Bullen. Darke Night, dread Night, the silence of the Night,
Wherein the Furies maske in hellish troupes,
Send vp I charge you from *Sosenus* lake,
The spirit *Ascalon* to come to me,
To pierce the bowels of this Centricke earth,
And hither come in twinkling of an eye,
Ascalon, Affenda, Affenda.
It thunders and lightens, and then the spirit
riseth vp.

Spirit. Now *Bullenbrooke* what wouldst thou haue me do?
Bullen. First of the *King*, what shall become of him?
Spirit. The Duke yet liues that *Henry* shall depose,
But him out liue, and dye a violent death.
Bullen. What fate awayts the Duke of *Suffolke.*
Spirit. By water shall he die and take his ende.
Bullen. What shall betide the Duke of *Somerset* ?
Spirit. Let him shun Castles, fafer shall he be vpon the fandie
plaine, then where Castles mounted stand.
Now question me no more, for I must hence againe.
He finkes downe againe.

Bullen. Then downe I fay, vnto the damned poule.
Where Pluto in his firie Waggon fits,
Ryding amidft the fingde and parched fmoakes,
The Rode of *Dytas* by the Riuer Stykes,
There howle and burne for euer in those flames,
Rife *Iordane* rife, and ftate thy charming Spels.
Sonnes, we are betraide.

Enter the Duke of Yorke, and the Duke of
Buckingham, and others.
Yorke. Come firs, laie hands on them, and bind them fure,
This tyme was well watcht. What Madame are you there?
This wil be great credit for your husband,
That your are plotting Treasons thus with Coniurers,
The King fhall haue notice of this thing.
Exet Elnor aboue.

Buc. See here my Lord what the diuell hath writ,

C

Go

The firſt part of the contention of the two famous

Go firs, ſee them faſt lockt in priſon.
Exeat with them.
Buckingham. My Lord, I pray you let me go poſt vnto the King,
Vnto S. Albones, to tell this newes.
Yorke. Content. Away then, about it ſtraight.
Buck. Farewell my Lord.
Exet Buckingham.
Yorke. Whoſe within there?
Enter one.

One. My Lord.
Yorke. Sirha, go will the Earles of Salsbury and Warwicke, to
ſup with me to night.
Exer Yorke.
One. I will my Lord.
Exet.

Enter the King and Queene with her Hawke on her fiſt,
and Duke *Humphrey* and *Suffolke,* and the *Carde-*
nall, as if they came from hawking.

Queene. My Lord, how did your grace like this laſt flight?
But as I caſt her off the winde did riſe,
And twas ten to one, old Ione had not gone out.
King. How wonderfull the Lords workes are on earth,
Euen in theſe ſilly creatures of his hands,
Vnckle Gloſter, how hie your Hawke did ſore?
And on a ſodaine ſouſt the Partrige downe.
Suffolke. No maruell if it pleaſe your Maieſtie
My Lord Protectors Hawke done towre ſo well,
He knowes his maiſter loues to be aloft.
Humphrey. Faith my Lord, it is but a baſe minde,
That can ſore no higher then a Falkons pitch,
Card. I thought your grace would be aboue the cloudes,
Humph. I my Lord Cardinall, were it not good
Your grace could flie to heauen,
Card. Thy heauen is on earth, thy words and thoughts beat on
a Crowne, proude Protector dangerous Peere, to ſmooth it thus
with King and common-wealth.
Humphrey. How now my Lord, why this is more then needs,
Church-men ſo hote. Good vnckle can you doate,
Suffolke. Why not Hauing ſo good a quarrell & ſo bad a cauſe,
Humphrey.

Houſes of Yorke and Lancaſter,
Humphrey. As how, my Lord?
Suffolke. As you, my Lord. And it like your Lordly
Lords Protectorſhip.
Humphrey. Why Suffolke, England knowes thy inſolence.
Queene. And thy ambition Gloſter.
King. Ceaſe gentle Queene, and whet not on theſe furious
Lordes to wrath, for bleſſed are the peace-makers on
earth.
Card. Let me be bleſſed for the peace I make,
Againſt this proud Protector with my ſword.
Humphrey. Faith holy vnckle, I would it were come to that,
Cardinall. Euen when thou dareſt.
Humphrey. Dare. I tell thee Prieſt, Plantagenets could neuer
brooke the dare.
Card. I am Plantagenet as well as thou, and ſonne to Iohn of
Gaunt.
Humph. In Baſtardie.
Cardi. I ſcorne thy words.
Humph. Make vp no factious numbers, but euen in thine own
perſon meete me at the Eaſt end of the groue.
Card. Here's my hand, I will.
King. Why how now Lords?
Card. Faith Coufin Gloſter, had not your man caſt off ſo ſoone,
we had had more ſport to day, Come with thy ſwoord
and buckler.
Humphrey. Faith Prieſt, Ile ſhaue your Crowne.
Cardinall. Protector, protect thy ſelfe well.
King. The wind growes high, ſo doth your chollour Lords,
Enter one crying, A miracle, a miracle.
How now, now firſha, what miracle is it?
One. And it pleaſe your grace, there is a man that came blinde
to S. Albones, and hath receiued his ſight at his ſhrine.
King. Goe fetch him hither, that wee may glorifie the Lord
with him.
Enter the Maior of Saint Albones and his brethren with
Muſicke, bearing the man that had bene blind,
betweene two in a chaire.
King. Thou happie man, giue God eternall praiſe,
C 2   Far

The first part of the contention of the two famous

For he it is, that thus hath helpest thee.
Humphrey. Where walt thou borne?
Poore man. At Barwicke sir, in the North.
Humph. At Barwicke, and come thus far for helpe,
Poore man. I sir, it was told me in my sleepe,
That sweet faint Albones should giue me my sight againe.
Humphrey. What art thou lame too?
Poore man. Indeed sir, God helpe me.
Humphrey. How cam'st thou lame?
Poore man. With falling off on a plum-tree.
Humph. Wart thou blind & wold clime plumtrees?
Poore man. Neuer but once sir in all my life,
My wife did long for plums.
Humph. But tell me, wart thou borne blinde?
Poore man. I truly sir.
Woman. I indeed sir, he was borne blinde.
Humphrey. What art thou his mother?
VVoman. His wife sir.
Humphrey. Hadst thou bene his mother,
Thou couldst haue better told.
Why let me see, I thinke thou canst not see yet.
Poore man. Yes truly maister, as cleare as day.
Humphrey. Saist thou so. What colours his cloake?
Poore man. Why red maister, as red as blood.
Humphrey. And his cloake?
Poore man. Why thats greene.
Humphrey. And what colours his hose?
Poore man. Yellow maister, yellow as gold.
Humphrey. And what colours my gowne?
Poore man. Blacke sir, as blacke as Ieat.
King. Then belike he knowes what colour Ieat is on. (one,
Suffolke. And yet I thinke Ieat did he neuer see.
Humph. But cloakes and gownes see this day many a
But tell me sirha, whats my name?
Poore man. Alasse maister I know not.
Humphrey. Whats his name?
Poore man. I know not,
Humphrey. Not his

Houses of Yorke and Lancaster.

Poore man. No truly sir,
Humphrey. Nor his name?
Poore man. No indeed maister,
Humphrey. Whats thine owne name?
Poore man. Sander, and it please your maister.
Humphrey. Then Sander sit there, the lyingest knaue in Chri-
stendom. If thou hadst bene born blind, thou mightest aswell haue
knowne all our names, as thus to name the seuerall colours we doo
weare. Sight may distinguish of colours, but sodenly to nominate
them all, it is impossible. My Lords, faint Albones here hath done a
Miracle, and would you nor thinke his cunning to be great, that
could restore this Cripple to his legs againe.
Poore man. Oh maister I would you could.
Humphrey. My Maisters of faint Albones,
Haue you nor Beadles in your Towne,
And things called whippes?
Mayor. Yes my Lord, if it please your grace,
Humph. Then send for one presently.
Mayor. Sirha go fetch the Beadle hither straight,
                                     Exet one,
Humph. Now fetch me a stoole hither by and by.
Now sirha, If you meane to saue your selfe from whipping,
Leape me ouer this stoole and runne away.
                                     Enter Beadle.
Poore man. Alasse maister I am not able to stand alone,
You go about to torture me in vaine.
Humph. Well sir, we must haue you finde your legges,
Sirha Beadle, whip him till he leape ouer that same stoole.
Beadle. I will my Lord, come on sirha, off with your doublet
quickly.
Poore man. Alas maister what shall I do, I am not able to stand,
After the Beadle hath hit him one girke, he leapes ouer
the stoole and runnes away, and they run after him,
crying, A miracle, a miracle.
Humph. A miracle, a miracle, let him be taken againe, & whipt
through euery Market Towne til he comes at Barwicke where he
was borne,
Mayor. It shall be done my Lord.   Exet Mayor,
                                          Suffolke,
                                          C 3

The first part of the contention of the two famous

Suffolke. My Lord Protector hath done wonders to day,
He hath made the blinde to see, and halt to go.

Humph. I but you did greater wonders, when you made whole
Dukedomes flie in a day.

Witnesse *France.*

King. Haue done I say, and let me here no more of that.

Enter the Duke of Buckingham.

What newes brings Duke Humprey of Buckingham?

Buck. Ill newes for some my Lord, and this it is,
That proud dame Elnor our Protectors wife,
Hath plotted Treasons gainst the King and Peeres,
By witchcrafts, sorceries, and coniurings,
Who by such meanes did raise a spirit vp,
To tell her what hap should betide the state,
But ere they had finisht their diuellish drift,
By *Yorke* and my selfe they were all surprisde,
And heres the answere the diuel did make to them.

King. First of the King, what shall become of him?

Readd. The Duke yet liues, that *Henry* shal depose,
Yet him out liue, and die a violent death.

Gods will be done in all.

What fate awaits the Duke of Suffolke?
By water shall he die and take his end.

Suffolke. By water must the Duke of Suffolke die?
It must be so or else the duel doth lie.

King. Let *Somerset* shun Castles,
For safer shall he be vpon the sandie plaines,
Then where Castles mounted stand.

Card. Heres good stuffe, how now my Lord Protector
This newes I thinke hath ruffde your weapons point,
I am in doubt youle scarsly keepe your promise.

Humphrey. Forbeare ambitious Prelate to vrge my griefe,
And pardon me thy gratious Soueraigne,
For here I sweare vnto your Maiestie,
That I am guiltlesse of these hainous crimes
Which my ambitious wife hath falsly done,
And for she vvould betraie her soueraigne Lord,
I here renounce her from my bed and boord,

And

House of Yorke and Lancaster.

And leaue her open for the law to iudge,
Vnlesse she cleare her selfe of this foule deed.

King. Come my Lords this night vveele lodge in S. Albones,
And to morrovv vve vvill ride to London,
And trie the vtmost of these Treasons forth,
Come vnckle *Gloster* along vvith vs,
My mind doth tell me thou art innocent.

Exet omnes.

Enter the Duke of Yorke, and the Earles of
Salsbury and VVarwike.

Yorke. My Lords our simple supper ended, thus,
Let me reueale vnto your honours here,
The right and title of the house of Yorke,
To Englands Crovvne by linall desent.

VVar. Then *Yorke* begin, and if thy claime be good,
The Neuils are thy subiects to command.

Yorke. Then thus my Lords.
Edward the third had seuen sonnes,
The first vvas Edward the blacke Prince,
Prince of Wales.
The second vvas Edmund of Langly,
Duke of Yorke.
The third vvas Lyonell Duke of Clarence.
The fourth vvas Iohn of Gaunt,
The Duke of Lancaster.
The fift vvas Roger Mortemor, Earle of March.
The sixt vvas fir Thomas of Woodstocke.
William of Winsore vvas the seuenth and last.
Novv, Edvvard the blacke Prince he died before his father, and left
behinde him Richard, that aftervvards vvas King, Crovvnde by
the name of Richard the second, and he died vvithout an heire.
Edmund of Langly Duke of Yorke died, and left behind him two
daughters, Anne and Elinor.
Lyonell Duke of Clarence died, and left behinde Alice, Anne,
and Elinor, that vvas after married to my father, and by her I
claime the Crovvne, as the true heire to Lyonell Duke
of

The first part of the contention of the two famous

of Clarence, the third sonne to Edward the third. Now fir. In the
time of Richards raigne, Henry of Bullingbrooke, sonne and heire
to Iohn of Gaunt, the Duke of Lancaster fourth sonne to Edward
the third, he claimde the Crowne, depofde the Merthfull King, and
as both you know, in Pomfret Castle harmeleffe Richard was
fhamefully murthered, and by Richards death came the houfe of
Lancafter vnto the Crowne.

Suff. Sauing your tale my Lord, as I haue heard, in the raigne
of Bullenbrooke, the Duke of Yorke did claime the Crowne, and
but for Owin Glendor, had bene King.

Yorke. True. But fo it fortuned then, by meanes of that monftrous rebel Glendor, the noble Duke of York was done to death,
and fo euer fince the heires of Iohn of Gaunt haue poffefled the
Crowne. But if the iffue of the elder fhould fucceed before the iffue
of the yonger, then am I lawfull heire vnto the kingdome.

VVaruicke. What plaine proceeding can be more plaine, hee
claimes it from Lyonel Duke of Clarence, the third fonne to Edward the third, and Henry from Iohn of Gaunt the fourth fonne,
So that till Lyonels iffue failes, his fhould not raigne, It failes not
yet, but florifheth in thee & in thy fons, braue flips of fuch a ftocke,
Then noble father, kneele we both togither, and in this pinate
place, be we the firft to honor him with birthright to the Crowni.

Both. Long liue Richard Englands royall King.

Yorke. I thanke you both, But Lords I am not your King, vntill
this fword be fheathed euen in the hart blood of the houfe of Lancafter.

Warw. Then Yorke aduife thy felfe and take thy time,
Claime thou the Crowne, and fet thy ftandard vp,
And in the fame aduance the milke-white Rofe,
And then to gard it, will I roufe the Beare,
Inuiron'd with ten thoufand Ragged-ftaues,
To aide and helpe thee for to win thy right,
Maugre the proudeft Lord of Henries blood,
That dares deny the right and claime of Yorke,
For why my minde prefageth I fhall liue
To fee the noble Duke of Yorke to be a King.
Yorke. Thanks noble Warwicke, and Yorke doth hope to fee,
The Earle of Warwicke liue to be the greateft man in England,
But

but the King, Come lets goe.

　　　　　　　　　　Exet omnes,

Houfes of Yorke and Lancaster.

Enter King *Henry,* and the Queene, Duke *Humphrey,* the Duke of
Suffolke, and the Duke of *Buckingham,* the *Cardinall,* and Dame
Elnor Cobham, led with the Officers, and then enter to them the
Duke of *Yorke,* and the Earles of *Salisbury* and *VVaruicke.*

King. Stand foorth Dame Elnor Cobham Duches of Glofter,
and here the fentence pronounced againft thee for thefe Treafons,
that thou haft committed againft vs, our States and Peeres.
Firft for thy hainous crimes, thou fhalt two daies in London do
penance barefoote in the ftreetes, with a white fheete about thy
bodie, and a waxe Taper burning in thy hand. That done, thou
fhalt be banifhed for euer into the Ile of Man, there to ende thy
wretched daies, and this is our fentence erreuocable. Away with
her,

Elnor. Euen to my death, for I haue liued too long.

　　　　　　　　　　Exet foine with Elnor.

King. Greeue not noble vnckle, but be thou glad,
In that thefe Treafons thus are come to light,
I eall God had pourde his vengeance on thy head,
For her offences that thou hedft fo deare.

Humph. Oh gratious Henry, giue me leaue awhile,
To leaue your grace, and to depart away,
For forrowes teares hath gripte my aged heart,
And makes the fountaines of mine eyes to fwell,
And therefore good my Lord, let me depart.

King. With all my hart good vnkle, when you pleafe,
Yet ere thou goeft, Humphrey refigne thy ftaffe,
For Henry will be no more protected,
The Lord fhall be my guide both for my land and me.

Humph. My ftaffe, I yeeld as willing to be thine,
As erft thy noble father made it mine,
And euen as willing at thy feete I leaue it,
As others would ambitioufly receiue it,
And long hereafter when I am dead and gone,

D　　　　　　　　　　　　May

The first part of the contention of the two famous

May honourable peace attend thy throne.
King. Vnkle Gloster, stand vp and go in peace,
No lesse beloued of vs, then when
Thou weart Protector ouer my land.   *Exet Gloster.*
Queene. Take vp the staffe, for here it ought to stand,
Where should it be, but in King Henries hand:
Yorke. Please it your Maiestie, this is the day
That was appointed for the combating
Betweene the Armourer and his man, my Lord.
And they are readie when your grace doth please.
King. Then call them forth, that they may trie their rightes.

Enter at one doore the Armourer and his neighbours, drinking
to him so much that he is drunken, and he enters with a drum
before him, and his staffe with a sand-bag fastened to it, and
at the other doore, his man with a drum and sand-bagge, and
Prentises drinking to him.

1. *Neighbor.* Here neighbor Hornor, I drink to you in a cup of
And feare not neighbor, you shall do well inough.   (Sacke.
2. *Neigh.* And here neighbor, heres a cup of Charneco.
3. *Neigh.* Heres a pot of good double beere, neighbor drinke
And be merry and feare not your man.
Armourer. Let it come, yfaith ile pledge you all,
And a figge for Peter.
1. *Prentife.* Here Peter I drinke to thee, and be not affeard.
2. *Pren.* Here Peter, heres a pinte of Claret-wine for thee.
3. *Pren.* And heres a quart for me, and be merry Peter,
And feare not thy maister, fight for credit of the Prentifes.
Peter. I thanke you all, but ile drinke no more,
Here Robin, and if I die, here I giue thee my hammer,
And Will, thou shalt haue my aperne, and here Tom,
Take all the mony that I haue.
O Lord blesse me, I pray God, for I am neuer able to deale with
my maister, he hath learnt so much fence alreadie.
Salb. Come leaue your drinking, and fall to blowes.
Sirha, whats thy name?
Peter. Peter forsooth.
Salbury. Peter, what more?   *Peter.*

Houses of Yorke and Lancaster.

Peter. Thumpe.
Salsbury. Thumpe, then see thou thumpe thy maister.
Armour. Heres to thee neighbour, fill all the pots again, for be-
fore we fight, looke you, I will tell you my minde, for I am come
hither as it were of my mans instigation, to proue my selfe an ho-
nest man, and Peter a knaue, and so haue at you Peter with downe-
right blowes, as Beuys of South-hampton fell vpon Askapart.
Peter. Law you now, I told you hees in his fence alreadie.
Alarmes, and Peter hits him on the head and fels him.
Armou. Hold Peter, I confesse, I confesse, Treason, treason.   (He dies.
Peter. O God I giue thee praise.   He kneeles downe.
Pren. Ho well done Peter God saue the King.
King. Go take hence that Traitor from our sight,
For by his death we do perceiue his guilt,
And God in iustice hath reuealde to vs,
The truth and innocence of this poore fellow,
Which he had thought to haue murthered wrongfully.
Come fellow, follow vs for thy reward.   *Exet omnis.*

Enter Duke *Humphrey* and his men, in
mourning cloakes.

Humph. Sirha, whats a clocke?
Seruing. Almost ten my Lord.
Harph. Then is that wofull houre hand at hand,
That my poore Lady should come by this way,
In shamefull penance wandring in the streetes,
Sweete *Nell,* ill can thy noble minde abrooke,
The abiect people gazing on thy face,
With enuious lookes laughing at thy shame,
That carst did follow thy proud Chariot wheeles,
When thou didst ride in triumph through the streetes.

Enter Dame *Elnor Cobham* bare-foote, and a white sheete about
her, with a waxe candle in her hand, and verses written on
her backe and pind on, and accompanied with the Sheriffes
of London, and Sir *Iohn Standy* and Officers, with billes and
holbards.
Seruing. My gratious Lord, see where my Lady comes,
Pleasit your grace, weele take her from the Sheriffes?
                                                          D 2
                                                      Humphrey

The first part of the contention of the two famous

Humph. I charge you for your liues stir not a foote,
Nor offer once to draw a weapon here,
But let them do their office as they should,

Elnor. Come you my Lord to see my open shame?
Ah Gloster, now thou doost penance too,
See how the giddie people looke at thee,
Shaking their heads and pointing at thee heere,
Go get thee gone, and hide thee from their sights,
And in thy pent vp studie rue my shame,
And ban thine enemies, Ah mine and thine.

Ham. Ah Nell, sweet Nell, forget this extreme grief,
And beare it patiently to ease thy heart.

Elnor. Ah Gloster teach me to forget my selfe,
For whilst I thinke I am thy wedded wife,
Then thought of this, doth kill my wofull heart.
The ruthlesse flints do cut my tender feete,
And when I start the cruell people laugh,
And bids me be aduisd how I tread,
And thus with burning Taper in my hand,
Maide vp in shame with papers on my backe,
Ah, Gloster, can I endure this and liue,
Sometime ile say I am Duke *Humphreys* wife,
And he a Prince, Protector of the land,
But so he rulde, and such a Prince he was,
As he stood by, whilst I his forelorne Duches
Was led with shame, and made a laughing stocke,
To euery idle rascall follower.

Humphrey. My louely Nell, what wouldst thou haue me do?
Should I attempt to rescue thee from hence,
I should incurre the danger of the law,
And thy disgrace would not be shadowed so.

Elnor. Be thou milde, and stir not at my disgrace,
Vntill the axe of death hang ouer thy head,
As shortly sure it will. For *Suffolke* he,
The new made Duke, that may do all in all
With her that loues him so, and hates vs all,
And impious *Yorke* and *Bewford* that false Priest,
Haue all lymde bushes to betraie thy wings,

And

Houses, of Yorke and Lancaster.

And flie thou how thou canst, they will intangle thee.

Enter a Herald of Armes.

Herald. I summon your Grace, vnto his highnesse Parlament
holden at saint *Edmunds-Bury,* the first of the next month.

Humphrey. A Parlament and our consent neuer craude
Therein before. This is sodeine.
Well, we will be there.

Exet, Herald.

Maister Sheriff, I pray proceede no further against my
Lady, then the course of law extends.

Sheriffe. Pleas it your grace, my office here doth end,
And I must deliuer her to sir *Iohn Standly,*
To be conducted into the Ile of Man.

Humphrey. Must you sir *Iohn* conduct my Lady?

Standly. I my gratious Lord, for so it is decreede,
And I am so commanded by the King.

Humph. I pray you sir *Iohn,* vse her neare the worse,
In that I intreat you to vse her well.
The world may smile againe and I may liue,
To do you fauour if you do it her,
And so sir *Iohn* farewell.

Elnor. What gone my Lord, and bid not me farewell.

Hamph. Witnesse my bleeding heart, I cannot stay to speake.

Exet Humphrey and his men.

Elnor. Then is he gone, is noble Closter gone,
And doth Duke *Humphrey* now forsake me too?
Then let me haste from out faire Englands bounds,
Come *Standly* come, and let vs haste away.

Standly. Madam lets go vnto some house hereby,
Where you may shift your selfe before we go.

Elnor. Ah good sir *Iohn,* my shame cannot be hid,
Nor put away with casting off my sheete:
But come let vs go, maister Sheriffe farewell,
Thou hast but done thy office as thou should.

Exet omne.

Enter to the Parlament.

Enter two Heralds before, then the Duke of *Buckingham,* and the

D 3   Duke

The first part of the contention of the two famous
Dukes of *Suffolke*, and then the Duke of *Yorke*, and the Cardinall of *VVinchester*, and then the King and the Queene, and then
the Earle of *Salisbury*, and the Earle of *VVarwike*.

King. I wonder our vnkle Gloster staies so long.
Queene. Can you not see, or will you not perceiue,
How that ambitious Duke doth vse himselfe?
The time hath bene, but now that time is past,
That none so humble as Duke Humphrey was:
But now let one meete him euen in the morne,
When euery one will giue the time of day:
And he will neither moue nor speake to vs.
See you not how the Commons follow him
In troupes, crying, God saue the good Duke Humphrey's,
And with long life, Iesus preserue his grace,
Honouring him as if he were their King,
Gloster is no little man in England,
And if he list to stir commotions,
Tys likely that the people will follow him.
My Lord, if you imagine there is no such thing,
Then let it passe, and call it a womans feare.
My, Lord of Suffolke, Buckingham, and Yorke,
Disproue my Alligations if you can,
And by your speeches, if you can reproue me,
I will subscribe and say, I wrong'd the Duke.
Suffol. Well hath your grace foretolen into that Duke,
And if I had bene licen't first to speake,
I thinke I should haue told your graces tale,
Smooth runs the brooke whereas the streame is deepest.
No, no, my soueraigne, Gloster is a man
Vnsounded yet, and full of deepe deceit.

Enter the Duke of *Somerset.*

King. Welcome Lord Somerset, what newes from France?
Somer. Cold newes my Lord, and thus it is,
That all your holds and Townes within those Territores
Is ouercome my Lord, all is lost.
                                                          King.

Houses of Yorke *and* Lancaster.

King. Cold newes indeed Lord Somerset,
But Gods will be done.
Yorke. Cold newes for me, for I had hope of France,
Euen as I haue of fertill England,
                    Enter Duke Humphrey.
Hum. Pardon my liege, that I haue staid so long.
Suffol. Nay, Gloster know, that thou art come too soone,
Vnlesse thou proue more loyall then thou art,
We do arrest thee on high treason here.
Humph. Why Suffolkes Duke thou shalt not see me blush
Nor change my countenance for thine arrest,
Whereof am I guiltie, who are my accusers?
York. T is thought my lord your grace tooke bribes from France,
And stopt the souldiers of their paie,
By which his Maiestie hath lost all France.
Humph. Is it but thought so, and who are they that thinke so?
So God helpe me, as I haue watcht the night
Euer intending good for England still,
That penie that euer I tooke from France,
Be brought against me at the iudgement day.
I neuer robd the souldiers of their paie,
Many a pound of mine owne propper cost
Haue I sent ouer for the souldiers wants,
Because I would not racke the needie Commons,
Car. In your Protectorship you did deuise
Strange torments for offendors, by which meanes
England hath bene defamde by tyrannie.
Hum. Why tis wel knowne that whilst I was protector
Pitie was all the fault that was in me,
A murtherer or foule felonous theefe,
That robs and murthers filly passengers,
I tortord aboue the rate of common law.
Suffolk. Tush my Lord, these be things of no account,
But greater matters are laid vnto your charge,
I do arrest thee on high treason here.
And commit thee to my good Lord Cardinall,
Vntill such time as thou canst cleare thy selfe.
King. Good vnkle obey to his arest,
                                                          I haue

The first part of the contention of the two famous

I haue no doubt but thou shalt cleare thy selfe,
My conscience tels me thou art innocent.
Hum. Ah gratious Henry these daies are dangerous,
And would my death might end these miseries,
And staie their moodes for good King Henries sake,
But I am made the Prologue to their plaie,
And thousands more must follow after me,
That dreads not yet their liues destruction.
Suffolkes hatefull tongue blabs his harts malice,
Bewfords fiue eyes showes his enuious minde,
Buckinghams proud lookes bewraies his cruel thoughts,
And dogged Yorke that leuels at the Moone
Whose ouerweening arme I haue held backe.
All you haue ioynd to betraie me thus:
And you my gratious Lady and soueraigne mistresse,
Causelesse haue laid complaints vpon my head,
I shall not want false witnesses inough,
That so amongst you, you may haue my life.
The Prouerbe no doubt will be well performde,
A faulte is quickly found to beate a dog.
Suffolke. Doth he not twit our soueraigne Lady here,
As if that he with ignomious wrong,
Had suborunde or hired some to sweare againſt his life.
Queene. I but I can giue the loſer leaue to speake,
Humph. Far truer spoke then ment I looke indeed,
Behooue the winners hearts, they plaie me false,
Buck. Hele wreſt the sence and keepe vs here all day,
My Lord of Winchester, see him sent away.
Car. Who's within there? Take in Duke Humphrey,
And see him garded sure vvithin my house.
Humph. O thus King Henry casts avvay his crouch,
Before his legs can beare his bodie vp,
And puts his watchfull shepheard from his side,
Whilſt vvolues stand snarring who shall bite him first,
Farewell my soueraigne, long, maiſt thou enioy,
Thy fathers happie daies free from annoy.
Exet Humphrey, with the Cardinals men.
King. My Lords what to your wisdoms shall seeme best,

Do

Houses of Yorke and Lancaster.

Do and vndo as if our selfe were here.
Queen. What wil your highnesse leaue the Parlament?
King. I Margaret. My heart is kild with griefe,
Where I may fit and sigh in endlesse mone,
For who's a Traitor, Gloster he is none.
Exet King, Salsbury and Warwicke.
Queene. Then sit we downe againe my Lord Cardinall,
Suffolke, Buckingham, Yorke and Somerset.
Lets us consult of proud Duke Humphries fall.
In mine opinion it were good he die,
For safetie of our King and Common-wealth,
Suffolke. And so thinke I Madame, for as you know,
If our King Henry had shooke hands with death,
Duke Humphrey then would looke to be our King:
And it may be by pollicie he workes,
To bring to paſſe the thing which now we doubt,
The Foxe barkes not when he would ſteale the Lambe,
But if we take him ere he do the deed,
We should not queſtion if that he should liue.
No, Let him die, in that he is a Foxe,
Leaſt that in liuing he offend vs more.
Car. Then let him die before the Commons know,
For feare that they do rise in Armes for him.
Yorke. Then do it ſodainly my Lords.
Suffol. Let that be my Lord Cardinals charge & mine.
Car. Agreed, for hee's alreadie kept within my house,
Enter a Messenger.
Queen. How now sirrha, what newes?
Meſſen. Madame I bring you newes from Ireland,
The wilde Onele my Lords, is vp in Armes,
With troupes of Iriſh Kernes that vncontrold,
Doth plant themſelues within the Engliſh pale,
Queene, What redreſſe shal we haue for this my Lorde
Yorke. Twere very good that my Lord of Somerſet
That fortunate Champion were sent ouer,
And burnes and ſpoiles the Country as they goe.
E   T.

The first part of the contention of the two famous

To keepe in awe the stubborne Irishmen,
He did so much good when he was in France.
Somer. Had Yorke bene there with all his far fetcht
Pollicies, he might haue lost as much as I.
Yorke. I, for Yorke would haue lost his life before
That France should haue reuolted from Englands rule.
Somer. I so thou might'st, and yet haue gouernd worse then I.
Yorke. What worse then nought, then a shame take all.
Somer. Shame on thy selfe, that wisheth shame.
Queene. Somerset forbeare, good Yorke be patient,
And do thou take in hand to crosse the seas,
With troupes of Armed men to quell the pride
Of those ambitious Irish that rebell.
Yorke. Well Madame sith your grace is so content,
Let me haue some bands of chosen soldiers,
And Yorke shall trie his fortune against those kernes.
Queene. Yorke thou shalt, My Lord of Buckingham,
Let it be your charge to muster vp such soldiers
As shall suffice him in these needfull warres.
Buck. Madame I will, and leaue such a band
As soone shall ouercome those Irish Rebels,
But Yorke, where shall those soldiers staie for thee?
Yorke. At Bristow, I will expect them ten daies hence.
Buc. Then thither shall they come, and so farewell.
                        Exet Buckingham.
Yorke. Adieu my Lord of Buckingham.
Queene. Suffolke remember what you haue to do,
And you Lord Cardinall concerning Duke Humphrey,
T'were good that you did see to it in time;
Come let vs go, that it may be performde.
                Exet omnes, Manet Yorke.
Yorke. Now York bethink thy selfe and rowse thee vp,
Take time whilst it is offered thee so faire,
Least when thou wouldst, thou canst not attaine,
T'was men I lacke, and now they giue them me,
And now whilst I am busie in Ireland,
I haue seduste a headstrong Kentishman,
John Cade of Ashford,

Houses of Yorke and Lancaster.

Under the title of Iohn Mortemer,
To raise commotion, and by that meanes
I shall perceiue how the common people
Do affect the claime and house of Yorke.
Then if he haue successe in his affaires,
From Ireland then comes Yorke againe,
To reape the haruest which that coystrill sowed,
Now if he should be taken and condemd,
He else nere confesse that I did set him on,
And therefore ere I go lie send him word,
To put in practise and to gather head,
That so soone as I am goine he may begin
To rise in Armes with troupes of country swaines,
To helpe him to performe this enterprise.
And then Duke Humphrey, he well made away,
None then can stop the light to Englands Crowne,
But Yorke can tame and headlong pull them downe.
                        Exet Yorke.

Then the Curtaines being drawne, Duke *Humphrey* is discouered
in his bed, and two men lying on his brest and smothering him
in his bed. And then enter the Duke of *Suffolke* to them.

Suffolke. How now sirs, what haue you dispatcht him?
One. I my Lord, hees dead I warrant you.
Suffolke. Then lie the cloathes laid smooth about him still,
That when the King comes, he may perceiue
No other, but that he dide of his owne accord.
2. All things is handsome now my Lord.
Suffolke. Then draw the Curtaines againe and get you gone,
And you shall haue your firme reward anon.
                        Exet murtherers.

Then enter the King and Queene, the Duke of *Buckingham,* and
the Duke of *Somerset,* and the Cardinall,
King. My Lord of Suffolke go call thither Gloster,
Tell him this day we will that he do cleare himselfe.
Suffolke. I will my Lord.   *Exet Suffolke.*

King. And good my Lords proceed no further against our vnkle
                                            (Gloster,
                                                Then

E 2

The first part of the contention of the two famous

Then by iust proofe you can affirme,
For as the sucking childe or harmlesse lambe,
So is she innocent of treason to our state.

Enter *Suffolke.*

How now Suffolke, where's our vnkle?
Suffolke. Dead in his bed, my Lord Gloster is'dead.
Queen. Ay-me, the King is dead, help, help, my Lords.
Suffolke. Comfort my Lord, gratious Henry comfort.
Kin. What doth my Lord of Suffolk bid me comfort?
Came he euen now to sing a Rauens note,
And thinkes he that the cheeping of a Wren,
By crying comfort through a hollow voyce,
Can satisfie my griefes, or ease my heart:
Thou balefull messenger out of my sight,
For euen in thine eye-bals murther sits,
Yet do not goe, Come Basaliske
And kill the silly gazer with thy lookes.
Queen. Why do you rate my Lord of Suffolke thus,
As if that he had causde Duke Humphreys deathe
The Duke and I too, you know were enemies,
And you had best say that I did murther him.
King. Ah woe is me, for wretched Glosters death.
Queen. Be woe for me, more wretched then he was.
What doest thou turne away and hide thy face?
I am no loathsome leoper looke on me,
Was I for this nigh wrackt vpon the sea,
And thrise by awkward winds driuen back from Englands bounds,
What might it bode, but that well foretelling.
Winds, said sicke n't a scorpions neast.

Enter the Earles of *Warwike* and *Salisbury.*

War. My Lord, the Commons like an angrie hiue of bees,
Run vp and downe, caring not whom they sting,
For good Duke Humphreys death, whom they report
To be murthered by Suffolke and the Cardinall here.
King. That he is dead good Warwick, is too true,
But how he died God knowes, not Henry.
War. Enter his priuie chamber my Lord and view the bodie.

Good

Houses of Yorke and Lancaster.

Good father stay you with the rude multitude, till I returne.
Salb. I will soone ——
Exet Salbury.
VVarwike drawes the curtaines and showes Duke
Humphrey in his bed.

King. Ah vnkle Gloster, heauen receiue thy soule.
Farewell poore Henries ioy, now thou art gone.
VVar. Now by his foule that tooke our shape vpon him,
To free vs from his fathers dreadfull curse,
I am reclou'd that violent hands were laid,
Vpon the life of this thrise famous Duke.
Suffolk. A dreadfall oth I swome with a solemne tooing,
What instance giues Lord Warwicke for these wordes?
VVar. Oft haue I seene a timely parted ghost,
Of ashie semblance, pale and bloodlesse,
But loe the blood is setled in his face,
More better coloured then when he liu'd,
His well proportioned beird made rough and sterne,
His fingers spred abroad as one that graspt for life,
Yet was by strength surprisde, the least of these are probable,
It cannot chuse but he was murthered.
Queene. Suffolke and the Cardinall had him in charge,
And they I trust sir are no murtherers.
VVar. I, but t'was well knowne they were not his friends,
And tis well seene he found some enemies.
Card. But haue you no greater proofes then these?
VVar. Who sees a butcher with an axe,
And sees hard-by a heifer dead and bleeding fresh,
But will suspect twas he that made the slaughter?
Who findes the partridge in the puttocks neast,
But will imagine how the bird came there,
Although the kyte soare with vnbloodie beake?
Euen so suspitious is this Tragidie.

Queene. Are you the kyte Bewford, where's your talants?
Is Suffolke the butcher, where's his knife?
Suffolke. I weare no knife to slaughter sleeping men,
But heres a vengefull sword rusted with ease,
That shall be scoured in his rankorous heart,
That slanders me with murthers crimson badge,

Say

E 3

The first part of the contentions of the two Famous

Say if thou dar'st proud Lord of Warwickshire,
That I am guiltie in Duke Humphreys death?

Warw. What dares not Warwicke, if false Suffolke dare him?

Queene. He dares not calme his contumelious spirit,
Nor cease to be an arrogant controwler,
Though Suffolke dare him twentie thousand times.

Warw. Madame be still, with reuerence may I say it,
That euery word you speake in his defence,
Is slaunder to your royall Maiestie.

Suffolke. Blunt-witted Lord, ignoble in thy words,
If euer Lady wrong'd her Lord so much,
Thy mother tooke vnto her blamefull bed,
Some sterne vntutor'd churle, and noble stocke
Was graft with crab-tree slip, whose fruit thou art,
And neuer of the Neuels noble race.

Warw. But that the guilt of murther bucklers thee,
And I should robb the deaths man of his fee,
Quitting thee thereby of ten thousand shames,
And that my soueraignes presence makes me mute,
I would false murtherous coward on thy knee
Make thee craue pardon for thy passed speech,
And say it was thy mother that thou meanst,
That thou thy selfe was borne in bastardie,
And after all this fearefull homage done,
Giue thee thy hire and send thy soule to hell,
Pernicious blood-sucker of sleeping men.

Suffol. Thou shalt be waking whilst I sheed thy blood,
If from this presence thou dare go with me.

Warw. Away euen now, or I will drag thee hence,
Vnworthie though thou art, ile cope with thee,
And doe some seruice to Duke Humphreys ghost.

*Exet Warwicke and Suffolke, and then all the Commons
within cries, downe with Suffolke, downe with Suffolke.
And then enter againe, the Duke of Suffolke and Warw.
meete, with their weapons drawne.*

King. Why how now Lords?

Suf. The Traitorous Warwicke with the men of Berry,
Set all vpon me maugre all my

The

Houses of Yorke and Lancaster.

The Commons againe cries, downe with Suffolke, downe
with Suffolke. And then enter from them, the Earle of
Salsbury.

Salb. My Lord, the Commons sends you word by me,
That vnlesse false Suffolke here be done to death,
Or banished faire Englands Territories,
That they will erre from your highnesse person,
They say by him the good Duke Humphrey died,
They say by him they feare the ruine of the realme.
And therefore if you loue your subiects weale,
They wish you to banish him from foorth the land.

Suf. Indeed this is like the Commons rude vnpollisht hinds
Would send such message to their soueraigne,
But you my Lord were glad to be imployd,
To trie how quaint an Orator you were,
But all the honour Salsbury hath got,
Is, that he was the Lord Embassador
Sent from a sort of Tinckers to the King.

The Commons cries, an answere from the King,
my Lord of Salsbury.

King. Good Salsbury go backe againe to them,
Tell them we thanke them all for their louing care,
And had I not bene cited thus by their meanes,
My selfe had done it. Therefore here I sweare,
If Suffolke be found to breathe in any place,
Where I haue rule, but three dares more he dies.

Exet Salsbury.

Queene. Oh Henry, reuerse the doome of gentle Suffolkes banishment.

King. Virginie Queene to call him gentle Suffolke,
speake not for him, for in England he shall not rest,
If I say I may relent, but if I sweare, it is irreuocable.
Come good Warwicke and go thou in with me,
For I haue great matters to impart to thee.

*Exet King and VVarwicke, Manet Queene
and Suffolke.*

Queene. Hell fire and vengeance go along with you,
Theres two of you, the diuell make the third,

Fie

The first parte of the contention of the two famous

Fie womanish man, canst thou not curse thy enemies?
Suffolke. A plague vpon them, wherefore should I curse them?
Could curses kill as do the Mandrakes groanes,
I would inuent as many bitter termes
Deliuered strongly through my fixed teeth,
With twise so many signes of deadly hate,
As leane fast enuy in her loathsome caue.
My toong should stumble in mine earnest words,
Mine eyes should sparkle like the beaten flint,
My haire be fixt on end, as one distraught,
And euery ioynt should seeme to curse and ban,
And now me thinkes my burdened hart would breake,
Should I not curse them, Poison be their drinke,
Gall worse then gall, the daintiest thing they taste.
Their sweetest shade a groue of Cypris trees.
Their softest tuch as smart as lyzards stings.
Their musicke frightfull, like the serpents hys.
And boding scrike-oules make the consort full.
All the foule terrors in darke seated hell.   (selfe.
    Queene. Inough sweete Suffolke, thou torments thy
    Suffolke. You bad me ban, and will you bid me leaue?
Now by this ground that I am banisht from,
Well could I curse away a winters night,
And standing naked on a mountaine top,
Where byting cold would neuer let grasse grow,
And thinke it but a minute spent in sport.
    Queene. No more sweete Suffolke bid me hence to *France*,
Or liue where thou wilt within this worldes globe,
Ile haue an Irish that shall finde thee out,
And long thou shalt not staie, but ile haue thee repelde,
Or venture to be banished my selfe.
Oh let this kisse be printed in thy hand,
That when thou seest it, thou maist thinke on me.
Away, I say, that I may feele my griefe,
For it is nothing whilst thou standst here,
    Suffolke. Thus is poore *Suffolke* ten times banished,
Once by the King, but three times thrise by thee.
        Enter Vause.

Queene.

Houses, of Yorke and Lancaster.

    Queene. How now, whither goes *Vause* so fast?
    Vause. To signifie vnto his Maiestie,
That Cardinall Beuvford is at point of death,
Sometimes he raues and cries as he were madde,
Sometimes he cals vpon Duke Humphries Ghost,
And whispers to his pillow as to him,
And sometime he calles to speake vnto the King,
And I am going to certifie vnto his grace,
That euen now he cald aloude for him.
    Queene. Go then good *Vause* and certifie the King.
            Exit Vause.
Oh what is worldly pompe, all men must die,
And vvoe am I for Beuvfords heauie ende,
But why mourne I for him, whilst thou art here?
Sweete Suffolke hie thee hence to France,
For if the King do come, thou sure must die.
    Suff. And if I go I cannot liue: but here to die,
What vvere it else, but like a pleasant slumber
In thy lap?
Here could I, could I breath my soule into the aire,
As milde and gentle as the new borne babe,
That dies with mothers dugge betweene his lips,
Where from thy sight I should be raging madde,
And call for thee to close mine eyes,
Or vvith thy lips to stop my dying soule,
That I might breathe it so into thy bodie,
And then it liu'd in sweete Elyziam,
By thee to die, vvere but to die in iest,
From thee to die, vvere torment more then death,
O let me staie, befall, vvhat may befall.
    Queene. Oh might I thou staie with safetie of thy life,
Then shouldst thou staie, but heauens deny it,
And therefore go, but hope ere long to be repelde.
    Suff. I goe.
    Queene. And take my heart with thee.
            She kisseth him.
    Suff. A ievvell lockt into the vvofull caske,
That euer yet comaunde a thing of vvoorth,

Thus like a splitted barke so sunder vie.
This way fall I to death.   Exet Suffolke.
Queene. This way for me.   Exet Queene.

Enter King and Salsbury, and then the Curtaines be drawne, and
the Cardinall is discouered in his bed, raning and staring as if he
were madde.

Car. Oh death, if thou wilt let me liue but one whole yeare,
Ile giue thee as much gold as will purchase such another Iland.
King. Oh see my Lord of Salsbury how he is troubled,
Lord Cardinall, remember Christ must saue thy soule.
Car. Why died he not in his bed?
What would you haue me to do then?
Can I make men liue whether they will or no?
Sirra, go fetch me the strong poison which the Pothecary sent me.
Oh see where duke Humphreys ghoast doth stand,
And stares me in the face. Looke, looke, come downe his haire,
So now hees gone againe: Oh, oh, oh.
Sal. See how the panges of death doth gripe his heart.
King. Lord Cardinall, if thou diest assured of heauenly blisse,
Hold vp thy hand and make some signe to vs.
                    The Cardinall dies.
Oh see he dies, and makes no signe at all
Oh God forgiue his soule.
Salb. So bad an ende did neuer none behold,
But as his death, so was his life in all.
King. Forbeare to iudge, good Salsbury forbeare,
For God will iudge vs all.
Go take him hence, and see his funerals be performde.
                    Exet omnes.

Alarmes within, and the chambers be discharged, like as it
were a fight at sea. And then enter the Captaine of the ship
and the Maister, and the Maisters Mate, & the Duke of Suffolke disguised, and others with him, and Water Whickmore.

Cap. Bring forward these prisoners that scornd to yeeld,
Vnlade their goods with speed and sincke their ship,
Here Maister, this prisoner I giue to you.

This other, the Maisters Mate shall haue,
And Water Whickmore thou shalt haue this man,
And let them paie their ransomes ere they passe.
Suffolke. Water!   He starteth.
Water. How now, what doest feare me?
Thou shalt haue better cause anon.
Suf. It is thy name affrights me, not thy selfe.
I do remember well, a cunning Wyzland told me,
That by Water I should die:
Yet let not that make thee bloudie minded.
Thy name being rightly founded,
Is Gualter, not Water.
VVater. Gualter or Water, als one to me,
I am the man must bring thee to thy death.
Suf. I am a Gentleman looke on my Ring,
Ransome me at what thou wilt, it shalbe paid.
VVater. I lost mine eye in boording of the ship,
And therefore ere I marchantlike sell blood for gold,
Then cast me headlong downe into the sea.
2. Priso. But what shall our ransomes be?
Mat. A hundreth pounds a piece, either paie that or die,
2. Priso. Then saue our liues, it shall be paid.
VVater. Come sir, haste, thy life shall be the ransome
I will haue.
Suff. Staie villaine, thy prisoner is a Prince,
The Duke of Suffolke, William de la Poull.
Cap. The Duke of Suffolke folded vp in rags,
Suf. I sir, but these rags are no part of the Duke,
Ioue sometime went disguisde, and why not I?
Cap. I but Ioue was neuer slaine as thou shalt be.
Suf. Base ladie groome, King Henries blood
The honourable blood of Lancaster,
Cannot be shead by such a lowly swaine,
I am sent Ambassador for the Queene to France,
I charge thee waste me crosse the channell safe.
Cap. Ile waste thee to thy death, go, Water take him hence,
And on our long boates side, chop off his head.
Suf. Thou dar'st not for thine owne.
                    F 2   Cap.

The first part of the contention of the two famous

Cap. Yes Poull.

Suffolke. Poull?

Cap. I Poull, puddle, kennell, sinke and durt,
Ile stop that yawning mouth of thine,
Those lips of thine that so oft haue kist the
Queene, shall sweepe the ground and thou that
Smildst at good Duke Humphreys death,
Shalt liue no longer to infect the earth.

Suffolke. This villain being but Captaine of a Pinnais,
Threatens more plagues then mightie Abradas,
The great Masadonian Pyrate,
Thy words addes fury and not remorse in me.

Cap. I but my deeds shall staie thy fury soone.

Suffalke. Haft not thou waited at my Trencher,
When we haue feasted with Queene Margret?
Haft not thou kift thy hand and held my stirrope?
And barehead plodded by my footecloth Mule,
And thought the happie when I smilde on thee?
This hand hath writ in thy defence,
Then shall I charme thee, hold thy lauish toong.

Cap. Away with him, Water, I say, and off with his hed

1.Prisn. Good my Lord, intreat him mildly for your life,

Suffalke. Firft let this necke ftoupe to the axes edge,
Before this knee do bow to any,
Saue to the God of heauen and to my King:
Suffolikes imperiall toong cannot pleade
To such a ladie groome.

Water. Come, come, why do we let him speake,
I long to haue his head for ranfsome of mine eye.

Suffalke. A Swordar and bandero slaue,
Murthered sweete Tully.
Brutus ballard-hand stabde Iulius Cæfar,
And Suffolke dies by Pyrates on the seas.

Exet Suffolke, and VVater.

Cap. Off with his head, and send it to the Queene,
And ranfomeleffe this prifoner fhall go free,
To fee it fafe deliuered vnto her,
Come lets goe.   Exet omnes.

Enter

Houfes of Yorke and Lancafter.

Enter two of the Rebels with long ftaues.

George. Come away Nick, and put a long ftaffe in thy pike, and prouide thy felfe, for I can tell thee, they haue bene vp this two daies.

Nicke. Then they had more need to go to bed now,
But firrha George whats the matter?

George. Why firrha, Iack Cade the Dar of Afhford here,
He meanes to turne this land, and fet a new nap on it.

Nick. I marry he had need fo, for its growne threedbare,
T was neuer merry world with vs, fince thefe gentle men came vp.

George. I warrant thee, thou fhalt neuer fee a Lord weare a leather aperne now a-daies.

Nick. But firrha, who comes more befide Iacke Cade?

George. Why theres Dicke the Butcher, and Robin the Sadler,
and Will that came a wooing to our Nan laft Sunday, and Harry
and Tom, and Gregory that fhould haue your Parnill, and a great
fort more is come from Rochefter, and from Maydftone, and Canterbury, and all the Townes here abouts, and we muft all be Lords
or fquires, affoone as Iacke Cade is King.

Nicke. Harke, harke, I heare the Drum, they be comming.

Enter Iacke Cade, Dicke Butcher, Robin, VVill, Tom,
Harry and the reft, with long ftaues.

Cade. Proclaime filence,

All. Silence,

Cade. I Iohn Cade fo named for my valiancie.

Dicke. Or rather for ftealing of a Cade of Sprat.

Cade. My father was a Mortemer,

Nicke. He was an honeft man and a good Brick-laier.

Cade. My mother came of the Braces.

VVill. She was a Pedlers daughter indeed, and fold many laces,

Robin. And now being not able to occupie her furd packe,
She walketh backes vp and downe the country.

Cade. Therefore I am honourably borne.

Harry. I for the field is honourable, for he was borne
Vnder a hedge, for his father had no houfe but the Cage.

Cade. I am able to endure much,

George. Thats true, I know he can endure any thing,
For I haue fcene him whipt two market daies together.

F 3   Cade.

The first part of the contention of the two famous houses

Cade. I feare neither sword nor fire.

Will. He need not feare the sword, for his coate is of proofe.

Dicke. But me thinkes he should feare the fire, being so often burnt in the hand, for stealing of sheepe.

Cade. Therefore be braue, for your Captain is braue, and vowes reformation: you shall haue seuen half-penny loaues for a penny, and the three hoop't pot, shall haue ten hoopes, and it shall be felony to drinke small beere, and if I be king, as king I will be;

All. God saue your maiestie.

Cade. I thanke you good people, you shall all eate and drinke of my score, & go all in my liuerie, and wee'le haue no writing, but the score & the Tally, and there shall be no lawes but such as comes from my mouth.

Dicke. We shall haue sore lawes then, for he was thrust into the mouth the other day.

George. I and stinking law too, for his breath stinks so, that one cannot abide it.

Enter *Will* with the Clarke of *Chatam.*

Will. Oh Captaine a prize.

Cade. Whose that *Will?*

Will. The Clarke of *Chatam,* he can write and reade and cast account, I tooke him setting of boyes coppies, and he has a booke in his pocket with red letters.

Cade. Sonnes, hees a coniurer bring him hither.

Now sir, whats your name?

Clarke. Emanuell sir, and it shall please you.

Dicke. It will go hard with you, I can tell you,
For they vse to write that oth top of letters.

Cade. And what do you vse to write your name?
Or do you as auncient forefathers haue done,
Vse the score and the Tally?

Clarke. Nay, true sir, I praise God I haue bene so well brought vp, that I can write mine owne name.

Cade. Oh hee's confest, go hang him with his penny-inckhorne about his necke.

Enter *Tom.*

Tom. Captaine, Newes, newes, sir Humphrey Stafford and his brother are comming with the kings power, and mean to kil vs wall.

Cade.

Houses of Yorke and Lancaster.

Cade. Let them come, hees but a knight is he?

Tom. No, no, hees but a knight.

Cade. Why then to equall him, ile make my selfe knight.
Kneele downe *John Mortemer.*
Rise vp sir *John Mortemer.*
Is there any more of them that be Knights?

Tom. I his brother.

Cade. Then kneele downe *Dicke Butcher,*
Rise vp sir *Dicke Butcher.*

Drumme sounds.

Now sound vp the Drumme.

Enter sir *Humphrey Stafford* and his brother, with Drumme and souldiers.

Cade. As for these silken coated slaues I passe not a pinne,
Tis to you good people that I speake.

Stafford. Why country-men, what meane you thus in troopes,
To follow this rebellious Traitor *Cade?*
Why his father was but a Brick-laier.

Cade. Well, and Adam was a Gardner, what then?
But I come of the *Mortemers.*

Stafford. I, the Duke of *Yorke* hath taught you that,

Cade. The Duke of *Yorke,* nay, I learnt it my selfe,
For looke you, Roger *Mortemer* the Earle of March,
Married the Duke of Clarence daughter.

Stafford. Well, thats true: But what then?

Cade. And by her he had two children at a birth.

Stafford. Thats false.

Cade. I, but I say, tis true.

All. Why then tis true.

Cade. And one of them was stolne away by a begger-woman,
And that was my father, and I am his sonne,
Deny it and you can.

Nicke. Nay, looke you, I know twas true,
For his father built a chimney in my fathers house,
And the brickes are aliue at this day to testifie.

Cade. But doest thou heare *Stafford,* tell the King, that for his fathers sake, in whose time boyes plaide at spanne-counter with French Crownes, I am content that hee shall be King as long

as

Houſes, of Yorke and Lancaſter.

King. Sir *Humphrey Stafford* and his brother is slaine,
And the Rebels march amaine to London,
Ile come to them, and tell them thus from me,
Ile come and parley with their generall.

Reade. Yet flaie, ile reade the Letter one againe.
Lord Say, Iacke Cade hath solemnely vowde to haue thy head.
Say. I but I hope your highneſſe ſhall haue his.
King. How now Madam, still lamenting and mourning for Suf-
folkes death, I feare my loue, if I had bene dead, thou wouldst not
haue mournde ſo much for me.

Queene. No my loue, I ſhould not mourne, but die for thee.
Enter a Meſſenger.

Meſſen. Oh flie my Lord, the Rebels are entered
Southwarke, and haue almoſt wonne the Bridge,
Calling your grace an vſurper,
And that monſtrous Rebell Cade, hath ſworne
To Crowne himſelfe King in Weſtminſter,
Therefore flie my Lord, and poſte to Killingworth.

King. Go bid Buckingham and Clifford, gather
An Army vp, and meete with the Rebels.
Come Madame, let vs haſte to Killingworth.
Come on Lord Say, go thou along with vs,
For feare the Rebell Cade do finde thee out.

Say. My innocence my Lord ſhall pleade for me.
And therfore with your highneſſe leaue, ile ſtae behind.

King. Euen as thou wilt my Lord Say.
Come Madame, let vs go.

Exet omnes.

Enter the Lord *Skayles* vpon the Tower
walles walking.

Enter three or foure Citizens below.

Lord Scayles. How now, is Iacke Cade ſlaine?
1. Citizen. No my Lord, nor likely to be ſlaine,
For they haue wonne the bridge,
Killing all thoſe that withſtand them.
The Lord Mayor craueth ayde of your honor from the Tower,
To defend the Citie from the Rebels,
Lord Scayles. Such aide as I can ſpare, you ſhall command,

The firſt part of the contention of the two famous

as he liues Marry alwaies prouided, ile be Protectour ouer him.
Stafford. O monſtrous ſimplicitie.
Cade. And tell him, weele haue the Lorde Sayes head, and the
Duke of Somerſets, for deliuering vp the Dukedomes of Anioy
and Mayne, and ſelling the Townes in France, by which meanes
England hath bene mainde euer ſince, and gone as it were with a
crouch, but that my puiſſance held it vp. And beſides, they can
ſpeake French, and therefore they are traitors.
Stafford. As how I prethie?
Cade. Why the French men are our enemies be they not?
And then can hee that ſpeakes with the tongue of an enemy be a
good ſubiect?
Anſwere me to that.
Stafford. Well ſirrha, wilt thou yeeld thy ſelfe vnto the Kings
mercy, and he will pardon thee and theſe, their outrages and rebel-
lious deedes?
Cade. Nay, bid the King come to me and he will, and then ile
pardon him, or otherwaies ile haue his Crowne tell him, ercit be
long.
Stafford. Go Herald, proclaime in all the Kings Townes,
That thoſe that will forſake the Rebell Cade,
Shall haue free pardon from his Maieſtie.
Exet Stafford and his men.

Cade. Come ſirs, faint George for vs and Kent.
Exet omnes.

Abrams to the battaile, and ſir *Humphrey Stafford*
and his brother is ſlaine. Then enter Iacke
Cade againe and the reſt.

Cade. Sir Dike Butcher, thou haſt fought to day moſt valiantly,
And knockt them down as if thou hadſt bin in thy ſlaughter houſe.
And thus I will reward thee. The Lent ſhall be as long againe as
it was, Thou ſhalt haue licence to kil for foure ſcore & one a week,
Drumme ſtrike vp, for now weele march to London, for to mor-
row I meane to ſit in the Kings ſeate at Weſtminſter.
Exet omnes.

Enter the King reading of a Letter, and the Queene, with
the Duke of Suffolkes head, and the Lord Say,
with others.

Kin

The first part of the contention of the two famous

But I am troubled here with my selfe,
The Rebels haue attempted to win the Tower,
But get you to Smythfield and gather head,
And thither I will send you Mathew Goffe,
Fight for your King,your Country,and your liues,
And so farewell for I must hence againe.
     Exeet omnes.

Enter Iacke Cade and the rest,and strikes his sword
     vpon London stone.

Cade. Now is Mortemer Lord of this Citie,
And now sitting vpon London stone,We command,
That the first yeare of our raigne,
The pissing Cundit run nothing but red wine.
And now hence forward,it shall be treason
For any that calles me any othervvise then
Lord Mortemer.

    Enter a souldier.

Sould, Iacke Cade,Iacke Cade.
Cade. Sounes,knocke him dovvne. (*They kill him.*
Dicke. My Lord,theirs an Army gathered togither
Into Smythfield.
Cade. Come then,lets go fight with them,
But first go on and set London bridge a fire,
And if you can burne dovvne the Tovver too.
Come lets avvay.   *Exeet omnes.*

Alarmes,and then Mathew Goffe is slaine,and all the
rest with him. Then enter Iacke Cade a-
gain,and his company.

Cade. So,sirs novv go some and pull dovvn the *Sauoy,*
Others to the Innes of the Court,dovvne vvith them all.
Dicke. I haue a sute vnto your Lordship.
Cade. Be it a Lordship Dicke,and thou shalt haue it
For that vvord.
Dicke. That vve may go burne all the Records,
And that all vvriting may be put dovvne,
And nothing vlde but the score and the Tally.
Cade. Dicke it shall be so, and henceforvvard all things shall be
in common,and in Cheapeside shall my palphrey go to grasse.
           Why

Houses, of Yorke and Lancaster.

Why ist not a miserable thing,that of the skin of an innocent lamb
should parchment be made,& then with a litle blotting ouer with
inke,a man should vndo himselfe.
 Some saies tis the bees that sting,but I say, tis their waxe,for I
am sure I neuer seald to any thing but once, and I was neuer mine
owne man since.
 Nicke. But when shall we take vp those commodities
Which you told vs of.
 Cade. Marry he that will lustily stand to it,
Shall go with me, and take vp these commodities following:
Item,a gowne,a kirtle,a petticoate,and a smocke.
     Enter George.
George. My Lord,a prize,a prize,heres the Lord Say,
Which sold the Townes in France,
Cade. Come hither thou Say, thou George,thou buckrum lord,
What answere canst thou make vnto my mightinesse,
For deliuering vp the townes in France to Mounsier bus mine cue,
the Dolphin of France?
And more then so, thou hast most traitorously erected a grammer
schoole, to infect the youth of the realme, and against the Kings
Crowne and dignitie,thou hast built vp a paper-mill,nay it will be
said to thy face, that thou keptst men in thy house that daily reades
of bookes with red letters,and talkes of a Nowne and a Verbe,and
such abhominable words as no Christian eare is able to endure it.
And besides all that,thou hast appointed certaine lustifies of peace
in euery shire to hang honest men that steale for their liuing, and
because they could not reade,thou hast hung them vp: Onely for
which cause they were most worthy to liue. Thou ridest on a foot-
cloth doest thou not?
 Say. Yes, what of that?
 Cade. Marry I say, thou oughtest not to let thy horse weare a
cloake, when an honester man then thy selfe, goes in his hose and
doublet.
 Say. You men of Kent.
 All. Kent,what of Kent?
 Say. Nothing but *bona,terra.*
 *Cade. Bonum terrum,*sounds whats that?
 Dicke. He speakes French.

       G 2

The first part of the contention of the two famous

Wid. No tis Dutch.

Nicke, No tis our talian, I know it well inough.

Say, Kent, in the Commentaries Cæsar wrote,
Termde it the ciuell't place of all this land,
Then noble Country-men, heare me but speake,
I fold not France, I loft not Normandie.

Cade. But wherefore doeft thou fhake thy head fo?

Say, It is the palfie and not feare that makes me,

Cade. Nay thou nodft thy head, as who fay, thou wilt be euen
with me, if thou geeft away, but ie make the fure inough, now I
haue thee. Go take him to the ftanderd in Cheapfide and chop of
his head, and then go to milende-greene, to fir Iames Cromer his
fonne in law, and cut off his head too, and bring them to me vpon
two poles prefently.   (Away with him.

Exet one or two, with the Lord Say.

There fhall not a noble man weare a head on his fhoulders,
But he fhall paie me tribute for it.
Nor there fhal not a mayd be married, but he fhal fee to me for her,
Maydenhead or elfe, ele haue it my felfe,
Marry I will that married men fhall hold of me in capitie,
And that their wiues fhalbe as free as hart can thinke, or toong can
                                                                        (tell.

Enter Robin.

Robin, O Captaine, London bridge is a fire.

Cade. Runne to Billingfgate, and fetche pitch and flaxe and
fquench it.

Enter Dicke and a Sargiant.

Sargiant. Iuftice, iuftice, I pray you fir, let me haue iuftice of this
fellow here.

Cade. Why what has he done?

Sarg. Alaffe fir he has rauifht my wife.

Dicke. Why my Lord he would haue refted me,
And I went and and entred my Action in his wiues paper houfe.

Cade. Dicke follow thy fute in her common place,
You horfon villaine, you are a Sargiant youle,
Take any man by the throate for twelue pence,
And reft a man when hees at dinner,
And haue him to prifon ere the meate be out of his mouth.
Go Dicke take him hence, cut out his toong for cogging, Hough

Hough him for running, and to conclude,
Braue him with his owne mace.

Exet with the Sargiant.

Enter two with the Lord Sayes head, and fir Iames
Cromers, vpon two poles.

So, come carry them before me, and at euery lanes ende, let them
kiffe together.

Enter the Duke of Buckingham, and Lord Clifford the
Earle of Cumberland.

Clifford, Why country-men and warlike friends of Kent,
Whar meanes this mutinous rebellions,
That you in troopes do mafter thus your felues,
Vnder the conduct of this Traitor Cade?
To rife againft your foueraigne Lord and King,
Who mildly hath his pardon fent to you,
If you forfake this monftrous Rebell here?
If honour be the marke whereat you aime,
Then hafte to France that our forefathers wonne,
And winne againe that thing which now is loft,
And leaue to feeke your Countries ouerthrow.

All. A Clifford,a Clifford.
                                        They forfake Cade.

Cade. Why how now,will you forfake your generall,
And ancient freedome which you haue poffeft
To bend your neckes vnder their feruile yokes,
Who if you ftir, will ftraightwaies hang you vp,
But follow me,and you fhall pull them downe,
And make them yeeld their fwings to your hands.

All. A Cade,a Cade.
                                They runne to Cade againe.

Cliff. Braue warlike friends heare me but fpeak a word,
Refufe not good whilft it is offered you,
The King is mercifull,then yeeld to him,
And I my felfe will go along with you,
To Winfore Caftle whereas the King abides,
And on mine honour you fhall haue no hurt,

All. A Clifford,a Clifford,God faue the King.

Cade. How like a feather is this rafcall company

                                    G 3   Blowne

The first part of the contention of the two famous

Blowne euery way,
But that they may see there want no valiancy in me,
My staffe shall make way through the midst of you,
And so a poxe take you all.

He runs through them with his staffe, and flies away.

Bull. Go some and make after him, and proclaime,
That those that can bring the head of Cade,
Shall haue a thousand Crownes for his labour.
Come march away.   *Exet omnes,*

Enter King Henry and the Queene, and Somerset.

King. Lord Somerset, what newes here you of the Rebell Cade?
Som. This, my gratious Lord, that the Lord Say is done to death,
And the Citie is almost sackt.

King. Gods will be done, for as he hath decreede, so must it bee:
And be it as he please, to stop the pride of those rebellious men.

Queene. Had the noble Duke of Suffolke bene aliue,
The Rebell Cade had bene suppreft ere this,
And all the rest that do take part with him.

*Enter the Duke of Buckingham and Clifford, with the
Rebels, with halters about their necks.*

Cliff. Long liue King Henry, Englands lawfull King,
Loe here my Lord, these Rebels are subdude,
And offer their liues before your highnesse feete.

King. But tell me Cliffordis there Captaine here.

Cliff. No, my gratious Lord, he is fled away, but proclamations
are sent forth, that he that can but bring his head, shall haue a thousand crownes.   But may it please your Maiestie, to pardon these
their faults, that by that traitors meanes were thus milled,

King. Stand vp you simple men, and giue God praise,
For you did take in hand you know not what,
And go in peace obedient to your King,
And liue as subiects, and you shall not want,
Whilst Henry liues, and weares the English Crowne.

All. God saue the King, God saue the King.

King. Come let vs haste to London now with speed,
That solemne processions may be sung,
In laud and honour of the God of heauen,
And triumphs of this happie victorie.

(Exet omnes,

Enter

Houses of Yorke and Lancaster.

*Enter Iacke Cade at one doore, and at the other, maister Alexander
Eyden and his men, and Iack Cade lies downe picking of hearbes
and eating them.*

Eyden. Good Lord how pleasant is this country life,
This little land my father left me here,
With my contented minde serues me as well,
As all the pleasures in the Court can yeeld,
Nor would I change this pleasure for the Court.

Cade. Sounes, heres the Lord of the foyle, Stand villaine, thou
wilt betraie me to the King, and get a thousand crownes for my
head, but ere thou goeft, ile make thee eate yron like an Aftridge,
and swallow my sword like a great pinne,

Eyden. Why sawcy companion, why should I betray thee?
Ift not inough that thou haft broke my hedges,
And entered into my ground without the leaue of me the owner,
But thou wilt braue me too.

Cade. Braue thee and beard thee too, by the best blood of the
Realme, looke on me well, I haue eate no meate this fiue dayes, yet
and I do not leaue thee and thy fiue men as dead as a doore nayle, I
pray God I may neuer eate grasse more.

Eyden. Nay, it neuer shall be faide whilft the world doth stand,
that Alexander Eyden an Efquire of Kent, tooke oddes to combat
with a famisht man, looke on me, my limmes are equall vnto thine,
and euery way as big, then hand to hand, ile combat thee.   Sirrha
fetch me weopons, and stand you all afide.

Cade. Now sword, if thou doeft not hew this burly-bond churle
into chines of beefe, I befeech God thou maift fal into some smiths
hand, and be turnd to hobnailes.

Eyden. Come on thy way.   *(They fight, and Cade fals downe.*

Cade. Oh villaine, thou haft flaine the floure of Kent for chiualrie, but it is famine & not thee that has done it, for come ten thoufand diuels, and giue me but the ten meales that I wanted this fiue
daies, and ile fight with you all, and so a poxe rot thee, for lacke
Cade muft die.   *(He dies.*

Eyden, Iack Cade, & wast it that monftrous Rebell which I haue
flaine. Oh fwordile honour thee for this, and in my chamber shalt
thou hang as a monument to after age, for this great feruice thou
haft done to me. Ile drag him hence, and with my fword cut off his
head and beare it   Enter

The first part of the contention of the two famous

Enter the Duke of *Yorke* with Drum and souldiers,
Yorke. In Armes from Ireland comes Yorke amaine,
Ring belles aloud, bonfires perfume the ayre,
To entertaine faire Englands royall King,
Ah *Sancta Maiestas*, who would not buy thee deare?

Enter the Duke of Buckingham.

But soft, who comes here *Buckingham*, what newes with him?
Buc. Yorke, if thou meane well, I greete thee so.
Yorke. Humphrey of Buckingham, welcome I sweare:
What comes thou in loue or as a Messenger?
Buc. I come as a Messenger from our dread Lord and soueraign,
Henry. To know the reason of these Armes in peace?
Or that thou being a subiect as I am,
Shouldst thus approach so neare with colours spred,
Whereas the person of the King doth keepe?
Yorke. A subiect as he is.
Oh how I hate these spitefull abiect termes,
But Yorke dissemble, till thou meete thy sonnes,
Who now in Armes expect their fathers fight,
And not farre hence I know they cannot be.
Humphrey Duke of Buckingham, pardon me,
That I answerde not at first, my mind vvas troubled,
I came to remoue that monstrous Rebell Cade,
And heaue proud Somerset from out the Court,
That basely yeelded vp the Townes in France.
Buc. Why that vvas presumption on thy behalfe,
But if it be no othervvise but so,
The King doth pardon thee, and granft to thy requeft,
And Somerset is sent vnto the Tovver.
Yorke. Vpon thine honour is it so?
Buc. Yorke, he is vpon mine honour.
Yorke. Then before thy face, I here difmiffe my troopes,
Sirs, meete me to morrovv in faint Georges fields,
And there you fhall receiue your paie of me.

Exet souldiers.

Buc. Come Yorke, thou fhalt go fpeake vnto the King,
But fee, his grace is comming to meete vvith vs.

Enter

Houses of Yorke and Lancaster.

Enter King Henry.

King. How now Buckingham, is Yorke friends with vs,
That thus thou bring'st him hand in hand with thee?
Buc. He is my Lord, and hath difchargde his troopes
Which came with him, but as your grace did fay,
To heaue the Duke of Somerset from hence,
And to fubdue the Rebels that vveere vp.
King. Then vvelcome coufin Yorke, giue me thy hand,
And thankes for thy great feruice done to vs,
Againft thofe traitorous Irifh that rebeld.

Enter maifter *Eyden* vvith *Jacke Cades* head.

Eyden. Long liue Henry in triumphant peace,
Lo here my Lord vpon my bended knees,
I here prefent the traitorous head of Cade,
That hand to hand in fingle fight I flue.
King. Firft thankes to heauen, & next to thee my friend,
That haft fubdude that vvicked traitor thus:
Ohler me fee that head that in his life,
Did vvorke me and my land fuch cruell fpight,
A vifage fterne, cole blacke his curled locks,
Deepe trenched furrovves in his frovvning brovv,
Prefageth vvarlike humors in his life.
Here take it hence, and thou for thy revvard,
Shall be immediatly created Knight.
Kneele dovvne my friend, and tell me vvhats thy name?
Eyden. Alexander Eyden, if it pleafe your grace,
A poore Eiquire of Kent.
King. Then rife vp fir Alexander Eyden knight,
And for thy maintenance, I freely giue
A thoufand markes a yeare to maintaine thee,
Befide the firme revvard that vvas proclaimde,
For thofe that could performe this vvoorthie act,
And thou fhalt vvaight vpon the perfon of the king.
Eyden. I humbly thank your grace, and I no longer liue,
Then I proue true and loyall to my king.   (*Exit.*
Enter the Queene vvith the Duke of *Somerfet.*
King. O Buckingham fee vvhere Somerfet comes,
Bid him go hide himfelfe till Yorke be gone.

H   Queene.

Queene. He ſhall not hide himſelfe for feare of Yorke,
But beard and braue him proudly to his face.
Yorke. Whoſe that, proud Somerſet at libertie?
Baſe fearefull Henry that tis diſhonor'ſt me,
By heauen, thou ſhalt not gouerne ouer me:
I cannot brooke that Traitors preſence here,
Nor will I ſubiect be to ſuch a King.
That knowes not how to gouerne nor to rule,
Reſigne thy Crowne proud Lancaſter to me,
For now is Yorke reſolu'd to claime his owne,
That thou vſurped haſt ſo long by force.
And riſe aloft into faire Englands Throane.
Somer. Proud Traitor, I areſt thee on high treaſon,
Againſt thy ſoueraigne Lord, yeeld thee falſe Yorke,
For here I ſweare, thou halt vnto the Tower,
For theſe proud words which thou haſt giuen the king.
Yorke. Thou art deceaued, my ſonnes ſhalbe my baile,
And ſend thee there in diſpight of him.
Hoe, where are you boyes?
Queene. Call Clifford hither preſently,
Enter the Duke of Yorkes ſonnes, Edward the Earle of March and
crook-backe Richard, at the one doore, with Drumme and ſol-
diers, and at the other doore, enter Clifford and his ſonne, with
Drumme and ſouldiers, and Clifford kneeles to Henry, and
ſpeakes.
Cliff. Long liue my noble Lord, and ſoueraigne King.
Yorke. We thanke thee Clifford.
Nay, do not affright vs with thy lookes,
If thou diſt miſtake, we pardon thee, kneele againe.
Cliff. Why, I did no way miſtake, this is my King.
What is he mad to Bedlam with him.
King. I, a bedlam franticke humor driues him thus
To leauy Armes againſt his lawfull King.
Clif. Why doth not your grace ſend him to the Tower?
Queene. He is areſted, but will not obey.
His ſonnes he faith, ſhall be his baile.
Yorke. How ſay you boyes, will you not?
Edward. Yes noble father, if our words will ſerue.   Richard.

Richard. And if our words will not, our ſwords ſhall.
Yorke. Call hither to the ſtake, my two rough beares,
King. Call Buckingham, and bid him Arme himſelfe.
Yorke. Call Buckingham, and all the friends thou haſt,
Both thou and they, ſhall curſe this fatall houre.
Enter at one doore, the Earles of Salsbury and VVarwicke, with
Drumme and ſouldiers. And at the other, the Duke of Bucking-
bam, with Drumme and ſouldiers.
Cliff. Are theſe thy beares? weele bayte them ſoone,
Diſpight of thee, and all the friends thou haſt.
War. You had beſt go dreame againe,
To keepe you from the tempeſt of the field,
Cliff. I am reſolu'd to beare a greater ſtorme,
Then any thou canſt coniure vp to day,
And that ile write vpon thy Burgonet,
Might I but know thee by thy houſhold badge.
VVar. Now by my fathers age, old Nevels creſt,
The Rampant Beare chain'd to the ragged ſtaffe,
This day ile weare aloft my burgonet,
As on a mountaine top the Cædar ſhowes,
That keepes his leaues in ſpight of any ſtorme,
Euen to affright the with the view thereof.
Cliff. And from thy burgonet will I rend the beare,
And tread him vnderfoote with all contempt,
Diſpight the Beare-ward that protects him ſo.
Yoong Cliff. And ſo renowned ſoueraigne to Armes,
To quell theſe Traitors and their complotters.
Richard. Fie, Chairite for ſhame ſpeake it not in ſpight,
For you ſhall ſup with Ieſus Chriſt to night.
Yoong Cliff. Foule Stigmaticke thou canſt not tell.
Rich. No, for if not in heauen, youle ſurely ſup in hell.
                                              Exet omnes.
Alarmes to the battaile, and then enter the Duke of Somerſet
and Richard fighting, and Richard kils him vnder the ſigne of
the Caſtle in ſaint Albones,
Rich. So. Lie thou there, and breathe thy laſt,
Whats here, the ſigne of the Caſtle?
Then the prophetie is come to paſſe,
                                          H 2   For

For Somerset was forewarned of Castles,
The which he alwaies did obserue.
And now behold, vnder a paltry Ale-house signe,
The Castle in faint Albones,
Somerset hath made the Wissard famous by his death.
                                 Exet.

    Alarme again, and enter the Earle of
        Warwike alone.

VVar. Clifford of Cumberland, tis Warwicke calles,
And if thou doest not hide thee from the Beare,
Now whilst the angry Trumpets found Alarmes,
And dead mens cries do fill the emptie aire:
Clifford I say, come forth and fight with me,
Proud Northerne Lord, Clifford of Cumberland,
Warwicke is hoarse with calling thee to Armes.
         Clifford speakes within.

Warwicke stand still, and view the way that Clifford hewes with
his murthering Curtelaxe, through the fainting troopes to finde
thee out,
Warwicke stand still, and stir not till I come.
                     Enter Yorke.

VVar. How now my Lord, what a foote?
Who kild your horse?

Yorke. The deadly hand of Clifford, Noble Lord,
Fiue horse this day slaine vnder me,
And yet braue Warwicke I remaine aliue,
But I did kill his horse he lou'd so well,
The bonnie gray that ere was bred in North.
    Enter Clifford, and Warwicke offers to
         fight with him.

Hold Warwicke, and seeke thee out some other chafe,
My selfe will hunt this deare to death.
VVar. Braue Lord, tis for a Crowne thou fights,
Clifford farewell, as I intend to prosper well to day,
It grieues my soule to leaue thee vnassaild.
              Exet VVarwicke.

Yorke. Now Clifford, since we are singled here alone,
                                      Be

Be this the day of doome to one of vs,
For now my heart hath sworne immortall hate
To thee, and all the house of Lancaster.
Clifford. And here I stand, and pitch my foot to thine,
Vowing neuer to flit, till thou or I be slaine.
For neuer shall my heart be safe at rest,
Till I haue spoyld the hatefull house of Yorke.
    Alarmes, and they fight, and Yorke kils Clifford.

Yorke. Now Lancaster sit sure, thy sinowes shrinke,
Come fearefull Henry groueling on thy face,
Yeeld vp thy Crowne vnto the Prince of Yorke.
                         Exet Yorke.

    Alarmes, then enter yoong Clifford alone.

Yoong Clifford. Father of Cumberland,
Where may I seeke my aged father forth?
O disinall fight, see where he breathlesse lies,
All smear'd and weltred in his luke-warme blood,
Ah aged pillar of all Cumberlands true house,
Sweete father, to thy murthred ghoast I sweare,
Immortall hate vnto the house of Yorke,
Nor neuer shall I sleepe secure one night,
Till I haue furiously reuengde thy death,
And left not one of them to breath on earth.

           He takes him vpon his backe.

And thus as old Ankyses sonne did beare
His aged father on his manly backe,
And fought with him against the bloodie Greeks,
Euen so will I. But staie, heres one of them,
To whom my soule hath sworne immortall hate.
    Enter Richard, and then Clifford laies downe his father,
         fights with him, and Richard flies away againe.

Out crookt backe villaine, get thee from my fight,
But I will after thee, and once againe
When I haue borne my father to his Tent,
Ile trie my fortune better with thee yet.
      Exet yoong Clifford with his
                    father.
                        H 3
                                Alarmes,

The first part of the contention of the two famous Houses of Yorke and Lancaster.

Alarmes againe, and then enter three or foure, bearing the Duke of *Buckingham* wounded to his Tent.

Alarmes still, and then enter the King and Queene.

Queene. Away my Lord, and flie to London straight,
Make haste, for vengeance comes along with them,
Come stand not to expostulate, lets go.
King. Come then faire Queene to London let vs haste,
And sommon a Parlament with speede,
To stop the fury of these dyre euents.

Exet King and Queene.

Alarmes, and then a flourish, and enter the Duke of
Yorke and *Richard.*

Yorke. Howe nowe boyes, fortunate this fight hath bene,
I hope to vs and ours, for Englands good,
And our great honour, that so long we loft,
Whilst faint-heart Henry did vsurpe our rights:
But did you see old Salsbury, since we
With bloodie mindes did buckle with the foe,
I would not for the losse of this right hand,
That ought but well betide that good old man.
Rich. My Lord, I saw him in the thickest throng,
Charging his Lance with his old weary armes,
And thrise I saw him beaten from his horse,
And thrise this hand did set him vp againe,
And still he fought with courage gainst his foes,
The boldest spirited man that ere mine eyes beheld.

Enter *Salisbury* and *Warwike.*

Edward. See noble father, where they both do come,
The onely props vnto the house of Yorke.
Salf. Well haft thou fought this day, thou valiant Duke,
And thou braue bud of Yorkes encreasing house,
The small remainder of my weary life,
I hold for thee, for with thy warlike arme,
Three times this day thou haft preseru'd my life,
Yorke. What say you Lords, the King is fled to London?
There as I heare to hold a Parlament,

What

Houses, of Yorke and Lancaster.

What faies Lord Warwicke, shall we after them?
War. After them, nay before them if we can.
Now by my faith Lords, twas a glorious day,
Saint Albones battaile wonne by famous Yorke,
Shall be eternest in all age to come,
Sound Drummes and Trumpets, and to London all,
And more such daies as these as to vs befall.   Exet omnes.

FINIS.

LONDON.

Printed by Thomas Creed, for Thomas Millington,
and are to be sold at his shop vnder Saint Peters
Church in Cornwall.
1594

APPENDIX 2
Q1 AND Q3 VARIANTS

Q1 / F variants

Appendix 1 reproduces in reduced facsimile the whole of Q1.
The following extracts from Q1, preceded by the relevant parallels where this edition follows F, offer examples of the more
interesting or substantial variants. The extracts, and through–line
numbering references, are taken from William Montgomery's
facsimile edition published by Malone Society Reprints (for
Montgomery's contribution to the textual study of Q1 see
Introduction, pp. 131–5).

1.1. This edition

QUEEN
    Great King of England, and my gracious lord,
    The mutual conference that my mind hath had
    By day, by night, waking and in my dreams,
    In courtly company, or at my beads,
    With you mine alderliefest sovereign,
    Makes me the bolder to salute my king
    With ruder terms, such as my wit affords
    And overjoy of heart doth minister.

                        (1.1.24–31)

1.2   Q1

> *Queene.* Th'excessiue loue I beare vnto your grace,
> Forbids me to be lauish of my tongue,
> Least I should speake more then beseemes a woman:
> Let this suffice, my blisse is in your liking,
> And nothing can make poore *Margaret* miserable,
> Vnlesse the frowne of mightie Englands King.
>
> (TLN 51–6)

2.1   This edition

CARDINAL
> My Lord of Gloucester, now ye grow too hot:
> It was the pleasure of my lord the King.
>
> (1.1.134–5)

2.2   In Q1 the dialogue below directly follows a truncated version of Gloucester's speech, ll. 70–98.

> *Card[inal].* Why how now cosin *Gloster*, what needs this?
> As if our King were bound vnto your will,
> And might not do his will without your leaue,
> Proud Protector, enuy in thine eyes I see,
> The big swolne venome of thy hatefull heart,
> That dares presume gainst that thy Soueraigne likes.
>
> (TLN 114–19)

3.1   This edition

2 PETITIONER   Marry, the Lord protect him, for he's a good
man, Jesu bless him.

(1.3.4–5)

3.2   Q1

    2. *Peti[tioner]*. I pray God saue the good Duke *Humphries*
life,
For but for him a many were vndone,
That cannot get no succour in the Court,

(TLN 296–8)

4.1   This edition

Enter ELEANOR *aloft* [, HUME *following*].

(1.4.12 SD)

4.2   Q1

Enter *Elnor*, with sir *Iohn Hum, Koger Bullenbrooke* a Coniurer,
and *Margery Iourdaine* a Witch.

    Elnor. Here sir *Iohn*, take this scrole of paper here,
Wherein is writ the questions you shall aske,
And I will stand vpon this Tower here,
And here the spirit what it saies to you,
And to my questions, write the answeres downe.

She goes vp to the Tower.

    Sir Iohn. Now sirs begin and cast your spels about,
And charme the fiendes for to obey your wils,
And tell Dame *Elnor* of the thing she askes.

    Witch. Then *Roger Bullinbrooke* about thy taske,
And frame a Cirkle here vpon the earth,
Whilst I thereon all prostrate on my face,
Do talke and whisper with the diuels be low,
And coniure them for to obey my will.

She lies downe vpon her face.
Bullenbrooke makes a Cirkle.

    Bullen. Darke Night, dread Night, the silence of the Night,
Wherein the Furies maske in hellish troupes,

410

Send vp I charge you from *Sosetus* lake,
The spirit *Askalon* to come to me,
To pierce the bowels of this Centricke earth,
And hither come in twinkling of an eye,
Askalon, Assenda, Assenda.

It thunders and lightens, and then the spirit
riseth vp.

(TLN 481–507)

5.1   This edition

BOLINGBROKE

Descend to darkness and the burning lake!
False fiend, avoid!

(1.4.39–40)

5.2   Q1

Bullen. Then downe I say, vnto the damned poule.
Where Pluto in his firie Waggon sits.
Ryding amidst the singde and parched smoakes,
The Rode of *Dytas* by the Riuer Stykes,
There howle and burne for euer in those flames,
Rise *Iordaine* rise, and staie thy charming Spels.
Sonnes, we are betraide.

(TNL 519–25)

6.1   This edition

CARDINAL [*aside to Gloucester*]
Marry, when thou dar'st.
GLOUCESTER [*aside to Cardinal*]
Make up no factious numbers for the matter,
In thine own person answer thy abuse.

(2.1.38–40)

6.2 Q1

> *Cardinall.* Euen when thou darest.
>
> *Humphrey.* Dare. I tell rhee Priest, Plantagenets could neuer brooke the dare.
>
> *Card.* I am Plantagenet as well as thou, and sonne to John of Gaunt.
>
> *Humph.* In Bastardie.
>
> *Cardin.* I scorn thy words.
>
> (TLN 585–91)

7. The following dialogue in Q1 replaces York's lines at 2.2.67–76, 'And that's not suddenly . . . prophesy'.

> *War[wick].* Then Yorke aduise thy selfe and take thy time,
> Claime thou the Crowne, and set thy standard vp,
> And in the same aduance the milke-white Rose,
> And then to gard it, will I rouse the Beare,
> Inuiron'd with ten thousand Ragged-staues
> To aide and helpe thee for to win thy right,
> Maugre the proudest Lord of Henries blood,
> That dares deny the right and claime of Yorke,
> For why my minde presageth I shall liue
> To see the noble Duke of Yorke to be a King.
>
> (TLN 788–97)

8.1 This edition

POST
> Great lords, from Ireland am I come amain
> To signify that rebels there are up
> And put the Englishmen unto the sword.
> Send succours, lords, and stop the rage betime,
> Before the wound do grow uncurable;
> For, being green, there is great hope of help.

CARDINAL

    A breach that craves a quick expedient stop! –

    What counsel give you in this weighty cause?

YORK

    That Somerset be sent as regent thither.

    'Tis meet that lucky ruler be employed;

    Witness the fortune he hath had in France.

SOMERSET

    If York, with all his far-fet policy,

    Had been the regent there instead of me,

    He never would have stayed in France so long.

YORK

    No, not to lose it all, as thou hast done.

    I rather would have lost my life betimes

    Than bring a burden of dishonour home

    By staying there so long till all were lost.

    Show me one scar charactered on thy skin;

    Men's flesh preserved so whole do seldom win.

QUEEN

    Nay, then, this spark will prove a raging fire

    If wind and fuel be brought to feed it with.

    No more, good York. Sweet Somerset, be still.

    Thy fortune, York, hadst thou been regent there,

    Might happily have proved far worse than his.

YORK

    What, worse than naught? Nay, then a shame take all!

SOMERSET

    And in the number thee, that wishest shame.

CARDINAL

    My Lord of York, try what your fortune is.

    Th'uncivil kerns of Ireland are in arms

    And temper clay with blood of Englishmen.

    To Ireland will you lead a band of men

    Collected choicely, from each county some,

    And try your hap against the Irishmen?

YORK

    I will, my lord, so please his majesty.

SUFFOLK

    Why, our authority is his consent,

    And what we do establish he confirms.

    Then, noble York, take thou this task in hand.

YORK

    I am content. Provide me soldiers, lords,

    Whiles I take order for mine own affairs.

SUFFOLK

    A charge, Lord York, that I will see performed.

    But now return we to the false Duke Humphrey.

                                   (3.1.281–321)

8.2   Q1 Hattaway points out the Marlovian echo from *Edward*
     II – 'The wild O'Neill, with swarms of Irish kerns, /
     Lives uncontroll'd within the English pale' (2.2.164–5) – in
     the following lines (TLN 1125–7) which are usually
     regarded as evidence of memorial contamination.

                     Enter a Messenger.

   Queene. How now sirrha, what newes?

   Messen. Madame I bring you newes from Ireland,

The wilde Onele my Lords, is vp in Armes,

With troupes of Irish Kernes that vncontrold,

Doth plant themselues within the English pale.

   Queene. What redresse shal we haue for this my Lords?

   Yorke. Twere very good that my Lord of Somerset

That fortunate Champion were sent ouer,

And burnes and spoiles the Country as they goe.

To keepe in awe the stubborne Irishmen,

He did so much good when he was in France.

   Somer. Had Yorke bene there with all his far fetcht

Pollices, he might haue lost as much as I.

   Yorke. I, for Yorke would haue lost his life before

That France should haue reuolted from Englands rule.

    Somer. I so thou might'st, and yet haue gouernd worse then I.

    Yorke. What worse then nought, then a shame take all.

    Somer. Shame on thy selfe, that wisheth shame.

    Queene. Somerset forbeare, good Yorke be patient,

And do thou take in hand to crosse the seas,

With troupes of Armed men to quell the pride

Of those ambitious Irish that rebell.

    Yorke. Well Madame sith your grace is so content,

Let me haue some bands of chosen soldiers,

And Yorke shall trie his fortune against those kernes.

    Queene. Yorke thou shalt. My Lord of Buckingham,

Let it be your charge to muster vp such souldiers

As shall suffise him in these needfull warres.

                              (TLN 1122–50)

9.1   This edition

SUFFOLK

    But now return we to the false Duke Humphrey.

CARDINAL

    No more of him; for I will deal with him

    That henceforth he shall trouble us no more.

    And so break off, the day is almost spent.

    [*aside*] Lord Suffolk, you and I must talk of that

       event.

                              (3.1.321–5)

9.2   Q1

    Queene. Suffolke remember what you haue to do.

And you Lord Cardinall concerning Duke Humphrey,

Twere good that you did see to it in time,

Come let vs go, that it may be performde.

                          (TLN 1158–61)

10.1 The following is displaced by Q1

ALL

No, no, and therefore we'll have his head.

BROTHER

Well, seeing gentle words will not prevail,

Assail them with the army of the King.

(4.2.162–4)

10.2 Q1

Stafford. Well sirrha, wilt thou yeeld thy selfe vnto the Kings mercy, and he will pardon thee and these, their outrages and rebellious deeds?

Cade. Nay, bid the King come to me and he will, and then ile pardon him, or otherwaies ile haue his Crowne tell him, ere it be long.

(TLN 1674–9)

11. Added after 4.7.117 'tongue can tell' is the following sequence.

Enter *Robin.*

Robin. O Captaine, London bridge is a fire.

Cade. Runne to Billingsgate, and fetche pitch and flaxe and squench it.

Enter *Dicke* and a Sargiant.

Sargiant. Iustice, iustice, I pray you sir, let me haue iustice of this fellow here.

Cade. Why what has he done?

Sarg. Alasse sir he has rauisht my wife.

Dicke. Why my Lord he would haue rested me,

And I went and and entred my Action in his wiues paper house.

Cade. Dicke follow thy sute in her common place,

You horson villaine, you are a Sargiant youle,

Take any man by the throate for twelue pence,

And rest a man when hees at dinner,
And haue him to prison ere the meate be out of his mouth.
Go Dicke take him hence, cut out his toong for cogging,
Hough him for running, and to conclude,
Bra[n]e him with his owne mace.

> *Exet* with the Sargiant.
> (TLN 1834–53)

12. 4.9 is completely rewritten and almost halved in Q, as follows:

> Enter King *Henry* and the Queene, and *Somerset.*
> *King.* Lord Somerset, what newes here you of the Rebell Cade?
> *Som.* This, my gratious Lord, that the Lord Say is don to
> death, And the Citie is almost sackt.
> *King.* Gods will be done, for as he hath decreede, so must it be:
> And be it as he please, to stop the pride of those rebellious men.
> *Queene.* Had the noble Duke of Suffolke bene aliue,
> The Rebell Cade had bene supprest ere this,
> And all the rest that do take part with him.
> Enter the Duke of *Buckingham* and *Clifford*, with the
>   Rebels, with halters about their necks.
> *Cliff.* Long liue King Henry, Englands lawfull King,
> Loe here my Lord, these Rebels are subdude,
> And offer their liues before your hignesse feete.
> *King.* But tell me Clifford, is there Captaine here.
> *Cliff.* No, my gratious Lord, he is fled away, but proclamations
> are sent forth, that he that can but bring his head, shall haue a
> thousand crownes. But may it please your Maiestie, to pardon
> these their faults, that by that traitors meanes were thus misled.
> *King.* Stand vp you simple men, and giue God praise,
> For you did take in hand you know not what,
> And go in peace obedient to your King,
> And liue as subjects, and you shall not want,
> Whilst Henry liues, and weares the English Crowne.
> *All.* God saue the King, God saue the King.

King. Come let vs hast to London now with speed,
That solemne pro[f]essions may be sung,
In laud and honour of the God of heauen,
And triumphs of this happie victorie.   (*Exet omnes.*
                                        (TLN 1898–1926)

13.1 This edition

OLD CLIFFORD
    What seest thou in me, York? Why dost thou pause?
YORK
    With thy brave bearing should I be in love,
    But that thou art so fast mine enemy.
OLD CLIFFORD
    Nor should thy prowess want praise and esteem,
    But that 'tis shown ignobly and in treason.
YORK
    So let it help me now against thy sword
    As I in justice and true right express it.
OLD CLIFFORD
    My soul and body on the action both!
YORK
    A dreadful lay! Address thee instantly.
            [*They fight, and Old Clifford falls.*]
OLD CLIFFORD
    La fin couronne les oeuvres. [*Dies.*]
YORK
    Thus war hath given thee peace, for thou art still.
    Peace with his soul, heaven, if it be thy will!   [*Exit.*]
                                        (5.2.19–30)

13.2 Q1

    Yorke. Now Clifford, since we are singled here alone,
Be this the day of doome to one of vs,

For now my heart hath sworne immortall hate
To thee, and all the house of Lancaster.
    Cliffood. And here I stand, and pitch my foot to thine,
Vowing neuer to stir, till thou or I be slaine.
For neuer shall my heart be safe at rest,
Till I haue spoyld the hatefull house of Yorke.
      Alarmes, and they fight, and *Yorke* kils *Clifford.*
    Yorke. Now Lancaster sit sure, thy sinowes shrinke,
Come fearefull Henry grouelling on thy face,
Yeeld vp thy Crowne vnto the Prince of Yorke.
                           Exet Yorke.
                      (TLN 2153–65)

14.1 This edition

YOUNG CLIFFORD
    Shame and confusion! All is on the rout,
    Fear frames disorder, and disorder wounds
    Where it should guard. O war, thou son of hell,
    Whom angry heavens do make their minister,
    Throw in the frozen bosoms of our part
    Hot coals of vengeance! Let no soldier fly.
    He that it truly dedicate to war
    Hath no self-love; nor he that loves himself
    Hath not essentially, but by circumstance,
    The name of valour. [*Sees his dead father.*]
                  O, let the vile world end,
    And the premised flames of the last day
    Knit earth and heaven together!
    Now let the general trumpet blow his blast,
    Particularities and petty sounds
    To cease! Wast thou ordained, dear father,
    To lose thy youth in peace and to achieve
    The silver livery of advised age,
    And, in thy reverence and thy chair-days, thus

To die in ruffian battle? Even at this sight
My heart is turned to stone, and while 'tis mine
It shall be stony. York not our old men spares;
No more will I their babes; tears virginal
Shall be to me even as the dew to fire,
And beauty, that the tyrant oft reclaims,
Shall to my flaming wrath be oil and flax.
Henceforth I will not have to do with pity.
Meet I an infant of the house of York,
Into as many gobbets will I cut it
As wild Medea young Absyrtus did.
In cruelty will I seek out my fame.
Come, thou new ruin of old Clifford's house;
  [*He takes him up on his back.*]
As did Aeneas old Anchises bear,
So bear I thee upon my manly shoulders;
But then Aeneas bare a living load,
Nothing so heavy as these woes of mine.
                              [*Exit with the body.*]
                                   (5.2.31–65)

14.2 Q1

  Yoong Clifford. Father of Comberland,
Where may I seeke my aged father forth?
O! dismall sight, see where he breathlesse lies,
All smeard and weltred in his luke-warme blood,
Ah, aged pillar of all Comberlands true house,
Sweete father, to thy murthred ghoast I sweare,
Immortall hate vnto the house of Yorke,
Nor neuer shall I sleepe secure one night,
Till I haue furiously reuengde thy death,
And left not one of them to breath on earth.

          He takes him vp on his backe.

And thus as old Ankyses sonne did beare
His aged father on his manly backe,
And fought with him against the bloodie Greeks,
Euen so will I. But staie, heres one of them,
To whom my soule hath sworne immortall hate.
    Enter *Richard*, and then *Clifford* laies downe his father,
      fights with him, and *Richard* flies away againe.
Out crooktbacke villaine, get thee from my sight,
But I will after thee, and once againe
When I haue borne my father to his Tent,
Ile trie my fortune better with thee yet.
            Exet yoong *Clifford* with his
                father.

                        (TLN 2167–90)

Q3/Q1 variants

In the *Textual Companion* (180, 182, 186) William Montgomery discusses the major variants of Q3 from Q1. He believes that the Q3 variants which contaminate F either came about through compositorial copy-stretching, or that Q3 had access to a supplementary report not available to Q1. For further discussion of Q3 see the Introduction, pp. 129–35.

1.1   This edition

GLOUCESTER
    Methought this staff, mine office-badge in court,
    Was broke in twain; by whom I have forgot
    But, as I think, it was by th' Cardinal;
    And on the pieces of the broken wand
    Were placed the heads of Edmund, Duke of Somerset,
    And William de la Pole, first Duke of Suffolk.

                        (1.2.25–30)

1.2   Q1

> *Humphrey.*
> (. . .) This my staffe mine Office badge in Court,
> Was broke in two, and on the ends were plac'd,
> The heads of the Cardinall of *Winchester*,
> And *William de la Poule* first Duke of *Suffolke.*

(TLN 221–4)

1.3   Q3

> *Hum.*
> (. . .) That this my staffe, mine Office badge in Court,
> Was broke in twaine, by whom I cannot gesse:
> But as I thinke by the Cardinall. What it bodes
> God knowes; and on the ends were plac'd
> The heads of *Edmund* Duke of *Somerset*,
> And *William de la Pole* first Duke of *Suffolke.*

(8)

2.1   This edition

ELEANOR
> Yes, my good lord, I'll follow presently.
> > [*Exeunt Gloucester and Messenger.*]
> Follow I must; I cannot go before
> While Gloucester bears this base and humble mind.
> Were I a man, a duke and next of blood,
> I would remove these tedious stumbling-blocks
> And smooth my way upon their headless necks.
> And, being a woman, I will not be slack
> To play my part in Fortune's pageant. –

(1.2.60–7)

2.2 Q1

> *Elnor.* Ile come after you, for I cannot go before,
> But ere it be long, Ile go before them all,
> Despight of all that seeke to crosse me thus,
>
> (TLN 251–3)

2.3 Q3

> *Elnor.* Ile come after you, for I cannot go before,
> As long as Gloster bears this base and humble minde:
> Were I a man, and Protector as he is,
> I'de reach to'th crowne, or make some hop headlesse.
> And being but a women, ile not behind
> For playing of my part, in spite of all that seek to crosse me thus:
>
> (9)

3.1 This edition

QUEEN
> Strangers in court do take her for the Queen.
> She bears a duke's revenues on her back
> And in her heart she scorns our poverty.
>
> (1.3.80–2)

3.2 Q1

> *Queene.*
> (. . .) As strangers in the Court takes her for the Queene.
> The other day she vanted to her maides,
>
> (TLN 353–4)

3.3   Q3

Queene.

(. . .) As strangers in the Court take her for Queene:
She beares a Dukes whole reuennewes on her backe.
The other day she vanted to her maides,

(12)

4.1   This edition

SUFFOLK
(. . .) My Lord Protector's hawks do tower so well,
They know their master loves to be aloft,
And bears his thoughts above his falcon's pitch.
GLOUCESTER
My lord, 'tis but a base ignoble mind
That mounts no higher than a bird can soar.

(2.1.10–14)

4.2   Q1

Suffolke.

(. . .) My Lord Protectors Hawke done towre so well,
He knowes his maister loues to be aloft.
Humphrey. Faith my Lord, it is but a base minde
That can sore no higher then a Falkons pitch.

(TLN 561–4)

4.3   Q3

Suff.

(. . .) My Lord Protectors hawkes do towre so well.
They know their master sores a Faulcons pitch.
Hum. Faith my Lord, it's but a base minde.
That sores no higher then a bird can sore.

(18)

5.1 This edition

YORK

> (. . .) To make commotion, as full well he can,
> Under the title of John Mortimer.
> In Ireland have I seen this stubborn Cade

(3.1.357–9)

5.2 Q1

> *York.*
> (. . .) Vnder the title of Iohn Mortemer,
> To raise commotion, and by that meanes
> I shall perceiue how the common people

(TLN 1170–2)

5.3 Q3

> *Yorke.*
> (. . .) Vnder the title of *Iohn Mortimer,*
> (For he is like him euery kinde of way)
> To raise commotion, and by that meanes
> I shall perceiue how the common people

(35)

APPENDIX 3
'RECOLLECTIONS' IN Q1

Offered below is a selection of examples which some critics and scholars have claimed are memorial recollections or echoes of other plays, inadvertently included by the reporters of Q1 (*The Contention*).[1] Given the acknowledged commonplace nature of humanist writing and the fact of authorial imitation, however, some contemporary experts remain sceptical and have reinvestigated the whole issue of memorial report.[2] I have deliberately included what seem to me weaker instances, as examples for the reader of the variety of 'evidence' cited in this area of textual criticism. The persuasive instances, for example from *3H6* (1.2), *Tit* (1) and *Edward II* (3), suggest the likelihood of memorial influence, but the highly doubtful quotations (see *R3* (1) and *Arden of Feversham* (1)) support the need for scepticism in assessing scholars' claims for the extent of such 'recollection'.

The following sequences below lay out, for each play, the dialogue recollected, followed by the 'echoes' in *Q1*, then the relevant passage from *2 Henry VI* for comparison. Quotations are from editions of first quartos, as indicated in the notes.

1.   *1 Henry VI*

1.1 But all the whole inheritance I giue
      That doth belong vnto the House of *Yorke*,
      From whence you spring, by Lineall Descent.

                                        (*1H6*, F TLN 1381–3)

---

1. See Alexander (91 ff), Cairncross (182–5), Hattaway (236–4) and Hart *Copies* (354–61).
2. See Maguire, particularly 159–67.

The right and title of the house of Yorke,
To Englands Crowne by liniall desent.

(Q1, TLN 738–9)

In crauing your opinion of my Title,
Which is infallible, to Englands Crowne.

(*2H6*, F TLN 963–4)

1.2 What ransome must I pay before I passe?

(*1H6*, F 2510)

And let them paie their ransomes ere they passe.

(Q1, TLN 1473)

Heere shall they make their ransome on the sand,

(*2H6*, F TLN 2179)

2.   *3 Henry VI*

2.1 And he that casts not vp his cap for ioie,
Shall for the offence make forfeit of his head.

(*True Tragedy*, O 2.1.196–7)

That he that breakes a sticke of *Gloster's* groue,
Shall for th'offence, make forfeit of his head.

(Q1, TLN 226–7)

That he that breakes a sticke of Glosters groue,
Shall loose his head for his presumption.

(*2H6*, F TLN 307–8)

2.2 As I bethinke me, you should not be king
Till our *Henry* had shooke hands with death,

(*True Tragedy*, O 1.4.101–2)

And so thinke I Madame, for as you know,
If our King Henry had shooke hands with death,

(Q1, TLN 1107–8)

(Not in *2H6*, see 3.1.233–40)

2.3 Awaie my Lord for vengance comes along with him:
Nay stay not to expostulate make hast,

(*True Tragedy*, O 2.5.134–5)

Away my Lord, and flie to London straight,
Make hast, for vengeance comes along with them,
Come stand not to expostulate, lets go.

(Q1, TLN 2194–6)

Away, my Lord, you are slow, for shame, away.

(*2H6*, F TLN 3297)

3.   *Richard III*[3]

As I intend to prosper and repent,
So thriue I in my dangerous attempt,

(*R3*, Q1 4.4.397–8)

Clifford farewell, as I entend to prosper well to day,

(Q1, TLN 2150)

As I intend Clifford to thriue to day,

(*2H6*, F TLN 3237)

4.   *Titus Andronicus*[4]

4.1 Which dreads not yet their liues destruction.

(*Tit*, Q1 2.3.50)

---

3. *Richard the Third 1597* (Oxford, 1959).
4. *Titus Andronicus 1600*, A Facsimile by Charles Praetorius (London, n.d.).

And thousands more must follow after me,
That dreads not yet their liues destruction.

(Q1, TLN 1064–5)

For thousands more, that yet suspect no perill,

(*2H6*, F TLN 1452)

4.2 Oh reuerent Tribunes . . .

reuerse the doome of death . . .

My euerlasting doome of banishment.

(*Tit*, Q1 3.1.23–4, 51)

Oh Henry, reuerse the doome of gentle Suffolkes banishment.

(Q1, TLN 1347–8)

Oh *Henry*, let me pleade for gentle *Suffolke*.

(*2H6*, F TLN 2003)

4.3 Then sit we downe and let vs all consult,
My sonne and I will haue the wind of you:
Keepe there, now talke at pleasure of your safety.

(*Tit*, Q1 4.2.132–4)

Then sit we downe againe my Lord Cardinall,
Suffolke, Buckingham, Yorke, and Somerset.
Let vs consult of proud Duke Humphries fall.
In mine opinion it were good he dide,
For safetie of our King and Common-wealth.

(Q1, TLN 1102–6)

This *Gloster* should be quickly rid the World,
To rid vs from the feare we haue of him.

(*2H6*, F 1535–6)

4.4 . . . lay hands on them, / . . . binde them sure,

(*Tit*, Q1 5.2.159, 161)

> . . . laie hands on them, and bind them sure,
>
> > (Q1, TLN 528)

> . . . Lay hands vpon these Traytors, and their trash:
>
> > (*2H6*, F TLN 671)

5.   *The Spanish Tragedy*[5] (Thomas Kyd)

> I saw more sights then thousand tongues can tell,
> Or pennes can write, or mortall harts can think.
>
> > (*The Spanish Tragedy*, Q1 TLN 60–1)

> . . . as free as hart can thinke, or toong can tell.
>
> > (Q1, TLN 1833–4)

> . . . as free as heart can wish, or tongue can tell.
>
> > (*2H6*, F 2756–7)

6.   *Edward II*[6] (Christopher Marlowe)

6.1 Nay, all of them conspire to crosse me thus,
> But if I liue ile tread vpon their heads,
>
> > (*Edward II*, TLN 940–1)

> But ere it be long, Ile go before them all,
> Despight of all that seeke to crosse me thus,
>
> > (Q1, TLN 252–3)

> Follow I must, I cannot go before
>
> > (*2H6*, F TLN 336)

6.2 The wilde Oneyle, with swarms of Irish Kernes,
> Liues vncontroulde within the English pale,
>
> > (*Edward II*, TLN 1012–13)

5. *The Spanish Tragedy (1592)*, The Malone Society Reprints (Oxford, 1948).
6. *Edward the Second by Christopher Marlowe 1594*, The Malone Society Reprints (Oxford, 1925).

The wilde Onele my Lords, is vp in Armes,
With troupes of Irish Kernes that vncontrold,
Doth plant themselues within the English pale.

(Q1, TLN 1125–7)

Th'vnciuill Kernes of Ireland are in Armes,

(*2H6*, F TLN 1615)

6.3 My lord, I see your loue to *Gaueston*
Will be the ruine of the realme and you,
For now the wrathfull nobles threaten warres,
And therefore brother banish him for euer.

(*Edward II*, TLN 1058–61)

They say by him they feare the ruine of the realme.
And therefore if you loue your subiects weale,
They wish you to banish him from foorth the land.

(Q1, TLN 1328–30)

They say, in him they feare your Highnesse death . . .
Makes them thus forward in his Banishment.

(*2H6*, F TLN 1961, 1965)

6.4 Did you regard the honor of your name?. . .
As though your highnes were a schoole boy still.
And must be awde and gouernd like a child.

(*Edward II*, TLN 1397, 1410–11)

And nere regards the honour of his name,
But still must be protected like a childe,
And gouerned by that ambitious Duke,

(Q1, TLN 347–9)

What, shall King *Henry* be a Pupill still,
Vnder the surly *Glosters* Gouernance?

(*2H6*, F TLN 432–3)

6.5 And leuie armes against your lawfull king?
$$\textit{(Edward II, TLN 1605)}$$

To leauy Armes against his lawfull King.
$$\textit{(Q1, TLN 2073)}$$

Makes him oppose himselfe against his King.
$$\textit{(2H6, F TLN 3130)}$$

6.6 But hath your grace no other proofe then this?
$$\textit{(Edward II, TLN 2821–2)}$$

But haue you no greater proofes then these?
$$\textit{(Q1, TLN 1268)}$$

Than you belike suspect these Noblemen,
As guilty of Duke *Humfries* timelesse death.
$$\textit{(2H6, F TLN 1890–1)}$$

6.7 I, lead me whether you will, euen to my death . . .
Nay, to my death, for too long haue I liued,
$$\textit{(Edward II, TLN 2506, 2864)}$$

Euen to my death, for I haue liued too long.
$$\textit{(Q1, TLN 815)}$$

Welcome is Banishment, welcome were my Death
$$\textit{(2H6, F TLN 1067–8)}$$

7.   *Dr Faustus*[7] (Christopher Marlowe)

7.1 . . . of this centricke earth . . .

. . . in twinckling of an eie.
$$\textit{(Dr Faustus, TLN 666, 1356)}$$

---

7. W. W. Greg (ed.). *Marlowe's Doctor Faustus 1604–1616* (Oxford, 1950). The *Dr Faustus* references were first pointed out to Hattaway by Eric Rasmussen.

To pierce the bowels of this Centricke earth,
And hither come in twinkling of an eye,

(Q1, TLN 503–4)

(Not in *2H6*, cf. 1.4.15–22.3)

7.2 Now *Faustus*, what wouldst thou haue me do?
(*Dr Faustus*, TLN 280)

Now *Bullenbrooke* what wouldst thou haue me do?
(Q1, TLN 508)

Aske what thou wilt; that I had sayd, and one.
(*2H6*, F TLN 653–4)

8. *Arden of Feversham*[8] (Anon.)

8.1 Ah neighbors a sudden qualm came ouer my heart
(TLN 2331)

Pardon my Lord, a sodain qualme came ouer my hart,
(Q1, TLN 79)

Pardon me gracious Lord,
Some sodaine qualme hath strucke me at the heart,
(*2H6*, F TLN 59–60)

8.2 Hell fyre and wrathfull vengeance light on me,
(TLN 347)

Hell fire and vengeance go along with you,
(Q1, TLN 1356)

Mischance and Sorrow goe along with you . . .
And three-fold Vengeance tend vpon your steps.
(*2H6*, F TLN 2014, 2018)

---

8. *Arden of Feversham 1592*, The Malone Society Reprints (Oxford, 1947).

APPENDIX 4
DOUBLING CHART

Actor	Role	1.1	1.2	1.3	1.4	2.1	2.2	2.3	2.4	3.1	3.2	3.3
1	King	26		9		35		27		43	76	15
2	Queen†	9	17	58		10		12		68	128	
3	Gloucester	59		22		71		14	40	69	0	
	Cade											
4	Eleanor†				4				55			
5	York	56	51	7	30		58	1		115		
6	Suffolk	20		15		13		10		62	97	
	Young Clifford			45				2				
7	Warwick	16		7			17			0	64	3
	Butcher											
8	Cardinal	31		3		24				30	2	14
	Old Clifford											
9	Salisbury	30		0			9			0	28	1
	Saye											
10	Buckingham	8		8	8	12				4		
	Lieutenant				3							
11	Hume		28			Si23		11				
12	Peter			13	St*					At*		
13	Bolingbroke				22	T*			C*	At*	At*	
14	Horner			10		T*		9	C*			

Actor	Role	1.1	1.2	1.3	1.4	2.1	2.2	2.3	2.4	3.1	3.2	3.3
15	Somerset	7				B2			Sy7	7	1	
16	2 Petitioner		3	5		F*		D*	0f*		1M5	
17	Messenger			6		T4			Of*	P6	2M2	
18	1 Petitioner			10		MB*		1N3	Sh4	H*	C*	
19	Servant				Gu*	MB*		Gu*	2		C2	
20	Guard	0		0	0	Ma2		0	Se*		V11	
21	Attendant/Other					T*		2N2	C*		C2	
22	Guard	0		0	So*	F*		3H2		H*		
23	Attendant			G*	Sc*	T*		D*	H*	0	0	
24	Spirit†				9			1A†1				
25	Jourdain†				4			2A†2				
26	Simpcox's Wife†					8		3A†3				

#	4.1	4.2	4.3	4.4	4.5	4.6	4.7	4.8	4.9	4.10	5.1	5.2	5.3	Lines
1				17					31		32	1		312
2				14							9	11		319
3										41				292
4														238
5	59	82	13			10	65	27			90	13	12	118
6											3	42		399
7		28	4	7		4	11	0	0		8	12	6	298
8				5				27	3		21	5		45
9							41	10	3		14		7	133
10	64									142	16			47
11		R*	R*				R*	R*	R*		19			104
12		St16	St*								Ri10	Ri6	Ri9	56
13		G21	G*				G1	G*	G*		E1			89
14		Ni17	Ni*				Ni6	Ni*	Ni*					48
														74
														64
														105
														65
														23
														42

	4.1	4.2	4.3	4.4	4.5	4.6	4.7	4.8	4.9	4.10	5.1	5.2	5.3	Lines
15	0*	Br7	Br*				Go*		2		3	0		41
16	W19	S*		11	Gi*		On*				S*		S*	30
17		Cl3	Mi*			S1	S*	Mi*		Im*				29
18		Mt6	Sa*				Mi*	Sa*			S*	0*	S*	14
19	0*	Sa*			Gi*		Me6			Im*		0*		10
20	1G7	We17		Me5		R*	We4		Me8		At*	0		42
21	2G1	R*			Sc8		R*				0		S*	18
22	Mr1	S*			1Ci4		S*				S*		S*	11
23	Mt1	D*					D*				D*		D*	6
24														10
25														6
26														11

KEY

†boy's part   *non-speaking part

A Apprentice	E Edward	Im Iden's man	Mt Mate	R Rebel	Si Simpcox
At Attendant	F Falconer	M Murderer	N Neighbour	Ri Richard	So Southwell
B Beadle	G Gentleman	Ma Mayor	Ni Nick	S Soldier	St Stafford
Br Brother	Go Gough	MB Mayor's Brother	O Other	Sa Sawyer	Sy Stanley
C Commoner	Gu Guard	Me Messenger	Of Officer	Sc Scales	T Townsman
Ci Citizen	H Herald	Mi Michael	On One	Se Servant	V Vaux
D Drummer	I Iden	Mr Master	P Post	Sh Sheriff	W Whitmore
					We Weaver

APPENDIX 5
SOURCES

There is general agreement among editors and critics that Shakespeare drew primarily upon the chronicles of Hall and Holinshed, sometimes turned to Grafton, used Foxe specifically for the Simpcox miracle scene, and occasionally took from Fabyan and Hardyng. The main endeavour of scholarship has been to try to establish a primary, or leading, historical source. Cairncross (xl) considered Hall the chief source and was followed by Bullough (90) who also favoured Grafton. More recently Hattaway (68–9) considered the 1587 second edition of Holinshed as the primary source. In his original research work Brockbank (*Myth*, 30) noted that 'Seventeen of the twenty-three scenes of *2 Henry VI* can be illustrated at choice from Holinshed, Grafton or Hall.' Law ('Chronicles', 19–20) provided a useful tabulation which aligns the act and scene divisions of the play, plus the historical chronology, against the page numbers of the source materials in Hall and Holinshed. Brockbank anticipated Hattaway by arguing that the second edition of Holinshed, not the first of 1577, was Shakespeare's source. His argument in part derived from his recognition of the error of McKerrow's evidence ('Note') for Shakespeare's use of the first edition.

By McKerrow's time the established authority on the sources of the English histories was W. G. Boswell-Stone's *Shakespeare's Holinshed* (1896). Boswell-Stone's volume reprinted the relevant sections of the chronicle above an impressive foundation of learned footnotes. But as far as one particular detail of *2 Henry VI* is concerned, Boswell-Stone's procedure went beyond what today would be considered acceptable scholarly practice. In act 2.3, the Duke of Gloucester bids farewell to his wife Eleanor, who is being escorted by Sir John Stanley to the Isle of Man as punishment for her crime (see LN 2.3.13). The name of Sir John Stanley appears in both the first and second editions of Holinshed. When Boswell-Stone compiled his volume he knew that this was an error and silently emended his copy with the correct name of the official, Sir Thomas Stanley: though he provided a footnote he did not make clear what he had done. McKerrow accepted the amended name as an accurate record of the 1587 edition and took what he considered to be the discrepancy in the 1577 edition as evidence towards his argument that Shakespeare used this earlier text as a source for *2 Henry VI*.

There is a scholarly consensus, then, that Shakespeare relied chiefly on Hall and Holinshed for the documentary facts. The editions quoted throughout this work are as follows: Edward Hall, *The Union of the Two Noble and Illustre Families of Lancaster and York* (rep. 1809); Raphael Holinshed, *The Chronicles of England, Scotland and Ireland* (rep. 1809, 6 vols, references are to vol. 3 of this edition, unless otherwise stated). The major question of the artistic and critical response to the inherent ideology of Tudor historiography, then and now, has been dwelt on extensively in the Introduction. The way in which Shakespeare variously used historical materials is illustrated throughout the commentary, and may be further touched on here under three convenient categories. First, although Shakespeare relied on Hall and Holinshed, he was occasionally eclectic and would draw on small detail from other sources. Second, Shakespeare recognized the dramatic potential to be gained from the need to telescope selected historical events. Third, his modifications of and additions to historical sources gave him the opportunity to experiment with stage business and scenic development. Some examples will illustrate these categories.

Consider the detail of Jack Cade's 'sallet', the military headgear that is named at 4.10.11, in Iden's garden, just before the rebel's end. Earlier in the rebellion, when Cade defeats the Staffords, we learn from Hall that Cade 'apparaled hym selfe in their rych armure' (220), whereas Holinshed gives a particular detail; Cade 'apparelled himselfe in sir Humfries brigandine set full of guilt nailes' (224). Fabyan, however, following fifteenth-century prede- cessors (see 4.3.9–10n.), goes further: 'he . . . did on hym his bryganders set with gylt nayle, and his salet and gylt sporis' (623). As Shakespeare took the name of the armourer, Thomas Horner (1.3.25–6) (which does not appear in Hall or Holinshed), from Fabyan's identification of one of the sheriffs at the combat ('Robert Horne', 618), it seems reasonable to assume that he had looked over other parts of the chronicle and the 'salet' stuck in his mind. In Cade's soliloquy (4.10.1–15) before Iden's entry, the pun on sallet as headgear and sallet as food serves as a dramatic focus for place, body language and actual speech, as the exhausted and starved rebel leader loosens and removes his helmet. The semiotic catalyst naturally enacts a situation which might otherwise be rendered as biographical statement, as the audience shares in Cade's revealing reverie rather than merely listening to a speech. The actor's face is an automatic focus for an audience. In Shakespeare's visual imagination, the dynamic utility of a prop associated with the head to negotiate the responses of actor to audience is fully realized, and is developed further with the crown of *2 Henry IV* (4.5) and the mirror in *Richard II* (4.1), and is at its most pungent with Yorick's skull in *Hamlet* (5.1).

Bullough (98) provides some discussion of the complex tele- scoping of the historical events of 1452–55 in 5.1, which leads to the battle of St Albans in the following scene. Another example is Shakespeare's decision to integrate into the drama the affair of Eleanor's witchcraft, trial and banishment, which actually took place in 1441, four years before the arrival of Queen Margaret and six years before the parliament at Bury St Edmunds. This dramatic licence created the opportunity for multiple dramatic possibilities, not least the enmity between these noble ladies. The technique which Shakespeare developed to accommodate such material was that of scenic contrast by interspersing different groups and actions. Consider the close of Act 2 and the opening of Act 3.

In Hall (202) and Holinshed (203), the public penance of Eleanor is accounted for in a couple of lines (see 2.4 headnote). Shakespeare's scene, of little more than one hundred lines, does so much with this. The shock of Eleanor's entry derives from the indignity of her penitential white sheet (the garb of a punished prostitute), in contrast with her earlier splendid costumes, to which she refers at l.108. But the deeper drama explores the tension between justice, politics and simple human emotion. At the beginning and end of the scene the cue word for Gloucester is 'tears' (ll. 16, 86). Private emotion is in conflict with public office, as the Duke is now completely compromised in his dual role of husband and former dignified Protector, both bidding farewell and observing that justice is done. The audience recognizes that Eleanor's warning here about the traps set by York, Suffolk and the cardinal does not come from personal bitterness, just as we recognize that Gloucester's reply asserting the inviolability of personal probity is fatally naive. Further, when the herald enters to announce the parliament at Bury, an arrangement Gloucester describes as 'close dealing' (l.73) since it has been made without consultation, we recognize the full danger to the Duke, whereas he appears to see only the insulting failure of protocol.

With the historical telescoping of the next scene at Bury (3.1), Suffolk in the welter of accusation voices the charge that Gloucester suborned the 'devilish practices' of Eleanor. In contrast to the pathos of the preceding scene, here all is ruthless machiavellianism as the King is pressured by those around him. On his entry Gloucester is arrested for treason, then murdered shortly after. Using the freedom of artistic licence combined with the necessity of selection, Shakespeare dramatizes the paradox that humanity and faith in justice can create circumstances in which inhumanity and injustice thrive. Shakespeare was fascinated by the Eleanor story and considerably developed her role throughout Acts 1 and 2. The fate of Eleanor is closely tied to that of Gloucester, as we have seen.

To sustain a balanced dramatic development, Shakespeare always links seemingly secondary or minor scenes to major characters, and we can see this in the relationship of York to the chroniclers' report of the armourer, which is modified and expanded to contribute to something larger than local action. The 'History, justice, drama' discussion within the Introduction looks closely at the culmination of the armourer story in the combat of 2.3. Here I shall look at the related events of 1.3.

Once more the report of the armourer and his man takes up just a few lines in Hall (207-8) and Holinshed (210). As we have seen above, Shakespeare turned to Fabyan and used the further detail he found there. The whole business of the treason trial could have been confined to the one combat scene, like that of the St Albans miracle affair (2.1), but Shakespeare chose to alternate the Eleanor and armourer stories. As the Eleanor plot implicates Gloucester, so Shakespeare chose to implicate York, but linking his name to the armourer; he has no association with the armourer in the chronicles.

With the group of petitioners at the opening of 1.3 Shakespeare's invention introduces the disaffected commoners who are to have such a large part in the play. They seek justice from the Lord Protector against the Cardinal and the Duke of Suffolk for various kinds of criminal appropriation. Peter, the armourer's man, bears a petition against the treason of his master for declaring York to be rightful heir to the crown. Unfortunately, the commoners encounter the scornful Margaret and Suffolk rather than Gloucester. Shakespeare anticipates the grievances of the later rebels led by Cade, who is suborned by York, but here Margaret takes such protest as a sign of Gloucester's power, and alone with Suffolk she reveals her resentment of all court factions around the piously uncomprehending Henry. Suffolk's reply confirms the clerk Hume's words in the preceding scene concerning the entrapment of Eleanor, and sets up an expectation of what is to follow. With the entry of the King and his chief courtiers, faction increases with the division over who should take up the regency in France, Somerset or York; Suffolk challenges the authority of Gloucester and Margaret boxes Eleanor's ear. Gloucester supports York for the regency and Suffolk, at this crucial point in court and national politics, having already challenged the Protector, plays his trump card to discredit York (and thus advance his and Margaret's power) by having the armourer and his man brought on stage. The treason charge against York is heard by the King who accepts Gloucester's judgement: York loses the regency to Somerset and the armourer and his man will stand trial by combat. The following scene takes up Eleanor's witchcraft and entrapment. Thus we see how Shakespeare takes a discrete, minor incident from the chronicles and by modification and expansion integrates it into the major movements of plot and history, namely those of class and society, justice and morality, politics and power.

In current historical writing on the late medieval and early modern period there is considerable interest in the representation of rebellion (see Steven Justice). As the commentary and Introduction show, Shakespeare chose in large part to model Cade's uprising on that of the Peasants' Revolt of 1381, but Cade's own 'supplication' is mentioned at 4.4. Reproduced here from Holinshed (222–4) is that supplication (see Caldwell, Appendices A, B and C), for those who wish to compare historical documentation with the late Tudor dramatic representation.

> *The complaint of the commons of Kent,*
> *and causes of their assemblie on the Blackheath*

1.   INPRIMIS, it is openlie noised that Kent should be destroied with a roiall power, & made a wild forrest, for the death of the duke of Suffolke, of which the commons of Kent thereof were neuer giltie.

2.   Item, the king is stirred to liue onelie on his commons, and other men to haue the reuenues of the crowne, the which hath caused pouertie in his excellencie, and great paiments of the people, now late to the king granted in his parlement.

3.   Item, that the lords of his roiall bloud beene put from his dailie presence, and other meane persons of lower nature exalted and made chéefe of his priuie councell, the which stoppeth matters of wrongs done in the realme from his excellent audience, and maie not be redressed as law will; but if bribes and gifts be messengers to the hands of the said councell.

4.   Item, the people of this realme be not paid of debts owing for stuffe and purueiance taken to the vse of the kings houshold, in vndooing of the said people, and the poore commons of the realme.

5.   Item, the kings meniall seruants of houshold, and other persons, asken dailie goods and lands, of impeached or indicted of treason, the which the king granteth anon, yer they so indangered be conuicted. The which causeth the receiuers thereof to inforge labours and meanes applied to the death of such people, so appeached or indicted, by subtill meanes, for couetise of the said grants: and the people so impeached or indicted, though it be vntrue, maie not [b]e committed to the law for their deliuerance, but held still in prison, to their vttermost vndooing & destruction, for couetise of goods.

6.   Item, though diuerse of the poore people and commons of the realme, haue neuer so great right, truth, and perfect title to their land: yet by vntrue claime of infeoffement made vnto duierse states, gentles, and the kings meniall seruants in maintenances against the right, the true owners dare not hold, claime, nor pursue their right.

7.   Item, it is noised by common voices, that the kings lands in France béene aliened and put awaie from the crowne, and his lords and people there destroied with vntrue meanes of treason; of which it is desired, inquiries thorough all the realme to be made how and by whome; & if such traitors maie be found giltie, them to haue execution of law without anie pardon, in example of others.

8.   Item, collectors of the fiftéenth penie in Kent be greatlie vexed and hurt, in paieng great summes of monie in the

excheker, to sue out a writ called Quorum nomina, for the alowance of the barons of the ports, which now is desired, that hereafter in the lieu of the collectors, the barons aforesaid maie sue it out for their ease at their owne costs.

9. Item, the shiriffes and vndershiriffes let to farme their offices and bailiwickes, taking great suertie therefore, the which causeth extortions doone by them and by their bailiffes to the people.

10. Item, simple and poore people that vse not hunting, be greatlie oppressed by indictements feined & doone by the said shiriffes, vndershiriffes, bailiffes, and other of their assent, to cause their increase for paieng of their said farme.

11. Item, they returne in names of inquests in writing into diuerse courts of the king not summoned nor warned, where through the people dailie léese great summes of monie, well nigh to the vttermost of their vndooing: and make leuie of amercements called the gréene wax, more in summes of monie than can be found due of record in the kings books.

12. Item, the ministers of court of Douer in Kent vex and arrest diuerse people thorough all the shire out of Castle ward, passing their bounds and libertie vsed of old time, by diuerse subtill and vntrue meanes and actions falselie feined, taking great fées at their lust in great hurt of the people on all the shire of Kent.

13. Item, the people of the said shire of Kent, maie not have their frée election in the choosing of knights of the shire: but letters béene sent from diuerse estates to the great rulers of all the countrie, the which imbraceth their tenants and other people by force to choose other persons than the cōmons will is.

14. Item, whereas knights of the shire should choose the king collectors indifferentlie without any bri[b]e taking, they haue sent now late to diuerse persons, notifieng them to be collectors: wherevpon gifts and bribes be taken, & so the collectors office is bought and sold extortionouslie at the knights lust.

15. Item, the people be sore vexed in costs and labour, called to the sessions of peace in the said shire, appearing from the

furtherest and vttermost part of the west vnto the east; the which causeth to some men fiue daies iournie: wherevpon they desire the said appearance to be diuided into two parts; the which one part, to appeare in one place; an other part, in an other place; in reléeuing of the gréeuances and intollerable labours & vexations of the said people.

The requests by the capteine of the great assemblie in Kent

INPRIMIS, desireth the capteine of the commons, the welfare of our souereigne lord the king, and all his true lords spirituall and temporall, desiring of our said souereigne lord, and of all the true lords of his councell, he to take in all his demaines, that he maie reigne like a king roiall, according as he is borne our true and christian king annointed: and who so will saie the contrarie, we all will liue and die in the quarell as his true liege men.

Item, desireth the said capteine, that he will auoid all the false progenie and affinitie of the duke of Suffolke, the which beene openlie knowne, and they to be punished after the custome and law of this land, and to take about his noble person the true lords of his roiall bloud of this his realme, that is to saie, the high and mightie prince the duke of Yorke, late exiled from our said souereigne lords presence (by the motion and stirring of the traitorous and false disposed the duke of Suffolke and his affinitie) and the mightie princes & dukes of Excester, Buckingham, and Norffolke, and all the earles and barons of this land: and then shall he be the richest king christian.

Item, desireth the said capteine and commons punishment vnto the false traitors, the which contriued and imagined the death of the high, mightfull and excellent prince the duke of Glocester, the which is too much to rehearse; the which duke was proclaimed as traitor. Vpon the which quarell, we purpose all to liue and die vpon that that it is false.

Item, the duke of Excester, our holie father the cardinall, the noble prince the duke of Warwike, and also the realme of France, the duchie of Normandie, Gascoigne, and Guion, Aniou, and Maine, were deliuered and lost by the meanes of the said traitors: and our true lords, knights, and esquiers, and manie a good yeoman lost and sold yer they went, the which is great pitie to heare, of the great and gréeuous loose to our souereigne lord and his realme.

Item, desireth the said capteine and commons, that all extortions vsed dailie among the common people, might be laid downe, that is to saie, the gréene wax; the which is falselie vsed, to the perpetuall destruction of the kings true commons of Kent. Also the kings Bench, the which is too gréefefull to the shire of Kent, without prouision of our soueriegne lord and his true councell. And also in taking of wheat and other graines, béefe, mutton & all other vittels, the which is importable to the said councell, they maie no longer beare it. And also vnto the statue of labourers, and the great extortioners, the which is to saie the false traitors, Sleg, Cromer, Isle, and Robert Est.

APPENDIX 6
GENEALOGICAL TABLES

1 The House of Lancaster

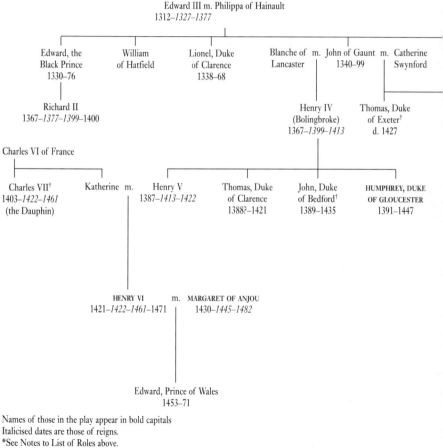

Edward III m. Philippa of Hainault
1312–*1327–1377*

Edward, the
Black Prince
1330–76

William
of Hatfield

Lionel, Duke
of Clarence
1338–68

Blanche of m. John of Gaunt m. Catherine
Lancaster   *1340–99*   Swynford

Richard II
1367–*1377–1399*–1400

Henry IV
(Bolingbroke)
1367–*1399–1413*

Thomas, Duke
of Exeter[†]
d. 1427

Charles VI of France

Charles VII[†]
1403–*1422–1461*
(the Dauphin)

Katherine m.

Henry V
1387–*1413–1422*

Thomas, Duke
of Clarence
1388?–1421

John, Duke
of Bedford[†]
1389–1435

**HUMPHREY, DUKE
OF GLOUCESTER**
1391–1447

HENRY VI   m.   **MARGARET OF ANJOU**
1421–*1422–1461*–1471   1430–*1445–1482*

Edward, Prince of Wales
1453–71

Names of those in the play appear in bold capitals
Italicised dates are those of reigns.
*See Notes to List of Roles above.
[†]Indicates characters only in *Part One*

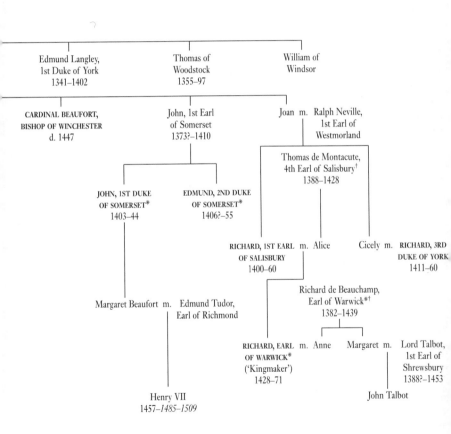

Edmund Langley,
1st Duke of York
1341–1402

Thomas of
Woodstock
1355–97

William of
Windsor

CARDINAL BEAUFORT,
BISHOP OF WINCHESTER
d. 1447

John, 1st Earl
of Somerset
1373?–1410

Joan m. Ralph Neville,
1st Earl of
Westmorland

Thomas de Montacute,
4th Earl of Salisbury†
1388–1428

JOHN, 1ST DUKE
OF SOMERSET*
1403–44

EDMUND, 2ND DUKE
OF SOMERSET*
1406?–55

RICHARD, 1ST EARL m. Alice
OF SALISBURY
1400–60

Cicely m. RICHARD, 3RD
DUKE OF YORK
1411–60

Richard de Beauchamp,
Earl of Warwick*†
1382–1439

Margaret Beaufort m. Edmund Tudor,
Earl of Richmond

RICHARD, EARL m. Anne
OF WARWICK*
('Kingmaker')
1428–71

Margaret m. Lord Talbot,
1st Earl of
Shrewsbury
1388?–1453

Henry VII
1457–*1485–1509*

John Talbot

2 The Houses of York and Mortimer

Edward III m. Philippa of Hainault
1312–1327–1377

Edward, the
Black Prince
1330–76

William
of Hatfield

Lionel, Duke
of Clarence
1338–68

John of Gaunt
Duke of Lancaster
1340–99

Richard II
1367–1377–1399–1400

Philippa m. Edmund Mortimer,
3rd Earl of March

Elizabeth m. Henry Percy
(Hotspur)
1364–1403

Roger Mortimer,
4th Earl of March
1374–98

Sir Edmund
Mortimer,
1376–1409?

John, 7th   m. Elizabeth
Lord Clifford

Edmund Mortimer,
5th Earl of March†
1391–1425

THOMAS, 12TH BARON CLIFFORD
(OLD CLIFFORD)
1414–55

EDWARD IV   m. Elizabeth Woodville
1442–1461–1483   (Lady Grey)
1437?–1492

JOHN, 13TH BARON CLIFFORD
(YOUNG CLIFFORD)
1435?–1461

Edward V
1470–*1483*

Richard
1472–1483

Elizabeth   m.
1465–1503

Henry VII
(Richmond)
1457–1485–1509

Names of those in the play appear in bold capitals
Italicised dates are those of reigns.
*See Notes to List of Roles above.
†Indicates characters only in *Part One*

450

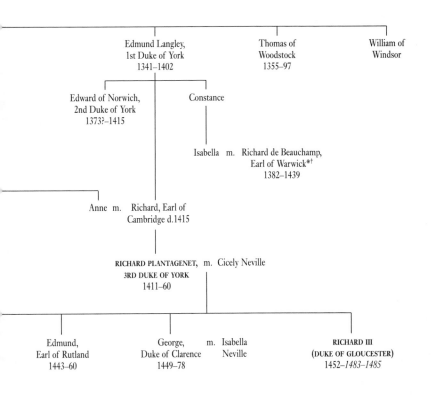

ABBREVIATIONS AND REFERENCES

Unless otherwise stated, the place of publication is London. All references to Shakespeare's works, other than *2H6*, are to *The Riverside Shakespeare*, ed. G. Blakemore Evans (Boston, 1974), with exceptions as indicated. Abbreviations of parts of speech follow the conventions of the *OED*. The Geneva Bible is quoted throughout, unless otherwise noted.

ABBREVIATIONS

ABBREVIATIONS USED IN NOTES

*	precedes commentary notes involving readings altered from the early editions on which this edition is based
anon.	anonymous
conj.	conjectured (by)
ed., eds	editor, editors
edn	edition
LN	longer notes
n.	(in cross-references) commentary note
n.d.	no date
n.p.	no pagination
om.	omitted
opp.	opposite
SD	stage direction
SP	speech prefix
subst.	substantially
this edn	a reading adopted for the first time in this edition
TLN	through line numbering in either Charlton Hinman's Norton Facsimile of *The First Folio of Shakespeare* (New York, 1968) or William Montgomery's edition of Q1, *The First Part of the Contention* (Malone Society Reprints, Oxford, 1985), as indicated
t.n.	textual note
( )	surrounding a reading in the textual notes indicates original spelling; surrounding an editor's or scholar's name indicates a conjectural reading

SHAKESPEARE'S WORKS AND WORKS PARTLY BY SHAKESPEARE

AC	*Antony and Cleopatra*
AW	*All's Well that Ends Well*
AYL	*As You Like It*
CE	*The Comedy of Errors*
Cor	*Coriolanus*
Cym	*Cymbeline*
E3	*King Edward III*
Ham	*Hamlet*
1H4	*King Henry IV, Part 1*
2H4	*King Henry IV, Part 2*
H5	*Henry V*
1H6	*King Henry VI, Part 1*
2H6	*King Henry VI, Part 2*
3H6	*King Henry VI, Part 3*
H8	*King Henry VIII*
JC	*Julius Caesar*
KJ	*King John*
KL	*King Lear*
LC	*A Lover's Complaint*
LLL	*Love's Labour's Lost*
Luc	*The Rape of Lucrece*
MA	*Much Ado About Nothing*
Mac	*Macbeth*
MM	*Measure for Measure*
MND	*A Midsummer Night's Dream*
MV	*The Merchant of Venice*
MW	*The Merry Wives of Windsor*
Oth	*Othello*
Per	*Pericles*
PP	*The Passionate Pilgrim*
R2	*King Richard II*
R3	*King Richard III*
RJ	*Romeo and Juliet*
Son	*Shakespeare's Sonnets*
STM	*Sir Thomas More*
TC	*Troilus and Cressida*
Tem	*The Tempest*
TGV	*The Two Gentlemen of Verona*
Tim	*Timon of Athens*
Tit	*Titus Andronicus*
TN	*Twelfth Night*
TNK	*The Two Noble Kinsmen*
TS	*The Taming of the Shrew*
VA	*Venus and Adonis*
WT	*The Winter's Tale*

REFERENCES

EDITIONS OF SHAKESPEARE COLLATED

Alexander	*The Complete Works*, ed. Peter Alexander (London and Glasgow, 1951)
Ard[1]	*The Second Part of King Henry the Sixth*, ed. H. C. Hart, The Arden Shakespeare (1909)
Ard[2]	*The Second Part of King Henry the Sixth*, ed. Andrew S. Cairncross, The Arden Shakespeare (1957)
Cairncross	See Ard[2]
Cam	*Works*, ed. William George Clark and William Aldis Wright, 9 vols (Cambridge and London, 1863–6)
Cam[1]	*The Second Part of King Henry VI*, ed. John Dover Wilson (Cambridge, 1952)
Cam[2]	*The Second Part of King Henry VI*, ed. Michael Hattaway (Cambridge, 1991)
Capell	*Mr. William Shakespeare His Comedies, Histories and Tragedies*, ed. Edward Capell, 10 vols (1767–8)
Collier	*The Works of William Shakespeare*, ed. John Payne Collier, 8 vols (1842–4)
Delius	*Shakesperes Werke*, ed. Nicolaus Delius, 7 vols (Elberfeld, 1844–53)
Dyce	*The Works of William Shakespeare*, ed. Alexander Dyce, 6 vols (1857)
Dyce[2]	*The Works of William Shakespeare*, ed. Alexander Dyce, 9 vols (1864–7)
Evans	*The Riverside Shakespeare*, ed. G. Blakemore Evans (Boston, 1974)
F, F1	*Comedies, Histories and Tragedies*, The First Folio (1623)
F2	*Comedies, Histories and Tragedies*, The Second Folio (1632)
F3	*Comedies, Histories and Tragedies*, The Third Folio (1663)
F4	*Comedies, Histories and Tragedies*, The Fourth Folio (1685)
Farmer	Richard Farmer, in Johnson Var.
Hanmer	*The Works of Shakspear*, ed. Thomas Hanmer, 6 vols (1743–4)
Harbage	*The Complete Works*, general editor Alfred Harbage (Pelican, rev. edn, 1969)
Hart	See Ard[1]
Hattaway	See Cam[2]
Hudson	*The Complete Works of William Shakespeare*, ed. Henry N. Hudson, 11 vols (1851–6)
Johnson	*The Plays of William Shakespeare*, ed. Samuel Johnson, 8 vols (1765)

Johnson Var.	*The Plays of William Shakespeare*, ed. Samuel Johnson and George Steevens, 10 vols (1773)
Kittredge	*The Complete Works of Shakespeare*, ed. George Lyman Kittredge (Boston, 1936)
Knight	*The Pictorial Edition of the Works of Shakespeare*, ed. Charles Knight, 8 vols (1838–43)
Malone	*The Plays and Poems of William Shakespeare*, ed. Edmond Malone, 10 vols (1790)
Malone[2]	*The Plays and Poems of William Shakespeare*, ed. Edmond Malone, 21 vols (1821)
New Penguin	See Sanders
Oxf	*The Complete Works*, ed. Stanley Wells and Gary Taylor (Oxford, 1986)
Pelican	See Turner & Williams
Pope	*The Works of Shakespear*, ed. Alexander Pope, 6 vols (1723–5)
Q, Q1	*The First Part of the Contention betwixt the Two Famous Houses of York and Lancaster* (1594), facsimile of the Folger Shakespeare Library copy by William Montgomery (Malone Society Reprints, Oxford, 1985)
Q2	*The First Part of the Contention betwixt the Two Famous Houses of York and Lancaster* (1600)
Q3	*The Whole Contention between the Two Famous Houses, Lancaster and York* (1619), facsimile ed. Charles Praetorius (1886)
Qq	Q1, Q2 and Q3
Riv	See Evans
Rowe	*The Works of Mr William Shakespeare*, ed. Nicholas Rowe, 6 vols (1709)
Rowe[2]	*The Works of Mr William Shakespeare*, ed. Nicholas Rowe, 2nd edn, 6 vols (1709)
Rowe[3]	*The Works of Mr William Shakespeare*, ed. Nicholas Rowe, 3rd edn, 8 vols (1714)
Sanders	*The Second Part of King Henry the Sixth*, ed. Norman Sanders (New Penguin, 1981)
Singer	*The Dramatic Works of William Shakespeare*, ed. Samuel Weller Singer, 10 vols (1826)
Steevens	*The Plays of William Shakespeare*, ed. George Steevens, 10 vols (1778)
Steevens[2]	See Johnson Var.
Theobald	*The Works of Shakespeare*, ed. Lewis Theobald, 7 vols (1733)
Turner & Williams	*The Second and Third Parts of King Henry the Sixth*, ed. Robert K. Turner Jr and George Walton Williams, in Harbage

Warburton	*The Works of Shakespeare*, ed. William Warburton, 8 vols (1747)
Wells & Taylor	See Oxf
White	*Works*, ed. Richard Grant White, 12 vols (1857–66)
Wilson	See Cam¹

OTHER WORKS

Abbott	E. A. Abbott, *A Shakespearian Grammar*, New Edition (1881)
Addenbrooke	David Addenbrooke, *The Royal Shakespeare Company* (1974)
Aesop	Aesop, *Fabellae Aesopicae*, transl. J. Camerarius (Lugduni, 1571)
Alexander, 'Henry VI'	Peter Alexander, *Shakespeare's 'Henry VI' and 'Richard III'* (Cambridge, 1929)
Alexander, 'Restoring'	Peter Alexander, 'Restoring Shakespeare: the modern editor's task', *SS* 5 (1952), 1–9
Allen	J. W. Allen, *A History of Political Thought in the Sixteenth Century* (London and New York, 1928)
Altman	Joel B. Altman, *The Tudor Play of Mind* (Berkeley, 1978)
Anglo	Sydney Anglo, *Spectacle Pageantry and Early Tudor Policy* (Oxford, 1969)
Appelbaum	Stanley Appelbaum, *The Triumph of Maximilian I* (New York, 1964)
Apuleius	Apuleius, *The Golden Ass*, trans. William Adlington (1566), Abbey Classics, n.d.
Armstrong, E. A.	E. A. Armstrong, *Shakespeare's Imagination* (1963)
Armstrong, I.	Isobel Armstrong, 'Thatcher's Shakespeare', *Textual Practice*, 3 (1989), 1–14
Artaud	Antonin Artaud, *The Theatre and its Double* (1958)
Augustine	St Augustine, *The City of God*, transl. John Healey, 2 vols (London and New York, 1968)
Babb	Lawrence Babb, *The Elizabethan Malady* (East Lansing, 1951)
Babcock	Barbara Babcock (ed.), *The Reversible World: Symbolic Inversion in Art and Society* (Ithaca and London, 1978)
Bacon	Francis Bacon, *The Philosophical Works of Francis Bacon*, ed. John M. Robertson (1905)
Baldwin, E., *Legislation*	E. Baldwin, *Sumptuarie Legislation and Personal Regulation in England* (Baltimore, 1926)
Baldwin, T. W., *Genetics*	T. W. Baldwin, *On the Literary Genetics of Shakespeare's Plays 1592–1594* (Urbana, 1959)
Baldwin, T. W., *Organisation*	T. W. Baldwin, *The Organisation and Personnel of the Shakespearean Company* (New York, 1927)

Baldwin, T. W., *Small Latine*	T. W. Baldwin, *William Shakspere's 'Small Latine & Less Greeke'*, 2 vols (Urbana, 1944)
Baldwin, W.	William Baldwin, *A Treatise of Moral Philosophy* (1547)
Bale	John Bale, *King Johan* (1548), ed. Barry B. Adams (San Marino, 1969)
Bale's Chronicle	In Flenley, 114–53
Barber	C. L. Barber, *Shakespeare's Festive Comedy* (Princeton, 1959)
Barron	Caroline M. Barron, 'The Government of London and its Relationship with the Crown', unpublished Ph.D., University of London, 1970
Bartholomeus	Bartholomeus Anglicus, *On the Properties of Things*, transl. John of Trevisa, 3 vols (Oxford, 1975)
Barton & Hall	John Barton and Peter Hall, *The Wars of the Roses* (1970)
Baskervill	C. R. Baskervill, *The Elizabethan Jig* (Chicago, 1929)
Bate, *Constitutions*	Jonathan Bate, *Shakespearean Constitutions: Politics, Theatre, Criticism 1730–1830* (Oxford, 1989)
Bate, *Ovid*	Jonathan Bate, *Shakespeare and Ovid* (Oxford, 1993)
Bate, *Titus*	William Shakespeare, *Titus Andronicus*, ed. Jonathan Bate, The Arden Shakespeare (1995)
Beer	Barrett L. Beer (ed.), '"The commoyson in Norfolk, 1549": a narrative of popular rebellion in sixteenth-century England', *Journal of Medieval and Renaissance Studies*, 6 (1976), 73–99
Beier	A. L. Beier, *Masterless Men: The Vagrancy Problem in England 1560–1640* (1985)
Bellamy	J. G. Bellamy, *The Law of Treason in England in the Later Middle Ages* (Cambridge, 1970)
Berry, E. I.	Edward I. Berry, *Patterns of Decay: Shakespeare's Early Histories* (Charlottesville, 1975)
Berry, R.	Ralph Berry, *Shakespearean Structures* (1981)
Bingham	Dennis Bingham, 'Jane Howell's first tetralogy: Brechtian break-out or just good television?', in Bulman & Coursen, 221–9
Blackstone	Sir William Blackstone, *Commentaries on the Laws of England* (1829)
Blake	N. F. Blake, 'Fume/fury in *2 Henry VI*', *N&Q*, 38 (1991), 49–51
Boorde	Andrew Boorde, *The First Book of the Introduction of Knowledge* (*c.* 1548)
Born	Hanspeter Born, 'The date of *2, 3 Henry VI*', *SQ*, 25 (1974), 323–34
Boswell-Stone	W. G. Boswell-Stone, *Shakespeare's Holinshed: The Chronicle and the Historical Plays Compared* (1896)
Boyce	Charles Boyce, *Shakespeare A–Z* (New York, 1990)

Brandes	Georg Brandes, *William Shakespeare: A Critical Study* (1911)
Brecht	Bertolt Brecht, 'The street scene', in Willett, 121–9
Brewer	E. Cobham Brewer, *Dictionary of Phrase and Fable* (London, Paris and Melbourne, 1897)
Bristol	Michael Bristol, *Carnival and Theater: Plebeian Culture and the Structure of Authority in Renaissance England* (New York and London, 1985)
Brockbank, 'Frame'	J. P. Brockbank, 'The frame of disorder – *Henry VI* ', in Brown & Harris, 73–99
Brockbank, 'Myth'	J. P. Brockbank, 'Shakespeare's Historical Myth: A Study of Shakespeare's Adaptations of his Sources in Making the Plays of *Henry VI* and *Richard III* ', unpublished Ph.D. dissertation, University of Cambridge, 1993
Brooke, C. F. T.	C. F. Tucker Brooke, *The Tudor Drama* (1912)
Brooke, N.	Nicholas Brooke, *Shakespeare's Early Tragedies* (1968)
Brown	John Russell Brown, 'Three kinds of Shakespeare', *SS 18* (1965), 147–55
Brown & Harris	John Russell Brown and Bernard Harris (eds), *Early Shakespeare*, Stratford-upon-Avon Studies, 3 (1961)
Browne	Sir Thomas Browne, *Pseudodoxia epidemica*, in *The Works of Sir Thomas Browne*, ed. Charles Sayle, vols 1 and 2 (1904)
Brownlee	Alexander Brownlee, *William Shakespeare and Robert Burton* (Reading, 1960)
Brut	*The Brut; or, The Chronicles of England*, ed. Friedrich W. D. Brie, Early English Text Society, Original Series, No. 131 (1906)
Bullough	Geoffrey Bullough, *Narrative and Dramatic Sources of Shakespeare*, 8 vols (1957–75)
Bulman & Coursen	J. C. Bulman and H. R. Coursen (eds), *Shakespeare on Television* (Hanover, NH, 1988)
Burke	Peter Burke, *The Renaissance Sense of the Past* (1969)
Burt & Archer	Richard Burt and John Michael Archer (eds), *Enclosure Acts* (Ithaca and London, 1994)
Bush	Douglas Bush, 'Notes on Shakespeare's classical mythology', *PQ*, 6 (1927), 295–6
Calderwood	James L. Calderwood, 'Shakespeare's evolving imagery: *2 Henry VI* ', *ES*, 48 (1967), 481–94
Caldwell	Ellen C. Caldwell, 'Jack Cade and Shakespeare's *Henry VI, Part 2* ', *SP*, 42 (1995), 18–79
Calendar	*Calendar of the Patent Rolls, V. Henry VI AD 1446–1452* (1909)
Calvin	John Calvin, *Institutes of the Christian Religion* (Grand Rapids, n.d.)

Camden *Remains*	William Camden, *Remains of a Greater Worke, concerning Britaine* (1623)
Camerarius	See Aesop
Campbell	Lily B. Campbell, *Shakespeare's Histories: Mirrors of Elizabethan Policy* (San Marino, 1947)
Capell	Edward Capell, *Notes and Various Readings to Shakespeare* (1793)
Carroll, D. A., *Groatsworth*	D. Allen Carroll (ed.), *Greene's Groatsworth of Wit* (1592), Medieval and Renaissance Texts and Studies, 114 (New York, 1994)
Carroll, D. A., 'Upstart'	D. Allen Carroll, 'Greene's "vpstart crow" passage: a survey of commentary', *Research Opportunities in Renaissance Drama*, 28 (1985), 111–27
Carroll, W. C., *Fat King*	William C. Carroll, *Fat King, Lean Beggar: Representations of Poverty in the Age of Shakespeare* (Ithaca and London, 1996)
Carroll, W. C., 'Nurse'	William C. Carroll, ' "The nurse of beggary": enclosure, vagrancy, and sedition in the Tudor–Stuart period', in Burt & Archer, 34–47
Carter	Charles H. Carter (ed.), *From the Renaissance to Counter-Reformation* (1966)
Cercignani	Fausto Cercignani, *Shakespeare's Works and Elizabethan Pronunciation* (Oxford, 1981)
Chambers, E. K.	E. K. Chambers, *William Shakespeare: A Study of Facts and Problems*, 2 vols (Oxford, 1930)
Chambers, R. W.	R. W. Chambers, *Man's Unconquerable Mind* (1939)
Champion	Larry S. Champion, ' "Havoc in the commonwealth": perspective, political ideology and dramatic strategy in *Sir John Oldcastle* and the English chronicle plays', *Medieval and Renaissance Drama in England*, 5 (1991), 165–80
Chapman	George Chapman, *Caesar and Pompey* (1603?)
Charlton	H. B. Charlton, *Shakespeare, Politics and Politicians*, The English Association, Pamphlet No. 72 (April 1929)
Charney	Maurice Charney (ed.), *'Bad' Shakespeare: Revaluations of the Shakespeare Canon* (London and Toronto, 1988)
Cheke	Sir John Cheke, *The Hurt of Sedition* (1549), in Holinshed, vol. 3
Cibber	Theophilus Cibber, *Henry VI* (1723)
Cicero	Cicero, *De Officiis* (Loeb, 1937)
Clark	Peter Clark, *The English Alehouse: A Social History 1200–1830* (Harlow, 1983)
Clarke	Mary Clarke, *Shakespeare at the Old Vic* (1958)
Clemen, 'Aspects'	Wolfgang Clemen, 'Some aspects of the *Henry VI* plays', in Edwards *et al.*, 9–24
Clemen, *Development*	Wolfgang Clemen, *The Development of Shakespeare's Imagery* (1951)

Cloud   Random Cloud [Randall McLeod], 'The marriage of good and bad Quartos', *SQ*, 33 (1982), 421–30

Cohn   Norman Cohn, *The Pursuit of the Millennium* (1962)

Collingwood   R. G. Collingwood, *The Idea of History* (Oxford, 1946)

Collinson   Patrick Collinson, 'The English conventicle', in Sheils & Wood, 223–60

Comenius   Joannes Amos Comenius, *Orbis sensualium pictus*, ed. James Bowen (Sydney, 1967)

Contre-League   *Contre-League*, transl. 'E. A.' (1589)

Corbin & Sedge   Peter Corbin and Douglas Sedge (eds), *The Oldcastle Controversy: 'Sir John Oldcastle, Part I' and 'The Famous Victories of Henry V'* (Manchester and New York, 1991)

Courthope   W. J. Courthope, *A History of English Poetry*, vol. 4 (1903)

Craig   Hardin Craig, 'Shakespeare and the history play', in McManaway *et al.*, 55–64

Crane   Milton Crane, 'Shakespeare on television', *SQ*, 12 (1961), 323–7

Cranmer   *Miscellaneous Writings and Letters of Thomas Cranmer, Works*, ed. John Edmund Cox, The Parker Society (Cambridge, 1846), vol. 3

Crowley   Robert Crowley, *The Way to Wealth* (1550), in *Select Works*, Early English Text Society (1872)

Crowne, *Henry*   John Crowne, *Henry the Sixth, the First Part* (1681)

Crowne, *Misery*   John Crowne, *The Misery of Civil War* (1681)

Cruden   Alexander Cruden, *A Complete Concordance to the Old and New Testament* (n.d.; first published 1737)

Culpeper   *Culpeper's Complete Herbal* (Ware, 1995)

Cunnington   C. Willett Cunnington and Phillis Cunnington, *A
 & Cunnington   Handbook of Medieval Costume* (1973)

Cunnington   Phillis Cunnington and Catherine Lucas, *Occupational
 & Lucas   Costume in England from the Eleventh Century to 1914* (1967)

Daniel   Samuel Daniel, *The Civil Wars between the Two Houses of Lancaster and York* (1595)

Daniell   David Daniell, 'Opening up the text: Shakespeare's *Henry VI* plays in performance', in Redmond, 247–77

Davies   Christie Davies, *Ethnic Humour around the World* (Bloomington, 1990)

Dean   Leonard F. Dean, *Tudor Theories of History Writing*, University of Michigan Contributions in Modern Philology, No. 1 (1947)

Dent   R. W. Dent, *Shakespeare's Proverbial Language: An Index* (Berkeley, Los Angeles and London, 1981)

Dessen   Alan C. Dessen, 'Oregon Shakespeare Festival', *SQ*, 28 (1977), 244–52

Dick   Hugh G. Dick, 'Thomas Blundeville's *The true order and Method of writing and reading Histories* (1574)', *The Huntington Library Quarterly*, 2 (1940), 149–70

Dillenberger   John Dillenberger, *God Hidden and Revealed: The Interpretation of Luther's 'Deus absconditus' and its Significance for Religious Thought* (Philadelphia, 1953)

Dodson   Sarah Dodson, 'Caterpillars, sponges, horseleeches in Shakespeare and in Holinshed', *Shakespeare Association Bulletin*, 19 (1944), 41–6

Dollimore   Jonathan Dollimore and Alan Sinfield (eds), *Political
& Sinfield   Shakespeare* (Manchester, 1994)

Doran   Madeleine Doran, *'Henry VI, Parts II and III': Their Relation to the 'Contention' and the 'True Tragedy'* (Iowa City, 1928)

Drayton,   Michael Drayton, *The Battle of Agincourt* (1627)
  Agincourt

Drayton,   Michael Drayton, *Polyolbion* (1612, 1622)
  Polyolbion

Du Boulay   F. R. H. Du Boulay (ed.), *Documents Illustrative of Medieval Kentish Society* (Kent Record Society, 1964)

Dugdale   Sir William Dugdale, *The Baronage of England* (1675)

E3   Giorgio Melchiori (ed.), *King Edward III* (Cambridge, 1998)

Edwards *et al.*   Philip Edwards, Inga-Stina Ewbank and G. K. Hunter (eds), *Shakespeare's Styles* (Cambridge, 1980)

ELR   *English Literary Renaissance*

Elton   W. R. Elton, *King Lear and the Gods* (San Marino, 1966)

Elyot   Sir Thomas Elyot, *The Book Named The Governor*, ed. S. E. Lemmberg (London and New York, 1962)

English   *An English Chronicle of the Reigns of Richard II, Henry IV,
  Chronicle, An   Henry V, and Henry VI. Written before the year 1471*, ed. John Silvester Davies (1856)

Erasmus, *Adages*   Desiderius Erasmus, *Adages*, transl. and annotated R. A. B. Mynors, *Collected Works of Erasmus*, vols 31–4 (Toronto, 1982–92)

Erasmus,   Desiderius Erasmus, *Preparation to Death* (1538)
  Preparation

Erskine-Hill   Howard Erskine-Hill, *Poetry and the Realm of Politics: Shakespeare to Dryden* (Cambridge, 1996)

ES   *English Studies*

Evans,   G. Blakemore Evans, review of Prouty, *JEGP*, 53 (1954),
  Prouty review   628–37

Fabyan   Robert Fabyan, *The New Chronicles of England and France* (1516; reprinted 1811)

Fairfield   S. Fairfield, *The Streets of London* (1983)

Faith	Rosamond Faith, 'The "Great Rumour" of 1377 and peasant ideology', in Hilton & Aston, 43–73
Famous Victories	*The Famous Victories of Henry the Fifth*, in Corbin & Sedge
Fenwick	Henry Fenwick, 'The production', in *Henry VI, Part 2*, BBC TV Shakespeare (1983)
Fleay	F. G. Fleay, *A Chronicle History of the Life and Work of William Shakespeare* (1886)
Flenley	Ralph Flenley (ed.), *Six Town Chronicles of England* (Oxford, 1911)
Fletcher	Anthony Fletcher, *Tudor Rebellions* (1983)
Florio	John Florio, *A Worlde of Wordes* (1598)
Fox-Davies	A. C. Fox-Davies, *A Complete Guide to Heraldry* (1925)
Foxe	*The Acts and Monuments of John Foxe*, ed. Josiah Pratt, 8 vols (1877)
Freeman	Arthur Freeman, 'Notes on the text of "2 Henry VI", and the "upstart crow" ', *N&Q*, 213 (1968), 128–30
French, 'Henry VI'	A. L. French, '*Henry VI* and the ghost of Richard II', *ES*, 50 (1969), xxxvii–xliii
French, 'Mills'	A. L. French, 'The mills of God and Shakespeare's early history plays', *ES*, 55 (1974), 313–24
Frey	David L. Frey, *The First Tetralogy: Shakespeare's Scrutiny of the Tudor Myth* (The Hague, 1976)
Froissart	*The Chronicles of Froissart*, transl. John Bourchier, Lord Berners, ed. 6 vols (1903)
Fulke	William Fulke, *A Defence of the Sincere and True Translation of the Holy Scriptures into the Mother Tongue* (Cambridge, 1843)
Fuller	David Fuller (ed.), *Tamburlaine the Great Parts 1 and 2*, see Marlowe
Fussner	F. Smith Fussner, *The Historical Revolution: English Historical Writing and Thought 1580–1640* (1962)
Gabel	Leona C. Gabel, *Benefit of Clergy in England in the Later Middle Ages*, Smith College Studies in History, 14 (Northampton, MA, 1928–9)
Gabrieli & Melchiori	Vittorio Gabrieli and Georgio Melchiori (eds), *Sir Thomas More* (Manchester and New York, 1990)
Gaus	F. Gaus, 'Social utopias in the Middle Ages', *Past and Present*, 38 (1967), 3–19
Gaw	Allison Gaw, 'John Sincklo as one of Shakespeare's actors', *Anglia*, 49 (1925), 289–303
Geneva Bible	*Holy Bible* (1560; edition quoted 1597)
George	David George, 'Shakespeare and Pembroke's Men', *SQ*, 32 (1981), 305–23
Gervinus	G. G. Gervinus, *Shakespeare Commentaries* (1875)
Goldberg	Jonathan Goldberg, 'Textual properties', *SQ*, 37 (1986), 213–17

Golding	See Ovid
Gower	John Gower, *Confessio amantis* (1889)
Grafton	Richard Grafton, *A Chronicle at Large of the History of the Affairs of England*, 2 vols (1569; reprinted 1809)
Grafton, *Continuation*	*See* under Hardyng
Greene, *Groatsworth*	Robert Greene, *Greene's Groatsworth of Wit* (1592), ed. D. Allen Carroll (New York, 1994)
Greene, *Menaphon*	Robert Greene, *Menaphon* (1589), ed. Edward Arber, The English Scholar's Library, No. 12 (1880)
Greene, *Web*	Robert Greene, *Penelope's Web* (1587)
Greg, *Folio*	W. W. Greg, *The Shakespeare First Folio* (Oxford, 1955)
Greg, *Problem*	W. W. Greg, *The Editorial Problem in Shakespeare* (Oxford, 1942)
Gregory	*The Chronicle of William Gregory, Skinner*, in James Gairdner (ed.), *The Historical Collections of a Citizen of London in the Fifteenth Century*, Camden Society, New Series, 17 (1876)
Griffiths	Ralph A. Griffiths, *The Reign of King Henry the Sixth: The Exercise of Royal Authority, 1422–1461* (1981)
Gurr, *Companies*	Andrew Gurr, *The Shakespearean Playing Companies* (Oxford, 1996)
Gurr, *Playgoing*	Andrew Gurr, *Playgoing in Shakespeare's London* (Cambridge, 1987)
Hall	Edward Hall, *The Union of the Two Noble and Illustre Families of Lancaster and York* (1548; reprinted 1809)
Halliwell	J. O. Halliwell (ed.), *The First Sketches of the Second and Third Parts of King Henry the Sixth* (1843)
Hamilton	A. C. Hamilton, *The Early Shakespeare* (San Marino, 1967)
Hammond	William Shakespeare, *Richard III*, ed. Antony Hammond, The Arden Shakespeare (1981)
Hampton	Christopher Hampton (ed.), *The Radical Reader* (Harmondsworth, 1984)
Hardyng	John Hardyng, *The Chronicles of J. H.* (1543; reprinted 1811). With a *Continuation* by Richard Grafton
Harriss, 'Beaufort'	G. L. Harriss, 'Cardinal Beaufort – patriot or usurer?', *Transactions of the Royal Historical Society*, Fifth Series, 20 (1970), 129–48
Harriss, *Cardinal*	G. L. Harriss, *Cardinal Beaufort* (Oxford, 1988)
Hart, A. L., *Copies*	Alfred Hart, *Stolne and Surreptitious Copies* (Melbourne and London, 1942)
Hart, A. L., *Homilies*	Alfred Hart, *Shakespeare and the Homilies* (Melbourne, 1934)
Hart, H. C., *1H6*	William Shakespeare, *King Henry VI, Part 1*, ed. H. C. Hart, The Arden Shakespeare (1909)

Hart, H. C., *3H6*	William Shakespeare, *King Henry VI, Part 3*, ed. H. C. Hart, The Arden Shakespeare (1909)
Harte	N. B. Harte, 'State control of dress and social change in pre-industrial England', in D. C. Coleman and A. H. John (eds), *Trade, Government and Economy in Pre-Industrial England* (1976), 132–65
Harting	James Edmund Harting, *The Ornithology of Shakespeare* (1871)
Harvey	I. M. W. Harvey, *Jack Cade's Rebellion of 1450* (Oxford, 1991)
Hattaway, *Theatre*	Michael Hattaway, *Elizabethan Popular Theatre* (1982)
Haydn	Hiram Haydn, *The Counter Reformation* (New York, 1950)
Hazlitt	William Hazlitt, 'Characters of Shakespeare's plays', in Howe, 165–361
Helgerson	Richard Helgerson, *Forms of Nationhood: The Elizabethan Writing of England* (Chicago and London, 1992)
Heriot	D. B. Heriot, 'Anabaptism in England during the 16th and 17th centuries', *Transactions of the Congregational Historical Society*, 12 (1913), 256–71, 312–20
Hibbard, 'Emendation'	G. R. Hibbard, 'An emendation in "2 Henry VI", I. iv', *N&Q*, 210 (1965), 332
Hibbard, *Making*	G. R. Hibbard, *The Making of Shakespeare's Dramatic Poetry* (Toronto, Buffalo and London, 1981)
Hill	Christopher Hill, 'The many-headed monster in late Tudor and early Stuart political thinking', in Carter, 296–324
Hilton & Aston	R. H. Hilton and T. H. Aston (eds), *The English Rising of 1381* (Cambridge, 1984)
Hinchcliffe	Judith Hinchcliffe, *King Henry VI, Parts 1, 2, and 3: An Annotated Bibliography* (London and New York, 1984)
Hobday	Charles Hobday, 'Clouted shoon and leather aprons: Shakespeare and the egalitarian tradition', *Renaissance and Modern Studies*, 23 (1979), 63–78
Hodgdon, *End*	Barbara Hodgdon, *The End Crowns All: Closure and Contradiction in Shakespeare's History* (Princeton, NJ, 1991)
Hodgdon '*Wars*'	Barbara Hodgdon, '*The Wars of the Roses*: scholarship speaks on stage', *Shakespeare Jahrbuch* (Heidelberg), 108 (1972), 170–84
Holderness, 'Agincourt'	Graham Holderness, 'Agincourt 1944: readings in the Shakespeare myth', *Literature and History*, 10 (1984), 24–45
Holderness, 'Radical'	Graham Holderness, 'Radical potentiality and political closure: Shakespeare in film and television', in Dollimore & Sinfield, 206–25

Holderness & McCullough	Graham Holderness and Christopher McCullough, 'Shakespeare on the screen: a selective filmography', *SS 39* (1986), 13–38
Holdsworth	W. S. Holdsworth, *A History of English Law*, vol. 3 (1903)
Holinshed	Raphael Holinshed, *The Chronicles of England, Scotland and Ireland* (2nd edn, 1587; reprinted, 6 vols, 1808). References are to vol. 3 unless otherwise specified.
Homilies	*Certain Sermons or Homilies* (Oxford, 1844). This volume includes the editions of 1547 and 1571, with much guidance and information concerning the complex bibliographic history.
Homily	*An Homily against Disobedience and Wilful Rebellion*, see *Homilies*
Honigmann, *Impact*	E. A. J. Honigmann, *Shakespeare's Impact on his Contemporaries* (1982)
Honigmann *Lost Years*	E. A. J. Honigmann, *Shakespeare: the 'Lost Years'* (Manchester, 1985)
Honigmann, 'Re-enter'	E. A. J. Honigmann, 'Re-enter the stage direction: Shakespeare and some contemporaries', *SS 29* (1976), 117–26
Honigmann *Stability*	E. A. J. Honigmann, *The Stability of Shakespeare's Texts* (1965)
Hook, *Edward I*	Frank S. Hook (ed.), *Edward I*, see Peele
Hook, *Tale*	Frank S. Hook (ed.), *The Old Wives Tale*, see Peele
Hooper	Wilfrid Hooper, 'The Tudor sumptuarie laws', *English Historical Review*, 30 (1915), 433–9
Horace	Quinti Horatii Flacci, *Opera*, transl. Christopher Smart (n.d.)
Howard & Rackin	Jean E. Howard and Phyllis Rackin, *Engendering a Nation* (London and New York, 1997)
Howe	P. P. Howe (ed.), *The Complete Works of William Hazlitt*, vol. 4 (London and Toronto, 1930)
Hughes & Larkin	Paul L. Hughes and James F. Larkin, *The Tudor Proclamations*, 3 vols (New Haven and London, 1969)
Huizinga	J. Huizinga, *The Waning of the Middle Ages* (1924; New York, 1954)
Humphreys, *2H4*	William Shakespeare, *The Second Part of King Henry IV*, ed. A. R. Humphreys, The Arden Shakespeare (1966)
Hunt *et al.*	R. W. Hunt, W. A. Pantin and R. W. Southern (eds), *Studies in Medieval History Presented to Frederick Maurice Powicke* (Oxford, 1948)
Hunter, 'Henry VI'	G. K. Hunter, 'The Royal Shakespeare Company plays *Henry VI*', *Renaissance Drama*, 9 (1978), 91–108

Hunter, 'Seneca' G. K. Hunter, 'Seneca and the Elizabethans: a case-study in "influence"', *SS* 20 (1967), 17–26

Hutchinson Roger Hutchinson, *The Image of God* (1550), in John Bruce (ed.), *The Works*, The Parker Society (Cambridge, 1842)

Irace Kathleen O. Irace, *Reforming the 'Bad' Quartos* (Newark, 1994)

Iser Wolfgang Iser, *Staging Politics: The Lasting Impact of Shakespeare's Histories* (New York, 1993)

Jackson, B. Sir Barry Jackson, 'On producing *Henry VI*', *SS* 6 (1953), 49–52

Jackson, MacD. P. MacD. P. Jackson, '*The Wars of the Roses*: the English Stage Company on tour', *SQ*, 40 (1989), 208–12

Jack Straw *The Life and Death of Jack Straw* (1594), ed. K. Muir, The Malone Society Reprints (Oxford, 1957)

JEGP *Journal of English and Germanic Philology*

Jewel John Jewel, *An Apology of the Church of England* (1564), in *The Works of John Jewel*, vol. 3 (Cambridge, 1848)

Jones Emrys Jones, *The Origins of Shakespeare* (Oxford, 1977)

Jonson *The Works of Ben Jonson*, C. H. Herford and P. and E. Simpson (eds), 11 vols (Oxford, 1925–52)

Jordan John E. Jordan, 'The reporter of *Henry VI, Part 2*', *PMLA*, 64 (1949), 1089–1113

Justice Steven Justice, *Writing and Rebellion: England in 1381* (Berkeley and London, 1994)

Kelly H. A. Kelly, *Divine Providence in the England of Shakespeare's Histories* (Cambridge, MA, 1970)

Kemp, T. W. T. W. Kemp, 'Acting Shakespeare: modern tendencies in playing and production with special reference to some recent productions', *SS* 7 (1954), 121–7

Kemp, W. Will Kemp, *Kemp's Nine Days' Wonder*, Camden Society, Old Series, 11 (1840)

Kenny Thomas Kenny, *The Life and Genius of Shakespeare* (1864)

King T. J. King, *Casting Shakespeare's Plays* (Cambridge, 1992)

Klibansky & Paton Raymond Klibansky and H. J. Paton (eds), *Philosophy and History: Essays Presented to Ernst Cassirer* (Oxford, 1936)

Knowles, *Carnival* Ronald Knowles (ed.), *Shakespeare and Carnival: After Bakhtin* (Basingstoke, 1998)

Knowles, 'Farce' Ronald Knowles, 'The farce of history: miracle, combat, and rebellion in *2 Henry VI*', *YES*, 21 (1991), 168–86

Knowles, '*Henry IV*' Ronald Knowles, *Henry IV Parts 1 & II* (Basingstoke, 1992)

Knutson Roslyn L. Knutson, 'Henslowe's naming of parts', *N&Q*, 228 (1983), 157–60

Kocher Paul H. Kocher, 'Contemporary pamphlet backgrounds for Marlowe's *The Massacre at Paris*', *MLQ*, 8 (1947), 151–73

Kökeritz	H. Kökeritz, *Shakespeare's Pronunciation* (New Haven, 1953)
Korniger	Siegfried Korniger (ed.), *Studies in English Language and Literature* (Stuttgart, 1957)
Kott	Jan Kott, *Shakespeare Our Contemporary*, transl. Boleslaw Taborski (1964)
Kunzle	David Kunzle, 'World upside down: the iconography of a European broadsheet', in Babcock, 39–94
Kyd, *Cornelia*	Thomas Kyd, *Cornelia*, in F. S. Boas (ed.), *The Works of Thomas Kyd* (Oxford, 1901)
Kyd, *Tragedy*	Thomas Kyd, *The Spanish Tragedy*, ed. J. R. Mulryne (1970)
Lander	J. R. Lander, *Conflict and Stability in Fifteenth-Century England* (1969)
Langland	William Langland, *Piers Plowman*, ed. A. V. Schmidt (1995)
Latimer, *Remains*	Hugh Latimer, *Sermons and Remains*, ed. George Elwes Corrie, The Parker Society (Cambridge, 1845)
Latimer, *Sermons*	*Sermons of Hugh Latimer*, ed. George Elwes Corrie, The Parker Society (Cambridge, 1844)
Laver	James Laver, *A Concise History of Costume* (1972)
Law, 'Chronicles'	R. A. Law, 'The chronicles and the Three Parts of *Henry VI*', *University of Texas Studies in English*, 33 (1955), 13–32
Law, 'Cycle'	R. A. Law, 'Shakespeare's historical cycle: rejoinder', *SP*, 51 (1954), 39–41
Law, 'Links'	R. A. Law, 'Links between Shakespeare's history plays', *SP*, 50 (1953), 168–87
Lee	Jane Lee, 'On the authorship of the Second and Third Parts of *Henry VI*, and their originals', *The New Shakspere Society's Transactions*, Series I, No. 4 (1875–6), 219–92
Leech	Clifford Leech, *Shakespeare: The Chronicles* (1962)
Leishman	J. B. Leishman (ed.), *The Three Parnassus Plays* (1949)
Liturgies	*Liturgies and Occasional Forms of Prayer set forth in the Reign of Queen Elizabeth*, ed. William Keatinge Clay, The Parker Society (Cambridge, 1847)
Longstaffe	Stephen Longstaffe, ' "A short report and not otherwise": Jack Cade in *2 Henry VI*', in Knowles, *Carnival*, 13–35
Lyle	H. M. Lyle, *The Rebellion of Jack Cade*, Historical Association Pamphlet G16 (1950)
Lyly	John Lyly, *Endymion* (1591)
McFarlane	K. B. McFarlane, 'At the death-bed of Cardinal Beaufort', in Hunt *et al.*, 405–28
McKerrow, 'Bad Quartos'	R. B. McKerrow, 'A note on the "Bad Quartos" of *2 and 3 Henry VI* and the Folio text', *RES*, 13 (1937), 64–72

McKerrow, 'Note'   R. B. McKerrow, 'A note on *Henry VI, Part II*, and *The Contention of York and Lancaster*', *RES*, 9 (1933), 157–69

McKerrow, 'Treatment'   R. B. McKerrow, 'The treatment of Shakespeare's text by his early editors, 1709–1768', *Proceedings of the British Academy* (1933), 89–122

McManaway   James G. McManaway, '*The Contention* and *2 Henry VI*', in Korniger, 143–54

McManaway *et al.*   James G. McManaway, Giles E. Dawson and Edwin E. Willoughby (eds), *Joseph Quincy Adams Memorial Studies* (Washington, 1948)

McMillin   Scott McMillin, 'Casting for Pembroke's Men: the *Henry VI* Quartos and *The Taming of a Shrew*', *SQ*, 23 (1972), 141–59

McMullan   Gordon McMullan, ' "Our whole life is like a play": collaboration and the problem of editing', *Textus*, 9 (1996), 437–60

Maguire   Laurie Maguire, *Shakespearean Suspect Texts* (Cambridge, 1996)

Mandeville   *The Travels of Sir John Mandeville* (1586 translation), Everyman's Library (1928)

Manheim, 'Plays'   Michael Manheim, 'The Shakespeare plays on TV', in Bulman & Coursen, 294–5

Manheim, *Weak King*   Michael Manheim, *The Weak King Dilemma in the Shakespearean History Play* (New York, 1973)

Marder   Louis Marder, 'History cycle at Antioch College', *SQ*, 4 (1953), 57–8

Marlowe, *Dido*   Christopher Marlowe, *Dido Queen of Carthage and The Massacre at Paris*, ed. H. J. Oliver, The Revels Plays (1968)

Marlowe, *Poems*   Christopher Marlowe, *The Complete Poems and Translations*, ed. Stephen Orgel (Harmondsworth, 1971)

Marlowe, *Tamburlaine*   Christopher Marlowe, *Tamburlaine the Great Parts 1 and 2, The Complete Works of Christopher Marlowe*, Vol. 5 ed. David Fuller (Oxford, 1998)

Masefield   John Masefield, *William Shakespeare* (London, 1911)

Maxwell   J. C. Maxwell, 'Three notes on *2 Henry VI*', *N&Q*, 218 (1973), 133–4

Medvedev & Bakhtin   P. N. Medvedev and M. M. Bakhtin, *The Formal Method in Literary Scholarship* (Baltimore, 1978)

Merivale   J. H. Merivale, *Richard Duke of York; or, The Contention of York and Lancaster* (1817)

Merrix   Robert P. Merrix, 'Shakespeare's histories and the new bardolaters', *SEL*, 19 (1979), 179–96

Meyrick   Sir Samuel Rush Meyrick, *A Critical Inquiry into Ancient Armour*, 3 vols (1842)

Middleton	Thomas Middleton, *Women Beware Women*, ed. Roma Gill (1968)
Mirror	William Baldwin, *Mirror for Magistrates*, ed. Lily B. Campbell (Cambridge, 1938)
Miola	Robert S. Miola, *Shakespeare and Classical Tragedy: The Influence of Seneca* (Oxford, 1992)
MLN	*Modern Language Notes*
MLQ	*Modern Language Quarterly*
Montgomery, 'Critical Edition'	William Montgomery (ed.), '*The Contention of York and Lancaster*: A Critical Edition', unpublished D.Phil., University of Oxford, 1985
Montgomery 'Staging'	William Montgomery, 'The original staging of *The First Part of the Contention* (1594)', *SS 41* (1988), 13–22
More, *Dialogue*	Sir Thomas More, *Dialogue . . . Wherein be treated divers matters as of the veneration and worship of images and relics, praying to Saints and going on pilgrimage*, 2nd edn (1530)
More, *Utopia*	Sir Thomas More, *Utopia*, ed. Edward Surtz S.J. and J. H. Hexter (eds), *The Complete Works of St Thomas More*, vol. 4 (rev. transl. by G. C. Richards, 1923; New Haven, 1965)
MP	*Modern Philology*
Müntzer	*Revelation and Revolution: Basic Writings of Thomas Müntzer*, transl. and ed. Michael G. Baylor (1993)
Murray	Margaret Alice Murray, *The Witch-Cult in Western Europe* (1921)
N&Q	*Notes and Queries*
Nashe, *Traveller*	Thomas Nashe, *The Unfortunate Traveller* (1594), in J. B. Steane (ed.), *The Unfortunate Traveller and Other Works* (Harmondsworth, 1972)
Nashe, *Works*	Thomas Nashe, *Works*, ed. R. B. McKerrow (1904–10), rev. F. P. Wilson, 5 vols (1958)
Neale	J. E. Neale, *Elizabeth and her Parliaments 1584–1601* (1957)
Neilson	G. Neilson, *Trial by Combat* (Glasgow, 1890)
Nichols	John Nichols, *Illustrations of the Manners and Expenses of Ancient Times in England* (1797; reprinted 1973)
Noble	Richmond Noble, *Shakespeare's Biblical Knowledge and Use of the Book of Common Prayer* (1935)
Norman	Charles Norman, *So Worthy a Friend: William Shakespeare* (New York, 1947)
North's Plutarch	T. J. B. Spencer (ed.), *Shakespeare's Plutarch* (Harmondsworth, 1964)
Odell	George C. D. Odell, *Shakespeare from Betterton to Irving*, 2 vols (New York, 1920)
ODEP	*The Oxford Dictionary of English Proverbs*, see F. P. Wilson
OED	*The Oxford English Dictionary*, 13 vols (Oxford, 1933)
Oliver	See Marlowe, *Dido*

Onions	C. T. Onions, *A Shakespeare Glossary* (1911), rev. Robert D. Eagleson (Oxford, 1986)
Orgel	Stephen Orgel, 'What is a text?', *Research Opportunities in Renaissance Drama*, 24 (1981), 3–6
Ornstein	Robert Ornstein, *A Kingdom for a Stage* (Cambridge, MA, 1972)
Orsini	N. Orsini, '"Policy" or the language of Elizabethan Machiavellianism', *Journal of the Warburg and Courtauld Institutes*, 9 (1946), 122–34
Ovid	Ovid, *Metamorphoses*, transl. Arthur Golding (1567), ed. John Frederick Nims (New York, 1965)
Palgrave	F. Palgrave, *The Ancient Calendars and Inventories of the Treasury of His Majesty's Exchequer* (1826)
Palmer	J. Palmer, *Political and Comic Characters of Shakespeare* (1961)
Partridge	Eric Partridge, *Shakespeare's Bawdy* (1968)
Patch	Howard R. Patch, *The Goddess Fortuna in Medieval Literature* (Cambridge, MA, 1927)
Patterson	Annabel Patterson, *Shakespeare and the Popular Voice* (Oxford, 1989)
Peele, *Eclogue*	George Peele, *An Eclogue Gratulatory* (1589)
Peele, *Edward I*	George Peele, *Edward I*, Frank S. Hook (ed.), in *The Dramatic Works of George Peele*, general editor Charles Tyler Prouty, vol. 2 (New Haven and London, 1961)
Peele, *Tale*	George Peele, *The Old Wives' Tale*, Frank S. Hook (ed.), in *The Dramatic Works of George Peele*, general editor Charles Tyler Prouty, vol. 3 (New Haven and London, 1970)
Pettitt	Thomas Pettitt, '"Here comes I, Jack Straw": English folk drama and social revolt', *Folklore*, 95 (1984), 3–20
Philips	Ambrose Philips, *Humfrey Duke of Gloucester* (1723)
Plantagenets, The	William Shakespeare, *The Plantagenets* (London and Boston, 1989), with 'Introduction', vii–xv, by Adrian Noble
Pleasant	*The Pleasant and Stately Moral of the Three Lords and Ladies of London* (1590)
PMLA	*Publications of the Modern Language Association of America*
Pocock	J. G. A. Pocock, *The Ancient Constitution and the Feudal Law* (1957)
Pollard, A. F.	A. F. Pollard, *Tudor Tracts* (1903)
Pollard, A. W.	A. W. Pollard, *Shakespeare's Folios and Quartos* (1909)
Polychronicon	Ranulph Higden, *Polychronicon Ranulphi Higden monarchi Cestrensis; together with the English Translations of John of Trevisa and of an unknown writer of the fifteenth century*, ed. Churchill Babington, 9 vols (1865–86)

Popper	Karl Popper, *The Poverty of Historicism* (1957)
Porter	Henry Porter, *The Too Angry Women of Abington* (1599), The Malone Society Reprints (Oxford, 1912)
Potter, *TNK*	John Fletcher and William Shakespeare, *Two Noble Kinsmen*, ed. Lois Potter, The Arden Shakespeare (1997)
Potter, 'Recycling'	Lois Potter, 'Recycling the early histories: "The Wars of the Roses" and "The Plantagenets"', *SS 43* (1991), 171–81
PQ	*Philological Quarterly*
Prayer Book	*King Edward's Second Prayer Book* (1552), in *The First and Second Prayer-Books of King Edward the Sixth* (London, Toronto and New York, 1910)
Presson	Robert K. Presson, 'Two types of dreams in Elizabethan drama, and their heritage: somnium animale and the prick-of-conscience', *SEL*, 7 (1967), 248–9
Price, 'Mirror'	Hereward T. Price, 'Mirror scenes in Shakespeare', in McManaway *et al.*, 101–14
Price, 'Review'	Hereward T. Price, review of Prouty, *MLN*, 70 (1955), 527–9
Prior	Moody E. Prior, *The Drama of Power* (Evanston, 1973)
Prouty	C. T. Prouty, *'The Contention' and Shakespeare's '2 Henry VI'* (New Haven, 1954)
Pugliatti	Paola Pugliatti, *Shakespeare the Historian* (Basingstoke, 1996)
Puttenham	George Puttenham, *The Art of English Poesy* (1589), ed. Edward Arber (1906)
Quinn	Michael Quinn, 'Providence in Shakespeare's Yorkist plays', *SQ*, 10 (1959), 45–52
Raab	Felix Raab, *The English Face of Machiavelli* (London and Toronto, 1964)
Rackin	Phyllis Rackin, *Stages of History: Shakespeare's English Chronicles* (New York, 1990)
Ralegh [Raleigh]	*The Poems of Sir Walter Ralegh*, ed. Agnes Latham (1951)
Raleigh	Sir Walter Raleigh, *The History of the World* (Edinburgh, 1820)
Redmond	James Redmond (ed.), *Drama and Society*, Themes in Drama, 1 (Cambridge, 1979)
Reed	Robert Rentoul Reed, *Crime and God's Judgement in Shakespeare* (Lexington, 1984)
Reese	M. M. Reese, *The Cease of Majesty* (1961)
Replogle	Carol Replogle, 'Shakespeare's salutations', *SP*, 70 (1973), 172–86
RES	*Review of English Studies*
Rhetorica	[Cicero], *Ad C. Herennium*, ed. Harry Caplan, Loeb Classical Library (London and Cambridge, MA, 1964)

Ribner	Irving Ribner, *The English History Play in the Age of Shakespeare*, rev. edn (1965)
Richmond	H. M. Richmond, *Shakespeare's Political Plays* (Gloucester, MA, 1977)
Riggs	David Riggs, *Shakespeare's Heroical Histories: Henry VI and its Literary Tradition* (Cambridge, MA, 1971)
Robbins	Russell Hope Robbins (ed.), *Historical Poems of the XIVth and XVth Centuries* (New York, 1959)
Rossiter, 'Ambivalence'	A. P. Rossiter, 'Ambivalence: the dialectic of the histories', in *Angel with Horns* (1961), 40–64
Rossiter, 'Tragedy'	A. P. Rossiter, 'Shakespearian tragedy', in *Angel with Horns* (1961), 253–73
Rossiter, *Woodstock*	A. P. Rossiter (ed.), *Woodstock* (1946)
Rothery	G. C. Rothery, *The Heraldry of Shakespeare* (1930)
RP	Richard Proudfoot, private communication
Sabine	George Sabine, *A History of Political Theory* (1937)
Salgado	Gamini Salgado, *Eyewitnesses of Shakespeare* (Brighton, 1975)
Sandoe	James Sandoe, '*King Henry VI, Part 2*: notes during production', *Theatre Annual*, 13 (1955), 32–48
Saunders	Claire Saunders, ' "Dead in his bed": Shakespeare's staging of the death of the Duke of Gloucester in *2 Henry VI*', *RES*, 36 (1985), 19–34
Saxl	Fritz Saxl, 'Veritas filia temporis', in Klibansky & Paton, 197–222
Scattergood	V. J. Scattergood, *Politics and Poetry in the Fifteenth Century* (1971)
Schafer	Elizabeth Schafer, *Ms-Directing Shakespeare* (1998)
Schelling	Felix E. Schelling, *The English Chronicle Play* (New York, 1902)
Schlegel	August Wilhelm Schlegel, *Lectures on Dramatic Art and Literature* (1900)
Schoenbaum	S. Schoenbaum, *Internal Evidence and Elizabethan Dramatic Authorship* (1966)
Scott	Margarite Scott, 'Machiavelli and the Machiavel', *Renaissance Drama*, 15 (1984), 147–74
Scott-Giles	C. W. Scott-Giles, *Shakespeare's Heraldry* (1950)
Segar	Sir William Segar, *The Book of Honour and Arms (1590) and Honour Military and Civil (1602)* (New York, 1975)
SEL	*Studies in English Literature*
Shaheen	Naseeb Shaheen, *Biblical References in Shakespeare's History Plays* (Newark, 1989)
Shakespeare's England	Sidney Lee and C. T. Onions (eds), *Shakespeare's England: An Account of the Life and Manners of his Age*, 2 vols (Oxford, 1916)

Sharp	Buchanan Sharp, *In Contempt of All Authority* (Berkeley, 1980)
Sheils & Wood	W. J. Sheils and Diana Wood (eds), *Voluntary Religion* (Oxford, 1986)
Shirley	Frances A. Shirley, *Swearing and Perjury in Shakespeare's Plays* (1979)
Siemon	James R. Siemon, 'Landlord not king: agrarian change and interarticulation', in Burt & Archer, 17–33
Simpson	Richard Simpson, 'The politics of Shakespeare's plays', *The New Shakspere Society's Transactions*, Series I, No. 2 (1874), Pt II, 419–23
Sinfield	Alan Sinfield, 'Royal Shakespeare: theatre and the making of ideology', in Dollimore & Sinfield, 182–205
Sisson	C. J. Sisson, *New Readings in Shakespeare*, 2 vols (Cambridge, 1956)
Slack	Paul Slack (ed.), *Rebellion, Popular Protest and the Social Order in Early Modern England* (1984)
Sledd	James Sledd, 'A note on the use of Renaissance dictionaries', *MP*, 49 (1951–2), 10–15
Smallwood	Robert Smallwood, 'Shakespeare of Stratford-upon-Avon, 1988', *SQ*, 40 (1989), 83–94
Smidt	Kristian Smidt, *Unconformities in Shakespeare's History Plays* (1982)
SP	*Studies in Philology*
Spelman	Sir Henry Spelman, *Archaeologus* (1626)
Spencer	Hazelton Spencer, *Shakespeare Improved* (Cambridge, MA, 1927)
Spenser	Edmund Spenser, *The Faerie Queene*, ed. A. C. Hamilton (London and New York, 1977)
Sprague	Arthur Colby Sprague, *Shakespeare's Histories: Plays for the Stage* (1964)
Spurgeon	Caroline Spurgeon, *Shakespeare's Imagery and What It Tells Us* (Cambridge, 1935)
SQ	*Shakespeare Quarterly*
Squibb	G. D. Squibb, *The High Court of Chivalry* (Oxford, 1959)
SS	*Shakespeare Survey*
Stahl	E. L. Stahl, *Shakespeare und das deutsche Theater* (Stuttgart, 1947)
Stanyhurst	Richard Stanyhurst, *A Treatise containing a Plain and Perfect Description of Ireland* (1587), appended to Holinshed, vol. 6
Statutes	*The Statutes at Large*, vol. 6 (Cambridge, 1763)
Sternhold & Hopkins	T. Sternhold, J. Hopkins *et al.*, *The Whole Book of Psalms, collected into English Metre* (1562)

Stirling	Brents Stirling, *The Populace in Shakespeare* (New York, 1949)
Stow, *Annals*	John Stow, *Annals of England* (1592)
Stow, *Survey*	John Stow, *The Survey of London* (1603)
Stubbes	Philip Stubbes, *Anatomy of Abuses* (1583), Part II, *The New Shakspere Society's Transactions*, Series VI (1882)
Suetonius	C. Suetonius Tranquillus, *The Lives of the Twelve Caesars*, transl. Alexander Thomson (1914)
Surtz & Hexter	Edward Surtz S. J. and J. H. Hexter (eds), *Utopia*, see More, *Utopia*
Sutcliffe	Christopher Sutcliffe, 'Kempe and Armin: the management of change', *Theatre Notebook*, 50:3 (1996), 122–34
Svendson	Kestor Svendson, *Milton and Science* (1956)
Swander	Homer D. Swander, 'The rediscovery of *Henry VI*', *SQ*, 29 (1978), 146–63
Talbert	E. W. Talbert, *Elizabethan Drama and Shakespeare's Early Plays: An Essay in Historical Criticism* (Chapel Hill, 1963)
Taming of a Shrew	*The Taming of a Shrew* (1594), ed. Stephen Miller, Malone Society Reprints (Oxford, 1998)
Thomas	Keith Thomas, *Religion and the Decline of Magic* (1971)
Thomson, J. A. K.	J. A. K. Thomson, *Shakespeare and the Classics* (1952)
Thomson, W. H.	W. H. Thomson, *Shakespeare's Characters: A Historical Dictionary* (Altrincham, 1951)
Tilley	M. P. Tilley, *The Proverbs in England in the Sixteenth and Seventeenth Centuries* (Ann Arbor, 1951)
Tillyard, 'Cycle'	E. M. W. Tillyard, 'Shakespeare's historical cycle: organism or compilation?', *SP*, 51 (1954), 34–9
Tillyard, *History Plays*	E. M. W. Tillyard, *Shakespeare's History Plays* (1944)
Tillyard, *Picture*	E. M. W. Tillyard, *The Elizabethan World Picture* (1943)
True Tragedy	*The True Tragedy of Richard Duke of York, and the Death of Good King Henry the Sixth* (1595)
Tuck	Anthony Tuck, *Richard II and the English Nobility* (1973)
TxC	Stanley Wells and Gary Taylor, with John Jowett and William Montgomery, *William Shakespeare: A Textual Companion* (Oxford, 1987)
Ulrici	Hermann Ulrici, *Shakespeare's Dramatic Art*, 2 vols (1876). Originally *Shakespeare's dramatische Kunst* (1839). The English translation by L. Dora Schmitz is of the third edition, which has additions by Ulrici often taking into account German and English Shakespeare scholars' comments on the first edition.
Urkowitz, 'All things'	Steven Urkowitz, '"All things is hansome now": murderers nominated by numbers in variant texts of *2 Henry VI* and *Richard III*', in G. W. Williams, 101–19

Urkowitz, 'Good news'	Steven Urkowitz, 'Good news about "Bad" Quartos', in Charney, 189–206
Urkowitz, 'Mistake'	Steven Urkowitz, ' "If I mistake in those foundations which I build upon": Peter Alexander's textual analysis of *Henry VI Parts 2 and 3*', *ELR*, 2 (1988), 230–56
Vaughan	Henry H. Vaughan, *New Readings and Renderings of Shakespeare's Tragedies*, 3 vols (1886)
Venezky	Alice S. Venezky, *Pageantry on the Shakespearean Stage* (New York, 1951)
Vice	Sue Vice, *Introducing Bakhtin* (Manchester and New York, 1997)
Vickers, B.	Brian Vickers, *Shakespeare: The Critical Heritage*, vol. 2, *1693–1733* (1974); vol. 5, *1765–1774* (1979); vol 6, *1778–1803* (1981)
Vickers, K. H.	K. H. Vickers, *Humphrey, Duke of Gloucester* (1907)
Virgil	P. Vergili Maronis, *Opera*, ed. Otto Ribbeck (Lipsiae, 1894)
Virgoe, 'Death'	Roger Virgoe, 'The death of William de la Pole, Duke of Suffolk', *Bulletin of the John Rylands Library*, 47 (1964–5), 489–502
Virgoe, 'Indictments'	Roger Virgoe, 'Some ancient indictments in the King's Bench referring to Kent, 1450–1452', in Du Boulay, 214–65
Walker	William S. Walker, *Critical Examination of the Text of Shakespeare*, 3 vols (1860)
Walsingham	Thomas Walsingham, *Historia anglicana*, ed. Henry Thomas Riley, 2 vols (1863)
Walter & Wrightson	John Walter and Keith Wrightson, 'Dearth and the social order in early modern England', in Slack, 108–28
Walton	J. K. Walton, *The Quarto Copy for the First Folio of Shakespeare* (Dublin, 1971)
Warren, 'Comedies'	Roger Warren, 'Comedies and histories at two Stratfords, 1977', *SS 31* (1978), 141–53
Warren, 'Contrarieties'	Roger Warren, ' "Contrarieties agree": an aspect of dramatic technique in *Henry VI*', *SS 37* (1984), 75–83
Weimann	Robert Weimann, *Shakespeare and the Popular Tradition in the Theatre*, ed. Robert Schwartz (Baltimore and London, 1978)
Wells, R. H.	Robin Headlam Wells, 'The fortunes of Tillyard: twentieth-century critical debate on Shakespeare's history plays', *ES*, 66 (1985), 391–403
Wells, S.	Stanley Wells, 'The history of the whole contention', in Bulman & Coursen, 292–4
Welsford	Enid Welsford, *The Fool* (1968)

Wentersdorf	Karl Wentersdorf, 'Shakespeare chronology and the metrical tests', in *Shakespeare-Studien*, ed. W. Fischer and K. Wentersdorf (1951)
Werstine	Paul Werstine, 'Narratives about printed Shakespeare texts: "Foul Papers" and "Bad" Quartos', *SQ*, 41 (1990), 65–86
West	Gillian West, 'Shakespeare's "Edmund Mortimer"', *N&Q*, 233 (1988), 463–5
Whitney	Geoffrey Whitney, *A Choice of Emblems* (1586)
Wiggins	Martin Wiggins, *Journeymen in Murder: The Assassin in English Renaissance Drama* (Oxford, 1991)
Wilders	John Wilders, *The Lost Garden* (London and Basingstoke, 1978)
Wiles, *Clown*	David Wiles, *Shakespeare's Clown* (Cambridge, 1987)
Wiles, *Robin Hood*	David Wiles, *The Early Plays of Robin Hood* (Cambridge, 1981)
Willcock	Gladys D. Willcock, 'Language and poetry in Shakespeare's early plays', *Proceedings of the British Academy* (1954), 103–18
Willett	John Willett (ed.), *Brecht on Theatre* (New York and London, 1964)
Williams, G.	Gordon Williams, *A Dictionary of Sexual Language and Imagery in Shakespearean and Stuart Literature*, 3 vols (1994)
Williams, G. W.	George Walton Williams (ed.), *Shakespeare's Speech-Headings* (Newark and London, 1998)
Willis	Deborah Willis, 'Shakespeare and English witch-hunts', in Burt & Archer, 96–120
Wilson, F. P., *Marlowe*	F. P. Wilson, *Marlowe and the Early Shakespeare* (Oxford, 1953)
Wilson, F. P., *ODEP*	F. P. Wilson, *The Oxford Dictionary of English Proverbs* (Oxford, 1970)
Wilson, R.	Richard Wilson, '"A mingled yarn": Shakespeare and the cloth workers', in *Will Power* (1993), 22–44
Woodstock	See Rossiter, *Woodstock*
Woudhuysen	William Shakespeare, *Love's Labour's Lost*, ed. H. R. Woudhuysen, The Arden Shakespeare (1998)
Wright	George T. Wright, *Shakespeare's Metrical Art* (Berkeley, Los Angeles and Oxford, 1988)
YES	*Yearbook of English Studies*
Young	Alan Young, *Tudor and Jacobean Tournaments* (1987)
Zall	P. M. Zall (ed.), *A Hundred Merry Tales and Other English Jestbooks of the Fifteenth and Sixteenth Centuries* (1963)

INDEX

The index covers the Preface, Introduction, Commentary and Appendices. It omits *OED* references other than to ante-datings, first citations and only citations.

Index